An End to
Murder

An End to
Murder

*A Criminologist's View of
Violence Throughout History*

Colin Wilson and Damon Wilson

A Herman Graf Book
Skyhorse Publishing

First published in 2015 in the UK by Robinson
Copyright © Colin Wilson and Damon Wilson, 2015

This North American edition published in 2015 by Skyhorse Publishing

The moral right of the authors has been asserted.

Skyhorse publishing books may be purchased in bulk at special discounts
for sales promotion, corporate gifts, fund-raising, or educational purposes.
Special editions can also be created to specifications. For details, contact
the Special Sales Department, Skyhorse Publishing, 307 West 36th Street,
11th Floor, New York, New York 10018 or info@skyhorsepublishing.com.

Skyhorse® and Skyhorse Publishing® are registered trademarks of
Skyhorse Publishing, Inc.®, a Delaware corporation.

Visit our website at www.skyhorsepublishing.com.

10 9 8 7 6 5 4 3 2 1

Library of Congress Cataloging-in-Publication Data is available on file.

Cover design by Brian Peterson

Print ISBN: 978-1-62914-812-0
Ebook ISBN: 978-1-63220-238-3

Printed and bound by CPI Group (UK) Ltd, Croydon, CR0 4YY

I find myself in an odd position. The death of my father and co-author, Colin Wilson, has left me having to dedicate this book – containing his last original writing – for both of us.

But I am quite certain who the dedication from Dad should go to, even though I never got the chance to discuss the matter with him. On behalf of my father, I would like to dedicate this book to Joy Wilson. My mother stood beside my father throughout his writing career, gave him children that he loved and cherished, filled his life with a quietly smug happiness, and was the first sounding-board for all of his ideas. Without my mother, I'm sure Colin Wilson would have been a much less optimistic and a much less creative author.

For myself, I would like to dedicate this book to my own wife, Lucy. She is doggedly and long-sufferingly fulfilling the same role for me that my mother did for my father. It is my dearest wish that my much-loved wife will eventually tuck me into my grave, just as Mum did for Dad.

Damon Wilson, Friday 6 March 2015

Contents

A Beginning

There is something essentially wrong with the human race. And, ironically, it is in the light of our astonishing achievements that this wrongness is so clearly visible.

We are the dominant life form on the planet. Creatively and intellectually there is no other species that has ever come close to equalling us. Our ability to adapt to any environment is surpassed only by our ability to change any environment to meet our needs. Human society is dynamic, ever-evolving and tremendously multifaceted. Our humanitarianism empathises not only with the troubles of other people, but even with the suffering of competing species of animal. And the very fact that most, or perhaps all, of the above statements will have been questioned by the average reader could also be seen as evidence of the uniquely probing and Socratic nature of the human mind.

Yet, while no other species on Earth can hold a candle to human achievements, no other species is as suicidally prone to internecine conflict. Human history is a catalogue of cold-hearted murders, mindless blood-feuds, appalling massacres and devastating wars. We are the only species on the planet whose ingrained habit of conflict constitutes the chief threat to our own survival: in Darwinian terms we are an enigma – a species so successful that we threaten our own existence.

The question as to why our species is so exceptionally prone to violence is, of course, often asked; but usually rhetorically. The answers given are generally politically or religiously motivated, and are usually more reliant on unconsidered dogma than on scientific deduction.

For a politician the cause is always the failure of political opponents to deal with crime, and the solution is always to place more power into his or her hands. For the priest it is always failure to follow the commands of their god, as necessarily expressed through the priesthood. And for everyone, it seems, violence is never totally wrong: there are always expedients that allow for a violent solution. Terrorists who have to be killed, wars that have to be fought, children who need to be spanked – none of us are free from at least the inclination to do violence to other human beings.

It's natural enough, on hearing such a statement, to think that that may be true of other people, but that you yourself hate all violence. Consider the following true story from the Second World War[1].

A young soldier was captured by the enemy. They discovered that he was an excellent pianist, so they sat him at a piano and told him to play. He was also told that the moment that he stopped playing, he would be taken outside and shot. The young man played continuously for over twenty-two hours, until his arms and fingers were in agony. Eventually he collapsed in tears, unable to play another note. His captors heartily congratulated him for such a Herculean effort. Then they took him outside and shot him.

Examine your emotional reaction at this moment. How much do you empathise with him? With his fear, pain, and his final despair when he realised that his captors' laughter and slaps on the back did not mean that they were going to spare him. How do you feel about the men who tortured and murdered the young soldier? Can there ever be any justification for such heartless cruelty?

Now consider the following additional facts: the young man was a member of the Waffen SS – the Nazi Party's elite shock troops, who ruthlessly carried out some of the worst atrocities of the war. The Russians who tortured and killed him had just fought their

---

1 From Antony Beevor's *Berlin: The Downfall 1945* (2007)

way across hundreds of miles of scorched earth, and knew of compatriots by the thousand – non-combatant men, women and children – who had been murdered by the retreating Nazis.

How much did your emotional reaction to the story just change? You would be a remarkable person if you found that your moral indignation had not reduced, if only by a fraction. You don't know that the young Nazi ever personally committed any crime, yet the fact that he died wearing the most hated uniform in modern history moved you at least a step closer to approving of his horrific murder.

This is a typical human trait: we almost automatically start to rationalise and justify any violence that happens to serve purposes of which we approve. On an instinctual level we act as if the ends justify the means; even if, intellectually, we reject that repugnant excuse. The ongoing mystery of unnecessary human violence is a classic case of not being able to see the wood for the trees: we tend to concentrate on individual crime cases – the trees – and fail to consider the vast forest of our apparently habitual brutality.

And yet, compared with any other period of human history, our generation is the most compassionate and non-violent that has ever walked the planet. Official report after official report, for almost twenty years, has clearly shown a steady downswing in violence, right across the globe. Certainly there are eruptions of brutality – serial killers, crime waves and, of course, wars – but these are brief reversals when compared to the general passivity that seems to be settling on the human race. And that recent trend is actually a continuation of gradual reduction of violence, both criminal and military, that has been taking place over the past three hundred years. The risk of you being stabbed by a thug, or killed by an invading army, is less now than it has been for any previous generation in history.

It is true that today we are constantly worried by violent crime but, unless the reader is quite unlucky, the chances are that their only point of contact with non-fictional violence is on the news. The twenty-four-seven TV news channels (plus, of course, the ever-present internet) exposes us to crimes that, back in the days of one or two newspaper perusals a day, we would never have been told about.

Petty local crimes and obscure national and international acts of violence – which previously wouldn't have made it past the newspaper editor's spike – are now automatically thrown into the mix, simply to fill twenty-four hours of news every day with as little repetition as possible. But that repetition is still necessary, and TV screens are everywhere, so you may hear about the same crime a dozen times a day. Given this carpet-bombing of bad news, it's hardly surprising that most people feel we are living in one of the most violent periods of human history; not, as is the case, the most pacific.

(Coincidentally, I was listening to the radio a few minutes after writing the last paragraph and heard an interviewee say: 'There's violence all over the place; you just have to turn on the TV or the radio . . .')

Consider the fact that the planetary population is now over seven billion. That's more than seven thousand million humans. Yet the vast majority of those people will never commit a violent act in their entire lives. If we were anywhere near as habitually violent as our forebears were just a few hundred years ago, the planet would be soaked in human blood.

In 1981, the political scientist Ted Robert Gurr published a simple but shocking study[2]. He had compared court and parish records in England and found that in the town of Oxford in the thirteenth century, there was an average of 110 murders per 100,000 citizens per year. That compares with one murder per 100,000 a year in twentieth-century London (a murder rate that has gone down further since the date of Gurr's study). Put simply, you were 110 times more likely to have been murdered in medieval Oxford than you would be in modern London.

And medieval England was not a particularly violent place compared with the rest of Europe. Oxford avoided bloody

---

2 'Historical Trends in Violent Crime in Europe and America: A critical review of the evidence', by Robert Ted Gurr, in *Crime and Justice* (volume 3) (University of Chicago Press, 1981)

involvement in the Second Baron's Rebellion (1264–67) and England was otherwise peaceful in that century; so any violent deaths were entirely on the heads of the Oxford citizenry going about their daily lives.

Remember that for most of history almost everyone went about armed – carrying a knife at the very least. And that killing was generally accepted as a proper remedy to someone 'insulting your honour'. Such killings were still seen as homicide by the law, but defending one's honour was regarded as a mitigating circumstance by most courts, much as temporary insanity is today.

Our ancestors – from the dawn of civilisation to up to a few generations ago – were habitually brutal in a way that is unimaginable today. Wife and child-beating was the norm. Killing to settle petty arguments was commonplace. Slavery and/or serfdom was the backbone of most economies. Torture and public execution were standard judicial practices. And war for political gain was considered the righteous and noble calling of both kings and aristocrats.

Ted Gurr's figures made a simple graph that indicated a steady, if spiky, drop in homicides in England between the medieval and modern periods. And virtually every other study since then has indicated a similar drop in violence worldwide over the same period. Some regions, like western Europe, are leading the trend; while others, like certain states in the developing world and in the USA, are slowly but clearly trailing along behind. In the past eight hundred years, murder has started to end.

Why?

To try to answer this question, we will need to consider the fundamental question of whether humans are naturally violent. Are people born killers; or are they trained by life, and the people around them, to attack when faced with a problem? The 'nature versus nurture' debate is one of the oldest in modern science. Shakespeare even mentions it in his 1611 play, *The Tempest*:

A devil, a born devil, on whose nature nurture can never stick.[3]

---

3 William Shakespeare, *The Tempest* (Act 4, Scene 1)

In the case of unnecessary human violence, the question has never come close to being settled.

Yet this is probably one of the most important questions of the modern age. For more than half a century, human beings have possessed the technology to make weapons of mass destruction. Individually, or in combination, these weapons – atomic, chemical and bacteriological – could destroy cities, civilisation, humanity or all life on the planet.

For fifty years, in the Cold War, we lived under the shadow of total destruction; never certain if those controlling the opposing side were willing to risk destroying the planet, simply to win a political argument. Did we survive because we and our enemies allowed reason to control fear, hatred and paranoia? Or did we just get lucky?

The political crisis that brought the world to the edge of total annihilation (on at least two occasions) during the Cold War may be over; but the weapons of mass destruction are still out there.

This book was originally started by my father – Colin Wilson – in 2011, and was aimed at considering his more than fifty years of interest in criminology. He suffered a stroke in the spring of 2012 and, although mentally unharmed, he was left unable to speak or write.

I, his son, have also been writing books about criminology for a number of years – some in collaboration with my father. So I offered to take over the project and was delighted when the publisher, Constable & Robinson – through their editor, Duncan Proudfoot – kindly agreed.

My immediate problem was that what Dad had already written could not be continued as it was by me. As you will see, he was writing a form of autobiography – centring around his fascination with crime and his philosophical wish to understand criminality. I simply don't know what he was planning to write in the rest of the book.

But I do know that his most in-depth study of criminology and human violence was his *A Criminal History of Mankind*, originally published in 1984, and updated by him in 2005. I've read this book at least half a dozen times over the years, and know that

I'm not alone in regarding it as one of the most influential and insightful books on crime ever written.

Dad concluded that book with these words:

Looking back over three million years of human history, we can see that it has been a slow reprogramming of the human mind, whose first major turning point was the moment when the mind became aware of itself. When man learned to recognise his own face in a pool and to say I, he became capable of greatness, and also of criminality.

But if this history of human evolution has taught us anything, it is that 'criminal man' has no real, independent existence. He is a kind of shadow, a Spectre of the Brocken, an illusion. He is the result of man's misunderstanding of his own potentialities – as if a child should see his face in a distorting mirror and assume he has changed into a monster.

The criminal is, in fact, the distorted reflection of the human face, the 'collective nightmare of mankind.' And this insight is in itself a cause for optimism. As Novalis says: 'When we dream that we dream, we are beginning to awaken.'

So I've attempted to write a sister book to Dad's *A Criminal History of Mankind*, if not a sequel. I've included everything that he wrote for the original manuscript – his last original writing – but have then built a book around it that I hope is in step with his lifelong intent to understand the reasons for needless human violence.

The opinions in my sections are my own, of course, not Dad's. But I had the tremendous luck to have spent decades talking to, and writing with my father – an man I believe was one of the great optimist philosophers. A few of my opinions, expressed in this book, I'm fairly sure he would not agree with. But that was never a problem when working with Dad: he was always willing to consider other people's opinions, and I never heard him flatly reject any argument without giving it fair consideration.

One of the reasons why unnecessary human violence remains such a mystery, to its perpetrators as well as to its victims, are the tools that we use to try to understand it: other than our own gut instincts, these are mainly evolutionary biology, historical analysis, behavioural psychology and forensic psychiatry. These all offer conclusions that are too open to argument and rely too much on individual interpretation. And a similar problem occurs with our understanding of history – the resource from which we gather almost all our research data.

In the following pages I, and later Dad, will chart the rise of the human species from ancestral ape to the present day, noting the historical trends of violence and the theories around why that violence happened. Much of what follows is controversial – in scientific circles as much as anywhere else. I devote most of the third chapter to aquatic ape theory, for example, knowing full well that the orthodoxy of evolutionary science presently regards the very idea as pure heresy. But I happen to know that Dad believed that the evidence supported this theory, as do I; so I'm glad to include it, despite being sure that it will alienate some readers.

The final aim of the book is to suggest reasons why humans are so violent and, more importantly, why we recently seem to have become less violent.

Is this an ongoing trend?

Are we at last seeing the beginning of an end to murder?

The reader, and future history, will decide.

And it is partly because the tools that we use to understand our history can lead to such uncertain results, that I'll begin with a brief overview of some of the blood feuds and gang fights that regularly take place within the hallowed halls of science . . .

Damon Wilson, March 2013

Part 1
The Long Bloody Road to Now

Damon Wilson

Chapter 1

'The Great Tragedy of Science'

It is a matter of heated scientific debate as to whether our earliest ancestors were – or were not – violent killers; but you might never guess that if you only read the standard textbooks on paleoanthropology or evolutionary biology.

Professor Raymond Dart's 'killer ape' theory of early hominid development presently holds sway in university lecture halls and on archaeological dig sites, and has done so for most of the past fifty years. This is despite several problems with the theory and the fact that an apparently competing idea – Elaine Morgan's 'aquatic ape' theory – seems to answer many of these quandaries. Yet if you mention Elaine Morgan or her theory in academic circles you are likely to be patronised, jeered at or simply howled down. Why is this? To understand, it is necessary to have an idea of just how theoretic and recently developed much of our scientific knowledge is.

By the start of the twentieth century, human civilisation had ostensibly reached its zenith. The French later referred to this period as *La Belle Époque*; English speakers called it a golden age. Great passenger liners crossed stormy oceans with speed and ease. Huge standing armies ensured peace – especially in Europe, a former hotbed of warfare. The British Empire securely held sway over much of the globe – continuing its selfless task of civilising primitive peoples, while helping them to exploit their natural resources to the full. And in most civilised countries democracy held sway – paternally guided by the hand of plutocrats (as in the USA) or monarchs (as in most of Europe).

At this time it was a commonly held belief – among men of learning as well as the general public – that science had achieved almost all it would ever achieve. The wonderful and bewildering rush of discoveries of the previous century had convinced many people that everything that *could* be discovered already *had* been discovered. Men flew like birds, travelled faster than galloping horses, and easily prevented lethal diseases like small-pox and cholera. So, when a young musician called Max Planck mentioned in 1875 that he was thinking of studying physics, a leading physics professor told him: 'In this field, almost every-thing is already discovered and all that remains is to fill a few holes.' In his opinion physics had become a scientific backwater. Planck ignored his gloomy advice.

Fifty years later – in which time the *Titanic* had sunk, the First World War had devastated Europe, the British Empire was tottering and totalitarianism was on the rise – Planck's quantum theory of subatomic particles had fundamentally changed the way that human beings understood the universe. And, as with physics, so with virtually every other branch of science – a cata-ract of discoveries rewarded researchers' efforts. Yet academic complacency, myopia and dogmatism could continue to block areas of scientific development.

For example, the science of palaeontology – the study of prehistoric life through the examination of fossils – had thrown up an odd conundrum. It appeared that certain species were to be found in, say, both South America and Africa: yet how had two continents, separated by thousands of miles of ocean, managed to host almost identical types of creatures? Darwinism stated that each separated continent would be populated by species that had evolved independently. These would be well-adapted to local conditions, but should not be found on other, physically disconnected continents. To a large extent this seemed to have happened. Giraffes had evolved in Africa to feed on the upper leaves of trees, for example, while in South America an elephant-sized sloth called a megatherium had once exploited the same hard-to-reach food source. There were no giraffes in the Americas and there had never been any giant sloths in Africa or Asia. In fact, most mammals and plants were restricted to their local region and had presumably evolved there.

Yet there were anomalous finds that skewed this neat hypothesis. Primitive horses, for example, had once existed on both sides of the Atlantic – before dying out in the Americas, while surviving in Africa and Asia. Bears and canine species – like wolves, jackals and dingoes – were almost universal around the planet. Monkeys, too, were found across the globe (apart from in Australia) but apes, their close cousin, did not make it to Australia, Europe, Asia or the Americas except in the form of human beings. Bewilderingly, it also appeared that the ancestors of the marsupials originated in South America, but had somehow crossed over 9,000 miles of ocean to colonise Australia. And the fossils of lemurs were found in Madagascar and India, but not in any of the lands around and in between. It was all very odd.

Yet it was not the naturalists or the palaeontologists who successfully proposed an answer to this dilemma, but the geologists. These had recently come to realise that some areas of the Earth's surface had been forced upwards by unimaginably powerful subterranean forces – explaining, for example, why sea shells were sometimes found on the tops of mountains. Likewise, other areas of land had apparently sunk beneath the sea; thus North Sea fishermen, many miles from any sight of land, sometimes dredged up mammoth bones and tusks.

In 1861 the influential geologist Eduard Suess suggested that isthmus links between the continents – what he called 'land bridges' – might have once risen from the oceans, allowing an intercontinental traffic of animals and plants. These bridges, undoubtedly unstable by their very nature, later collapsed back into the sea, he said, separating venturesome species from their respective native continents. Suess suggested that these land bridges had, at one time, linked every continent, effectively making all of the world's landmasses one great (if rather disjointed) continent that he named 'Gondwanaland'. This was a neat and creative answer to the question of anomalous species spread and was widely accepted for nearly a hundred years . . . until it was proved to be utter rubbish.

What Eduard Suess had not known – and to be fair to him could not have imagined, given the knowledge available at the time – was that the continents are not fixed in position. In fact, they skate about across the surface of the Earth with, in geological terms, breakneck speed. Despite what seems to us the inconceivable weight of the planet's landmasses, their substance is – relatively speaking – little more than slag floating on the surface of the molten metal in a foundry vat; where the vat itself is the vast mass of magma and the iron core that make up the majority of our planet.

A theory of 'continental drift' had in fact been suggested by a German meteorologist called Alfred Wegener as early as 1912. But, largely because he was not a geologist by profession, his theory was either ignored or downright ridiculed by specialists in the field. It was not until studies of oceanic trenches in the late 1950s – and the subsequent discovery of the shifting tectonic plates on which all landmasses have their foundation – that mainstream geologists seriously considered Wegener's arguments and, eventually, accepted them.

It was now seen that land bridges were not necessary to explain the spread of plants and animals over separated continents. Gondwanaland – Suess's super-continent – had indeed existed, but it had not needed any land bridges because what are now separate landmasses had then (from 570 million to 180 million years ago) been pressed together into a single landmass.

Ancient species had not had to cross seas and oceans at that time, because those bodies of water had not then existed. Later on, as the continents started to drift apart, they had still been close enough together to allow some species to fly, drift on debris, or to island-hop from one landmass to another; journeys that would now be impossible due to the sheer distances involved. This rather hit-and-miss method of travel might explain why very few living species are found on separate continents, and most are only found on one.

The now-universal acceptance of Wegener's theory of continental drift (and scientists' mortified rejection of Suess's land bridge theory) is a classic example of what the American physicist and philosopher Thomas Kuhn called a 'paradigm shift'.

Kuhn pointed out that established thinking in any scientific discipline will doggedly hang on to old ideas until anomalies and inconsistencies built up to an almost ludicrous degree. Then – often forced to it by some new and apparently incontrovertible piece of evidence – the establishment will suddenly undergo a 'revolution': a sea change, after which trend-setting scientists will start believing ideas that, sometimes only months before, they had been contemptuously deriding.

The image of scientific consistency presented by experts in any field is all too often just that: an image or even an illusion. A theory, no matter how 'well-established', is just a structure of interconnected ideas; a structure that can be damaged or even brought crashing down by contrary evidence. As the biologist Thomas Huxley noted ruefully: 'The great tragedy of science [is] the slaying of a beautiful theory by an ugly fact.'

Even eminent scientists suffer from the same petty and self-serving temptations as the rest of us. Just imagine discovering that a theory you have professed for decades, and built your career and reputation on, is under assault – maybe from some whippersnapper who has barely a tenth of your academic achievements to his or her name. Could you consider their views with a completely open mind?

Too often, those with academic reputations to protect will use their political clout within a speciality to jealously attack, or even deliberately obfuscate evidence that might undermine their pet theories – ignoring the actual scientific merits of that evidence. Certainly this sort of contemptible behaviour isn't the norm within scientific endeavour (or we would still be bleeding patients with leeches and travelling by horse and cart) but few would claim that it never happens.

This over-defensive attitude can lead to an ossification of ideas and the forming of an effective pseudo-religion around 'established' theories; with senior experts behaving like high priests and heretical thinkers being cast into the outer darkness (by having their research funding cut). Knowing this tendency all too well, Thomas Huxley also said that: 'Science commits suicide when it adopts a creed.'

And even after a Kuhnian revolution of ideas has overthrown such resistance, the newly accepted theory can quickly fossilise into something as inflexible as the orthodoxy it replaced. Just because it's new and it beat the old theory, that doesn't necessarily mean that a fresh idea is any more true to reality. And in rejecting old theories (and hitching their careers to the new ones) scientists risk throwing out ideas that still have value. As the author George Orwell pointed out, in his introduction to his 1945 novel *Animal Farm*: 'To exchange one orthodoxy for another is not necessarily an advance.'

For example, despite their fall from grace, Eduard Suess and the proponents of 'land bridges' were not entirely wrong: in fact there was once a land bridge between Siberia and North America – called 'Beringia' by geologists – across what is now the sea called the Bering Strait.

Around twelve thousand years ago, during the last Ice Age when ocean levels were lower, Beringia had stood high enough above the sea ice to allow the migration of humans from Asia to America. Then, as the weather warmed and the seas were swelled by huge amounts of melting ice, Beringia vanished beneath the waves, cutting off the intercontinental link.

And there is another great land bridge that you can see in any atlas today: the link between the northern and southern American continents called the Isthmus of Panama and Central America. This land bridge began when undersea volcanoes formed a chain of islands between the two continents. Then, over the period of fifteen million to three million years ago, the grinding collision of two plates of the Earth's crust forced these islands upwards to make a chain of mountains and, eventually, an isthmus that linked the two landmasses. Just as Eduard Suess had theorised, animal species used the land bridge to cross backwards and forwards between the continents – and are still doing so today.

This forming of the Isthmus of Panama had a profound effect on the planet. By cutting off the Pacific from the Atlantic, the new landmass broke the flow of the great ocean currents. This combined with the rise of the Himalayan Mountains – caused by the slamming of the island of India into the continent of Asia – to change the climate drastically. Northern Asia and Europe became much colder and Africa underwent a very long drought – one that is still, to a large extent, going on today. This multi-million-year African dry season was probably responsible for the rise of a bizarre and unique genus of ape: our original hominid ancestor.

The earliest known apes split from their monkey cousins between fifteen million and twenty million years ago (in the Miocene period). At that time Africa was almost entirely covered by tropical jungle and rainforests – a habitat to which arboreal apes and monkeys were perfectly adapted. Primates were like rodents in the Miocene Epoch: widespread, highly varied and frighteningly prolific. We have found over forty genera of fossil-ised Miocene ape alone – eight times those that exist today. And, given the haphazard nature of both fossilisation and archaeological discovery, it is likely that there were many other families of early ape that we still haven't found.

Then, as the weather patterns changed and Africa began to dry out, savannah grassland replaced most of the jungles. The fossil record shows that between nine million and five million years ago, a great number of ape and monkey species died out – just what you would expect to happen when a highly specialised group of creatures find their habitat vanishing. What you would also expect is that some of those creatures would evolve to take advantage of the new circumstances, which is apparently just what our ancestors did.

The trouble is that we have virtually no evidence for what happened next. There is, at present, what is called the 'Miocene fossil gap', in which we have found no certain fossils of our earli-est ancestors. There are plenty of quadrupedal apes; starting from around twenty million years ago. Then, at around 6.1 million to 5.7 million years ago, we find an upright, Central African, fully bipedal ape species (*Orrorin tugenensis*) that may well be (but isn't definitely) our remote ancestor. Within that multi-million-year gap, we have no clear idea of what our ances-tors looked like, because they didn't lay their bones anywhere that we have, so far, been able to find them. This evidence gap is particularly ironic since the idea of a 'missing link' between apes and humans has haunted the debate over evolution ever since Darwin first expounded the theory. Sceptics asked where the 'half-man, half-ape' fossils were, and all that Darwin could reply was that that these 'ape-men' must have existed, and that fossil evidence might still be found one day.

Over a hundred years later we have found early ape fossils – which were clearly arboreal, curved-back, quadrupedal knuckle-walkers like modern apes. And we have found *Orrorin tugenensis* – which evidently walked upright, because its hip bones were evolved to bear the weight of a torso balanced vertically above the legs, just like ours. (Bipedalism is the key here, since the other main difference between apes and humans – big brains – came millions of years after we started to walk upright.) Yet we still haven't found a fossil ape that had a back and hips indicating development somewhere *between* knuckle-walking and human-style bipedalism. All we can say, like Darwin before us, is that this missing link ape-man must have existed, but that he's still proving annoyingly elusive. (A possible candidate as a missing link, *Sahelanthropus tchadensis*, dates to around seven million years ago; but we only have a partial skull, so we can't be sure if it was bipedal, quadrupedal or somewhere in between.) But at least we can now put a more solid date on *when* our mysterious missing link ancestor split from the ancestors of the chimps; but that discovery has also been the cause of considerable scientific controversy.

Mitochondrial DNA (mtDNA) is part of the human genome. Because it mutates at a regular pace over the centuries, we can study mtDNA 'mutation markers' and compare the differences between population groups or even related species. This allows the reconstruction of early human development and migration.

For example, everyone shares mtDNA markers from the period of human history just before early modern humans left Africa to explore the rest of the world. But those groups that stayed behind, and those roving groups that travelled west and east after that first migration, have different *subsequent* mtDNA markers, because they were no longer interbreeding. So all you have to do is count the mtDNA mutation markers back from the present to the point where any differences vanish, then multiply by the right number of years. That will give you a rough date – to within a few millennia – of when that particular branching of humanity took place.

A comparison study of chimp and human mtDNA, made by Alan Wilson and Vincent Sarich in 1967, indicated that we only split off from our arboreal cousins between three million and five million years ago; not the nine million to thirty million years then estimated by the palaeontologists. Unsurprisingly, the report threw the paleontological community into a fury of denial and denunciation, but the mtDNA evidence could not be debunked.

Another human/chimp mtDNA study in 2005 – made by Sudhir Kumar and a team from Arizona State University – has closed the gap between the geneticists and the palaeontologists somewhat: they estimated that the splitting of human ancestors from chimp ancestors took place between seven million and five million years ago. This would just allow *Orrorin tugenensis* (and even *Sahelanthropus tchadensis*) to be a human ancestor – which the Wilson–Sarich study would not have done.

Of course all this may seem an academic point: Wilson and Sarich's genetic study conclusively proved that we are indeed descended from the same ape root-species as chimps and bonobos (although not gorillas and orangutans, whose ancestors branched off from the ape 'super family' – *Hominoidea* – several million years earlier). So what does it matter how we got from there to where we are now?

The answer is that what happened to our ancestors, after they branched away from the ancestors of chimps and bonobos, may explain much about our inherited psychological make-up: specifically, if we are natural born killers or something else entirely.

Chapter 2

'The Inheritance of Cain'

To understand how the evolution of the human body might have also affected our intellectual development – and our apparent instinct towards committing unnecessary violence – it is first necessary to consider just how weird our bodies are.

A key difference between humans and the other types of primate (and, indeed, every other creature on the planet) is our method of walking. We are fully bipedal, where apes and monkeys are knuckle-walking quadrupeds. But our method of bipedalism is *very* strange. If you want to see an efficiently evolved large biped, look at an ostrich or an emu: these creatures have a low centre of gravity that always remains directly above their legs, even when running at full tilt. Humans, on the other hand, have a painfully high centre of gravity and a heavy upper body that leans in the direction of travel.

This means that our centre of gravity is swung precariously forward when we move. The faster we go, the more we lean, and the less well-balanced we become – which is why running people often trip over. In fact, humans don't so much sprint, as dextrously manage a continuous controlled fall. Even when standing still we can easily be pushed off our feet, or at least made to stagger, because of our top-heavy build. It would take a blow from a battering ram to make an ostrich stagger.

Largely because of our odd construction, humans are also very slow runners compared with just about any mammal of comparable size. It is certainly true that we are among the best long-distance runners on the planet; but that wouldn't have helped much when trying to outrun a sprinting leopard or sabre-tooth cat, back when a swift escape was our ancestors' main means of defence. Then there is the fact that our practice of standing upright exposes the belly, throat and genital region to attackers – damage to any of which is likely to incapacitate or kill us immediately. No other surviving land animal has made this reckless evolutionary gamble: they, by walking with their bellies pointed towards the ground, largely shield them from attack.

Finally there is the grim truth that human bipedal movement has made childbirth insanely painful and dangerous. This is the reason why we are the only species of mammal that almost invariably screams when giving birth. The balancing of the entire torso above the human hips demanded that the pelvis re-evolve into a much more weight-bearing structure: quadrupedal apes' pelvises are very lightweight in comparison. This change greatly narrowed the pelvic outlet, through which the birth canal passes, and has condemned an appalling percentage of mothers and newborns to birth complications. Up to the age of modern medicine, the biggest killer of women was always childbirth.

In short, their inefficient way of walking should have doomed our ancestors to extinction in the early days of human development – long before their intelligence developed beyond anything more than the animal level. Yet they somehow survived and clambered their way to the top of the food chain (where lions, tigers and bears could no longer threaten our species' survival).

The man whose theory is now most widely believed to have explained how we got through the late Miocene extinction bottleneck was Raymond Arthur Dart; but he had to endure decades of ridicule from the scientific establishment before that same establishment accepted his ideas wholesale. Dart, born in 1893, was an Australian medical doctor with a special interest in anatomy. In his twenties he broke off from his medical training to serve as a medical officer during the First World War. It was then that he seems to have concluded that humans are inherently violent and aggressive – a war veteran's grim outlook that may well have coloured his later scientific thinking.

In 1922 Dart became the head of the Department of Anatomy

at the University of the Witwatersrand in South Africa. It was there, in 1924, that he was presented with the fossilised skull of an infantile extinct primate. The skull, about as big as a fist, had been dug out of the lime quarries at Taung in the savannah region in the north-west of South Africa, and was remarkably complete – including the braincase, face, lower jaw and teeth. Dart immediately saw that it was a tremendously important find. The brain was comparable in size to that of a young chimp, but the teeth were very small for an ape. And the angle of the skull's connection to the spine suggested that the 'Taung Child' had walked upright.

He named the creature *Australopithecus africanus*, and announced that it was the earliest known bipedal ape and therefore a likely ancestor of humankind. (*Australopithecus africanus* dates to around 3.3 million years ago. The 5.7 million-year-old *Orrorin tugenensis* (*see Chapter 1*) would not be discovered until the year 2000.)

This earth-shaking discovery was treated with, at best, indifference by the scientific establishment. Why? Well for a start Raymond Dart was not a paleoanthropologist (one trained in the study of the fossil remains of human and pre-human ancestors): he was just a medical doctor.

Secondly, the Taung Child's skull did not fit with the known evidence because it had human-like teeth and a relatively small brain. A skull found in 1912 in Piltdown, Sussex, was then considered the most likely candidate as the earliest known link between apes and humans: 'Piltdown Man' had also been bipedal, but had a human-sized brain and an ape-like jaw and teeth – the exact opposite of Dart's find.

And finally there was the fact that the *Australopithecus africanus* had been found in Africa: if it was indeed our ancestor, then that would mean we were all descended from Africans. It may now sound ridiculous, but in the 1920s – in the utterly white-skinned, Euro-centric realms of paleoanthropology – the thought that we were all descended from (probably) black ancestors was all but unthinkable. It was much more comfortable to believe that we had descended from Sussex ape-men (who probably had nice white skin).

Dart – shocked by the icy reception of his discovery – went back to teaching anatomy, probably vowing not to shove his head over the paleontological firing line again. Yet by the early 1940s other fossil examples of *Australopithecus* had been found, all vindicating Dart's original conclusions.

At the same time, the Piltdown skull (and the belief that humans had originated in England) was being regarded with increasing scepticism by paleoanthropologists. This was because no other examples of the species had ever come to light. (Nor could they: the 'Piltdown Man' was a crude hoax – a modern human cranium attached to an orangutan lower jaw. But it was not conclusively proved to be so until 1953, forty-one years after its discovery.)

So a Kuhnian paradigm revolution took place in paleoanthropology over the 1940s. Dart's *Australopithecus africanus* was accepted as a possible human ancestor and Africa as the probable birthplace of our branch of the primate family.

You may have noticed that there are a lot of 'probablys' and 'possiblys' here. The fact is that the science of early human evolution is based on very little physical evidence and a huge amount of educated speculation. The total number of early hominid fossils found (as opposed to the painted plaster copies generally seen by the public) could barely stock a small museum. In fact there seems only one thing in paleoanthropology that outweighs the mass of sheer guesswork necessary to link up our early family tree: that is the bitterness of the attacks that seem to be routinely levelled against every new discovery or theory by rivals from within the field.

Raymond Dart of course knew this only too well, but his next venture into paleoanthropology was to prove as contentious as his last. In 1953 Dart published a paper titled: 'The Predatory Transition from Ape to Man'. In it he observed that *Australopithecus* apes (and their still undiscovered 'missing link' ancestors, who Dart labelled 'proto-humans' for convenience) were highly unlikely to have lived on a vegetarian diet.

Modern apes are generally vegetarians (chimps are known to occasionally hunt and kill small animals for meat, but this nutrition source only makes up about 3 per cent of their diet). But apes live in fruit-abundant jungles and rainforests, so vegetarian-ism is, for them, the most efficient method of survival.

On the other hand our ancestors, in their food-scarce savannah habitat, would have been more likely to have been omnivores, like modern baboons. Certainly humans moved from vegetarianism to regular meat-eating at some point after split-ting from other apes – Dart was simply speculating that the savannah was a likely place to have demanded this change.

Furthermore, with too few trees on the savannah to hide in, our knuckle-walking ancestors would have needed to watch out for predators all the time. Long grasses would make this hard to do, so ape-men that could stand upright for longer periods would be more likely to survive to pass on their genes.

The resultant evolution towards full bipedalism would also have freed their arms and hands from knuckle-walking activity. Idle hands are evolution's plaything, so to speak; so our ancestors started to use sticks, rocks and bones as utensils – much as chimps occasionally do today. This development of tool-use would have, in turn, influenced their evolution towards greater intelligence, as well as evolving increasingly dexterous hands with better opposable thumbs. So out of a jungle ape template, savannah life formed proto-human beings.

None of this, in itself, was too contentious; but Dart took his ideas further. He suggested that the meat-eating ancestors of *Australopithecus* would have had to have been much more aggressive than any previous species of ape, simply to survive.

This is certainly true of baboons. Although not very closely related to us, baboons are similarly aggressive creatures with a more complex social structure than other types of primate. This is almost certainly because they evolved in a tougher environ-ment than their tree-living cousins.

So, Dart extrapolated, in learning to defend themselves from predators on the harsh savannah, proto-humans became preda-tors themselves. And, having their hands freed by becoming partly bipedal, Dart believed, proto-humans went the rest of the way to full human bipedalism because they needed to wield weapons more effectively.

Hunting and killing game would have also given our ancestors the bonus that regular meat-eating offers all carnivores: time. Vegetarian animals need to gather food and eat through most of their waking hours. On the other hand raw meat has a high energy-to-weight ratio and releases that energy more slowly than raw vegetables. This is why carnivores like lions and dogs can spend so much of their time napping. But a proto-human – with opposable thumbs, a developing intelligence and spare time on its hands – might have also used that digestion time to create simple social structures, basic communication and better tools.

Meat, Dart suggested, became an addiction that, in turn, fuelled proto-human evolution. And to get meat, our ancestors had to be killers – not just of other animals, but of other proto-humans. Ape-men, he thought, killed their own species to secure better hunting and living territory. Dart also suggested that, on killing other ape-men, our ancestors overcame the instinct against cannibalism that seems inherent in most mammals: proto-humans, he believed, were cannibalistic warriors.

This savage trait, Dart suggested, remains in modern humans as a genetic inheritance. We cover it with a veneer of civilisation and can generally suppress it (since modern life rarely calls on us to fight for our lives). But it remains there, just under the surface; and it explains all the brutality and monstrosity of which humankind is so ashamed. From domestic violence; through all the wars of history; to the gas chambers of Auschwitz – there, hovering in the background, is the shadow of the violent and cannibal proto-human.

Raymond Dart was not the first person to describe this bleak view of human instinct. Seventeen years earlier, in 1936, the ageing H. G. Wells had published a dark novella called *The Croquet Player*. The previously optimistic science-fiction writer could see that the world was tipping into a second world war, and he was beginning to lose his hope for humanity.

In the novella, a foppish young croquet player is told a disturbing story about a Norfolk village called Cainsmarsh. Everyone in the village is haunted by a constant but nebulous fear, and they react with unpredictable violence and madness. The 'haunting' is, in fact, a recurring ancestral memory of our brutal ape-man forebears. At the end of the story, the croquet player admits that he too has become infected with a horror of our murderous genetic inheritance – and that he finds a reflection of that heritage in every newspaper – but that he feels powerless to do anything about it.

The story was partly H. G. Wells's attempt to use allegory to warn against the calculated savagery that he saw being utilised by regimes like the Nazis (who had recently banned, then burned, his books). But Wells – like Dart – clearly believed that such brutality originally stemmed from our shared proto-human ancestry.

Both Wells and Dart illustrated this shared belief by reference to the same biblical character: Cain. In the Abrahamic religions, Cain was the first murderer and ancestor of all mankind. In *The Croquet Player*, one of the maddened inhabitants of Cainsmarsh screams that the haunting is 'The doom of Cain! [. . .] The punishment of Cain!'

This is a reference to the belief that all people are tainted with the first murder – that we all inherited Cain's propensity for killing. And, in his paper, Raymond Dart described the 'blood-bespattered, slaughter-gutted archives of human history from the earliest Egyptian and Sumerian records to the most recent atrocities of the Second World War' as indicating 'this mark of Cain' that all humans have inherited from our proto-human forebears.

Dart's 'Predatory Transition from Ape to Man' received a cold reception from most of the paleoanthropological community. Even the editor of the scientific journal that published his paper – *The International Anthropological and Linguistic Review* – washed his hands of it. In an attached disclaimer, he wrote: 'Of course [*Australopithecus africanus*] were only the ancestors of the modern Bushmen and Negroes, and of *nobody else*.' This was, in fact, the opposite of what Dart had argued in the paper: that we are all descended from the same violent proto-human ancestors.

The *Review* editor's attitude proved typical: a knee-jerk reaction that Dart's theory was simply too distasteful and horrid to be considered seriously. (Their attitude boiled down to: 'Dr Dart might be correct to suggest that the ancestors of black Africans were violent cannibals; but surely, my dear, that can't be true of the forebears of the sort of people who write for scientific journals . . .')

On a more scientific note, it was pointed out that Dart's thesis was based on little physical evidence (mostly the bone fragments of *Australopithecines*) and a lot of surmise. But, as we saw above, this is reasonable criticism of almost all paleoanthropology. Dart was simply describing the brutality he saw in modern humans, and was looking for its origin in the lives of our proto-human ancestors. As such, his theory carried as much weight as anything else in the uncertain world of paleoanthropology; but his scientific colleagues continued to treat him as a troublesome and eccentric outsider.

Yet, once again, Raymond Dart's views won out in the end – and in a very modern fashion: they got popularised. An American playwright and movie scriptwriter called Robert Ardrey had an interest in paleoanthropology, and came across Dart's paper in his hobby reading. He became so enthused with the idea that he expanded Dart's theory into a whole book: *African Genesis*, published in 1961. In it he gave Dart's supposition a catchy new name – 'killer ape theory' – and the book became an international bestseller.

Under Ardrey's influence – and the grim zeitgeist engendered by the Cold War – killer ape theory soon became widely accepted among non-scientists. The runaway success of Freudian psychoanalysis in the 1950s had taught people to believe that they all had a monstrous other self – an oedipal and irrational Mr Hyde figure – lurking in their subconscious minds. Killer ape theory gave them a plausible (and guilt-free) origin for that monster.

The idea that all humans shared a savage instinctual inheritance became a popular theme in the public imagination. Stanley Kubrick's 1968 cult movie *2001: A Space Odyssey* actually begins by depicting proto-humans surviving and flourishing through learning to utilise violence. Soon shades of killer ape theory were to be found in everything from comic books to political philosophy. (For example, the dominant Pentagon Cold War strategy called 'game theory' was partly based on the belief that all people are ultimately selfish and ruthless.)

Under this steady social pressure, non-believers in the paleo-anthropology community almost universally became converts to Dart's theory. And – although another classic case of a Kuhnian paradigm revolution – arguably this time it was a process that was even more unthinking than their previous rejection of the hypothesis.

One scientist who was utterly won over by the Dart/Ardrey killer ape theory was the English zoologist Desmond Morris. In his 1967 book *The Naked Ape*, Morris argued that a large proportion of modern human attitudes – and especially our sexual attitudes – stem from the hunter-gatherer evolution of our savannah ancestors.

For example, Morris suggested that a proto-human male needed to know which of the clan were his own children (carrying his genes) so that he could dedicate his energy towards protecting them, and not some other bloke's kids. So he pair-bonded with a single female and could therefore be sure that her children were also his own. But how to be sure that she was faithful to him while he was away hunting? Evolution provided the answer by causing ape-man fur to largely disappear. Skin-on-skin sex was therefore more pleasurable and proto-humans learned to be utterly affectionate to a single partner. Thus early humans became 'naked apes' and the emotion of exclusive love was evolved.

Although very popular with the general public, *The Naked Ape* did not overly impress evolutionary biologists. Morris's popularised explanation of evolution struck them as 'teleological' – that is, that it suggested that evolution was somehow 'goal-oriented'. Evolution isn't a targeted, intelligent development. It's a gradual refinement, filtered over multiple generations by the need to survive in a changing environment long enough to bear and raise children.

To deconstruct the above example: even if pair-bonding did improve a male's chance of immortalising his genes, what was in it for the female? (Or, for that matter, for the other males who hung around when Daddy went off hunting?) Surely, from the female's evolutionary point of view, the more males willing to protect her and her kids the better. Her interests would lie in increasing the ambiguity about fatherhood by mating with as many potential protectors as possible, not in exclusive pair-bonding with just one male. As an explanation for the development of the pair-bonding instinct, Morris's theory was rather incomplete.

The Naked Ape also failed to impress a Welsh TV scriptwriter called Elaine Morgan. In the book Morris depicts dominant male hunters, standing silent and upright to spot predators and prey. Women proto-humans were given a rather less heroic position: child-rearing and berry-gathering – with enlarged breasts, not to better feed children, but to remind males of buttocks and thus encourage mating. Morgan, a feminist, disliked this servile image of early femininity.

To give him his due, there is no reason to believe that Desmond Morris set out in his book to demean our mutual female ancestors. In *The Naked Ape* he was simply popularising the theory that almost all anthropologists then shared: that modern humans inherited much of our physical and psychological make-up from our savannah-bred ancestors and that the driving force of early human evolution was the violent male hunter, not the servile female gatherer.

Elaine Morgan fumed quietly. Then she set about shaking this self-congratulatory and complacent male theory to its foundations.

Chapter 3

Darwin on the Beach

The groundbreaking and controversial idea popularised by Elaine Morgan has got a bad name. Just saying 'aquatic ape theory' in public is enough to cause at least half your audience to snigger – the almost automatic thought of chimps wearing snorkels and rubber flippers is not a good start if you want to impress people with the seriousness of your scientific approach.

On a BBC radio programme on the subject (*Scars of Evolution*, 2005) the eminent paleoanthropologist Professor Phillip Tobias commented that: 'Regrettably the name is its own worst enemy, I believe. That's what makes people laugh. Let's just talk about water and human evolution.'

Of course, as we saw in the last chapter, Morgan's original motivation to enter the minefield of human evolutionary theory had nothing to do with water: she simply wanted to rebuff the apparently phallocentric views depicted in Desmond Morris's book *The Naked Ape*.

In the evolutionary scheme that Morris described, there seemed little reason for female proto-humans to have become bipeds. After all, the males did all the hunting and guarding, which demanded an upright posture; the designated activities of the females – berry-picking, mating and child-carrying – could have been done just as well by a knuckle-walker.

This again highlighted the question of just *why* proto-humans became bipeds. Mammal skeletal structure forms in the womb before the sexual characteristics, so both sexes will always be built largely the same way. But that does not explain why humans evolved so far towards full bipedalism, to the detriment of the female sex. Given the pain and danger that human bipedalism causes pregnant women one might suspect that, as an evolutionary driving force, safer childbirth might outweigh the need to hunt for meat as a dietary supplement.

Had the females also been hunting game, and thus also needed to utilise Dart's 'killer ape' posture? This seemed unlikely as female great apes, due to their long gestation period, tend to spend much of their lives either pregnant and/or child-rearing. (A female chimp, probably the closest modern creature to our proto-human female ancestor, gives birth on an average of once every five years and carries the pregnancy for nine months, but her children remain dependent for up to ten years after being born.) That's a bit of a hindrance to chasing down and beating to death the following prey animals, whose remains Raymond Dart had found in what he believed was an *Australopithecus* cave midden:

> ... *the grotesque and extinct tree-bear (or Chalicothere), the extinct horse (Hipparion), the extinct giraffe (Griquatherium), the elephant, the rhinoceros, hippopotamus, pigs and fourteen or more species of antelopes (eight of which appear to be extinct) from the largest like the kudu to the smallest like the duiker and gazelle, and even carnivores like the lion, hyenas (two species), hunting dog and jackal.*

So, whatever it was that caused proto-humans to evolve into bipeds, it seemed unlikely to Morgan that it was simply hunting and weapon use. Then, re-reading *The Naked Ape*, she found reference to a hypothesis for which Desmond Morris had (very unfortunately) coined the name 'aquatic ape theory'.

The basic proposition went like this: some time after our ape forebears split from the ancestors of bonobos and chimpanzees – but before they became hairless, big-brained bipeds – they went to live on the beach. Regular contact with water, over possibly millions of years, caused evolutionary changes that made them markedly different from their forest-dwelling kin.

Most notably, the buoyant body-support of standing and swimming in water encouraged evolution into a long-legged biped. Then, as the environmental demands changed, they left the beach and went back to living a fully land-based life. But the evolutionary mutations that had started to turn them into aquatic mammals came with them, and have marked us ever since.

Morris himself seemed fairly enthusiastic about this explanation of early human evolution. But he also noted that it was not considered seriously by paleoanthropologists, so he only gave it three paragraphs (*The Naked Ape*, pp. 39–40) and failed to mention who had originally devised the idea.

Intrigued, Elaine Morgan wrote to Desmond Morris to ask for more details about aquatic ape theory. He replied, pointing her to an article in the March 1960 issue of the *New Scientist Magazine*. Although written by one of the world's leading experts on marine biology, Professor Sir Alister Clavering Hardy, it had barely caused a ripple in the scientific community; and since then it had been totally ignored, until briefly noted by Morris.

This lack of reaction by evolutionary biologists to Hardy's theory was odd in itself, since what he suggested was both revolutionary and gave reasonable explanations for some elements of human development that had always baffled anatomists. For example, it is an unfortunate fact that humans are easy to skin. Almost every culture that has invented knives has also, at some point, used flaying alive as a punishment or torture. This is not simply sadism, but practicality: human skin is quite easy to remove, even if the subject is still alive. The reason is our abundance of subcutaneous fat.

In 1930, Hardy had read a book on anatomy by the naturalist Frederic Wood Jones. Wood Jones noted that when removing a human cadaver's epidermis, the thick subcutaneous fat layer always came away with the skin. In all other animals that he had seen skinned, the fat stayed with the muscle and the skin came away clean.

Alister Hardy had just returned from an expedition to the Antarctic, in which it was his job, as expedition zoologist, to study South Atlantic whales. The main way he had done this was to cut up dead whales, and he instantly saw the answer to Wood Jones's mystery about human skin: the blubber on sea animals, like whales and seals, also comes away with the skin; thus human subcutaneous fat had probably evolved in the same way as blubber, not land-animal fat.

Looking into the question more closely, Hardy realised that there was more evidence that pointed to early humans having gone through a semi-aquatic phase. For a start, we are very prone to getting overweight compared with other primates. Human babies are born swaddled in fat, while chimp and gorilla babies are born with virtually no fat at all. And for the rest of our lives we are inclined to building up excessive fat reserves in our bodies – feed an orangutan as much as you like but, unlike a human, it will never get so overweight that it needs a mobility scooter to get about. For land mammals, too much fat is as risky as having unnecessary limbs – it just gets in the way – but aquatic mammals absolutely need layers of fat to keep warm and buoyant.

As a marine biologist, Hardy also thought he saw why we lost our fur and became 'naked apes'. Followers of killer ape theory said that it was because hunting under the savannah sun made fur too hot. But no other large savannah predators are bald. Hardy knew that for the smaller semi-aquatic mammals, like otters and beavers, oily fur is a sufficient insulator and demands less food to maintain than subcutaneous fat reserves. But for larger mammals, like seals and hippos, fat reserves are a more efficient way to keep a broad surface area warm. Only one insulating system would have been necessary, so our ancestors lost the less efficient fur.

Then there is the direction that our hair follicles point on our backs. Human back hair – such of it that remains to us – points in the opposite direction of that of all other primates. It does, however, point the same way that you find it on semi-aquatic creatures like beavers and sea-otters. It seemed to Hardy that our fur, before we lost most of it, had been evolving towards maximum aqua-dynamic efficiency.

Finally, he noted that human hands are much more sensitive

that those of other primates: we have thinner skin and a greater abundance of nerve-endings in our extremities. This, he thought, might be because our ancestors had needed to find food by touch alone, in muddy river beds or sandy sea shallows.

Hardy became totally convinced that proto-humans had spent a long period evolving into aquatic animals – just as otters have partially; seals more thoroughly; and whales and dolphins have completely. But he didn't publish his theory. He knew that it was 'poaching' into a scientific field – human evolution – in which he had no specific training; and he could wreck his academic career if he tried to publish such an outlandish idea outside his officially designated area of expertise.

By 1960, however, Alister Hardy was considered one of the most eminent men in British science – a knight and a Fellow of the Royal Society. So he risked mentioning his theory during a talk that he gave to the British Sub-Aqua Club. A journalist was there and splashed the bizarre-sounding idea over the next day's front page. With the cat out of the scientific bag, Hardy published his theory in the next issue of *New Scientist*, but the result was what he had feared for decades. If he had not been so well respected, Sir Alister might have been directly attacked for such a breach of scientific etiquette. As it was, his fellow scientists acted as if he had gone temporarily insane and refused to give his theory any serious debate.

Almost a decade later, Hardy was contacted by a very enthusiastic Elaine Morgan, who wanted to write a book on human evolution based around his theory. After some initial uncertainty he agreed and the result was *The Descent of Woman*, published in 1972, and provocatively titled as a parody on Darwin's *The Descent of Man*.

Morgan had expanded on Hardy's original hypothesis. But she had also maintained her own essential aim of countering what she saw as the scientific establishment's male-centric view of early human evolution. For example, the reason that women usually have softer-feeling skin than men is that they typically have more subcutaneous fat. Morgan saw this as an indication that female proto-humans might have spent more time in the water than the males. Why? Because water is an ideal defence against most land-based predators, few or none of which could have out-swum a proto-human, then successfully managed to attack them. Such a passive defence – sitting or standing in the relatively warm African shallows – would have been very attractive to pregnant or nursing mothers, just as sitting high in a tree is for forest apes. The more active (less baby-burdened) male proto-humans might have spent less time hiding in the water, because that allowed them more time to hunt or scavenge the shoreline. Thus they had less need for subcutaneous fat.

And, from the point of view of our study of human violence, this might also explain why men are typically more brutal than women. A beach-scavenging male would have a greater natural inclination towards aggressive defence. A water-protected female would incline to passive defence.

Hardy had noted that the one place where we didn't lose our fur – but indeed seem to have grown it much longer than for a typical primate – is on the crown of our heads. This, he believed, was to protect against sunburn; a creature in the water has little opportunity to find shade. Elaine Morgan disagreed with him on this last item. She pointed out that sunburn isn't a big problem for semi-aquatic creatures, who can cool their skin as often as they need to. She felt that long head hair had served another purpose: as a handhold for babies and young children.

Primate children typically hang on to their mother's torso fur when her hands are busy elsewhere, but what if that fur was underwater for much of the day? Long head hair would be a safe place to hang on, without overly inconveniencing the parent. And since mothers do most of the tending to nursing infants, it might be expected that female head hair would evolve to be thicker and longer than that found in males – something that we indeed find in humans. In fact it is worth noting that pregnant mothers' hair tends to grow longer, thicker and (in the case of curly-headed mothers) straighter in the months before the birth of their baby.

And, on the subject of birth, there is the odd fact that human babies are born with traits that help them to survive immersion in water. Water-birthing (a mother giving birth in a shoulder-deep pool or bath) is growing increasingly popular in developed countries. (Two of my own children were born this way.) Many mothers find the water buoyancy reduces the contraction pains, and the baby is in little danger of drowning: it will automatically hold back on trying to take its first breath until it is lifted and its head breaks the water surface (a survival trait also seen in newborn sea mammals, like dolphins).

The extra fat a baby puts on in the month before birth makes it naturally buoyant and helps to insulate it in water; as does the waxy skin covering, called *vernix caseosa*, that many babies are born slathered in. The reason for the existence of vernix has long been uncertain: no other land animal is born with this coating and it serves no obvious purpose. But vernix certainly resembles the goose grease that long-distance swimmers cover themselves with as a lightweight insulator. Then, in 2005, it was found that several species of seal – most notably harbour seals – are born covered in the same substance. It would seem that vernix is another aquatic trait that has found its way into the human genome.

(The definition of a successful scientific theory is one that can make accurate predictions about, as yet, unverified data. In this case, if human vernix was indeed an adaptation to a semi-aquatic life, then one could predict that other semi-aquatic mammals might also have that adaptation. Harbour seal vernix does not win the argument for aquatic ape theory; but it certainly strengthens its position.)

Apes sink like rocks if they fall into water because they have so little body fat, and they start drowning at once because they can't hold their breath. (Apes tend to fear water so much that they are often confined in zoos by simply surrounding them with a shallow moat.) But a human baby will automatically close its larynx – holding its breath – and will float, making swimming motions if it falls into deep water, allowing a few vital moments for rescue by an adult. This affinity with water continues past the neonate stage for our offspring – indefinitely if they are given regular supervised contact with deep water. In fact, swimming could be said to be a skill that most of us lose by lack of water exercise as babies, and then reacquire later in life.

The evolution of human hands and feet also suggests an aquatic history. Flat and paddle-like, there are no exact equivalents to their structure among any other land animals. But look at the bone-structure within the flippers of whales, seals and dolphins, and you can immediately see a similarity. It can be said with some confidence that – at an earlier stage of their evolution from land to water – these creatures must have had part-evolved flippers much like our extremities. And on the human side, it is a relatively common malformation for babies to be born with webbed fingers and/or toes: is this just a deformity, or a throwback to an earlier genetic blueprint?

The term 'killer ape theory' has recently fallen out of fashion; now replaced with the more scientific-sounding 'savannah theory'. But, in essence, it remains the same hypothesis postulated by Raymond Dart and popularised by Robert Ardrey. It also remains the 'established' explanation for early human evolution.

Sir Alister Hardy died in 1985, having never found the necessary courage to publish his own theory in a full academic work. But Elaine Morgan has soldiered on over the decades, publishing half a dozen books on the aquatic ape theory – each more academically targeted than the last – and she has met with almost universal derision and contempt from evolutionary biologists and paleoanthropologists. Aquatic ape theory has remained on the fringes of the evolutionary debate, not because its theories have been disproved, but because the scientific establishment has consistently refused – for almost half a century – to investigate it objectively. It is simply dismissed as 'unscientific', 'crackpot' and 'populist'.

It is depressing to see that the vehement critics of aquatic ape theory don't seem to understand how they appear to anyone outside their enclosed fields of academically sanctified specialisation. They sound pompous, vindictive, territorial, self-serving and, worst of all, unscientific – especially since they pointedly refuse to hold up savannah theory to the same level of criticism.

Detractors of aquatic ape theory cite a lack of fossil evidence, not taking into account the fact that shore animals very rarely get fossilised because of the caustic and shifting nature of the environment. And for that matter, thanks to the 'Miocene fossil gap' (*see Chapter 1*), there is no conclusive fossil evidence to support the belief in killer ape/savannah theory either. In fact, a proto-human evolutionary period on the fossil-destroying shoreline might actually explain the Miocene fossil gap.

Aquatic ape theory has been said to rely too heavily on supposition, ignoring the fact that the savannah theory is heavily based on the suppositions of Raymond Dart (for which he was heartily criticised, before his theory became evolutionary gospel). Savannah theory is just as reliant on wishful thinking as aquatic ape theory – how could it not be, with both ideas based precariously on the same sparse fossil evidence. But on several unanswered evolutionary questions the establishment theory falls down, where aquatic ape theory offers plausible explanations for the same anomalies.

We saw in the last chapter just how bizarre and ungainly human bipedalism is when seen in terms of evolutionary survival. The savannah explanation – that proto-humans evolved this method of movement as the most efficient way to run and use weapons simultaneously – is undermined by two facts. First, that human bipedalism is fairly *in*efficient, for all the reasons given in Chapter 2, and as indicated by the fact that no other species in known zoological history has ever utilised it.

Second, the first proto-humans don't seem to have been using tools or weapons: the earliest basic tools discovered (to date) are from around 3.4 million years ago – at least 2.3 million years *after* we became bipedal (if we accept the upright ape, *Orrorin tugenensis*, as our ancestor). If we can't be certain that tools were part of the proto-human environment, we can't insist that tool use influenced proto-human evolution.

The aquatic ape explanation of human bipedalism is that it is the evolutionary result of defensively swimming, walking, standing and sitting in shallows, utilising the buoyant water to support much of the body's weight. And that it has survived to the present day, after we again became land animals, only as a fluke. This idea is partially supported by the fact that other primates are also known to walk upright in water for protracted periods. Gorillas and chimps, although usually terrified of water, have been known to overcome their fear and have been seen to play – sitting or standing upright – in shallow water for hours. And the proboscis monkey of Borneo (*Nasalis larvatus*) is a positively ardent swimmer and also wades bipedally in water for long periods.

In passing, it should also be noted that humans and proboscis monkeys share another apparent water adaptation: big noses. Most primates hate swimming because their shallow, upturned nostrils allow water straight into their sinus cavities. Humans and proboscis monkeys have noses that trap air in a natural airlock, and thus can partly resist incursion by water.

Then there is the matter of human breath-control. We can hold our breath as a conscious act – something that is vital for both diving and the controlled release of breath that allows us to talk. No other land animal can do this – they breathe totally automatically and so start to drown immediately when their heads sink in water. Sea mammals on the other hand – like dolphins and whales – breathe entirely through conscious effort (so much so that even when they sleep, alternating halves of their brains remain awake to ensure their regular surfacing for air). Humans are like semi-aquatic animals, in that we can voluntarily hold our breath when we want to, but can also drop into automatic breathing when there is no need for breath control.

A harbour seal can hold its breath underwater for up to thirty minutes, and a sperm whale for forty-five minutes. The average human can only manage between one and two minutes, and even the world's best free-diver can manage only eleven and a half minutes; but that's not bad for a species that, as a land mammal, has no more evolutionary need for extended breath control than a cat or a chicken.

Savannah theory explains away breath control as a side-effect of our learning to communicate with complex sounds – but this seems to be putting the cart before the horse. Complex sounds are a result of breath control, so how did we start to develop them before we could control our breathing? And, again, why are we the only land animal to have evolved this trick?

But perhaps the most remarkable support for aquatic ape theory comes from our medical knowledge of the brain. To grow a normal, fully functional brain, human babies and children need regular doses of omega-3 fatty acids and of iodine – as do pregnant mothers for the foetus. It seems likely that, at some point in our proto-human past, we were getting a lot of these dietary elements. And having become physiologically dependent on them, we need them still.

Before the invention of modern transport, preservatives or refrigerated storage, such food sources were vanishingly rare in inland areas. In fact, populations raised in inland regions have traditionally suffered a high incidence of the brain development dysfunction called 'cretinism' – a condition caused by iodine deficiency. But cultures on sea shores suffered almost no cretinism, because all seafood has a high iodine content. Plus fish meat has a good concentration of omega-3 fatty acids, making it literally a 'brain food'. On the beach, where food like seaweed and shellfish are always lying around, collecting a healthy diet would have been a less risky process for our ancestors than on the harsh savannah plains.

(It may also be noted that the other species that have a high brain-to-body-size ratio – porpoises and dolphins – also have a high iodine and omega-3 intake though their diet.)

Adherents to the savannah theory suggest that the elements necessary to fuel infant brain growth in proto-humans must have come from eating the brains and bone marrow of prey animals – including those of other early humans. But if this is so, then why have no other carnivores developed big brains? In fact, even scavenger carnivores – such as jackals, wolves and hyenas – which eat a lot of brain tissue and bone marrow, still have a low brain-to-body-size ratio.

Today even some senior paleoanthropologists have questioned whether our proto-human ancestors were savannah creatures at all. Professor Phillip Vallentine Tobias was a distinguished paleoanthropologist who had worked under Raymond Dart himself (and who was also instrumental in finally exposing the 'Piltdown Man' skull as a hoax). In 1995 Tobias revealed that digs at various south and east African *Australopithecus* sites had shown that, far from being a savannah when inhabited by Australopithecines, these had uniformly been forested areas. Dart had assumed that these areas had always been savannah, because they had been savannah throughout recorded human history, but he had no access to the modern archaeological techniques that can detect and analyse tiny plant and seed fossils.

With the evidence of both tool use and a savannah environment under question, the savannah/killer ape explanation of human physical evolution now looks a bit anaemic. In fact, Professor Tobias's exact words, at a London conference in 1995, were: 'The savannah hypothesis is no more. Open that window and throw it out!'

Having read the above history, objective readers can postulate a different sequence of events, and then ask themselves a question. Imagine if the situation had been reversed: if Hardy's aquatic ape theory had been presented and accepted *first* and then later followed by Dart's killer ape theory. Would the consensus in evolutionary biology then have thrown out the aquatic ape theory for the killer ape theory?

The answer – given their track record on dealing with new ideas – is that the same paleoanthropologists and evolutionary biologists would be just as vehement in their defending of aquatic ape theory as they are now in defending the killer ape/savannah theory. Although 'getting your shot in first' should not be a decisive factor in scientific analysis, it clearly carries a lot of weight where there is little physical evidence to tether the debaters to specific facts.

When all the heat and fury is removed from the debate, it seems most likely that *both* sides contain elements of the truth – just as proved true in the land bridge versus continental drift dispute (*see Chapter 1*). Our proto-human forebears almost certainly did spend a lengthy period on the beach, evolving towards an aquatic life. The evidence for this is clearly imprinted in the odd evolution of our bodies. But we also know that this phase didn't last (because we aren't now living underwater and frolicking with the dolphins). Having returned to dry land, our ancestors' upright posture, increasingly efficient brains and dextrous hands made them very dangerous predators – evidence for which we will see in the next chapter. This predatory edge started us towards the position of dominance that our species holds in the world today.

And as with our bodies, so with our minds . . .

The aquatic ape was essentially a defensive creature – using the shallow water as a means of escape and protection. But we didn't stop there. Back on land we became Dart's killer ape, and it is perfectly possible that he was right to say that we carry the spectre of that aggression in our mental make-up to this day.

Chapter 4

Killing Cousins

The novelist George MacDonald Fraser noted sardonically that 'there's nothing like ignorance to fuel argument', which is probably why the field of proto-human evolution is such a hotbed of furious debate. We are certain about a few key facts, but the rest of our 'knowledge' is really just creative guesswork surrounded by a mire of uncertainty.

To illustrate the problem, imagine trying to depict the USA to someone who doesn't share a language with you and who knows nothing about the place. And imagine that all you have to help you is a handful of photos from an old road trip: say, one photo of New York, several of the Rocky Mountains, one of the Grand Canyon and one of Disneyland. They might reasonably conclude that the USA is highly urbanised where it isn't almost insanely mountainous and is at least partly peopled by worshipers of some sort of mouse god. Those conclusions contain some elements of the truth, but what is missed out of the overall picture makes them all but useless.

That's where we stand when it comes to understanding pre-human evolution. The incomplete fossil hominids that we have found so far are just too scattered across millions of years of otherwise darkened history. So, argue and rearrange the fossils as much as you like, they simply can't give a reliably consistent picture of early human evolution. We can make educated guesses, but it's almost certain that our guesses are wide of the mark almost as often as they are correct.

We don't even know for sure if any of the early bipedal

hominid fossils that we have found, to date, are from species that
are actually our direct ancestral forebears. We are the sole biped
primate species on the planet *now*, but several million years ago
it is likely, even probable, that there were a number of them in
Africa. Some of the fossilised creatures we've found are probably
our direct forebears, but others are likely to be only distantly
related: parallel side-branches of the proto-human family line, or
cousin species.

(I will use the term 'cousin species' a lot in this chapter. By it,
I mean a pair of species that are superficially different, but
might still be genetically close enough to interbreed and
produce offspring. Some contemporary examples are lions and
tigers, dogs and wolves, horses and donkeys, and sheep and
goats: all can and have produced hybrid children. Humans and
chimps, despite their closeness on a genetic level, are not
cousin species, because no amount of interbreeding could
produce a hybrid offspring.)

For example, *Paranthropus boisei* was a gorilla-like biped
hominid which died out around 1.2 million years ago. Once
classed as a breed of *Australopithecus africanus*, it is now generally thought to be a separate branch of our ancestral tree that
became extinct about the same time that our direct ancestors –
Homo habilis – came into competition with it.

Since million-year-old fossils can't provide DNA, all we have
to go on is whether a discovered biped ape *looks* like it might be
in our ancestral line. It's rather like going through an unlabelled
nineteenth-century family photo album, trying to guess who
your direct relatives were by judging if their faces look a bit like
your own.

So here then is a sketch of what we can say with reasonable
certainty about pre and early human development – including
any attached evidence of violent inclinations . . .

We know, thanks to studies of our mitochondrial DNA, that
we split from the ancestors of chimps and bonobos about five
million to seven million years ago. We know that at some point
after this split – although whether it was thousands or millions of
years, we still can't be sure – our forebears had become partly

carnivorous and probably more aggressive than other great apes. We also know that within a relatively short time, in evolutionary terms, our ancestors evolved to their environment in such a way as to be physically very different to our nearest ape cousins, while remaining genetically almost identical to them.

(One of the great shocks of twentieth-century science was the discovery that our DNA is at least 95 per cent identical to that of chimpanzees and bonobos. In fact, a controversial study by Detroit's Wayne State University School of Medicine in 2002 found our DNA to be a staggering 99.4 per cent the same as that of chimps; the researchers suggested, in the light of their findings, that the chimp should be re-categorised as a branch of the human family, with their species' name changing from *Pan troglodytes* to *Homo troglodytes*.)

We further know that one of the first of the physical changes from ape to early proto-human was the development of human-style bipedalism – with all the disadvantages and, as we will see, a few key advantages that it provided. This cannot have happened later than 5.7 million years ago, as proved by the existence of the bipedal *Orrorin tugenensis*. This period – ranging in length somewhere between 700,000 and 1.3 million years – was presumably when we went through the aquatic ape stage of our evolution. We also believe that bipedal apes existed for millions of years before they started to use tools, and that it took even longer for brains much bigger than a chimp's to grow in any proto-human's skull.

By four million years ago we find the earliest known examples of Raymond Dart's *Australopithecus africanus*. These creatures were highly successful, and spread across Africa for over two million years before being superseded. They had roughly chimp-sized brains and bodies, but walked upright. Ironically, given that *Australopithecus africanus* was the basis of Dart's killer ape theory (*see Chapter 2*), studies of their fossil teeth indicate that they probably lived mainly on fruit, nuts and seeds. Recent discoveries, however, suggest that they were at least occasionally eating meat.

Animal bone fossils found in Dikika, Ethiopia, dating to

around 3.4 million years ago, indicate evidence of butchery. Someone – it is presumed the local Australopithecines – had been using rocks to smash open the bones to get at the marrow inside. But whether they were hunting living animals or just scavenging dead carcasses is, as yet, unproven.

We've yet to find *Australopithecus africanus* fossils that are from later than two million years ago. It is open to question as to whether they were eradicated by a cousin species – *Homo habilis* – or if *Australopithecus africanus* simply evolved to become this new branch of the genus.

Homo habilis – the earliest example found, to date, hailing from around 2.2 million years ago – was typically smaller in body than the Australopithecines. But unlike earlier hominids they *made* tools rather than just picking up convenient sticks or rocks. (*Homo habilis* is Latin for 'handy man'.) Evidence of rock flaking (or 'knapping') has been found at various *Homo habilis* sites, indicating that they were making basic hand axes. Whether these hand axes helped them to kill off competing hominid species, like *Australopithecus africanus* or *Paranthropus boisei*, remains a matter of debate.

We dubbed this species with the genus name 'Homo' – the same as our own subspecies, *Homo sapiens sapiens* – thus nominating them as the first creature that was more human than ape. This was because *Homo habilis* had a bigger brain than any known anthropoid.

Ask most people what differentiates us from other animals, and they will usually say our big brains. This is somewhat based on a misconception, as brain-size is not necessarily an indication of brain efficiency. An elephant has a brain almost four times larger than that of a human, for example, but it isn't noticeably more intelligent than a dog, or even a rat. (You can argue about 'different types of intelligence' until you are blue in the face; but the deciding factor, as far as genetics is concerned, is how well a species' use of intelligence has aided its survival and spread into different environments: on that score, a rat beats an elephant every time.)

Brain efficiency is largely governed by the potential

complexity of the neural pathways. However, brain size *is* an indicator of intelligence, if taken into account with the relative size of the body that houses it. Humans have a big brain in relation to our body size – 2 per cent of our overall body weight. A blue whale, on the other hand, has a brain almost five times bigger than that of a human, but that's only 0.007 per cent of its overall weight. And (at the risk of sounding tactless) *who* hunted *who* to the point of extinction? (Our friend the rat, by the way, has a brain that is 0.5 per cent of its body weight. An elephant's brain averages at 0.1 per cent of its body weight.)

An outsized brain is an expensive luxury – which is why so few species have successfully used it as an evolutionary gambit. For we humans, that 2 per cent of our bodyweight devours 20 per cent of our energy reserves. The extra food gathering that this demanded was, for most of human history, a life-or-death problem for a species that also had to worry about becoming dinner for less brainy, but more brawny animals.

The way that our ancestors seem to have overcome the diner-not-dinner problem was to become Raymond Dart's killer apes – with meat becoming a key part of our diet. Bigger brains allowed more complex defensive and hunting strategies and, probably, the beginnings of language. At the same time their bipedal posture gave them more hunting and combat tools than any other primate has ever had available to them. Because, for all the numerous failings of human bipedalism (*see Chapter 2*) it has several advantages that our forebears' growing brain-capacity must have used to great advantage.

First there is the fact that it allows us to run continuously for hours or, at peak fitness, even for days at a time. Against this a quadruped's running endurance is greatly limited by its front legs. This is because its lungs are compressed every time one of its forefeet hits the ground, so a four-legged animal has to time its breathing to match its running pace. The faster it runs, the faster it has to breathe, so that its legs and lungs don't get out of synchronisation. A sprinting quadruped automatically breathes fast and shallowly. It can't get enough oxygen to its brain and muscles, so it quickly gets out of breath and has to slow to a walk.

The proto-human biped had no such problem. It could take slow, deep breaths when running, aided by the conscious breath control it had acquired as an aquatic ape. It could thus maintain a mercilessly continuous pace up to the point of muscular exhaustion – not running very fast, compared to most big quadrupeds, but much *further* than any animal they happened to be chasing. As Aesop noted: 'slow and steady wins the race'; as long as the prey was in sight or could be tracked, our ancestors could literally run it to death.

Of course, it would have helped if the prey was already wounded, and that's where proto-human hand-eye coordination came into play. Although other primates are very accurate at throwing (shockingly so, as many people who have visited the monkey enclosure at a zoo can testify) they don't seem to have ever used it as anything other than a defensive tactic. Early humans developed throwing as a form of attack. Our tall upright posture, bifocal vision, free-swinging arms and dextrous hands made for a lethal combination, either with stones or, much later, with spears and arrows. Humans are the only mammals to have mastered killing at range.

Hunting in cooperative groups, or packs, was another evolutionary leap forward for the early meat-eating hominids. In fact very few land mammals actually do this. Wolves and their relatives, wild dogs, hunt in packs; as do female lions and their distant cousins, the hyenas. Wild chimps and bonobos also hunt cooperatively but, as meat is only 3 per cent or less of their typical diet, they do this quite rarely. We can be sure, however, that our ancestors acted cooperatively when scavenging for the kills of other predators, or when hunting for themselves, because *we* inherited the habit from somewhere down the line.

Cooperative hunting of meat had another interesting effect on our ancestors: they learned to share their food. Some species of social herbivores also hunt cooperatively – spotting and communicating where good feeding grounds like ripe fruit trees are to be found. But they don't share the food once they've got it – after all, there is usually plenty of food back on the tree, so 'go get your own' is a natural enough response to someone filching from your collection. A pack of hunting carnivores, on the other hand, will usually only have one kill to share – so everyone has to get a bite. Certainly there will be a dominance hierarchy that rules who gets to eat when, but this sharing of food – from the strongest in the pack to the weakest – creates a social cohesion and bonding that is not found in most other large mammals.

So if *Homo habilis* were hunting, rather than just scavenging for scraps of meat, then they had potential killing techniques to make a success of the endeavour, and probably a nascent eusocial (that is, socially complex) pack society. Unfortunately our knowledge of *Homo habilis* – arguably the first true human to appear on the planet – is minimal to say the least. They seem to have survived in Africa up to about 1.4 million years ago, but the wide variation found in their few surviving fossils has caused a lot of controversy.

Some leading paleoanthropologists are even cautious about accepting *Homo habilis* as a distinct subgenus at all. They have been called a 'wastebasket' species; optimistically reconstructed from partial fossils that don't fit any pattern and that could, in fact, be totally unrelated to each other. (To illustrate the problem, imagine a far-future paleoanthropologist finding a few incomplete human, gorilla and chimp fossils, and trying to reconstruct a single creature out of them.)

Fortunately, the next (generally accepted) rung of human evolution is much better documented in the fossil record. The first *Homo erectus* found, to date, is from eastern central Africa and is around 1.8 million years old. The last known example was from around 143,000 years ago (just yesterday, by evolutionary standards).

They were prolific explorers – *Homo erectus* fossils have been found in Kenya, Spain, Georgia (in Eastern Europe, not the American state) Indonesia, Vietnam and China. And there has been evidence discovered of their flint tool-making in Suffolk in England, dating to 700,000 years ago. (This is ironic since Suffolk was the county chosen by an unknown hoaxer to plant the fake 'Piltdown Man' skull (*see Chapter 2*) that misled paleoanthropologists for decades.)

Erectus was clever: despite having a relatively unimpressive brain by our standards, they seem to have mastered both the use of fire, and better tool-making than anything seen on the planet to that time. They were also hefty; growing up to 6 ft tall, with bones that indicate a more muscular physique than modern humans. Alan Walker, one of the leading experts on *Homo erectus* fossils, has described the species as 'the velociraptor of its day'.

Circumstantial evidence of their ferocity can be found in their successful spread across the globe. *Homo erectus* must have encountered some of the most terrifying carnivores in human history – everything from sabre-toothed cats and pony-sized dire wolves to giant cave bears – yet they could not be stopped. And keep in mind that, apart from the orangutan, no other known great ape species has managed to even get out of Africa.

So was *Homo erectus* Raymond Dart's brutal and cannibalistic 'killer ape'? Evidence found in caves in Gran Dolina in northern Spain indicates so. Amid butchered animal bones found in the cave, archaeologists discovered the bones of children. The human bones had been split to get at the marrow and the skulls had been shattered to allow the brains to be eaten. The human bones were found to range in age from 300,000 to 780,000 years ago; this indicated that the cannibalism was not an act of desperation, caused by a season of starvation, but was a relatively regular practice by the *Homo erectus* of the Gran Dolina caves. And the fact that the human bones were thrown away with the trash of other dead animals indicates that there was probably no cultural significance to the killings: the victims were just food to their murderers.

Against this evidence of ancestral savagery, we need to consider another aspect of behaviour that *Homo erectus* may have introduced to the planet: human empathy, otherwise known as altruism. (Seen in scientific terms, altruism strictly means more than just empathising with and helping others. To be altruistic a creature must help another at some immediate cost to their own interests. Giving away food that you don't need is charitable, but it is not altruistic. Giving away food when you yourself are hungry and short of food *is* altruistic.)

In 1973 an expedition led by Richard Leakey (arguably the greatest name in twentieth-century paleoanthropology) surveyed the area around Lake Turkana in north-west Kenya. Leakey's team found a remarkably complete *Homo erectus* skeleton of a boy of about ten years old who had died 1.54 million years ago.

The completeness of the remains allowed for a remarkable discovery. The boy's skull had space for a Broca's area – a part of the frontal lobe of the brain that, in modern humans, is associated with our speech functions. This brain feature is not found in apes, nor is it seen in any known proto-human previous to *Homo erectus*. Although it is a supposition not accepted by all paleoanthropologists, this could be an indication that *Homo erectus* could talk.

Near to the Turkana boy the Leakey team found parts of an older *Homo erectus* skeleton: a woman who had died around 1.7 million years ago. She had evidently suffered – her bones were covered in growths, indicating that she had probably died while afflicted with a condition called 'hypervitaminosis A'. This is a form of poisoning that causes long-term nausea, vomiting, dizziness, blurred vision, clumsiness and malforming bone growths.

Interestingly, the probable cause of the Turkana woman's agony was successful hunting. Hypervitaminosis A is caused by the liver being asked to process too much vitamin A. The most likely source of such a massive overdose of the vitamin would have been though eating the liver of a big carnivore. (The condition first came to the attention of western medicine in 1597, when a group of Dutch explorers made the mistake of eating a polar bear's liver.) She may have found the liver while scavenging a corpse, but since the guts are usually the first thing to be eaten from a dead animal in the wild, it is more likely that she and her fellows hunted and killed a large and dangerous meat-eater.

However, what is more striking – and heart-warming – is the fact that, to live long enough to have developed this extent of bone growth, the Turkana woman must have been cared for. She would have been in no fit state to look after herself in the wilds of primordial Africa, so someone else must have protected and probably fed, watered and possibly even carried her.

This fact might seem insignificant; but remember that we are talking about *Homo erectus*, a creature that was probably much closer to a wild animal than to a modern human. For such a creature, or group of creatures, to show genuine altruism is remarkable to say the least.

Animals – for all our sentimental anthropomorphism over them – are not caring creatures; they can't afford to be. For non-humans, life is largely governed by what some scientists have dubbed the 'Red Queen effect'. The name is taken from the novel *Through the Looking Glass*, where the Red Queen tells Alice that sometimes 'it takes all the running you can do, to keep in the same place'.

Wild creatures must spend almost all their energies on survival and procreation. Under the whip of evolutionary competition, animal species must 'run' – that is, maintain themselves at maximum efficiency – just to hold on to their position in the pecking order of nature. Predators and evolutionary rivals have no mercy for laggards. Slow down just a little – by becoming instinctually complacent or wasting efforts on non-essential activities – and they can fall into extinction: butchered like the dodo and the Carolina parakeet; or pushed out of the good living areas by a rival species to die off slowly, as almost happened to the European red squirrel over the past hundred years. Then some more pushy and energetic species below or beside them on the food chain will take their place. This is really what is meant by the phrase 'survival of the fittest'.

This is why even intelligent animals, like dogs, dolphins and apes, don't show more than a modicum of sympathy, much less altruism, for other creatures, even of their own species or their direct kin. They certainly don't endanger their own lives to take care of a sick fellow for weeks or months, as the Turkana woman was evidently nursed. Being left to die was nature's only medicine, until the advent of humans.

So why did our ancestors – while they were still in constant danger of becoming food for other animals – risk being altruistic to others? The answer might well be to do with their enlarged brains, their developing linguistic skills, and the social development that came of both. But it is also, almost certainly, the result of yet another side-effect of our odd method of bipedalism.

We noted, in Chapter 2, that the proto-human birth canal was constricted by the evolution of the pelvis into a bipedal, weight-bearing structure. This made childbirth an outrageously dangerous process for both mother and baby. It also meant that human (and presumably proto-human) babies had to be born at an earlier developmental stage than other big mammals. The baby's skull has to be small and soft-boned enough to get through the narrow confines of the mother's pelvis, so the infant is born at a stage where it is entirely helpless and remains so for many months. Think of a horse foal staggering to its feet while still wet from birthing, if you want a telling comparison with a human newborn.

From this fact we get a more likely origin of the human pair-bonding instinct than Desmond Morris over-complicated naked ape theory (*see Chapter 2*): two parents can look after a baby better than one, so it's in the interest of Dad's genes that he sticks around. Mutual love for Mummy and the baby makes this much easier, if not automatic.

A clan group of these nuclear families is a good defensive structure and, coupled with the lethal biped hunting techniques noted above, such a *Homo erectus* tribe could be the most dangerous predators in any local area. Empathy for others within that clan group (who almost certainly shared some of your genes, even if not as much as your actual children) was another way of bolstering the chance of your genes' survival and spread. Conversely, of course, those from outside your clan (who did not share any of your genes) were an automatic threat. Xenophobia, jingoism and racism all stem from a primitive urge not to empathise with those who don't share our genes.

This basic, close-knit clan structure might be seen as the earliest indication of human civilisation. Individuals within wolf packs and chimp troupes also look out for each other, but not to the extent that they will nurse a sick female who can't hunt or even move very fast. It may or may not be true that the Turkana woman was cared for to this extent by her fellow *Homo erectus*; but we know that the instinct to protect others and empathise with their suffering took a strong hold on our ancestors, because we inherited the traits.

So, the present scientific consensus is that *Homo erectus* conquered most of the globe by being clever, forceful, cooperative, affectionate, talkative . . . cannibals. All but the last are traits that are certainly to be found in us, their descendants. If we have outgrown the killer ape instinct to eat people who don't belong to our immediate family or clan, then maybe it is also possible to escape our other inherited inclinations to excessive violence.

But now we come to the great scientific murder mystery – a prehistoric Cain and Abel legend, and maybe our evolutionary 'original sin': Did our immediate ancestors, *Homo sapiens*, exterminate our closest relatives, *Homo sapiens neanderthalensis*?

(We, modern humans, are the subspecies *Homo sapiens sapiens*. People often shorten this title to *Homo sapiens*, but that is a misnomer: the species equivalent of calling you by your parent's given name.)

The Neanderthals arose between 500,000 and 200,000 years ago, and were probably descended (via an intermediate stage: *Homo heidelbergensis*) from the *Homo erectus* who had remained in Africa when the others went globetrotting. The early Neanderthals moved first to North Africa and the Middle East – around 130,000 years ago – then went on to colonise the whole of Europe, the Caucasus, and a good section of Central Asia. At the time the planet was in the grip of the quaternary ice age, so Neanderthals evolved a large, heavy-set, heat-retaining body to better deal with the ice and snow.

Our *Homo sapiens* ancestors – sometimes called 'Cro-Magnons' or simply 'early modern humans' – split from the same African precursor species as the Neanderthals about 250,000 years ago and evolved into a separate, but very closely related cousin species. (Both are named for the region where they were originally unearthed by archaeologists – the Neander Valley in Germany and the Cro-Magnon cave in France).

Early modern humans started to migrate out of Africa much

later than the Neanderthals – between seventy thousand and sixty thousand years ago – during an interglacial stage when the planet was, for a time, as temperate as it is today. They thus evolved bodies to suit a warmer climate; our ancestors were taller but only three-quarters the weight of an equivalent Neanderthal. Yet it was the 25 per cent weedier Cro-Magnons that survived and the Neanderthals that became extinct.

Somewhere between seventy-seven thousand and sixty-nine thousand years ago, there was a volcanic explosion in Indonesia: the Toba super-eruption. Atmospheric dust clouds caused the planet to fall under a ten-year, continuous winter (on top of the quaternary ice age that was already going at full blast). Genetic studies suggest that early modern humans almost died out at this stage. The total population of the ancestors of all modern humans fell, at one point, to around fifteen thousand people. To this day humans are more prone to epidemics than most other animal species, because of this genetic bottleneck – we're all too closely related, we share many immune system vulnerabilities and we are thus too likely to pass around diseases.

So it was not until sixty thousand years ago that our ancestors had recovered their numbers enough to seriously start pushing into Neanderthal territory. But they moved slowly; the most recent study suggests that early modern humans did not colonise Europe in significant numbers until forty-five thousand years ago. And by thirty-nine thousand years ago there were apparently no Neanderthals left: we arrived and they died.

So did our ancestors murder them? Once again we run into the problem of having discovered too little evidence to make a conclusive decision. But there is one fossil find that seems to indicate hostile interaction between Cro-Magnons and *Homo sapiens neanderthalensis*: a Neanderthal child's jawbone, found in at the Les Rois excavation in south-west France in 2009.

The head of the archaeological team, Fernando Rozzi of the Centre National de la Récherche Scientifique, believes that cut marks on the bone indicate that the owner had been killed, butchered and eaten by the early modern humans who lived in the Les Rois caves. The cuts were identical to those made by stone meat-scrapers on deer bones, examples of both of which were also found at the site.

But, of course, evidence of one murder does not prove that a genocide took place. Some paleoanthropologists believe that our ancestors simply out-evolved the Neanderthals; that early modern humans gradually pushed the hulking Neanderthals out of the good hunting areas. *Homo sapiens neanderthalensis* died out, they suggest, just as the European red squirrel almost died out when pushed out of the lush woodlands by the invading American grey squirrels over the course of the twentieth century. The grey squirrels didn't actually attack the red squirrels, they just edged them out by being better at 'Red Queen' survival tactics.

In fact, some scientists believe that the Neanderthals were already dying out when our ancestors first hove over the horizon. They too must have been hit by the effects of the Toba super-eruption, and ice-age weather was doubtless brutally changeable and unforgiving. The physically specialised Neanderthals might have found it impossible to adapt to new conditions – rather as polar bears are finding it impossible to deal with global climate change today.

Then there was the catastrophic eruption of the Campi Flegrei supervolcano – in what is now southern Italy – thirty-nine thousand years ago. This would have devastated the continental weather patterns for decades. Perhaps that event pushed the already teetering Neanderthals over the edge. After all, it has been estimated that there might never have been more than seventy thousand Neanderthals in existence, even at the peak of their success. So it wouldn't have taken too much of a push to finish them off.

Nevertheless, the theory that Neanderthals left the stage of history peaceably – gently replaced by a more advanced branch of the species – is partly undermined by evidence that the Neanderthals were at least as intelligent as our invading forebears. They had a similar brain-to-body ratio, made clever tools, used fire and were socially complex enough to ceremonially bury flowers with their dead. Such intellectual creatures are likely to have been highly adaptable which, in turn, increases the likelihood that our ancestors had to 'force the issue' of territorial disputes . . . perhaps to the point of murdering and eating them, as the jawbone found at Les Rois suggests.

The very fact of the extinction of a whole human subspecies, in an area and time when an almost identical subspecies flourished, suggests that intra-species violence may have been a key factor in that extinction. We may only be here today because our forebears were more brutal than the Neanderthals.

There is a third, and perhaps more charming, explanation of where the Neanderthals went: that they are in *us*. Neanderthal remnants are to be found in the DNA of many modern humans: those whose ancestors migrated from Africa when the Neanderthals were still around. Modern people of unbroken African heritage have no Neanderthal blood.

Some Neanderthal fossil bones are recent enough for geneticists to have extracted partial DNA strands. Those modern peoples who are descended from the Cro-Magnons that left Africa – and thus came into contact with Neanderthals – share between 1 per cent and 4 per cent of Neanderthal DNA coding. In other words, those human ancestors successfully interbred with Neanderthals.

The idea of human–Neanderthal cross-breeding was long rejected by most scientists, on the grounds that any offspring would be 'mules' – that is, infertile hybrids, like actual mules (the product of cousin species breeding between horses and donkeys). It now seems that those scientists might have been exactly half right.

The key thing to understand here is that part of our DNA coding – what is called mitochondrial DNA (or just mtDNA for short) – is *only* passed down through the female line. Males are all a dead end for mtDNA researchers, and for mtDNA itself. The fact that no modern human shares mtDNA with Neanderthal ancestors shows that only a certain type of cross-bred baby survived long enough to breed in their turn. Those were the children of female Cro-Magnons who had sex with male Neanderthals.

The fact that the DNA some of us inherited from Neanderthal ancestors lacks any element of mtDNA tells us something specific: that any offspring of the female Neanderthals, who were impregnated by male Cro-Magnons, did not manage to pass their genes (and mtDNA) back into the Cro-Magnon population. That might be because they were born as infertile mules, or because they died (or were killed) before they could re-initiate the cultural/genetic exchange.

These would have been small local populations involved in this interspecies contact – probably only dozens or, at the most, a few hundred on each side at any one time. And remember that we are talking about a maximum of 4 per cent Neanderthal DNA in any modern human. It is therefore unlikely that there was much sexual interaction between the species: if there had been regular cross-breeding, the Neanderthal DNA percentage in modern humans would be higher. And given the tens of thousands of years since then – of humans happily intermixing our DNA and spreading around the smidgen of Neanderthal – we may be talking about only a handful of first-generation Cro-Magnon/Neanderthal hybrids who survived long enough to pass their genes on to posterity.

This low level of interbreeding might have been a good thing. A taste for rape, after all, is another perennial aspect of human conflict that might also have been found in male Neanderthals. (We will consider the human, and possibly proto-human, habit of rape in greater depth in the last chapter of this book.)

Certainly there is no indication that the Neanderthals were entirely peaceful creatures, who were ruthlessly destroyed by cruel Cro-Magnons. A study of their bone chemistry, conducted in the year 2000, indicated that the Neanderthals were almost entirely carnivorous. So they must have been expert hunters and, as such, they would have known how to fight. It would seem likely that if there was intra-species hatred, violence and even cannibalism, then it was almost certainly a two-way exchange.

The ancient and universal myth of demons, ogres and troll-like monsters – lurking in remote caves and gloomy forests, just waiting for tasty human victims to fall into their hands – may be a very old cultural memory of a war to the death between early modern humans and *Homo sapiens neanderthalensis*. Given the evident physical prowess and high intelligence of the Neanderthals, that might have been a conflict that our ancestors won against heavy odds.

Chapter 5

'Why We Fight'

The death of the Neanderthals left our ancestors as the effective rulers of the planet. No competing species could threaten us with extinction. Wolves, bears and sabre-toothed cats might kill a few individuals. Whole tribes might be wiped out by bad winters, starvation or disease outbreaks. But our forebears were now too numerous and too spread out across the globe to ever again face total extermination by anything less than a universal planetary catastrophe.

By thirty thousand years ago our ancestors had made it to the top of the food chain. Humans had become Earth's apex predators: the killers of killers. And we had physically evolved into the subspecies *Homo sapiens sapiens* – also known as 'anatomically modern humans', or simply *us*.

But matters were still far from perfect. Man-eating predators were common and much of the planet was buried under the snow of the quaternary ice age. People lived in what the seventeenth-century philosopher Thomas Hobbes described as the 'state of nature': a life with few or no elements of organised civilisation, and where Mother Nature wasn't just outside the door, but all around you. This may sound idyllic now – to people who live comfortably distanced from it – but for our ancestors life was, as Hobbes put it: 'poor, nasty, brutal and short'.

Individual survival for people in this world of cold and danger was a matter of toughness, luck and inventiveness. They took flint-knapping and bone-whittling beyond the level of survival technology and into the realm of art; their barbed flint spearheads and bone fishhooks were marvels of intricate dexterity. And where spears were not enough, they used their brains.

At the bottom of the Ouaisne cliffs on the Channel Island of Jersey, for example, archaeologists discovered the remains of woolly mammoths and woolly rhinos. These huge and dangerous animals had apparently been deliberately stampeded to their deaths over the precipice, then butchered where they fell. The quantity and position of the fossil carcasses suggests that this was not a one-off event, but a regular occurrence: local humans had used both geography and gravity to create a slaughterhouse.

The late Palaeolithic inhabitants of western Europe, around 22000 to 17000 BCE, are known to archaeologists as the Solutreans. This people discovered one of the most underappreciated inventions of all time: the eyed-needle. Being able to pull threads of dried sinew through hides allowed them to sew together clothes that didn't fall off if they moved vigorously. Try making your way through knee-deep snow, carrying a heavy spear and dressed only in separate sheets of tarpaulin, if you want an idea of just what a leap forward this was for human survival during an ice age.

Our caveman ancestors were even greater travellers than their forebears, the *Homo erectus*. Braving the same brutal terrain, lousy weather and terrifying carnivores, they covered the same territories as their now (probably) extinct ancestor species. But they also managed to colonise the far-flung Pacific islands, Australia and the Americas – lands that had never seen an ape before, let alone a human being. And, strangely enough, the last of these land conquests was almost certainly made possible by the use of the eyed needle.

As we saw in Chapter 1, some humans arrived in the American north-west, via the Beringia land bridge from Siberia, around twelve thousand years ago. But the Clovis people, as they are known, almost certainly met other humans as they spread across the North American continent. Various sites – in Maryland, Pennsylvania, Virginia, Florida and Delaware – have revealed evidence of habitation which carbon dating has placed as early as twenty-six thousand years ago; fourteen thousand years before the arrival of the Clovis people. Since the *Homo erectus*, *Homo heidelbergensis* and the Neanderthals never made it that far, the only other people who could have colonised the North American Eastern Seaboard at that period were the western European Solutreans.

How did cavemen make it across thousands of miles of storm-wracked, ice-age ocean? They could have done it by using eyed needles to sew together interleaved hides. These could then be used to make layered waterproof clothes and canoe hulls. Those, in turn, would have allowed the Solutreans to hop from ice sheet to ice sheet across the Atlantic – fishing with bone fish hooks and skewering seals with barbed stone spearheads. After all, this is what the Inuit peoples did regularly – hunting across the ice floes of the Arctic North Atlantic using essentially the same stone-age technology – right into the early twentieth century.

The 'Solutrean-first' hypothesis of human colonisation of the Americas remains highly controversial, partly because the believers in the dominant 'Clovis-first' hypothesis refuse to consider it, whatever the supporting evidence. It is also a sore point for Native Americans, who naturally dislike the idea of being pre-dated by Europeans – especially since post-Columbian European colonisers almost managed to eradicate their people.

It is a grim irony that that attempted genocide may have also destroyed the main potential strand of evidence for the Solutrean-first hypothesis. Mitochondrial DNA studies could have proved the matter conclusively: if *any* modern Native Americans could be shown to possess Solutrean mtDNA (samples of which we have recovered from European sources) then some of their ancestors *must* have come from Europe before 10000 BCE. But the extermination of so many Eastern Seaboard Native American tribes probably eradicated any such chance. If there were surviving descendants of Solutrean colonisers of North America when Columbus landed in 1492, they would have been the first to die of European diseases and European colonial aggression.

Our late-Palaeolithic ancestors had to be tough and resourceful just to survive long enough to procreate, let alone conquer and colonise a savage planet. But were they as prone to committing homicide as we, their civilised descendants? There are those who believe that early modern humans were more peaceful than modern humans – for reasons that will soon become apparent, we will call this the 'bonobo theory'. Against this stands the 'chimp theory': that early modern humans were territorial, murderous and probably downright sadistic.

Bonobos and chimps are our closest genetic relatives (now that the Neanderthals are all dead). Bonobos (also known as pygmy chimpanzees) are sweet little apes who live in small matriarchal groups, have sex in the same way that sheep excrete (casually and copiously) and hardly, if ever, fight other bonobos – even those from rival troupes. This is why they've been nick-named 'the hippy apes'.

Bonobo theory suggests that early modern humans were similarly peaceful, and were corrupted into excessive intra-species violence by the unnatural aspects of complex civilised living. Although this might sound like wishful thinking – as we have absolutely no direct evidence of early *Homo sapiens sapiens'* social habits – but it might indeed be possible. Zoologists have shown conclusively that wild animals, kept in unnatural and stressful conditions, exhibit behaviour that, in a modern human, would be considered criminality.

In 1958 the American ethnologist John B. Calhoun ran a groundbreaking experiment. He set up four large, equally sized and interlinked animal pens. Then he introduced a colony of Norwegian rats. Two of the pens had two exits each, leading to other pens. The other two had only one exit each. The one-exit pens were more defendable and therefore were more desirable from a rat point of view. These were immediately annexed by the two most dominant males and their harems of females. All the other rats had to live in overcrowded conditions in the pens with two exits.

The little communities in the one-exit pens behaved perfectly naturally (for rats). But the rats in the increasingly overcrowded 'slum' pens quickly underwent behavioural decay. Gangs of male rats stole more than their share of the food and often killed rats who stood up to them. Sexual behaviour also deteriorated

– mating rituals were all but abandoned, with the gangs of male rats forcing their way into the burrows of females, whom they would rape. If the female victim had a litter, the rat pack would also kill and eat her babies.

It is always a risk to extrapolate animal behaviour on to humans (because humans are such bizarrely unique animals) but here there is a comparison that cannot be ignored. Consider any city slum in history and you will see similar behavioural deterioration as seen in Calhoun's rats. Bullying gangs, theft, murder and rape are all common among groups of deprived, stressed and over-crowded people.

One might argue that selfishness and brutality are normal reactions to slum life, but to a disinterested alien observer this would seem inconsistent. As intelligent, pack-forming animals, the typical human reaction to disaster is to immediately pull together to escape or at least better the situation for as many people as possible. But where the calamity is a result of continuous squalor, this does not often happen.

One explanation might be that the unnatural living conditions undermine our natural responses, creating a downward behavioural spiral: a bad environment encourages criminal conduct, which makes the situation more stressful, and that stress increases the likelihood of antisocial behaviour, and so on . . .

In policing, this is known as 'broken window syndrome'. This theory states that rundown areas typically have a higher crime rate, partly because locals feel that they have no way to better themselves in so grim and effectively lawless a situation. If the area is improved – even just cosmetically by, say, replacing broken windows in derelict buildings – it has been found that the crime rate usually drops and local civic self-help groups start to spring up automatically. As the area is improved further, the crime rate drops further. Negating or even just reducing the antisocial behavioural influences, it is argued, allows the socially optimistic side of human nature to re-assert itself.

One can see apparent evidence of this in any big city, simply by visiting the former slum areas that have gone upmarket. For example, have a look at Hogarth's eighteenth-century engraving

Gin Lane – a seemingly irredeemable world of drunks, filth, depravity and degradation. Hogarth also created a companion and comparison engraving to sit beside *Gin Lane*. This was titled *Beer Street*, and depicted happy prosperous people, drinking beer and reading the King's latest proclamation. The city buildings around them are recognisably the same crumbling slums as shown in *Gin Lane* – although seen from another angle and, presumably, a later time – but here they are being industriously repaired and renovated.

Now consider modern Bloomsbury: the London district which was the model for Hogarth's *Gin Lane*, and is now one of the most pleasant parts of the city. Bloomsbury's conversion from a hellish *Gin Lane* to an idyllic *Beer Street* was the result of steadily increasing prosperity over only a few decades.

Broken-window theory has been seized upon, largely by the political right, as evidence that it is weak policing policies that create criminal black spots, not poverty or disenfranchisement. Simply crush the crime, they say, and an area will improve automatically. But this seems to be a misreading of the evidence. Innovative studies in the town of Groningen in Holland have shown that it is the environment itself – not police action or even visibility – that most influences criminal behaviour. For example, researchers found that both littering and petty theft doubled in the same town street immediately after the researchers had painted graffiti on the walls. We seem to react strongly to the social expectation impressed on us by the relative disorder of the local environment: 'I wouldn't want my neighbours to see me doing that,' is a powerful incentive to a pack-minded animal like a human.

It was once thought that chimpanzees were almost as peaceful as bonobos: their violence being restricted to screaming and macho posing when rival chimp troupes met, but with little or no physical conflict. This illusion was shattered by the pioneering zoologist Jane Goodall. She spent months at a time living with wild chimps – until her presence was taken for granted and their behaviour was, as far as we can tell, totally natural. She reported that raiding and murder were both typical chimp behaviours.

It is true that when two chimp troupes of equal size meet in the wild, they just shout and threaten – because the risk of an equal battle is too great for both sides. But Goodall discovered that male chimps also go out on raiding parties about once a fortnight, hunting the no-chimp's-land between troupe territories for smaller groups of 'enemy' chimps. Any females they meet they will surround, then the dominant male in the raiding party will groom her in an attempt to initiate mating – this is as close as the mating-ritual-dominated instincts of male chimps can bring themselves to rape. But any infants that they find with females from another troupe, they will kill and eat. Enemy males they beat, torture (by biting off extremities), kill and cannibalise. The attrition of this opportunistic raiding can eventually wipe out entire troupes of chimps – this would be called 'ethnic cleansing' if we accepted that chimps were a branch of humanity.

So, why are male chimps such brutal bastards? Scientifically, it comes down to a simple matter of maximising the potential survival and spread of their genes. Female mammals don't generally behave like sex maniacs, because they can only be pregnant once at any one time – the spreading of their genes is therefore, necessarily, slow and steady. As a result, females don't have to dedicate a significant part of their time to competing for mates, so they are less likely to be sexually aggressive.

A male mammal, on the other hand, can impregnate, willing or not, any number of available females at almost the same time, thus greatly increasing the spread of his genes. So, genetically, it's in a male's interests to splurge his efforts – so to speak – to dedicating much of his spare energy to mating (and, in youthful male humans, to also thinking about mating). All that stops him doing so is opportunity and the competition of other males. Which is why the males of most mammal species are bigger and more aggressive than the females: males are in a continuous evolutionary arms race with all the other males of their species, while females don't need to compete with the other females anywhere near as much.

(There is of course a natural limit placed on the supersizing of the ever-competing males: famine. For most species, through most of history, food famine – for various reasons – has been a regular part of the environment. Big males can steal food from weaker creatures as long as there *is* food available. But when there is none, hulking and thus energy-inefficient bodies tend to die off quickly. After the time of famine the smaller males – those who can survive on less rations – can have their pick of the surviving females, thus creating a short-term counter tide in the evolutionary development of a species, moving towards smaller body size.)

A male chimp kills the babies of other (non-closely related) males as a part of that arms race – reducing the spread of competing genes. He kills other males for the same reason. And schmoozing with enemy females obviously increases the chance of spreading his own genes.

This is the underlying behavioural drive that was highlighted by the biologist Richard Dawkins in his seminal 1976 book *The Selfish Gene*. Nobody is suggesting that animal behaviour is *consciously* aimed at the successful spreading of genes, but it seems that it is the core motive for most of their competitive instincts.

You, for a parallel example, might be totally unaware that your dietary instincts are dangerously skewed by a long period in our shared prehistory (probably on the savannah and the beach) in which carbohydrates, like sugars, were hard to glean in the local environment. But you *are* likely aware of the urge to eat more dessert than is good for you. As suggested by Desmond Morris in his book *The Naked Ape* (*see Chapter 2*), it seems likely that our sexual desires, and resultant social choices, are subconsciously directed by primordial proto-human impulses . . . much like your (illusory) need for pudding.

It is uncomfortable to think that we – sophisticated thinking creatures that we are – might just be a carrying mechanism for our mindless genetic coding. As Dawkins himself neatly illustrated the idea: 'The chicken is only an egg's way for making another egg.' But it is a fact that our genes undoubtedly affect our behaviour, but not vice versa. In fact, the only way that your behaviour can directly impact on your genetic legacy is through a refusal to have children: the genetic equivalent of committing suicide in order to spite your parents.

Dawkins also suggested that the 'selfish gene' was the core motivation for our altruism instinct: that we are kind for genetically selfish reasons, of which we are largely unaware.

We tend to show greatest empathy towards those who are from our direct family, or who are second or third-tier genetic relations: 'blood is thicker than water', as the old saying goes. Nepotism is a knee-jerk tendency to unfairly favour kin. Bigotry is a similarly unthinking process that causes people to prefer strangers who are similar to themselves – often through nationality, culture or race – and, conversely, to dislike or hate those who don't match those prerequisites. These prejudiced attitudes could be seen as subconscious attempts to identify those who might share some of your genetic code. Likewise, altruism could be seen as a long-term strategy, by our genes, to maximise the survival chances of the copies of themselves that are stored in other living bodies.

The Turkana woman – the *Homo erectus* who was apparently protected while suffering a debilitating illness (*see Chapter 4*) – was almost certainly nursed by blood relatives. They had little to gain personally by risking themselves in this way but, from the point of view of their genes, the risk was worth it: there was a chance that she might have survived long enough to bear a child, thus creating a new carrier for their shared gene-set.

Just why male chimps commit torture and cannibalism when raiding is more difficult to explain, even in genetic terms. It's tempting to conclude that they're simply brutal bastards, but the real reason is probably to do with their high intelligence. Sadly, chimps seem to be bright enough to get caught in the tribalism-and-vengeance downward spiral that we will discuss shortly.

Chimp theory holds that raiding, rape and territorial murder are also basic human characteristics – the echo of Raymond Dart's proto-human killer ape instinct. Certainly it is true that virtually every recorded pre-municipal culture regularly indulged in territorial raiding, institutionalised rape and murderous feuds. In fact, the violent death rates in purely pastoral or hunter-gatherer cultures was (and is) higher than in any modern inner-city, gang-and-drug ravaged slum.

An overall comparison between such diverse societies is actually fairly is easy to make. Most authorities (legal, bureaucratic and academic) define the violence in any given group as a basic numeric measurement – that is, the number of violent crimes over a set time, in a set number of people. The most typically used equation is the number of violent killings per 100,000 people within a population, averaged over a year. (These figures include murders, war casualties and deaths through criminal negligence; but not state executions, or deaths caused by unavoidable accidents.) This gives the overall percentage probability of a person, within that given group, being murdered, or otherwise illegally killed, within any given year. This basic figure can then be compared with any other population (or the same population during a different year). Even those populations numbering under 100,000 can be studied this way, if you multiply the figures correctly.

So, for example, the United Nations Office on Drugs and Crime reported that the illegal death rate in the UK in 2011 averaged at 1.4 unlawful deaths per 100,000 members of the population. That meant that – leaving aside all the subtleties of circumstance, demographics, economics and location within the UK – the overall chance of being murdered or being a victim of manslaughter in the UK in 2011 was 0.0014 per cent. The UNODC gave the illegal death rate in the USA in 2011 as 4.7 per 100,000 people; which equals 0.0047 per cent chance of being illegally killed. And in China in 2011, your chance of being illegally killed was 0.001 per cent.

So one can roughly conclude that the UK was almost half again more dangerous than China in that year. At the same time the USA was more than three times more dangerous than the UK and almost five times more dangerous than China. (Of course, the UNODC figures do not include state executions. Inclusion of these legal killings would push both the USA and China's risk of violent death higher, while leaving the UK unchanged.)

Similar calculations for what are sometimes referred to as

'non-state societies' (pre-municipal hunter-gatherers and agrarians) give striking results. In *The Better Angels of our Nature* – his 2011 landmark study of the decline of human violence – Steven Pinker gives a simple, combined homicide figure for non-state societies. Such cultures have an average of 524 violent deaths per 100,000 of population. That is a 0.524 per cent chance of being murdered each year: and that's 111 times worse than the USA in 2011, 374 times worse than the UK and 524 times more dangerous than China.

But, a bonobo theorist might argue, all these once-called 'primitive cultures' have been studied by modern anthropologists, and have – by definition – been in contact with 'civilised' cultures. Were they influenced towards violence by that (often violent and traumatising) contact?

An interesting case study came from deep in the Venezuelan rainforest. A research team led by a professor from the University of Missouri, Napoleon Chagnon, spent years studying a tribe called the Yanomami. This people had remained uncontacted by the outside world until the late 1960s. Chagnon reported that the Yanomami were a habitually 'fierce people', living in 'a state of chronic warfare'.

In a film of a village-wide battle that he made in 1971 (which he titled *The Ax Fight*) Chagnon was able to show that most of the brutality was directed by Yanomami at other Yanomami who had no direct blood links to them. In other words, the violence was an unconscious strategy to maximise the potential of the attacker's genes. So, we might see this as evidence that the Yanomami were just as driven by genetic imperatives as any chimp raiding party.

To this day *The Ax Fight* remains a standard part of most university anthropology courses. However, Napoleon Chagnon's study has recently come under attack within the anthropological community, because he himself may have contaminated the research.

The fierceness of the Yanomami, it is claimed, was increased when Chagnon's team arrived and offered machetes, shotguns and axes as bribes to get people to cooperate with the study. The ax fight itself, it has been suggested, only broke out when a group from outside the village turned up to see if they too would be given weapons – and were then driven off by the jealous villagers. As such, it would be hardly surprising if most of the violence in the film was directed at non-blood relatives, as the interlopers were all outsiders.

Professor Chagnon has always denied compromising his research by accidentally influencing the Yanomami. In 2007 he was asked by the documentary maker Adam Curtis, 'You don't think a film crew in the middle of a fight in a village had an effect?' Chagnon replied curtly, 'No, I don't,' and immediately terminated the interview (*The Trap*, BBC2, 2007).

Of course, even if the bonobo theorists are right – that any contact with civilisation can corrupt human behaviour to become more violent – that doesn't prove that humans were less violent *before* the advent of civilisation. So, perhaps the easiest way to judge whether pre-literate, non-state people are habitually violent is to look at those cultures that remained as hunter-atherers or basic agrarians for the longest historical period before they were touched by outside influences ... such as well-meaning anthropologists or (more commonly) invasion by land-hungry people carrying guns.

The northern Native American tribes, the rainforest dwellers of South America (like the Yanomami), the Aboriginal Australians, the Pacific Islanders, and isolated inhabitants of South and Central Africa: all were at the hunter-gatherer or basic agrarian stage of technological development when they first made contact with literate, municipal-culture civilisations. And all were noted to be in a continual state of low-level warfare with their neighbours. Intertribal feuds, raiding and rape were at least as common in their cultures as in any city-builder civilisation; just as they were in the Middle East, Asia and Europe before their populations developed complex civilisations that took warfare to a higher, and more destructive, level.

Steven Pinker gives the following figures for non-state hunter gatherers: 65–70 per cent of such groups are at war with their neighbours at least every two years. Ninety per cent go to war at least once in a generation and almost all non-state peoples have cultural memories of wars from the recent past.

Pinker also gives statistics for skeletons found at archaeological dig sites of hunter-gatherer and basic agricultural cultures from around the world, dating from between 14000 BCE to 1770 CE. Forensic analysis of such bones gives a fair indication of how many died by violence: essentially a bone broken while the owner was still alive, but with no sign of subsequent healing, indicates that the person died at the time that the bone was broken. Some may have died in natural accidents but, in a world devoid of high structures and automobiles, broken human bones were generally the result of combat, either with dangerous animals or with other humans.

Between zero and 60 per cent of the skeletons found at the various sites showed signs of violent death – with an average of 15 per cent. That equates to 15,000 probable murders in every 100,000 members of the population – or a life that was 3,191 times more dangerous than that in the USA in 2011.

In fact, the percentage of violent deaths in ancient non-state societies was certainly higher than those given above, as at least a proportion of the skeletons found without broken bones probably died of soft-tissue wounds that left no archaeological indications. And we should also reiterate that none of the ancient cultures in the analysis had come into contact with any state-based, municipal civilisations. They were simply people living in the 'state of nature', making each other's lives poor, nasty, brutal and short.

In perusing history, it is possible to be misled by scales of violence. Most people would think that civilised war is more destructive than tribal conflicts. Images leap to mind: the men killed while charging machine guns during the First World War; the carpet-bombing of civilians in the Second World War; the smoke billowing from furnace chimneys over Nazi death camps; the fiery napalm destruction of fields and villages during the Vietnam War . . .

But in even the most brutal of modern wars, the percentage of the populations involved who are actually harmed directly is always relatively small. This is because the excess resources that civilisation creates allows the birth and survival of vast populations – most of whom are non-combatants throughout their entire lives.

In his 2004 book, *War Before Civilisation*, Lawrence H. Keeley points out that, since hunter-gatherer and basic agrarian cultures can't sustain large populations (because they can't gather and store enough food), *any* homicide will destroy a significant proportion of the population. For example, in 2011 the South American Yanomami tribes were thought to number approximately twenty thousand people in total. The 2011 population of the UK was 63 million. One single Yanomami death would therefore have been, in comparative terms, the equivalent of 3,150 deaths in the UK. Or 15,650 deaths in the USA. Or 67,550 deaths in China.

To match a population impact equal to, say, Britain's military and civilian losses during the entire Second World War (believed to be close to 388,000 deaths from a 1939 population of 46.5 million), the Yanomami would have to lose only 167 people to violence. According to Napoleon Chagnon's 1968 book *The Fierce People*, almost 50 per cent of Yanomami men die in feuds, fights and inter-village raids. So 167 violent deaths would be typically racked up in much less time than the five years of Britain's involvement in the Second World War. Tribal warfare may be on a much smaller scale than civilised conflicts, but its impact is still devastating to the small populations involved.

The two main reasons for this high homicide rate in pre-literate cultures seem to be tribalism and revenge. Tribalism is a fundamental part of human nature and elements of it can be seen in almost every aspect of our lives – from your political or religious allegiance; to your support of a sports team; to the chilling sentiment on the wall of the Buchenwald concentration camp: '*Recht oder Unrecht mein Vaterland.*' (A translation of a quote by the American reformer Carl Schurz: 'My country, right or wrong.') What the Nazis left out was the second, modifying part of the statement: 'If right, to be kept right; and if wrong, to be set right.'

By 'tribalism' a psychologist means an allegiance that may

initially be carefully thought out and rational; but then – after gaining their heartfelt loyalty – will have a powerful hold on a person, even in the face of evidence that should rationally make them abandon that allegiance. More often, however, tribal allegiances are beliefs that you are born into: inherited from your family and community. Political and religious affiliations commonly cause people to desperately 'defend the indefensible' for reasons of tribal allegiance – to 'stand by their beliefs,' after those beliefs have been comprehensively disproved or debased. This instinct is, arguably, the motivation behind the scientific intransigence that leads to the Kuhnian paradigm revolutions that we considered in Chapter 1. But such tribalism can also be seen in the mother of a serial rapist 'standing by her son', or an abused spouse loyally defending the very person who is making their life a misery.

In actual tribal societies, tribalism is both a social glue and a life-motivator. It is also a major cause of mortality. Here again we can turn to the philosopher Thomas Hobbes for possible clarification. Hobbes said that there are three core reasons for basic human conflict: aggression, anticipation and prestige.

Aggression as a motivation is fairly self-explanatory. It is the seizure of resources that will increase the survival chances of you and the group to which you are affiliated – be it yourself, your family, your clan, gang, tribe, nation, racial group, religion or political party. Like chimps going raiding, we essentially fight and kill to better our own lives at a cost to others who are not of our group. Economists call this a 'zero-sum game' – indicating that the ownership of resources is moved, through theft and violence, but nothing new is created. In a zero-sum game, for every winner there has to be a loser.

Anticipation as a motivator to violence can be a major cause of ongoing feuds and rivalries. Regardless of how peaceful you are yourself, you might still fear attack by others. It is logical to decide to attack them before they attack you – thus weakening the danger of counter-attack, or possibly annihilating the threat altogether. Of course, many people consider pre-emptive strikes to be unethical and dishonourable, but they might not believe that strongly enough to stop them from attacking anyway. The predicament is illustrated by the story of 'the prisoner's dilemma'.

This short parable can be told in different ways, but essentially comes down to this: the authorities hold two guilty prisoners in separate cells. Each prisoner is offered freedom if they will implicate the other prisoner in their crime, but only one of them can be freed. How can an isolated individual be sure that the other prisoner isn't selling him out? No matter how noble his own inclinations, the logical conclusion is to accuse the other person immediately to win freedom, before the other prisoner can do the same to him. The worst case scenario (for the prisoners) is that they both go to jail because the authorities welshed on the deal as soon as they got the two accusations; but it is logically worth risking this, and betraying the other prisoner, for the chance of personal freedom (the only possible positive outcome). In warfare there is the same dilemma of logic versus honour, but the stakes are even higher.

A further problem is that, in the case of tribal warfare, it rarely stops with one raid. The people attacked first will have their own anticipation of assault increased by the pre-emptive strike and are thus more likely to try a surprise attack themselves as soon as they are able. This can quickly deteriorate into a downward spiral of tit-for-tat feuding, where both sides are losing more than they can ever gain. This is what an economist would call a 'negative-sum game'.

Like the feuding Grangerfords and Shepherdsons in Mark Twain's 1884 novel, *The Adventures of Huckleberry Finn*, both sides can eventually be so weakened that they risk mutual destruction. In the novel, both Kentucky families initially strike the wandering Huck as paragons of civilised gentility, but then Buck Grangerford explains the situation:

> 'Well,' says Buck, 'a feud is this way: A man has a quarrel with another man, and kills him; then that other man's brother kills him; then the other brothers, on both sides, goes for one another; then the cousins chip in—and by and by everybody's

killed off, and there ain't no more feud. But it's kind of slow,
and takes a long time.'

Later, the twelve-year-old Buck tries to murder Harney
Shepherdson, shooting at him from behind a tree in an ambush.
Then Buck and another Grangerford boy are hunted down
before Huck's horrified gaze:

All of a sudden, bang! bang! bang! goes three or four guns
– the men had slipped around through the woods and come
in from behind without their horses! The boys jumped for
the river – both of them hurt – and as they swum down the
current the men run along the bank shooting at them and
singing out, 'Kill them, kill them!' It made me so sick I most
fell out of the tree. I ain't a-going to tell all that happened
– it would make me sick again if I was to do that. I wished
I hadn't ever come ashore that night to see such things. I
ain't ever going to get shut of them – lots of times I dream
about them.[1]

Twain based the fictional Grangerford—Shepherdson war on
the real blood feud between the Hatfields of West Virginia and
the McCoys of Kentucky. The infamously savage quarrel lasted
twenty-six years (between 1865 and 1891) and devastated both
clans. At one point the Governor of West Virginia even threatened to invade Kentucky to restore order. In the end it took both
state militias, the US Supreme Court and a number of executions for murder to end the dispute.

Prestige, Hobbes's third motivator to violence, is a problem for
any culture that is habituated to conflict. Where prowess at fighting is a necessity for everyday survival, a pecking order of warriors
will automatically develop. The more senior the warrior, the more
respect he will demand, because signs of respect further cement
his position in society. But old victories are soon forgotten and
prestige will fade over time. So new victories are needed to

---

1 Mark Twain, *The Adventures of Huckleberry Finn* (1884)

maintain a warrior's status. Therefore new conflicts are regularly initiated – whether the tribe needs such fights or not.

If allowed to run free – as they usually are in non-state societies – the influences of aggression, anticipation and prestige can lead to almost constant conflict – internal and external. Tribal leaders initiate wars to seize valuable resources – like food, women or a fresh water source. Young bucks dream of war as a way to prove their manhood and will fight each other if no enemy is available. Tough old warriors start fights to prove that they still have what it takes. And everyone is on a hair-trigger in case a surprise raiding party from another tribe appears out of the night.

Along with the killing of men, the theft of resources and the raping of women, eventually comes a lust to torture. This is because of the other main psychological element – together with tribalism – that creates non-state conflict: revenge.

We will look more closely at sadism – pseudo-sexual pleasure in causing or witnessing the suffering of others – in both Chapters 21 and 23. But for now we will concentrate on the conflict escalation that can embed sadism within a culture.

Animals do not indulge in revenge: that is, the dedication of much of your resources – and maybe even your life – to the misery or destruction of someone or something against whom you hold a grudge. An animal, further down the food chain, must utilise most of its energies to 'Red Queen' daily survival (*see Chapter 4*). As part of that survival strategy they might target a particular threat for destruction, but an animal simply doesn't have the spare energy or mental capacity to hold more than a passing grudge. Long-term revenge planning is a human speciality.

Even in the most regulated or ceremonious forms of warfare, escalation is inevitable. Someone will always go too far in the heat of the moment, and the victim's almost automatic reaction to such an outrage is to retaliate in kind, plus a bit extra as punishment. Most cultures have some proscription against killing helpless children, for example. But this taboo will often be dropped as soon as your own children are killed by an enemy, whether that killing was accidental or not.

Likewise, most people have a revulsion towards torture. Yet, there are few long-running conflicts that have not led, sooner or later, to the torturing of enemy prisoners. Degrees of torture can vary enormously, of course. Many things are torturous, from vivisection – as found in the medieval British tradition of hanging, drawing and quartering – to simply denying people adequate food and water. But here we are considering just the basic idea of deliberately going beyond societal bounds in order to satisfy the need for revenge on an enemy.

Everybody, child and adult, has used the rationalisation 'well, they did it first' as an excuse for unacceptable behaviour. But when that excuse is accepted by the local authority figure – be it Mummy, the tribal chief or the law (as defined by a mandate by a majority of the voting public) – that previously unacceptable behaviour can become part of everyday life.

An example. The deliberate bombing of civilian targets is illegal under the Geneva Convention. On 24 August, 1940, a few German bombers became lost on a night raid that was originally aimed at the London docks (a legitimate target under the convention). The crews, running low on fuel and fearful of attack by British night fighters, released their bombs over unidentified territory and headed for home. The bombs fell on civilian houses and killed twenty-four of their occupants. Unaware that the bombing of civilians had been accidental, the British government ordered a small retaliatory night bomber raid on Berlin. It was largely a failure, in which little damage was done and no people were killed. The Nazis were infuriated nevertheless, and ordered the mass-bombing of British cities: what came to be called the Blitz. Civilians were not officially specified as targets in the Blitz, but their killing in thousands was guaranteed by this strategy: 28,556 people were killed in London alone during the thirty-seven weeks of the Blitz. Later in the war, British and American bombers levelled virtually every German city, killing an estimated 410,000 non-combatant men, women and children.

In 1939 even Hitler had publicly condemned the indiscriminate bombing of civilian targets. By 1945 the destruction of civilian areas was accepted, by all sides, as an unpleasant but necessary act of war. And all because a bomber squadron's lead navigator became lost and scared.

As mentioned above, chimpanzees are probably just intelligent enough to be caught in this behavioural downward spiral. A chimp may have no language to pass on atrocity stories, but finding a dead relative with toes, fingers, lips and penis bitten off will create enough of an impression on its own. Such a bereaved ape may not be subtle enough to feel complex urges towards revenge, but they may well conclude that this is the proper way to treat an enemy. Allied subordinate chimps see them using torture on captured enemy chimps, and decide that this behaviour is also expected of them. A chimpanzee cultural norm for torture and cannibalism thus becomes cemented into the troupe for as long as it is continued to be passed on by either friends or enemies.

The concept of revenge is a side-effect of the unusual human mental habit of living 'outside the moment', as are the mental processes that lead to both fear of retaliation and rationalisation of our own morally dubious actions.

If you consider it carefully, a large proportion of your day is spent away from the immediate moment, adrift in your mental inner world. Other relatively intelligent animals, like dogs or apes, clearly have memories and can anticipate potential events in the future. But it is doubtful, from their behaviour, that they dedicate as much time to thinking about these things as humans do. If it wasn't for our tendency to mentally 'drift', car accidents would be almost unknown: because all people would have their minds entirely on the road when driving. When you add the ability to think about abstract ideas – given to us by the symbology inherent in our use of language – it is easy to see how most of a person's life can be spent mulling over past events and considering future possibilities . . . or just daydreaming.

And two of the things we are painfully prone to thinking about are resentment at the actions of others and self-justification for our own actions. Both are the motivational parents of murders, feuds and, ultimately, wars.

It is probably true, as the bonobo theorists believe, that the stress associated with civilisation and urban life can erode our pacific instincts and can make us habituated to unnecessary violence. But the chimp theorists also seem to be correct when they say that the urge to commit unnecessary violence is something that predates civilisation.

Our remote forebears were killer apes and our nearer ancestors evolved into killer humans. Far from reducing the urge to kill for no good reason, the evolution of human intelligence has just given us a perfect tool to motivate and self-justify unnecessary violence. The truth seems to be that in becoming the most intelligent species on the planet, we also became the most self-destructive.

Chapter 6

'A Paradise Inhabited by Devils'

For most of human history we have been totally uncivilised. Even if we start the clock from the sprouting of the early modern human branch of the hominid family, *Homo sapiens*, we are looking at around 240,000 years of being simple, unsophisticated and – to be frank – brutal hunter-gatherers. Against this long period of savagery we can hold up, at the very most, twelve thousand years of relatively cultured living.

The first concrete step towards civilisation was basic agriculture, but we can't really claim much credit for its invention: that probably goes to the weather and our ancestors' inability to be tidy.

The Earth is normally warmer than it has been lately, but we've been suffering an ice age for 2.6 million years. We saw in Chapter 4 that the northern continents were buried under snow and ice when our ill-fated cousins, the Neanderthals, first emigrated from Africa. Our *Homo sapiens* ancestors left Africa as a warmer, interglacial period was just ending, so they too suffered increasing cold and resultant deprivation as they gradually spread north, west and eastwards.

Our forebears survived by living in caves wherever possible, but they couldn't stay in such shelters permanently. The herds of wild animals that they relied on (for food, for skins for making clothing, and bone for making utensils) were always on the move – migrating to find seasonal grazing not blighted by the bitter cold. So nomadism was the only way to survive for our Mesolithic (Middle Stone Age) ancestors; and that rootlessness – and the terrible weather – made agriculture and the domestication of livestock out of the question.

But not art. It would be a mistake to think of the Mesolithic peoples as 'stupid cavemen'. Surviving cave paintings and bone carvings show that they had well-developed intellectual, technical and imaginative skills. While living under appalling conditions, they nevertheless managed to produce some quite astonishing art.

From these paintings and carvings we can get something of a window into their minds. Their art was typically representational – that is, of the animals in their territory. There are very few depictions of people that we have found and these are invariably less detailed than the animal pictures. They also played about with dot patterns and with the kindergarten trick of painting around their hands to leave a silhouette, but they were essentially pragmatic in their artistic outlook. There are no imaginary monsters, ghosts or – as far as we can tell – gods in their depictions: just food animals. If they painted and carved what they were most interested in, then they were probably thinking about their next meal most of the time.

Nevertheless one could argue that these down-to-earth cave folk were at least the creative equals of modern humans. After all, as we saw in the last chapter, they invented many things that people would continue to use right up to the modern day: eyed needles, fitted clothing, boats, shafted spears, fish hooks and that first weapon of mass destruction, the bow and arrow. (It may be notable that it was after the invention and spread of the bow and arrow, some time around eighteen thousand years ago, that most giant mammals – like woolly mammoths, sabre-toothed cats, giant sloths and woolly rhinos – went extinct.) Mesolithic art may seem limited by our standards, but that was because those artists didn't have all the life and creation-enhancing tools that we take for granted – like writing, pottery, the wheel, summers without snow, and surviving past the age of twenty.

Around twelve thousand years ago the weather started to improve as another interglacial – the Holocene period that we are still enjoying – began to take hold. Warmer weather meant that grazing areas lasted longer, instead of disappearing under snow for six or nine months of a year. The herds of prey animals thus began to migrate less fervently, and Neolithic (Latter Stone Age) humans could stay in one place for more than a few weeks at a time. Further south – for example, around the Mediterranean Sea and beside the Tigris, Euphrates and Nile rivers – they could even set up full-time homes.

Permanent and semi-permanent grazing areas also offered a new food source to our ancestors. Grass seeds could be chewed as an extra source of nourishment but, on a practical level, only those few types of grass that helpfully produced their seeds bunched together inside husks. Carrying armfuls of these husks home meant that you could roast them on a stone by the fire and eat them in comfort and greater safety. However, having no pots or woven baskets, a lot of seeds must have been dropped and trodden into the dirt around those homes. Thus, archaeologists believe, the first fields of crops sprang up; but entirely by accident.

The discriminatory picking of the meatier types of grass seed, and the discovery that you could plant fields of crops deliberately, led to staple foods being selectively bred. The ancestors of modern wheat, millet and barley – and, later on, chickpeas, rice and maize – were the basis of what is sometimes called the 'Neolithic Agricultural Revolution'. This discovery of basic agriculture happened almost simultaneously – at unconnected points of habitation around the globe – starting from the very beginning of the Holocene period. The food plants that our ancestors produced during that revolutionary phase are still the basis of most human nutrition today.

The making of fire had already been a key factor in human survival during the ice age, but now clay soil got inadvertently baked under permanent fire pits and the making of pottery was discovered. Clay pots allowed both the storage of food and the cooking of combinations of meat, fruit and grains into health-giving stews. Better nutrition – that didn't even require teeth to eat – increased life expectancy and this, in turn, created the world's first data storage system: the wise old man or woman.

Unearthed ice-age bones indicate that up to around twelve thousand years ago, humans generally lived into their twenties or, at best, their thirties before the climate, disease, accidents, predators or other humans killed them. And most of that short life would have been dedicated to 'Red Queen' borderline survival: to making it through just one day at a time while trying to protect yourself and your offspring. Then, as the Holocene interglacial began, humans could enjoy gentler weather and better food. They might survive an additional ten or twenty years under these conditions – chattily passing on what they had learned in that time to the next generation.

This accumulation of knowledge within a clan allowed for yet more improvements: to the building of superior shelters, to better food-gathering knowledge, to improved tool and weapon making, to advanced language skills, and to the domestication of animals like dogs, ponies and cattle. But it would be a mistake to think that all these improvements came easily or quickly. In the modern world we are used to groundbreaking innovations taking place every couple of years. For tribal peoples the development period for creating and spreading the use of an invention tended to run in the hundreds or thousands of years. The domestication and cultural ubiquity of dogs, for example – from foundling wolf cub to man's best friend – took between ten thousand and twenty thousand years.

This prehistoric era of human history – following the beginning of the Holocene interglacial – could be vital to our understanding of the recent decline in unnecessary violence across the globe. If the bonobo theorists (*see Chapter 5*) are right – that humans were markedly less violent before the advent of civilisation – then this time could have been a comparative golden age. Good food, good weather, friendly neighbours, cool new inventions and longer lives that gave the chance to really get to know your kids before either you or they were killed off in some unpleasant (but wholly natural) way: a Neolithic Heaven on Earth. If this were true, then we could believe that our present civilisation may have at last matured to the point where our naturally peaceful natures are allowed free rein for the first time in over ten thousand years.

But of course, as we also saw in Chapter 6, although the bonobo theorists can point to clear evidence that the stress of civilised life can make humans behave savagely, they cannot show any proof that pre-civilised humans were not at least equally brutal. Here the weight of circumstantial evidence favours the chimp theory.

The basic number of murders in tribal societies were and are lower, because the number of people in such pre-industrial societies have always been low. Yet the individual, per capita chance of being murdered in such 'natural' cultures has always been notably higher than in even the most over-populated and socially decayed town-based society. The enlightenment philosopher Jean-Jacques Rousseau speculated that uncivilised peoples were naturally kind and decent 'noble savages' (*bon sauvage*). Unfortunately, as we saw in the previous chapter, such peoples are often more savage than noble.

But what were early Holocene humans likely to have been fighting about? As already mentioned, they were living in a better climate than any species of human had enjoyed for tens of thousands of years. And they had vast areas of uninhabited land to colonise. Why not just leave each other alone?

One probable cause of conflict was the habitual enmity between nomads and settlers. Some Neolithic humans would have permanently settled in the more luscious areas, raising crops and cattle. Others would have stuck to the hand-to-mouth lifestyle of nomad hunter-gatherers. To these often hungry nomads, the hoards of stored food (and healthy, well-fed women) of the settlers would have been a constant temptation.

Entirely nomad cultures are usually patriarchal, with women often treated as little better than chattel or, during raids, booty. Such societies are also typically based around the leadership of a warrior elite, whose skill at hunting and/or fighting is often regarded as the sole necessary ability for headship. (Historical examples of patriarchal nomad societies are legion: ranging from the Native American Plains tribes or the Arabian Bedouin clans, through the pirates of the Caribbean, to the late twentieth-century biker gangs.) Such cultures would invariably outgun settlers, because a settler spends so much time tending crops and cattle that their hunting and combat skills become blunted. Raiding such rich weaklings has never proved an enticement that nomads have resisted for very long.

This pattern has repeated throughout human history – nomad raiders plunder settlers, then leave to return to the hunting life or, where available, to plunder other communities of settlers. (For a graphic illustration of this relationship, see Kurosawa's classic movie, *Seven Samurai*.) Provided the parasitic nomad bandits don't rob the settlers too often – causing their victims to either starve to death or to give up and become rival nomads themselves – the equilibrium is maintained.

Sometimes settlers hired other nomad warriors to protect them, but this solution was generally worse than the original problem – using wolves to guard sheep rarely works for long. Bored warriors will generally cause trouble, and start extorting greater and greater payment from their helpless employers. The only other answer was to gather into larger settled communities, perhaps surrounded by natural defences or – where there were no suitable rivers, hills or ravines – building walls around the community. Thus the first towns sprang up.

The earliest town discovered to date is Jericho, situated in the modern-day Palestinian Territories: a walled community that dates back almost eleven thousand years, to around 9000 BCE. Jericho had such impregnable walls that, according to the Bible, it took a musical act of the god Yahweh to shatter them, allowing the nomad Israelites to break in and massacre all the citizens but one. Biblical scholars date this destruction to around 1400 BCE. Archaeologists have indeed shown that Jericho was ruthlessly sacked and never fully recovered, but radio-carbon dating of the burned layer of the city has placed the massacre to around 1550 BCE.

Early towns consisted of no more than a few dozen families to begin with. But they were a huge leap forward for creatures who, for all of their previous history, had lived more like wild dogs than what we would now consider a human existence. Not only were towns a food store and a defensive fortress, but they were also a centre of barter and creative innovation. It was in towns that wheeled vehicles, numeracy, carpentry, metallurgy, engineering, architecture and writing were invented; not in a nomad's yurt.

Unfortunately walled towns also created new problems for the inhabitants. Cramped groups of people – with little or no sense of basic hygiene – spread diseases very quickly. The water also became a big problem: even where there was enough to go around, it was usually contaminated by poor sewerage management. So a carrier of endless disease vectors was made a central part of each community.

Archaeologists report that although early town dwellers seem to have been better fed and longer-living than contemporary nomad cultures, their bones indicate that they were also smaller in stature and often crippled by disease. Life for a nomad might have been nasty, brutish and short (as the philosopher Thomas Hobbes predicted it would be) but life for an early town-dweller was nasty, sickly and only marginally longer.

A partial answer to the water problem – utilised by every early settled culture we know of (and by most others ever since) – was alcohol. Storing fruit in pots naturally leads to the discovery of fermentation and – quite aside from the warm glow the resulting drink gives the imbiber – even weak alcohol will act as a disinfectant and sterilising agent. Drinking booze, instead of 'pure' water, reduced the risk of disease for town dwellers.

In fact some of the oldest writing yet discovered – five-thousand-year-old cuneiform, written on clay tablets in the city states of Mesopotamia – details the paying of city workers in set measures of beer. The Ancient Egyptian pyramid builders were also part paid in beer. Alcohol was the glue of early civilisation, keeping townies comparatively healthy and happy.

The drinking of booze has even influenced human evolution. Cultures with a long history of town-dwelling – and the necessity of drinking alcohol instead of the tainted water – typically have a higher tolerance to alcohol addiction. People from these communities inherit genetic instructions to produce more of a particular enzyme (*alcohol dehydrogenase*) that tries to break down alcohol before it can do them lasting harm.

Descendants from long-standing rural and nomad cultures have a lower tolerance to alcoholism, because their ancestors could safely drink local, sewage-free water, so they never needed to over-produce the alcohol dehydrogenase enzyme. Such cultures – including, for example, the once nomadic Native Americans and Aboriginal Australians, and also, arguably, traditionally rural peoples like the Irish and Russians – have a notably higher alcoholism problem than other, more historically urbanised cultures.

The trouble was (and is) that alcohol is also an emotional de-inhibitor: it makes people drunk and prone to committing violence. It is no overstatement to say that alcohol has caused more unnecessary violence than any other environmental influence on human behaviour. The sheer number of murders, beatings, rapes and acts of vandalism throughout history, where alcohol was a contributory factor, is beyond calculation.

And perhaps here we see some circumstantial support for the bonobo theory of human violence: if humans had been immune to the adverse affects of this particular organic compound, we certainly would have had a much less sanguinary past. Without civilisation there would have been no booze, no raging drunks and no grinding hangovers.

Another unexpected mixed blessing that came with agrarian town-dwelling was the food surplus that each town created. It's already been seen that stored food was a constant temptation to nomad bandits to raid settlements, but such wealth also created what might be seen as internal robbers. Where there is spare food, some people will not be needed to work in the fields producing more food. Some of those people fulfilled new and useful roles – such as crafting, trade, administration and basic civic maintenance. Even a humble rat-catcher was well worth his pay in food and beer, given the ongoing disease problems in any crowded town. But town life invariably seems to have produced two other classes of non-food workers, and these were arguably less useful than the rat-catchers: the nobles and the priests.

Each municipality needed warriors to fend off nomad raiders and other threats. Clearly these men could not work full time on the farms, when weapon training and guard patrols were a more important use for their time. But – as we saw with the small communities that hired nomad mercenaries to fend off thieves – men who can use weapons tend to demand excessive privileges from those who can't defend themselves. And a municipal warrior elite invariably became, in a few generations, a hereditary aristocracy.

Warrior fathers passed their weapons, armour and skills on to their sons. Those sons in time did likewise, along with the family's wealth – accumulated from the spoils after successful battles and also by extorting goods from those at home who wouldn't dare fight back. Mafia-style protection rackets have a very long and ignoble history. This open extortion in early civilisations, dignified by time and custom, was eventually redefined as taxation. Certainly some or much of that taxation was fairly earned by the fighting men of the towns and cities. But fairly or unfairly taken, any non-perishable wealth tended to be hoarded by warrior families.

Multiply this passing on of well-guarded wealth over several generations and it became inevitable that the family in question would take on a posh-sounding title. By then such a family would certainly believe itself to have 'better blood' than neighbours with less wealth and fewer weapons. They would thus be tempted to intermix and interbreed only with other 'noble' families. This created the two enduring aristocratic traits of elitist exclusivity and disastrous inbreeding.

Early on in this ennobling process the richest, the most powerful and the most ruthless of the aristocratic families would have begun to contest for the position of hereditary chief, overlord or king. Most of the civil wars in history have been the result of such feuds and power games between members of the nobility.

Nomad cultures, as we saw above, were hardly free of swaggering bullies, eager to boss everyone about and take the best of what's available. But the general shortage of food meant that these men kept their position by being good hunters and fighters. A well-fed, town-supported aristocrat was, by and large, free of such menial demands. So complacent nobles might, sooner or later, lose most of their fighting skills. But by that time they would have become wealthy and powerful enough to be able to either employ or force others to go into battle on their behalf.

So eventually these chinless descendants of a town watchman were talking about their right and duty to levy higher taxes, so that they could employ more soldiers, so as to 'keep the lower orders in their place'. Civilisation seems to automatically produce a parasitic 'upper' class, whose main purpose in life is to maintain and increase their prestige, privileges and power. This is as true today, in the international 'global village', as it was in Neolithic Jericho.

Obviously such an elite level of society would be undermined if it were not both exclusive and restricted in numbers. The hoi polloi, the proletariat, the peasants, the bourgeoisie, the nouveau riche and the scumbags had to be kept out and kept down; either through social snubs, socially conservative laws or by armed troops. Otherwise, if the mere rich or the popularly celebrated were allowed to act as if they were from noble families, the illusion of aristocratic superiority would be diluted and weakened.

(There have been societies that, nominally, were almost entirely made up of nobles – for example, the ancient Greek Spartans – but such cultures survived on the backs of multitudes of slaves. If those slaves were seen as included as part of the society, the ratio of nobles to non-nobles could be recognised as being close to the norm for old-world oligarchies.)

We will look more closely at the concept of class barriers in the next chapter. Here we will simply note that the modern problem of 'glass ceilings' – cultural, legal and discriminatory barriers to people of minorities, disabilities or non-dominant genders achieving their full value in society – are not a new phenomena. For much of civilised history the blocks against entering the ruling noble class were not so much a glass ceiling, more a concrete ceiling . . . with nails sticking out of it. This is why so many aristocratic families date their ennoblement back to wars: their ancestors broke into the nobility holding a battle axe.

Where nobles were a product of civilisation – and some might say decadence – priests undoubtedly predated town living. The ice-age man or woman who invented stories to explain the inexplicable terrors beyond the cave mouth was a sort of proto-priest. And there was so much that needed explaining.

Up until several hundred years ago, virtually everything was beyond the understanding of humankind. Where does the wind come from? Why does the moon change shape? How does having sex make a woman pregnant? Why is my wounded leg turning green? Virtually any existential question that could be asked had no definitive answer before the Enlightenment and the subsequent age of science that we now inhabit. So people made up stories to fit the bewildering facts as best they could.

Faced with a world in which apparently arbitrary pain and death were never more than a moment away, and in which titanic forces like storms, earthquakes and wolf packs could strike out of nowhere, it was only natural to suspect that someone, somewhere out of sight, was making it all happen. Belief in spirits and demons leads to belief in gods, and every culture seems to accumulate gods like a stray dog collects fleas. Propitiation of these apparently unpredictable and often malevolent beings could be a full-time job: a job for a shaman or priest, that is.

Town life, and access to potentially aristocratic lifestyles, made the priest more than the local wise man, however. Increasingly numerous and urbane worshipers wanted sophisticated religions, so religious hierarchies and dogmas proliferated. Impressive temples were also needed and sacrifices to the gods had to be made regularly – although it was rarely the priests who did the actual temple building, or provided the materials to be knifed or burned. So religious tithes were added to the taxation demanded by the nobles; generally to be paid by the merchant and peasant classes.

It may seem odd to look at religion as part of a history of unnecessary human violence, but that is because we all grew up with comparatively modern-thinking religions. Present-day faiths do not gut people every morning to make the sun rise, as the Aztec priests did. Nor do they instigate holy wars to eradicate other religions: as the Catholic Church did to the Cathars in the thirteenth century, and tried to do to Islam throughout the Crusades.

But, on the other hand, the present-day Catholic dogma – that the spouses of HIV sufferers can't protect themselves against infection with condoms – could be seen as a form of human sacrifice in the name of an inscrutable faith. And many believers in the twenty-first-century Islamic fundamentalist jihad ultimately hold that the whole planet *must* convert to Islam – renouncing all other beliefs, either willingly or at the point of a gun.

No historian can deny that religion, whatever its many positive roles in society, is nevertheless a regular motivator of violence. In this context we tend to think of the religious wars, the crusades, the jihads and the occasional mass persecution of heretics. Yet the main attrition of religion around the world, for thousands of years, was blood sacrifice – the ritual killing of animals or people.

Just when it was that blood sacrifice started and ended is a moot point. Certainly it was mentioned in the *Epic of Gilgamesh* – one of the earliest written stories yet found – dating from perhaps as early as 3000 BCE. However, what archaeological evidence we have may point to blood sacrifice being at least as old as the Neolithic origin of organised religion itself. Altar stones with carved blood gutters – as may have stood at Mystery Hill in New Hampshire, USA (dating from perhaps as early as 2000 BCE); at Stonehenge in Wiltshire (3000 BCE); and at Gobekli Tepe in Anatolian Turkey (9000 BCE) – may be evidence of such vigorous theological activity.

A clay tablet (Pylos TN 316) was unearthed from the remains of a Mycenaean palace at Pylos, in southern Greece, and has been dated to some time in the twelfth century BCE. It reads:

Perform the rituals at the shrine of Zeus and bring the gifts: to Zeus one gold cup and one man. To Hera, one gold cup and one woman.

It is believed to be the orders for a human sacrifice to the gods, made at a time of invasion and extreme peril. The clerk's initially neat writing becomes a scrawl towards the end, and the tablet itself was baked rock hard in the fire that destroyed the palace.

(Certainly the Mycenaeans might have had a tradition of human sacrifice. King Agamemnon was said to have sacrificed his own daughter, Iphigenia, in order to ensure good winds to launch his thousand-ship invasion of Anatolia.)

In 264 BCE, the Roman Republic buried four slaves alive in the marketplace, as a sacrifice to the gods, when the city was in imminent danger of invasion by Hannibal the Carthaginian. Maybe they believed that the human sacrifice worked – as Hannibal never took Rome – but the Romans felt shame ever afterwards for sinking so low. (Although, of course, they were perfectly happy to watch people being killed in the arena in the name of entertainment.)

Blood sacrifice was largely abandoned in Europe – mainly due to the rise of Christianity – by the second century CE. Unless, that is, one counts the multitude of accused witches and heretics, executed from the thirteenth to eighteenth centuries CE (*see Chapter 15*).

'Suttee', the ritual burning to death of Hindu widows, was commonplace in India until the mid-nineteenth century CE. Then the religious rite was repressed by the conquering British Empire. Sir Charles Napier, the British Commander-in-Chief of India, met complaints that he was trampling on Indian tradition with a memorable diplomatic comment:

This burning of widows is your custom; by all means, prepare the funeral pyre. But my nation has also a custom. When men burn women alive we hang them, and confiscate all their property. My carpenters shall therefore erect gibbets on which to hang all concerned when the widow is consumed. Let us all act according to national customs.

Faced with this risk to their own lives – if they wanted to maintain the custom of suttee – the male priests and community leaders decided that it was best to let the tradition lapse.

Of course most religious sacrifice was not of people, but came in the destruction of animals and other foodstuffs. This was bad enough in itself because, even in towns with food stores, the likelihood of starvation for the poor was usually only a few lost meals away. But human sacrifice is present in the DNA of most religions, both ancient and modern.

For example, modern Judaism and Christianity seem the perfect examples of wise, kindly faiths. But just outside the old city walls of Jerusalem lies the Valley of Hinnom – better known by its Greek name from the Gospels: *Gehenna*. There is a reason why this pleasant valley is a synonym for Hell.

It was there a tribe called the Ammonites once burned children to death as a sacrifice to their god, Moloch (later co-opted by the Christians as an arch demon). The tribes of Israel, after driving the Ammonites away from Hinnom, took up the horrific practice themselves – offering their own children as sacrifices. The Valley of Hinnom/Gehenna was a place of fiery child-sacrifice from the reign of 'wise' King Solomon, in the tenth century BCE, to the Babylonian invasion over four hundred years later. The Prophet Jeremiah railed against the practice in the final days before that invasion:

> *They have built the high places of Baal[1] to burn their children in the fire as offerings to Baal – something I did not command or mention, nor did it enter my mind. So beware, the days are coming, declares the Lord, when people will no longer call this place Topheth or the Valley of Ben Hinnom, but the Valley of Slaughter.[2]*

All this horror may have been less insane than it sounds. Child killing has been an essential part of human life for many millennia. Throughout history and back into prehistory, killing excess

---

1 Jeremiah is probably referring here to the god Moloch. *Ba'al* was an ancient Levantine title meaning 'Lord', and was used much as Jeremiah later uses 'Lord' to refer to his own god, Yahweh.
2 Jeremiah 19: 5–6

children was the main method of population control in all societies. Better an unneeded baby die than everyone else go short on food, was the ruthless logic. One more mouth to feed is, first and foremost, one more mouth to feed.

It is now thought by some that this horrible necessity is actually ingrained into our genes. Many mothers, just after birth, feel an odd emotional disconnection with their new baby, just when they expect to be flooded with feelings of love and attachment. This upsetting symptom is often linked to post-natal depression and usually passes within a few days – after which mother and child bond lovingly. Some scientists now think that this feeling of detachment might be the body's way of creating a neutral emotional window, in which the mother can decide whether to kill her newborn without enormous emotional trauma resulting.

Remember, for most of human history, and all human pre-history, we have usually had too little food available to comfortably maintain our big bodies and king-sized brains. Starvation was never far from most human, and all proto-human, lives. A newborn might take up so much of a family's time and resources that other family members could be put at risk. And the family may have already invested huge efforts into nurturing and protecting previous children; as such, it might be illogical to risk their lives for a new baby. So the period immediately after birth might be the time when a mother had to assess their overall chances of survival with another baby to feed and protect. If the chances were bad, she would need to be able to kill her baby without becoming an emotional wreck.

So, the child murderers in the Valley of Hinnom were perhaps making a virtue out of a necessity by dedicating the killings as a sacrifice to gain the favour of a god; while also maintaining sensible population control.

Back on the subject of human sacrifice, consider the Jewish tradition of Passover – in which the god Yahweh personally killed all the Egyptian first-born sons. And there is the Christian faith in the literal self-sacrifice of Jesus of Nazareth. Both of these beliefs echo precursor religions, where angry gods could only be pacified by the deliberate killing of a beloved child.

Before putting all this down to ancient world savagery – that we have now safely outgrown – it is worth remembering present-day 'honour killings'. This is where family members – usually the fathers, brothers or uncles – murder teenage girls or young women for being too interested in boys, or for being gay, or for surviving after being raped.

In areas of the world with lax policing of honour crime, burning alive is a favoured method. In areas with stricter policing, enforced suicide is often used in an attempt to cover up the murder. In 2013 the BBC reported an estimate of between five thousand and twenty thousand murders of women and girls every year. Convicted honour killers almost invariably justify their actions by reference to their religion. Islam is notably plagued by honour killing, but there are examples to be found from most other faiths.

The pragmatism of population control (or defence of family honour) was rarely the conscious motivation for human sacrifice in the ancient world. As we will see in Chapter 8, one of the motivations for the creation of human slavery was to find expendable sacrificial victims who weren't from your family or local neighbourhood.

This was because killing people to please a god was often an habitual and even routine religious practice, and it was sometimes done on an industrial scale. The fifteenth-century CE Aztecs killed between 300 and 250,000 people a year (depending on which historian's estimate you accept). But even the low figure of three hundred would mean that on almost every day of the year a human being would have his or her belly cut open with an obsidian knife, and their still beating heart ripped out by a doubtless well-meaning and conscientious group of priests. That number rises to an average of over seven hundred daily sacrifices – or one fatal disembowelment every two minutes – if you believe the higher estimate.

As with the damage caused by human alcohol abuse, the sheer amount of suffering caused by religious sacrifice, worldwide and throughout history, defies calculation or even imagination. And all to pacify beings whose favour or existence was, by definition, beyond the ability of people to verify other than through blind faith. Even if you are a devout believer in a modern-thinking and humane religion, you would have to accept that all that sacrifice – to what you presumably believe to be false gods – was an appalling waste of resources, time and human lives.

Chapter 7

Civilised Cannibals

So far we have only lightly touched on a particularly disgusting aspect of human violence which, although fortunately rare, cannot be ignored in a history of brutality – that is cannibalism.

Up until fairly recently anthropologists and historians have treated the subject of cannibalism in much the same way that criminologists treated it. The eating of people was seen as a bizarre and disgusting anomaly: a form of madness that overtook certain cultures, just as it can obsess some murderers.

The causes of cannibalism were often seen as environmental: such as overpopulation in a limited area and shortages of meat animals for hunting. This happened on Easter Island in the Pacific after overpopulation, and the religious making of giant stone heads, had wrecked the environment: to make log rollers to move the heads, the carvers felled too many of the island's trees, thus tipping the environmental balance towards total deforestation. So the Easter Islanders could eventually make no log canoes and they were trapped over 2000 miles from any other habitable land. With the tree screen gone, farming became harder in the harsh wind and the lack of canoes made fishing all but impossible. Food became increasingly scarce.

Radio-carbon dating suggests that Easter Island was first colonised by Polynesian explorers around 1200 CE. Over the next four hundred years the islanders constructed a complex – giant stone head building – culture. But the environmental collapse led to starvation, war and, finally, to institutionalised cannibalism. When Europeans discovered Easter Island, in

1722, only around two thousand islanders remained – a fall from around fifteen thousand just a century before, and a population drop of 87 per cent. Cannibalism, by then, had ceased to be practised; but only because the island's population had reached an environmentally supportable number.

Certainly it is true that cannibalism most commonly survived into the modern age in isolated cultures with limited food resources: such as the pre-Columbus Carib people of the Caribbean, isolated Polynesian cultures (like the Easter Islanders), or the Korowai people of Papua New Guinea (who were still reported to be eating human meat as late as 2006).

Anthropologists also saw the eating of people as an essentially ritualistic and fetishistic behaviour. So, warriors who ate their enemies – like the pre-seventeenth century Maoris of New Zealand – often believed that they were also ingesting some of their courage and strength. When the British explorer Captain James Cook was murdered on the Pacific island of Hawaii, in 1779, the local chiefs ate his heart during an elaborate funeral service, to distribute his courage.

The Hawaiian chiefs were also motivated by respect and regret, and this was another key motivator of ritual cannibalism. The esteemed people within a tribe would be eaten after they had died of natural causes: something once practised by the South American Yanomami people and is reputedly still practised by the previously mentioned Korowai people. This 'endocannibalism' was always an indication of esteem, but might also be an attempt to magically retain a loved one's knowledge within the tribe: 'eaten with honour', as the pioneer Egyptologist, Sir Flinders Petrie, described the practice.

Quite often anthropologists have dismissed unsubstantiated reports of cannibalism as negative propaganda, put about by competing peoples for their own ends. For example, there was the widespread belief among Europeans, from the seventeenth through to the early twentieth century, that the Native Americans on the US western frontier were cannibals. This is now known to be utterly untrue; it was a folktale, spread by European colonists who had a vested interest in depicting the Native Americans as monsters.

However, as far as prehistory goes, human cannibalism is now thought to have been much more widespread than we previously believed. In Chapter 4 we saw evidence from Gran Dolina in Spain and Les Rois in France that indicated that both *Homo erectus* and *Homo sapiens* seem to have been eating human flesh, possibly as a regular part of their diet. And recent genetic discoveries support the belief that cannibalism has always been a common, if not necessarily a typical human behaviour.

Human prion diseases of the brain, like Creutzfeldt-Jakob (a.k.a. 'mad cow disease') and kuru are passed on through the eating of already infected brains. In the case of mad cow disease, the cause was eating the brains of cows that had been forced – through dubious factory-farming methods – to eat the dried but still infected brains of dead cows. With kuru, it was human cannibalism.

It has recently been discovered that having a particular variation of the prion gene (PRNP) confers some resistance to prion diseases, and this mutation has been found to be prevalent in many population groups (although just how globally widespread remains a matter of scientific controversy). The most likely cause of the success of such a mutation is an evolutionary favouring of those groups who were willing to utilise cannibalism as an extra food source. But the evolution of such an immunity would entail a lot of cannibalism, taking place over many generations.

As an illustrative comparison, consider milk-drinking by adults. Newborn babies are obviously capable of digesting milk, but it is certain that most grown-ups in human history were lactose intolerant – that is, incapable of properly digesting the complex lactose sugars found in dairy products. This was because – like all other species of mammal – as soon as they stopped being breastfed, humans automatically lost the ability to produce the lactase enzymes that break lactose down into digestible sugars. Yet the chances are reasonable that the reader of this book, like the authors, can drink milk with wild abandon, should they so wish.

The Neolithic domestication of cattle – typically ponies or goats – made dairy products available to humans. But only a few groups – notably in Europe, North Africa, the Middle East and India – took advantage of it for long enough to evolve the ability to host lactase enzymes into adulthood. In fact, most early herding cultures seem to have used cattle only for meat and blood – the latter taken from the living animal and used in stews or drunk raw.

Consequently, even after nearly ten thousand years of cattle herding, only about 25 per cent of the present world adult population are entirely lactose tolerant[1]. So how many millennia of cannibalism and brain-eating were necessary to allow even a proportion of our ancestors to develop a resistance to prion diseases?

Of course, cannibalism might be seen to be an academic subject when studying the greater overall picture of human violence. After all, it is the act of killing that is the key part of a murder – not what was done with the body afterwards. But what we are most interested in is the *mind* of a killer, and how that might have culturally changed to the extent that the murder rate is now falling sharply around the globe.

So it is worth considering here the basic mindset of a predatory cannibal: that they are willing to destroy another person's life in order to feed themselves. In economic game theory this is called a 'negative-sum game' – the cannibal takes, and the victim loses, but the overall production of the event is less than zero because the cannibal only stays fed for a short time, while the victim has lost their entire life. The world is self-evidently made poorer; yet that is a cost that the cannibal is willing to see others pay, provided that they themselves end up with a full belly.

For a traditional cannibal – like the sixteenth-century Caribs and the stranded Easter Islanders – the gain from murder was essentially nutritional. But it certainly also had a psychological aspect; often as the ultimate act of revenge. Professor Paul Moon noted of the New Zealand Maoris: 'If you can chop [your enemy]

---

1 Figures from Hertzler, Huynh and Savaiano – 'How much lactose is low lactose?', *The Journal of the American Dietetic Association* (1996)

up and eat them and turn them into excrement that is the greatest humiliation you can impose on them.'[2]

For a cannibal serial killer – like Jeffrey Dahmer or Albert 'the Werewolf of Wysteria' Fish – the act of killing in order to eat human flesh is essentially a pseudo-sexual-control game; it is the ultimate extension of the dominance obsession that is the key drive of serial rape and serial murder alike. Forcing sex on an unwilling partner 'proves' a serial rapist's power over their victim. And when that ceases to be enough, thanks to the law of diminishing returns, they might try to demonstrate their dominance by killing the victim. Eating the corpse afterwards is usually seen as going too far – even by serial killer standards – but for a few murderers it feels like the ultimate act of domination.

(Originally an economic principle, the *law of diminishing returns* is now commonly used to refer to any situation in which continued effort returns less and less result. For example, increasing tolerance to heroin is a common problem for drug-users, as is pushing a particular political policy too far for political leaders. In the case of a serial killer, a psychological law of diminishing returns means that the initial thrill of murder wanes over time – and further murders. This often drives them to greater acts of monstrosity, simply to get any thrill at all.)

The ironic fact is that, for the perpetrator, even the most desperate atrocities essentially don't work: rape, torture, murder or cannibalism can't silence the nagging insecurity that seems to hound all serial criminals. The British serial killer Dennis Nilsen once complained to biographer Brian Masters that the fictional serial cannibal, Hannibal Lecter, was fantastically unrealistic. Nilsen said that: '[Lecter] is shown as a potent figure, which is pure myth . . . My offences arose from a feeling of inadequacy, not potency. I never had any power in my life.'[3]

In this chapter I'm going to argue that there is another form of cannibalism, identified by a cannibalistic mindset, but not by the

---

2 Paul Moon, *This Horrid Practice: The Myth and Reality of Traditional Maori Cannibalism* (2008)

3 Brian Masters, *Killing for Company* (1995)

actual act of eating human flesh. Anyone who is willing to destroy the lives of others in order to enrich their own life should be called a cannibal.

For example: the Ancient Roman patrician or the Deep South plantation owner who starved and worked their slaves to death, because it was cheaper to replace slaves than it was to feed them properly. Or the company executives who cover up evidence that their product has lethal side-effects, in order not to damage sales, and thus their own salaries and bonuses. Or a politician who deliberately starts an unnecessary war in order to enhance their own power and prestige. All, I suggest, are psychologically as cannibalistic as any blood-soaked, child-eating *Homo erectus* in the Gran Dolina caves. They are 'socio-economic' or 'civilised' cannibals.

We've already seen how the Neolithic birth of civilisation probably created an increase in human conflict. It would be reasonable to guess that the earliest walled towns, like Jericho, were under regular threat of attack, because the inhabitants went to all the trouble of building walls. You don't need stone defences to keep out wolves and bears – but to keep out humans. Raids by nomad bandits were probably the original problem for town dwellers. But as those towns prospered and grew in size – and developed militias and armies – inter-town warfare became a regular aspect of civilised life. As did social unrest within the town walls.

In the last chapter we also saw how town watchmen soon evolved into a warrior nobility. And how the tribal shaman became a temple priest. Giving up nomadism also had another side-effect: the creation of excesses of wealth, poverty and political power.

Ownership was never a key issue for people living a purely nomadic, hand-to-mouth existence. There were doubtless fights over who got the biggest portion of food after a hunt, and who slept with which sex partner. And, of course, the local definition of 'rich' and 'poor' is entirely relative to the resources available.

(There is a B. Kilban cartoon of a man and woman dressed in filthy rags, facing a shabby, one-room shack with just a tattered blanket for a door. The woman is smiling delightedly and saying: 'Wow! I know you said that you were rich. But I didn't think that you meant *this* rich.')

Yet on the whole, in a wandering tribe, fortunes and misfortunes were shared by all. Everyone got fat when there was game, and got thin when the hunting was poor. There was only so much that a bullying chief could do to feather his own nest in these circumstances – if he ate while the rest of the tribe starved, they would simply kill him and choose a new leader.

Secure town living, food storage and the crafting of non-perishable goods changed all that. Even before the invention of money, towns had created the 'haves' and the 'have-nots'. Storing food in granaries and cold rooms greatly reduced spoilage, for example, but also meant that whoever was in charge of food distribution was in a position to line their own pockets and bellies. Noble warriors were able to collect wealth through battle with foreigners and extortion from compatriots. Holy men often demanded more than their fair share, on the understanding that thin or poorly dressed priests made the gods angry. And then there were the traders and craftsmen who earned their wealth fairly – or not, as the case may be.

All these comparatively rich people, because they had permanent homes, could store their possessions securely – unlike a nomad who had to carry their wealth with them and defend it while they did so. For the well-off townie, display of their wealth became an essential method of gaining prestige. And, of course, these original nouveau riche were resented, to greater or lesser degrees, by their less well-to-do neighbours.

Robbery, and the harsh punishment of thieves, has always been an obsession within settled societies. But, from the very beginning, there have been 'blue-collar' thieves and 'white-collar' thieves. A robber who is willing to kill during a burglary or mugging is arguably as bad as an exploiting rich man who impoverishes others until they starve. Yet as a civilisation grew and became more multifaceted, the scope for the latter type of socio-economic cannibalism also grew; while the homicidal bandit has always had limited opportunities . . . and life expectancy.

The invention of money – to at least partially replace barter – dates from around 3000 BCE, and a was a side-effect of the invention of both writing and numeracy. The 'shekel' was originally a standardised unit of weight used to separate out divisions of food (usually barley) in Mesopotamia, five thousand years ago. Someone obviously needed to be able to both count and write to be able to manage such a precise system, and using non-perishable tokens to represent a collection of shekels was an obvious time-saving device. A man could then hold the representative value of his farm's entire yearly harvest in his hand, and exchange his shekels for whatever he might need or want, provided he was trusted to deliver the actual food to his buyer.

From this basic monetary system (copied or invented independently in almost all town-based cultures throughout history) there ultimately came long-distance trade, accountancy, money lending, interest on debt, and banking. It also created the first super-rich, which in early civilisations meant someone who was not reduced to a hand-to-mouth existence or starvation by crop failures (provided there was someone else with a food surplus available to buy).

We've already discussed the warrior-noble families, who stored wealth in the form of weapons, armour and captured non-perishables like jewellery and land. But the invention and spread of money not only gave the nobles something else to capture and hoard, but also created a non-aristocratic merchant class who could, and often did, wield more wealth than the nobility.

Generally the nobility of any civilisation regarded such upstarts as usurpers and interlopers – they were dismissed as 'jumped-up tradesmen'. But the nobility could be pragmatic as well as snobbish. Where they couldn't politically suppress the merchant class (as in Republican Ancient Rome) or legally steal their money through unfair taxation (as in pre-revolutionary France) the nobility would allow the richest merchants to buy their way into the aristocracy, thus effectively absorbing and assimilating the leading families of the merchant class.

Either way, the aristocracy held the whip hand on most civilisations' finances – and thus legislation – right up to the invention of modern income tax and inheritance tax systems in the nineteenth century. When these laws were adopted, in combination, they efficiently gutted the bank accounts of the idle rich over a few generations. The aristocracy, in most countries, went from plush and secure comfort, to permanent debt and bankruptcy in less than a hundred years. This left the merchant class – who actually made or traded things, rather than inherited their wealth, and thus had a regular stream of profits – to take the reins of power.

And wealth *is* power when used correctly. Political power is, necessarily, a much more nebulous concept than money: if only because each culture manifests its power in different ways, dependent on its circumstances and traditions. In medieval Christian Europe, for example, ruling power was almost entirely restricted to hereditary noble families and the Church. Rich merchants had some influence, but were generally seen as mere cash-cows by their rulers. In Periklean Athens in the fifth century BCE, on the other hand, the nobles and the merchant-adventurers were generally one and the same; and all sought to wield power by manipulating the votes of the democratic assembly through both rhetoric and bribery.

However, political power in *any* culture almost invariably boils down to getting a better deal, and privileges, for those wielding that power. This is not necessarily a bad thing for the rest of society – use of power can potentially right wrongs and improve the lot for everyone across the board – but it usually means robbing somebody else's Peter to pay your Paul.

It is very rare for a leader – be they an ancient-world king or a modern-day president – to die poorer than when they first took power. And as with leaders, so too with the clan, class or caste with which they associate themselves. The benefits produced by limited resources – be they food, water, gold, oil or intellectual property rights – almost always float upward in any society.

This book is about unnecessary human violence, not social or economic exploitation; but where personal enrichment demands the death of others, we are again considering civilised cannibalism. This might also be seen as circumstantial evidence for the

bonobo theory of human nature, as such inhumane greed was
rarer in smaller communities with less complex civilisations.

In the early town societies there was limited scope for exploitative abuse. The rich lived within a stone's throw of the poor,
because *everyone* lived within a stone's throw of everyone else.
In a community of a few hundred or even several thousand
people, you are still likely to know the names of anyone you
harm, and shame as well as social condemnation have a real
power. But where the community is big enough to allow the
affluent to isolate themselves into separate, well-guarded districts
– and thus there is little chance of them personally knowing the
victims of any exploitative actions – the scope for socio-economic
cannibalism by the rich grows proportionately.

Slaves can be overworked on starvation rations. Employees
can be underpaid and trapped in debt bondage. Weaker (or
more moral) business competitors can be driven to the wall by
shady or outright illegal tactics. Extortion and shameless theft
can be justified by the ancient rule of 'might makes right'. And if
you are ever caught and condemned, the authorities can be
bribed to see things your way.

Indeed, officialdom's corrupt sanctioning of antisocial acts by
the privileged parts of society – while rightly prohibiting similar
or identical acts for everyone else – is an essential element that
allows civilised cannibalism to take place. White-collar cannibals
will generally make sure that they have the protection of the law
before they begin their feast; but it's in nobody's interest that
everyone in society be allowed such latitude, or there would be
chaos. As the novelist Joseph Conrad commented in *Heart of
Darkness* (1899):

> *By heavens! there is something after all in the world allow-
> ing one man to steal a horse while another must not look at
> a halter.*

Each of the above 'business practices' are almost as old as
civilisation itself. All, except large-scale slavery, are still prevalent
in the free markets of today. And each has cost human lives when

taken to their level of 'maximum profitability'. Of course, such exploitation can build up social resentment among the exploited, and that risks a backlash against the rich and powerful. So why are revolutions by the oppressed so rare in history?

One reason harks back to our days as pack-minded animals. The creation of a nobility, a priestly hierarchy and people with markedly different levels of wealth within a society inevitably led to a stratification of a culture into social classes and/or religious castes. This was often a form of direct social control that could become virtually totalitarian – as in the late period Western Roman Empire where the lower classes were forbidden to change professions, on pain of death. Or in India, where almost 20 per cent of the population – the Dalits – were defined as 'untouchable,' because merely touching them could ritually pollute a higher caste Indian.

It can be hard to improve your social status if nobody in a position to help you is willing to risk going near you. Or if the full weight of the law will fall on you if you try to get a better job. Yet, once social stratification is well established, it doesn't need such ham-fisted intervention by the ruling classes. Almost everyone in such a stratified culture sets up as a social border guard, even – and often especially – those who have most to gain by social climbing.

One of the worst insults a middle-class British Victorian could level at another middle-class person, for example, would be to call them a 'counter-jumper'. This implied that they had started out as a shop assistant (or in an equally lowly position) and, 'because they didn't know their place', they had sought to climb the social ladder. Such upwardly mobile 'counter-jumpers' were despised at least as much by those who they left behind the shop counter, so to speak, as the class they were trying to invade. The very people one might logically expect to have been seen as revolutionary, groundbreaking heroes, were often seen as 'class-traitors' or 'no better than they ought to be' by the labouring or servant class that they had been born into.

The early feminists, in the nineteenth and twentieth centuries, ran into the same problem. The chief advocates against female rights might have been patriarchal men; but they were supported in their opposition by a sizable number of non-socially-active, yet influential women. The Suffragette movement was held back by the apathy and trepidation of women, as much as it was by the active opposition and ridicule of men. It was not until after the First World War – when many women had proven that they could do 'a man's job' (and there was a small but significant reduction of the male population due to machine guns) – that a strong popular movement for female emancipation took wing.

George Orwell noted in *The Road to Wigan Pier* (1937) that it was the financially struggling section of the middle class – what he called the 'shabby-genteel' – that hung on to class distinction most desperately. Yet it was exactly this class that suffered most from the irrational demands of the British class system.

On an income that was sometimes not much higher than that of a working-class family, the lower-middle-class family had the extra financial burden of 'keeping up appearances': that is, trying to look as if they were financially 'respectable', with good clothes, a nice house with 'decent' furniture, posh schools for their children and so forth. The fear that they might 'slip back' into the working class – on losing their job or suffering some other financial mishap – only added further stress to the embittering struggle. But their chief fear was of the shame and social ostracisation caused by 'not keeping up with the Joneses' and being seen as 'jumped-up guttersnipes'.[4]

Class – and caste – distinction is a key factor in maintaining the status quo in a non-egalitarian civilisation; much more than armed soldiers, or a draconian legal system designed to serve the ruling class. There is an automatic human deference to established power that is probably a hangover from our days as pack-minded animals – civic authority being the civilised version of the alpha-male pack leader. This unthinking deference can even make people vehemently fight against their own interests. And over time this habit can become thoroughly entrenched,

---

4 George Orwell, *The Road to Wigan Pier* (pages 109–13)

because even the most blatant forms of abuse will eventually become 'honoured traditions'.

The philosopher and novelist Robert Anton Wilson once wrote up an illustrative parable about the destructive interplay between tradition and class deference:

> [Once upon a time there was] *a king who decided that every time he met somebody he would kick them in the butt, just to emphasize his power . . . Since this maniac wore a crown and had an army, people soon learned to tolerate being kicked fairly often, and even began to accept it philosophically or stoically, as they accept taxation and other impositions of kings and governors. They even learned to bend over as soon as they saw the king coming.*
>
> *Eventually, the king died and his successor naturally continued the tradition and kicked anybody he chanced to meet. Centuries passed, and, in the usual course of things, the nobility as a whole had demanded, and acquired, the same 'right' as the king: any baron could kick anybody of lesser rank, and the knights could kick anybody except the barons or the royal family, etc. A large part of the population spent most of its waking hours facing a wall, crouched over, waiting for the next boot in the bottom.*
>
> *The coming of democracy, in that amazing parallel universe, could only be understood according to the traditional thought-forms or acquired mental habits of the strange people there. Democracy therefore meant to those peculiar folks that anybody could kick anybody else as long as the kicker could prove that he (or she) had a bigger bank balance than the person receiving the boot in the rump. Within the context of the gloss or grid or reality-tunnel in that world, 'democracy' could not have any other thinkable meaning.*[5]

---

5 Robert Anton Wilson, 'The Semantics of "Good" & "Evil"' (essay in *Critique: A Journal Questioning Consensus Reality*)

But if all this suggests that religion and nobility have always acted together to control the rest of society, then think again. Almost as old as the feud between nomad and settler, there is the rivalry between aristocrat and priest.

As noted in the last chapter, a noble's main interests lie in protecting their family's prestige and privileges, while looking to expand the range of both wherever possible. Anyone born into such a position of privilege is likely to be at least a little paranoid, simply by being aware that there are so many people beneath them on the social ladder, most of whom must be jealous of all that they have. Social and political conservatism are a natural response to this constant background fear, and a prevalence of this attitude in the ruling class inevitably leads to repression of the poor.

An aristocrat's social and political manoeuvring to improve their family's position is another way to secure their noble inheritance. Of course the more successful they are at these power games – and the higher up the greasy pole that they climb – the more their paranoia (as a sort of social vertigo) risks building up to dangerous levels: 'Uneasy lies the head that wears a crown.'[6]

A simple, if short-term way to reduce the rulers' fear of social insurrection is militarism. Most noble families originally got and kept their exalted positions by being warriors or – later on – by employing soldiers. Raising troops to repress the peasants was a natural reaction for them. US Vice-President Elbridge Gerry noted that a standing army is like an erect penis: 'An excellent assurance of domestic tranquillity, but a dangerous temptation to foreign adventure.' But in fact, like an erection, permanent armies could cause trouble anywhere, even on home ground.

The problem with keeping military forces around home territory permanently was that the grunts tended to get bored and troublesome. Visit a pub or bar near a military base if you want a graphic illustration. And, like the Imperial Roman Praetorian Guard, under-employed soldiers can become prone to starting *coup d'état* to replace the ruler with someone more exciting or profitable.

---

6 William Shakespeare, *Henry IV: Part II* (Act III, scene i) (1597)

So an aristocratically run culture tended to be on a permanent war footing. This kept the professional soldiers too busy to either start brawls or to overthrow the government, but also meant that they were usually available to fight insurrections or civil wars at home. As a result aristocrats often regarded war as a noble calling; although fighting in the front line – in the mud with the common squaddies – was generally seen as rather ignoble. And, as a bonus, if the soldiers won any battles or wars with foreign enemies, there would be spoils to divide among their employers. Cultures next to this sort of state quickly became equally war-like themselves . . . or became conquests.

Priests, on the other hand, usually won their social position through merit or favour. There have been, and are, such things as priestly castes – entire hereditary sections of society, like the Brahmins in India and the Tribe of Levi in Ancient Israel – but most religions have recruited mainly on potential from any section of society. A noble who became a priest was usually a second or third son – without much or any inheritance – and thus likely to give most of their loyalty to the faith, not their family. For anyone else in society, becoming a priest was generally a step up in the world, which again guaranteed loyalty to the religious hierarchy.

Like the noble families, a priesthood was mostly concerned with maintaining the status quo in society, but for different reasons. Priests had little or no fear of the underclass, because that was where the majority of their loyal flock originated. On the other hand, a priest lived in constant fear of losing his congregation – and their tithes – to another religion. Bitchy sectarianism has always been a major facet of religious life in states where multiple religions compete; this sometimes escalating into full-scale rioting, death-squad terrorism or outright religious civil wars.

This sort of unrest angered the aristocracy, as the last thing they wanted was domestic trouble that might further ignite the resentment of the lower orders. Priests, on the other hand, often turned their face against the war-mongering militarism of the nobles. After all, it was their congregations that stood to be killed in battle, and influxes of conquered foreigners generally brought their damnable foreign gods with them.

This dynamic tension between two key sections of the ruling class has caused some of the worst bloodshed in history. Think of Europe's sixteenth-century Reformation wars – between the forces of the priestly Catholic Church and nobility-supported Protestant reformers: central and western Europe were devastated and partly depopulated before they came to an end. Then consider China's nineteenth-century Taiping Rebellion – between the decaying government of Manchu nobles and a sect of Christian revolutionaries: in just fourteen years, between twenty and thirty million people died as a result of the conflict. Or read the *Epic of Gilgamesh*, the almost four-thousand-year-old tale of a feud between the egotistical king of Uruk (in Mesopotamia) and the Gods themselves. Again and again in history, beyond the religious dogma and political rhetoric, one can see evidence of an essential power struggle between the secular and the religious hierarchies.

This chapter had concentrated on the cannibalistic abuse of power: be it a Palaeolithic warrior using stone weapons to kill and eat his victims, or a twenty-first-century multinational company improving its profit margins by cutting back on workplace safety. Chief among these abusers, throughout history, have been members of the ruling class. This is not because they are somehow born less humane than the rest of the population, but simply because they have always had the most power available to misuse. The ruler is gifted with the power to feather his own nest . . . at a cost to others . . . and must live with the constant temptation to do so.

Yet it is from the ruling class that perhaps civilisation's greatest invention emanated: law-making and justice.

Pre-literate societies certainly had laws; in fact, they could be positively riddled with rules and taboos. But maintaining these laws, via local oral traditions alone, could make social regulation both parochial and too open to manipulation by those given the job of 'remembering' past rulings. A complex society simply can't function with such a rickety legal system.

It takes a literate culture to create a code of law and a legal system. And it has always taken a ruling class to run that legal system. (The English words 'judge' and 'judgement' derive from the Biblical *Book of Judges* – but that book's title is referring to tribal war chiefs like Samson, not to trained legal experts.) People who have to work from dawn to dusk, like farmers or traders, never had time to devise and police the laws; but a king, or some other type of aristocrat, generally had plenty of spare time to dedicate to these activities.

Even in a modern, internet-linked democracy, the responsibility of law-making is routinely handed over to a group of specialists – the politicians, lobby groups and civil servants – because the general public are too busy, or too lazy, to manage the state on a day-to-day basis. These specialists are the active arm of the modern ruling class. And, of course, the ruling class has always had a vested interest in maintaining peace among the lower orders.

Think of justice from the point of view of a ruler in an early or primitive civilisation. Disputes among his people will rarely help or enrich him – quite the reverse, in fact. If two farmers came to blows over a boundary stone position, for example, the result might have been, at best, a local feud; and at worst a disruption of food production and tax revenues. People might get hurt or killed as well, of course. So the king, or the local noble, had a vested interest in smoothing the matters over as quickly as possible. And if he did so with evident justice and fair-mindedness, the litigants would be less prone to resenting the fines that he might impose (and pocket).

It is only recently, since the European Enlightenment in the seventeenth century CE, that any legal system on the planet was specifically designed to separate the ruler's and the judge's vested interests. In fact, up to then, the two roles were generally filled by the same person. In most cultures it was only in the past three hundred years that the idea of an independent and politically neutral judiciary was even imagined, much less expected by the general populace.

What the judicial nobility didn't often have – up until comparatively recently – was the education (or patience) to record and arrange their legal rulings. A life that was a mixture of leisure, hunting and war did not match up well with endless and humdrum bookkeeping. This was so much true that the few genuinely academic rulers in history – like King Ashurbanipal of Babylon (who died in 627 BCE) and the Roman philosopher-emperor, Marcus Aurelius (121 to 180 CE) – were invariably seen as remarkable (not to say freakish) by both their contemporaries and by later historians.

Here the nobility and the priesthood sometimes put aside their differences and worked in tandem: a noble had the time and inclination to give rulings over their underlings, and a priest had the time and the literacy to record and order the legal precedents. A priest, after all, needed to be able to read and write to be able to learn, preach and elaborate on their religious doctrine. Later on professional scribes did this work, then actual lawyers; but for much of civilised history the man holding the stylus and clay tablet, sitting respectfully below the judge's dais, was a priest.

Today it is a common complaint that we live in an over-legalised society: that spurious litigation and excessive legal controls surround us at every turn. This, however, is nothing new. For example, the Ancient Romans were even more litigious than modern Americans or Europeans. Reading Roman history, it is hard not to conclude that the Roman ruling class were essentially all amateur lawyers – with access to one of the most lethal armies on the planet. The Roman historian Tacitus, writing in the first century CE, lamented: 'Once we suffered from too much crime. Now we suffer from too much law.'

It is tempting to say that civilised humans are as acclimatised to laws as a fish is to water. From the moment of birth we are socialised by our parents; schools continue the process; and our definition of adulthood is largely based around legal concepts such as the age of sexual consent and being old enough to vote. A vast and intricate network of laws defines not only what we can and can't do, but also comforts us with the security that our fellow citizens are also, by-and-large, restricted and protected by the same legal network.

Thomas Hobbes (1588–1679) called the legal control of the state over the individual the 'Leviathan'; a reference to the gigantic sea monster mentioned in the Old Testament book of Job. He used this frightening image to indicate the great power that, he believed, must be exerted by the government to prevent humans falling back into what, he believed, was the sheer savagery of 'the state of nature'. But it should be remembered that Hobbes had just lived through the brutal English Civil War (1642–51) so it was hardly surprising that he thought even the tiniest tear in the social fabric could potentially plunge civilisation into chaos.

Yet Hobbes was no totalitarian. He stressed that legal government was a 'social contract' between rulers and ruled. Without this continuous strand of mutual agreement, the law could not hold society together. In fact, Hobbes clearly understood that the English Civil War had been caused by a breaking of this contract between the king and the English parliament.

(The pompous and rather stupid Charles I had ignored the demands of the elected representatives of the people, who had asked not to be ruthlessly taxed to finance unnecessary and glory-hunting foreign wars. Parliament rebelled and King Charles declared war on them. The resulting bloodbath killed at least 190,000 people (3.8 per cent of an English population of approximately five million). One of the last to die because of the conflict was Charles I himself.)

For Hobbes, what better example could there be that *everyone* – rulers and ruled – needed to be held within the leviathan grip of the social contract? The chopping-off of a king's head had conclusively showed that nobody can be allowed to put themselves above the law.

It is a legal truism that law and justice are two separate things – it is preferable that their paths coincide, but that can't always be arranged. Corruption, ignorance, bigotry or simple disagreement about what is or is not fair can derail the wheels of justice; especially when lawmakers and judges suffer a combination of these shortfalls. Yet continuous oversight of the legal process by an empowered population can generally keep justice and law running in roughly the same direction. This is why the principle of a free press has become so essential to a modern, well-functioning civilisation.

It is notable that the great revolutions of the modern era – the American, French, Russian and Chinese to name just the most world-shaking – all came after the ruling class had begun to behave as if they were above the law *and* there had been a technological leap in communication technology. For the birth of the USA and the (first) fall of the French monarchy, it was cheap pamphlet printing. For the fall of the Tsar it was telegraphy and for the rise of Red China it was radio. And in 2011, some of the most stable dictatorships in the Middle East – Tunisia, Egypt and Libya – fell with the key help of internet communications.

Civilised cannibalism may be as prevalent today as it has always been. But since the development of easy-to-access mass communication, the cannibals are finding it increasingly hard to hide the evidence of their monstrous diet.

Chapter 8

'Everywhere in Chains'

There is an old children's story that you've probably heard at one time or another. It's about a prince who is kidnapped from his native land. He, and thirteen other abducted young men and women, are taken to an island kingdom to be fed to a monster. The prince is called Theseus of Athens, the island is Crete in the south-eastern Mediterranean and the monster is the Minotaur – a man with the head of a bull. Thrown into the Labyrinth – the maze that houses the Minotaur – Prince Theseus fights and kills the monster, then escapes with his companions (and an amenable Cretan princess). Some versions of the story add that Theseus later returned to take his revenge on Crete as a pirate raider.

For most of the past three millennia that was all that the tale of Theseus was thought to be: a mythic children's story. Then, in 1900, the British archaeologist Arthur Evans unearthed the remains of a vast palace at Kephala Hill, four miles outside the northern port of Heraklion, on Crete. The palace complex consisted of over 1300 interconnected rooms, spread over six acres. Ranging from palatial apartments and a regal audience chamber, to ordinary workshops and storerooms, the palace-city must have been literally labyrinthine.

Evans named his discovery 'Knossos', after the capital of the Cretan empire in the myth of Theseus and the Minotaur. Certainly the site was ancient, with the earliest signs of basic village habitation dating back to the Neolithic period, at around 6000 BCE. Over the next four thousand years Knossos had grown into the fabulous complex unearthed by Evans. At its height it must have been one of the greatest habitations on the planet. In a world where a building with a dozen rooms would have been seen as a mansion, Knossos represented vast wealth, great technical knowledge and a rich culture. Yet this palace-city, full of potential plunder as it must have seemed to its neighbours, had no defensive walls. It was evidently kept safe by the powerful Cretan navy, just as described in the tale of Theseus.

Yet Arthur Evans also discovered that Knossos had been shattered repeatedly. Some time between 1600 and 1570 BCE the island volcano of Thera – 70 miles north of Crete – had exploded. The eruption of ash into the atmosphere was so great that it caused a 'volcanic winter': a decade-long period of continual cold and bad harvests. This was so tremendous in its effect, that it might even have brought about the fall of the (semi-legendary) Xia Dynasty in China, over 4000 miles away. Certainly Thera's eruption, the rain of ash, and the associated earthquakes and tsunamis, would have devastated the entire region of the eastern Mediterranean.

Almost all of the Cretan navy was undoubtedly destroyed by tsunamis, as were Crete's northern ports and many or most of the inhabitants on that coast. Knossos was too far inland and uphill to be drowned by tidal waves, but the earthquakes, volcanic ash fall and bad harvests from the Thera eruption must have brought the palace-city to its knees.

This breaking of Cretan imperial power had another consequence. The fledgling city-states of Mycenaean Greece must also have been devastated by the Thera eruption, but evidently recovered more quickly. Archaeological evidence shows that from at least 1450 BCE, the rulers of Knossos were not native Cretans, but conquering Mycenaean Greeks – the culture of Theseus of Athens.

The palace-city suffered another catastrophe when it was ravaged by fire around 1375 BCE. Yet – so strong was the cultural memory of one of the greatest living structures on Earth – the patched-up ruins of Knossos remained inhabited until as late as 1100 BCE.

Arthur Evans's discoveries, and his bringing to life of an ancient fairy story, enchanted the world. But it was what he found on the walls of Knossos that was truly dumbfounding. Among gorgeous frescos of dolphins, griffons and courtly men and women, there was an illustration of a Cretan sport: young men are shown vaulting over the back of a charging, long-horned bull. Arthur Evans felt sure that he had uncovered the true face of the Minotaur.

He suggested that the Cretan sea empire – which he dubbed the 'Minoans' after the mythical ruler of the Labyrinth, King Minos – must have enslaved people from surrounding lands. Some of these unfortunates then had to learn and perform the lethally dangerous game of 'bull-leaping' for their Minoan masters. The fresco shows the athletes as quite unarmed and unarmoured – the only things that kept bull-leapers alive would have been their skill, their wits and their agility. And, given the hefty size of the bull pictured, fatal goring and trampling must have been a regular spectacle in the Minoan bullring. Rumours of this savage entertainment probably made their way back to Greece where, Evans suggested, they were twisted into the story of a bull-headed, man-eating ogre.

Of course the real ogre in the story of Theseus was the enforced human bondage. Be it performing and dying in the bullring, sweating in the fields, or pulling the oars that powered the Cretan navy, slavery was a key element of Minoan prosperity. But, if he ever really existed, the heroic Prince Theseus would certainly have owned slaves of his own and would have considered slavery as part of the natural order of things. In fact, slavery has existed for so long that it might be tempting to agree with Theseus; but slavery is no more natural to human beings than blacksmithing or kite-flying. Without civilisation, slavery would never have existed.

Slavery was unknown in hunter-gatherer societies, because of a cardinal rule of survival: 'One more mouth to feed is, first and foremost, one more mouth to feed.' A hand-to-mouth existence meant that people had enough trouble providing for themselves. In such a basic economy, a kidnapped and enslaved stranger would necessarily eat at least as much as their enforced labour produced. Taking on a work slave would therefore have been like adopting a new family member against their will – and there are less dangerous and more pleasant ways to create new family members.

Women-stealing and sexual enslavement was another matter: all hunter-gatherer societies habitually kidnapped women from enemy tribes. Indeed, as we saw in Chapter 5, wild chimps regularly go raiding to kill the males of other troupes, and to kidnap their females. And believers in killer ape theory suggest that our pre-civilised ancestors were also doing so, all the way back to before we started walking upright. Certainly, for as long as males have been the bigger and more aggressive sex, the sexual enslavement of females could be said to be a typical part of mammalian behaviour; so much so, that many zoologists would say it is over-emotive to call it slavery and rape in the first place.

Our disgust at sexual slavery might be seen as a by-product of our civilisation's fairly recent adoption of the belief that a woman can always, and in any circumstances, say no to sex. Laws against rape may be ancient, but so is the tradition of a father choosing his daughter's husband, irrespective of her feelings in the matter. And in fact most rape laws originally defined the crime as a destruction of property: that is the woman's valuable virginity or chastity, which was seen as the property of her father or husband. But we are not looking at domestic-level slavery in this chapter, but at slavery as an industry.

Of course, technically speaking, you can't be an unpaid slave when *nobody* is paid. Civilisation has to create surplus food or goods first. You could then pay others to do work for you from that surplus. Only then could you be a slave master, by making people work without recompensing them with anything other than their survival needs. Later, with the development of coinage, a slave was someone you imprisoned, forced to work and didn't pay in coins. But you still had to provide food and shelter for them, and prevent their escapes and/or attempts to kill you. All told, a civilisation had to be comparatively advanced for slavery to be a practical proposition.

Economically speaking – beyond surplus food, spare housing,

reliable guards and a ready source of replacement slaves – you also needed access to lucrative work that, nevertheless, you wouldn't want friends or relatives to have to do. For example, many of the slaves kidnapped around the ancient eastern Mediterranean were forced to make linen ropes and cloth. Linen was an expensive product, because it was so time-consuming and exhausting to make. First you had to crush and then soak the cut stems of the flax plant for weeks in stagnant ponds. After wading in and dragging the stuff out, workers then laboriously cleaned and combed the plant fibres until they were ready to weave. It was stinking, backbreaking work; so a pirate industry sprang up, kidnapping foreigners to enslave to the task of linen-making.

Women were generally preferred for this sort of slave work, which demanded more endurance than strength. This was mainly because they cost less to feed than men. Women were also less likely to rebel (especially if they had children in tow) and could be forced to prostitute themselves to their owner and guards; which free perk of the job, presumably, further reduced the slave-master's expenses. And, of course, female slaves produced baby slaves – who, when they were old enough, could also be forced to work or sold. As such, a slave-master's job wasn't so far different from that of a cattle farmer; only more risky, much more profitable and with a more self-gratifying husbandry aspect.

So widespread was the industry of woman-stealing during the Mycenaean period (c.1600 to 1100 BCE) that some historians have suggested it may have been the true cause of the Trojan War. Once thought a myth, the story of the destruction of the Anatolian city of Troy (known as *Ilium* to the Greeks and *Wilusa* to the neighbouring Hittite Empire) is now generally accepted to be based on historical fact. Certainly an impressively walled town, at roughly the right place in Turkish north-eastern Anatolia, was unearthed by the pioneering archaeologist Heinrich Schliemann in 1871. Archaeological evidence showed that the town had been devastated and burned, probably due to war, in both 1275 and 1180 BCE. The layout of the town that was ravaged in 1275 BCE is startlingly close to that of the Ilium described by the epic Greek poet Homer; right down to the towered walls, splendid palaces and the great, ramped gate.

Homer, writing the *Iliad* around 750 BCE, described the long siege and savage sacking of the city as the Greek attempt to rescue the beautiful Queen Helen from her Trojan kidnappers. But this may be a poetic metaphor for a more pragmatic *casus belli*: a Greek punitive expedition to try to stop the regular theft of their women by the Trojans. Certainly Troy, situated on the Anatolian Dardanelles with access to both the Black and Aegean Seas, was in an excellent position to act as a centre for the regional slave trade.[1]

Whether the above theory is true or not, slave trading was already an ancient occupation at the time of the Trojan War. For example, the Sumerians – dating from around 4000 BCE – were a culturally linked group of Mesopotamian city-states and are the earliest known literate culture; and they were also slave owners. As, indeed, were the Ancient Egyptians (who became a definable nation around 3000 BCE), the Ancient Indians (2600 BCE) and the Ancient Chinese (2100 BCE). Northern Europe, the Americas, Central and Southern Africa, Australia and the island cultures of the Pacific had no definable slave trade until much later, but that was because they took much longer to crawl out of the hunter-gatherer level of human development.

Early slavery was equally a result and a motivator of early warfare. We've already noted in Chapter 7 how the ruling class of a growing city-state would automatically build a standing army, both for defence from outside raiders and to keep the lower orders in line at home. War for profit and territorial expansion – usually against other city-states – followed whenever there seemed an opportunity. But what was to be done with the captured enemies?

In the case of conquered farmers and craftsmen, the answer was easy enough. They were left to get on with their lives, provided they paid taxes and tithes to their new rulers. But captured soldiers and nobles were another matter; since the

1 Michael Wood, *In Search of the Trojan War* (2005)

victorious state already had an army – and nobles – these prisoners were self-evidently surplus to requirements.

Ransoming them back to their relatives paid nicely in the short term, but ran the risk of rebuilding the enemy's fighting force with experienced and vengeful men.

Killing them was another option – often as sacrifices to the gods. The Aztecs, for example, were constantly starting wars with their neighbours – mainly with the aim of securing prisoners of war that they could then sacrifice to the gods. Given the possible scale of human sacrifice in the ancient world (*see Chapter 6*) this need for expendable victims was a major economic and military problem for cultures with bloodthirsty gods.

But then the victorious (and sacrificial) state had to be fairly secure in its military prowess. Because of the principle of escalation (*see Chapter 5*) any savage or inhumane practice adopted by one side in a conflict almost automatically became standard practice with their enemies. No general, high priest or king much liked the idea that they themselves might end up on a sacrificial altar, just because they made a few tactical errors and lost a battle or two. The obvious halfway house was to enslave military prisoners.

The impact of slavery on the development of civilisation should not be underestimated. Having the possession of slaves – especially former enemies – a slave owner's natural inclination was to tire them out with heavy labour, so they would cause less trouble. Digging irrigation ditches, carrying trade goods over long distances, labouring to build large constructions, and rowing galleys across the sea were obvious ways of doing this. So better farms were built, trade expanded, great palaces and temples were erected, and the world was explored – all on the back of the slave.

The earliest slavery seems to have been largely a state-run operation. Even the richer nobles could not afford the high set-up costs and ongoing maintenance of a slave industry; that took a taxpayer-supported royal family. Plus, easy access to an army was necessary to put down slave revolts and to capture replacement slaves.

For example, some of the clay tablets found in a Mycenaean palace unearthed at Pylos in the south-west Peloponnese (dating to around 1200 BCE) described the administration and feeding of slaves. Organised into batches of five hundred people, they were employed in local linen production – most of them being women kidnapped from Asia Minor. All of these slaves were evidently owned and controlled by the royal family of Pylos.

Eventually, however, other noble families in a culture would build up enough financial and military power to set up their own slave industries. So human exploitation for profit would, sooner or later, cease to be a state monopoly and become a free market-place – for the slave owners, at least.

Most slaves in history have been industrial or agricultural workers – and by industrial, one should think of a semi-skilled, high-production trade; from the making of ancient-world clay amphorae to modern-day high-tech sports shoes. With enough upfront and ongoing investment, such projects will eventually pay very high dividends. After all, how could competing non-slave industries survive, when they had the additional expense of paying wages to their workers? In the long run, the slave owners were virtually guaranteed monopoly status.

Of course, this favouring of slave industries malformed local economies. Perfectly healthy, non-slave businesses were driven to the wall, and widespread unemployment became a chronic social problem for the first time in history. As slave plantations spread, gobbling up neighbouring smallholdings and family farms, entire agricultural communities were uprooted. The dispossessed farm workers headed for the nearest city in the hope of finding work and, joining the unemployed industrial labourers there, became the urban poor. The slums in which they found themselves living became crime black spots. Seeing this degradation – from the comfort of their uptown villas – confirmed the opinion of the slave-owning rich that the lower classes were little better than immoral animals, and thus deserved whatever happened to them.

A major cause of social friction in the time of Julius Caesar (100 to 44 BCE) was the unemployment being caused among the Roman *capite censi* (the impoverished 'head count' class) by the increasing use of mass slavery. Caesar himself turned against his fellow Patrician aristocrats – who were now rich enough to run huge slave plantations and industries as family concerns. Throughout his career he championed the rights of the underemployed, and thus underfed, lower classes. It was this, more than anything else, that motivated his enemies in the Roman Senate; leading to civil war and Caesar's eventual assassination.[2]

However – laudable as he was as a social reformer – it should be noted that when he became the absolute Roman dictator, Julius Caesar apparently never even contemplated freeing the slaves and did nothing to make their slavery any easier. He presumably realised that Roman civilisation would collapse without the economic underpinning provided by brutal slavery.

Writing before Julius Caesar's rise to power, the lawyer-orator Cicero once wrote to a friend about a mutual acquaintance:

> *As for our friend Cato, you do not love him more than I do: but after all, with the very best intentions and the most absolute honesty, he sometimes does harm to the Republic. He speaks and votes as though he were in the Republic of Plato, not in Romulus's shit pit.*

Heartless pragmatism was the norm in Romulus's shit pit, and was not reserved to just the ruling class. Everyone – in Roman and indeed in all other slave-owning societies – gave at least tacit agreement to slavery's continuation, even the very poor and the ex-slaves. As an illustrative comparison, consider our society's attitude to the internal combustion engine. You are probably aware of the catastrophic damage that petrol-driven vehicles do to the environment. And the fact car crashes kill and injure more people than any other type of accident: indeed, cars are probably the most dangerous thing in your everyday life.

---

2 Michael Parenti, *The Assassination of Julius Caesar: A People's History of Ancient Rome* (2004)

Yet it is highly unlikely that you refuse to have anything to do with cars, buses or lorries. Much less that you actively campaign against the use of the internal combustion engine. Or sneak out to sabotage parked vehicles at night. Why not? You have plenty of moral motivation to do so. But the fact is that the petrol engine is the economic backbone of our society. The car, for all its faults, is simply too useful to you . . . and to me.

That's how slave-owning societies felt about slavery. The horror of it was fully understood – which is why very few people ever volunteered to become slaves, no matter how poor and desperate they were. But rather than abolish that horror, most people chose to live with it either by ignoring the misery, or justifying it through self-serving rationalisations.

Almost all major religions also have a history of turning a blind eye to slavery. Hinduism, Judaism, Taoism, Zoroastrianism, Buddhism, Confucianism, Mithraism, Christianity, Islam and Mormonism all accepted slavery in societies where slaves were commonplace; doing so in the face of their own humanitarian teachings and creeds. Many early Christians, for example, were slaves themselves (which was one of the reasons why snobbish Patrician Romans abhorred the religion). Yet early Christian teaching only disapproved of excessive cruelty to slaves, not to slavery itself.

For example, the first coordinator of the Christian religion, Saint Paul of Tarsus (c.5–67 CE), simply advised Christian slaves to be humble and obedient:

> *Tell slaves to be submissive to their masters and to give satis-*
> *faction in every respect; they are not to talk back, not to pilfer,*
> *but to show complete and perfect fidelity, so that in everything*
> *they may be an ornament to the doctrine of God our Saviour.*[3]

Christian slaves were told to forget earthly freedom in return for a promise of freedom in Heaven and (inferred) torment in Hell for their masters.

---

3 'The Epistle to Titus', Paul 2:9–10

So, throughout history, religions did very little to effectively oppose slavery – with the honourable exception of the Quakers, who were instrumental in achieving the total abolition of slavery in the British Empire by 1833.

Over the past two centuries, most governments in the world have followed suit in passing anti-slavery laws – at least in the case of (highly visible) industrial-level slavery. Some states were rather late, of course: Saudi Arabia only outlawed slavery in 1962, Oman in 1970, Niger in 2003 and Mauritania in 2007. (4.3 per cent of the Mauritanian population are still believed to be slaves.) And, as of 2014, only 123 of the 192 member nations had ratified the United Nations' 1956 Supplementary Convention on the Abolition of Slavery. But we will look more closely at modern slavery later.

Domestic slaves were relatively rare in the ancient world, compared with the vast numbers enslaved on plantations and in manufacturing industries. But domestic slavery was more geographically widespread. This was why any individual slaves mentioned in surviving ancient writings – like the letters of Marcus Tullius Cicero (106 to 43 BCE) – were almost always domestic slaves.

The vast majority of slaves throughout history sweated and died out of sight of anyone but their illiterate overseers. These were the uncounted millions who lived the cruel lives of beasts of burden, yet on whose backs civilisations grew and prospered. But the slave who dressed you, swept your floors, cooked your food, minded your children and peeled your grapes was a part of everyday life for the literate classes. Some of those few slaves might earn a passing mention by their masters.

A noble or a merchant might not be able to afford a slave-stocked plantation, but they could certainly own a few household slaves. Indeed, the house slave has always been a key sign of social respectability in slaver societies. Towards the end of the Roman Republic, even the poorest plebeians felt it was necessary to own at least one domestic slave – just as lower-middle-class Victorians pinched pennies in order to employ a house-maid, thus to maintain their precious air of respectability.

Domestic slaves certainly lived better – and longer – lives than plantation or industrial slaves, and stood a much greater chance of being manumitted (that is, voluntarily freed by their master). But throughout history they have also had few or no legal rights, and suffered untold physical, sexual and psychological abuse by their masters. A few – like Cicero's slave secretary Tiro – were essentially treated as beloved members of the family. But most were basically seen as subhuman by their owners.

For example, in 2 CE the Emperor Augustus (63 BCE to 14 CE) exiled and imprisoned his only daughter, Julia, for promiscuity with numerous well-born lovers. But what seems to have most outraged Roman Patrician sensibilities at the time was the rumour that Julia had also copulated with her male domestic slaves.

Like an aristocrat's seemingly automatic fear and loathing of the 'lower orders', a slave owner apparently *needed* to believe that the people he owned somehow deserved their fate: that morally or mentally they were less than him, and therefore somehow destined to be his slaves. It is probable that Julia's unforgivable social gaffe was not that she had sex with slaves – many Romans probably did that – but that she was *known* to do so. A slave was thought of as so utterly inferior, that sex with them was regarded as only a step above bestiality – something shameful and to be kept hidden.

Humans are a naturally empathic species. Since at least the time of the *Homo erectus*, we have psychologically felt the pain of others simply by witnessing it. But such empathy, or resultant shame, can get in the way if we have to harm others for our own purposes.

As the novelist John Steinbeck concisely noted in his travelogue *Travels with Charley* (published in 1962):

> *If by force you make a creature live and work like a beast, you must think of him as a beast, else empathy would drive you mad.*

We get around this problem by convincing ourselves that those we harm are unworthy of our compassion or mercy. And it is easy to hate those we hurt, because we can subconsciously blame them for making us feel shame for hurting them. This bitter little conundrum has been the cause of untold suffering for uncounted slaves for thousands of years.

Chapter 9

'I'm Spartacus'

It should be plain to anyone why the subject of slavery needs to go into a study of unnecessary human violence and homicide. Slavery unavoidably combines all the worst elements of human behaviour: unjust imprisonment, theft (of bodies and labour), rape, racism (by the better-travelled slavers) and – to maintain order – brutalisation and punishment murder.

So why did the slaves stand for it? In the later slave-owning societies – like Imperial Rome and in the US Deep South – the slaves in some areas outnumbered the free population. Certainly agricultural and industrial slaves generally outnumbered their guards and overseers – and slaves often had access to makeshift weapons like spades and kitchen knives. So why have slave revolts always been so rare in history?

Pack dominance is a central reason, as is social programming. The philosopher H. G. Wells neatly summed up this key factor of human behaviour in his book *The Outline of History*:

> *All animals – and man is no exception – begin life as depend-ants. Most men never shake themselves loose from the desire for leading and protection. Most men accept such conditions as they were born to, without further question.*[1]

We are all aware of the role of dominance in human society. There are some people who can get away with bossing us around,

---

1 H. G. Wells, *The Outline of History* (1920), (Chapter 17, page 229)

and others from whom we would not stand such treatment. Social position is certainly a factor in these matters: the employer who pays your wages, the powerful government official, the mugger with a gun – such people receive automatic deference (from most people). But there are also bullies, and there are people with charm and charisma: both can be given deference by those around them who are – in all other ways – on the same social level.

As H. G. Wells pointed out, this is partly because we are genetically and socially programmed to be dependent on others. After all, as a baby, child and even as a young adult, we depend on our parents or guardians for protection, sustenance, shelter and social guidance. But just how far this communal programming runs in all people, of whatever age, was not discovered until the early 1950s. Then the Chinese discovery of 'brainwashing' changed our understanding of the deep mechanisms of the human mind.

During the Korean War (1950–53) – in which both the US and China sent troops to fight supporting opposite sides – the Americans became concerned at the comparatively high number of their soldiers who were converting to Maoist communism in Chinese prisoner-of-war camps. The Nazis had also tried to indoctrinate Allied prisoners to their side during the Second World War, less than a decade before. But the Germans had failed almost completely – a failure that was humorously illustrated in a scene in Kurt Vonnegut's semi-autobiographical novel, *Slaughterhouse-Five*. So what were the Red Chinese doing that the Nazis – masters of propaganda and mental manipulation – had failed to do?

First they undermined the prisoner's mental defences through brutal treatment, sleep deprivation and sensory deprivation. The latter especially damaged the victim's psyche: being locked in isolation – with no sound or visual stimuli – can cause terrifying hallucinations within a matter of hours. After days of such treatment, the victim often suffered a mental and emotional breakdown.

The prison guards would then try to 'rebuild' the prisoner's mind in a shape that better suited their purposes. Extensive indoctrination sessions, coupled with much kinder treatment, could prove fantastically successful: the victims sometimes converted wholeheartedly to Maoism. Like the tortured Winston Smith, in George Orwell's dystopian novel *Nineteen Eighty-Four*, they truly 'loved Big Brother'.

It was almost as if the mental breakdown had washed away the prisoner's previous beliefs and even elements of their personality; like chalk wiped off a blackboard. The owner of that 'clean' mental blackboard was then desperate to be filled with any belief that the (socially dominant) guards wanted to give them. Humans are social creatures and we largely define ourselves by our status with those around us. The Maoist interrogators believed they had removed their victims' pre-existing beliefs, so that they then had no reference points to define their social position. As such, the brainwashing victim's need for indoctrination was no different to a scared child's need for guidance on their first day at school. Provided that indoctrination, the prisoners clung to Maoist ideas like a drowning man clings to a rescuing lifeguard.

One explanation of how brainwashing works is that it takes advantage of the basic learning processes hardwired into our brains. The initial assault on the victim's identity – through the deliberate causing of an emotional breakdown – resets their mind to a toddler-level openness to new knowledge. Small children learn and assimilate new information much faster than adults, partly because it is more of a survival necessity for them to do so. An adult knows that they already have the essential skills they need to get by. A child's ability to learn totally new facts – like crossing the road safely or not eating the red berries – can be a matter of life and death: they have little or no previous experience to fully understand degrees of danger, so they must learn *everything* as if it were vital.

It's notable, for example, that children or adults dropped into a totally alien culture tend to learn the new language and subtleties of custom much faster than people sitting in a classroom. This is because they feel isolated and lost; learning and integration suddenly become key survival techniques, to which the brain dedicates maximum concentration and information processing.

Violent psychological, physical and social trauma – as was used during Chinese brainwashing – makes even an adult feel that they are totally lost in a world that they can't control. Their instincts then kick in, believing that the only way to survive the situation is to learn as much as possible about their new environment. If the trauma is violent enough, their previous social programming is wiped by the powerful need to learn the new data: the victim's instincts have essentially decided that their previous programming is a danger in the new situation, and must be replaced. This is especially true if your torturers are forcefully telling you that your old ideas and social attitudes are the reason why they are torturing you.

The brainwashing victim's total conscious acceptance of the enforced ideology is an overreaction to the psychological torture of the first stage of the reprogramming. This is because they mentally attach themselves to the main local authority figure – in this case the Chinese brainwasher – as a pseudo-parent figure. The victim's instincts decide that the authority figure must know how best to survive; so they learn all they can from them. Millions of years of mammalian instinct – in which the parental nurturing of infants was a key species survival skill – drives this conclusion home.

In psychology this is a recognised flash-learning process called 'filial imprinting'; a process that can cause a hatchling goose to accidentally become convinced that a rubber boot is its mother, because that is the first thing that it saw as it broke out of the egg. The mis-programmed creature will follow the boot around (ignoring the actual wearer of the mother-substitute), will try to sleep beside it and, on reaching adulthood, may be sexually attracted to rubber boots.

The gosling, and the broken brainwashing victim, are imprinted to a figure that seems to offer protection and social boundaries. The result is instinctual acceptance, trust and even adoration of the authority figure. This is no matter what one's previous opinions of them were, because those opinions are now as invalid as if they had been held by someone else entirely.

However, brainwashing in Chinese POW camps was by no means fully successful. Many prisoners resisted mental breakdown, or any attempt to indoctrinate them. It seemed that those with a strong personal image of themselves – a mental imprint of just who and what they believed themselves to be – were almost unbreakable. And even those who did convert to Maoism generally abandoned the beliefs as soon as they were repatriated to the US after the war.[2]

On this basis, the US Department of the Army announced in 1956 that brainwashing was a myth: victims could be forced to say anything under torture, they said, but true conversion to a totally new set of ideas could not be forced on people.

But they were wrong: in the decades since then, numerous religious cults and totalitarian regimes have shown that brainwashing – sometimes on a mass basis, as in North Korea – is a reality. The US prisoners returning from China had simply reacclimatised to a culture where Maoism had no place – but that didn't mean that they hadn't fully converted when in Chinese hands. Notably those who freely chose to remain in China after the war – some twenty Americans and one Briton – stayed true to communism for much longer; sometimes for life.

On 4 February 1974, the nineteen-year-old heiress to an American newspaper publishing fortune, Patty Hearst, was kidnapped by a Maoist terrorist group called the Symbionese Liberation Army. In fact the SLA were just a small group of radical young Californians. 'Symbionese' referred not to a country, but to 'symbiosis' – meaning the positive interaction between different (communist) political factions. Like the contemporary West German Baader-Meinhof terrorist group, the SLA believed that urban warfare could bring about a fairer society by catalysing a popular revolution.

Thirteen days after her abduction from her Berkley

2 Robert Jay Lifton, *Thought Reform and the Psychology of Totalism* (1962)

apartment, Patty Hearst tape-recorded the SLA's ransom demands. But what slightly disturbed investigating police was the fact that Hearst seemed to be making SLA political statements spontaneously, and without evident coercion, during that recording. Was she so terrified that she was trying to butter up her captors? She didn't sound that scared, so why did she do it?

On 14 April, Patty Hearst helped the SLA to rob a bank in San Francisco. She was clearly free and was acting under her own volition – wielding an M1 carbine and making no attempt to escape. She left voluntarily with the other bank robbers and escaped with them. Eventually Hearst was captured by the FBI the following September, hiding out in a San Francisco apartment with another SLA member.

It now seems clear that Patty Hearst had been brainwashed – although whether the SLA deliberately did this, or it was accidental, is a moot point. In the first week after her kidnapping she was terrified, isolated (blindfolded and locked in a closet) and later was sexually assaulted. This, court-appointed psychiatrists agreed, had brought about the mental breakdown that is the first stage of the brainwashing process.

The leader of the group then started to feed and tend to the still blindfolded Patty, chatting with her as he did so. She may then have bonded with this authority figure. Patty was then welcomed into the wider group, re-cementing the new imprinting, but was also subjected to lengthy and often verbally abusive indoctrination sessions. These latter completely converted her to the SLA's belief system; the upper-class rich girl apparently became a wholehearted communist terrorist.

Hearst's bad luck continued, unfortunately, when the jury found her guilty and the judge sentenced her to thirty-five years for armed bank robbery. She was released twenty-one months later, on the orders of President Jimmy Carter. Her family is reported to have begged psychiatrists to restore her old mind and set of values, but were told that 'that Patty' was as gone as if she had died. She could be 'reprogrammed' to fit into her old ideas, they were told, but the family refused. They felt that re-brainwashing Patty would be almost as bad as what the SLA had done to her.

As it turned out, prison seemingly reformed her mind anyway. Although Patty Hearst could never truly become her old, pre-kidnapping self again, she abandoned SLA beliefs and eventually married her bodyguard – a former police officer.

Many of our institutions unconsciously brainwash the citizens under their control. Schools impart society's norms of behaviour, just as much as they teach facts. Prison reform programmes do just that – reform the prisoner's mind to make them less antisocial. Mental institutions heal patients partly by showing them which of their thoughts are acceptable, and which would be seen as crazy by the general public. And the army uses basic training to turn civilised people into disciplined killers. All these institutions combine different types of punishment, encouragement and indoctrination to achieve their ends. In a word, they brainwash.

Indeed, it might be argued that by originally manipulating the mental processes of their Korean War troops through basic training, the US Army had unwittingly prepared them for brainwashing by Chinese interrogators. Anti-cult activists suggest that 'reprogramming' brainwashed former cult members is often made easier, because they have been broken to the technique once already.

Just how far unintentional brainwashing can go was apparently shown during a bank robbery and subsequent siege in Sweden. On 23 August 1973, Stockholm police surrounded the Kreditbanken building after two investigating officers were fired upon by robber Jan-Erik Olsson. Four bank employees were then held at gunpoint by Olsson in the bank vault.

Five days later the siege was lifted as the police threw in tear gas and Olsson surrendered. But, during that time, the four hostages had started to behave oddly. Despite the fact that Olsson had threatened them, fired his weapon to scare them and had grabbed at least one in a stranglehold, they doggedly insisted on taking his side at the subsequent trial. In their testimony they said that Olsson had behaved reasonably; it was the

police who had endangered their lives by trying to force an end
to the siege prematurely. Some psychiatrists later suggested
that the hostages had been accidentally brainwashed by their
ordeal, and the theoretical phenomenon came to be called
'Stockholm syndrome'.

None of this would be possible if humans weren't particularly
open to mind control by others – whether you call it propaganda,
brainwashing, indoctrination or just schooling. Indeed, we're
open to mental manipulation to the extent of damaging our own
interests or even survival chances. How else could people be
persuaded to become suicide bombers? Or to embrace lifelong
celibacy? Or to wholeheartedly support political parties that are
evidently corrupt, incompetent or despise whole sections of
their own citizenry? As we saw in Chapter 5, the human habit of
tribalism can all too readily be exploited, especially when
combined with brainwashing.

Brainwashing also explains why slave owners, right through
history, have tended to be cruel, vicious swine. Quite aside from
the theft of other people's labour and freedom, the slaver has to
be willing to humiliate, torture and kill. They, of course, thought
of it as necessary discipline, but in reality they were undermining
their slaves' sense of identity, self-worth and self-determination.
In 'breaking in' their slaves, the slavers were forcing them
through the first stage of the brainwashing process. The second
stage – total obedience and loyalty to the master – was then
easier to enforce.

So it can be seen that people either born as slaves, or born free
and later enslaved, were likely – unless they had exceptionally
strong personalities – to surrender to the situation simply due to
an uncontrollable and largely subconscious survival instinct.
Indeed, they might then rationalise their submission to the
extent that they believed they deserved to be slaves, and actively
helped their owner to suppress other slaves.

Slave owning remained a risky business, nonetheless. Push
anyone too far and they will try to kill you, regardless of the
consequences. After seeing that, the other slaves might be
inspired to kill a few overseers themselves. Minor slave revolts

were so common in slave-owning societies that contemporary historians rarely mentioned them. But fatal car accidents often don't make it on to the news today, let alone into the pages of history books – that doesn't mean that car crashes don't happen. Besides, escaped slaves rarely did more than kill a few slave owners, before becoming common bandits and being hunted down by the authorities.

Major slave rebellions were far from impossible, of course. Slaves, having freed themselves, could inspire other slaves to escape and join them. The problem then was how to best organise themselves for the inevitable counter-blow by the slave owners. For example, the late Roman Republic suffered several such uprisings – the Servile Wars, as Roman historians called them.

The First Servile War was indirectly caused by a normal war, and then greed. Following the defeat of their chief rivals, the Carthaginians, in the Second Punic War, the Romans annexed the island of Sicily. Patrician speculators rushed in and bought up vast tracts of captured land at next to nothing from the Roman state. Slaves, at that time, were cheap and plentiful, thanks to the piracy that had become rife in the Mediterranean – again, thanks to the chaos caused by the Punic wars. Roman plutocrats became unbelievably rich by maximising the profits from their Sicilian grain plantations. They did this by working slaves to death on starvation rations, then buying cheap replacements from the pirate slavers.

In passing, it should be remembered that identical economic cruelty existed up to fairly recently. Nineteenth-century planta-tion owners in the Deep South – near to the great slave markets of the Caribbean – could also replace dead slaves more cheaply than keep their living slaves in survival conditions. This was why the phrase 'to be sold down the river' meant a slow death sentence to an American slave. The further down the Mississippi a slave was shipped, the more terrible the conditions were likely to be.

In 135 BCE, a Syrian conjurer and jester called Eunus told his fellow slaves that he was a prophet, and predicted that if they rose in rebellion, they would defeat the Romans and could set up their own nation in Sicily. He was right, initially. The slave uprising defeated the local Roman garrison troops and held on to Sicily for two years. Then, in 132 BCE, the Romans sent a large army and defeated the slaves. Eunus was taken alive, but died before his captors could torture and execute him.

The Second Servile War also took place on the island of Sicily, but this time it was sparked by an act of justice. The Roman consul and commanding general, Gaius Marius, had called for additional troops to be provided by Rome's Italian allies; but these were refused on the grounds that many of their people had been illegally forced into slavery.

The Roman Republic had privatised tax-gathering in their empire – outside Rome itself, that is. These private companies – called 'tax farmers' – would bid for a provincial tax contract and the company that offered to collect the most taxation would win. They then got to keep any money collected above the figure of their bid: so it was in their interests to screw every penny out of their allotted provinces, whatever the long-term consequences for the province, or for Rome.

Gaius Marius was told that tax farmers had been 'collecting' allied Italian citizens and selling them as slaves – an act that was illegal under the Italian treaties of allegiance. Over the howls of protest from their owners (many of whom would also have been partners in the tax-farming companies) the consul ordered all Italian-born slaves to be freed.

Unfortunately, on Sicily, the order from Marius became rather garbled. Eight hundred Italian slaves were indeed freed, but it wasn't made plain to the other slaves why this was happening. They, naturally, hoped that they too were about to be freed, and rose in revolt when their chains were not struck off.

Between 104 and 100 BCE, Sicily was held by an army of escaped slaves, numbering 2,000 cavalry and 20,000 foot soldiers. This is an indication of what a multitude of slaves must have been held on the Sicilian grain plantations, because the numbers recorded for the slave army would not have included the women, children and the male slaves too old, sick or scared to fight. The Romans eventually managed to beat the ex-slaves into surrender, but at a much greater effort and cost than during the First Servile War.

The third and last Roman Servile War started in 73 BCE, when a gladiatorial school near Capua, in southern mainland Italy, was overrun by its combat-trained slaves. The rebels, led by a Gaul called Crixus and a Thracian named Spartacus, then ran and hid in the verdant forests on the nearby (and then) extinct volcano called Mount Vesuvius. Other local slaves were inspired to escape and join the gladiators, swelling the numbers on Vesuvius into a small army. But they were only armed with kitchen knives, farm implements and the few weapons taken from the gladiatorial school's armoury. So they may well have felt trapped and doomed.

We now tend to think that gladiators must have been highly dangerous killers, whatever the opponent; but Spartacus and his men probably knew better. Gladiatorial combat to the death had originally been a religious ceremony, held at the funerals of rich and well-born Romans. Of course this was really a human sacrifice by another name, with the added thrill of not knowing which slave was going to die. Such matches had gradually lost much of their religious significance as they became a popular sport, displayed in public arenas to entertain roaring crowds. These public combats were often fought only to victory rather than to the death; thus to save on the loss of highly trained, and therefore expensive, slaves. But gladiatorial fights remained very symbolic and traditionalised. The gladiators were trained to fight with only a small set of time-honoured – and largely outmoded – weapons and armour. Put up against a shield wall of drilled Roman legionaries, even a skilled gladiator would be dead within moments.

And Roman legionaries were certainly coming for Spartacus and his people. As noted above, the crushing of minor slave uprisings was a standard and fairly commonplace police action for the Roman authorities. But the officer sent after the escaped gladiators, praetor Gaius Claudius Glaber, was lazy, stupid or both. He simply camped his 3000 men at the bottom of Vesuvius and waited for the rebel slaves to starve into surrender.

Spartacus and Crixus realised that they could not descend the mountainside directly, without facing a lethal formation of prepared Roman soldiers at the bottom. But the far side of the mountain had been left unguarded by the Romans, because it was so precipitous. Making ropes out of wild vines, the ex-slaves clambered down the cliffs one night, crept up on Glaber's unsuspecting camp and annihilated the Romans. They then had plenty of military-grade weapons and armour to share out and train with.

Even now, with the loss of an entire army, the Roman senate failed to see the growing threat in southern Italy. They sent out another relatively small attack force. This was led by another praetor, Publius Varinius, who was inexperienced or foolish enough to divide his forces within sight of the enemy. Spartacus and Crixus swiftly smashed one Roman force and then the other.

These victories set southern Italy ablaze – not only escaped slaves, but poor and downtrodden peasants flooded to the rebel army, swelling their numbers to over 70,000. But this, in itself, proved to be a problem. Feeding such a horde must have been a nightmare. All the neighbouring towns had closed their gates and granaries, so the rebels had to pick a precarious living by scavenging from the countryside and plundering farms and plantations. And thus freeing yet more hungry slaves in the process.

The rebel forces split up in 72 BCE, possibly in an effort to solve their supply problems by moving to separate regions. Crixus commanded the rebel army that remained in the south, while Spartacus led his army north, towards Rome.

On the march, word came that Crixus and his army of 30,000 had been defeated at Mount Garganus, 20,000 rebels and Crixus himself having been killed in the battle. On hearing the news, Spartacus forced his Roman prisoners, some three hundred men, to fight to the death in gladiatorial combat, as sacrifices to the ghosts of Crixus and his men. This may seem either hypocritical or ironic justice, depending on your point of view. He then pressed on, despoiling the country he passed through and rescuing more slaves as he went.

The Roman senate were now really alarmed. Their economy was reeling thanks to the slave rebellion; and no slave owner could have slept well in his bed, knowing that his own slaves might, at any moment, cut his throat and head off to join Spartacus. Rome sent out two large armies, commanded by that year's ruling consuls; but by the time they caught up with Spartacus, his horde had expanded to 120,000 people.

The consuls, Lucius Gellius Publicola and Gnaeus Cornelius Lentulus Clodianus, attempted to trap the rebels in a pincer movement. But Spartacus defeated Publicola's army before Clodianus could arrive. Clodianus was then thrashed. Both Publicola and Clodianus escaped on horseback as soon as they saw that their men were defeated and retreating.

It was at this moment that Spartacus could have attacked Rome itself. Certainly there was very little standing between him and the city of his oppressors. But he and his army continued northward, away from Rome.

It has been speculated that all Spartacus wanted to do was get his people over the Alps and out of Italy, where they could disperse and return to their home countries. It was also possible that he realised that attacking a gigantic walled city, with an army that knew nothing of siege warfare and had no siege engines, would be a gamble at best. Certainly he must have seen that his people, scavenging the countryside for food as it was, might starve before they could capture Rome. And Spartacus must have known that the Romans had other armies that were now heading back to Italy from across the empire. But the fact is that we have no idea why Spartacus marched past Rome, because he took that knowledge with him when he died.

The rebels defeated the consuls' weakened and disheartened armies again at Picenum, in northern Italy, but then made a fatal error. They could have escaped over the Alps, as there was nobody standing in their way, but instead they turned back into Italy. Possibly the fear of taking a horde of people across high mountain passes, to an uncertain welcome from the tribes on the other side, overcame their hopes of freedom.

It was now 71 BCE. The Romans, virtually panicking in the streets, handed the command of their available forces to one of the most ruthless men in the republic: Marcus Licinius Crassus. Possibly the world's first self-made multi-millionaire, Crassus had collected his fortune by inventing both the fire brigade and, simultaneously, a legal extortion racket. His fire-fighting slaves would turn up at one of Rome's many house fires and, before doing anything, Crassus would offer to buy the neighbouring houses at well below their actual value. Faced with a loss of everything if the fire was allowed to spread, the owners often sold. When Crassus had added enough to his property portfolio, he would order his slaves to put out the fire.

General Crassus was given six hurriedly recruited legions, plus the remains of the two consular armies that Spartacus had already defeated twice: in total, about 48,000 soldiers. Crassus then immediately reduced this number by performing a punishment decimation on the consular armies. That is, one in ten of the men were chosen by lot, then beaten to death by their own comrades. Publicola and Clodianus – the Patrician commanders who were actually responsible for the defeats – were not, of course, among the troops executed. Having thus indicated the price of failure – for common soldiers – Crassus marched to pursue Spartacus.

It may seem that the odds were heavily in Spartacus's favour: more than 120,000 to less than 48,000. But remember that all of Crassus's troops were trained (if green) legionaries. Most of Spartacus' horde were women, children and non-fighting men. His fighting men were the veterans of several battles, but were also only part-trained, under-equipped and probably badly underfed and tired from months of marching.

Nevertheless, the rebels managed to take advantage of the overconfidence of Crassus's second-in-command – a legate called Mummius – and routed part of the pursuing army. Crassus, true to form, had fifty common soldiers executed as a punishment for the army's cowardice. Mummius was not executed.

But that was Spartacus's last military victory. Crassus defeated the rebels in a string of minor battles, and eventually bottled them up in the toe of Italy, opposite the inviting island of Sicily. Spartacus is said to have made a deal with the Cilician pirates to ship his people across the narrow strait but, after taking his money, the pirates abandoned them to the Romans.

The rebels, starving and desperate, broke through the besieging Romans, then turned to fight beside the River Siler. Before the battle, Spartacus ordered his horse to be brought to him. He then killed it, telling his men that if they won, he could find another. If they lost he wouldn't need a horse as he had no intention of trying to escape. Unlike the Roman generals, he would share the fate of his men: bad as well as good.

Spartacus's 50,000 rebels almost won against Crassus's 32,000 legionaries, but lack of training and weakness through months of starvation eventually broke the ex-slaves. Spartacus was said, by Roman historians, to have come within sight of Crassus himself during the battle. Spartacus called a challenge and killed two centurions trying to get at the Roman general – nobody says that Crassus made much effort to get to Spartacus. The rebel leader was then stabbed in the leg, fell to his knees and was hacked down by Roman legionaries. His body could not later be identified.

Five thousand rebels escaped the slaughter, only to be destroyed by another Roman army coming from the north. The six thousand ex-slaves captured during the Battle of Siler River were all crucified on the orders of the vindictive Crassus. The line of crosses, with their agonised and dying victims, were spaced out to stretch all the way along the road from Capua to Rome: 130 miles.

Eighteen years later, Marcus Licinius Crassus was captured and killed during a shambolic campaign against the Parthians, in what is now eastern Turkey. Some accounts say that the millionaire general was executed, with brutal irony, by having molten gold poured into his mouth.

The Third Servile War was the last and greatest slave uprising of ancient history. After that the Romans made damn sure that any slave insurrection was smashed before it could gather any momentum. Yet the name Spartacus has remained one to run a chill down any slave owner's backbone over the next two millennia: the clear proof that slaves can fight back.

The Haitian slave revolution, starting in 1791, was the only slave uprising in known history to win a permanent victory. Like the Roman First Servile War, it began when a prophet – a vodou high priest called Dutty Boukman – called for an uprising by his fellow slaves. After initial rebel victories, the revolution bogged down into a guerrilla war of attrition that lasted for over a decade. The Haitian revolution was vicious on both sides; with vengeful ex-slaves raping, torturing and killing, and French colonial slavers taking equally brutal revenge.

But by 1804 the French colonial slave masters had finally been defeated and driven off the island – although this was partly because France itself was then in the throes of an egalitarian revolution, and could send little help. It has been estimated that between 24,000 and 100,000 Europeans, and between 100,000 and 350,000 Haitian ex-slaves, died in the revolution. However, these appalling figures are not as cut and dried as they may first seem. Tropical disease was a major factor in the number of deaths – which arguably would have happened anyway. And the racial element to the war was less simple than it would first appear. Many black and Caribbean people died fighting *for* white masters; and a large number of British and Spanish soldiers, deployed to neighbouring San Dominique, died aiding the rebels.

Three years after the creation of independent Haiti, Britain – up to then the main player in the selling of slaves in the western hemisphere – renounced the trade through an Act of Parliament. It seems unlikely that the news of the victorious Haitian revolution had no impact on this decision.

The Republic of Haiti is the only country in the world based on a triumphant slave revolution. Yet it has had an unhappy history, not least because France remained spiteful to their former slave colony. Despite having abolished slavery in France, and all its colonies, in 1794 (while the Haitian rebellion was still blazing), in 1825 the French government demanded 150 million francs (today's equivalent of US$21 billion) as reparation for its lost Haitian plantations . . . and slaves. Using warships and trade sanctions, France has managed to extort 90 million francs out of the impoverished Haitians over the years, in payment of this 'debt'.

Chapter 10

'They Can't Sell my Wife and Child No More. No More That. No More That. We're Free Now. Bless the Lord'

So what did bring about the end of industrial-level slavery? With all due respect to the ex-slaves and freeborn abolitionists who campaigned and fought to end slavery, it was not political or moral pressure. Nor was it the blood sacrificed on the battle-fields of the American Civil War, and on the British Royal Navy ships that blockaded the slave ports and boarded and captured the slave-running vessels. It was ended by technology and economics.

Adam Smith, the patron saint of modern Capitalism, wrote in 1776:

> . . . the work done by slaves, though it appears to cost only their maintenance, is in the end the dearest of any. A person who can acquire no property can have no other interest but to eat as much and to labour as little as possible. Whatever work he does beyond what is sufficient to purchase his own mainten-ance, can be squeezed out of him by violence only, and not by any interest of his own.[1]

---

1 Adam Smith, *The Wealth of Nations* (Book 3, Chapter 2) (1776)

Smith believed that the supposed efficiency of slavery was an illusion, and that the paid labour of free men – working to further their own interests through the success of their employing business or industry – must ultimately be superior to that of slaves.

On the face of it, Adam Smith was flying in the face of at least five millennia of contrary evidence. As noted in Chapter 8, slave-powered industries had always run non-slave competitors into the ground. Indeed, his argument was one that seemed based on faith and his personal dislike of slavery, rather than on an unadulterated economic judgement. But Smith was writing at the very beginning of the Industrial Revolution, and he may have foreseen the changes that were about to grip the world.

The growing mechanisation of agriculture improved crop yields and reduced the number of labourers needed to work the land. Up to that time, agricultural work had been the main employer of human effort since the Neolithic Revolution. The sheer effort of raising enough food to live had fully occupied most humans throughout history: only a minority of people in each civilisation could be spared for trades, such as craftsmen, merchants and soldiers (or to live lives of aristocratic ease). The mechanisation of farms changed that. With more food, the population levels rose at the same time that work on the land was becoming harder to find. Displaced country people moved to the towns where new, machine-powered factories were becoming the driving impetus of the Industrial Revolution. These growing numbers of unemployed, faced with starvation, clamoured for work – even for a pittance of a wage if it would keep them alive.

So, for the first time in history, waged workers became more economically viable than slaves. After all, they needed no support infrastructure or guards – they looked after themselves. And, if they got sick, died or found better work, they were easily replaced from the legions of unemployed in the streets.

This is why mass unemployment is always a part of any modern industrial economy, and why national economic strategies are partly designed to produce unemployment. Governments and employers see unemployment as the ultimate stick to pacify and control the workforce. If workers create trouble – such as demanding too high a proportion of the profits in return for their work – they can be sacked and replaced from the pool of the unemployed. Faced with the risk of joining the unemployed, and seeing their lifestyle collapse due to a lack of money, employees generally toe the line and knuckle under. But if full employment was ever allowed actually to happen – or worse, if there were more jobs than people to do them – then the ordinary workers would be free to behave much as senior executives do now. They could demand exorbitant remuneration for their work, or they would leave and go to an employer willing to pay them what they wanted.

This is what happened in fourteenth-century medieval Europe after the Black Death had killed, in different regions, between 30 and 60 per cent of the population. In the aftermath of the plague, the serfs – feudal peasants who had always been expected to work for nothing but the 'protection' of their overlord – realised that they could demand pay. There were more jobs to be done than people to do them. If their lord refused, the peasants simply walked until they found a lord who was desperate enough for workers to pay a wage. The nobility had always believed that they had ruled by 'divine right', but now discovered that it had only been their ownership and control of serfs that had made them the ruling class. A noble without any peasants had to hoe his own cabbages or starve. This development effectively marked the beginning of the end of western European feudalism.

From the beginning of the Industrial Revolution, when the socio-economic balance was moved to create permanent mass unemployment, mass slavery was doomed. And as mechanisation advanced and proliferated, the value of enslaved human muscles fell ever further in relative value. Even if the British Empire had not renounced the slave trade, and if the American Civil War had never been fought, industrial slavery would have been economically finished by the beginning of the twentieth century.

By the end of the First World War, the growing union movement was steadily improving the wages and the working conditions of paid employees, reducing their employers' profits accordingly. Some industrialists may have dreamed of a return to mass slavery (that was, of course, still within living memory in much of Europe and America), but by then the enormous support infrastructure needed to maintain any large-scale slave industry was gone.

The Nazis reintroduced mass slavery during the Second World War – kidnapping tens of thousands of foreign workers in conquered lands and working the inmates to death in their concentration camp factories. If they had won the war, the Nazis fully expected to maintain race-based slavery in all their territories. But that economic vision lasted only as long as their 'thousand-year Reich'.

Since Germany's defeat in 1945, there have arguably been several other outbreaks of mass industrial-level slavery in the world. There was the Soviet Gulag system in which criminals – many of them political dissenters – were forced to work at hard labour in isolated and unbelievably harsh locations like Northern Siberia. The Russian dissident author Aleksandr Solzhenitsyn estimated that between 1930 and 1975, fifty million people were forced to work in the Soviet work camps; sometimes for many years, or until they died of exhaustion or maltreatment. The most infamous Gulag, Perm-36, was not closed until 1987. Four years later Soviet communism collapsed, but the Russian penal system continues to use forced labour as a punishment to the present day.

Then there was 'the Great Leap Forward' in China, officially running between 1958 and 1961, but with repercussions lasting well into the 1970s. The Chinese leader, Mao Zedong, became convinced that China needed to 'collectivise' its agriculture: that meant ending all elements of private farm ownership and making agricultural workers labour on vast collective farms that were little better than prison work camps. This was in an attempt to create the equivalent of agricultural mass-production. The plan was an utter disaster – as Mao should have realised it would have be, before he started. He must have been aware that a similar policy in the 1930s Stalinist USSR had been the cause of famine, starvation, episodes of cannibalism, and hundreds of thousands of unnecessary deaths. Yet Mao pressed forward with the Great

Leap Forward. Some estimates place the death toll in China, during the three years of the massive reorganisation, at forty-five million premature fatalities – mostly due to needless starvation.

Following on from the Great Leap Forward, in 1966 Mao Zedong instituted the 'Cultural Revolution'; in which supposedly bourgeois citizens from China's towns – usually the college-age youths – were forced to work on the collective farms. This was less of a humanitarian disaster than Mao's previous deluded scheme, but during the ten years of the Cultural Revolution China was socially and developmentally crippled. Mao failed to see that educated city-dwellers are the driving force of a modern civilisation, not the permanently exhausted farmers. The young people forcibly uprooted and made to work on collective farms have been called China's 'lost generation'. But China as a nation lost almost as much, as millions of potential university graduates instead sweated over shovels and hoes.

More was to come. Following their victory in the Cambodian Civil War in 1975, the communist Khmer Rouge faction took power and, inspired by Mao's Cultural Revolution, forced virtually everyone in Cambodia's towns and cities out into the fields to slave as enforced peasants. Four years later, neighbouring communist Vietnam invaded Cambodia to oust the Khmer Rouge regime and end the slaughter. It is thought that at least 2.2 million people had died in Cambodia's 'killing fields' in that short time. Many were tortured and executed for the most minor infractions. For example, for wearing glasses: this was seen as a sign of bourgeois intellectualism and automatically made the wearer a 'class enemy of the people'. But most victims died of hunger and exhaustion as they slaved to fulfil the fantasy of a 'purely proletariat society'.

Yet none of these open attempts to bring back effective slavery – under the guise of revolution and political reformation – had any real chance of surviving indefinitely in the modern world. This was partly because of the loathing that they engendered in other countries, but mostly because mass industrial slavery seems no more practical now, in an economic sense, than it was after the American Civil War.

Yet the American political theorist James Burnham, in his widely read 1940 book *The Management Revolution*, had edged towards suggesting that a return towards mass slavery was actually inevitable in the modern world. He believed that the newly developing 'management class' of technocrats and bureaucrats would inevitably take control of what Karl Marx had called 'the means of production'. Armed with this exclusive power, they could form a permanent ruling class, with the rest of society living as increasingly powerless drones. As evidence of this already happening in major nations, Burnham pointed to Stalinist Russia and the (then) triumphant Nazi Germany. (Burnham, a former Trotskyist who had become a hard-line right-winger, tended to favour the latter form of government. He later retracted and apologised for his tacit support of Nazism, but only after the Stalinists and the liberal democracies had reduced the Nazi empire to smouldering rubble.)

The novelist and journalist George Orwell was horrified by Burnham's influential vision of a totalitarian future. So he satirised it, and totalitarianism in general, in his dystopian novel *Nineteen Eighty-Four* (written in 1948, and published in 1949). In the book, the ultra-totalitarian state of Big Brother icily proclaims, 'War is Peace. Freedom is Slavery. Ignorance is Strength.' And the relationship between the state and the free individual is described by O'Brien, a senior official, as 'a boot stamping on a human face – forever'.

Bleak as most people find George Orwell's *Nineteen Eighty-Four*, the book was meant to serve as a warning, and not as some pessimistic rant by a dying Jeremiah. Orwell spent much of his adult life battling both economic inequality in democratic Britain, and despotic totalitarianism abroad. He lived (if only just) to see a major victory on the first front – the setting up of the British Welfare State and the free National Health Service. (Indeed, his influential reportage on the misery of the poor and unemployed in the north of Britain – *The Road to Wigan Pier* (published in 1937) – was a key influence on that social development.)

He also lived to see one of the two great totalitarian states, once half-lauded by James Burnham, utterly obliterated. And

Orwell clearly believed that *all* totalitarianism could be stopped, if faced by brave and determined opposition from democratic and humane people. In a 1946 article, titled 'James Burnham and the Managerial Revolution', Orwell wrote:

> *The huge, invincible, everlasting slave empire of which Burnham appears to dream will not be established, or, if established, will not endure, because slavery is no longer a stable basis for human society.*

But now, finally, we should consider the one area where mass industrial slavery arguably survives into the present day: in our supposedly enlightened penal systems. Most visibly in the USA.

Acceptance of the last example of mass slavery might rather depend on your opinion of strict drug legislation and the so-called 'prison-industrial complex'. But it is undeniable that the profits of privatised US prisons – and the companies that contract to utilise prison labour – have rocketed in the past three decades. And the financial bonanza for such companies seems to parallel the increasing percentage of US citizens incarcerated.

In 2008, 0.52 per cent of the population of the USA were in prison. That was 1,610,446 people. US citizens represent 4.5 per cent of the total world population, but the USA houses a disproportionate 25 per cent of all the planet's prisoners.[2]

Institutionalised race discrimination is also a key issue. In 2008, 32.8 per cent of prisoners in the USA (528,200 people) were self-defined as 'non-Hispanic white', 36.8 per cent (519,900 people) classified themselves as 'black', 19.4 per cent (313,100 people) 'Hispanic' and 11 per cent (249,246 people) as 'other' (including Native Americans, Asian Americans, Pacific Islanders and anyone else who felt that they did not fit into the main three categories). This was with a total US population that defines itself as 64 per cent non-Hispanic white, 13 per cent black, 16 per cent Hispanic and 7 per cent 'other'.

---

2 *The New York Times*, 23 April 2008, 'US Prison Population Dwarfs that of other Nations', by Adam Liptak

Thus, from these official figures, a Hispanic American in 2008 was more than twice as likely to have been jailed as a white American – as was anyone defined under the categorisation 'other'. And a black American was five and a half times more likely than a white person to be in jail. But, in fact, 2008 was actually a relatively good year to be an indicted black citizen in America. The US Department of Justice themselves estimate that a black American is typically six and a half times more likely to be incarcerated than a white American.[3]

Even the most rabid white supremacist would find it hard to believe that the average black American is six-and-a-half times more likely than the average white American to be a criminal. Yet that is how the US judicial system functionally behaves. Either white Americans are less likely to be jailed for their crimes than black Americans, or a lot of innocent black people are being falsely imprisoned in the USA. Or both. However you look at it, it seems to be rampantly discriminatory.

The term 'Jim Crow Law' is used to describe a collection of racist and segregationist state-level statutes, passed in the USA between 1876 and 1965, that effectively barred African-Americans and other 'non-whites' from taking any significant part in public life. In the southern states the Jim Crow laws often made it very difficult – or effectively impossible – for non-whites to vote. There, and to a lesser extent in other states of the USA, the white majority maintained their disproportionate power, wealth and privileges through corruptly gerrymandering the democratic system.

Ten years after freeing the slaves at the end of the US Civil War, the northern states had begun to attempt an economic and political accommodation with the defeated southern states. Industrial reunification was, arguably, an utter necessity if the USA wasn't to collapse into economic recession. But the price was paid by the American black community as their bloodily won

---

3 Figures from the US Census Bureau; and from the US Department of Justice, 'The Bureau of Justice Statistics Bulletin' – Prisoners in 2008', by William J. Sabol PhD and Heather C. West PhD

rights were trampled by southern whites and their pleas for help were ignored by the northern states.

The Jim Crow laws were progressively repealed in the 1950s and 1960s, thanks largely to growing civil rights movement. But there is a contention that they remain – both in spirit and practice – hidden within the statutes of many states of the Union. Convicted felons, for example, are denied the right to vote in many of the United States, even after they have 'paid their debt to society' and been released from prison. And because of the higher proportion of non-whites being imprisoned, this has a 'Jim Crow' effect on voting results, with non-white communities losing a substantial part of their democratic power.

In the 2012 US presidential election, for example, various disenfranchisement laws prevented 5.85 million people from voting – most because of their previous prison record. This was 2.5 per cent of the overall potential voting population, but included a disproportionate 8 per cent of the African-American vote. In the state of Florida – a key 'battleground state' that has decided the swing of presidential elections on several occasions – 1.5 million African-Americans were legally denied the vote in 2012: that was 20 per cent of the state's black population. A fundamental element of slavery is the removal of the right to take an equal part in public life.

A strikingly high proportion of US internees are jailed for non-violent, and usually drug-related, offences. In 2014, for example, 25.4 per cent of prisoners held in US federal prisons had been convicted of violent crimes, which meant that 74.6 per cent of inmates had been incarcerated for non-violent crimes[4]. In the same year 48.8 per cent – almost half of all the inmates in federal prisons – had been convicted of drug-related offences.

The incarceration of many of these non-violent felons serves little purpose: they cost the tax-payer a fortune to house, and are effectively lost to their families and communities for the whole of their incarceration. Electronic tagging, local police and probation service oversight, and community service orders (the latter

---

4 Statistics from the Federal Bureau of Prisons

being what might be called socially acceptable slavery) would be a more effective and economic way to punish such criminals. But few states utilise these options to any significant degree. So one might indeed wonder if draconian US anti-drug laws might be primarily serving a purpose other than public order, considering the money being made off the backs of prisoners.

Convicts *are* paid for their work in US prisons. But their wages are well below the market rate for the non-incarcerated: between 23 cents and $1.15 per hour. The US federally set minimum wage is, in 2014, $7.25 an hour.

Obviously the prisoners do not have to pay for their own upkeep, like the non-incarcerated, but neither do the private companies that are making such large profits from prisoner labour. Such companies include household names like McDonald's, Starbucks, Boeing and Victoria's Secret – but there are many other, less well known industry beneficiaries of prison labour.

Because of financial confidentiality rules it is impossible to estimate the yearly profits made by companies utilising imprisoned workers (incidentally increasing unemployment in the outside world) but Federal Prisons Industries, a government-owned labour contracting company, made $900 million just in commissions in 2012 alone. Yet it is the US tax-payer who provides the upkeep costs, either directly or indirectly, for both the publically owned and the privatised prisons – $55 billion in 2013. (Privately run prisons in the USA even charge the tax-payer 'holding rent' for any empty cells they might have; in essence fining society for reducing crime.)

Prisoners are also prevented from forming official labour unions to defend their rights. And remember that unionisation and workers' legal rights were key elements that made a return to industrial-level slavery in the outside world impracticable.

US prison inmates have little choice about providing their labour since they get less food and increased sentences (through denial of parole) if they refuse to work. Plus they are obviously guarded; and they are threatened with violence and death if they rebel against their conditions. All the above controversial elements of prison life – gratuitous detention, racial inequality, democratic disenfranchisement, forced and exploitative labour, and violent punishment – could be said to also be the essential elements of slavery. And the USA is far from the only country to be doing this. Like modern Russia's continuation of Gulag work camps, almost all penitentiary systems around the world contain some or all of these elements of mass slavery.

As the poet James Whitcomb Riley once wrote:

When I see a bird that walks like a duck and swims like a duck and quacks like a duck, I call that bird a duck.

It is difficult for most present-day people to fully understand the slave owners' way of thinking: that human beings who in all essentials are identical to you are nevertheless to be treated as draft animals, or as faceless units of profit and loss. This is slightly easier to understand (if not condone) of slave-owning societies that specialised in enslaving foreigners – like Ancient Greece or Rome; or people of a different race – like the American Deep South. Human tribalism makes it easier to victimise strangers from over the hill, so to speak. Or to believe that 'people who have a different complexion with slightly flatter noses than ourselves' aren't really human. Yet, in most slaver societies in history, anyone – except the rich and powerful – could be forced into slavery if they fell sufficiently foul of the law.

It should be remembered that the law has worked with very limited tools throughout most of human history: long-term imprisonment, for example, is a fairly new invention. Up until just a few hundred years ago, a convicted felon would typically be executed, exiled, mutilated and released, or enslaved. Long-term prisons or dungeons were impractical, simply because of the difficulty and expense of holding a person in one place while keeping them alive. So most prisons in history were more like the police cells of today: holding pens where the arrested awaited either a worse fate, or to be exonerated and released.

Here we can make an illustrative comparison between the modern and past mindsets. In, say, eighteenth-century England, a man might be your respected neighbour and friend until he was convicted of some medium-level crime, such as theft, and was then sent into slavery – except, at that time, social and legal niceties dubbed it 'transportation to the colonies'. Transportation was and is rarely seen as a form of slavery, but the similarities make such a comparison obvious.

The British transported convicts to wild and dangerous outlands of the Empire; like Australia, the Andaman Islands in the northern Pacific and to New England in North America. The French transported convicts to Devil's Island, off French Guiana in South America – as was made infamous by the autobiographical prison novel (and movie) *Papillon*. Conditions were primitive, the work was brutal, and the convicts died like flies of disease, snakebites, beatings by the guards, and of simple exhaustion. Yet the domestication of these areas – to their civilised status today – was initially achieved through the forced labour of hundreds of thousands of unpaid convicts.

But now consider the point of view neighbour of someone transported to the colonies. The transported convict might continue to be your friend, as long as he remained in contact with you or as long as he remained in your thoughts. But you simply couldn't publicly acknowledge him as an equal any more without severely damaging your own social standing. Charles Dickens illustrated the problem in his novel *Great Expectations*. The protagonist, Pip, is mortified to discover that the transported convict Abel Magwich is the man who has secretly been paying for his education as a gentleman. The goodhearted Pip feels shame that he cannot acknowledge his debt to the escaped convict, but his social standing (ironically paid for by Magwich) prevents him from doing so. The act of being transported had transformed the frightening but benevolent Magwich into more of a possession of the state than a free human being.

A similar process happens today if a friend is convicted of a major and highly disreputable felony – say fraud, rape or murder. Up until the moment he or she is convicted, modern societies generally rule that the suspect is given the benefit of the doubt:

they are not officially seen as guilty until proven so in a court of law. But the instant that they are pronounced guilty, they become social pariahs. A few people might remain unchanged in their attitude to the convicted felon, but even that is usually because they are convinced that the person is actually innocent.

The modern felon is then not only punished, but even after the punishment is over they will find it very hard to rebuild their lives: former friends and family may refuse to acknowledge them, jobs are very hard to find and they remain one of 'the usual suspects' for the authorities whenever a similar crime is committed anywhere near them.

Similar contempt and distrust could await a returning transported convict – if he or she managed to get back to their home community after completing their term of state indenture. Most, in fact, chose to remain in the colonies, rather than suffer the indignity of a return to an alienated home.

This is not to morally equate modern and ancient attitudes – or, even less, to liken slavery-ridden societies to modern, relatively enlightened cultures. The point to note is the instant change in a person's social status the moment that they are convicted and their punishment begins. No matter how humane we become as a species, it seems that we can't fully escape the 'them and us' categorisation of basic human tribalism. 'One of us' who becomes, through their own actions, 'one of them', is transformed not only into a social pariah, but they also become a traitor to our social set. We may not deny them all human rights and human dignity – as slaves so often were – but we certainly find other ways to show our newfound disgust.

As we saw in the last chapter, exploitation for profit is certainly one way that the empowered in a society can show their scorn for those they feel are insignificant, contemptible, subhuman or otherwise inferior to themselves. And this attitude can quickly become a piece of circular logic: the self-serving belief that those we oppress, in some perhaps indefinable way, must be deserving of such treatment. As noted before, it's very easy to hate those that we harm. But legal slavery was not the only way in which this maltreatment could manifest itself.

The concept of wage labour is, as we saw in the last chapter, thousands of years old. Ideally it is what economists call a 'win-win' or a 'positive sum game': that is, a situation in which the employer and the employee gain more from the interaction than both the wages and the work effort that they provide. It is a moot point, however, how often this ideal equilibrium is reached and maintained.

If the employer is made to pay over the odds for their work-force, then they might be forced out of business by competitors who pay a lower wage for the same work. For example, British Fleet Street newspaper offices were chronically overstaffed in the late 1970s and early 1980s, mainly due to weak management and very powerful unions. Then the media mogul Rupert Murdoch bought first the *Sun* tabloid, and then the prestigious *Times* newspaper. In 1986 he moved the entire printing, journalism and distribution operation to Wapping, in the East End of London. Over six thousand people were made redundant by the move, and the much smaller number of replacement employees were made to sign up to much less generous contracts than their predecessors; but the *Sun* and *The Times*, as part of Murdoch's News International, started to make a consistent profit for the first time in decades. Faced with losing their own tenuous market share, other British newspapers followed suit: cutting wages and staffing in order to compete with the Murdoch papers. Or they went out of business.

Competitive wage bills are therefore in the long-term interests of both the employer and the wage earner, simply to maintain the business. But there is obviously a temptation for the employers to force wages down as far as possible, in order to maximise their financial security and, incidentally, their own take-home profits. If the employee's wage gets so low that they can only just survive – and they can find no work elsewhere – then they are what economists call a 'wage slave'.

If you personally are a low paid employee, it might be easy to bitterly suspect that you are also a wage slave. But in fact, thanks to labour unionisation and increasingly enlightened employment laws worldwide, actual wage slavery is, thankfully, rare in most economies. Barely being able to afford luxuries and barely being able to afford food are two very different things.

If you doubt this, consider the example of the Pullman Palace Car Company: a manufacturer of luxury railroad cars in the late nineteenth century. Pullman built an entire town – called 'Pullman' – outside Chicago, Illinois; including schools, shops, a library and homes for its six thousand employees. If you worked for the company, you *had* to live in Pullman. You also had to spend your wages in the company shops and pay rent to the company rent collector. To be caught shopping elsewhere, or to live anywhere out of town, meant instant dismissal to an outside world with few jobs and virtually no unemployment or poverty support.

Initially there was a pretence that Pullman was a 'model town'; like the idyllic community of Port Sunlight, created by the Lever Brothers soap company in Britain in 1887. But the fact was that the rents and the prices in the Pullman Company stores were deliberately set to eat up most of the employee's wage – so the cost of living in Pullman was noticeably higher than in neighbouring communities. This meant that almost all of the Pullman wage bill was pumped back into the company. Pullman still had to pay for the upkeep of the town and the goods in the stores; but, of course, even an overt slave owner had to pay for the accommodation and feeding of his slaves. So the functional difference between Pullman Palace Car Company and the recently outlawed southern state slavers was, at most, nominal. The employees of the Pullman Company were waged slaves, even if they might not have initially realised the fact.

Matters came to a head in 1893 during an economic downturn. The company lowered wages, but refused to lower the shop prices and rents. The desperate employees went on strike in 1894 and sympathetic railroad workers across the US refused to operate trains containing Pullman cars. The resulting chaos led to a federal investigation, and the exploitative behaviour of the Pullman Company was officially condemned as 'un-American'. Eventually the Pullman Company was forced to renounce its ownership of the entire town, along with its contractual enslavement of its employees.

Yet other companies, especially in the United States' indus-trial and mining belt, continued similar practices well into the twentieth century. Some refused to pay their employees in real money, but instead issued 'company scrip': an artificial coinage that could only be spent in the overpriced company stores. Under this fake economic system, growing debt and effective entrapment by the company was almost inevitable for the employees. This is the meaning behind the chorus from the 1930s coalminers' protest song, 'Sixteen Tons':

> *You load sixteen tons, what do you get?*
> *Another day older and deeper in debt.*
> *Saint Peter don't you call me 'cause I can't go.*
> *I owe my soul to the company store.*[5]

Why do these undoubtedly profitable industrial practices belong in a book about unnecessary human violence? Debt-ridden families starved and people died needlessly because of them. And, to maintain their systems of pseudo-slavery, companies employed thugs to beat up and sometimes kill malcontents and union organisers. This was civilised cannibal-ism – the deliberate destruction of lives, merely for personal profit – at its most blatant.

Matters may have improved over the past half-century in most countries, but even modernised capitalism in liberal nations tends to automatically create economic inequality, and a resulting exploitation of the poor. The fact is that, even with fairly and reasonably staggered income tax, it is the lower-paid workers who provide most of the economic strength of a nation, not the rich. Between direct taxes, like income tax, and indirect taxes, like sales tax or value added tax (VAT), the poor generally provide a higher proportion of their income to the state. For example, in 2014 a report by the UK Equality Trust revealed that the poorest 10 per cent of the British population were paying out an average of 43 per cent of their income in

---

5 'Sixteen Tons', recorded by Merle Travis (1946)

taxes. The richest British 10 per cent were paying only 35 per cent in taxation.[6]

Of course, on an individual basis the rich pay more tax per capita, because they have more possessions and income to tax. But the sheer number of the poor and low paid in a society more than counter-balances the difference. And also, by living on a low wage, the lowest paid workers boost the economy for everyone by freeing their employers to invest the spare cash into development and expansion. It would be hard to say this of senior company managers who, even after pocketing eye-wateringly huge salaries, then demand enormous bonus payments – whether their stewardship of the company led to profit or loss.

By 'poor' I don't necessarily mean just the unemployed or the low skilled and thus low paid employees. It is a simple fact that in the advanced economies the remuneration of senior company managers – the post-aristocratic-age ruling class – has at least doubled since the mid-1970s; and that's after adjusting the figures to remove the effect of inflation from the calculation. Meanwhile, the pay of the majority of workers – what used to be called the 'working class' – has fallen by up to a quarter; this again including calculations to remove the effect of inflation over the past forty years. The main reason for this change is the increasing financial and political inequality between the employers and the employed in modern societies.

The economic definition of the term 'working class' is a person or family who can never earn enough money to buy a property to live in. They must always rent, because they will never be able to earn enough money to start and service even a basic mortgage. Of course, as George Orwell pointed out in the 1930s, this meant that many well-educated, white-collar employees were actually working class, whether they liked to admit it or not. And, in these days of soaring property prices, many apparently middle-class people are also effectively working class, at least by this limited definition.

---

6 The Equality Trust: 'Unfair and Unclear: The Effects and Perception of the UK Tax System' by Madeleine Power and Tim Stacey (June 2014)

When I was a child, in the 1960s and 1970s, it was normal for a single earner (usually the father) to support a family in reasonable comfort. This situation is now increasingly uncommon and, in many communities, a rarity. Two earners (usually Dad *and* Mum) are needed to pay the rent or service a mortgage, plus pay rising food, transport, childcare and health costs. Families with only one low-wage earner, or with no jobs at all, are the new poor.

Even if your state provides generous benefits to the poor, it is normally true (except in times of major economic downturns) that the vast majority of this money does not go to the long-term unemployed 'benefit scroungers' and 'welfare queens'. It goes to supporting families that are earning low wages. State income support is therefore less of a crutch to the poor, and more of an indirect taxpayer-provided subsidy to employers, who can thus keep wages down and profits up.

The truth is that, without this financial support from the taxpayer, many of the low paid would become wage slaves, trying to survive on an income that is on or below the poverty line. Low-wage-paying employers – who often make large profits – are arguably holding the government and the nation to ransom, by putting their employees in this precarious position. In a truly free market companies wouldn't be given this indirect state subsidy: if they can't make a profit while paying a living wage then, according to the rules of *laissez-faire* capitalism, they should go bust and thus make room for a company that can.

Finally it is worth reiterating that the poor arguably support and maintain the economy more than the rich. The well off, and sometimes the middle class, can avoid paying tax by salting money away into offshore bank accounts – where it is out of circulation and therefore does their home economy little or no good. Such legal tax-avoidance schemes by rich individuals – and even more-so by influential multi-national companies – harm the ordinary taxpayers. Nations need taxes to run essential services – so every tax-avoidance scheme means a higher tax bill for the non-avoiders.

Meanwhile, those nations that implement any kind of value added tax or sales tax, are indirectly taxing the poor every day, almost every time they go out to buy something. The poor have to immediately spend every penny that they get, just to keep bread on the table. They can't use offshore banks if they have no money to save. Much of the day-to-day spending in the world is actually done by the poor, and it is that spending that keeps an economy revving along. After all, consumer spending accounts for around 70 per cent of the ongoing economy in most advanced nations. When consumer spending flags, for any reason, the economy instantly buckles and may crash.

If a selective plague were to wipe out all the rich in a nation (along with the knowledge of their Swiss or Cayman Island bank account security passwords) the economy would falter, but it would survive. If a similar plague wiped out the poor rather than the rich, the economy would immediately collapse.

Economists use the term 'free rider' to refer to any individual or group that takes more from their society than they give back. The term is most often pointed at the long-term unemployed and at blue-collar criminals – although, indeed, politicians on the right often seem to see no difference between the two. But, as we have seen in the past few chapters, it can also be historically levelled at the aristocratic class of most cultures. And the rich of any culture, even in our own enlightened times, might have a difficult time proving that they put more into the economy than they take out.

The concept of 'trickle down' economics was very popular with right-wing political parties in the late twentieth century. This states that tax cuts and financial incentives for the rich will ultimately trickle down to the rest of society, enriching all. In the nineteenth century this concept was known as 'horse and sparrow' theory – the idea being that if a (rich) horse is fed too many oats, the excess will fall to the ground and feed the (poor) sparrows. Unfortunately over thirty years of trickle-down policies in the United States, in western Europe and in many other countries have shown this hopeful theory to be largely false. The rich do not let excess wealth 'fall' to the poorer parts of society; they salt it away in foreign bank accounts to avoid tax and then hand it on as inheritance to their children. The result has been growing economic inequality in these societies, with all the cultural problems that stem from visible unfairness. And ultimately, if allowed to continue, the growth of state-protected inherited wealth will inevitably create a new aristocracy.

The free-riding of the rich on the backs of the poor is arguably another form of civilised cannibalism – especially in societies with inadequate social support for the poor. Certainly the lives of the poor, even today in the richest economies, are normally shorter than those of the rich. It is easy to blame this on unhealthy lifestyles – cigarettes, fatty foods and heavy drinking being more typical among the low paid. But the stress of living hand-to-mouth for decades, with nothing but a meagre state pension at the end of it, must also be a factor. Maybe if the wealth of society was more equitably distributed, life expectancy would increase across the board – as it did in Britain after the setting up of the welfare state in 1946.

Open slavery may be anathema to most modern people, and legal wage slavery is becoming increasingly uncommon; but indirect exploitation, through economic inequality, continues across the globe. And often this abuse of the powerless shades into functional slavery.

On 16 December 2013, the British Home Office released a report that estimated the slave population of modern Britain as at least 10,000 individuals[7]. On 29 November 2014, this number was revised upwards by another Home Office report, to as many as 13,000 slaves in Britain. From an overall population of 63 million, that constitutes 0.02 per cent of the populace.

This may seem staggering in a modern, comparatively enlightened democracy. But that is because the chains that enslave people today are rarely visible; they are, more often, purely mental shackles.

Modern slavers most often take advantage of national immigration policies to enforce bondage. They import illegal immigrants,

---

7 Baroness Butler-Sloss, Frank Field MP and Sir John Randall MP, 'Establishing Britain as a World Leader in the Fight Against Modern Slavery' (December 2013)

then threaten to report them to the authorities – to have them arrested and deported – if they don't slave for them. But they also take advantage of the under-educated, the drug-addicted, and even unprotected children within a society. They might also pay their slaves but that, in reality, is just another form of psychological fetter. A modern slaver makes sure that they pay less than they claim is the cost of the slave's room and board. Or, as often in the case of slave prostitutes, the cost of their healthcare, childcare and the illegal drugs that make their life bearable. The 'debt' therefore builds up constantly, and every day that the slave works, sees them sink more deeply into arrears and the slaver's control. They, in effect, soon owe their souls to the company store.

Prostitution, agricultural labour, low-skilled industrial labour and domestic work are the main areas where effective slavery is still rife in many economies. Industries that use child labour are especially prone to enslaving their helpless 'employees'. The *Global Slavery Index 2013* – produced by the non-profit Walk Free Foundation – conservatively estimated that there were 1,300 slaves in Sweden (that's 0.013 per cent of the overall Swedish population); 3,300 in Australia (0.014 per cent of the population); 4,600 slaves in the UK (0.007 per cent but, as seen above, this is just a third of the UK government's own figures); 6,300 slaves in Spain (0.014 per cent); 9,000 in France (0.014 per cent); 11,000 in Germany (0.014 per cent); 60,000 in Saudi Arabia (0.2 per cent of the population); 63,000 slaves in the United States (0.012 per cent); 540,000 in Russia (0.37 per cent); 2.2 million in Pakistan (1.17 per cent); 3.1 million in China (0.23 per cent); and a staggering 14.7 million slaves in India. So, in the second most populated country in the world, around 1.18 per cent of their entire population is functionally enslaved.

Essentially any lightly government-regulated, non-unionised work could be dabbling (or wading deeply) in the slave economy, because such work is less visible to outside oversight. The United Nations estimates that the number of slaves in the world today is around thirty million people. That's about 0.4 per cent of the entire world population.

How much each of us personally gains from this ongoing

slavery is hard to estimate precisely, because figures for such a hidden economy are naturally hard to collate. Certainly our food, clothes and many other goods would be much more expensive if national and international laws against slavery were properly enforced.

For example, many countries – including Britain and the USA – have minimum wage laws. Yet some companies deliberately employ illegal immigrants, precisely because they are willing to work off the books for less than the legal minimum wage – this often being barely enough money to survive, and therefore illegal wage slavery.

Our governments often seem unwilling to punish such employers to the maximum extent of the law, or to even investigate how far the problem has spread. Could it be that they guess just how badly our economies would stagger if covert slavery were genuinely outlawed?

Chapter 11

'Living in a Primitive State of Neurotic Irresponsibility . . . I Mean War'

By May 1941, the Nazi empire was almost universally victorious. Austria, Czechoslovakia, Poland, Denmark, Belgium, Luxembourg, Holland, France, Norway, Yugoslavia, Greece and most of North Africa had been conquered – incorporated into the largest European domain since the Napoleonic conquests. Britain was on her knees and must fall soon. America was keeping out of the new European war. Soviet Russia was a mistrustful friend of the Third Reich, while Romania, Hungary, Bulgaria, Italy and Japan were enthusiastic allies. The Nazi rulership of Germany was just eight years old, but they had already laid the foundation of their vaunted 'thousand-year Reich'.

At that time the dissident German playwright Bertolt Brecht was in hiding in Helsinki; but Finland was another Nazi ally. Extradition to Germany, torture by the Gestapo and death were staring him in the face – unless the USA granted him political asylum and he could get across the war-torn Atlantic.

It was then, when the Nazis seemed utterly unbeatable, that Brecht penned a strange epitaph, both optimistic and pessimistic, for Adolf Hitler and the German war machine. He wrote:

Do not rejoice in his defeat, you men.
For though the world has stood-up and stopped the bastard,
the bitch that bore him is in heat again.[1]

Exactly four years later the Third Reich was dead. The world had stood up and stopped the bastard. Yet Brecht's prophecy had also voiced the near-universal belief that war, and warmongers, are a permanent feature of human existence.

The American author Kurt Vonnegut once told film-maker Harrison Starr that he was writing a novelisation of his experiences of the Second World War. Starr asked him if it would be an anti-war book. Vonnegut's answer was coloured by a particular experience: he had been a prisoner of war in the German city of Dresden when it was incinerated by the Allies, using continuous heavy bomber raids over 13–15 February 1945. Between 23,000 and 25,000 people were killed by high-explosive bombs, incendiary devices and by the resulting firestorm. A firestorm is a conflagration so intense that it creates its own wind system. Thus fed as much oxygen as it can use, a firestorm will usually burn until all the local fuel is gone: in Dresden, the fuel was mainly buildings and human bodies.

In *Slaughterhouse-Five* (published in 1969) Vonnegut claimed that he was told by his guards that Dresden was an 'open city' – a town with no war industries and no military garrison – and was therefore exempt from attack. Certainly Dresden had been untouched by bomber raids up to that point in the war, and nobody taking shelter on 13 February can have expected a three-day continuous air raid. The city was packed with refugees, had comparatively few bomb shelters and, according to Vonnegut, no blackout rules were observed.

Just why the British and Americans decided to obliterate Dresden, with the Germans within three months of total defeat, remains one of the greatest controversies of the war. Certainly Dresden did have some war industries and was a rail nexus for German troop movements, but that doesn't seem to explain the

---

1 Bertolt Brecht, *The Resistible Rise of Arturo Ui* (written 1941; first produced 1958)

sheer overkill of the three-day raid. Perhaps the best explanation can be found in a memo given to British bomber crews just before they set out on the raid. It concluded:

The intentions of the attack are to hit the enemy where he will feel it most, behind an already partially collapsed front . . . and incidentally to show the Russians when they arrive what Bomber Command can do.

Many generals on the British and American side feared that the Soviet communists might try to continue their sweeping military victories, attacking their former allies and rolling on as far as the Atlantic. The destruction of Dresden, in their eyes, might have been a message that the Americans and the British could be just as cold-heartedly ruthless as the Russians or the Germans. Certainly the Soviets, who captured eastern Germany and the ruins of Dresden, did not then attack their allies. Of course that was cold comfort to the survivors of Dresden, including the young Kurt Vonnegut.

He survived the bombing raid in the very deep cold cellar of a slaughterhouse (the *Slaughterhouse-Five* of his book's title). Vonnegut was also lucky in that his shelter was on the outskirts of the city. Many of the casualties of the raid died in their bomb shelters of suffocation – the firestorm over the centre of the city literally sucked the air out of their lungs. Emerging after the raid, Vonnegut saw a 'moonscape' of scorched rubble, virtually devoid of all life and scattered with shrunken, heat-desiccated corpses. He also describes seeing Allied fighter planes strafing and killing survivors in the ruins. He and other surviving Allied prisoners were later forced by German soldiers to dig the rotting bodies out of the ruins – what Vonnegut called the 'corpse mines'.

So in reply to Harrison Starr's question, about whether his book would be anti-war, Kurt Vonnegut replied:

'Yes,' I said. 'I guess.'
'You know what I say to people when I hear that they're writing anti-war books?'

'No. What do you say, Harrison Starr?'
'I say, 'Why don't you write an anti-glacier book instead?''
What he meant, of course, was that there would always be
wars, that they were easy to stop as glaciers. I believe that,
too.[2]

A few utopian thinkers – philosophers like Immanuel Kant, novelists like H. G. Wells, religious visionaries like Mahatma Gandhi and cultural icons like John Lennon – have suggested, at one time or another, that human life without warfare *could* be possible. But until quite recent times, most people would have regarded this as unattainable – and many would have deemed universal peace as undesirable. Without war, after all, how could you defeat and destroy evil people?

Tribalism – our intrinsic need to define most other people as *them*, so that we can define ourselves and a few others as *us* – seems to naturally create distrust, fear and even paranoia. This nervousness all too often leads to aggression. That, coupled with the cultural phenomena of escalation of tension, sometimes leads to fighting. And if the groups fighting are big enough and vicious enough, you have a war.

Of course, intra-species warfare is hardly restricted to humans. Ant colonies battle for resources, dog packs fight over hunting territory and – as we saw in Chapter 5 – chimpanzee troupes raid each other in order to kill enemy males, kidnap females and to seize new feeding grounds.

Indeed for most of human history the chimp level was where human warfare remained: hit-and-run raids and malicious blood feuds. Then, about ten thousand years ago, our ancestors got all sophisticated. Better agriculture, walled towns, and developments in transport technology meant that bigger and better-fed populations could strike at more distant enemies. Instead of raiding to steal whatever they could carry, an army might actually conquer enemy territory – annexing farmland, taking towns and forcing enemy populations into vassalage.

---

2 Kurt Vonnegut, *Slaughterhouse-Five* (1969)

Common foot soldiers armed with spears and long knives would tramp along in rough formation behind the aristocrats, who usually rode in chariots. These latter were drawn by oxen, donkeys, mules or horses – where they were available – and by people where they were not. Pitched battles became the norm. This was where both sides arrived the day before and pitched camp overnight. Then they lined up to fight the next morning at a prearranged spot – after breakfast like civilised people. The area chosen to fight upon was generally an open bit of plain or farmland, without intervening structures: thus the English term 'battlefield'.

Archers and slingers were also there in the early wars, but the increasing use of armour and shields meant that missile wounds were rarely fatal. So archers were used mainly as skirmishers, spreading fear and confusion in the enemy ranks before the armies clashed. Necessarily lightly armed and armoured, the archers generally retreated if charged by regular soldiers, and were often run down and scattered by enemy cavalry units.

The larger-scale battles soon developed a degree of strategy and tactics. The gods were generally on the side of the big battalions; but a skilful use of terrain, surprise attacks and outflanking tactics sometimes meant that a smaller force could defeat an overconfident enemy. Such use of strategy usually demanded that only one person be in overall command – as a battlefield is no place for debates – so the role of general came into existence. That in turn demanded a hierarchy of lesser officers to convey his orders.

Yet most battles remained tactic-free slugging matches; fought until one side broke and ran, to be pursued by the victors. Foot soldiers did most of the killing and dying, and the troops with the best nerve had a better chance of winning. Thus training, battle experience, decent leadership and confidence from former victories could be telling factors. So could the basic physical fitness of the soldiers; the difference between defeat and victory might be as simple as which side had marched the least distance the day before and then remembered to eat a good breakfast before the battle.

This last point was important in another way: alcohol was almost invariably used as a spur to combat by armies, right up and into the nineteenth century CE. Many armies in history went into battle literally fighting-drunk – but let the men get too drunk, on an empty belly, and a general risked chaos in the ranks, panic and defeat.

The practical use of a chariot in early warfare was questionable at best. As often as not, a chariot warrior would ride to battle, then dismount to actually fight – as Homer, in *The Iliad*, described the heroic champions doing during the battles of the Trojan war. Moreover, a battle chariot needed two able-bodied soldiers, only one of whom could fight because the other was busy driving.

A chariot's main use in battle was to disquiet the opposite side by charging at them full tilt, then turning away at the last moment, shooting arrows or throwing javelins. This was because even well-trained horses simply would not charge into a battle line of spearmen. And the chariots themselves were too fragile to risk much rough handling; if an axle or wheel broke on the battlefield, the charioteers would be stranded – and probably surrounded by a group of vengeful enemy spearmen.

The military cavalry unit was invented after the chariot. This was because it is extraordinarily difficult to fight from the back of a pony, horse or camel if you are riding bareback: any kind of bump or blow can knock you off the animal. And everyone rode bareback until around 700 BCE, when the Assyrians invented the basic girthed saddle. The horned saddle, which actually reduced the chance of falling off, was not seen until 200 BCE in China and was being used by the Romans from around 100 BCE. The stirrup – which allowed a rider a firm enough footing to kill with a lance – was not invented until around 400 CE, again in China. Its use did not spread to the Middle East or Europe until the seventh century CE. So, even though the horse had been domesticated as early as 4500 BCE, the cavalryman spent most of history on the fringes of battles.

This is not to say that the cavalry and chariots did little damage to the enemy. In fact most of the killing might actually take place *after* a battle, when one side broke and ran. Mounted troops were very good at riding down and slaughtering defenceless, fleeing enemies.

Of course, the best mounted warriors were not townsmen or even farmers, but their traditional enemy: the nomads. Wandering peoples had good reason to master the horse, if only to save on shoe leather. Fighting from horse or camelback became their speciality – most notably on the wide plains of Eastern Europe, the bleak Asian steppes and the deserts of the Middle East. Not that being born in the saddle, so to speak, did them a great deal of good. A horse nomad would still have no chance against a line of spearmen, no matter how daring he was, and mounts weren't much use when storming a town's stone walls. So, while townsmen got on with fighting set-piece battles and organising sieges, nomads generally kept to the borders of civilisation, making hit-and-run raids.

Generally. Until there was a population boom out in the wilds, and a horde of nomads got on the move. Over and over again, throughout recorded history, an inundation of nomad peoples has crashed over established civilisations. The largest civilised armies were nothing to a barbarian horde. Strung out in a undisciplined mob of warriors, women, children and domestic animals, an approaching horde could stretch from horizon to horizon, making terrified observers feel that the whole world was avalanching towards them.

One of the earliest recorded examples of an invading barbarian horde were the *Hyksos* who, according to Ancient Egyptian inscriptions, swept out of Asia and over the Middle East around 1800 BCE. Horse nomads who worshipped a storm god, the Hyksos eventually conquered Egypt, and settled there as a ruling race. They were thrown out by a revolt of the native Egyptians around 1550 BCE.

In passing it is interesting to note the opinion of the third-century BCE Egyptian historian, Manetho.[3] He suggests that the biblical story of *Exodus* – about the enslaving of the Hebrew

---

3 Josephus, *Against Apion* (Book 2)

tribes in Egypt and their subsequent escape north to freedom – might actually be a gloss on the expulsion of the Hyksos. Certainly the dates could match: although there is little academic or theological agreement on the subject, most authorities are prepared to date the possible events of Exodus as some time before the thirteenth century BCE. And the usually punctilious Egyptian records make no mention of escaping tribes of slaves; just the defeat of the barbarian Hyksos. Manetho even mentioned that the fleeing Hyksos settled around the area of Jerusalem. If it were true that the Hyksos and the Hebrews were one and the same people, it might have been an understandable temptation for the later biblical authors to describe their ancestors as escaping slaves, rather than as routed overlords.

India may also have suffered a barbarian horde invasion from the north, starting around 1500 BCE. The *Aryan* peoples are thought, by some historians, to have conquered and subjugated the native (and darker skinned) *Dravidian* population. This, it has been suggested, may have been the origin of the Indian caste system[4] – where the lighter the skin, the more likely a person was accepted to be of a higher caste. Yet the theory of the Aryan horde invasion of India remains highly controversial, due to a paucity of both archaeological evidence and of academic agreement. And the temperature of the debate was not helped by the Nazis building their racist fantasies on the idea of a white-skinned 'Aryan master race'.

From what little we know of both of the above barbarian invasions, they were comparatively slow, taking hundreds of years to reach their full extent. They are therefore seen not as invasions by some historians, but as migrations or colonisations. But this was certainly not true of the warlike hordes of first the Huns, and later the Mongols.

The Hunnic people originated somewhere in eastern Asia; some historians trace their origins to China's northern border in the third century BCE. Like the Hyksos, they were barbaric horse-riding nomads. As their population grew too big for their

---

4 H. G. Wells, *The Outline of History* (pages 242–3)

homeland to support they moved ever westwards, driving other tribes before them. This tide of peoples struck Europe and the eastern borders of the Roman Empire around 400 CE. Displaced and desperate tribes such as the Goths, Vandals, Angles, Saxons, Lombardi, Frisii and Franks defeated and rode over the armies of the Western Empire. Outlying parts of the empire, like Britain, were cut off and abandoned by the Romans. The refugee conquerors then settled across Germany, northern Italy, France, southern Britain, Spain, Portugal and North Africa. The former owners of those lands were driven out, killed, subjugated or enslaved.

Meanwhile the Huns themselves had, by 370 CE, conquered most of Eastern Europe and the Balkans. Under their infamous war leader, Attila, they beat the Eastern Roman Empire into a grudging treaty and attempted an invasion of Persia. Yet the Hunnic Empire did not survive Attila the Hun by more than a year. He died in 453 CE, of a haemorrhage at his wedding feast. We have no idea how old he was at his death, because we don't know when he was born.

In 454 CE the Huns were defeated at the Battle of Nedao, by a rebel alliance of the tribes that they had subjugated. With little or no central organisation to help them recover from this blow, the Huns collapsed as an imperial power and were absorbed by the tribes they had once conquered. (The modern Hungarians are not the blood descendants of the Huns; they just live on the heartland of the former Hunnic Empire.)

The Mongols were rather more successful than the Huns. Originally from the Mongolian Asian steppes, the Mongols were also great horse-warriors. And by the time their population had swelled to become a horde, at the beginning of the thirteenth century CE, the invention of the saddle and stirrup had turned the cavalryman into a lethal battlefield killer.

Inspired by their ruthlessly ambitious leader, Genghis Khan, the Mongol hordes swept across Central Asia, China, Russia, the Middle East and Eastern Europe, ultimately creating the greatest contiguous land empire that the world has ever seen. The Mongols were utterly ruthless when faced with opposition. They ravaged the countryside that they passed through and decimated conquered populations. (Decimation was originally a Roman military term, indicating the killing of one person in every ten.) The Mongols' fall-back policy, if faced by a city that refused to instantly surrender, was to leave a smoking ruin and three sickening pyramids: the severed heads of all the town's men, women and children.

Armies that stood in their way were destroyed by mounted Mongol lancers, and by horse-archers wielding powerful composite bows. Both weapons could instantly kill even a heavily armoured man; so the military tactics of the past ten thousand years – mainly reliant on armoured foot soldiers manoeuvring in formation – were all but worthless against Mongol cavalry. Even plate-armoured formations of mounted knights – the medieval European super-weapon – had little chance against massed Mongol horsemen.

And there was another terrifying weapon that the Mongols utilised in their ruthless expansion: gunpowder. Discovered in China, by Taoist alchemists who were experimenting to create a compound that would grant eternal life, gunpowder turned out to do exactly the opposite. Chinese armies used primitive gunpowder weapons against the Mongol hordes, but with mixed success.

The Mongols were a remarkably open-minded people – when they weren't slaughtering entire cities. They were impressed by these noisy weapons, but were not actually held back from rolling over all of China. They acquired the secret of gunpowder during their Chinese conquests and then spread its use as far as Europe.

Mongol expansion was stopped by bad luck rather than military opposition. Their sea invasion of Japan was scotched when a typhoon sank most of their fleet in 1274. The Japanese called this lucky storm 'the divine wind', or *kamikaze*. A second attempted invasion, in 1281, was also destroyed by a typhoon.

(The unfortunate long-term side-effect of these auspicious storms was to convince the imperialists, running the country during the Second World War, that Japan was invulnerable to foreign invasion. They honestly believed that the Shinto gods, and the suicidally patriotic *kamikaze* pilots, would throw their American foes back from the shores of the sacred homeland. Modern science, in the form of two atomic bombs and a number of devastating conventional bomber raids, brutally re-educated them.)

The Mongol Empire's westward expansion pushed as far as eastern Germany. The Kingdom of Hungary was totally defeated at the Battle of Mohi in 1241, smashing the last effective opposition in Eastern Europe. Given the effectiveness of Mongol numbers, tactics and weapons, there seemed little reason for them not to roll on to conquer all the way to the Atlantic – and that was certainly their proclaimed intention. But then news came of a power struggle for the rulership of the empire.

Genghis Khan had died of old age in 1227. His son Ögedei took over, but died himself in 1241. So the leaders of the European invasion force hurried back to place their claims for power and, fortunately for Europe, took their armies with them as support in the inheritance debate. Surviving Europeans were left wondering where the hell the Mongol hordes had vanished to, and generally gave the credit for their miraculous escape to prayer.

By 1264, just fifty-eight years after Genghis Khan had come to power, the Mongol Empire had broken into factions and petty kingdoms. Yet the so-called *Pax Mongolica* lasted another hundred years: the remnants of Genghis's empire maintained a level of civilisation and communication across Asia that had been unknown since the brief days of Alexander the Great in the fourth century BCE.

As soon as they settled down to ruling – rather than conquering – the Mongols proved to be comparatively reasonable and decent overlords. And under Mongol protection the Silk Road – running from China to Europe – enriched the whole continent through international trade. Not a bad legacy from a horde of illiterate barbarians who slaughtered an estimated thirty million people during their years of empire-building.

The last great horde invasion in history is rarely seen as such;

mainly because it originated not from a barbarian wilderness, but from one of the most advanced civilisations on the planet. European conquest and colonisation – from 1492 to the present day – rolled over both American continents, Siberia, and Australia. It also temporarily subjugated the Indian subcontinent, Africa, China, the Far East and the islands of the Pacific; although in those places the demographic impact of the European host was ultimately less pronounced.

Just like previous horde invasions, Europe's explosive expansion was triggered by a boom in population that the homeland could not support. Also like previous horde invasions, the Europeans conquered foreign lands and occupied them – often displacing, dominating or killing the original inhabitants. Their invasions were successful because they utilised new technologies – travelling in huge ocean-going ships and introducing gunpowder and cavalry to those parts of the world that knew nothing of horses or firearms. And like previous hordes, they colonised in an unceasing stream of people that overwhelmed opposition by sheer force of numbers.

European invaders committed mass slaughters, enslaved native populations, set themselves up racial overlords, and forced their alien culture and religions on to their oppressed subjects. Indeed, from a certain point of view, Europe's Age of Imperialism differed from the Mongol Empire only in that the Mongols were noticeably less self-righteous as rulers.

Apologists for Europe's colonial period point out that Europeans spread industrial development, modern medicine, ordered government and Enlightenment thinking around the globe: and they are right. But the negative side of the scale remains hard to counter-balance.

The cost to human life of this phase of history is impossible to accurately calculate. Think of all the seemingly endless colonial and imperial wars – from the Carib Islands and India to Vietnam and Afghanistan; the global slavery industry; the attempted genocide of the native American and Australian populations; the racist segregation, miscegenation and apartheid laws; the spread of lethal diseases around the planet, like smallpox, syphilis and

HIV; the famines caused by incompetent imperial bureaucracies – or as a deliberate policy to 'thin out' native populations; the rape of natural resources to enrich countries on the other side of the planet; the hard-selling of dangerous and addictive substances like alcohol, tobacco, opium and cocaine; and even the appalling cost to those millions of Europeans forced to emigrate from their birthplaces – driven out by poverty, injustice and wars at home.

Given that the European racial hegemony is still the most powerful cultural and military force on the planet, one could say that the 'butcher's bill' for the mass migration of the European horde is still ratcheting upward.

But can aggressive war ever be seen as necessary or even heroic? Certainly that is how many of our ancestors felt. (Although generally not those ancestors who were on the front-lines of battlefields; as George Orwell noted, the rarest sight in war is a jingoist with a bullet hole in him.) Well into the twentieth century, warmongers and nationalists regarded territorial expansion, and resulting wars, as a cultural necessity. Indeed, many people saw imperial wars as destined to happen; provided their own side happened to be winning. Phrases like '*Pax Romana*', 'the white man's burden', 'manifest destiny' and '*lebensraum*' were used to justify the theft of territory, vital resources and even the bodies of enslaved populations.

Above all, in the modern age, there is one name synonymous with 'glorious warfare'. A man whose magnificent achievements as a battlefield general almost, for some people, obscure the fact that he was a totalitarian dictator who betrayed his early principles and caused millions of unnecessary deaths.

In the late winter of 2002, workmen bulldozing an abandoned army barracks outside Vilnius, the capital of Lithuania, stumbled on a mass grave. The bodies had not been thrown in haphazardly; they were laid out in rows and layers with military neatness. And many of them were still covered by the shreds of dark blue uniforms.

The dead men were the remains of one of the most successful armies in European history: the French *Grand Armée* of Napoleon Bonaparte. They had defeated larger armies again and again, winning France an Empire that, at one time or another, stretched from Egypt to Sweden and from Portugal to Russia. And there, in the frozen Lithuanian earth, lay two thousand of them – none showing evidence of death through violence. All had died of a combination of starvation, disease, exhaustion and, especially, bitter cold. They had followed the tremendous vision of their commander, only to be killed by an enemy that his strategic genius could not out-manoeuvre: the Eastern European winter.

At the height of his power, Napoleon had been nicknamed 'the Monster' by his many enemies in foreign nations – so frightening was his reputation. Yet he died suddenly on his exile island of Saint Helena at the age of just fifty-two. Little surprise, then, that some still believe that he was murdered to prevent his escape to terrorise the world again.

Napoleon di Buonaparte was born on Corsica in 1769, the son of a petty aristocrat. In his teens Napoleon was sent to the Parisian Military Academy (and changed his surname to the more French-sounding, less provincial 'Bonaparte'). He rose rapidly through the ranks of the French Army, joining the republicans during the revolution and becoming a national hero after he led the Revolutionary army to victory over the Austrian occupying forces in Northern Italy.

He then invaded Egypt, seeking to strike from there at British territories in India; but he was defeated by Admiral Nelson at the Battle of the Nile and was forced to return to France. There he seized power over the flagging revolutionary government and made himself First Consul – dictator in all but name – in 1799. Napoleon, the former radical republican, had himself crowned Emperor of France in 1804.

Bonaparte and his *Grand Armée* smashed the Austrians and their Russian ally at the Battle of Austerlitz on 2 December 1805. Then, in 1806, he annexed the Kingdom of Naples and the Republic of Holland, crowning his brothers Joseph and Louis as their new kings. In the same year Prussia (what is now northern Germany and western Poland) joined the anti-French coalition, but Napoleon destroyed the Prussian armies at the battles of

Jena and Auerstadt. The Russian army was also decisively defeated at the Battle of Friedland and, in 1807, Tsar Alexander I signed a peace treaty with the French. Napoleon then destroyed what remained of Austria's fighting strength at the Battle of Wagram. His generals had also captured Spain and most of Portugal, so Napoleon was the absolute ruler of almost all of Western Europe by 1809.

Then came the defeats. The unconquered British sent armies under the future Duke of Wellington to the Iberian peninsula and, by 1814, Napoleon's generals had been driven all the way back over the Pyrenees into France. But, by then, things were much worse in the east of Napoleon's empire.

France invaded Russia in 1812. After being defeated at the Battle of Borodino the Tsar's armies fell back and refused to fight. Napoleon captured Moscow, but the retreating Russians burned much of the city, making it useless as a base of operations for the French. Napoleon tried to organise a fighting retreat, but his army was all but destroyed by the Russian winter and by Russian guerrilla attacks. On the retreat from Moscow to France, 570,000 of the 600,000 soldiers of the *Grand Armée* died in the snow.

The French Empire was evidently finished. Napoleon's own generals persuaded him to surrender and hand himself over to the victorious allied nations. He was sent into exile on the Mediterranean island of Elba with a ceremonial guard of 2000 men. But within a year he and his tiny army escaped and marched on Paris. The French royalist armies sent to kill him instead joined him, and within weeks Napoleon was master of France again.

Napoleon now asked his enemies for peace, but they would not trust him. So he attacked their forces in Belgium before they could invade France. He almost won the Battle of Waterloo; defeated only by a combination of thick mud, the Duke of Wellington's generalship and the doggedness of British, Dutch and Prussian troops.

His new island of exile was Saint Helena – off the African coast in the mid-Atlantic. Somewhere so remote that even Napoleon could not escape.

When he died in 1821, aged just fifty-two, the autopsy described Napoleon's cause of death as 'stomach cancer'. Certainly this sounded convincing at the time. Paintings of Napoleon famously showed him habitually holding his right hand under his waistcoat, cradling his stomach, because he suffered from peptic stomach ulcers – a condition brought on by a childhood bacterial infection and then the constant stress of leadership, but later made worse by the terrible cold on the retreat from Moscow. Such severe ulcers are often a precursor to stomach cancer.

Yet tests on samples of Napoleon's hair, conducted in 2007, found significant amounts of the poison arsenic. Death by slow arsenic poisoning and death by stomach cancer are very similar, right down to the damage done to the stomach lining by both afflictions. Then, in 2008, further tests on hair samples of Napoleon's family and other, unrelated contemporaries found similar amounts of trace mineral arsenic. The poison was used in many commercial products in the eighteenth and nineteenth centuries, so natural environmental seepage seems a likely cause of the high levels of arsenic found in Napoleon's hair. Of course, it is still possible that his British jailors assassinated Napoleon with slow arsenic poisoning but, because of the high levels of the poison in his environment, we will probably never be able to prove it.

Of all the dictators mentioned in this book, Napoleon was arguably the most benign. His rule generally improved the lives of his subjects, if only because France's *Code Napoleon* – a civic legal structure on a par with the USA's enlightened constitution – created and spread the most egalitarian system of justice that Europe had yet seen. The Emperor Napoleon was more than a warlord; he was a patron of scholarship, a shrewd reformer and, above all, an adventurer on a par with Alexander the Great. Little wonder that, within a decade of his defeat at Waterloo, Lord Byron was poetically describing Napoleon as 'the lightning'.

Yet it should be remembered that his wars of conquest were not even primarily for the good of France, but to serve Napoleon's own self-esteem. Contemporary accounts, by those who knew him personally, make it plain that Napoleon had a strong streak of egomania. He also had gnawing feelings of inadequacy – as shown in his often miserable and humiliating domestic life.

(There is a true story concerning one of Napoleon's more wretched moments. He wanted to have a day's rabbit hunting with his courtiers; so hundreds of rabbits were bred and released on the day, to ensure plenty of targets. But the rabbits were all hand-reared and thus quite tame. Regarding humans as providers of food, the rabbits all lolloped hopefully towards Napoleon and his hunting party as soon as they arrived. The emperor – who had a lifelong aversion to cats – saw the advancing carpet of small furry animals and panicked, hurrying back to his carriage and demanding to be returned home. For a man who had always remained calm under cannon fire – and later faced down an entire army that had been sent to kill or capture him – it was a nasty embarrassment.)

In the early days Napoleon's brilliant generalship served France well, but after he made himself emperor his endless need for victories and plaudits drove France's dominion first to over-expand, and then to catastrophic defeats.

At the turn of the eighteenth century France did not need a European empire. It needed a period of social recuperation following the chaos of the Revolution – but the Emperor Napoleon's ceaseless ambition demanded conflicts in which he could further prove himself. Despite his undeniable glory years, he left France much worse off than before he took power.

When all is said and done, Napoleon Bonaparte was a brilliant war leader; but that was all he was. In the absence of war he evidently felt this inadequacy keenly: so he started unnecessary wars. Those wars cost Europe around seven million lives.

The seemingly eternal military arms race is a key part of the history of warfare. Gaining superior weapons, before your enemy does, has always been an essential factor to human survival.

Think of one of the most basic of weapons: the spear. A man with a spear could easily kill a man with a hand axe or club, because he could stab him before the other man could get into striking range. If both men had spears, then the difference between the length and fragility of the spear shaft, and the sharpness of the spearhead could mean the difference between life and death. A fair proportion of your ancestors will have died due to such apparently small military engineering factors.

The constant development and counter-development of weapon technology has proved a decisive factor throughout history. The invention of the stone hand axe was countered by the striking range of the spear. The spear was countered by missile weapons like spear-throwers, slings, javelins and bows. Missile weapons were countered by hide armour and shields. Men forming a shield-wall – the most basic, yet effective military formation – could protect each other while still striking at an enemy. Chariots and flanking skirmishers armed with missile weapons could break up an enemy formation, allowing your own men to do greater damage. Well-drilled soldiers commanded by knowledgeable officers were less likely to break formation or panic in battle. Heavy cavalry, secured on their horses by saddles and stirrups, could shatter even disciplined infantry formations. Developments in metallurgy allowed the creation of longer, sharper swords and tougher, better-fitted armour. Superior missile weapons, like the Italian crossbow, the English longbow and the Mongol composite bow, could kill even a plate-armoured knight at a hundred paces. Gunpowder weapons developed from noisy panic-inducers (as likely to harm your own side as the enemy) into decisive battlefield weapons. Artillery – originally only good for destroying town walls during sieges – came into its own with the invention of explosive-filled shells; meaning that nobody could feel completely safe anywhere on (or near) a battlefield. Soldiers using rifle-barrelled guns could fire accurately at longer range and could therefore massacre troops using unrifled muskets. A single machine-gunner could slaughter hundreds of rifle-armed troops. Airplanes carrying bombs – or armoured vehicles like the tank – could smash even entrenched machine gun nests. Heavily armed fighter planes could destroy large numbers of bombers or tanks.

Then we came to the weapons of mass destruction (WMD): chemical, biological and atomic. From August 1945 onwards

– following the nuclear destruction of Hiroshima and Nagasaki – the endless historical arms race fundamentally changed in character. The only way that you can effectively counter a WMD is to nullify the enemy before they have a chance to use it. Otherwise the cost of the conflict to your side will be too great, whatever it is that you hoped to gain by starting the fight.

(J. Robert Oppenheimer was the lead scientist on the Manhattan Project: the US military's operation to research, build and test the first fission atom bomb. In 1945 he was sent to the White House to be enthusiastically congratulated on the project's success by President Harry S. Truman. But Oppenheimer replied that he felt haunted by shame that he had helped create science's own original sin – that he could not help feeling that the science of physics now had blood on its hands. After the meeting Truman – the man who had given the order to drop atom bombs on two helpless enemy cities – told his aides that he never wanted to see Oppenheimer again.)

Even the most brilliant thinkers of the late 1940s and early 1950s – like the scientist Albert Einstein, the journalist George Orwell, the historian Arnold Toynbee and the philosopher Bertrand Russell – believed that nuclear war was almost inevitable. After all, when had a new and highly effective weapon *not* been immediately used by its inventors to gain a military and political advantage? Yet we're still here, and no city since Nagasaki has been annihilated by a weapon of mass destruction.

There are only two ways to nullify a WMD-armed enemy. The first is to utterly destroy them before they can attack you – the annihilating pre-emptive strike – but the risk of this strategy is appalling. Fail to shatter *all* of their WMD strike capacity and your side will, at the very least, pay a heavy price. How many leaders are willing to implement a war strategy that might actually kill them personally – or might see their own vengeful people lynch them if they happen to survive that long?

Then, in the mid-1950s, scientists discovered the likely global side-effects of even a 'limited' nuclear war, using the newly developed and deployed thermonuclear 'hydrogen' bombs. Such high-yield blasts would not only obliterate entire cities and the surrounding countryside; they would also hurl vast amounts of radioactive ash all the way to the stratosphere. High-level atmospheric winds would then carry the radioactive fallout around the planet, poisoning, genetically damaging or killing everything it landed on. For a moving illustration of the shock of that discovery, read Nevil Shute's 1957 novel, *On the Beach*, in which a terrified Australia waits for agonising months as the result of a northern hemisphere nuclear war blows certain death towards them.

Yet the Cold War and the nuclear arms race continued unabated. Indeed it did so even after the early-1980s discovery that a hot war using nuclear warheads would almost certainly cause a 'nuclear winter'. That is, the dust from nuclear explosions would cut out most of the sunlight, globally, for a number of years. This, in turn, would create a short but particularly brutal ice age. Combined with the effects of radioactive fallout, the cold would certainly destroy all human life, and probably all planetary life bigger than microbes.

At least twice during the Cold War (1947–91) political brinkmanship brought the world to the edge of a total nuclear exchange between the superpowers – officially called MAD by the US Military: short for 'mutually assured destruction'.

In July 1983, Soviet premier Yuri Andropov warned the United States that the two superpowers were dangerously close to the 'red line' of a nuclear war. But US president Ronald Reagan, angered over the Soviet invasion of Afghanistan, rejected the warning as Russian 'huffing and puffing'. In March 1983 he had publicly called the Soviet Union an 'evil empire': a piece of political rhetoric that infuriated the Soviets, who saw themselves as the heroes of humanity. Tensions racked up further in September 1983, when a South Korean civilian airliner strayed into Soviet airspace and was shot down, killing all 269 people on board, including a US congressman for Georgia.

Later that month *Oko* – the Soviet early-warning radar system that tracked potential incoming nuclear intercontinental missiles – reported a single missile launch from the continental United States. Lieutenant Colonel Stanislav Petrov, the senior officer on duty, decided that the report was a false alarm and ignored it. His certainty must have wavered a few minutes later when Oko reported four more launches from the USA. But he bravely refused to pass the warning on to his superiors, fearing that they would launch a full-scale nuclear retaliation out of blind panic. Petrov was in fact correct – the 'launches' were just the result of technical glitches in the system – but he was nevertheless demoted to 'non-vital duties' and later suffered a nervous breakdown.

Then, in November 1983, NATO (a military alliance of countries that opposed the Soviets) staged *Able Archer*: a full-scale military exercise in which military forces and command HQs practised their procedures for fighting a ground war and nuclear conflict in Europe. Considering the tensions that were then rampant, this was a highly dangerous thing to do. Soviet generals came close to being convinced that Able Archer was a cover for a NATO first strike against them. The sick and (as it turned out) dying Andropov was almost too weak to rein in his panicking generals, and it is now generally agreed that nuclear war was avoided more by luck than leadership. Although the world public were aware of the deadly tensions throughout 1983, it was not until the end of the Cold War – and the publication of Soviet military documents – that it was realised just how close to annihilation we'd come.

More publicly recognised, at the time, was the infamous Cuban Missile Crisis of October 1962. Here I want to pay tribute to three men – Jack Kennedy, Nikita Khrushchev and Oleg Penkovsky – who between them saved the entire world. Oleg Penkovsky was a colonel in the GRU (the Soviet intelligence agency). In 1960 he had spontaneously offered to spy for the British Secret Service (MI6) and became one of their highest-ranked and thus most valuable secret agents in the USSR.

Two years later the Cuban Missile Crisis had brought the Americans and the Russians to the brink of war over the placing of Soviet nuclear missiles on communist Cuba. Positioned so close to the American mainland, such missiles could launch and strike too fast for the USA to be able to fire back – making Cuba the perfect pre-emptive strike base for the USSR. From the moment of this discovery, the Pentagon pushed US President John F. Kennedy to approve a full-scale US invasion of Cuba to counter the Soviet move once and for all.

Penkovsky risked his life to get urgent information to the west. He reported that the Soviet missiles already on Cuba were not yet ready to fire. That gave Kennedy a vital breathing space. The president used the time to rein in his gung-ho Joint Chiefs of Staff, and allowed a diplomatic solution to solidify.

The then Soviet premier, Nikita Khrushchev, was sometimes seen as a bit of a joke in the west. The British Prime Minister, Harold Macmillan, had once asked: 'How can this fat, vulgar man with his pig eyes and ceaseless flow of talk be the head – the aspirant Tsar – for all those millions of people?' In fact Khrushchev had stayed alive during the later Stalin years, partly by appearing to be a twit. The homicidally paranoid dictator had enjoyed watching him get drunk and making a fool of himself at parties, so never had him executed.

After Stalin's death in March 1953, Khrushchev spent two years clawing his way to the Soviet leadership; but he was no small-minded party hack. At a 'secret speech', given at the 20th Party Conference in 1956, he denounced purges of the past two decades and even Stalin himself – who, he said, 'often chose the path of repression and physical annihilation, not only against actual enemies, but also against individuals who had not committed any crimes against the party or the Soviet government'. In other words, he called Stalin a murderer. Khrushchev then ushered in a noticeably less repressive era of Soviet governance.

Nikita Khrushchev always maintained the air of a jolly, slightly dopey peasant – discomforting pompous snobs like Macmillan – but he was, at heart, a very clever and pragmatic man. He once joked about international politics: 'I'm no Tsarist officer who has to shoot himself if I fart at a masked ball. It's better to back down than to go to war.' So, when Jack Kennedy offered to withdraw America's secret missiles stationed in Turkey in return for a public Soviet missile withdrawal from Cuba, Khrushchev eventually accepted. But the world teetered on the brink of a nuclear war for thirteen days before this diplomatic answer took hold and worked. Unaware of the American side of the bargain, the world public thought that the Soviets had suffered a humiliating climbdown.

Kennedy was assassinated just over a year later. Although it was clear even by that time that the Pentagon's Cuban invasion plan would certainly have sparked World War Three, senior members of the US military had still not forgiven Kennedy for 'chickening out'. This makes them, in the eyes of conspiracy theorists, among the prime suspects in his murder.

(For those who still believe that Kennedy was killed by 'lone gunman' Lee Harvey Oswald, I recommend reading the 1978 report by the United States House Select Committee on Assassinations. That concluded that at least four bullets were fired during the assassination, of which only three could possibly have been fired by Oswald. If there was more than one assassin then that is, by legal definition, a criminal conspiracy.)

Penkovsky was already dead by the time Kennedy was murdered. Arrested by the Soviets while the Cuban Missile Crisis was in full swing, he was convicted of spying and was executed in May 1963. A nuclear holocaust was avoided through Kennedy's cool head, and the pragmatism of Nikita Khrushchev; who was willing to be publicly humiliated, rather than risk war. But they probably could not have done it without the time bought for them by Penkovsky's leaked information. Most sources agree that Penkovsky was shot. But some have claimed that he was strapped to a stretcher and thrown – alive – into a furnace, as a warning to other would-be traitors.

As was seen during the Cuban Missile Crisis, the second way to counter a WMD-armed enemy is diplomacy. Against all expectations, it was this second strategy that kept us alive through the forty-four years of the Cold War and is now gradually reducing the stockpiles of WMDs around the world.

Diplomacy: work done by grey-suited men and women, who constantly and tediously adjust the minutiae of international relations in places like the United Nations. If not for those people the Earth might now be a radioactive rock, devoid of life.

There is a reason that diplomacy has become such a powerful

tool in the Atomic Age. The post-Second World War period of comparative peace has been called the Balance of Terror. The great national powers – most notably the USA and the USSR – used espionage, made threatening moves and instigated conventional wars, civil wars and *coups d'état* in other nations. But the WMD-armed nations were too scared to risk fighting each other directly or decisively: their mutual terror of the consequences balanced out into a nervous status quo. And it is possible that this long period in which warmongering was throttled back, if not actually stopped, has had a long-term effect on the human race.

For three generations, the whole planet has lived with the knowledge that one political mistake could burn us alive, or sentence us to a slow and excruciating death by radiation poisoning. Or that a single broken test-tube might release a manmade virus as lethal as Ebola and as contagious as the common cold. It would be inconceivable that the human race as a whole had not become habitually more cautious about starting jingoistic conflicts under such circumstances.

Anyone who has read archives of pre-Cold War newspapers could confirm that unquestioning patriotic nationalism – so prevalent before 1947 – has become a noticeably less influential political force in the last half-century. In August 1914, young men across Europe ran to the enlisting stations, celebrating as if a public holiday had been declared, not a world war. In 1939, scarred by the experience of the Great War, people were noticeably less gung-ho about the encroaching Second World War; but few actively protested against taking part in the conflict. In February 2003, over fifteen million people protested worldwide against the oncoming US-led war on Iraq. *Guinness World Records* noted that this was the largest protest in human history.

(The 2003 Iraq War may seem a break from the historical pattern set by the WMD-influenced 'balance of terror'. The US and its allies stated that Iraq owned illegal weapons of mass destruction: indeed, that was the official reason for the invasion. Over the previous half-century no such attack, by WMD-armed nations on another WMD-armed nation, had ever been risked. It was almost as if the leaders of the US, the

UK and the other allies *knew* that Iraq in fact had no weapons of mass destruction – as, indeed, turned out to be the case when Iraq was defeated and searched. But, of course, that would have made the war illegal under international law, and the leaders who instigated the invasion might be charged as war criminals for waging a war of conquest.)

It may be, at last, that the risk and inhumanity of war has started to break the habit of our species resorting to mass conflict to resolve our disputes. In *The Outline of History* – his 1920 book that vividly reviewed the record of life on the planet – the writer H. G. Wells concluded that:

> *Human history becomes more and more a race between education and catastrophe . . . New falsities may arise and hold men in some unrighteous and fated scheme of order for a time, before they collapse amidst the misery and slaughter of generations.*
>
> *Yet, clumsily or smoothly, the world, it seems, progresses and will progress.*

The recent fall in violent crime, and the absence of global conflict for over two-thirds of a century, may indicate that our educated intelligence may at last be edging us ahead of our catastrophically brutal inclinations. But war and warmongering remain far from being defeated.

Bertolt Brecht's bitch is still in heat.

Kurt Vonnegut's glaciers are still grinding.

Chapter 12

'My Brother's Keeper'

To an alien observer, civil war might seem to be the most typical type of human conflict. On the lowest level one might say that a family fist fight is a form of civil war. Or, at the other end of the scale, a humanitarian might say that *all* conflicts are civil wars, since the human race is – philosophically and genetically speaking – just one big, diverse family.

The majority of people would say that a civil war is a conflict dividing a nation; but remember that the idea of nationalism is comparatively new. Up until the Enlightenment, most people would have defined their loyalties by stating their family, religion, ethnic group, local town and/or ruling aristocrat. Their overall country was a vague and distant idea that rarely, if ever, impinged on their daily existence. Most people lived their whole lives within a mile or two of where they were born, and only heard about foreigners in fanciful stories. It was not until the eighteenth century – with increased international travel, the spread of education, the reading of newspapers, and a resultant widening of political horizons – that the concept of the 'nation state' became widely accepted as coming above people's basic allegiances.

Absent a strong and defining concept of nationalism, a civil war more resembles a political turf war or an overblown feud. Indeed, on one level, any civil war *is* just an extension of the endless tribal feuding that cursed all pre-literate, pre-municipal societies. Yet, petty and nonsensical as it so often is, we have yet to come close to eradicating it. Civil war is generally the most vicious and vindictive type of warfare, and it is also the most common type of war in the modern, post-imperial world.

Indeed, under the broadest definition of civil war – that of people fighting and killing those they would normally call countrymen, kin or fellow believers – then we should also include revolutions, rebellions, and internal religious conflicts over heretical sects. Seen from this point of view, a revolution is just a civil war in which the ruling power is toppled. A rebellion is a civil war where the rulers survive. And the forming, persecution and victory of heretical sects is an essential part of a religion's evolution: without such doctrinal civil wars, all faiths would still be conducting human sacrifices to appease nature spirits.

The Syrian Civil War is raging as I write this. Beginning in March 2011, it is now three years old. In that time one of the most urbane, if totalitarian, nations in the Middle East has been reduced to savagery and chaos. At least 100,000 citizens have been killed. Over 2.3 million refugees have fled to neighbouring countries. Cities like Homs are under continuous shellfire. Sarin nerve gas has been used in attacks on urban areas. Torture and execution without trial are common practices by both sides. And sniper squads have been reported to run competitions in which they win cigarettes for hitting different types of victim in specific parts of the body: for example, shooting heavily pregnant women through the belly. Yet the Syrian Civil War, even if it continued as it is for another decade, would be barely noticeable if placed next to the great civil wars of recorded history.

Indeed, civil war can destroy entire civilisations. For example, the Mycenaean Greek culture – sometimes known as the Age of Heroes, and dating from roughly 1600 to 1100 BCE – was shattered only a few generations after their greatest military victory. The civilisation that gave us the tales of Theseus and the Minotaur, the Twelve Trials of Hercules, Jason and the Argonauts, Helen and the Thousand Ships, and the Voyages of Odysseus, went down in a welter of blood worthy of the darkest Greek tragedy.

Ironically, it may have all begun with an engineering and agricultural triumph. The city of Orchomenus, in central Greece, drained the nearby Lake Copais by building canals and cyclopean dykes – the remains of which can still be seen today, over three thousand years later. The Orchomeneans then produced vast amounts of grain from the rich new farmland. The population of the Mycenaean city states boomed after that, giving them the manpower to launch a seaborne invasion of Anatolia in the late thirteenth century BCE. These were the thousand ships launched, Homer says, to rescue and avenge the kidnapped Queen Helen; the invasion led to a ten-year war that culminated with the sack of Troy in 1275 BCE (*see Chapter 8*).

Three generations later, around 1200 BCE, Orchomenus was sacked and burned; legend says in a war with the neighbouring city of Thebes. Either through subsequent neglect, or because of deliberate Theban sabotage, the great dykes were wrecked and the grain fields of Orchomenus flooded.

What happened next is a matter of archaeological interpretation, as very few written records survive from that period. But what we do know is that almost all the cities of Mycenaean Greece, including Thebes and Mycenae itself, were destroyed.

Smaller regional centres of power, like Pylos in the south-west Peloponnese, were hit so fast that the clerks were still writing out instructions for defensive troop dispersments – and ordering propitiatory human sacrifices to the gods – when the enemy stormed the walls and burned the palace to the ground (*see Chapter 8*). But the last cities to fall – like Tiryns 'of the great walls' and 'golden' Mycenae – had evidently known full well that destruction was coming: archaeological evidence shows that they hastily built extra defensive walls and dug deep water cisterns to help to withstand a siege. But even that could not save them. They too were despoiled and burned.

The myth of Theseus tells that, in his later life, he eloped with Antiope, the queen of the Amazon tribe of the Caucasus, a region north-east of Greece. This all-female warrior tribe then vengefully invaded Greece and besieged Theseus's native city of Athens for four months, but the Amazons were eventually repulsed.

That tale may stem from a folk memory of an actual siege of Athens during the Mycenaean *Götterdämmerung*. The archaeology suggests that only Athens, of all the great Mycenaean cities, escaped the storm of destruction; and that was almost certainly due to a lucky trick of geology. Athens' great stone promontory – called the *Acropolis* or 'upper city' – was probably too steep-sided to assault using Bronze Age siege technology. So the Athenians, who had also dug siege cisterns, managed to hold out when all the nearby cities were obliterated.

Around the same time neighbouring nations – like the Anatolian Hittites, the Cretans and the Egyptians – were attacked by sea raiders. The Egyptians called these pirates 'the People of the Sea' and were clearly terrified of them. It remains a contentious issue among historians just who the People of the Sea actually were; the Egyptians described them as a heterogeneous 'conspiracy' of different peoples and tribes. But it seems likely that Mycenaean Greeks, fleeing chaos and destruction at home, formed a large contingent of the sea-going horde.

By 1100 BCE, Greece had collapsed into a dark age that lasted three hundred years. But why? What threw an entire literate and thriving civilisation into savagery and darkness in less than a century? The answer was almost certainly not an invasion by Amazon warriors – or, indeed, by any outside force. A more likely cause was hunger.

The flooding of the grain fields of Orchomenus, the 'Mycenaean grain basket', may have created a chronic food shortage for the over-populated Greek city states, quickly tipping the balance into chaos. We can guess that Mycenaean Greece was over-populated because, as Homer noted in *The Iliad*, during the Trojan War there were Greek colonies set up on the coast of Anatolia. And as we saw in the last chapter, a typical way for a culture to try to deal with an unsustainable population boom is to send out the excess people as a horde of colonists.

But colonisation and opportunistic war weren't enough to save the Mycenaean Greeks. As the food crisis escalated, desperate raids to steal provisions from neighbouring cities may have spiralled into a civil war of all against all. One less mouth to feed is one less mouth to feed: so old allegiances were forgotten as cities sought to destroy their neighbours before their neighbours could destroy them.

The conflagration was so violent that nearby civilisations were hit by the shrapnel: the People of the Sea savaged Egypt and despoiled Crete. And the Hittite Empire saw Boğazköy, its capital, destroyed. Eternal Egypt survived, but the Cretans and Hittites collapsed into the same Dark Age that enveloped the Greeks.

Classical Greek historians, writing over half a millennium later, claimed that a northern barbarian horde, the Dorians, swept over Greece around this time; but there is no archaeological evidence of such a culture-changing invasion. Historians are now inclined to believe that the all-destroying 'Dorians' were actually the common people of the Mycenaean city states. Once starvation and all-out civil war had caused the social infrastructure to fall apart, the peasants and slaves may have risen up to sack the palaces of their aristocratic rulers. The grandchildren of the nobles who burned Troy may have been killed or enslaved by their own desperate people.

And with the downfall of the overly centralised Mycenaean palace culture, so too went all knowledge of writing, art, cyclopean architecture, mechanical technology and overseas trade. Only the nobles, priests and clerks had been allowed to learn about such things – as is plain from Homer's description of Mycenaean society – and now they were gone. When Greek civilisation arose again, three hundred years later, they were essentially rebuilding from scratch.

So the Greek Heroic Age died choking in the smoke of its own burning cities. The vindictive brutality of that all-encompassing destruction was echoed, six hundred years later, in a line from Aeschylus's play *Agamemnon*:

They raped our queen, so we raped their city. And we were right!

Many other pivotal moments of history have turned on civil wars, but they were rarely quite so apocalyptic. For example, almost two centuries of internecine wars – dating from 133 BCE to 30 CE – wrecked the Ancient Roman Republic, but probably had a death toll only in the tens of thousands. That was because most of the dead were soldiers killed in set-piece battles. The deliberate targeting of civilian populations, and the mass execution of political enemies, certainly took place during the Roman Civil Wars, but nowhere near the scale as seen in more modern conflicts.

Yet those wars changed European history and led the way to the world's first imperial dictatorship – the Caesars. Absolute rulers who governed with the rubberstamp support of an elected senate, the Roman emperors may not seem much of a political improvement to modern eyes. But – corrupt, decadent and insane as they often were – the emperors claimed that their right to rule sprang primarily from the will of the people, not from divine favouritism. To a small degree our modern democracy grew from the ideals of the Roman Empire . . . if not its usual practices.

Likewise, the English Civil War (1642 to 1651) led to the creation of the first modern parliamentary democracy. And the US Civil War (1861–65) put the final nail into the coffin of industrial-level slavery. The cost of both these wars was appalling: around 190,000 deaths for the English Civil War, and 750,000 deaths for the US Civil War. Yet these figures pale into insignificance when compared with the two most terrible civil wars in history – both fought in China.

The *An Lushan* Rebellion began on 16 December, 755 CE. That day was when General An Lushan, commander of the northern provinces of the Tang Empire, renounced his old loyalty and declared himself Emperor of the new Yan Dynasty. He then struck south with a huge army, intending to absorb the rest of the Tang Empire. After several brutal battles, the rebel army moved on to capture Chang'an, the imperial capital. The population of the city and surrounding lands, almost two million people, fled in terror while the city was sacked. With no food or shelter, a large number died.

An Lushan, who had been showing increasing signs of homicidal paranoia, was murdered by his own son in January 757. The neonate Yan Dynasty then began to implode. As leaders and would-be leaders of the rebellion killed each other off, the Tang armies slowly drove the Yan armies back. The last Yan Emperor committed suicide to avoid capture in 763, and the Tang Dynasty began the slow job of reconstruction.

There is no official death toll for the An Lushan Rebellion, but it is known to be almost unimaginable. The Tang imperial census for 755 gave the entire population of the empire as 52,919,309 people. In 764 the census recorded 16,900,000 people: a loss of 36,019,309 citizens. As a death toll this figure is almost certainly too high, as not all the missing people were necessarily dead. The Tang Empire still had not regained certain northern provinces at the time, so naturally could not retrieve census data from those areas. And a census taken just after a devastating civil war is not likely to be as accurate as one taken during a time of peace and plenty. Yet even the most conservative estimate of the An Lushan civil war death toll is a staggering thirteen million. That was around 6 per cent of the entire world's population at that time.

So why did so many people die in an eight-year squabble between spoiled and overambitious aristocrats? The reason was that the highly organised Tang Empire communal structure had been shattered by the marauding armies, leaving millions to die of starvation and disease. The very civilisation of the Chinese counted against them, since very few people knew how to survive without the support of a working infrastructure. Uncivilised barbarians could live through terrible adversity, because they grew up knowing that they had to fend for themselves. Civilised people – like you and me – may well die before working out how to survive in the midst of disaster.

During and immediately after the An Lushan Rebellion, destroyed farms and transport networks meant that not enough food was available to the surviving Chinese population. These were faced with a grim choice between death, banditry or cannibalism. The latter expedient was most horribly evident during the brutal siege of Suiyang, in 757 CE. There 'after the horses ran out, the [Tang garrison] turned on the women, the old, and the young . . . the people traded their children to eat, and cooked bodies of the dead . . . 30,000 people in total were eaten . . . by the time that the city fell, only 400 people were left alive.'[1]

The second great Chinese civil war was more recent and almost certainly killed more people. It all began when a middle-aged would-be bureaucrat failed his civil service exams and had a holy vision – or went totally mad, depending on your point of view.

Hong Xiuquan was thirty-seven, in 1836 CE, when he failed the examination that would have ushered him into the ranks of the Chinese intellectual elite. In fact only 5 per cent of candidates ever passed the exam to become *mandarins*, but Xiuquan took his failure to heart. He went to bed with both a fever and an evangelical pamphlet given to him by a Protestant missionary. Hong arose convinced that he was the younger brother of Jesus Christ, sent by God to China to cast out the twin 'devils' of Manchu rulership and the teachings of Confucius.

Xiuquan proved a charismatic speaker, and his odd interpretation of Christian doctrine caught on like wildfire – although it must have horrified the Protestant missionary who had accidentally contributed to Xiuquan's beliefs. The revolt against the Manchu government began in Xiuquan's native Guangxi Province in the south of China and spread steadily, especially among the oppressed peasant class. They named their reform movement the Taiping – a word meaning 'great peace'.

The governing Manchu Dynasty was ancient and corrupt. They had ruled China from Beijing since the mid-fifteenth century, having invaded from their native Manchuria and displaced the rulers of the Ming Dynasty. In the two hundred years of their rulership of China, the Manchu had taken on all the failings typical to a racial overlord aristocracy: they believed themselves infallible when they were in fact incompetent; they saw themselves as mentally and physically superior, while they wallowed in decadence; they hated and feared the native Han Chinese, so they oppressed them to the point of mass rebellion (non-Manchus were forced to wear their hair in a long pigtail, as

---

1 *The Book of Tang* (first published 941 CE)

a sign of their racial inferiority); and they refused to see that any reform that might impinge on their many privileges was either desirable, or even possible.

As a result, by 1851, the Taiping had grown from a kooky religious sect into a powerful military force, and routed the large government army set against them. They then conquered a sizable area of south-east China, including the great city of Nanking.

The resulting Taiping 'Heavenly Kingdom' was a bizarre place; they used a communist sharing of all resources as the basis of their socio-economic system, but they were ruled from palaces by autocratic 'princes' and an increasingly reclusive god-king. Their armies, captained by former shopkeepers or peasants, were highly organised, very disciplined and believed that they were the holy warriors of God. The opposing Manchu armies, on the other hand, were badly led, badly treated and had terrible morale. So the Taiping won battles consistently.

It was failures in politics and diplomacy that proved the downfall of the Taiping. Their anti-Confucian beliefs estranged the Chinese middle-class and their pseudo-Christian communism alienated the European imperial powers: both of whose support they desperately needed to consolidate their victories. In 1861 the Taiping attempted to capture the port city of Shanghai, but they were repulsed by Manchu loyalists who were led by European officers and an American sailor called Frederick Townsend Ward. This 'Ever Victorious Army' then marched out of Shanghai, swelled in numbers, and proceeded to smash the Taiping Heavenly Kingdom.

Hong Xiuquan, the 'younger brother of Jesus', died in his palace in 1864 as his new religion collapsed around him. It is uncertain whether he died of illness, poisoning or suicide.

The Taiping Rebellion cost between twenty and thirty million lives – most deaths caused by famine and disease, because the armies of both sides habitually despoiled the countryside that they passed through. But combat was still a major cause of death: at the Third Battle of Nanking, for example, 100,000 people were killed over three days of fighting. That's as many as in the three *years* of the present Syrian Civil War, and was an average of twenty-three deaths a minute.

The Taiping conflict is now largely forgotten outside China. The American Civil War – which took place at the same time – is much better remembered by historians, the media and by the public. Yet, in fatalities alone, the Taiping Rebellion was the equivalent of up to forty US Civil Wars. It was also equivalent to around twice the total death toll caused by the First World War, or half the entire global death toll caused by the Second World War. It's surprising, the things that can slip the public memory.

Why are civil wars almost always so hellish? The very brutality and hate that seems to epitomise civil conflicts – more so than is typical of even the most embittered of international wars – may be a clue in itself. Civil war, by its very nature, involves a fundamental breakdown of social norms and etiquette. Sharing a language with your enemy just allows you to understand their taunts and insults better. And when your nation is tearing itself apart around you, when members of your own family might be fighting for your mortal enemies, it is harder to remember and maintain the rules of war.

But how can such a reversal of the normal social consensus – on a subject as important as who it is acceptable to vilify, attack and kill – take place within a civilised society? Why do people, who should be bound together by myriad social ties, start to murder one another? To understand, it is necessary to consider just how flexible and unselfconscious the social consensus is . . .

An example. At some point in the not too distant past, a European traveller to faraway and exotic lands returned insisting that he had seen a unicorn. Naturally anyone with any education discounted this tale: unicorns were known to be mythical creatures, as proved by the fact that nobody (reputable) had ever seen one. But then other people started reported seeing unicorns in the same distant regions. A few more people back in Europe may have become convinced of the existence of such fabulous animals, but the educated consensus remained solid: unicorns simply didn't exist.

Then, on 20 May 1515 CE, a Portuguese ship arrived in Lisbon from India carrying a living unicorn. The animal was sent on towards Italy, as a gift for Pope Leo X, but the ship carrying it was wrecked. Fortunately a sketch had been made of the fantastic creature before it was lost at sea. A Dutch engraver called Albrecht Dürer, despite never having seen the animal himself, elaborated on the rough sketch; his print of the Indian unicorn became one of the first international bestsellers. You can see unicorns today in their natural habitat, and also in many zoos and wildlife parks. But we now call them rhinos.

Up to and including 19 May 1515, unicorns were mythical creatures to most educated Europeans. After that date, a creature had undeniably turned up that fitted most of the main attributes ascribed to traditional unicorns – it was horse-sized, had a single horn jutting from its head, had cloven feet, and was untameable, evil-tempered and dangerous. But instead of admitting they were wrong, people simply re-ascribed the new creature as a rhinoceros, and unselfconsciously carried on telling their children stories about mythical unicorns. A total reversal of accepted understanding had gone effectively unnoticed.

Now consider a different consensual flip; but this time over the sanctity of a ruling monarch. In the past four hundred years, England, America, France and Russia all underwent bloody civil wars, fought essentially to decide the rightful powers of their respective monarchs. And – in all but the case of the American Revolution – they travelled in a few short years from believing that a monarch was a wondrous creature, second only to God . . . to brutally killing the inbred bastard. Those countries changed fundamentally during their civil wars, but not so much that they didn't all – again apart from the USA – reinstitute monarchy again within a few years: France and England brought back kings and Soviet Russia made Joseph Stalin an absolute monarch in all but name.

But this flip-flopping of society's accepted ideas rarely carries everyone with it all the way. At every point of change – at every revolution, innovation and modernisation – some people are shocked and disgusted by the new social trend; and they fight it when and where they can. In most cases this is just normal political wrangling, but sometimes it ends in blood.

The seed of all human social consensus is the family. It is in the family that we learn the essentials of right and wrong – as defined by our local society. We naturally feel love and trust towards family members because of a bond of mutual protection. So an apparent betrayal of shared social values by family members, or by our compatriots, cuts us deeper than betrayal by a mere enemy.

This feeling of betrayal lies at the heart of all the cruelty of civil wars. The fact that people that you think should share your beliefs and loyalties clearly don't do so – to the point of trying to kill you – wounds an individual's sense of a just and well-ordered universe. Then the twin human habits of reprisal and conflict escalation can make the situation a downward spiral into violence, chaos and monstrosity. Forgiveness and mutual reconciliation are much harder at the end of a civil war, because both sides feel betrayed.

As the poet William Blake noted sadly:

It is easier to forgive an enemy than to forgive a friend.

Chapter 13

'Smelled like . . . Victory'

There is a popular homily of the US gun lobby – a pressure group who insist that every citizen has a right to own and carry firearms (up to and including semi-automatic rifles that can fire fifty high-velocity bullets a minute). It runs:

Guns don't kill people. People kill people.

It is certainly true that a weapon of any sort is generally harmless until wielded by a person willing to use it. But, of course, someone owning a gun is statistically much more likely to kill than someone denied access to a firearm. So the above argument is actually self-defeating if considered in any depth; and the gun lobby certainly hasn't convinced all Americans . . .

Batman: 'A gun is a coward's weapon. A liar's weapon. We kill too often because we've made it easy. Too easy. Sparing ourselves the mess and the work.'[1]

In the United States private gun ownership is relatively common, with between 39 and 50 per cent of American households owning at least one of an estimated 300 million legal firearms. But figures also indicate that for every one person deliberately shot by a homeowner in an act of self-defence,

---

1 Frank Miller, *The Dark Knight Returns* (1986)

around four people are shot in household gun accidents[2]. Between the beginning of 2001 and the end of 2010, 6,739 people were killed in accidental shooting incidents in the USA.

This compares unfavourably with the United Kingdom, which has very restrictive gun-ownership laws, with only 1.8 million licensed firearms in the hands of the public. In the UK, forty-five people died in accidental shootings over the same decade[3]. The US population is five times greater than that of the UK but, even taking that into account, an American's individual risk of being accidentally shot was almost thirty times higher than a Briton's over that ten-year period.

Of course those figures largely relate to untrained civilians wielding guns. The people most often armed with lethal weapons in the modern world are soldiers: men, and occasionally women, trained to kill on the orders of military or political leaders. Of course a soldier's duties include much else – other than killing, that is – but killing, or the willingness to kill, forms the bedrock of most of their official activities. Fighting, standing guard, training, maintaining weaponry and even peace-keeping duties all boil down to soldiers being willing and able to kill if the situation calls for it. Other servants of the state – like fire-fighters, bureaucrats, or school teachers – are rarely called upon to use the threat of lethal force.

In passing it should be noted that the police are a specialised form of soldier, but they are soldiers nonetheless. When Sir Robert Peel created the first modern police force, in London in 1829, he was conscious that the public feared that a 'domestic army' was being set up as a dictatorial arm of the state. So he made their uniforms blue (instead of British military red) dispensed with all military titles (other than 'sergeant') and he insisted that the police were to be a non-political arm of the judicial system. Few people were fully convinced. The men in blue uniforms still had the right to bear and use arms in the

---

2 A. L Kellermann, 'Injuries and Deaths due to Firearms in the Home' published in the *Journal of Trauma* (1998).

3 Figures from www.gunpolicy.org

pursuance of their duties; many of the first policemen were ex-soldiers with experience of the Napoleonic wars; and the new constabulary were soon put to the forefront of suppressing any anti-government protests. It took decades for the 'bobbies' to be fully accepted in England as law officers, rather than being seen as government thugs.

The non-politicisation of the police has varied widely in different states across the globe, as has the degree to which national police forces are prepared to use lethal force. For example the Nazi *Schutzstaffel* – better known as the SS – was originally set up as a small bodyguard unit for senior party members like Hitler. (*Schutzstaffel* translates as 'protection squad'.) That unit eventually metastasised into a paramilitary police force of almost a million men and women; and then, during the war, transmuted into the *Waffen SS* (translation: 'armed protection squad'). But even when they were acting as a military battle force, the SS maintained their policing duties. For example, during the desperate last battle to defend Berlin, there were SS units who were wholly devoted to catching and executing deserters from the frontlines (and thus, incidentally, avoided the fighting themselves). Over the sixteen years of their existence, the SS killed millions of people, acting largely in their role as a political police force.

All police organisations, no matter how benign, maintain the legal right to kill – to maintain order and to protect the public. As such, the police are essentially soldiers under another name with specialised duties.

This book is about the human habit of unnecessary violence; and it may be said that violence by soldiers, or the police, is generally legal and can therefore be seen as necessary. But that only works from a single point of view: that of the nation or governmental body that orders the violence to be done. For a victim of military violence, be they a civilian or a fighting soldier themselves, that violence is always very, very wrong.

The modern attitude to our military forces is that they are mainly there to deter aggression by other nations; this is why in the UK, the USA and in many other nations, the governmental

Department of War has been renamed the Department of Defence. But if we were all as non-aggressive as we would like to imagine ourselves, then wars would never happen.

Offering intellectual support for a war often becomes a matter of philosophical semantics: a conflict can be rationalised as a 'war of retribution' (as many slavery abolitionists saw the US Civil War), or a 'just war' (as the US Catholic Church called the First World War), a 'great patriotic war' (as the Soviets called the Second World War), a 'holy war' (as with almost *any* religiously inspired conflict), or even a 'police action' (the US military's description of their Vietnam, Afghan and Iraq wars). But all this is cold comfort to someone dying from a bullet wound.

In his novel about the Crimean War, *Flashman at the Charge* (1972), George MacDonald Fraser – himself a former soldier – has the eponymous hero bitterly witness the aftermath of the 1854 Battle of Alma:

> *The Russian wounded lay in piles by the hundred round our bivouacs, crying and moaning all through the night – I can hear their sobbing 'Pajalsta! pajalsta!' still. The camp ground was littered with spent shot and rubbish and broken gear among the pools of congealed blood – my stars, wouldn't I just like to take one of our Ministers, or street-corner orators, or blood-lusting, breakfast-scoffing papas, over such a place as the Alma hills – not to let him see, because he'd just tut-tut and look anguished and have a good pray and not care a damn – but to shoot him in the belly with a soft-nosed bullet and let him die screaming where he belonged. That's all they deserve.*

It needs to be remembered that wars are the recourse that nations and other powers take when legal and diplomatic efforts have failed to get them what they want. France's warmongering Sun King, Louis XIV, had *'Ultima Ratio Regum'* stamped on to his cannons: 'The Conclusive Argument of Kings'. Almost by definition, war is the weapon used when more civilised recourses have failed. And the soldier is the cutting edge of that weapon.

Most soldiers in history were part-timers, who lived as civilians when there was no war. Full-time soldiering is mostly a modern profession. Up until the Enlightenment (and the growth of Europe's global colonial ambitions) wars were too infrequent or short lived, and state economies were too poor, to allow the maintenance of anything more than a token standing army supported, at need, by conscripted local militia units. States like Imperial Rome, that always maintained huge standing armies, were definitely the exception to the rule; and they paid for it with constant financial instability and regular *coups* and civil wars.

The problem with the ancient world, non-professional soldier was that his fighting performance could be unpredictable. The same troops might fight like tigers to protect their homeland from invasion, but might be lacklustre and cowardly if marched far from home to invade the enemy's territory. The reason for this is that unless there is a direct threat to their genetic stock (that is, their children, mate and/or compatriots) humans are generally disinclined to fighting and dying when running away is a potential alternative.

The answer to this problem was training and discipline. Luckily – for those with military ambitions – human beings are terribly open to brainwashing (as discussed in Chapter 9). Basic training – a process of endless exercise drills, marching in formation, weapons training and, above all, fierce discipline – is essential to creating a reliable soldier.

(In August 2014, a study conducted at the University of California asked test subjects to walk 244 metres down a campus path with a companion. Some subjects were randomly told to walk at their own pace; others to march in step with the other person. They were all then shown a mugshot photo of a threatening-looking man. The ones who had marched in step all estimated that the pictured man was smaller, and therefore less threatening, than those who had strolled at their own pace. Dr Daniel Fessler noted: 'Thus, synchrony diminished the perceived relative fighting capacity of the foe.' In other words, square-bashing and marching into battle might make soldiers braver.)

The new military recruit is essentially broken down and psychologically rebuilt during basic training. Physical exhaustion, emotional domination by non-commissioned officers, and the alien environment of a training camp all combine to 'remould' the green soldier. The process aims to overwrite his or her taboos against killing, and also their overpowering reaction against placing themselves in lethal danger. The military replaces these social and instinctual reactions with a set of instilled, semi-utomated responses to orders, plus a powerful taboo against disobeying orders from a superior.

The recruit's previous civilian upbringing is largely wiped away and replaced with a smart military outlook. Those who have passed through this martial brainwashing process – and show themselves suitably dedicated to their new programming – are eventually promoted and may be used to indoctrinate new recruits, creating an ongoing 'military tradition'.

This process is partially why teenagers – even today – are preferred as army recruits, and candidates over twenty-five are often seen as too old. A teenager, fresh from family and school training, is still quite open to yet another set of mental rules being imposed on them. Older recruits will usually have developed a stronger sense of self over the years, and are less happy to have that submerged by military dogma.

Fully trained (and reprogrammed) to perform their military duties, a professional soldier will do so automatically and efficiently under almost all circumstances; including fighting to the death to defend such abstract ideas as regimental honour, national pride or a colourful piece of cloth fluttering from a flagpole.

Military organisation also takes advantage of the 'selfish gene' social instincts mentioned in Chapter 5. Most mammals have some natural inclination to protect blood kin because, on a genetic level, they thus are protecting gene sets similar to their own. But since this inclination is purely instinctual and subconscious, humans think of it as a form of love and family loyalty. We also stretch it to cover friends and compatriots who don't share our family genes. This is because, for most of human history, your only acquaintances would have been those in your tribe or village – and they would almost certainly be blood relations of one sort or another.

Fortunately for civilised life, our nepotistic instincts are lagging well behind our social and urban development: otherwise you couldn't be friends with anyone who wasn't directly related to you. This is the primal reason for human camaraderie – your instincts think that someone who will stick beside you through thick and thin must be a blood relation, and that they are therefore worthy of your protection. The military have always utilised this misdirected genetic impulse to create *esprit de corps* in its units. Men are kept together in squads and put through hells of danger and tedium. They soon come to rely on each other and become what Shakespeare called a 'band of brothers'. A soldier might not love his country; he might hate his commanding officers; he might loathe everything that his flag stands for; but he will often fight to the death to defend the men standing on either side of him in the battle line.

A trained soldier's natural inclinations to avoid unnecessary danger are subsumed by the automatic responses of military discipline – provided that they can be stopped from questioning their orders. This is why one of the supplementary instructions to be heard in all armies across history was: 'Don't think! Just do it!'

Having already noted the preference of most armies to take younger, less psychologically rounded recruits, it is here worth considering one of humankind's more contemptible traditions: the use of child soldiers.

The Brookings Institute (an American political think tank) published a report in 2003, claiming that children were being used as soldiers in around three-quarters of the world's ongoing conflicts. The report's author, Peter W. Singer, estimated that over 300,000 under-eighteen-year-olds were serving as combatants around the globe. But this figure does not include young recruits to many national armies; in the UK, for example, you can join up at sixteen (or even at fifteen if you have a permission note from your parents) but you can't be deployed to a frontline fighting unit until you are eighteen.

The use of kids in war is certainly not a new phenomenon. In the ancient world children often served as auxiliaries to the fighting soldiers – doing menial tasks such as hauling and caring for weapons and armour. But children were generally used only if adult auxiliaries weren't available (or if the grown-ups were all fighting).

Often such work was seen as an apprenticeship to becoming a soldier; for example, like the squires to feudal knights. A squire was often the knight's own son, and was thus in line to inherit the title and the military responsibilities – as well as the horse and armour – when Daddy got killed. More recently, in the Napoleonic wars for example, boys were used as drummers to march the troops into battle. It was hoped that their small size might reduce the risk that they might be shot on the battlefield. But many died anyway.

Nevertheless, the sheer size and strength needed to wield old-world weapons – like swords, spears, bows and muskets – meant that children were rarely recruited to actually fight and kill. One medieval exception was the Children's Crusade of 1212 CE. In that year a hysterical belief swept Europe (most notably France and Germany) that Jesus wanted children to go to Palestine to forcibly convert the Muslims to Christianity. Large numbers of children – possibly up to 30,000 – are thought to have been sent off by their parents towards the east; many presumably dying on the march for lack of provisions, shelter and adult protection. Other crusading children ended up in Genoa where two merchants – remembered as William the Pig and Hugh the Iron – offered to transport them to the Holy Land for free. But instead they shipped them to Muslim Tunisia, in North Africa, and sold them as slaves. The fairy tale of the *Pied Piper of Hamelin* – that ends with the town losing all its children but one – is thought to be based on a folk memory of the Children's Crusade.

The late twentieth century fundamentally changed the role of children in warfare. Modern weapons – like handguns, grenades and sub-machine guns – are usually light enough, and easy enough to operate, to allow even a small child to kill with comparative ease. Naturally children initially find such a prospect terrifying; but the rigours of basic training work at least as well on kids as they do on adults. So any sufficiently ruthless military organisation can utilise children as soldiers.

The most infamous user and abuser of child soldiers (at the time of this writing) is the Ugandan paramilitary rebel group and religious cult, *the Lord's Resistance Army*. In 1987 the LRA was born out of the brutal repression of the northern Ugandan Acholi peoples by the government of President Yoweri Museveni. Initially set up to defend the repressed people of the region, the LRA quickly began themselves to oppress the locals in order to cement their power base.

The LRA leader, Joseph Kony, is said to believe that he is a holy prophet: personally instructed by God to create a theocratic state, to be ruled by the 'principles of the Ten Commandments'. And ruled by Joseph Kony too, of course. To help bring this about the LRA use murder, rape, torture, slavery and the enforced recruitment of child soldiers. In over a quarter of a century of terrorist rule, the LRA have expanded their field of operations out of Uganda and into the neighbouring countries of South Sudan, the Democratic Republic of Congo and the Central African Republic. In that time they are believed to have kidnapped between twenty and thirty thousand children.

The Lord's Resistance Army's atrocities are too numerous to be even estimated: it's believed that, at the height of their activity, the LRA were causing over a thousand deaths a week. The following are three of their better reported actions. In 1995, the LRD forced Ugandan government troops to retreat from the small town of Atiak. The LRA then rounded up the civilian population and handpicked young boys to be soldiers and young girls to be sex slaves. After these had been marched away, the children's families – some two to three hundred people – were murdered. A year later, the LRA kidnapped 139 girls from a school in the town of Aboke – again to be used as sex slaves. On Christmas Day, 2008, the LRA attacked villages in the Democratic Republic of Congo. Over the next three days 620 people were killed – mostly with machetes – and around

180 children were kidnapped. Several survivors had had their lips cut off for daring to criticise the rebels. And at all of the above events, LRA child soldiers – carrying guns and knives – took part in the butchery.

The LRA's military training of children, some as young as seven years old, typically includes the killing of another recruit – child or adult – who has disobeyed orders or tried to escape. This indoctrination is meant to bond them to Kony's cause, and to the other recruits who have also passed the killing initiation. Mutilation is another commonly used form of punishment in the LRA.

The use of those under eighteen in combat is a crime under international law, as is the recruiting of children under the age of fifteen to act as non-combatant auxiliaries. Some progress has been made in shaming national governments out of fielding child soldiers, but many insurgent, revolutionary and terrorist groups – like the LRA – still use children as and when they see fit.

The charity Child Soldiers International reports that between 2010 and 2012, there were children fighting in conflicts in (or for) at least twenty countries worldwide[4]. The countries they listed were Colombia, Myanmar (formerly Burma), the Philippines, Thailand, Yemen, Syria, Afghanistan, Iraq, Israel (where, on several occasions, UN personnel have witnessed the Israeli Defence Forces using Palestinian children as human shields), Libya, the Democratic Republic of Congo, the Central African Republic, Sudan, South Sudan, Chad, Ivory Coast, Eritrea, Somalia, Rwanda and the United Kingdom (the UK sent five seventeen-year-olds to combat areas in Iraq and Afghanistan between 2007 and 2010).

The overall circumstances of these different conflicts may have varied greatly, but in each there remained one basic fact: adults sent children into danger in order to serve their own strategic, political or religious ambitions.

---

4 Child Soldiers International, 'Louder than Words: An Agenda for Action to End State Use of Child Soldiers' (2012)

As we saw in the last chapter, the officer class of soldier was a natural development from the tribal chief shouting instructions to his men during a fight. As fighting forces got bigger, and eventually developed into armies, a hierarchy of officers had to also develop to allow even basic tactical coordination on the battlefield. More often than not these early officers were also the local aristocracy, who commanded the same men during peacetime. This tradition – of officers being appointed because of their birth, rather than their ability – has arguably caused more military disasters than any other factor in warfare.

The problem was that, up until the mid-nineteenth century or later, these men 'born to command' rarely if ever went through the discipline of military training themselves. It was accepted, by their peers and commanders, that their better education and cultural superiority was all that they needed to be officers. This is not to say that military officers were undisciplined – army life and senior officers saw to that – but an officer's quality in battle was generally a matter of his previous experience, his character and his (men's) luck. Official training was rarely, if ever, a factor.

Provided an officer knew how to gain favour at court, had enough money to spend on fine uniforms and behaved impeccably at regimental banquets, he might ignore the fact that he was as fat as a pig, as stupid as an ox and as cowardly as a chicken. His military qualities might only be tested when he was in battle – and then it was generally the lower ranks who paid for his incompetence.

There was a reason for this; other than upper-class complacency, that is. It was recognised that rigid military training undermined an individual's ability to think for themselves. Indeed, as seen above, that was largely the point of the exercise. But an officer *had* to be able to think; and the higher his rank, the more lives hung on his ability to make quick and correct decisions. But it was only with the invention of officer training schools, less than two hundred years ago, that these specialised skills were formally passed on and candidates were actually tested and sometimes rejected for lack of ability.

Most armies in history simply didn't allow common soldiers

– 'men from the ranks' – to become officers, no matter how brilliant their experience and capabilities were. Getting a sergeant's stripes were as high as they were allowed to be promoted. This was generally excused with claims that the other common soldiers would become jealous and rebellious under a 'jumped-up' officer. But the main reason was upper-class snobbery and an unspoken fear that an oik from the ranks might prove himself better than his 'betters'.

This military class division was proved fatuous by the example of arguably the most respected national army in history: the Spartans. Situated in the southern Greek Peloponnese, Sparta was not a great country or even a grand city like their traditional rival, Athens. It was a cooperative of five rural villages with literally no money – the Spartans regarded the use of currency as decadent. But Sparta had a unique social system – aristocratic militaristic communism – and they had a land army that was the terror of their enemies.

The Spartan way of living was invented by the law-giver Lycurgus, some time around 770 BCE. This was as an attempt to reinvent civilisation after the Greek Dark Age that had followed the cataclysmic destruction of the Mycenaean culture (*see Chapter 12*). All of Sparta became a military camp, with luxuries outlawed and all citizens expected to be tough, disciplined and self-denying. The Spartans took to this new way of life wholeheartedly, and maintained it for over four hundred years.

The Spartans had two royal families whose senior men ruled as kings in cooperating partnership, together with a council of elders called the *ephors*. Beneath them came the citizens, called *spartiates*. Male spartiates referred to each other as *homoioi* (peers) because all were seen as social equals, except in military rank. But nobody could become a Spartan except by birth, so their whole society was effectively one big hereditary aristocracy. Then there were the slaves – the *helots* – who were kept in ruthless subjugation. Sparta was one of those slave societies where the helots often outnumbered the free citizens.

At age seven, a Spartan boy was taken from his family and placed in the *agoge*: the Spartan military training regime. From that age he would barely ever see his family, unless some of them happened to be among his teachers. He would only eat in public mess halls and sleep in barracks, both provided by the state. And he would train continuously to be a heavy infantry-man – a *hoplite*.

At the age of twelve a Spartan child would have even those meagre privileges removed: he was given one item of clothing – a red woollen cloak; he was expected to sleep on the streets and in the countryside, wherever he could find shelter; and he was deliberately given a starvation ration to eat. The last was to force him to steal food – a vital military skill when campaigning in enemy territory. But if he was caught stealing he was flogged – usually until blood ran down his back. A fairly high percentage of Spartan youths died in their teens, often under the lash.

By the time he was twenty, if he survived, a spartiate joined a military company and could go back to living and working on his family estate. But he was also expected to be ready to march off to war at any moment. And by the time he graduated from the agoge, a spartiate might well have already killed someone. Every autumn the Spartan leadership declared a short war on their own slaves – a spartiate could kill any malcontent helot he could find during this 'open season' and, indeed, was expected to.

In 425 BCE, for example, the helots were told to pick out among themselves those who they felt were most worthy of freedom. Two thousand were put forward. They were then butchered for their presumption. This Spartan destruction of their own property served a dual purpose: it reduced the chance of helot revolts when the army was away on campaign, and it taught the young men to kill ruthlessly . . . sometimes people that they had known all their lives.

However – elitist, callous and brutal as they may seem to modern eyes – the Spartans were also almost entirely egalitarian in military matters. Only the royal families got any special privileges above those of the common spartiates, and only the kings were given automatic command positions. Everyone else had to earn promotion the hard way – by sweat, blood and abil-ity. So every spartiate officer had started out as a common soldier in the ranks. The value of this system was shown at the Battle of Thermopylae.

In 480 BCE the king of the Persian Empire, Xerxes I, invaded Greece from the north with an enormous army: he wanted revenge for the utter defeat of his father by the Athenians at the Battle of Marathon, ten years before. Accounts of actual Persian numbers vary widely. The Greek historian Herodotus claimed the Persian force numbered 2.6 million fighting men, and as many support auxiliaries. Modern historians point out that it would have been impossible to feed and water over five million people (roughly equivalent to the entire population of modern-day Washington DC), especially on a march through difficult terrain. They suggest a more conservative 70,000 to 150,000 soldiers in the Persian invasion force.

Against them stood one of the two Spartan kings, Leonidas I, commanding three hundred Spartans and around six thousand Greek allies: the odds were at least ten to one. But the Greek force were not hoping to defeat the Persians; they simply needed to delay them long enough to allow the rest of Greece to mobilise their troops. Nevertheless, all of them must have realised that it was a probable suicide mission.

The Greeks chose to fight at the Pass of Thermopylae – the 'hot gates', so called because there was a thermal spring and a health spa located there. But, washing facilities aside, Thermopylae offered a unique battlefield. With a cliff and apparently impassable mountains to the south and a sheer drop into the sea on the north, only a few dozen men could march through the pass abreast. With their advantage in numbers and cavalry thus largely nullified, the lightly armoured Persians had to face a serried battle line of Greek hoplites – men armoured in heavy bronze and thick leather, carrying large round bronze and oak shields called *hoplons*.

The result was a slow massacre. Thousands of Persians moved up the pass in waves, only to be butchered or thrown back at the Greek shield wall. The Greeks were armed with 8-foot spears, and the Persian troops were often killed before they could get within the striking range of their shorter weapons. The Greeks also rotated their frontline men between and often during attack waves, reducing the risk of exhaustion and getting their wounded to doctors behind the lines. At the same time the Persians had to labour up a hill, clambering over mounds of their own dead and dying, and slogging through a thick slurry composed of dust and blood.

Meanwhile, King Xerxes sat on a throne – a safe distance away from and above the battlefield – and spectated as his best troops marched into a meat mincer. During the first day of the battle, the forty-year-old Xerxes was noted to have leapt to his feet in impotent fury no fewer than three times. But that was apparently the full extent of his physical exertions that day.

In striking contrast King Leonidas of the Spartans, who was over sixty years old, took his turns on the frontline, fighting side by side with his men. The Greeks couldn't win at Thermopylae, but their morale held in the face of insane odds. That was at least partly because their officers and leader fought beside them, while the noble-born Persian officers herded their men ahead of them like sheep.

On the morning of the third day of the battle, the Greeks realised that the Persians had found a way through the mountains to the south, and were rapidly outflanking them. Most of the Greek troops withdrew out of the trap; but Leonidas, all the surviving Spartans, and over a thousand Greeks from other city states decided to fight to the end. It took the rest of the day for the surrounding Persians to kill them all; and by that time Persian morale had been badly damaged and the invasion timetable was in tatters. Xerxes was so furious that he had Leonidas's dead body decapitated and crucified. Later, feeling ashamed of this petulant action, Xerxes executed the men who had carried out his order.

The delaying force's sacrifice at Thermopylae worked. The Greek city states allied, rallied and shattered the invading Persian forces; first at a sea battle in the Bay of Salamis, then at a land battle at Plataea. Most of the defeated Persian army died of starvation, exposure and bandit raids on the long march back to home territory. King Xerxes, however, was already safely back in

Persia – he went home in a regal huff after the defeat at Salamis. Indeed, if the king had not taken a large proportion of the invading army back with him as personal protection, the Persians might still have conquered Greece.

The Persian invasion of Greece should have worked. Greece was a tiny and divided country compared with the vast and well-organised Empire of Persia. Good military leadership on the Greek side and bad leadership on the Persian side proved one of the decisive factors in turning the war. This was a point that was further emphasised when the culturally backwards nation of Macedonia – situated between Greece and Persia – defeated both nations just over a century later. King Philip of Macedonia conquered most of the internally warring Greek city states; and his son, Alexander the Great, conquered the entire Persian Empire and led his army as far as India. Both men had a genius for leadership and habitually led their troops from the front.

(It might be noted, however, that the Macedonians never invaded Lacedaemon, the Spartan homeland. King Philip sent them a threat, saying: 'If I conquer Lacedaemon, I will burn Sparta.' The Spartan ephors replied – laconically – with one word: 'If.')

Yet often in the history of war, decisive engagements were not won with the help of good leadership defeating bad leadership: more typically, it was a matter of inept leaders on the winning side being slightly less incompetent than their enemy counterparts. The Second World War Battle of Stalingrad was an example.

The city of Stalingrad (now Volgograd) sat on the west bank of the Volga River in southern Russia. In June 1942, the German/Nazi empire moved to conquer the region – a blow that would have simultaneously crushed much of the Soviet Union's industrial power, given the Germans access to extensive and much-needed oil fields, and effectively cut Russia in two. If they had done it, the Nazi Empire might still be in existence today.

But as with their sneak attack on their Soviet allies the year before, the Germans began the 1942 eastern offensive with massive overconfidence. The German leader, Adolf Hitler, had been convinced that the USSR would collapse long before Christmas 1941 – but he had been wrong. Tens of thousands of Germans on the Eastern Front had suffered crippling frostbite or were frozen to death, mainly because Hitler had said that issuing the troops with winter uniforms and equipment would be a waste of resources. The 1941 campaign, between the cold and the fighting, had cost Germany over a million men – killed or severely injured.

Despite this experience, the Germans kicked off their 1942 eastern offensive far too late in the year. The terrible cold of the Russian winter was less than six months away but Hitler, comfortably far away from the fighting, insisted that his ambitious plans could all be achieved before the first snow fell.

The Nazi Führer – his egomania bloated by Germany's conquest of most of western Europe and North Africa – believed that the German army was utterly invincible under his leadership. Yet, within a year, German soldiers were bitterly joking that Hitler must be a secret agent for the Allies: so disastrous had all his recent decisions been for the German military.

On Hitler's orders, the city of Stalingrad was carpet-bombed into smoking rubble before the German army attacked. Thousands of Russian civilians died unnecessarily in the bombing because the Soviet leader, Joseph Stalin, had refused to allow them to evacuate. Stalin argued that Soviet soldiers would fight all the harder if they could see women and children sheltering on the battlefield.

This cold cruelty was typical of Stalin. Indeed, he was arguably the greatest mass-murderer in history: approximately twenty to thirty million Soviet citizens died unnecessarily during his rule, all thanks to decisions directly attributable to 'Papa Joe'. Stalin was the prime example of what happens if a paranoid sociopath is given absolute power: he felt no compunction against destroying any and all enemies in his power . . . and his paranoia made him see enemies everywhere.

Of course there is no evidence that Stalin ever killed anyone personally: he was essentially a bureaucratic murderer and used totalitarian state institutions as his weapons. In the above twenty to thirty million death toll, modern historians include all those executed in his regular purges of supposed 'enemies of the state', those starved to death in the avoidable famines that his policies knowingly caused, prisoners worked to death in Gulag concentration camps, and those who died of cold and exhaustion when Stalin ordered entire regional populations to march, on foot, to Siberia. But they do not include those people killed in the Great Patriotic War by his brutal, overbearing and ill-thought-out decision-making. After all, a leader can't be blamed for everything.

On the Nazi side, Hitler's ordered saturation bombing of Stalingrad proved to be a major mistake for the Germans – heaps of rubble are much more defendable than intact buildings, and allow for a more effective use of ambush and sniping tactics. Over the late summer and autumn of 1942, Soviet troops made the enemy fight for every square foot of the ruins, knowing that if they could delay the Germans until the onset of winter, the odds would swing dramatically against the invaders. The fighting in Stalingrad often came down to savage hand-to-hand combat in bombed-out buildings, with neither side taking prisoners. Realising with shocked horror that they were losing around twenty thousand men a week, the Germans were forced to call in reinforcements – conscripting large proportions of the armies of their Croatian, Rumanian and Italian allies.

The first snow fell on Stalingrad on 16 November. Few could have guessed it at the time, but it heralded the beginning of the end of the Nazi empire.

But things were going badly for the defending Russians too. Stalin deliberately starved the Stalingrad army of supplies and reinforcements, to tempt the Germans into thinking that victory was near. As a result, Russian casualties – among the military and the sheltering civilians – were appalling. Soviet figures compiled after the war suggest that over 750,000 Red Army soldiers were reported killed, or missing-presumed-dead, during the battle. Trapped on the battlefield by Stalin's orders, between twenty-five thousand and forty thousand Russian civilians were also killed.

Another problem was that most Soviet military officers were

terrified of being seen to make any bad decisions. In 1937 Stalin had convinced himself that there was a huge conspiracy against his rule, forming within the Soviet Red Army. He arrested thirty-five thousand officers, from field marshals down to humble lieutenants. Many were executed, others were sent to the Gulag work camps, and others were simply expelled from the army. Over half of the Red Army's officer corps had been lost, during peacetime, as a result of Stalin's paranoia – and just when another world war was looming on the horizon.

By 1942, the Soviet army had yet to fully recover its numbers, and the new officers were utterly cowed by the threat of the secret police. Scared that any bad decision might lead to execution as a traitor, they were often too frightened to make any risky decisions at all. Such decisions ended up being made over-cautiously; or by slow-moving committees; or by default. And, as usual, the common soldiers paid the price for bad leadership.

The flagging resistance within Stalingrad further convinced a jubilant Hitler that the entire Soviet military was on the verge of collapse. He believed that all the Red Army reserves were gone and their command structure was breaking down. Of course he was wrong; the German 6th Army, that was engaged at Stalingrad, was pushing itself further and further into a trap. While sending minimum support to the troops holding the shattered city, Stalin built up two huge forces to the north and south of Stalingrad, hidden behind the uncaptured eastern bank of the Volga River.

On 19 November, three days after the first snowfall, the Red Army launched Operation Uranus. Sweeping through the 6th Army's flank guards, the two Soviet forces went right past Stalingrad. They then moved towards each other, encircling the entire Axis force and cutting them off from their supplies and the route back to friendly territory.

The Soviets thought that they had cut off about seventy-five thousand enemy soldiers. In fact they had trapped just under a third of a million men: around 265,000 Germans, Romanians, Italians and Croatians, plus some forty thousand Russian 'volunteers'. These last were often slaves; forced to fight for the Germans, but knowing that they had no alternative: on Stalin's orders, all Russian soldiers were to be shot without trial if they were found with the enemy.

General Von Paulus, the 6th Army's commander, asked to be allowed to concentrate his forces to break through the Russian lines and back to safety. Hitler refused permission; partly because he still believed, idiotically, that the USSR was about to collapse, but mainly because he couldn't stand the idea that 'his army' might ever be forced into a retreat.

Some in the 6th Army dubbed their city-wide prison the '*Kessel*', meaning 'the cauldron'. Others simply called it 'the mass grave'. The German air force attempted to fly in supplies, but could only deliver a fraction of the needed ammunition, food and medicine. The troops, who had once triumphantly captured Paris, now found themselves in a frozen Hell, starving and under continuous sniper fire and artillery barrages.

By mid-January 1943, Von Paulus was sure that the 6th Army could not hold out much longer. The under-strength relief force, sent by Hitler to break them out, had been thrown back by the westward advancing Soviet forces. Von Paulus again asked for permission to surrender, but Hitler again refused. He insisted – from the comfort of Berlin – that the men of the 6th Army would die gloriously, 'fighting to the last bullet', rather than surrender ignominiously. On 30 January Von Paulus surrendered anyway.

The loss of such a huge military force nearly gutted the German war machine. Combining the Axis losses for the entire battle, historians estimate that Stalingrad cost between 500,000 and 850,000 men killed or captured. And of those taken prisoner by the Soviets, very few survived to see release at the end of the war. Most died of starvation and disease in Soviet prison camps.

The Nazi empire fought doggedly on until May 1945, but their failure to break the Soviet Union in both 1941 and 1942 – when the odds were still heavily on Germany's side – meant that their *Götterdämmerung* was increasingly inevitable.

And the foremost man responsible for the defeat of Germany was Adolf Hitler himself. Reviewing his military decisions from 1941 onwards, it is hard not to agree with his embittered soldiers: Hitler might as well have been acting as an agent for the Allies, considering all the unintentional damage he did to his country's war effort. Egotistical to the point of mania – and thus unwilling to listen to expert opinions, or to a word of criticism – Hitler did more than anyone else to destroy his beloved Nazism.

Chapter 14

'What Makes the Grass Grow?'

A mass execution took place in Vietnam on 16 March 1968. At 7.30 a.m. US Army troops of Company C of the 1st Battalion, 20th Infantry Regiment, 1st Brigade of the 23rd Infantry Division, landed by helicopter in a network of hamlets and villages in the Quang Ngai province of South Vietnam. One of those villages was called My Lai, and later its name was given to the entire massacre.

The American soldiers' mission was to eradicate enemy – North Vietnamese – activity that had been rife in the area. After taking a number of casualties over recent weeks, thanks to booby-traps and ambushes, the US grunts had taken to calling the area 'Pinkville' – suggesting that they believed that most of the inhabitants were working with the communist 'reds'.

It was a market day when the GIs arrived. ('GI' is a slang acronym for US troops, said to be short for 'galvanised iron,' 'general infantryman' or simply 'government issue'.) Most of the villagers were peaceably getting their goods ready for market when the men of 'Charlie' Company began rounding them up. There was no resistance and very few men of fighting age were found. Nevertheless the Americans almost immediately began to kill people. Victims were shot, bayoneted, pushed down wells, burned in their huts, and killed in groups with grenades. Some men, suspected of being pro-communists, were tortured before being summarily executed. The GIs also gang-raped many women before killing them.

At 11 a.m. Captain Ernest Medina – coordinating Charlie

Company on the ground – radioed that the soldiers should cease fire. But, after pausing to eat their lunch, Charlie Company continued killing unarmed civilians and raping women well into the afternoon, presumably with Medina's approval. All this took place in front of US Army journalists, who took photographs of the less gory scenes. The Pentagon later used those photographs to illustrate the total success of their Quang Ngai 'counter-terrorist' operation.

The Vietnamese government now believes that 504 people were murdered in and around the villages in Quang Ngai Province on 16 March 1968. The US Army claims that its troops caused a mere 347 civilian deaths.

The following statement was given in evidence to a subsequent public inquiry by one of the US soldiers present: 'They were shooting women and children just like anybody else. We met no resistance and I only saw three captured weapons. We had no casualties. It was just like any other Vietnamese village – old Papa-Sans, women and kids. As a matter of fact, I don't remember seeing one military-age male in the entire place, dead or alive.'

Another soldier testified: 'He fired at [a baby] with a .45 [pistol]. He missed. We all laughed. He got up three or four feet closer and missed again. We laughed. Then he got up right on top and plugged him.'

Captain Medina had reportedly told his troops that: 'They're *all* VC [Viet Cong insurgents]. Now go and get them!' So shooting babies might have been seen by his men as being officially sanctioned.

The Vietnamese government now insists that My Lai was only one of many other civilian massacres, committed by US troops and their South Korean allies, during the twelve years of the American police action in Vietnam – although My Lai was certainly one of the most blatant and savage. Only one American soldier made an official complaint over the massacre – helicopter pilot Hugh Thompson Junior. His statement automatically caused an investigation, and the cancellation of similar counter-terrorist operations which had been planned to take place in the same region over the next few days. So Thompson's outspoken feeling of outrage possibly saved hundreds of lives.

After a lengthy inquiry, conducted by the US military, the My Lai Massacre was finally blamed on a single man: 2nd Lieutenant William Calley Junior. There is certainly no doubt that Calley murdered many civilians that day. He openly admitted to shooting infants in their mothers' arms because he 'was afraid the babies might be carrying concealed grenades'. He was eventually given a life sentence – of which he served only three and a half years – for most of which he was under house arrest, not in prison.

But Calley was also the lowest-ranking officer present at the massacre, and certainly can have had little or no role in planning, coordinating or commanding the attack. Captain Ernest Medina – who had certainly coordinated the fighting on the ground (and who was reported by pilot Hugh Thompson to have shot at least one unarmed civilian) – was fully exonerated by a military court martial that lasted only an hour. Lieutenant Colonel Frank Baker, in overall command of the operation, was never even tried. US President Lyndon B. Johnson had no direct involvement in the massacre, so was never called to give evidence to the inquiry; but his hard-line policy over fighting communism in Vietnam certainly contributed to US military being willing to conduct such an operation. Finally, the non-commissioned soldiers of Charlie Company – who committed most of the actual murders, torture and rapes – were not tried either. They were just doing their duty and obeying orders.

The men of Charlie Company were not war-maddened battle veterans. They had been 'in-country' – on combat tour – for only three months; for most of which time they had seen no fighting. Many of them, like most American civilians called up to fight in the Vietnam War, were either in their early twenties or were teenagers not long out of high school. Yet they committed atrocities that would have sickened a hyena. It is doubtful that they were given specific orders to do this; they just followed the example of their officers, or they did it of their own volition when they realised that no officer would stop them.

Much as we might like to think that young men, especially unwilling draftees, might only commit war crimes when forced to do so by heartless officers – and by distant political leaders in overall command – the evidence does not generally support this. A young man given a gun, and unarmed people to lord it over, is subject to temptations that he will never feel in civilian life. In fact, history seems to show that soldiers most often commit atrocities when the military command structure is weak or non-existent.

Horse troopers have been particularly linked, down through time, with brutality and cruelty. For example, the French Napoleonic cavalry, called Lancers, committed numerous massacres during their occupations of Spain and Portugal between 1807–14. The Peninsular War was particularly embittered, especially between the French and the Spanish. This was because France and Spain had formerly been allies against Portugal and Britain; until the Emperor Napoleon betrayed Spain, occupied the whole country and put his brother on the Spanish throne.

The incompetently led Spanish armies collapsed in the face of the French invasion, but common Spaniards took to the hills and fought a brutal *guerrilla*. (Translation: 'little war'. It was from this conflict that the term 'guerrilla warfare' originated.) The French lost numbers of men to hit-and-run raids by the guerrillas – who specialised in torturing captured soldiers to death, then leaving the mutilated bodies to be found. So the invaders reacted with equal savagery: in an attempt to stamp out the insurgency, they targeted the families of any men who were missing from their villages, and therefore suspected of being away with the guerrillas. Rape, torture and the murder of women and children became almost commonplace military exercises. Mounted troops were most often used for these operations, because they could get away after an atrocity with greater ease. And such horse soldiers usually operated in small units, often without the oversight of a senior officer, so they felt freer to indulge in lavish acts of revenge. The French were eventually driven out of Spain by the British, the Portuguese, the reconstituted Spanish armies, and the Spanish guerrillas – but they left behind a devastated land.

Ease of movement is an important, if often ignored, element in the history of military atrocities. The French Lancers in Spain. The US 7th Cavalry: who committed indiscriminate slaughters against Native Americans at Washita River in 1867 and Wounded Knee in 1890 – and would undoubtedly have done so at the Little Bighorn River, in 1876, if their attack force hadn't themselves been annihilated. The truck and tank mounted units of the German Waffen SS: who committed innumerable atrocities across Nazi-occupied Europe between 1939 and 1945. And the helicopter-transported troops of Charlie Company at My Lai. All had the freedom to get the hell out after they had finished.

Foot soldiers couldn't get away so easily. They can march at most twelve or fifteen miles a day – provided they don't spend too much time killing. So pedestrian grunts have to live, and sleep, near to the consequences of their actions; and they are thus less likely to run wild.

Antony Beevor, in his history *Berlin: the Downfall 1945* (2007) estimated that there were 1.4 million rapes of German women by conquering Soviet troops in eastern Germany in late 1944 and early 1945. He also noted that the frontline Red Army troops (the *frontoviki*) were reported to be less involved in the rapes than the rear-echelon, support troops. Frontoviki were generally travelling on foot and were often too involved in combat to pause to attack terrified women. The auxiliaries arrived after the fighting had passed on – usually in trucks – and indulged in an orgy of pillage and gang-rape.

It is also interesting to note that, whenever the fighting allowed, the frontoviki were often reported to have been decent and even kind to enemy civilians. The Soviet support troops, on the other hand, arrived feeling that they had a duty of revenge. In their eyes – and presumably in the eyes of their commanding officers, who disciplined very few soldiers for attacking civilians – Nazi war crimes in the Soviet Union fully justified any and all assaults on helpless German women and girls. Indeed, some of the rapists seem to have regarded the taking of unwilling women as a privilege of war, with no revenge motivation being necessary. How else can you explain the reports, noted by Beevor, of freed

Soviet girls – formerly enslaved by the Nazis – being raped by Red Army troops, along with the German women who had held them captive?

It seems likely that both expectation and social pressure were deciding factors in whether a Red Army soldier gave a German woman food and help, or called his comrades over to help rape her. Frontoviki rarely had the opportunity to behave like beasts, so they developed an *esprit de corps* that maintained the normal civilised taboo against attacking helpless women. Support troops, conversely, had all the time in the world to ravish and pillage, so developed a unit *esprit de corps* that all but demanded that they behave like monsters.

After the war was over, those same monsters returned home and behaved like decent brothers, husbands and fathers, because peace had reacclimatised them to a civilised norm of behaviour. Even meeting a helpless German woman would not have renewed their old habits, because the predatory social climate that originally allowed them to become conscienceless rapists had been expunged with the war.

Unfortunately the same cannot be said for the victims of that barbaric time and place – Beevor reports that East German society suffered long-term trauma as a direct result of the wartime mass rapes. The women were of course emotionally damaged, but so were many German men. These had failed to protect their women – as many saw it – and suffered the after-effects of both guilt and denial. And the children born after the war to rape victims often suffered bullying and ostracisation, if there was any suspicion that they were a result of 'their mother's shame'.

It's a commonly quoted 'fact' that in the two hundred years leading up to the twentieth century, 90 per cent of war casualties were military men, and only 10 per cent were civilians; from the First World War, it is said, those percentages reversed. In fact, for once, the truth is rather less grim.

The fatal casualty figures for the First World War (1914–18) were, at most, 40 per cent civilian to 60 per cent military. The high civilian body count in that conflict was mainly due to the side-effects of warfare: in this case illness and starvation through famine, plus a proportion of the deaths caused by the 1918 Spanish Influenza pandemic. (While it is true that the flu pandemic was certainly made worse by armies of soldiers passing it around the globe, the historically regular fluctuation of lethal influenza outbreaks means that the Spanish flu would almost certainly have happened anyway.) Despite hysterical propaganda by both sides, civilians were rarely shot or otherwise killed directly by the conflict.

The civilian death toll for the Second World War (1939–45) was rather worse: at between 60 per cent and 67 per cent of the total number of deaths. This was mainly because both sides soon came to regard civilian populations as 'targets of opportunity' – that is, civilians were not officially targeted (very often) but both sides believed that killing enemy non-combatants damaged the other side's morale and war-making capability. In fact this was only partly correct. Attacking civilian areas – especially by ground artillery or aerial bombing – indeed caused disarray in war industries; but not significantly, or for any length of time. And it certainly didn't weaken morale to any significant degree. In fact, thanks to the twin human motivations of the need for revenge, and the resulting escalation of violence, both sides may have come to realise that they had ultimately lost much more than they gained by killing so many non-combatants. But by then it was too late.

Neither was the lesson well-learned. In the Korean War (1950–53) the civilian death rate was the same as for the higher estimate for Second World War – 67 per cent. That's two civilians for every one military death. Some estimates place the loss of North Korean civilians at 20 per cent of the entire population. In the First and Second Indochina Wars – generally lumped together in the public mind as 'the Vietnam War' – (1946–75) the civilian death toll – for the Vietnamese alone – was again at around 67 per cent.

This latter fact is striking, as it shows that it was not the brutality of particular nations that caused the high civilian casualty rate. The Vietnam War involved a rainbow of combatant countries – North and South Vietnam, France, the United States,

Korea, Australia, New Zealand, Laos and Cambodia – and all, to a greater or lesser degree, targeted civilian areas in the combat zones. Most of the Vietnamese civilian deaths, however, were caused by artillery and the aerial bombing of villages and cities, and were thus classed as 'collateral damage'.

In more recent times the figures are more controversial – as they related to ongoing political situations. The First Chechen War (1994–96), in which Russia tried to suppress an independence movement, killed 17,391 rebel fighters; the Russian Army lost 5,732 men[1]. That's 23,123 military deaths in total. At the same time and in the same region, between 50,000 and 100,000 civilians were killed or went permanently missing. That means that between 54 per cent and 77 per cent of the butcher's bill were civilians.

The American and British invasion of Iraq, in 2003, officially caused a mere 33 per cent civilian death toll. But if the deaths caused by the subsequent decade of chaos in Iraq, between 2003–13, are also taken into account, the figure soars to 77 per cent being civilian deaths.

So are *all* soldiers potential monsters? In this book we have perhaps considered more than enough evidence to lead a neutral judge to conclude so. Ordinary people, put into uniform, can be pressured into behaving in a way that they themselves believe to be cruel, savage or just plain wrong. They can also commit atrocities of their own volition, simply because 'everyone else was doing it' or because 'nobody ordered me not to'.

Such ethical crimes can be found at every level of military life; from the common soldier or policeman who uses weapons on unarmed civilians, to the leaders who callously give orders that they know will unnecessarily destroy lives. And in a modern state even the ordinary, unarmed citizens can be implicated because, without the tacit (or vocal) support of a majority of the public, such military crimes would be rare or unknown.

A ray of hope, against this bleak conclusion, was offered just after the Second World War by the American military historian,

---

1 Figures from an official Russian government report in 2001

Colonel S. L. A. ('Slam') Marshall. He and his small team interviewed US soldiers on the battlefield, just after battles had taken
place. His conclusion, published in 1947 in the book *Men Against
Fire: The Problem of Battle Command*, shook the military establishment – particularly in the USA, but also around the world.

Marshall believed that, taken down to its most simple level of
tactical analysis, combats are won by the side that can concentrate the greatest degree of gunfire on the enemy. And the
effectiveness of that firing is defined by how well the soldiers
were trained. He said that commanders needed to ask what
proportion of their troops were accurate shots. And did they
fire in a coordinated and controlled fashion? And did soldiers
take every opportunity to fire, even if they did so at the risk of
being shot at themselves?

To illustrate the point, Marshall and his team simply asked a
cross-section of US combat soldiers if they had fired a weapon
while in any recent battle. He was amazed to discover that an
average of 75 per cent said that they either hadn't fired persist-
ently, or that they hadn't let off a single shot – even when their
own lives depended on fighting back. He also noted that of
those who did fight with full commitment, only about 5 per
cent did so constantly in every battle. The men who didn't fire
were not cowards – they had marched into battle bravely and
were willing to return to combat – but they had found it hard
or impossible to actually attack, even when perfect enemy
targets presented themselves.

'SLAM' Marshall was no pacifist. The main aim of his study
was to make the US Army more efficient in killing enemy
soldiers. Yet he concluded that US GIs were so thoroughly
socially conditioned against killing that a majority literally
couldn't fight, even in self-defence. Their military basic training
had failed, in all but 25 per cent of cases, to break their taboo
against killing. If Marshall was right – that the side that fires the
most bullets is the side most likely to win skirmishes, battles and
wars – then it could be argued that the main reason the Americans
won their Second World War battles was that they ultimately had
a much greater pool of troops to call upon. The failure of up to

75 per cent of GIs to fight, was made up for by the sheer numbers of the remaining 25 per cent.

The results of the study were not deliberately fallacious, nor was it flippantly conducted: Marshall and his team interviewed hundreds of US soldiers in both the European and Pacific theatres of war, and were evidently convinced by their candour. These men were not proud of their involuntary pacifism, and nor were they misleading the researchers for the fun of it. The soldiers' self-perceived reasons for their unwillingness to fight varied widely: from panic; low morale; post-traumatic stress disorder ('shell shock', as it was then known); suddenly strengthened religious or humane conviction; or simply not being sure what had been happening in the battle and wanting to avoid firing on friends. But beyond these reasonable and rational explanations, Marshall believed, was the subconscious influence of their American cultural upbringing:

> [The American ground soldier] is what his home, his religion, his schooling, and the moral code and ideals of his society have made him. The Army cannot unmake him. It must reckon with the fact that he comes from a civilization in which aggression, connected with the taking of life, is prohibited and unacceptable. The teaching and the ideals of that civilization are against killing, against taking advantage. The fear of aggression has been expressed to him so strongly and absorbed by him so deeply and pervadingly – practically with his mother's milk – that it is part of the normal man's emotional makeup. This is a great handicap when he enters combat . . . A revealing light is thrown on this subject through the studies by Medical Corps psychiatrists of the combat fatigue cases in the European Theatre. They found that fear of killing, rather than fear of being killed, was the most common cause of battle failure in the individual, and that fear of failure ran a strong second.[2]

---

2 S. L. A. Marshall, *Men Against Fire* (Chapter 6, page 78) (1947)

Following the Second World War, and for over twenty years afterwards, *Men Against Fire* was highly influential and was required reading at most military command schools. Yet today S. L. A. Marshall's work is widely believed to be discredited. It has been pointed out that his research style was journalistic, not scientific: that, in battlefield circumstances, he could do little or no corroborative work to support his conclusions. Indeed, when he himself conducted a similar study during the Vietnam War in 1967, he found that close to 100 per cent of the combat GIs that he interviewed said that they had fired their weapons, aiming to kill, with little or no compunction.

But was S. L. A. Marshall's Second World War study totally worthless? Or worse: misleading? Half a century of studies – conducted by a discomfited military establishment – have since shown that most soldiers, and especially non-conscripted 'regular army' soldiers, generally overcome any psychological block against killing once they have been socially reprogrammed by basic training. In fact most modern studies seem to show that only around 20 per cent of soldiers ever 'freeze up' or otherwise refuse to fight.

Yet, reading *Men Against Fire,* it is hard not to be quickly convinced that Marshall himself was quite certain of his research, despite being personally horrified by its military implications. Is it possible that he was right in his 1944–45 study; but was also correct in his 1967 Vietnam study, that found an almost casual willingness to kill among US soldiers?

If it is true that it was the social taboos of Second World War GIs that held them back from killing, then maybe it is the social taboos that have changed in subsequent years, decreasing the American need to avoid killing. Certainly many of the GIs who fought in the Second World War were likely to have suffered a moral conflict over their military role.

After the First World War, the USA had suffered a strong national revulsion, caused by the horrific reports of slaughter in the trenches. Many Americans had come to feel that it had been a mistake to become involved in a European war – a feeling that was widely renewed in the populist *America First* movement,

when Britain declared war on Germany in 1939, and began calling for American military aid and troop support. The overall
result was a swing away from militarism in the American national
culture between the wars. Under political and economic pressure, the American Army shrank to a virtual skeleton force;
which was partially why the Japanese felt confident enough to
attack Pearl Harbor in December 1941.

Between the wars there was also a strong American Christian
revivalist movement – especially in the Midwest and southern
states: those areas that were eventually to provide a hefty proportion of the US troops who were conscripted to fight in the Second
World War. For many 1930s farm boys and provincial townsmen,
the Bible was about the only form of easily obtained entertainment; and its main message – at least in the New Testament –
was brotherly love and 'thou shalt not kill'.

At the same time US popular culture – in the form of movies,
newspapers and books – was also swinging away from any glorification of violence. The main source of regular trouble on the
streets of America, at that time, was the turf wars of the
Prohibition crime mobs. Such gangsters were universally vilified
as worthless hoodlums; but so too, sometimes, were the lawmen
who fought against them. It is now largely forgotten that the
fledgling FBI was heavily criticised for its violent methods.
About the only thing that could popularise ruthless killers like
Bonnie and Clyde, and menacing bank robbers like John
Dillinger, was the fact that the authorities gunned them down.

So it is likely that the average twenty-something conscripted
US soldier in the Second World War had a strong social and
ethical taboo against killing, indoctrinated – in one form or
another – since childhood. Marshall himself noted that the Axis
powers didn't seem to have this problem with their soldiers.
Germany, Italy and Japan had been fostering martial ardour in
their popular and political cultures for at least a decade before
the war. Many of their young men had been brought up to
believe that killing the enemies of their nation was their highest
possible goal in life.

But what of the American baby boomers – children born

immediately after the war – who seemed happy to kill in Vietnam and in subsequent conflicts? What happened to their taboo against homicide?

The aftermath of the Second World War was not the same for Americans as the aftermath of the First World War. The revelation of Axis war atrocities convinced almost everyone that smashing such a despicable enemy had been a worthy cause, or even a sacred endeavour. The Hollywood propaganda machine, that had produced jingoist movies by the dozen throughout the war, continued after the fighting was over – lionising the GIs who had fought in the conflict and achieving reliably good box office returns as a result.

The production of affordable television sets soon brought these movies into people's homes, along with many TV programmes that also had a selectively glorifying attitude to violence. For example Professor Leo Strauss, the forefather of the modern American Neoconservative movement, was reported by his students in the 1950s to be fascinated by the TV cowboy series *Gunsmoke*. In this show Matt Dillon, a fictional Dodge City Marshal in a white Stetson hat, gunned down black-Stetson-wearing bad guys each week. Strauss was particularly impressed by the mythic elements to the programme: the good guy was easily identifiable and sympathetic to the audience; the bad guys were all very villainous and their defeat naturally delighted the viewers.

Strauss argued to his students (some of whom eventually went on to become senior government officials and policy pundits) that contemporary American society needed such uncomplicated myths – even if those myths reduced their subject to almost idiotic oversimplification. The threat of the Soviet Union, Red China and the Cold War put the United States' very existence at risk. Yet many Americans still sympathised with their former anti-Axis allies, and regarded communism with similar sympathy. The American public, Strauss argued, needed to be presented with a simple 'us or them' depiction of Cold War politics. The communists were the 'black hats', and America and her allies were the 'white hats'. And the destruction of black hats by white hats was always a just and noble endeavour: *QED*.

In this opinion, Leo Strauss was largely echoing the American political zeitgeist of the time. McCarthyism – which flourished in America between 1950–56 – made anti-communist paranoia and right-wing bullying highly fashionable. This socio-political witch-hunt was undoubtedly fanned by the bloody and inconclusive war that America had helped the United Nations fight in Korea. Between June 1950 and July 1953, US GIs fought beside British Tommys and capitalist South Koreans, against communist North Koreans and their Red Chinese allies. The war cost approximately three million lives, civilian and military. And the cultural and racial difference of the troops on either side underlined their political differences; both sides undoubtedly felt that their enemies were the 'black hats'.

S. L. A. Marshall was also there in Korea, again interviewing soldiers just after battle. He found that just over 50 per cent now said that they had fired to kill without significant qualms. This – for the US Army – was a considerable improvement on the 25 per cent reported in the Second World War. But it still meant that at least 45 per cent of US GIs were potentially ineffective soldiers in combat.

If we accept Marshall's three studies of US combat soldiers (Second World War, Korea, and Vietnam) at face value, then add the result of subsequent studies, we can draw a lopsided bell curve graph. Beginning in 1944 with around 25 per cent of infantrymen fighting consistently well; passing through the 1950s Korean War with a rise to 55 per cent being effective; peaking in 1967 Vietnam with more than 95 per cent claiming to have no qualms against shooting to kill; then dropping to about 80 per cent of present day US soldiers avoiding 'freeze-up' in combat.

And what can this ugly graph tell us, other than that American great-grandfathers were less prone to causing massacres than American grandfathers, fathers, or the present generation? It tells us what we could already have guessed – that social trends in violence can go up as well as down. That a happy period of peace is no guarantee of its continuation.

S. L. A. Marshall's statistics, and the research methods he used when compiling the data for *Men Against Fire,* may now be seen as discredited; but it would be a mistake to completely throw out his conclusions. It is certainly hard to believe that as many as 75 per cent of US GIs were ineffective during combat in the Second World War. But Marshall and his team did seem to be accurately detecting a culturally instilled taboo against killing that was genuine, and can be traced to the upbringing of many American boys during the 1920s and 1930s. The very fact that Marshall himself clearly didn't want to believe that this was possible, but surrendered in the face of what he believed to be overwhelming evidence, tends to add verification to that conclusion.

It is certainly true that the armies of different cultures have strikingly different attitudes to their combat roles. Some armies are aggressive and nationalistic, and sometimes force their civilian rulers to start unnecessary wars to satisfy their martial urges. Other armies crave internal power, take over the government of their nation in a *coup d'etat*, and set up a military dictatorship. Most armies, in the modern world, see themselves as peacekeepers and defenders of the defenceless: but some, in following this noble calling, find themselves slipping into atrocity – like the fresh-faced young troops of Charlie Company at Mai Lai.

Chapter 15

'The Madness of Crowds'

Can something as vague as 'popular culture' be credited with sea changes within a nation's outlook over a comparatively short time? Say a generation or two, as seemed to happen with the US soldiers in S. L. A Marshall's studies of combat efficiency. Certainly the believers in tighter media censorship might believe it. Their argument is that increased access to material like pornography, gory movies, risqué television and violent video games degrades the mental and moral integrity of audiences, ultimately leading to more sex assaults and to other violent crime. And certainly, up until the mid-1990s, the evidence seemed all on the side of those who wanted to restrict or ban such entertainment.

Beginning in the mid-1960s – around the same time that the hippy and anti-authoritarian movements were gaining huge support in the younger generation in western countries – the violence rate in the USA began to rise sharply. For example, there was an average of 5.1 murders per 100,000 US citizens in 1960. This had risen to 7.9 killings by 1970. The rape statistics followed a similar pattern: 9.6 rapes per 100,000 US citizens in 1960, almost doubling to 18.7 by 1970.

Over the next third of a century the US violent crime rate continued to drift upwards. It peaked in 1980 at 10.2 killings per 100,000 – exactly twice the homicide rate of twenty years before. The US rape statistics for 1980 reached 36.8 per 100,000 people – almost four times higher than in 1960. Over that same period, cheaper printing methods, home video technology and the advent of home computers (and basic computer games) made access to pornographic and violent material easier and more widespread than it ever had been before: clear proof, for some, that smut and brutality were closely linked, and lack of proper censorship was undermining civilisation.

Yet, since the mid-1990s, the American violence rate has fallen considerably, with the rest of the planet by and large mirroring the fall. In 2014 the US was back to around the same murder rate as in 1960. The American rape statistics have fallen less quickly – to just over double those of 1960. But there too the trend is an almost continuous fall since 1993, with the higher recorded rate of rape attacks possibly due to the fact that rape is now more often reported than it was in the early 1960s.

This fall in violence happened just after the communication revolution that came with the creation and spread of the internet: an anarchistic medium that is largely self-regulating and successfully defies almost all governmental attempts at control or censorship. Today – largely due to the internet – hardcore pornography is more widespread than ever before. At the same time movies often depict extreme violence; television screens more audacious content than ever before; and many computer games allow people to play out acts of brutal savagery. So why hasn't civilisation collapsed?

The answer – from psychologists working with the sort of brutal criminals that the pro-censorship lobby believed would be epidemic by now – is that such materials rarely, if ever, inspire antisocial acts. It *is* true that many serial killers, serial rapists and other habitually violent people addictively view pornography and sadomasochistic entertainment. But the research of those trying to rehabilitate such violent criminals – and often the opinion of those criminals themselves – indicates that porn and violent entertainment does little more than support antisocial attitudes and habits that are already well established.

Certainly cutting violent people off from such amusements – usually in prison or in mental institutions – does little or nothing to resocialise them; which surely would be the case if media filth was a key factor in motivating their antisocial acts. Smut is unlikely to do them much psychological good; but it wasn't what made them into monsters, nor did it directly inspire their acts of monstrosity. Watching slasher movies never made anyone into a serial killer, and masturbating over porn doesn't turn people into rapists. It's not the same as, say, food advertising causing you to eat between meals. The inducements and causes of violent crime are too complex to yield to such straightforward pressures.

We will look more closely at what might induce or inhibit individuals from committing acts of violence in the final chapters of this book. Here we are considering what can make entire cultures, civilian or military, swing from having a taboo against bloodshed to embracing combat and aggression as a noble calling. Or vice versa.

And once again we touch on the key question of this book: are humans – as a species – naturally cruel and brutal, or are we instinctually humane? Is murder normal, or an aberration? Acceptance of either answer raises questions. If we are natural killers, like tigers or wolves, then why do most of us – and indeed, most people throughout history – never kill other humans? If we are naturally humane, then why is so much of our shared history a catalogue of bloodshed?

This question echoes back to the debate over the 'chimp' and 'bonobo' theories of early human development (see Chapter 5). Chimp theory holds that prehistoric humans were naturally prone to committing violence; that they were essentially Raymond Dart's 'killer apes'. While bonobo theory says that human violent tendencies were forced on them through the stress of living in an unnatural environment – essentially from becoming civilised. We are asking if human unnecessary violence is a matter of nurture or nature: is it a learned response to a stressful and difficult world, or are some people just *born* more likely to be monsters?

The issue is complicated by the fact that humans – civilised or not – are such social creatures. And, as we saw in Chapter 9, we are terribly prone to psychological peer pressure, and even to brain washing by the cultural forces that surround us. Much as we treasure our sense of individuality and free will, part of us is always under the control of the social groups to which we give our allegiance. And if those cultural forces lose their sense of proportion, then we can be dragged along without being fully or even partially aware that our behaviour is becoming radicalised.

Consider the German people in the early 1930s. Many were socialists or even communists. Charitable Christianity was a key factor in almost all German communities, and many Germans – after the horrific experiences in the trenches in the First World War – were inclined towards pacifism. And yet, ten years later, effectively the entire nation was supporting a fascist government in a total war of ruthless conquest and genocidal 'race purification'. Seen from the point of view of both before and after the Nazi period, the German people went collectively insane.

A similar martial psychosis overtook the Japanese nation at the same time. The 1983 movie *Merry Christmas Mr Lawrence* (based on the semi-autobiographical prison camp novel, *The Seed and the Sower*, by Laurens van der Post) laconically summed up the Japanese cultural decay towards ruthless empire-building:

> Colonel Lawrence: *'They're a nation of anxious people, and they could do nothing individually. So they went mad, en masse.'*

But the truth is that the Japanese and Germans were, and are, no more prone to national insanity than everyone else. Given the right circumstances, any nation, culture or clique can condone inhumane behaviour, and can even regard it as the height of civilisation. We've already mentioned McCarthyism: the all-American witch-hunt that polarised the country in the 1950s. McCarthyism saw thousands of people – sometimes only on the suspicion that they harboured left-wing sympathies – blacklisted from working and debarred from taking any part in public life.

And then what of the actual witch-hunts that ran for at least three centuries across Europe? Most historians date the Christian witch craze as beginning in the late fifteenth century CE, because a book – *Malleus Maleficarum* ('The Hammer of the Witches') – was published in 1486 by two Dominican monks. This book became a medieval bestseller and helped whip up a storm of paranoia about Satanic witchcraft. (Saint Augustine, writing in the fifth century CE, had ruled that witches were in fact not fully human, but were the offspring of humans and demons.)

Malleus Maleficarum's essential argument was that witches were everywhere and caused all sorts of misfortune, from bad weather to male impotency. The monastic authors clearly felt that the threat of witches was so dire that just an accusation of witchcraft should be seen as tantamount to being conclusive proof of guilt. If any further proof were needed, then a liberal use of torture would surely produce a confession.

The book's popularity might also have been fanned by the fact that it was also, for the medieval period, a work of sadomasochistic pornography. It droolingly detailed witches' sexual antics with demons, and carefully described how to strip and torture suspects until they confessed to being witches. Despite this content, *Malleus Maleficarum* was fully condoned and recommended by the Catholic Church; but if readers became sexually aroused while studying the book they, of course, had to confess the sin to their priest.

The Pope at the time, Innocent VIII, had fanned the flames of the hysteria by issuing a papal bull, *Summis desiderantes affecti-bus*, authorising the Inquisition's prosecution of accused witches in Germany. Innocent VIII is also historically interesting on two other counts: it was he who ruled that the slave trade was a Christian enterprise, provided the slave owners made some effort to convert any non-Christian slaves that they bought from the Barbary pirates. He also made medical history, receiving on his deathbed the first known attempt at a blood transfusion. He drank the blood of three ten-year-old boys, but it failed to save his life. All three boys died as well; presumably of either blood loss, or septicaemia from their wounds.

The historians can't agree on how many people accused of witchcraft were executed. Estimates run between 300,000, suggested by Voltaire, and the figure of nine million deduced by Gottfried Christian Voigt (both writing in the eighteenth century). Victims were tortured to death, beheaded, hanged or burned alive. A small but still shocking proportion of the executed 'witches' were children or even infants, and around 80 per cent of all those killed were female. Of course, in such a patriarchal society, the witchfinders, inquisitors, judges, torturers and executioners were all men. So it is hard not to suspect that the repressed sexuality of celibate priests, and the opportunity to strip women to search for 'Devil's marks', was an essential factor that drove the witch-hunting hysteria.

(In 1431, when Joan of Arc was burned for heresy and cross-dressing, the executioner reportedly waited until her dress had partly burned away, then tamped down the fire. Having allowed the crowd to enjoy the sight of her naked lower body, he got the fire going again and burned her to death.)

Yet a more basic reason for the witch hysteria – beyond sadistic voyeurism – was ignorance and the natural human inclination to blame anyone but themselves for their misfortunes. People didn't know why their crops failed, why the earth quaked and knocked down their house, why they got boils, or why their wife ran off with a tinker. They were unwilling to accept that it might be because they were bad farmers, who built shoddy houses, only washed their skin when they got drunk and fell in the pond, and beat their wife every day. No, it was demonic witches who made it all happen with their wicked spells. And if you could get your hands on someone that you didn't like very much – like, say, a vagabond tinker – it was easy to convince yourself that they were the malevolent witch in question.

Priests, as we noted in Chapter 6, had always filled the gaps of ignorance within human knowledge with believable and entertaining stories. These tales might have been the result of deliberate invention, self-delusion, divine revelation, or a combination of all three. But, in essence, they sprang from the same wellspring: the universal human ignorance about how most of the mechanics of the universe worked. The pre-Enlightenment priest knew as little as anyone else about why crops failed, why earthquakes happened, what basic hygiene might achieve, or (in many cases) why mistreating women made them want to run away. But saying that it was all God's will, or the work of the

Devil, generally plugged the gap of ignorance to most people's satisfaction.

And like all professional entertainers, the priest had to be aware of the mood of his audience – or, in this case, his congregation. If his parishioners demanded a human sacrifice – in the form of a witch burning – then he was unlikely to stand in their way for long; even if, in the case of Christian churchmen, it went against almost everything that their ostensibly humane religion advocated.

There were also financial reasons why the witch craze destroyed so many lives. As the astronomer Carl Sagan pointed out in his 1995 book, *The Demon-Haunted World*, the Europe-wide witch-hunt was also a massive expenses fiddle. While an accused witch was awaiting trial, they and their family were expected to pay for the cost of their upkeep. This would not only include room and board in a prison cell, but also the pay for the guards (including wine rations) and decent meals for the presiding judges, lawyers and priests. In many cases the accused was also made to pay for the procurement and maintenance of the torture implements used on them, and for the wood used to burn them alive. If anything was left of their property after their execution, it was divided equally between their prosecutors and the Church. So persecuting witchcraft could be a nice little earner; provided the stream of 'witches' didn't run dry.

But, in fact, the number of witches to be profitably prosecuted rarely ran short. The accused were tortured not only to force a confession to their own crimes, but also to get the names of other witches in the neighbourhood. Sometimes whole areas were almost depopulated by this domino method of collecting accusations. And if you criticised the inhumanity and corruption of the whole process, you might end up on a burning pyre yourself. After all, Mother Church endorsed witch burning. If witch burning was an error, then Mother Church would have been committing a monstrous crime. That was unimaginable and impossible; so critics of witch burning must be, through circular reasoning, heretics and probable witches themselves.

The European witch-hunt went on rather longer than most

people would believe – almost to the nineteenth century, in fact. The last recorded witch execution was in 1782 when a maid servant, forty-eight-year-old Anna Goeldi, was beheaded in Switzerland. Modern researchers believe that she was judicially murdered, to prevent her revealing that she had been committing adultery with her influential employer.

It is even possible that Gottfried Christian Voigt's estimate of nine million people killed by religious hysteria, during the Middle Ages and Renaissance, might be seen as too low. The witch craze had its roots in the Catholic Church's persecution of heretics; and that arguably began with the thirteenth-century Albigensian Crusade to destroy the Cathar faith in southern France.

Previous acts of heretic persecution had taken place sporadically: during straightforward – and often bloodless – theological turf wars between slightly different Christian sects. But heresy became a full-scale obsession with the Church authorities when the growth of the Cathar faith – centred in the French Languedoc region – became a threat to their hegemonic power.

Catharism was a pacifist, Gnostic and dualist form of Christianity that held that Satan was an equal deity to God. But the Cathars did not worship the Devil (whatever their enemies claimed). They did, however, believe that all material things were the creation of Satan, and were therefore intrinsically evil. This did not sit well with the grandees of the Church and nobility, who owned an awful lot of material possessions, and resented the Cathar implication of spiritual impurity.

Pope Innocent III called a crusade against Catharism in 1208; ironically, it was one targeted solely at fellow Christians. Catholic kings from across Europe sent troops to 'defend' the 'true faith', and by 1228 virtually every Cathar had been forced to recant their beliefs. Or they had been killed. The strategy and ethical stance of the crusade was set at the sack of the town of Beziers, in 1209: the papal legate was asked how to tell the good Catholics from the heretical Cathars. He replied, in priestly Latin: '*Caedite eos. Novit enim Dominus qui sunt eius.*' ('Kill them all. For God will know those who are His own.') In religious and cultural terms, the Albigensian Crusade was a successful act of genocide.

Following the eradication of the Cathars, the Catholic Church could not break the habit of killing almost anyone who openly questioned the smallest detail of Catholic theology. One heretical Christian sect – born in 1517 out of a protest against Church financial corruption – managed to escape the persecution and control of the Catholicism: it came to be called Protestantism. But Protestant Christians could, in turn, be equally keen on killing their own heretics and witches. And certainly Catholics and Protestants, in the late-medieval and Renaissance periods, often killed each other with wild abandon – even if it was for carefully argued theological reasons.

So the victims of the wars between Catholic and Protestant states that ravaged Europe – especially the catastrophic Thirty Years' War of 1618 to 1648 – might also be added to the butcher's bill of Christian theological hair-splitting. Add to that figure the numerous pogroms against European Jews over that period – for being 'the murderers of Christ' – and the witchcraft persecution starts to look like just the tip of a monstrous iceberg.

A chief motivator of much of this religious controversy and bloodshed was the belief in an afterlife and, more specifically, in Hell and damnation. The belief that people of the 'true faith' would be sent to Heaven, and everyone else to Hell, has been very influential in most societies; but mainly in the past two millennia. Tribal and pre-urban cultures certainly believed in life after death; but their faiths, like their lives, were typically less complicated and dogmatic than those of their civilised kin. Most often their beliefs were based around ancestor worship. This was coupled with the faith that those same dead ancestors spiritually inhabited the physical world after they died, and could be prayed and sacrificed to, in order for their descendants to obtain guidance or miraculous help.

The idea of a separate and invisible world, coexisting with our own and inhabited by super spirits called gods, was a natural development of this belief. But even then most BCE religions believed that the realm of the gods was actually part of our physical world. The Ancient Greeks, for example, thought their gods lived on top of Mount Olympus – a real mountain, but inaccessibly high and remote; so nobody (that we know of) ever tried to climb up to celebrity-stalk the gods in person. Even today if you ask most people to indicate Heaven they will, jokingly, point upwards. This is a hangover of many early religions thinking that the clouds look remote, peaceful and restful – an ideal place for the gods to live.

Hell, for most pre-monotheistic religions, was also part of the physical world, but was often thought of as being underground somewhere – like Tartarus, the realm of Hades, the Greek god of the dead. Anyone who has entered a cold, damp cave – or seen an eruption of lava – might guess why religious hells were often imagined as one or the other, or both.

Yet early ideas of Hell were not often judicial – places of hellish suffering reserved only for the wicked. They were seen as more of a holding area for the souls of *all* dead people, to stop them wandering the Earth as ghosts. Penitentiary hells – afterlife realms specifically designed to make the dead suffer for their crimes in life – did not enter religion until relatively late in history. The gods might punish particular criminals to eternal torments – like the titan Prometheus, who was tied to a rock and alternately eviscerated and healed for the crime of giving fire to the humans. But ordinary people were generally seen as too unimportant to feature on a god's pet hate list.

However, there were two old-world religions that went further than this. The first were the polytheists of Ancient Egypt: they believed that the souls of the wicked were boiled in the underground lake of fire through which the Sun god, Ra, rode his solar boat at night. But after a suitable period of suffering, the agonised souls were fed to a crocodile-headed monster and thus annihilated.

The dualist Zoroastrianism of Ancient Persia also held that the souls of the dead were tortured with heat: in this case an underground lake of molten metal. But they believed that it was a purging process rather than a ruthless punishment. Souls would eventually emerge from the fire cleansed of wickedness and worthy to enter Heaven.

Ancient Judaism had no concept of an afterlife – their philosophical attitude being more or less summed up by the modern
tragicomic complaint: 'You're born. Life's a bitch. Then you die.'
But by the dawn of the first century CE, the beliefs of the neighbouring Greeks, Zoroastrians and Egyptians had started to stain
into Judaism. One particular religious innovator and rebel,
Jeshua of Galilee, was apparently deeply influenced by the
concept of an afterlife. And, in another break with his cultural
traditions, he was probably outspokenly pro-Greek – as opposed
to traditionalist Jewish – because he seems to have introduced
himself by the Greek version of his name: Jesus.

(The Greek Seleucid Empire had, two centuries before,
conquered Judea and tried to suppress Judaism; and the political, religious and cultural repercussions were still very much
alive in the first century CE. So Jesus's choice of name was
roughly the equivalent of a Frenchman called Jacques insisting
on being called Johann, not long after the Second World War.)

Among the many groundbreaking and humane teachings
expressed by Jesus was an entirely new concept of a penitentiary
afterlife; but here he was rather less generous and humane. In
fact, he took the worst aspects of the Greek and Egyptian beliefs
and combined them. Hell was now to be a punishment for the
wicked, like the Egyptian lake of fire; but it was also to last
forever and ever, like the Greek afterlife. There was to be no
reincarnation to get a second chance at life, and certainly no
eventual purification and ascension to Heaven[1].

Whether Jesus was divine (as believed by Christians); was
divinely inspired (as believed by Muslims); or was making it up
as he went along (as believed by almost everyone else); his
doctrine of Hell profoundly changed religious thought, especially in Europe after the triumph of the Christian Church over
all competing religions.

Most of the medieval burners of heretics and witches honestly
believed that they were struggling to save their victim's soul from

---

1 Mark 9:43–50, where Jesus repeats three times that Hell is the place where
'the worm dies not, and the fire is not quenched'

an eternity of torment. This was why the call to repent was always part of any Christian persecution of sinners. Of course, even complete confession and repentance did not often turn away the executioner. The sinner, after all, must be punished for their crimes. Yet the death of the condemned person's body – in some agonising but crowd-pleasing fashion – was of little consequence to people who believed that an eternity of agony was being averted for the victim's soul.

And even if the sinner failed to confess and repent, guaranteeing their damnation, at least their judges and torturers were ensuring their own escape from Hell. For surely God smiled and blessed the persecution of His enemies. After all – thanks to the venerated writings of early Christian thinkers like Tertullian and Saint Augustine – it was generally believed that one of the many pleasures of Heaven would be to look down on Hell, so as to enjoy watching the tortures taking place there. And certainly God Himself must take pleasure in the torture of sinners, since it was He who created these viewing platforms on the bottom of Paradise.

In so much religiously inspired chaos, and with such inconsistent legal record keeping at the time, there is no way to even estimate how many people were killed for heresy and/or witchcraft – by their fellow Christians – between 1208 and 1782. Even if Gottfried Christian Voigt's figure of nine million witches killed is accurate, then it might be just a small percentage of those murdered to defend Jesus Christ. And of course the bitter irony is that there never was a secret cult of satanic witches. The whole 'witchcraft menace' was a hysterical fantasy, supported and maintained by the secular and religious authorities out of paranoia. And, of course, for their own political and financial purposes.

Similar bloody and groundless hysterias still break out in the modern world. Witness the witch panic that occasionally breaks out in areas of West and Central Africa. Rumours of witches stealing away men's penises have led to the persecution of scapegoats, riots and to murders. (Ironically, *Malleus Maleficarum* made an identical claim about penis-stealing by witches; but then its authors showed a marked obsession with all forms of male impotency.) The fact that it is physically impossible to 'magic away' any part of someone's anatomy, and that there is absolutely no medical or police evidence of men with vanished penises, has yet to eradicate the belief.

Or consider the satanic ritual child abuse panic that gripped some authorities in Britain and America in the late 1980s and early 1990s. Dozens of people were accused of sexually abusing children in their care, and even of secretly killing (unidentified) children as part of a widespread satanic cult. When the fuss finally subsided it was realised that there was no ritual Satanism: at worst there was the common or garden child abuse that takes place in some unhappy homes, but without any evidence of inspiration by supernatural fantasies. Indeed, the supernatural fantasists all seemed to be working for the investigating authorities.

Fundamentalist or Born-Again Christians (who were often the only people charitable enough to work in underfunded and overworked social work departments) believed that Satan was a real being. Since he was real, he must be active and trying to tempt people into sin. From there it was easy for some of them to believe that any evidence of child abuse, real or imagined, was a sign of a satanic cult. Disturbed children were extensively interviewed and some revealed astonishing stories of satanic abuse; including the ritual sacrifice of hundreds of newborn babies and, in one memorable case, a giraffe.

It was only afterwards, when full interview transcripts were revealed, that it was seen just how much coaching by investigators was taking place. A child might initially claim to only being disturbed or frightened by an unpleasant but otherwise normal event. The interviewer would then gently ask supplementary questions, many of which subconsciously pointed to their own personal obsession with Devil worshipers. The child would quickly pick up on this and elaborate their stories to please the nice adult. These elaborations were put down by the interviewers to 'repressed memory syndrome', to explain why such shocking details had not been mentioned before. Between the interviewer and child, a highly elaborate story might organically evolve, with neither being conscious of straying into falsehood or outright fantasy. When these well-meaning but deluded investigators pooled their various case histories – often through the media of tabloid news reports – a picture of an international satanic network of child-raping, baby-killing cultists was formed.

Naturally, true-believing investigators felt that this cult must be battled at all costs. Unfortunately those costs were often borne by innocent families. People were accused and jailed, and families were sometimes permanently split up with their children sent for adoption; all on the flimsiest of misapplied evidence. And add to that the openness of young children to brain washing, deliberate or accidental. Some of the child witnesses were later reported to have become deeply disturbed by the satanic abuses that they had described to investigators. By inadvertently being pushed into creating the stories, they had utterly convinced themselves that the terrible events had actually happened. They were as traumatised as if they had actually witnessed the ritual murder of babies.

Authoritarian support is not actually necessary to inspire or sustain these periods of national madness and inhumanity. Popular culture can spontaneously produce its own monstrosities . . .

At the Midsummer fair in mid-sixteenth century Paris, cat-burning was a regular attraction. A special stage was built so that a large net containing several dozen cats could be lowered into the bonfire beneath. The spectators, including kings and queens, shrieked with laughter as the animals, howling with pain, were singed, roasted, and finally carbonised. Cruelty was evidently thought to be funny. It played a part in many of Europe's more traditional sports, including cock-fighting, bear-baiting, bull-fighting, and fox hunting.[2]

Cruelty to animals has been a regular form of entertainment in many – perhaps most – cultures up until very recently. Human societies seem to routinely divide themselves up as 'in groups'

2 Norman Davies, *Europe: A History* (1996)

and 'out groups' – also known as 'decent people' and 'scum', 'good guys' and 'bad guys', or, most commonly, as 'us' and 'them'. And – until the humane psychological development that generally started with the European Enlightenment in the late seventeenth century CE – sympathy and empathy was typically withheld from 'them'.

Animals, our natural prey and slaves since we climbed to the top of the food chain, almost automatically fell into the 'them' category. (Only pet animals are regularly given the honorary 'us' status – and that is usually because of a recognisable likeness to infantile human beings.) From habitually seeing animals as alien to humanity and to our interests, it was often just a short step to torturing them for fun.

The same was true of public torture and public execution of criminals. Society's judicial system – and their own actions – had placed such people into the out-group 'them' category. And remember that for most of human history, human communities tended to be small and personal: so the people thus socially redefined were often 'one of us', right up to the moment of judgment. The man from down the road who killed his wife; the woman from the other side of town who stole from a rich house; or the next door neighbour that you yourself, for whatever reason, accused of witchcraft. These might be acquaintances or friends one day, and a screaming and bloody form of mass entertainment the next. Such public executions were always officially seen as a deterrent to other would-be lawbreakers – but the cries of sadistic delight from the watching crowds should not be forgotten.

This form of community sadism was so normalised that it even found its way into popular children's stories:

At first [the wicked queen] did not want to go to the wedding, but she found no peace. She had to go and see the young queen. When she arrived she recognized Snow-White and, terrified, she could only stand without moving. Then they put a pair of iron shoes into burning coals. The shoes were brought forth with tongs and placed before her. She was forced to step into the red-hot shoes and dance until she fell down dead. The end.[3]

Think of the innate contradiction here. The sort of person who loved their children enough to read them a bedtime story would also think nothing of telling them that a hideous death by torture was a just and decent thing: a happy ending, in fact. It is even fairly indicative that the fictional Queen Snow-White might believably demand such a bloody and cruel execution take place during her wedding celebration. (And, indeed, why did Snow-White's palace have a set of iron shoes ready and waiting, unless red-hot shoes could be seen as a normal form of execution in fairytale land?)

But public torture and execution was still commonplace over much of the world in the early nineteenth century CE (when the Grimms were collecting and collating traditional German folk-tales like that of Snow-White). Certainly there must always have been plenty of people who felt that such sadism was despicable but, for most of history, they must also have felt that they were swimming against the tide of public opinion. It was only gradually that enlightened education, public opinion and, finally, statute law dismantled the public gibbets and scaffolds.

The Ancient Romans raised public cruelty to an art form. We've already considered the Roman tradition of gladiatorial combat in Chapter 9. In forcing slaves to fight to either injury or death, the Romans combined sport with religious human sacri-fice: the gladiatorial combats were invariably dedicated solemnly to the gods, but that didn't dampen the pleasure of the roaring – and betting – arena crowds.

The spectacle of condemned people being fed alive to wild beasts (*damnatio ad bestias*) probably grew out of the Roman gladiatorial tradition. We know that some early variations of gladiatorial shows involved armed men 'hunting' and killing dangerous animals in an arena (much like modern-day Hispanic bullfighting). From there it was a simple progression to

---

3 Jacob and Wilhelm Grimm, 'Little Snow-White' from *Children's Household Tales* (1812)

experiment with changing the odds in such fights; to the extent of sending unarmed victims to battle starved animals, or by simply tying the condemned to stakes for the lions, attack dogs, bears or wild bulls to savage at will.

(It might also be worth noting that some of the arena animals were trained to rape bound victims. So the sexual element of sadism was also catered to in the Roman arena.)

The Romans used this form of execution, and entertainment, from the second century BCE, through to the third century CE – in other words, for half a millennium. By comparison, in the 500 years up to our own time, human beings have moved from armoured horse cavalry to cruise missiles; from bleeding patients with leeches to brain surgery; from the discovery of the Americas to landing on the Moon. *Damnatio ad bestias* was no passing fad for the Romans.

The people typically condemned to die in this grotesque way were recaptured army deserters, murderers who used poison or sorcery, coin counterfeiters, kidnappers of children, rebellious slaves, parricides and, most infamously today, religious trouble-makers like the early Christians. Being fed to the lions was the way that Rome showed its utter contempt for a criminal – maybe even more so than through death by crucifixion.

Defenders of the nobility and civilisation of the Ancient Romans have pointed out that neighbouring cultures – the Germans, Gauls, Spaniards, Carthaginians, Egyptians and Parthians, for example – could be just as savage in their entertainments and executions. The Romans were just, characteristically, rather more organised about it. But that argument misses the fact that Ancient Roman civilisation saw itself as an offshoot of Classical Greek civilisation – and looked to Grecian culture as the basis of their religion, political system and artistic endeavours.

Yet the Greeks didn't force men to fight to the death; nor did they watch with delight as people were eaten alive by animals. The Classical Greek idea of good family fun was a poetry recital, an athletic competition, or an afternoon at the theatre. Of course the Romans also enjoyed these pastimes – they just added the homicidal blood sports of the arena to the schedule of events.

So why were the Romans so bloodthirsty and callous, when their cultural forebears and mentors, the Greeks, were not? The reason was partly a matter of deliberate policy. The Romans sincerely believed that watching gladiatorial combat instilled a martial ardour into the audience – that it made them into a more warlike people. They also thought that seeing screaming victims being torn apart by lions toughened men for the sights of the battlefield while, at the same time, instilling a healthy and deterrent fear of the forces of the law.

An element of this spirit of the arena was found in everything that the Romans did and thought. The highest quality to be found in a Roman was believed to be *virtus*; a concept derived from their word for 'man' – *vir* – and from which we derive the English word 'virtue'. A willingness to fight and conquer – in every aspect of life – was thought to be essential to a truly *virtus* Roman, man or woman. Patrician Roman parents were even loath to show affection to their own children, until the kids were old enough to show solid evidence of *virtus*. More than one ancient world writer mentioned the general Roman dislike of babies, mainly because infants could not show much *virtus*.

The Romans believed that this carefully nurtured warrior spirit was what had created and maintained their empire when, by comparison, all the Greek attempts at empire-building had collapsed within a few decades of beginning. Roman aggression and cruelty was not a matter of individual madness, or even of perpetuated mass hysteria like the European witch craze. It was a carefully nurtured national outlook, created by rulers and ruled, with a specific aim of enforcing Roman will on the world.

It was essentially the same inhumane set of national beliefs that created Nazi Germany and Imperial Japan in the 1930s. A self-serving justification of cruelty and exploitation was also what powered the British Empire in the nineteenth century. Some might also believe that a similar, cannibalistic outlook built the pseudo-imperial 'sphere of interests' of today's superpowers; like China, Russia, the European Union and the USA.

There is a key difference between the cultural influence of frivolous entertainment and the influence of national obsessions. It is the difference between violent computer games and state propaganda; between pornography and religious dogma; between novels and news stories. People rarely, if ever, kill over the former examples. But they will lay waste whole regions when motivated by the latter.

Chapter 16

'Willing Executioners'

So what of the people who carry out the ruthless orders to brutalise, torture or kill other human beings? Orders issued by distant chiefs who refuse to get their own hands dirty and then try to weasel out of any blame when it all comes into the public eye. As clearly illustrated by the Nazi death camp guards, men or women with military training will generally carry out inhuman and even monstrous orders if they are issued by a superior officer. The troops who fed people into the gas chambers seemed to suffer no debilitating pangs of shame while they beat, starved and murdered millions. The rate of depression *was* apparently high among SS concentration camp guards, but the cause seems to have been boredom and frustration at a tedious job, rather than horror at what they were being ordered to do to fellow human beings.

In 1963, the political theorist Hannah Arendt published a study titled *Eichmann in Jerusalem: A Report on the Banality of Evil*. It was based on the extensive interviews that she had conducted with the war criminal Adolf Eichmann, while he awaited execution in an Israeli prison cell.

During the war, Eichmann had been the *SS-Obersturmbannführer* who had been the bureaucratic architect of the Final Solution. In 1942 he had helped to host the secret Wannsee Conference; where Nazi second-tier bigwigs spent a pleasant couple of hours, in luxurious comfort, working out and approving the details of the greatest orchestrated act of mass murder in human history.

Immediately afterwards, Eichmann was given the near-impossible task of organising the finer technical details of the Holocaust. Overseeing the production of death lists, co-ordinating millions of arrests, amassing transport and seeing that the death camps were well-fed with both supplies and victims; all had to be done by an empire that was beginning to lose the war and needed all its resources just to survive. In the eyes of his Nazi superiors, Eichmann managed the task magnificently. Without his logistical planning, the Holocaust might have become just another badly organised pogrom, in which all but a few thousand of the victims escaped.

Hannah Arendt's surprising conclusion was that Eichmann wasn't a Jew-hater, any more than a typical policeman would hate all criminals. He simply saw himself as a loyal servant of the German state. That state had required him to eradicate a certain problem. The fact that that problem had consisted of millions of human beings had not been, he thought, his concern.

At the Wannsee Conference Eichmann had seen some of the most senior officials in the country wildly applauding the policy of mass murder: so who was he to disagree? (It should be noted that Eichmann was painfully aware that he was an academic failure, without even high school qualifications. He thus had a certain awe for anyone with a university education.) *Obersturmbannführer* Eichmann had felt neither significant hate nor pity when he had helped to send a multitude of people into the gas chambers. He had just, he said, been obeying orders. Eichmann personally regarded the arrest, transport and murder of millions of people as a knotty work problem that he was rather proud to have solved.

Nor was Eichmann mad. Indeed, six eminent psychologists had examined him while he was awaiting trial in Israel, and all concluded that he was exceptionally well balanced, with an enviably pleasant attitude towards those he regarded as friends and family. The worst that could be said of him – leaving aside his key role in the greatest crime in modern history – was that he had been an unimaginative and mildly corrupt bureaucrat.

Even when confronted, at his trial, with the horror that his organising skill had created, Eichmann felt no responsibility for his pivotal part in implementing the Holocaust; any more than a

guard does for delivering prisoners to jail. The people killed in
the genocide, with his help, were deemed criminals by the state
that he had served. So 'he not only obeyed *orders*, he also obeyed
the *law*'[1] in helping to destroy them. And as such he regarded
himself as totally innocent of any crime.

He also said that he felt no personal shame for all the deaths
caused by the Final Solution. If there was any shame, he believed,
it lay entirely with those who had ordered the Holocaust to take
place; and, ultimately, with Adolf Hitler himself. Yet even there
Eichmann equivocated. He, through his defence council,
insisted that the resolution to exterminate the Jews, and other
undesirables, had been an act of state. The decision about what
to do with a large number of 'criminals', in time of war, had been
an internal German political issue. As such, he believed, it was a
sovereign matter and, under international law, lay outside the
scope of any external judicial system. He simply seemed not to
understand the horror and rage that the revelation of the
Holocaust had caused to most of the people on the planet.

Adolph Eichmann was hanged on 31 May 1962, insisting to
the end that he was innocent of any crime and proclaiming love
for Germany, his family and God.

Arendt's subtitle – *A Report on the Banality of Evil* – has sometimes been misunderstood. She was in no way suggesting that the
Holocaust, or Eichmann's part in it, was a banal event. She was
commenting on Eichmann's bland stupidity – his lack of imagination and empathy; his largely self-imposed intellectual
underachievement; and his automatic and spineless subordination
to any authority figure. It was these factors – Eichmann's fundamental banality – that allowed him to slip so thoughtlessly into
monstrosity and then to exonerate himself of all blame afterwards.

A key element of Eichmann's dull ruthlessness was his uncritical deference to authority. Certainly his military training, in one
of the most pitiless organisations in history, must have been a
factor in this. The SS used to use live ammunition in all training

---

1 Hannah Arendt, *Eichmann in Jerusalem: A Report on the Banality of Evil*
(page 135) (1963)

exercises, for example, rationalising that the resultant wounds and fatalities were just weeding out those unworthy to serve in their ranks. Questioning and disobeying inhumane orders was another way to get yourself out of the SS . . . and into a grave.

The typical military 'Don't think! Just do it!' indoctrination, seems to be very effective in giving individual soldiers an excuse to forget or ignore their moral responsibilities. Certainly the claim that they were 'just obeying orders' is the excuse most often given by military war criminals. But the human pack-minded instinct to bow to a dominant leader type can take over *anyone's* reactive thinking – military or civilian.

In 1963, Yale University psychology professor Stanley Milgram conducted a groundbreaking and very disturbing experiment. A test subject was put in a room with a white-coated experimenter. In front of them was a console consisting of a numbered dial and a loudspeaker. The experimenter told the test subject that turning the dial administered an electric shock to another person in a distant room. Their pained reaction could be heard over the speaker. The experimenter also informed them that the highest setting of the dial – marked 450 volts – was a potentially fatal shock.

The test subject was then told to give an increasing series of shocks to the person in the other room – while over the loud-speaker came their complaints, then calls for mercy and eventually their agonised screams. If the person administering the shocks balked, the experimenter was instructed to give a scripted instruction at each refusal:

> *'Please continue.'*
> *'The experiment requires that you continue.'*
> *'It is absolutely essential that you continue.'*
> And *'You have no other choice, you must continue.'*

The experiment was halted on the fifth refusal, or after the dial had been turned to 450 volts three times – at which time the screams would have invariably stopped and only a deathly silence came over the speaker.

What the test subject didn't know was that the dial was a harmless dummy and the 'victim' in the other room was an actor, pretending to be in pain. What was being tested was their willingness to inflict torture and potential death on instruction by an authority figure, who gave no explanation or justification for their orders.

What Professor Milgram was trying to determine was whether the 'I had no choice, I was just obeying orders' defence had any basis in psychological reality. Did the brutal guards of Auschwitz and the Burma Railway really feel that they *had* to do what they did? Or were they just sadistic monsters who were too cowardly to confess to their personal guilt? The result of the experiment was deeply shocking.

No one seemed to guess that the shocks were fake, and most were badly upset by what they were being 'forced' to do. Yet no coercion was offered, other than the scripted verbal prompts. No test subjects tried to escape to alert the authorities, and none attacked the experimenter other than verbally. Only seven out of forty people (17.5 per cent of the test subjects) refused to obey orders before the 150 volt level was reached – where the 'victim' was invariably screaming. Touchingly, several test subjects *did* offer to trade places with the victim – to save them by sacrificing themselves. But 65 per cent of the test subjects – 26 out of 40 ordinary people – turned the dial to 450 volts. The overall result was clear: a high proportion of people are quite capable of torturing or killing on demand.

The 'Milgram' experiment has been retried several times and under different conditions in the half-century since 1963, not least by Professor Milgram himself. The results have been remarkably consistent with the original experiment. In 2008, for example, Professor Jerry Burger reproduced the original experiment – except that new rules on human testing meant that he could only get permission to use a dial that was marked zero to 150 volts (for fear of the psychological damage done to test subjects who, however briefly, might think that they had actually killed someone). Burger's team found that twenty-eight out of forty test subjects, 70 per cent, turned the dial to 150 volts. This is obviously 5 per cent higher than Milgram's results, but it is reasonable to deduce that, if Burger's dial had turned to 450 volts, another couple of people might have refused. On a more positive note, 30 per cent (twelve people) balked before the dial reached 150 volts – almost double Milgram's results – suggesting that compassion and intelligent anti-authoritarianism might have increased in the intervening half-century.

However: the age, social group, race, educational level, religious beliefs and even the sex of the subject seemed to make no difference to their reaction to the experiment. No group showed itself to be more or less willing to be cruel than any other. Whatever was reacting to the experimenter's apparently inhuman orders, it was clearly very deep in the psyche of the test subjects, countermanding any social training not to harm helpless people. But, after trying variations on the experiment, Milgram noted that people were more likely to refuse if the experimenter was not wearing a white lab coat. The presence of a respected uniform, however meaningless in the context of the experiment, undermined their ability to make a humane decision for themselves. Voltaire, the Enlightenment philosopher, was quoted as saying that: 'Those who can make you believe absurdities, can make you commit atrocities.' In fact it seems that belief can be replaced with uniformed authority, and the end result will be much the same.

Eight years after the original Milgram experiment, in 1971, an even more disturbing experiment was conducted at Stanford University by Professor Philip Zimbardo. He set up a fake prison in the basement of the psychology department building, then selected the twenty-four of the apparently most stable of seventy young male applicants. They were then randomly allocated as either guards or prisoners. The twelve guards were given uniforms, batons and sunglasses; and the twelve prisoners were told to wear prison smocks and beanie hats. To further enhance the illusion, Zimbardo asked the Palo Alto police department to 'arrest' the prisoners and throw them into the 'jail'.

The aim of the experiment was to accurately recreate a prison atmosphere for a fortnight. Zimbardo wanted to see if the inherent personality traits in his subjects would cause them to start living their roles, rather than just acting them. But he ended the experiment after only six days, having become fearful that, if left to run for the full two weeks, something terrible might happen.

The 'prisoners', locked up day and night, very quickly began to act in a submissive fashion. One appeared to temporarily lose his mind, hysterically screaming and cursing, and was released after it became plain that he wasn't pretending. The 'guards' on the other hand, who worked in shifts, very quickly – and without any direct orders from Zimbardo – began to brutalise their charges. Prisoners were made to sleep on the concrete floors; had to do press-ups with a guard standing on their backs; were forced to use a public bucket instead of the toilet; and were then forced to clean the bucket with their bare hands. Others were stripped naked and guards pretended to sodomise them. Most of this took place in the first two days of the experiment.

Professor Zimbardo later estimated that at least a third of the guards had started to behave in a genuinely sadistic fashion and the rest were abusing their power in different ways. He ruefully included himself in this appraisal, because it was him – in his role of 'prison superintendent' – who had told the guards to do whatever was necessary to maintain order. This included moving the entire 'prison' to another floor of the building, when he and the guards became paranoid that the released 'crazy' prisoner might try to organise a break-out.

The young men in the experiment had no previous record of neurotic or criminal behaviour – in fact they were picked specifically because they seemed well adjusted. Most were typical middle-class American youths, and all were quite aware that it was a fake prison and that in two weeks they would be back to living their normal lives. They were also aware that there were cameras recording what happened in the 'cells'. Yet, in less than forty-eight hours, they had fallen into the roles of victims and victimisers; and there was nothing fake about the cruelty that took place.

Zimbardo noted that most of the guards seemed disappointed

that the experiment ended early; and that the prisoners – although they had the opportunity to 'parole' themselves at any time (forfeiting their payment of $15 a day) – had so internalised their role that not one of them used this method of escaping their awful situation. He concluded that the concept of prison institutionalisation and the expectations of the authority figure (himself, in fact) had subsumed their personalities in a way that was beyond their control. They helplessly became victims and thugs because that was what they thought was expected of them, and the illusion was reinforced by their environment. This converting of normal, thinking humans into unthinking extensions of the institution that they inhabit is, almost certainly, even more pronounced in *real* prisons, mental institutions and army bases.

A striking confirmation of both professors Milgram and Zimbardo's findings can be found in a book by Dr Mika Haritos-Fatouros – *The Psychological Origins of Institutionalized Torture* (2002). She had studied the men who were recruited, trained and deployed as torturers by the right-wing military junta – known as the 'Regime of the Colonels' – that held power in Greece between 1967–74.

Dr Haritos-Fatouros notes that the Greek junta had not employed drooling sadists or power-mad egomaniacs – who might be expected to throw themselves wholeheartedly into their work. Neither had they picked rabid political supporters or petty 'little Hitler' types. They 'were not looking for recruits with authoritarian personality traits or indeed any authoritarian tendencies . . . rather, what was important to them was conformity and conventionalism'. They wanted ordinary, man-on-the-street, people.

Sadists, egomaniacs, fanatics and martinets are simply too emotionally unsound to be professional torturers, mainly *because* of their governing passions. The Greek colonels had found that the best torturers were men who could spend the day tearing out fingernails or beating arrestees to a pulp, then could go home and have a pleasant evening with their families. Such men, by their very stability and normality, could subsume the horror of their working lives and rationalise it as simply obeying the orders of their superiors. (It should also be noted that the regime's 'torturer training' consisted of a particularly brutal form of military basic training that often bordered on torture for the trainees themselves.)

Mika Haritos-Fatouros concludes that 'torture, in one form or another, is not too different from the infliction of pain that occurs in everyday life. Institutionalised torture is at the extreme of a continuum, rather than something qualitatively different from everyday action.'

In other words, saying something deliberately hurtful to a loved one and crushing a political prisoner's toes with a pair of pliers are much the same psychological reaction to circumstance, except in degree. One happens fairly regularly in a normal life, while the other is very rare; but both spring from the same human capacity to ruthlessly hurt others if there is a perceived need to do so. Torture is an atrocity that almost anyone can be trained to commit, just as a soldier can be trained to fight.

But is there anything that differentiates those normal, sane people who are willing to torture and kill on command, and those normal, sane people who refuse? A basic problem in understanding this question is that both normality and sanity are not fixed points either in time or in human society. The very reason that this book was written is because attitudes to violence in society have changed fundamentally over just a few hundred years.

Consider the homicide statistics given in Chapter 5. The chance of a modern-day Briton being illegally killed is around 1.4 in 100,000; the chance for a contemporary US citizen is approximately 4.7 in 100,000. In Oxford in the thirteenth century CE, the murder rate averaged at 110 in 100,000. For a human being living in a pre-literate hunter-gatherer society before the sixteenth century CE, the chance of dying by violence was roughly 15,000 in 100,000. These variations are simply too great to be the result of a simple change in physical circumstances – the human attitude to violence itself must have changed over the centuries.

And, furthermore, attitudes to violence may radically vary

within a short time period or even within a seemingly homogeneous culture. Remove any single individual from their native society, and drop them into a culture with different necessities and goals, and they might well appear weird or crazy. This is partially why minority immigrant groups have always had trouble when first arriving in a new country . . . unless, of course, they arrive with superior weapons and the will to use them. But either way, somebody will have to re-evaluate many of the preconceived ideas that they had previously taken for granted, or suffer the consequences.

Not being a cannibal in New Zealand, prior to the invasion of Europeans in the seventeenth century, might have set one apart as a social outsider – much as vegetarians were often ridiculed during the early twentieth century in Europe and America. The arriving European settlers were horrified at the thought that the Maoris sometimes ate their dead enemies; yet such colonists often showed small taboo against eradicating their own enemies – including many Maoris and, in neighbouring Tasmania, the entire native population. The Europeans' disgust at Maori cannibalism was therefore less an ethical stance than a strong reaction to a clash of cultures. You might even describe it as a culinary disagreement.

That the Maoris soon gave up cannibalism – or that the European settlers did not take it up – might simply have been a matter of the Europeans having better weapons to reinforce the export of their cultural views. One might speculate that if the early colonists on New Zealand had been somehow cut off from Europe, with its cultural influence and its re-supplies of gunpowder, they might have soon 'gone native' when faced with the greater population numbers of the Maoris. Then the national dish of New Zealand might not have become lamb with mint sauce.

A scientific attempt to define whether a person was prone to either committing or ordering atrocities was made in 1947, at Berkeley University, with the *California F-Scale* test. This was a sheet of multiple-choice questions that each asked test subjects to rate their reaction to a single statement. For example: 'Science has its place, but there are many important things that can never be understood by the human mind'; 'No sane, normal, decent person could ever think of hurting a close friend or relative'; and 'Homosexuals are hardly better than criminals and ought to be severely punished.'

The intention was to use emotive phrases and ideas to try to engender a visceral, unintellectualised reaction. The questions were all indirect, and the test subject was never told the purpose of the test beforehand. In fact, the 'F' in the F-scale stood for 'fascism' and the test was designed to 'yield an estimate of fascist receptivity at the personality level'. Remember that the F-scale test was created just after the Second World War, when there was a justifiable fear of a resurgence of right-wing totalitarianism. Maybe the test designers wanted to know if there might be death camps built in California, some time in the near future.

The F-scale test is now often seen as being flawed, for several reasons. Some commentators were annoyed that the testers automatically connected unquestioning religious belief with fascist tendencies. Others pointed out that the test risked being socially divisive, since well-educated people often guessed the purpose of the test before completing it – thus invalidating their results. How could the test give an accurate result if some sections of society, through their better education, could escape proper study?

Certainly the poorly educated seemed to uniformly score higher on the F-scale test, apparently indicating a greater inclination towards fascism. But this result reflected the known fact that most of those who gave their unquestioning and fanatical support to the Nazi Party, in the late 1920s and early 1930s, were from the poorly educated lower-middle class of German society; like Adolf Eichmann.

Nevertheless, the California F-scale was interesting in one aspect: it tried to ascertain the test subject's attitude to authority of any sort: political, religious and cultural. As was clearly shown by Adolph Eichmann, an unquestioning attitude towards authority seems to be a strong determining factor over a person's willingness to carry out orders that they should consider unethical or barbaric. So it might be hoped that the fall in the public's automatic deference to authority, that has been notable in many cultures across the world since the 1960s, might indicate a reduction in the numbers willing to commit atrocities.

But, of course, a government only needs a few people who are willing to get their hands really dirty. The Waffen SS, for example, never numbered more than a million men – out of a German wartime population of around eighty million. And by no means were all the members of the SS either German or war criminals. So the Nazis managed to commit some of the worst atrocities in recorded history, with the active participation of probably less than 1 per cent of their native population.

Rare as such ruthless people may be, they are often regarded as valuable assets by governments of all shades. In 1945 British intelligence (SIS) recruited a certain German citizen to help identify fleeing war criminals in the newly conquered Germany. In 1947 the US Army Counter Intelligence Corp (CIC) employed this same agent to investigate communist infiltration of the French intelligence service in occupied Germany. This man – also utilised by the West German intelligence agency (BND) and codenamed 'Adler' ('Eagle') – proved so useful that when, in 1950, the French discovered his true identity and demanded his extradition to France, the Americans refused. Instead they secretly spirited him out of Europe to a new life in Bolivia. There, in 1966, he helped the CIA-run operation to hunt down and kill the Marxist rebel leader, Che Guevara. He also dealt in arms and befriended General Hugo Banzer: the man who, in 1970, overthrew the democratic government of Bolivia in a bloody coup, then set up a right-wing dictatorship.

This very helpful German was Klaus Barbie: a former SS *Hauptsturmführer* and commander of the Gestapo in Nazi-occupied eastern France through most of the Second World War. The Gestapo were an arm of the SS, and acted as the Nazi secret police. Barbie's Lyon-based unit were tasked with stamping out the French Resistance in the entire region, catching Allied spies, and locating Jews to send to the death camps.

Klaus Barbie was not the sort of leader who liked to delegate unpleasant tasks – in his three years as the head of the Lyon Gestapo, he is believed to have been directly involved in the execution of fourteen thousand people, many of whom he killed personally. But Barbie's speciality was torture. In order to discover the identities and location of French Resistance saboteurs, Jews and other 'criminals', he used beatings, dental torture, electroshock, sexual abuse, partial drowning and skinning alive. He smashed hands in door frames, immersed arrestees' heads in buckets of caustic ammonia and used attack dogs – sometimes to rape his victims.

Barbie tormented men, women, and even children. For example, Simone Lagrange was arrested by the Gestapo after a French neighbour denounced her family of being Jewish. When she first met Klaus Barbie, he was playing with a kitten:

> He was caressing the cat. And me, a child of thirteen years old, I couldn't imagine that he could be evil because he loved animals. I was tortured by him for eight days.

The British, American, West German and Bolivian authorities were all quite aware of Klaus Barbie's past crimes. But all protected him from justice after the war, because he was such a useful agent in their cold war on communism. But after taking part in the so-called 'Cocaine Coup' – in which yet another right-wing dictatorship overthrew Bolivian democracy in 1980 – Barbie paid the price. In 1983 a newly reinstated democratic government finally extradited him to France. He was tried and sentenced to life imprisonment. He refused to speak for much of the trial, stating: 'When I stand before the throne of God, I shall be judged innocent.' In 1991 he died in jail, aged seventy-seven, of leukaemia.

Klaus Barbie had had a fairly normal, middle-class German upbringing and was originally hoping to become an academic theologian. Acquaintances saw him as quite shy, fairly intelligent and reasonably pleasant company. And after the war there is no evidence that Barbie ever tortured or murdered anyone – other than those he indirectly helped to kill through his helpful advice to various intelligence agencies, and to two Bolivian fascist dictatorships. Yet, in the three years that he headed the Gestapo in eastern France, he truly earned the nickname: 'the Butcher of Lyon'.

It seems likely that if Klaus Barbie had not been influenced by Nazi indoctrination, SS training, and the war itself, he might have lived the life of a quiet academic and never harmed anyone. He, himself, would certainly have claimed that he was just as much a victim of circumstance as the people that he ruthlessly tortured and murdered. So perhaps the most chilling thing about Klaus Barbie wasn't that for a few years he was a sadistic monster, but that for the majority of his life he behaved as a relatively normal human being. Much as we might want to reject any connection with *Hauptsturmführer* Klaus Barbie, he was one of us.

Chapter 17

'When Evil-Doing Comes Like Falling Rain'

On 19 December 1937, the Reverend James McCallum wrote in his diary:

> *Never I have heard or read [of] such brutality. Rape! Rape! Rape! We estimate at least 1,000 cases a night, and many by day. In case of resistance or anything that seems like disapproval, there is a bayonet stab or a bullet.*

He was witnessing the aftermath of Japanese capture of Nanking; that ill-fated city that, less than eighty years before, had been besieged and ravaged during the Taiping Rebellion (*see Chapter 11*).

The Japanese Imperial Army had invaded China in July 1937, believing that the conquest of their vast but disorganised neighbour would be relatively easy. They were wrong. They immediately ran into dogged Chinese resistance in the port city of Shanghai, and became bogged down in vicious street fighting. It took the Japanese – with more troops, and with much better weapons and air-support than the Chinese – three agonising months to capture the city. Bloodied and humiliated, they marched on Nanking – the capital of the Chinese Republic – feeling that they had a right to take revenge for Chinese resistance.

Two Japanese officers – Tsuyoshi Noda and Toshiaki Mukai

– were proudly reported by Japanese newspapers at the time to be waging a killing contest: the first to kill a hundred Chinese with their guntō ceremonial swords would win. It was also claimed that they were killing in battle, but this seems highly unlikely – neither would have survived for long, fighting against rifle-armed soldiers with just swords. They must have been executing unarmed captives to achieve such numbers. Both men surpassed the one hundred mark without noting the time, so a winner could not be decided. Officers and gentlemen that they were, they agreed to hold another contest when they got to Nanking: the first to kill 150 Chinese with the blade would be declared the winner.

The Chinese defence of Nanking was a debacle. Surrounded and outgunned, the Chinese army in the city was defeated in only six days of fighting. After that the victorious Japanese Army – who saw themselves as noble warriors in the spirit of the ancient samurai – behaved like blood-maddened ogres.

The death toll of what came to be called 'the Rape of Nanking' has never been officially agreed upon, partly because the Japanese army carefully destroyed the records of their occupation when they were losing the war. Even today, many Japanese have yet to fully come to terms with the evidence of their nation's war crime record during the Second World War, and the controversy over the Rape of Nanking remains a bitter bone of contention.

In 2007, the mayor of the Japanese city of Nagoya was reported to have told a visiting delegation of Nanking citizens that the murder of thousands of their compatriots 'probably never happened', and that 'there was no massacre that resulted in the murders of several hundred thousand people'.

But the mayor of Nagoya was not only crashingly undiplomatic, he was also wrong. There is a mountain of evidence that the Imperial Japanese Army indulged in an orgy of killing in the defeated and helpless city. Even the German fascist government were shocked by the reports of their ally's savagery, and the Nazis offered to mediate diplomatic talks between China and Japan. This was after the Japanese ambassador to Berlin had bragged to his hosts – within the hearing of the US ambassador – that the Japanese Imperial Army had killed half-a-million Chinese even *before* they took Nanking. It seems that Mukai and Noda's playful contest of five hundred sword-killings was just a drop in a lake of spilled blood.

At least forty thousand, and maybe as many as 300,000 people were murdered over the six weeks following the fall of Nanking. That means that an average of between one thousand and eight thousand people were killed every day. Initially claiming to be searching for disguised Chinese soldiers hiding among the civilian population, the Japanese summarily executed any man of military age. But even this pretence of legality was soon dropped in favour of unashamed slaughter.

Independent foreign witnesses, like the Reverend James McCallum, saw Japanese soldiers pillaging, torturing, raping and killing with vicious abandon. Most of the structures of Nanking had been unharmed during the six-day siege; but, after the massacre, a third of the city had been burned down and the rest had been completely looted by Japanese troops. The tens of thousands of dead were burned in pyres, thrown into the Yangtze River, or were piled into mass graves. To save time – and for their own amusement – Japanese soldiers also buried some of their victims alive.

After the war, the International Military Tribunal for the Far East found that at least twenty thousand women and children had been raped during the Nanking massacre. Witnesses testified that many were gang-raped and killed after being violated, often by being bayoneted in the vagina or anus. It was also reported to the tribunal that children too young or small to accommodate the adult penis of their attacker were stabbed, and the wound was then raped.

All this was not a just a matter of common soldiers running amok – the headquarters of Prince Yasuhiko Asaka, the army commander, had issued specific orders to 'kill all captives'. The Rape of Nanking was therefore officially sanctioned; and certainly Japanese officers did little to rein in the slaughter, as most of them were pillaging, raping and murdering on their own account. Prince Asaka escaped trial after the war, because US General Douglas MacArthur had insisted on a blanket pardon for all the members of the Japanese imperial family. Asaka became fanatical about both golf and Roman Catholicism in later life. He died peacefully in 1981, at the age of ninety-three.

Tsuyoshi Noda and Toshiaki Mukai, the officers who had waged the sword-killing competition, were not so lucky. Both were extradited back to China after the war and, in 1948, they were executed for war crimes. They were each killed with a bullet to the back of the neck.

War crime is a surprisingly complicated issue for historians, because different cultures in history have abhorred different things at different times. The mass rape of women, for example, was long considered, by all cultures, as a natural and undeniable privilege of conquering soldiers – a perk to top up their meagre pay just like any other sort of plunder. So, arguably, the rapists of Nanking were just resurrecting a lost military tradition.

However, before writing this off as old-world barbarism, remember that there are patriarchal societies today that regard a female rape victim as a *de facto* criminal – for allowing herself to be raped. At the same time these societies see the rapist as someone who simply lost control of himself for a moment, due mainly to the wicked temptations of the woman in question.

Indeed, so relaxed are the authorities in Pakistan on the subject of female rape, that it was possible there for a woman to be *sentenced* to be gang-raped, in order to expiate the shame of a crime committed by her brother. This happened in June 2002 to Mukhtaran Bibi, a thirty-year-old woman who then shocked her local community by refusing to do the decent thing. That was, of course, to commit suicide to remove her own supposed shame from their sight.

So, it is fair to ask that if left entirely to themselves (and considering their dismal track records) would modern Sudan, Congo, Pakistan, Oman, Saudi Arabia, or indeed the Vatican, regard the rape of women as a war crime?

Insults to enemy political leaders or an enemy nation's cultural beliefs are now a standard part of an opposing nation's propaganda efforts. ('Hitler has only got one ball, Göring has two but very small, Himmler has something sim'lar, But poor old Goebbels has no balls at all.' – Second World War Allied marching song, to the tune of 'Colonel Bogey'.) Few people today would see humorous disrespect as a war crime, yet such abuse has been the *cause* of wars in the past.

In Athens, in 415 BCE, someone spent a night knocking the cocks off the sacred *Hermai* – traditional public good luck statues that sported erect penises. Comical as that petty vandalism may now seem, the Athenians regarded the act as a capital war crime; especially since they were about to embark on an invasion of Sicily. Denied any nearby Sicilians to blame, however, the Athenians became so hysterical that they nonsensically accused Alcibiades, their own invasion fleet's commander. To avoid execution by his countrymen Alcibiades defected to the enemy, and the Sicilian expedition became an unmitigated disaster for Athens.

We've already looked (in Chapter 5) at the phenomenon of escalation in any conflict. Both sides generally start a war with a set of shared rules – ranging from traditional tribal taboos to diplomatic written rules of war. But the hate and resentment fostered by a long-running conflict is likely to lead to an escalation of aggression that breaks those rules one by one. And once one side breaks a rule of war – whether by accident; as an unthinking overreaction to a lesser crime by the enemy; or simply as a rogue action by a sociopathic sadist – then the other side generally feels justified in breaking that rule too, as a punishment, of course.

After victory, the winning side will usually indict the defeated side with a list of war crimes, often as a prelude to demanding reparations: this is commonly known as 'winner's justice'. But they might not be so zealous in listing their own infractions. If the Nazis had somehow won the Second World War, for example, they would certainly have tried and executed the Allied political leaders and military commanders who authorised the mass bombing of German cities – killing around 410,000 civilian men, women and children. German propaganda often stated that intention during the war. But the Allies won, put up statues to honour the men that the Nazis would have hanged, and got on with convicting the German war criminals.

The Geneva Conventions are something of an icon of hope to the modern mind. They are a set of international laws, drawn up and expanded on between 1864 and the present day, which prohibit violence or other cruelty to civilians, and also to enemy combatants who have surrendered or have otherwise been made incapable of fighting. Of course you can do what you like – short of using internationally proscribed weapons like napalm or nerve gas – to anyone still holding a gun. But like many icons, the Geneva Conventions have too often proved to be little more than a hollow statue – representing an ideal, but incapable of enforcing it.

For example, the kidnapping and torture of non-combatants is strictly prohibited under the Geneva Conventions – and the USA is a signatory to those conventions. Yet, since 2001 and the commencement of the War on Terror, US security forces have committed numerous acts that seem very like kidnapping and torture – they themselves defining such actions as 'extraordinary rendition' and 'enhanced interrogation techniques'. How history will judge this is a matter for the future, but there is presently little debate that the US has lost a lot of friends and respect in the international community by implementing such policies. Yet that is apparently as far as international law can go in this situation; nobody in power has seriously considered placing indictments for war crimes against US politicians, security personnel or soldiers. On the global stage, might is usually equated to right.

Of course the ultimate war crime is genocide: the deliberate attempt to murder all, or a significant proportion of, an ethnic, social, racial, religious or national group. 'Ethnic cleansing' is related but different to genocide; it may only involve the forced movement of an unwanted population out of the cleanser's territory and not, necessarily, the murder of a large number of them. Genocide is mainly a modern phenomenon, because it takes a high degree of political control, long-distance organisation and military technology to have any chance of eradicating entire populations of people: men, women and children. Before the invention of invasive propaganda, fast telecommunications and machine guns, attempts at genocide generally deteriorated into chaotic pogroms, where most of the targeted victims could get away. That being said, there are several clear examples of genocide in ancient history.

The Bible contains at least one genocide. Following their escape from Egypt, the prophet Moses and the Israelite tribes are said to have wiped out a people called the Midianites – killing every man, boy and non-virgin woman. The virgin girls – thirty-two thousand of them – they kept as slaves. Some historians would describe this as 'gendercide' or 'androcide' rather than genocide, because only the male Midianites were totally exterminated; but the end result would have been the same. The surviving female Midianites were presumably kept alive to be used or sold on as sex slaves, since their virginity was the key factor in their stay of execution. But there was no chance of those miserable, scattered and oppressed girls ever rebuilding their tribe.

If we accept the Bible's figures as gospel truth, the massacre of the Midianites must have produced a very high body count – especially for the Bronze Age, when regional population levels were very low compared with today. Even if we allow for a generous proportion of the tribe being underage or unattached girls – say 20 per cent of the whole population – that still means that around 128,000 people were killed; most of them, as the Bible tells us, in cold blood after the fighting was over.[1] Moses zealously oversaw this butchery under the direct orders of his god, Yahweh. Yet it is possible that the prophet was secretly unhappy about the slaughter, as his own wife was a Midianite.

In 416 BCE the Athenian Greeks, during the Peloponnesian War with Sparta, committed a much smaller-scale genocide. They attacked the island of Melos, killing all the fighting-age men – around 1,500 of them – and selling the rest of the population into slavery. The Melians' crime was to have insisted on

---

1 Numbers 31

remaining neutral in the mainland war. The question here is not one of numbers – the Melians were a tiny island population of probably no more than six thousand people – but rather of the Athenians' genocidal intent. The enslavement and resultant scattering of the survivors effectively destroyed the Melians as an ethnicity. In a culture obsessed with ancestral heritage and traditions of the home, the Athenians were sending a clear message to all the other neutrals in the war: side with us, or see everything that you hold sacred destroyed. The Athenians eventually lost the Peloponnesian War.

The Ancient Roman Republic's destruction of the North African city of Carthage has also been described as a genocide. For over a hundred years, starting in 264 BCE, the city-states of Rome and Carthage had fought a series of brutal wars – the Punic Wars – with Rome coming close to being conquered by Hannibal the Carthaginian in 216 BCE. In 146 BCE, following a three-year siege, the Romans broke into Carthage and massacred the inhabitants. Of a city population between 100,000 and 200,000, only about forty thousand survived to be sold into slavery. The Romans then levelled all the buildings and placed a ritual curse on the rubble and scorched ground. The once mighty Carthaginian civilisation, that had stood for over six hundred years, was systematically wiped from the world.

As with the Athenians' attack on Melos, the Roman destruction of Carthage was *meant* to be genocidal: the deliberate killing of an entire culture. For years before the final Punic war, Cato the Elder – a leading Roman Statesman – had ended every speech, on whatever subject, with the ringing demand: '*Carthago delenda est*' ('Carthage must be destroyed'.)

In 146 BCE Cato got his way. Yet the Romans later seem to have become ashamed of their ruthless action. The shadow of what they called 'the Punic Curse' hung over them for generations. They understood that a worthy enemy had been ignobly destroyed – a fate that they themselves might have suffered if Hannibal had not turned away from the gates of Rome. The dictator Julius Caesar even tried to recreate Carthage, using

Roman colonists. But Roman Carthage remained just a pale copy of the original Carthage.

It's worth noting here that the Romans indulged in a similar slaughter at the Greek city of Corinth, in the same year that they annihilated Carthage, but that they apparently felt little or no shame about that. At Carthage they had deliberately and genocidally murdered a whole civilisation, while the death of Corinth left the rest of Greek culture unharmed.

This national-level shame seems to automatically follow on the heels of genocide; although it may take a couple of generations. For example, many and probably most Germans, before and during the Second World War, were quite aware of the Nazi policy to eradicate all 'undesirables' from German-occupied territory. There was certainly genuine horrified shock immediately after the war, when the Allies showed the German population films of what they had discovered in concentration camps like Dachau, and in death camps like Auschwitz. But, sickened as they clearly were, Germans' subsequent claims of ignorance – that only the SS (the elite Nazi troops) had known about the Holocaust – rang very hollow.

Indeed, after the war it was hard to find a German who didn't insist they had always been an anti-Nazi. (So where did all the fanatically pro-Nazi Germans – who had been in such evidence before the defeat – disappear to? We will consider this question later on in this chapter.) German claims not to have understood how serious the Nazi leadership were in their often proclaimed goal of 'purifying the Fatherland', or that they had not guessed the inhuman methods that were used in that purification, were simply unconvincing. The mass arrest and the disappearance of millions of people simply cannot go unnoticed, even during wartime. And someone who suspects that a murder is taking place, and yet does nothing to stop it, is at least morally culpable.

The unexpected result of the post-war German denial of their own past was a fracturing of German society in the late 1960s. Many of the new generation of Germans, born during or after the war, repudiated their parents' claims to innocence in the

Holocaust. The hippy revolution, which was sweeping western society at that time, took on a darker tinge in West Germany, where anti-government protests were violently put down by the police. Radical students and activists suspected a secret resurgence of Nazism in the German ruling class and started calling for a popular revolution.

In fact there was no real move back towards fascism in the West German government. But the younger generation – brought up by parents who generally refused to even talk about the war or the Holocaust – could not be expected to believe that. Older Germans did certainly feel a collective shame over the Holocaust, and of their own largely passive assistance in the genocide. But by suppressing that shame, and by fatuously denying the facts of their self-evident past, they made their own children distrust and fear them.

The result was that groups of left-wing radicals like the Red Army Faction – better known as the Baader-Meinhof Gang – felt justified in directly attacking the society that had produced them. Department stores were burned down, banks were robbed, a leading industrialist was kidnapped and murdered, and West German police stations and US military bases were bombed.

The self-justification for this urban terrorism was neatly summed up in an outburst by Gudrun Ensslin – made at a student meeting in 1968 – shortly before she absconded to help found the Red Army Faction:

> They'll kill us all. You know what kind of pigs we're up against. This is the Auschwitz generation. You can't argue with the people who made Auschwitz. They have weapons and we don't. We must arm ourselves!

Ensslin was paranoid and broadly wrong; but it's hard not to sympathise with her misunderstanding, remembering the mendacious world that she grew up in. And it was the German baby boomers of her generation who finally faced up to their nation's shame. By fully admitting to it, they radically changed their national outlook and character for the better. Modern

Germany is almost unrecognisable as being just over two generations away from Adolf Hitler, the Nazi Party, and the Final Solution.

European Jews were the majority of the victims of the Holocaust (originally a Middle English word, meaning a fiery religious sacrifice). But anti-Nazis, religious non-conformists, Communists, Romanies, homosexuals, the congenitally disabled, certain conquered ethnic groups and Soviet prisoners of war were also murdered on an industrial scale by the Nazis.

Although most victims were shot or gassed, many were simply imprisoned in concentration camps and allowed to die of sickness and starvation. A large number were forced into slavery – in German munitions works, in mines and in privately owned factories like those of I. G. Farben and Alfried Krupp – there to work on starvation rations until they died of exhaustion. A few were used in lethal and inhuman medical experiments. And many were beaten or tortured to death, often for the entertainment of their captors.

No final, definitive death toll for the Holocaust can ever be reached, because the defeated Nazis deliberately destroyed most of the records of the arrest, transportation and execution of their victims. The often quoted figure of six million Jewish murders is actually something of a guess: based on the nine million Jewish citizens recorded on European censuses before the war, and the three million after the war. Holocaust deniers enthusiastically point out that neither figure was terribly accurate in the first place, and the 'six million' figure does not take into account the uncounted number of Jews who escaped abroad during the conflict.

Of course this misses the basic point about genocide, and that which differentiates it from simple mass murder: genocide is not essentially a matter of numbers, but of intent and result. Athens, for example, was guilty of genocide at Melos after killing just 1,500 men and selling maybe three times that number of Melians into slavery. Six thousand people were murdered every twelve hours at the Auschwitz death camp alone, in May and July 1944 when it was at the height of its slaughterhouse efficiency. In both cases the killers were trying to eradicate an entire culture. Genocide is genocide, regardless of the final count of dead bodies.

The Jews, the chief Nazi scapegoats, were the main target of the Holocaust; but others were also seen as a danger to the Aryan gene stock. At least a million Romanies were murdered. And around two million Ethnic Poles. And twenty-five thousand Slovenes. And between two and three million Soviet prisoners of war. All these people were regarded as subhuman by the Nazis, but were still capable of interbreeding with, and thus genetically undermining, the 'Aryan master race'.

Also murdered in the Nazi attempt at communal decontamination were around ten thousand homosexuals; 100,000 Freemasons; 250,000 congenitally disabled German citizens; five thousand Jehovah's Witnesses; and maybe 1.5 million dissidents of all political hues. A rough and fairly conservative estimate of the Holocaust death toll would be around thirteen million people. And that figure leaves out the many thousands of civilians executed in Nazi-occupied territories as part of the German efforts to maintain their conquests through oppression and terror. Such deaths were not officially part of the orchestrated Nazi attempt at mass genocide; they were just the victims of German imperial megalomania.

The Nazi concept of 'racial hygiene' was an extension of the theory of eugenics: an assumption that the human species could be fundamentally redesigned and improved through selective breeding – in essence, treating people as if they were domesticated animals like milk cows or race horses. But the eugenicists in other countries never went much further than suggesting tax breaks to encourage the 'better people' to have more children. (And by 'better people', they essentially meant those who had shown their genetic superiority by becoming wealthy.) At worst, in the USA, state governments implemented policies to medically sterilise thousands of 'undesirables' to prevent them from having children – those included the congenitally disabled, habitual criminals and Native Americans.

Nazi racial hygiene efforts went a logical step further than this: they believed that those they deemed unworthy to breed were also unworthy to breathe. Exterminating those they deemed subhuman, decadent or subversive was seen as an act of social cleanliness as much as anything else; like killing rats to prevent the spread of disease to humans. And of course in a time of national emergency or war, one less mouth to feed is one less mouth to feed.

For intellectual justification, the Nazis pointed to carefully selected parts of the evolutionary work of Charles Darwin and the mystic philosophy of Friedrich Nietzsche. But both these men would have been horrified if they had lived to see Nazism. Darwin was a lifelong humanitarian and opponent of slavery. And it is known that Nietzsche broke off his close friendship with Richard Wagner, in protest at the composer's vituperative anti-Semitism. Yet leading Nazis honestly believed that by killing millions – by cleansing Germanic humanity of its flotsam of scum, as they saw it – they were on the way to creating a race of godlike super humans.

Beyond this pseudo-scientific self-delusion, the Nazis also fervently believed that their 'Final Solution' to the race question was also justified by the fact that they, the Nazis, were the real victims of the story. They believed that their attempt at genocide was an act of justice. A carefully conglomerated myth of a 'great anti-German conspiracy' psychologically fuelled every area of Nazi effort. The people they tortured and murdered were, in their eyes, the *real* criminals. Their every act of brutality, they insisted, could be fully justified by reference to the 'international Jewish conspiracy', and the political 'stab in the back' that supposedly defeated Germany in the First World War.

The Nazis believed that Jews, international capitalists, democrats, communists, and anyone else that they didn't like, had conspired to subvert the natural destiny of the German people: that was to rule a vast empire and, ultimately, the world. Germany's failure to win the First World War and subsequent economic collapse were, in their eyes, clear proof of this plot. Furthermore, they convinced themselves that they were in an ongoing life-and-death battle with these enemies because, they felt sure, the only way to prevent German world domination was to eradicate the German people entirely. So they convinced themselves that committing genocide was their ultimate defence against their own destruction.

There are several reasons for a modern, apparently enlightened society to tip into a downward spiral of paranoia and savagery. At the most basic, instinctual level there is misappropriation of disgust. The natural instinct of disgust has a specific purpose: to prevent you from eating bad food. Almost all of our feelings of genuine disgust are visceral – a gut feeling of sickening horror. We may often say that we are disgusted by something when we actually mean that we are feeling moral outrage or petty dislike, but this is mere hyperbole. Real disgust, in a scientific sense, is the feeling you experience when you accidentally bite into a rotten apple.

That we *do* feel genuine disgust for non-food-related things or ideas is because of the complexity of the human mind and culture. Remember, compared with most of human evolutionary history, even a basic tribal society is highly complex. While the multifaceted societies and lifestyles that we now inhabit allow for the misappropriation of instinctual reactions by even esoteric or ethereal ideas. You might feel genuine love for the concept of, say, free market capitalism, homosexual marriage, or Jesus of Nazareth. Or you might feel genuine disgust for any or all of these things. This reaction might be a result of your own carefully considered intellectual processes; but it might equally be something impressed on your subconscious mind by your upbringing, or by the tribalisms of your culture.

The feeling of visceral disgust is such a powerful force that it is often used by parents, teachers or political leaders as a control on people's behaviour. As a parent I toilet-trained my children, only partly because their crapping on the carpet might infect our food supply. There are a whole raft of reasons that occur to me why I forcefully modified their infantile behaviour patterns – not least because my own parents trained me to feel disgust at incorrect excretion habits. We may feel that such disgust is natural, but travel to anywhere in the world with non-existent sewage infrastructure, and you will see necessarily different cultural attitudes to the removal of body waste. Nobody likes the smell of shit, but your level of disgust generated by that smell in inappropriate places is governed by your cultural norms, and by how much choice you have in smelling it on a day-to-day, or hour-to-hour basis.

Disgust can also be used as an overall cultural control. The author and journalist George Orwell caused controversy when he published his 1937 report on poverty in the north of England: *The Road to Wigan Pier*. Ironically, his strident attack on free-market capitalism's exploitation of working-class miners and factory workers was not the chief cause of that controversy. It was the following statement:

> *Here you come to the real secret of class distinctions in the West – the real reason why a European of bourgeois upbringing, even when he calls himself a Communist, cannot without a hard effort think of a working man as his equal. It is summed up in four frightful words which people nowadays are chary of uttering, but which were bandied about quite freely in my childhood. The words were: The lower classes smell.*

> *That was what we were taught – the lower classes smell. And here, obviously, you are at an impassable barrier. For no feeling of like or dislike is quite so fundamental as a physical feeling. Race-hatred, religious hatred, differences of education, of temperament, of intellect, even differences of moral code, can be got over; but physical repulsion can-not. You can have an affection for a murderer or a sodomite, but you cannot have an affection for a man whose breath stinks.*

Orwell was roundly attacked, by critics on the political left, who read this as saying that he, George Orwell, thought that the working class were horrid and smelly. In fact anyone who has read the entire book will know that this is rubbish. Orwell records his admiration for working and unemployed people who, from his own observation, often managed to keep themselves as clean as any middle-class banker or upper-class mine owner. In fact, Orwell pointed out, due to the filthy state of the crumbling slums that they were forced to live in, such clean working-class people were necessarily more hygienic than their more comfortable contemporaries.

In fact, Orwell had previously lived as a pauper and tramp in Paris and London, so he was well aware of what real degradation smelled like. What he was in fact pointing out – to the discomfort of middle-class leftists – was that his (and their) generation were typically brought up to believe that some people – not of their class – were dirty and thus automatically worthy of visceral disgust.

Many modern societies have now consciously moved past this level of reactive and unthinking bigotry. But there is always a risk that those not of our tribe will be targeted with unreasoning disgust – just as the Nazis did, as a matter of policy, with all Jews, blacks and Slavic peoples. It is really this idea – that such people are rejected outsiders from our social group – that is being impressed on us when pundits, politicians or parents tell us that those people – perhaps enemy soldiers, terrorists, criminals, or illegal immigrants – are worthy of our abhorrence. And if it is impressed firmly enough, this social rejection can become a visceral disgust.

Think of the Nazi propaganda that depicted Jews being as filthy as sewer rats; or that suggested Jews secretly put excrement into the food that they then sold to 'good, clean Germans'. Or think of the three-word description of the Japanese people – 'dirty stinking Japs' – habitually used by Americans after the attack on Pearl Harbor. The fact that both the Jews and Japanese are famously among the most hygienic cultures in the world had no impact on this runaway train of thought. In both cases the addition of disgust to a tribal hate was partly automatic, but was certainly helped along by the propaganda machines of both, politically very different, nations. And it is so much easier to murder people who disgust you – a fact ruthlessly used by governments in their propaganda efforts to the public, and especially in their indoctrination of elite troops like, for example, the SS death camp guards.

A second contributory reason for an entire nation to lose control – to go into the equivalent of a berserk rage only to awaken, sometimes decades later, to the full horror of what they have done – is that humans are not telepathic. Or, at least, they have no way of knowing for certain what is going on around them in other people's heads – and they often make bad guesses at what the true situation is.

The reason that a lot of Germans, after the war, said that they had always harboured anti-Nazi sentiments was that it was generally true. Some Germans, perhaps even a large minority, were indeed rabidly pro-Nazi. But a lot of these were young men – the section of society that Nazism most lauded – and a lot of those were dead on the battlefield by the end of the war. Most Germans who survived the war had either harboured doubts about the Nazis from the beginning, or had developed doubts as the course of events had opened their eyes. So why did they tacitly support the Nazis with a lack of opposition? The reason was cleverly, and rather poetically, explained by the German political scientist Elisabeth Noelle-Neumann, in her 1974 Spiral of Silence theory.

Noelle-Neumann pointed out that in any society where open debate is limited – sometimes by firing squads – public opinion can be manipulated by a small and non-representative group, provided that group has the right to be vocal. When Adolf Hitler was appointed chancellor in 1933, for example, many Germans regarded him as a joke – a blundering windbag who looked like Charlie Chaplin. Hitler was, they thought, a short-term stop-gap to prevent disorder; as soon as he had served his purpose, President Hindenburg – the real ruler – would kick him out of office. What they didn't know was that Hindenburg was senile and dying, and that Hitler was no joke.

The new chancellor was swift and ruthless in the cementing of his power base. He dissolved the cabinet of ministers; he imposed martial law following the (suspiciously convenient) burning of the Reichstag; he outlawed the trade unions and all opposition parties; and then he murdered an entire section of his own party – the Brown Shirts – because it was politically expedient. Within a year, it was clear that directly opposing Hitler and the Nazis within Germany was tantamount to suicide.

With internal opposition voices silenced, and media from the outside world largely banned, the large but dispersed group of doubtful or downright anti-Nazi Germans felt isolated. They were fearful to speak out, even in private to others who they were sure agreed with them. What if you were overheard by a Nazi spy? And what if that sympathetic friend or relative was later arrested, and then betrayed you to save their own skin? Better to keep quiet and hope that it would all blow over eventually.

This is what Elisabeth Noelle-Neumann meant by a 'spiral of silence': limited or censored communication within a state leads to a negative cascade effect, in which rebellious people feel increasingly isolated and so cannot form practical opposition groups. And if this continues for too long, they begin to believe that opposition is impossible. From there it is a short step to just go with the apparently unanimous flow and do whatever you are told – even if you are told to commit atrocities.

This is why totalitarian governments can seem so strong to outside observers, and can apparently control their people like puppet-masters. But the moment such governments are seen to loosen their grip – by, for example, losing a war, wrecking the economy, or by not being able to fully censor internet access – the whole facade can crack and shatter.

Witness the death of the Soviet Union. On 26 April 1986, the Chernobyl nuclear power plant, in north-eastern Ukraine, melted down and exploded, jetting vast amounts of radioactive material into the atmosphere. Only thirty-one people died in the disaster, but as many as 985,000 people might eventually die prematurely, mostly of cancer, due to environmental radiation damage caused by the Chernobyl meltdown[2]. In the immediate aftermath of the disaster, Soviet Premier Mikhail Gorbachev

---

2 Alexey Yablokov, Vassily Nesterenko and Alexey Nesterenko, 'Chernobyl: Consequences of the Catastrophe for People and the Environment' (first published in Russian in 2007, and republished, in English, by the New York Academy of Sciences in 2009)

realised that lack of intercommunication and free speech within the USSR had been a key factor in causing the catastrophe. (Chernobyl was known by its managers to be on the verge of collapse, due to age and poor maintenance, but no one dared report such bad news to their superiors.) So Gorbachev allowed a partial relaxation of the Soviet Union's strict censorship laws. People gradually began talking to each other more freely, and quickly realised just how dissatisfied they all were with the underachieving Soviet communist system. What might be called a spiral of shouting led to increased anti-government opposition and, by 1991, the total collapse of the Soviet totalitarianism. But remember that in the sixty-five years of Soviet rule before Chernobyl, the spiral of silence had successfully served those who had ruled with an iron fist.

And before anyone living outside a totalitarian system becomes too self-congratulatory, it is worth remembering that big business interests, ambitious politicians, media barons and politically biased news sources – all of which are common in modern democracies – can also create spirals of silence. They do this by simply making sure that any genuine opposition to their pet interests rarely gets a fair hearing.

For example, the correlation between tobacco use and cancer has been known since 1937; when it was clearly indicated by a statistical analysis, made by a research team based in Cologne in Nazi Germany. Yet it was not until 1964 – when knowledge of the cancer risk was backed up by a mountain of medical research and an uncounted number of premature deaths – that the US government finally admitted tobacco was dangerous. Other nations then gradually followed suit. The tobacco industry (sometimes collectively referred to as 'Big Tobacco') has been fighting a rearguard action against safety legislation and lawsuits ever since; but with remarkable success, considering that lung cancer is one of the most horrible ways to die in the modern day.

Politicians have been extensively and expensively lobbied; genuine research has been rubbished and respected medical researchers slandered; anti-smoking campaign groups have been litigated against; and potentially vulnerable people have been targeted by hard-sell advertising campaigns. The latter have included – at different times – young women, countries with lax health regulations and even children. Tobacco companies have even been caught covering up their own medical research data, supporting the cancer link, in order not to undermine their case.

Tobacco smoking remains legal everywhere, despite being directly responsible for at least six million deaths worldwide every year[3]. This is about six times the number of accidental road deaths, worldwide, each year. Or, if you like, it is the equivalent of a new Holocaust death toll every couple of years. Tobacco use is generally supported by politicians and the popular media under the guise of 'individual freedom'. However, this is an excuse that they do *not* extend to narcotic drug use, which kills considerably fewer people each year, but makes no money for influential and well-connected industries.

Here again there is a glaring question raised by the subject of this chapter, and by all human monstrosity: how can normal people, with no evident mental aberrations, knowingly become part of something as clearly monstrous as war crime or genocide? We've looked at several social and psychological explanations in the past few chapters; but there is a simple one that we have yet to consider . . .

It is an essential truth about people that almost all of us see ourselves as the hero, or at least the protagonist, of our individual life stories. Our lifelong viewpoint – from just behind our eyes and just between our ears – tends to push us towards a solipsistic understanding of the world. Indeed, the first step towards adulthood could be said to be the overcoming of the childish and self-centred delusion that no other person in the world matters as much as we do. Yet total self-effacement – the ultimate spiritual goal of religions like Christianity and Buddhism – lies beyond the psychological power of most people. All of us harbour a degree of self-regard, and that tends to make us see ourselves as always centre stage.

Indeed the more culpable the individual, the more prone they

3 Figures from the World Health Organisation

seem to this self-aggrandising viewpoint. Serial killers, war criminals and child molesters are notorious for trying to justify themselves, and their crimes, by building teetering shrines of petty fantasy and embittered self-justification – and by placing most or all of the blame on their victims. The police confessions of these human predators can read like the autobiographies of misunderstood saints. They simply cannot accept that their crimes might be their own fault, because to do so would undermine the most important person in their life: themselves.

Very few people, of any sort, have the honesty and vision to blame themselves for their own faults . . . not without at least some reference to outside influences. Classic examples are: 'It's because of how I was brought up'; or 'It was my duty as I saw it'; or 'I was just doing my job'; or 'I did it, because *you* drove me to it'; or 'It's all the fault of the immigrants . . . or the unbelievers . . . or the traitors to our cause.' And then there are the ever-popular perennials: 'I was just obeying orders' and 'The Devil made me do it' and 'It was God's will'.

Absurdly weak as this self-justification usually seems in the clear light of day, it cannot be denied that it is a fundamental lubricator of human cruelty. The child-raping soldier, the concentration camp guard, the merciless official in a totalitarian state and the mendacious political lobbyist – all find a basic mental block in seeing themselves as a bad guy. Indeed they may deeply resent the very thought. And that resentment might later be inflicted on their next victim.

Bleak as all this may seem, there is plenty of evidence from history that can make us optimistic about the future. It should be remembered that, even from a Nazi point of view, the policy of the 'Final Solution' was a total failure. None of the targeted population groups were actually exterminated in German-held territory. And the tremendous cost in resources and manpower – dedicated to hunting, arresting, transporting, imprisoning and killing a largely harmless multitude of people – catastrophically undermined the German war effort. Indeed, one might argue that without the unnecessary expense of the Holocaust, the Nazis would have won the war.

The post-war revelation of the Holocaust also totally discredited totalitarian fascism as an acceptable political doctrine. Back in 1938 – just seven years before the death of Nazism – George Orwell was warning, in *Homage to Catalonia*, that fascism was becoming an unstoppable force. He feared a future world split between communist and fascist absolutism, with all remnants of democracy being crushed out of existence between the metastasising totalitarian regimes.

Yet, by mid-1945, fascist totalitarianism was finished as an open political doctrine. Certainly there have been many political leaders since the Second World War who have *behaved* like Nazis, but only the borderline insane would openly admit allegiance to specifically Nazi ideals and policies. One of the most virile (if brainless) political doctrines of the twentieth century was destroyed not by losing the war – ideas, after all, are bulletproof – but by worldwide revulsion over their attempt at mass genocide.

Mohandas K. Gandhi, the man who did more than anyone to free India from the British Imperial yoke, wrote the following in his autobiography (*The Story of My Experiments with Truth*: published in 1927):

> *When I despair, I remember that all through history the ways of truth and love have always won. There have been tyrants, and murderers, and for a time they can seem invincible, but in the end they always fall. Think of it – always.*

But before we get too pleased with ourselves for being the good guys who will always defeat the bad guys, it should be remembered what Mahatma Gandhi wrote in 1942, in *Non-Violence in Peace and War*:

> *What difference does it make to the dead, the orphans and the homeless, whether the mad destruction is wrought under the name of totalitarianism or in the holy name of liberty or democracy?*

Genocide is genocide; war crimes are war crimes; torture is torture; rape is rape; and murder is murder – whoever commits it and for whatever reason. Anyone who tells you anything different is selling something.

Chapter 18

Those Who Can Make You Commit Atrocities

So why do absolutist leaders – like Stalin, Hitler and Mao Zedong – often do so much unnecessary damage to the people that they rule? In fact, to a large degree, absolute power and delusional incompetence seem to run together. This is at least partly because a supreme leader's mistakes are magnified by the fact that so few of their underlings dare to tell them the truth about failures. A dictatorial leader lives in a bubble of unreality, generated by both the fear and the ambition of those around them. Criticism and bad news are banished, for fear of his reaction. Good news and false good news are overemphasised to put him into a generous mood. Small wonder that such leaders develop a tendency towards paranoia, not least because the one thing that they can be sure of is that many of their subordinates would very much like to step into their shiny parade boots.

And, like spoilt children, all-powerful leaders often make the situation worse through their immature self-indulgence. Hitler, for example, was infamous among his headquarters staff for never wanting to hear any casualty figures for his own troops – simply because he found such news annoying and depressing.

In his comprehensive and moving book *Stalingrad* (1999) the historian Antony Beevor mentions an incident in which Hitler's personal train was stopped for some time at a red signal. Next to it was a train full of wounded German soldiers returning from the Eastern Front. Hitler did not go over to comfort them, he didn't even give them a regal wave. He just slumped gloomily in his seat and ordered his flunkies to pull down his carriage's blinds.

Later in the war Hitler became a recluse, never leaving his Berlin bunker. His aides believed that this was because he didn't like to see the destruction of the city immediately outside. But this was not for reasons of pity for the bombed-out Berliners: indeed, at the end of the war, Hitler contemptuously told those around him that they were only losing because the German people had been unworthy of his leadership. Führer Adolf Hitler didn't like to see the ruin of Berlin, because the rubble was plain evidence that his carefully cultivated and essentially childish fantasies about still winning the war were all false.

There was an important military consequence of Hitler's refusal to face up to the consequences of his bad decisions: towards the end of the war he would often order army units into action that had actually been destroyed. Sometimes his staff hadn't dared to tell him the full truth about the casualty reports or, when they did, he refused to believe them. As a result, seeing counter-attack after counter-attack fail, Hitler became increasingly convinced that his orders were being undermined by traitors. And this paranoia further reduced the efficiency of his military oversight.

One of the most enlightening statements on the danger of the modern absolute dictatorship was made by Albert Speer: Hitler's one-time city architect, later his Armaments Minister, and one of the dictator's few close acquaintances. (Hitler didn't seem to have had any actual friends, in the normal sense of the word; but that was possibly another side-effect of his assuming absolute power. Who can be genuinely congenial with someone who has the power of summary execution over them?)

Speer stood trial for his life after the war – charged with complicity in the Nazi mass genocide of the Final Solution. Unlike the other defendants at the Nuremburg Trials, Speer freely admitted guilt. He said that although he had not specifically known about the Holocaust, he had seen evidence – when he was Armaments Minister – that had hinted at what was going on. He had chosen to do nothing at the time and now, having learned the truth, he felt damned. Speer said that he had taken on the trappings of power, so now he should take the responsibility: if the court sentenced him to death, he would see it as justice.

Speer was given twenty years in jail, during which he secretly wrote his memoirs on toilet paper. Even today, Albert Speer remains a controversial figure. Some historians believe that he was simply more clever than the other 'I was just obeying orders' war criminals tried at Nuremburg. Certainly it's true that the judges' sympathy for his courtroom self-accusation was a key reason why he wasn't hanged.

Trustworthy or not, Speer made a telling observation in his final speech to the Nuremburg judges, just before they passed sentence on him:

> *Hitler's dictatorship was the first dictatorship of an industrial state in the age of modern technology, a dictatorship which employed to perfection the instruments of technology to dominate its own people . . . By means of such instruments of technology as the radio and public-address systems, eighty million persons could be made subject to the will of one individual. Telephone, teletype, and radio made it possible to transmit the commands of the highest levels directly to the lowest organs where because of their high authority they were executed uncritically. Thus many offices and squads received their evil commands in this direct manner. The instruments of technology made it possible to maintain a close watch over all citizens and to keep criminal operations shrouded in a high degree of secrecy. To the outsider this state apparatus may look like the seemingly wild tangle of cables in a telephone exchange; but like such an exchange it could be directed by a single will. Dictatorships of the past needed assistants of high quality in the lower ranks of the leadership – men who could think and act independently. The authoritarian system in the age of technology can do without such men. The means of communication alone enable*

*it to mechanize the work of the lower leadership. Thus the
type of uncritical receiver of orders is created.*[1]

Advancing technology, quickening communications and
reducing the number of human links in a chain of command,
makes the time gap between decision-making and the execution of that decision shorter. Automation also removes some of
the humane and moral influences from decision-making, simply
by removing some people who might otherwise have expressed
a conflicting opinion. And by expediting the time between
decision and execution, technology leaves the remaining people
in the command chain less time to consider and object to an
order. In other words, increased automation increases the risk
of atrocity.

Speer, at the very dawn of the age of nuclear weapons, had put
his finger on one of the key risks of the modern world: that a
deranged or misinformed leader could theoretically kill thousands or even billions with a single command. It is mainly
because of this risk that the single 'big red button' to launch a
nuclear strike was always a paranoid Hollywood fantasy. No
government would take such a risk with weapons of mass destruction; a human chain of command is always put in place to reduce
the chance of mishaps.

But the most telling comment made by Speer is that even
insane or depraved orders 'because of their high authority . . .
were executed uncritically'. Not many officers, in any army,
would refuse an order radioed directly to them by the nation's
leader himself.

Of course leaders like Hitler and Stalin rarely gave morally
dubious orders directly to soldiers in the field. Nobody likes to get
their own hands dirty, if they can order someone else to do it; and,
after all, leaders have reputations to protect. Indeed, there remains
some question as to whether Adolf Hitler even knew about the
mass slaughter of the Holocaust. There is no documentational or
witness evidence that he did. So it is possible that his subordinates

---

1 Albert Speer, *Inside the Third Reich* (Chapter 35, page 520) (1970)

tried to protect him by giving him what is known in modern politics as 'plausible deniability'. The argument remains pointless, however, as Hitler himself deliberately created the national zeitgeist of fear and loathing that allowed the Final Solution to happen; and he would certainly have given the Holocaust his stamp of approval if he did indeed know about it.

Thanks to the chain of command, leaders can usually avoid direct intervention in morally dubious matters. Their orders are passed down and away from them, with each link in the chain thereafter feeling at least somewhat exonerated by the knowledge that 'they were just passing on orders'. And those who enact the order on the ground can comfort their consciences with the knowledge that many people above them must have sanctioned the action.

But that chain of command can also act as a brake on the more extreme, or insane, orders. Each person that the order is sent through – Speer's 'high-quality assistants' – might take moral authority on their own shoulders to destroy, misdirect or water down any questionable order given to them. And the very knowledge that maybe dozens of people will need to know about their decision, in order to simply pass it on, might give a leader pause. After all, every underling in the chain of command is also a witness. Even if he is egomaniac enough not to fear the chance of ever standing trial for his actions, a leader might still fear the judgement of history.

Consider the Wannsee Conference, held on 20 January 1942, where the Nazis' 'Final Solution to the Jewish question' ('*die Endlösung der Judenfrag*') was planned and set in motion. In fact the mass murder of the Holocaust had been running, unofficially and chaotically, for several years. But, over just a couple of hours, the attendees at the Wannsee Conference reorganised it, included the planned creation of purpose-made death camps, and gave it the official stamp of government policy.

Yet despite saying that they believed that history would glorify their decision – to exterminate all the Jews and the other 'undesirables' in German-occupied territory – the conference attendees were also there in strict secrecy. (A single transcript of the conference survived the war, but only because one of the attendees was himself sent to die in a concentration camp before he could destroy it.) Only one really senior Nazi was present: 'the Butcher of Prague' SS *Obergruppenführer* Reinhard Heydrich. All the other top Nazis circumspectly sent mere representatives to the conference.

At that time, in early 1942, the Axis powers were the most powerful military coalition on the planet, and were victorious on virtually every front. Yet the Nazi leadership clearly wanted to be able to claim that they had known nothing about the Final Solution, in case the unimaginable happened and they lost the war. And that, of course, is exactly what the surviving Nazi bosses did when they were captured: they pretended total ignorance of the Holocaust.

If, at the time of the Wannsee Conference, those Nazi leaders had been just a little more nervous about saving their own skins, the gas chambers at Auschwitz-Birkenau, Treblinka, Belzec, Sobibor, Lublin and Chelmno might never have been built, and millions of lives might have been saved.

So why do political leaders order their people to commit atrocities in the first place? Why do they restrict basic human rights; order the riot police to violently quell protestors; impose martial law; execute legitimate political opponents; declare unnecessary wars; and decide that genocide is the only way to solve a demographic problem?

The root of most of the wars and great atrocities in history can be traced back to the decisions of a few people – almost always leaders of one sort or another. One can argue about the forces of economics, demographics and history, or of the 'madness of crowds'; but somewhere in the move towards mass killing, there is usually a leader or leaders giving the go-ahead or leading the way. In his 1966 play *The Lion in Winter*, the writer James Goldman has Queen Eleanor of Aquitaine lament to her bickering, princeling children:

Oh, my piglets, we are the origins of war: not history's forces, nor the times, nor justice, nor the lack of it, nor causes, nor religions, nor ideas, nor kinds of government, nor any other thing. We are the killers. We breed wars. We carry it like syphilis inside. Dead bodies rot in field and stream because the living ones are rotten.

As we saw in Chapter 5, the seventeenth-century philosopher Thomas Hobbes believed that human conflict was motivated by three essential influences: aggression, anticipation and the need for prestige. In a leader who demands inhuman behaviour by their subordinates, all three motivations can easily be recognised.

Their aggressive tendencies are probably what made them a leader in the first place: defeating or subverting all opposition, then ruthlessly maintaining their position against all comers. Anticipation of trouble is also a key political skill, but can easily metastasise into the dangerous paranoia that seems to plague so many long-standing leaders – especially totalitarian dictators. And the constant need for prestige and public recognition could be said to be the essential character trait that puts many people into politics in the first place – if this wasn't so, then all politicians would be as anonymous as bureaucrats. Given that a typical leader might be particularly prone to the influence of Hobbes's three key motivators to bloodshed, then it's hardly surprising that many leaders seem to slip so easily into the ordering of unnecessary violence.

But for a less mechanistic explanation of the worst side of political leadership, we need to look to the work of a social theorist who wrote seventy years before Hobbes was born. A writer whose name, even today, is synonymous with cunning, treachery and the ruthless acquisition of power. Indeed, he is one of the only political philosophers to be specifically and regularly described as wicked, or even as downright evil.

Niccolo Machiavelli, born in 1469 CE, was at different times a military official, a general and an ambassador for the Republic of Florence – a rich northern Italian city-state that was at the heart of the Renaissance movement.

Italy, and all of Europe, had fallen into a dark age after the collapse of the Roman Empire; with culture, technology and learning grinding almost to a halt. It took a thousand years to crawl back to the stage where even a small proportion of the population had enough education just to read and write. And since very little had been written in the intervening period, what they read – especially in Italy – were the surviving books of the Greek and Roman classical writers. 'Renaissance' literally means rebirth or rediscovery; and the intellectual explosion caused by the resurrection of philosophical and scientific thinking in the thirteenth century took Europe from being a cultural backwater to the forefront of human creativity.

Italy might have been the birthplace of the Renaissance but it was also, at that time, one of the most chaotic countries on the planet. Split up into a number of petty dukedoms and kingdoms – constantly plagued by bickering internal wars, and by raiding invasions by stronger neighbours like France and the (German) Holy Roman Empire – Italy was a perfect example of what happens if aristocrats are given total power. The whole nation was a plaything for the over-privileged, the self-aggrandising and the incompetent. Machiavelli's native Republic of Florence was one of the better run Italian states, but even it was mostly ruled by a self-serving oligarchy of rich merchant families.

In 1494 Florence threw out the Medici family, who had controlled the supposed republic like a monarchy for the past sixty years. At different times between 1498 and 1512, Niccolo Machiavelli served as the organiser of the Florentine militia, as a victorious general, and as Florence's ambassador to the papacy. In the latter role he witnessed first hand the most controversial pope in history (to date): Alexander VI, known before his accession as Rodrigo Borgia.

The Borgia family were Spanish, and Pope Alexander was greatly resented by the other prelates ... who were almost all Italians. The Borgias were also ruthlessly ambitious, both for the Catholic Church and for themselves. Alexander dreamed of an earthly empire for the Church, a large proportion of which he intended to be governed by his three illegitimate sons.

Ambassador Machiavelli was particularly impressed by Pope

Alexander's eldest son, Cesare Borgia. Although initially earmarked by his father for a life in holy orders, Cesare became the first man in history to resign the post of cardinal. He then became the commander of the papal army, following the unsolved murder of the previous commander – Cesare's own brother, Giovanni. Few people at the time, or since, have doubted that Cesare either ordered the murder, or committed it himself. In many ways Cesare Borgia was the archetypal Renaissance aristocrat: devious, ruthless, ambitious, selfish and self-deluding. Niccolo Machiavelli took careful note of his career.

Pope Alexander VI has gone down in history as the most venal pontiff of all time, but this was partly because his story was written after his death by his enemies. Certainly he was deceitful, hypocritical and merciless to achieve his ends – but no more so than most of his political adversaries. Alexander died in 1503, aged seventy-two, of either malaria or poisoning. But this happened before he could cement the foundations of his religious pseudo-empire, so the Borgia clan fell from power.

In 1512 the Medici family re-conquered Florence, and set up as effective monarchs once again. Machiavelli was arrested and tortured after being accused of plotting against his new rulers. But he was eventually released and banished. Living on a provincial farm, and probably bored out of his mind, Machiavelli wrote a small book that was to shake Europe.

The Prince wasn't an unusual work in its presentation: many authors previous to Machiavelli had written what were known as 'mirrors to princes', that essentially told rulers how to rule. But all the previous duffer's guides to ultimate power had been written under the all-governing eye of the Catholic Church, and by the torturers of the Holy Inquisition. So they had invariably told rulers to be as Christian as possible – as Catholicism defined Christian ethics, that is. So, great wealth while others starved was fine, but due deference to the dignity of the Church was never to be forgotten. Rulers were also advised to be humble, peace-loving and meek; but Machiavelli clearly thought that this was dangerously idiotic rubbish.

In *The Prince*, he tells rulers to behave as they see fit at any one time, ignoring any dictates from outside the situation. This included Church doctrine and, if necessary, the pricking of their own consciences. Machiavelli didn't coin the axiom 'the end justifies the means'; but he might as well have done. The phrase is regularly misattributed to *The Prince*, and it neatly sums up his basic argument. The novelist Isaac Asimov also summed up the central idea of *The Prince* in a single sentence: 'Never let your sense of morals get in the way of doing what's right.'

For a statesman, Machiavelli insisted, catastrophe and failure was always near. Rivals for power, war, and rebellion were a constant threat. As such, he advises princes to appear virtuous but, behind the scenes, to do whatever was needed to get the job done.

It is best to seem merciful, faithful, humane, religious, and upright, and also to actually be those things; but the mind should remain so balanced that if it becomes necessary not to be [merciful, faithful, humane, religious, and upright] *you should be able and know how to act in a contrary way.*[2]

If the kind, decent and laudable course was obviously the best way, then certainly a leader should take it; but such niceties rarely won the day, in Machiavelli's considerable experience. Murder, treachery, lies and any other immoral action were all fair game, Machiavelli said, provided the necessity of the situation demanded it. If an immoral prince won in the end, who would dare question his methods of winning?

War, Machiavelli maintained, was an integral part of human life, and couldn't be avoided. A prince who tried to always be peaceful would soon be defeated by those who embraced this brutal truth. Thus war and conquest were an essential part of a prince's duties. It would be nice if such wars could serve a greater purpose – such as the political reunification of Italy, which was very dear to Machiavelli's heart – but conflict would happen anyway, for good or evil reasons.

---

2 Niccolo Machiavelli, *The Prince* (Chapter 18)

Machiavelli's overall view of humankind seemed particularly bleak. A prince must do evil, he said, because the people that he or she sought to rule were generally evil. But here, again, he was simply being practical. Advice to a prince ruling a happy, contented people would be largely redundant. Such advice would only be needed when dealing with an unhappy, resentful people – as such people were themselves willing to do evil, out of their own anger. He also noted that people were generally unhappy with their lot, as it is human nature to always target some further goal the moment that they achieve anything – and to blame their leaders if they can't immediately get what they want.

If this seems elitist, then it should also be noted that Machiavelli thought that the only group who were more malevolent and downright dangerous than the ordinary people were a prince's fellow rulers. He makes no bones that the leaders of men are generally untrustworthy, selfish and foolish. Most leaders in history had done a barely adequate job, he said, and often left their nations worse off than when they started. But such weak competition, he added, only allowed more scope for a sensible, well-advised prince to succeed.

In his advice on how best to deal with malcontents, Machiavelli said that 'people must either be flattered, or eliminated'. By this he meant that potential friends must be shamelessly buttered up, but enemies had to be ruthlessly crushed. If a prince did a minor injustice, the victims would always seek revenge. But if the same prince in the same situation was spectacularly cruel, his victims would either be too cowed to even think of striking back, or they would be safely dead.

Machiavelli believed that deliberate brutality and cruelty were key skills for a prince. This was despite having been tortured himself. (He was strappadoed, which involved tying his hands behind his back, then tying a rope around his wrists and winching it towards the ceiling. This agonisingly dislocated both shoulders. Weights were then strapped to the victim's feet, to increase their pain. A victim could be left hanging for hours, with little risk of actually killing them.) Machiavelli had even written a moving poem that described hearing the cries of others being tortured while he languished in his jail cell. Yet he insisted that a political leader should be as bestial and rapacious as a lion, when the situation called for it. And, equally, a ruler needed to be a fox: using subtlety and deception to get what they wanted. An ideal ruler could seamlessly combine both cunning and savagery; while giving full deference, publically, to the Christian moral codes that he or she was violating.

He gives many examples in the text, but there is one that stands out, as it concerns a personal acquaintance of Machiavelli's: Cesare Borgia. Through the political machinations of his father, the pope, Cesare became ruler of a region of Italy called the Romagna. Unfortunately the local population were less than thrilled by the change of ruler, and a rebellion threatened.

Cesare's answer was to appoint a notoriously cruel and ruthless man, Remirro de Orco, as governor of the region. De Orco was given *carte blanche* to crush the malcontents, and Borgia himself then left the region. After de Orco had smashed all resistance, with appalling acts of cruelty, Cesare Borgia returned. He ostentatiously condemned what had happened in his absence, and had de Orco cut in half in the town square of Cesena.

Machiavelli notes approvingly that the Romagna was peaceful thereafter, and the people regarded Cesare as a hero. Innocent people (including arguably de Orco himself) had certainly suffered and died as a result of Cesare's cunning plan. But not as many as would have suffered if there had been a rebellion or a civil war in the region. The end justified the means used to achieve it.

Indeed, Cesare Borgia might have hung on to power, as Count of the Romagna, even after the sudden death of his father, Pope Alexander VI. But, Machiavelli adds ruefully, Cesare made the mistake of trusting the newly appointed pontiff. Borgia was betrayed, impoverished, exiled and, in 1507, died of his wounds while acting as a mercenary general in Spain.

Machiavelli saw Cesare Borgia as an ideal prince – both cruel as a lion and clever as a fox – but generally able to maintain a public image of Catholic decency. (No one could ever prove, for example, that he murdered his brother and slept with his sister.) His fatal failing, in Machiavelli's eyes, was that of being virtuously over-trusting, when he should have guessed that the new pope would seek to destroy him.

Machiavelli's original manuscript of *The Prince* was dedicated to and sent to the Medici family – the very people who had conquered his beloved republic, and who had had him imprisoned, tortured and exiled. True to his pragmatic philosophy, Machiavelli was willing to ignore such evils to get what he wanted: access to power and riches. (With uncharacteristic heavy-handedness, Machiavelli advises that a prince should reward good advisors with wealth, honour and power.)

Yet there is no evidence that the ungrateful recipients ever read the book during Machiavelli's lifetime, and the Medici family certainly ignored his offer to return from banishment to work for them as a political adviser. The book was published for the general public in 1532, five years after Machiavelli's death. It was immediately banned by the Catholic Church, and became an underground sensation across Europe. People read bootleg copies with avid shame, as if it were pornography; and powerful men like Henry VIII's chancellor, Thomas Cromwell, carried the book about with them at all times, like priests carrying Bibles.

But it would be a mistake to say *The Prince* was ever popular. Its ruthless cynicism has seen it condemned by numerous public figures for the past half-millennium. Its suggestion that ethics and politics should be kept separate, and not be intermixed in policy, has seen the book attacked by every type of idealist and ideologue – from Marxists to Nazis; from liberal philosophers like Bertrand Russell – who called it 'a handbook for gangsters' – to religious fundamentalists of every shade. (An English pseudonym for Satan, 'Old Nick', is supposed to come from Machiavelli's first name.) Leo Strauss, the godfather of the modern American neo-conservative movement, flatly called Machiavelli 'a teacher of evil'.

Yet even Strauss admitted that Machiavelli himself was essentially a good man. He certainly didn't deny the human value of decency and virtue. Indeed, Machiavelli was one of the original humanists: a philosophy that puts the value of human life and reason ahead of any religious or political dogma.

Machiavelli's other works – and some of the less diplomatic sections of *The Prince* – make it plain that he was always a republican and a proto-democrat. He held that nations run by the people are generally superior, in organisation and general happiness, to those run by a monarch. Machiavelli just couldn't see how a planet of democratic republics could ever come about. And given the world that he knew – of power-mad churchmen, decadent aristocrats and a public that were almost all illiterate, parochial and chauvinistic – he was arguably just being pragmatic.

Practicality was the key element of Machiavelli's argument in *The Prince*. What good are inflexible morals, he says, if they were only likely to make the situation worse? For him the facts of a situation were all that mattered; ethereal ideas were given no room in his political analyses. His refusal to be swayed by unveri-fiable theology, or by purely ethical philosophy, has led to Machiavelli being numbered – along with Nicolaus Copernicus and Leonardo da Vinci – as a forefather of the modern scientific principle. (It should be noted that all three men were contem-poraries, and that Machiavelli and Da Vinci might have actually known each other – both being prominent Florentines.)

The inconsistency between Machiavelli's humane personal views, and the cynicism that he expresses in *The Prince*, suggests that he was actually writing a secret satire: a lampoon of the hypocrisy and immorality that he had witnessed in the rulers and churchmen of the Italian Renaissance states.

Antonio Gramsci, the twentieth-century Italian Marxist philosopher, believed that Machiavelli must have known that the Medici clan would probably spurn his book – after all, it told them what they already knew and self-evidently practised in their pursuit and use of political power. Indeed, the evidence of history seems to show that the entire ruling class of the Renaissance world was habitually educated to utilise Machiavellian-style ruth-less hypocrisy from birth. They had to be 'lions and foxes', because that was the only way to survive. Yet Machiavelli also made sure that his friends would publish and distribute the book after his death, thereby making its explosive revelations available to the non-princes of the world – when he himself was safe from the torturers of the Holy Inquisition.

Seen in this light, *The Prince* becomes a satire much like Jonathan Swift's 1729 essay: 'A Modest Proposal for Preventing the Children of Poor People From Being a Burthen to Their Parents or Country, and for Making Them Beneficial to the Publick'. Swift's 'proposal' was that the poor (especially in Ireland) should be made to eat their own children. Presented as a straight-faced answer to the population and poverty problems, the Modest Proposal caused furious anger in those who failed to understand that it was a black joke. Of course what Swift, an Irishman himself, was indirectly highlighting was the fact that poverty and social inequality were killing legions of poor children every year. Those who became angry over his suggestion of enforced cannibalism had to then face the fact that they themselves were doing nothing about such deaths.

Machiavelli may indeed have had a satiric sense of humour, much like that of Jonathan Swift. In a letter to a friend, he suggested that wicked priests were more theologically informative than righteous churchmen because:

I believe that the following would be the true way to go to Heaven: learn the way to Hell in order to steer clear of it.

So what does *The Prince* tell us, the common people, about our own rulers? Its systematic analysis essentially shows us that they have to be pragmatic, or they will fall from power very quickly. The wars, rebellions and assassination attempts of Renaissance Europe may seem a long way from the political life in most modern democracies; yet are battling for votes, party disunity and leadership challenges so very different? And in the case of modern dictatorships – or even of democratic leaders in times of national emergency – the similarities with Machiavelli's ruthless Renaissance princes become even more compelling.

A driving force of any political career is the necessity of the moment. Harold Macmillan, the British prime minister at the time of the Cuban Missile Crisis, was once asked what he feared most. He replied laconically: 'Events, dear boy. Events.' Read any leader's memoirs, and you will be given the impression that they spent much of their career lurching from one crisis to another. If many of those crises were – in hindsight – self-created, illusory or entirely meaningless to anyone outside the incestuous world of political infighting, that did not reduce the feeling of threat to those involved.

A sense of constant impending calamity hangs over those who hold significant political power. As noted at the beginning of this chapter, they may feel cut off from the everyday, non-political world by both their position and by the possible untrustworthiness of those around them. They probably resent the ungratefulness of those not in power who, nevertheless, complain and criticise endlessly. In multi-party democracies there is the deliberate and in-built threat of the opposition parties, who are seeking to defeat them at every turn. And for the dictator, there is the relatively high possibility that too many policy mistakes might end their career in front of a firing squad.

Of course most politicians thrive on this sort of life – most of the time – or they wouldn't do it. Many leaders claim to love the sham-violence of the 'cut and thrust' of political life. But it would be a rare human being who could take this sort of emotional attrition, for years or decades, and not show some negative effects.

One of the worst of these, which has been the cause of innumerable atrocities over the centuries, is the obsession that only they – the leader – can choose the correct course of action. Of course this is, to a large extent, exactly what leadership is: possession of this self-certainty is often why we, the people, delegate our authority to them in the first place. But the combination of power, isolation and the endless pressure of 'events' occasionally leads to disastrous decisions. And if the leader in question feels that they can't afford to show weakness or uncertainty, they might feel that they have to continue the policy, even when it has shown itself to be catastrophic.

Of course, the 'leader' in question might be a group of people. Perhaps a 'cabinet decision' of ministers; such as brought about the US/UK invasion of Iraq in 2003. Or maybe a succession of individual leaders; like the three US presidents who presided over America's involvement in the Vietnam War in the 1960s and early 1970s. By no means were all their decisions disastrous, in either of the above examples. And their overall intentions were almost certainly benign and humane. (As the comedian Spike Milligan once noted: 'Even Hitler meant well.') Yet history has increasingly come to see their general policy as being disastrous, both for those killed and maimed on both sides, and ultimately for the cause that their leadership was aiming to support.

Consider another example: it was the British Empire that invented concentration camps, during the Second Boer War, fought in South Africa between 1899 and 1902. The policy was originally aimed at controlling a thinly spread and rebellious population in a vast and hostile landscape. Burning farms and relocating all captured civilians – Boer and black – to centralised camps seemed a clever and fairly humane way to douse the insurrection. But it was mainly the non-combatant women and children who were interned – as the men took to the hills with their rifles – and the camps themselves were incompetently run and supplied. So the guerrilla war continued unabated, and twenty-six thousand people died of starvation and disease in the concentration camps.

The British government weathered the shock and anger when news of the concentration camp disaster was spread around the world by the press – to the extent that they continued the merciless and inept policy to the end of the war. But the long-term damage that the camps did to the image of the British Empire was incalculable. Enemies made much of British inhumanity; allies felt sickened and disillusioned; and the 'subject races' of the empire wondered if the British might be as ruthless to them, if they ever tried to secede. The Boer War concentration camp policy did much to hasten the British Empire's eventual collapse.

A key phrase in Machiavelli's *The Prince* is:

That war is just which is necessary.[3]

Whether he genuinely believed this; or he was writing what he thought the Medici wanted to hear; or he was lampooning their petty self-justifications; Machiavelli was here putting his finger on an essential element of leadership thinking: the unswerving belief that whatever they are doing is absolutely necessary. So, one of the most common excuses given by any leader is: 'It was a tough decision, but I felt I had no other choice.'

Think of Galileo Galilei: dragged before the Inquisition in 1633 to be 'shown the instruments of torture'. This frightened him into recanting his research that proved that the Earth was not the centre of the universe, but in fact orbited the Sun. The leaders of the Catholic Church were quite aware (unofficially) that Galileo was right; but his heliocentric explanation of the movement of the planets was an inconvenient truth for them. By showing that both the Bible and the Church's teachings were incorrect in matters of astronomy, he undermined their authority, just when they needed all the kudos that they could muster.

This was right in the middle of Catholic Europe's brutal Thirty Years' War to crush, or at least contain, Protestantism; plus a social and economic revolution that saw the educated merchant class rising to challenge the power of the noble ruling class. The authority, power and income of the Church rested on the established order of things, and that was shaking. Pope Urban VIII and the cardinals who bullied Galileo into recanting did an evil – as they saw it – in order to defend against greater evils.

But Protestantism was not defeated and the nobles continued to lose their power to the merchants – the collapse of feudalism under the growth of capitalism. The Church's gamble – to sacrifice the truth in order to hold their position as the final arbiters of reality in Catholic lands – failed. Today the Church has suffered almost four hundred years of ridicule for its decision to ruthlessly and hypocritically stifle scientific research. Before Galileo's recantation the Church was seen as a friend and patron

---

3 Niccolo Machiavelli, *The Prince* (Chapter 26)

of science; and, if it had reformed its dogmatism and embraced the new learning, that might have continued. But it didn't, and religion and science have been seen to be on increasingly divergent paths ever since.

Of course leaders who make hard decisions – like the unhappy Urban VIII – almost always mean well, and feel the hand of necessity forcing them to it. But the decision to deliberately order something monstrous – to, say, cover up the truth, to conquer another country, to order troops to fire on unarmed protestors, or to attempt to murder a whole ethnic group – is always going to be questioned by future generations. And generally they will decide that monstrosity, by its very nature, is unnecessary and unjust.

Part 2

Living with Killers

Colin Wilson

As I mentioned at the beginning of this book, my father, Colin Wilson, originally began work on this project several months before suffering a debilitating stroke in 2012. The following chapters were actually meant to be the beginning of an autobiographical study of his own interest in criminology. Naturally my completion of such a book, after his stroke, was impossible; not least because my father always wrote 'off the top of his head'. When working on a non-fiction project he would exhaustively read other people's books as research; then he would write out his own ideas with no preparatory notes.

So I wrote the chapters that you presumably have just read, aiming to create a sort of background setting into which my father's last original writing can be presented. Up until now the reader will have noticed that I have said little or nothing about crime as it is usually defined – that is, the careers of criminals. That's because Dad will now cover that subject in proper depth. He was fascinated by 'the problem of human criminality' for at least seven of his eight decades of life. I personally think that few, if anyone, can attack that problem with his depth of understanding. Certainly I can't.

Nevertheless, fans of my father's vast field of work will no doubt spot the odd parts in the following pages that don't sound like him. That's because I found these chapters as a working draft. Dad edited himself as he wrote, but here he was clearly planning to further expand each of these chapters when he had done some further thinking. Mostly I have just done basic copy-editing and tidying on these chapters. But here and there I have extended a point that seemed unfinished. All I can hope is that I've done so along the lines that he had planned.

Damon Wilson, January 2015

Chapter 19

Three Killers of Rotting Hill

If I write about a hill that is rotting it is because I deplore rot.
For the decay of which I write is not romantic decay . . . [1]

I moved to Notting Hill, west London, in the freezing winter of
1955; I was twenty-three at the time and had recently separated
from my wife – not because we had disagreements, but because
it was virtually impossible for a couple with a child (we had a son)
to find anywhere to live at a reasonable rent.

Gradually, the separation lengthened – as such separations
tend to – as it became clear to both of us that the marriage had
been a mistake. When it finally fell apart, I was working in a
coffee house near Trafalgar Square, on a wage so low that it
would certainly not have supported three of us. I decided it was
time to look for a room at a lower rent.

I had been living in a basement off Baker Street, but that cost
£2–10 shillings a week, (i.e. £36 in today's money) which was too
much. I was working on my first book, a study in literary 'outsiders',
and a publisher had agreed to pay me an advance of £25. Someone
suggested to me that rooms would be cheaper if I went further
west. So I took the Underground to Notting Hill Gate, and looked
at the advertisements in those glass-covered boards outside shops.
Many had been placed by prostitutes and said things like: 'Doris
and Judy, erection and demolition experts', or 'Mandy: ex-public
school girl, enjoys teaching the meaning of discipline'.

---

1 Wyndham Lewis, *Rotting Hill* (1951)

Then I noticed an advertisement for a room at £2 a week, which was closer to what I wanted to pay. When I rang, a woman with a pleasant upper-class voice explained that the house was virtually derelict, and that if I would agree to help with the repair and decoration I could have a bare room for thirty shillings a week. Naturally I agreed, and within ten minutes was standing outside a large but unprepossessing house with grimy windows and paint peeling off the front door.

My landlady proved to be a bohemian type with a wealthy mother who disapproved of her daughter's vagabond tendencies, but was willing to offer support to the extent of giving her a house and leaving her to find her own way to ruin. It was Chepstow Villas, and an earlier tenant had been the recently deceased Dylan Thomas. What Anne (her name was Anne Nichols) had to offer me at thirty shillings was an empty bathroom with an unconnected lavatory and bath, on whose bare floorboards I slept in a sleeping bag.

For me, Notting Hill was a descent down the social scale from Baker Street. Sherlock Holmes and Dr Watson had chosen Baker Street for its cheapness, according to Arthur Conan Doyle, but that was more than half a century before my time. Notting Hill had become the twentieth-century equivalent of Baker Street – that is, cheap and cheerless. This was some years before the advent of the now-famous Notting Hill Carnival. This annual celebration was instigated by arriving incomers from the Caribbean, who were also attracted by the low rents and by bohemian landlords who, unlike much of the rest of 1950s London, didn't hang up signs that said 'No Blacks'.

For non-Londoners the area's main association was with G. K. Chesterton's political satire novel, *The Napoleon of Notting Hill*; Chesterton's joke being that nobody could believe that anything world-shaking would ever come out of such a rundown backwater of a district. Although I was unaware of it at the time, it had another literary association: the painter and novelist Wyndham Lewis, who had lived there much of his life and would die there in 1957; his feelings about the place may be gauged from the title of his 1951 book *Rotting Hill*.

Not far from Chepstow Villas was the site of a notorious sex murder. The killer was a ruggedly handsome, thirty-year-old ex-RAF officer and con-man named Neville Heath, who was also a sadist. On the night of Thursday 20 June, 1946, he let himself and Margery Gardner into the room at the Pembridge Court Hotel, and knew he could simply release of all his sadistic impulses. His senior by two years, Margery was known to be a masochist who liked to be beaten. She lay passively as he tied her ankles and wrists, although she may have felt some misgivings as he tied a gag in her mouth. Then the sheer force of the first blows must have told her this was too savage to be consensual. After a frenzy of beating, he rammed a poker into her vagina and twisted it in an attempt to lacerate her. Then he tried to bite off her nipples. Margery suffocated to death while this was going on; perhaps accidentally from the over-tight gag. Shortly after that Heath left the hotel, slamming the door behind him.

The killing had probably been the climax of a lifetime of sadistic fantasies. Yet the fact that Heath simply left Margery to be found, in a place where his identity could easily be linked to the murder, strongly suggests that this was the first time he had killed anyone. A practised sex killer would have taken more care to cover his tracks. If he had planned the murder beforehand, Heath would almost certainly not have chosen a virtually public place to kill Margery. So it is likely that he himself did not know he was going to kill her, until he lost control during the flogging.

Indeed, Heath's conduct earlier the same week makes it almost certain that he wasn't plotting a sadistic homicide. On Saturday 15 June, five days before the murder, he went to a dance in Chelsea, where he met a girl named Yvonne Symonds, who was a virgin. The next day, Heath having promised marriage, she agreed to go and spend the night with him at the Pembridge Court Hotel, and she lost her virginity in the same room where, three days later, he killed Margery Gardner. He treated her, she agreed, 'perfectly courteously and decently'. She returned to her parents' home in Worthing, where Heath kept in touch with her by phone.

On Friday, the day after the murder, he went to Worthing

and took her to lunch. He met her parents and was introduced
as her fiancé. But when he saw her the next day he admitted
that he was having problems with the law. These were not
serious, he assured her. He had lent the key of his room at the
Pembridge Court to a man who wanted somewhere to sleep
with his girlfriend. It was this man, he insisted, who had
committed the murder.

Heath now moved on to Bournemouth, where on Sunday 23
June he booked a room under the name of Group Captain
Rupert Brooke. And for the next few days, while police all over
the country were looking for the killer of Margery Gardner, idled
pleasantly around Bournemouth, went to the golf club and the
Pavilion, where dances were held, and became acquainted with
a girl called Peggy. On the afternoon of Wednesday 3 June, he
met Peggy by chance, in the company of a shy nineteen-year-old
named Doreen Marshall. When Peggy left, he invited Doreen to
dinner and she accepted. She was staying at the Norfolk Hotel
– she had been in Bournemouth recovering from a severe bout
of influenza.

After a good dinner, which included champagne and liqueurs,
Doreen said it was time she went home and asked the waiter to
call for a taxi. Heath cancelled it and said he would walk her
home, but it was obvious she was not happy with this idea. Other
guests noticed that she looked tense and nervous. Both left the
hotel at fifteen minutes past midnight, Heath remarking that he
would be back in half an hour. Doreen added firmly: 'A quarter
of an hour.' This was the last time she was seen alive.

Wondering what had happened to Heath, the porter (with
whom he had become very friendly) checked on his bedroom
around 4 a.m. and found him fast asleep. Heath told the porter
later that he had entered his room up a builder's ladder that he
had found outside his window 'as a joke'.

On Saturday morning, the manager of the Norfolk Hotel
rang his opposite number at the Tollard Royal to ask if he
could shed any light on the non-return of Miss Marshall, who
had left all her belongings in her locked room. The manager of
the Tollard Royal in turn asked Heath about the young lady he

had dined with the previous Wednesday. Heath lied: 'Oh, I've known that lady for years.' But he offered no explanation for her odd disappearance.

Neville Heath then rang the local police station and offered to assist in finding the missing girl, asking if her photograph was available. When told there should be one later, he offered to call at the police station at 5.30 p.m. When he arrived there, Doreen Marshall's family were present – her father, mother and sister, the latter bearing such a distinct likeness to Doreen that it must have given Heath a bad shock.

A detective named Souter was struck by the resemblance between 'Group Captain Brooke' and the suspect pictured in the *Police Gazette*, wanted in connection with the Margery Gardner killing. When asked if he was Heath, 'Brooke' made his big mistake and said smoothly that several people had commented on the resemblance – an impossibility since no such photograph had appeared in the daily press. (The *Police Gazette* is a news magazine that is distributed to the British constabulary, but is not available to the public). Detective Souter immediately said: 'I am nevertheless detaining you for further questioning.' Heath shrugged indifferently and replied 'Oh all right.'

So by Saturday evening Heath was in custody, but still nobody knew what had become of Doreen. That Sunday a young waitress walking her dog noticed a cloud of buzzing flies over bushes in Branksome Dene Chine (a chine being a narrow valley). They were still there the next day, and when she sat down to eat with her parents she mentioned this. Since it was still daylight, she and her father walked to the spot, and he noticed that someone had cut off branches and piled them to form a screen near the bush with the buzzing flies. Behind this he found a body covered in clothes.

The corpse was naked except for one shoe: a black dress and yellow 'swagger' coat were thrown over the remains and pearl beads from a necklace were strewn everywhere. One stocking was found 21 feet away, hanging 7 feet from the ground. There were indications that the girl had been gagged and her wrists bound (a knotted handkerchief, blood and earth-stained, had been found in Heath's room at the Tollard Royal Hotel a day before the body's discovery). It is thought the murderer stripped naked, since none of his clothes bore signs of blood. Death was caused by the cutting of the throat above the larynx. There were also major mutilations to her body, but these had been inflicted after death.

With the forensic evidence, we can partly reconstruct what happened on the night of the murder. When they left the hotel, Heath turned the wrong way – the town centre and Doreen's hotel lay to the left, but he led her to the right. She appears not to have noticed. Soon they had left the hotel behind them and were walking into the darkness. They walked on for about a mile.

We are not sure what happened next – whether she noticed it and refused to go further, or asked where they were going. All we know is that he must have grabbed her by the throat to stop her crying out, then went on throttling until she passed out. He tied her wrists together with a handkerchief, then began to take off her clothes, flinging them away, at which point the stocking caught on a branch. He tore her panties in his haste to remove them. Then he undressed himself.

Once he was naked he could take the knife out of his pocket and stab her in the throat without danger of soiling his clothes. She struggled and it infuriated him, and he slashed her throat a second time – so deeply it almost severed the spinal cord. Now he was carried away by his frenzy, as he had been with Margery Gardner. He attacked Doreen's corpse with the knife, slashing the breasts, thighs and stomach, and slicing into the vagina and anus. He also bit off a nipple.

Now bloody all over, Heath made his way to the sea and washed himself. But he had not forgotten to remove her wrist watch, which he sold the next day for £3; the jeweller later identified him as the man who had pawned it.

The sheer extent of Doreen's injuries makes us aware of a basic puzzle: how can Heath have hoped to escape the hangman? Or did he? Had he come to accept that the killing of Margery Gardner was the end of the road, and that he may as well accept that his life was over?

His defence barrister, J. D. Caswell, would do his best to convince the jury that Heath was 'morally insane'; that he *had* been aware of what he was doing during the murders, but not that it was wrong. A similar defence is automatically applied to young children who commit major crimes – Caswell was essentially claiming that Heath had the moral development of a child, but the body and mind of an adult. In fact there is some reason, given the details of the case and of Heath's con-man life, to agree with Caswell's defence: Neville Heath might have been what we would now call a sociopath. However, Heath himself took trouble to undermine this argument in his evidence to the court, and the jury chose to ignore it as a mitigating circumstance.

Caswell was a brilliant lawyer, and might have saved his client from the noose, but Heath apparently didn't care if he lived or died. When Caswell had originally asked him how he intended to plead, Heath originally said 'guilty'. When Caswell asked if he was sure, Heath replied casually: 'Alright. Put me down as "not guilty", old boy.'

In the 1960s I knew an attractive woman named Heather Bradley who was a London editor on the *New York Times*, and she had met Heath on a number of occasions, before the murder of Margery Gardiner. Her theory about him was that his sadism arose from sexual boredom. He was so good-looking and charming, she said, that if he went into a party full of attractive women, he knew that he could have virtually anyone he wanted. His sadism, she thought, grew out of satiety.

I was dubious about this theory. If you are wealthy enough to eat any food you like, satiety does not tempt you to eat more and more highly flavoured or spiced dishes. My own view at the time was that confidence swindlers like Heath turn into actors whose lives are spent playing someone else, until all sense of sincerity is lost. Heath had been caught out so often and punished so often – cashiered from the army three times, no less – that when his final fling of murderous confidence trickery was found out, he was ready to give up. There was nowhere else to go.

There is another point that helps to throw some light on the murder. Doreen Marshall was not his type. Although pretty, she lacked self-assurance. He preferred self-assured girls with a certain sophistication, like Margery Gardner and Yvonne Symonds. Doreen was so shy she was almost tongue-tied. During an afternoon and evening when he pulled out all the stops in his seductive armoury, she was as reserved as ever. As they left the hotel, he could see that his chances of spending the night with her were as remote as ever. With the death of Margery fresh in his mind – and the growing certainty that he himself would soon be caught and hanged – Heath may have killed Doreen out of a combination of injured pride, sadistic frustration and the near-suicidal *ennui* that seems to have characterised his final days.

The evidence at his trial was overwhelming, and Neville Heath was hanged at Pentonville Prison on 16 October 1946. Offered the traditional shot of scotch by the prison governor, just before he was led to the gallows, Heath said: 'While you're about it, sir, you might make that a double.'

John Reginald Halliday Christie, 'the Nottting Hill Strangler', raped and choked women in a slum cul-de-sac called 10 Rillington Place. Christie was what used to be called a sex maniac. A sexually obsessed ex-policeman, his technique was to persuade women that he had invented the ideal cold-cure, which consisted of relaxing in a deck chair and breathing the steam from a strong decongestant with their heads inside a cloth bag, which Christie had attached to the gas outlet. When this induced unconsciousness he raped them, strangled them, then concealed the bodies inside a deep cupboard in the kitchen. Eventually, the cupboard being full, he solved the problem by moving out and leaving the next tenant to find his rotting leftovers.

Over nine years, between September 1943 and March 1953, Christie murdered at least six women and (by his own admission) a baby. The first victim was an attractive Austrian student nurse named Ruth Fuerst, who had been seventeen when she came to England just before the outbreak of war in 1939. She stayed on as a munitions worker, living in a single room not far from 10 Rillington Place. She was tall and pretty, with a shapely mouth, and may have supplemented her low income with occasional work as a prostitute. Christie met Ruth in a snack bar in

1943. After a life as a petty crook, he had enrolled in the War Reserve Police in 1939, at the age of forty, and came to know Ruth on his beat.

In August 1943, Christie's wife Ethel went to Sheffield to visit relatives, and he took the opportunity to invite the twenty-one-year-old Ruth Fuerst over to 10 Rillington Place. In his account of the murder that followed, Christie claimed they went to the front bedroom for sex, and that while this was happening he impulsively strangled her with a piece of rope. This is undoubtedly at least partly untrue. Christie knew he would be incapable of sex unless he killed Ruth first. So he strangled her, then he raped her dead body.

He was interrupted by a ring at the doorbell; it was a telegraph boy with a message saying his wife would be home early. Christie had to move the body quickly. He took it to the front sitting room and placed it in a space under the floorboards. Soon afterwards Ethel arrived with her brother Henry, who planned to stay overnight.

The next day, Henry left to take an early train back to Sheffield, and Ethel went off to her part-time job at the Osram light-bulb factory. Christie lost no time transferring the naked body to the wash house in the back garden, then he began digging her grave. That evening, he went to the wash house, and moved the body to the grave and covered it over. He burned Ruth's clothes in an old dustbin he used for burning garden rubbish.

Why did Christie commit this 'bestial and revolting crime'? asked Ludovic Kennedy in the best-selling account of the case: *Ten Rillington Place*. The answer is: because he was a sex maniac. Sex had been his lifelong obsession and frustration. The very thought of a naked girl threw him into a kind of fever. It was so powerful it made him impotent. This is why he had once been known as 'Reggie No-Dick' and 'Can't-do-it Christie'. The sheer force of the desire created a paralysing self-consciousness.

Yet he was not totally impotent – he could often perform with prostitutes, the anonymity of paid sex somehow overcoming his debilitating nervousness. But with women he knew – including his long-suffering wife Ethel – he was almost incapable of maintaining an erection. But again there was a telling exception – Reg Christie had no problem with sex, provided the woman he was with was fully unconscious . . . or dead.

At the end of 1943 Christie decided to leave the police force. He found himself a job with Ultra Radio, in the suburb of Acton. In the canteen there he met a girl from the assembly department called Muriel Amelia Eady. Unlike Ruth Fuerst, she was not pretty, and was inclined to plumpness. She was thirty-one and had a regular boyfriend. Christie invited her and her boyfriend to tea at Rillington Place. This happened several times, and both couples even went to the pictures together.

The fact that she was not pretty did not bother Christie; if anything, her ordinariness made the thought of taking off her clothes more exciting. And when she mentioned she suffered from chronic catarrh, the solution broke on him like a revelation: carbon monoxide.

In late September Ethel told him she wanted to go to Sheffield for a holiday. Now the plan took shape. The essential element lay in an inhalant named Friars' Balsam. Added to hot water it gave off a steam that smelled of angelica, a medicinal smell which would cloak the smell of coal gas. Mixed with carbon monoxide it should induce unconsciousness in about a minute.

So when Muriel came to call 'on invitation' in early October she was easily persuaded to sit in the deck chair with a cloth over her head as hot water was added to the Friars' Balsam in a square glass jar. Then the gas tap was connected up. Soon she was slumped in the chair. No doubt Christie took his time undressing both her and himself. He had waited for this all his life: to have an unconscious woman at his mercy; so there was no hurry.

After that he carried out the second part of the plan: to make sure she stayed unconscious, he moved her to the bedroom and strangled her to death. He later admitted entering her vagina as he strangled her. Afterwards, he said: 'Once again I experienced that quiet peaceful thrill. I had no regrets.' And by the time her disappearance was reported to the police, she was lying beside Ruth Fuerst, under the earth of the garden.

It was probably the most sexually satisfying experience of

Christie's life – killing Ruth Fuerst had been too much of a struggle, and he had been interrupted by the telegram boy. It was inevitable that, the sexually obsessed necrophile that he was, Christie should think about again achieving the 'quiet peaceful thrill' of killing for pleasure. We know he approached two more women at work to try his catarrh cure, but neither of them actually arrived as promised.

Life at 10 Rillington Place continued as usual for another five years until Easter 1948, when a young couple came to live in the upstairs flat. They were called Timothy and Beryl Evans. Their arrival would eventually lead to one of the most notorious apparent miscarriages of British justice of the twentieth century.

The Evanses were not a happy pair. Tim Evans was illiterate and mentally subnormal, with the IQ of a boy of eleven. Born at Merthyr Vale in South Wales, he was physically undersized and a born fantasist who lied for sheer pleasure, claiming that his father was an Italian count and that his brother owned a fleet of motor cars. He met Beryl, a pretty telephonist who was five years his junior, when he was twenty-three. They married in 1947, while he was working on a low wage as a van driver. In the following year they had their first baby, Geraldine, and they moved into 10 Rillington Place.

By then the strains of the marriage had begun to show. They were in debt for their hire-purchase furniture, and Beryl was a totally inadequate housekeeper who often left a sink-full of dishes for days. When she realised she was pregnant again, there was dismay and Evans reacted by drinking. He had a violent temper, and sometimes attacked Beryl physically. On one occasion she threw a jar at his head, and he had to go to his mother's to get the wound dressed.

On 2 December, 1948, Tim Evans walked into the police station in Merthyr Tidfil and voluntarily confessed to the accidental death of Beryl Evans at 10 Rillington Place. He said that he had given her something in a bottle to abort her pregnancy, but she had died. So he pushed her body down the drain outside the house. His story was checked by the Notting Hill police, who found nothing down the drain (it took three men to open the

manhole cover). After a further search they did find the dead
bodies of both Beryl and baby Geraldine in the outdoor wash
house of 10 Rillington Place . . . although they failed to notice a
human thigh bone being used to prop up the fence in the garden.
Both victims had been strangled to death about a month before.
The Christies were interviewed, of course, but said that they
knew nothing.

In the meantime Evans had changed his story. He now claimed
that it was Reg Christie who had accidentally killed Beryl during
an attempted abortion. He said nothing about the dead baby,
and was evidently shocked when he was asked who had killed
her. Indeed he was so shocked that he again changed his story,
reverting to his claim that it was he who had killed Beryl and the
baby. Evans's confession to the police was that he and Beryl had
argued, and that he hit her across the face with his flat hand. She
slapped back. The argument continued until he grabbed a piece
of rope which he had 'brought home in his van' and strangled her
with it. He had hidden her body and, two days later, he had
strangled the baby as well.

It is here that the controversy begins. Tim Evans's confession
is now widely believed to have been dictated not by him, but by
the arresting officers. Certainly it doesn't read as the words of a
man who, under the best of circumstances, could barely string a
sentence together. Certainly Evans later retracted the confession, but by then it was too late.

Ludovic Kennedy, in his book *Ten Rillington Place* (1961),
insisted that Evans was totally guiltless of both murders. He
reconstructed the death of Beryl as follows. Reg Christie offered
to induce a termination. Since she was already thinking along
these lines, she agreed immediately. Christie then approached
Evans when he returned from work. Evans was doubtful until
Christie assured him he had performed several successful abor-
tions; then he also agreed. Evans went to work that morning, on
Tuesday 8 November, and Beryl prepared for the abortion, lying
on a quilt before the fire. She had removed her knickers and lay
with her legs open. Christie advised her that a few sniffs of coal
gas would relax her and remove any pain. But when it came to it,

she panicked anyway, and he picked up his 'strangling rope' and killed her, then raped her body.

What happened to baby Geraldine? Ludovic Kennedy was quite certain Christie was solely responsible for her death. 'Sometime during that day [Thursday 10 November] Christie murdered her . . .' And, on the face of it, the weight of circumstantial evidence seems to agree with Kennedy. Evans was apparently surprised when told that Geraldine was dead too, which lent credence to his later claim that Reg Christie had promised to have her sent to a loving couple who would take care of her.

Indeed, Evans was evidently uncertain about all the events of the killings: his original confession suggested that Beryl had died of accidental poisoning – not self-evident strangulation – and he didn't even know where the body had been hidden. This all suggests that he might not have even seen the body – that Christie dealt with it alone. Add the questionable provenance of Evans's confession, which he later retracted, and the case against him looks highly uncertain. And finally there is the almost unbelievable coincidence that the very house in which Evans supposedly committed two murders by strangulation, contained a serial killer who liked to kill using a strangling rope.

But an alternative solution *is* suggested by Rupert Furneaux, in a book called *The Two Stranglers of Rillington Place* (also published in 1961). Furneaux revealed that while Evans was in Brixton Prison, he met an accused murderer named Donald Hume. A petty criminal and fraudster, Hume had been charged with the killing of a dealer in stolen cars called Stanley Setty, and of scattering parts of his body out of an aeroplane over the Essex marshes. Hume stuck to his story that he was merely an accomplice and was sentenced to twelve years, rather than being hanged.

But in 1958, when Hume was released early from prison, he confessed to the murder of Setty; he was aware that he was protected by Britain's double-jeopardy law, which meant a person could not be tried twice for the same offence under any circumstances. Hume also admitted to the *Daily Express* newspaper that it was he who had caused Tim Evans to change his

guilty plea. He had advised him: 'Don't put your head in a noose.
Make up a new story and stick to it.' When Evans asked his
advice on the 'new story', Hume asked him whether he murdered
his wife and Evans denied it. Hume then went on to make the
following strange statement:

> *He told me that when he and his wife went to live at Rillington*
> *Place, Christie came to an arrangement with his* wife [i.e. to
> abort her baby] *and that Christie had murdered her. Then he*
> *told me about the child. He said: 'It was because the kid was*
> *crying.' I said: 'So you did it?' He said: 'No, but I was there*
> *while it was done.' He told me that he and Christie had gone*
> *into the bedroom together, that Christie had strangled the kid*
> *with a bit of rag while he stood and watched.*

Here, at last, we can begin to glimpse a plausible outline of
what really happened. There seems to be no reason why Evans
should tell Hume that Christie murdered the baby – with Evans
looking on – unless it really happened. Evans, then, was an
accomplice in the murder, which would explain the sense of
guilt that led him to confess. The confession to the murder of
his own child is incomprehensible if Christie had committed
the murder alone.

But, Rupert Furneaux argues, if Evans stood by and consented
to the murder of Geraldine, then his claim that Christie killed
Beryl, and later told Evans that she had died in the course of an
abortion, becomes suspect. Even if Christie had assured Evans
that they would both go to jail if the truth should become known,
this would still not explain why Evans would allow Christie to kill
the baby.

Furneaux suggests that Evans killed his wife, exactly as he
confessed. That could be the only possible reason that he would
agree to Christie killing the baby. His neck was already at risk
because he had killed his wife. With a baby on his hands, he
stood no chance of remaining undetected. But if both bodies
could be concealed, he might escape. He went off to Merthyr
Vale believing that Christie would put both bodies down the

drain. In Merthyr, he was overcome by guilt and fear. The more he thought about it, the more obvious it was that the bodies must be found, and that he had admitted his own guilt by fleeing. His only chance lay in going to the police and telling a story in which he was only an accomplice. Such a story would, of course, put the blame squarely on Christie. But when he was taken back to London, and charged with the murder of his wife and child, he could no longer maintain the deception; he broke down and confessed to killing Beryl. This time he also admitted to killing the baby, for what point would there be in accusing Christie if he was already admitting to strangling his wife?

And so the tragedy played itself out; the bodies were refrigerated by the winter cold in the wash house. So Dr Donald Teare, the Home Office pathologist, could estimate with remarkable accuracy they had been dead for about three weeks. Teare observed Beryl's throat was bruised, and there was bruising inside the vagina. This latter must have seemed odd – how would her vagina have become bruised in the course of strangling her? Teare says that he thought of taking a swab to detect sperm 'but others thought it unnecessary'. That is, the police were fairly certain that only Evans could have caused the bruise, and that therefore it wasn't worth bothering with. Kennedy points out that Teare would almost certainly have found traces of Christie's spermatozoa, because Christie would have found her dead body irresistible, and would not have passed up this chance of raping her.

If Teare had followed through on his examination, he would have discovered that Beryl had been raped and, almost inevitably, identified Christie as the rapist. And three murders would have been prevented.

Evans went on trial on 11 January 1950. The prosecution had decided to only charge him with the death of baby Geraldine, not Beryl. This may seem odd, but it is common prosecution practice in states that have the death penalty: if the first murder trial fails, they can try again with a second count of murder – only one conviction will have to stick, as a person can only be executed once.

Tim Evans stuck to his story that Christie had committed both murders, when he, Evans, wasn't even in the house. (This may have been his attempt to follow Hume's advice to choose a story and stick to it.) But given the limited and targeted police investigation, and Evans's written confession, a guilty verdict was almost inevitable. In fact his attempt to blame Christie backfired. The judge praised and congratulated Christie – who coldly appeared as chief witness for the prosecution – and was evidently less prone to consider any plea for leniency after the guilty verdict was given by the jury on 13 January. An appeal was turned down on 20 February and Evans was hanged on the morning of 9 March 1950 at Pentonville Prison.

In 2004, the judges of the High Court of Justice refused an appeal by Timothy Evans's half-sister to send the case to the Court of Appeals. They did this entirely to avoid unnecessary public expense, adding that they did not personally believe that Evans was guilty of either murder. The main reason for this unofficial clearing of Tim Evans's name was Reg Christie's own confession. Just after the passing of his own death sentence for seven murders, on 25 June 1953, Christie is recorded as smugly saying that if the police only knew, they could have also charged him with the murder of Evans's baby girl.[2]

To round out the Christie case I quote my account from *An Encyclopedia of Murder*:

> *On 24 March 1953, Beresford Brown – a Jamaican tenant of 10 Rillington Place – was sounding the walls in the kitchen on the ground floor, previously occupied by Christie. One wall sounded hollow and the Jamaican pulled off a corner of wallpaper. He discovered that the paper covered a cupboard door, one corner of which was missing. He was able to peer into the cupboard with the help of a torch and saw the naked back of a woman. Hastily summoned policemen discovered*

2 Hon Mr Justice Brabin 'Rillington Place: Uncovered Editions', 'The Stationery Office' (page 212)

that the cupboard contained three female bodies. The first was naked except for a brassiere and suspender belt; the other two were wrapped in blankets and secured with electric wire. There was very little smell, which was due to atmospheric conditions causing dehydration. (Some of the more sensational accounts of the case state inaccurately that the tenant was led to the discovery by the smell of decomposition.) Floorboards in the front room appeared to have been disturbed, and they were taken up to reveal a fourth body, also wrapped in a blanket. This proved to be Christie's wife Ethel, who had been strangled.

Christie had left on 10 March, sub-letting to a Mr and Mrs Reilly, who had paid him £7, 13 shillings in advance. The Reillys had been turned out almost immediately by the owner, another Jamaican, Charles Brown, since Christie had no right to sub-let, and had, in fact, left owing rent.

The back garden was dug up, and revealed human bones – the skeletons of two more bodies. A human femur propped up the fence.

On 31 March, Christie was recognized by PC Ledger on an embankment near Putney Bridge and was taken to Putney Bridge Police Station. In the week since the discovery of bodies, the hue and cry had been extraordinary, and newspapers ran pictures of the back garden of 10 Rillington Place and indulged in speculations about the murders and whether the murderer would commit another sex crime before his arrest.

Christie made a statement admitting to the murders of four women in the house. In it he claimed that his wife had been getting into an increasingly nervous condition because of attacks from the coloured people in the house, and that on the night of 14 December 1952, he had been awakened by his wife's convulsive movements; she was having some kind of a fit; he could not bear to see her in this state, and strangled her with a stocking. His account of the other three murders – Rita Nelson, aged twenty-five, Kathleen Maloney, aged twenty-six, Hectorina McLennan, aged twenty-five, described quarrels with the women (who were prostitutes) in the course of which

*Christie strangled them. Later, he confessed to the murders of
the two women in the garden.*

*The first was an Austrian girl, Ruth Fuerst, whom Christie
claimed he murdered during sexual intercourse; then Muriel
Eady, an employee at the Ultra Radio factory in Park Royal
where Christie had worked in late 1944. A tobacco tin containing four lots of pubic hair was also found in the house.*

*There were many curious features in the murders. Carbon
monoxide was found in the blood of the three women in the
cupboard, although not in Mrs Christie. The three had semen
in the vagina; none was wearing knickers, but all had 'a piece
of white material between the legs in the form of a diaper'.*

*Christie admitted at his trial that his method of murder had
been to invite women to his house and to get them partly drunk.
They were persuaded to sit in a deck-chair with a canopy, and
a gas pipe was placed near the floor and turned on. When the
girl lost consciousness from carbon monoxide poisoning,
Christie would strangle her and then rape her. But since the
women were prostitutes, it would hardly seem necessary to
render them unconscious to have sexual intercourse. One theory
to explain this has been advanced by Dr Francis Camps, the
pathologist who examined the bodies. He suggested that Christie
had reached a stage of sexual incapability where the woman
needed to be unconscious before he could possess her.*

*The body of Rita Nelson, twenty-five, (no.3), was found to
be six months' pregnant. The other bodies were those of
Kathleen Maloney, twenty-six, last seen 12 January 1953, and
Hectorina MacLennan, age twenty-six, last seen alive on 22
March 1953.*

*Christie was tried only for the murder of his wife; his trial
opened at the Central Criminal Court on Monday 22 June
1953, before Mr Justice Finnemore; the Attorney-General, Sir
Lionel Heald, led for the Crown; Mr Derek Curtis-Bennett,
QC, defended.*

*Christie's case history, as it emerged at his trial, was as
follows: He was fifty-five years old at the time of his arrest. He
was born in Chester Street, Boothtown, Yorkshire, in April*

1898, son of Ernest Christie, a carpet designer. The father was a harsh man who treated his seven children with Victorian sternness and offered no affection. Christie was a weak child, myopic, introverted and jeered at by his fellow pupils as a 'cissie'. He had many minor illnesses in his childhood – possibly to compensate for lack of attention. He was occasionally in trouble with the police for trivial offences, and was beaten by his father whenever this occurred.

At the age of fifteen (this would be in 1933) he left school and got a post as a clerk to the Halifax Borough Police. Petty pilfering lost him the job. He then worked in his father's carpet factory. When he was dismissed from there, for petty theft, his father threw him out of the house.

Christie was a chronic hypochondriac, a man who enjoyed being ill and talking about his past illnesses. (His first confession starts with an account of his poor health.) In 1915 he suffered from pneumonia. He then went to war, and was mustard-gassed and blown up. He claimed that he was blind for five months and lost his voice for three and a half years. The loss of voice was the psychological effect of hysteria, for there was no physical abnormality to account for it.

The defence was of insanity, but the jury rejected it, following the medical opinions that Christie was sane, and he was sentenced to death, and executed on 15 July 1953.

Of Heath and Christie, only Reg Christie is officially seen as a serial killer – someone addicted to committing murders. Legally to be categorised as a serial killer, a person has to kill at least three people over a protracted period of time. A person might 'go postal' and slaughter dozens in an hour or two – but they are not a serial killer. To be a serial killer there has to be evidence of planning; of plotting to hunt and kill a fellow human being at least three times. Since there is rarely specific evidence of such planning, the courts see the time between killings as evidence of plotting. A serial killer rarely kills in wild abandon, but cold-bloodedly sets about destroying another person's life and, if they get away with it, eventually starts planning their next homicide.

Would Neville Heath have killed again – if he had not been caught – thus earning the necessary number of victims to categorise him as a serial killer? It seems likely. He might in fact have killed his first victim, Margery Gardner, by accident. But the damage he did to her suggests that he clearly had homicidal tendencies that he could no longer control. And he quite deliberately butchered Doreen Marshall, showing the savage glee of a man who has thoroughly taken to slaughtering women.

Yet Christie and Heath were opposites in a different way. Serial killers are often categorised, by psychological profiling investigators, as non-social/organised or asocial/disorganised. The terms were coined by the early FBI psychological profiler, John Douglas, and are somewhat self-explanatory: Heath was a disorganised killer who murdered on impulse and left numerous clues for the police. Christie was very organised, planning his murders and covering them up so efficiently that even his wife may have had no idea he was a murderer . . . up until the moment he killed her. During the investigation into the Evans killings, the police searched 10 Rillington place no fewer than three times, but found no evidence of the two murders that Christie had already committed.

Disorganised serial killers often 'blitz' their victims – that is, they build themselves up to an emotional peak, and then wildly attack, often killing with berserk violence – like Heath. An organised killer will often use charm and subterfuge to lure their victim to an isolated spot, or a hidden location, to be killed. And, like Christie, they might kill in a very cold and calculated fashion. Disorganised serial killers are often loners with weak social skills and below-average intelligence. Organised serial killers are often of above average intelligence, and often come over as being very charming and pleasant (as the Judge at the Tim Evans trial obviously found Reg Christie).

As we will see in the next chapter, the psychological profiling of serial killers is an essential tool used in catching them today. But in the 1950s and 1960s, even the term 'serial killer' had yet to be invented; and most policemen would have been flabbergasted to be told that some people can be as addicted to murder as a drunk can be to booze binges. This lack of police knowledge, and any understanding of the serial killer mindset, was possibly why one of the most notorious British serial killers of the period escaped capture . . .

In the two years or so in the mid-1950s when I lived at 24 Chepstow Villas, I graduated from the unconnected bathroom to a bare but fairly comfortable room overlooking the street; my circumstances having improved due to my first published book, a study in existential philosophy called *The Outsider*. My notion of an 'Outsider' was a potentially creative person trapped in a state of frustration; and since the dividing line between frustration and violence is a thin one, it followed that many of the 'Outsiders' I found most interesting – Poe, Baudelaire, Dostoevsky – were morbidly interested in crime.

My own interest in crime had started when I learned that in the world of my grandfather's childhood, children were often told to be home before dark 'in case Jack the Ripper gets you'. When I began writing in my mid-teens, it was almost inevitable that the subject of my first novel – *Ritual in the Dark* – should be a serial killer based on Jack the Ripper. And also on Peter Kürten, the Düsseldorf murderer on whom Fritz Lang based his film *M*. This novel finally appeared in 1960, by which time I, and my girlfriend Joy (who had steadfastly shared my Chepstow Villas bathroom), had moved to rural Cornwall: an equally cheap, but much more pleasant place to live.

But I still stayed in Notting Hill whenever I went to London, since friends like Bill Hopkins and Laura del Rivo lived in the area. And in 1959 there began another series of prostitute murders in west London centred around an unknown killer who became known as 'Jack the Stripper'.

Duke's Meadows is the southernmost point of Chiswick, where a bend in the river makes it impossible to go further south while keeping dry feet. Because it is dark and lonely, it was a favourite place for prostitutes whose clients had relatively peculiar outdoor demands, such as sodomy and fellatio; one chronicler, David Seabrook, referred to it as 'Gobblers Gulch'.

At 5.10 a.m. on 17 June 1959, a police patrol car noticed someone sitting against a tree in the area known as Riverside Lands, and since the figure made no movement, they looked more closely, and found it to be a dead woman wearing a blue-and-white-striped dress that looked new; it was open, revealing naked breasts. Two hours later, pathologist Dr Donald Teare noted that she seemed to have died of strangulation. Removed to Acton mortuary, she was photographed with her eyes propped open, and the picture released to the evening papers in the hope of identification.

It was recognised by a fellow prostitute with whom she shared a room, and who notified the girl's family. The corpse was Elizabeth Figg, who was twenty-one and had left home after quarrels with her father in Wales. She was a small girl, not much over 5 feet tall. Her professional alias was 'Ann Phillips', but she was generally known as 'Little Betty'. One of her teeth had recently been extracted and the place was still raw.

Little Betty died in June 1959. The next link to the Thames Nude Killer was uncovered by a mechanical digger more than three years later. A burst of newspaper publicity caused its echoes to reach our village in Cornwall.

In terms of distance it was not far from Duke's Meadows, except that it happened to be on the other side of the river, in Mortlake. On 8 November 1963, the driver of a mechanical digger sniffed disgustedly as the shovel unearthed a sickening smell and the lower half of a decaying corpse. A leg wearing only a rolled-down nylon stocking was jerked into the air. The top half of the body was still embedded in the ground. That afternoon, at Kingston Mortuary, Dr Arthur Mant estimated that the body had been buried for about six or so weeks, and had it not been uncovered by the digger, might never have been found. She had been strangled with a ligature and several of her front teeth had been knocked out.

The chief problem was identification. The decaying flesh seemed to rule out fingerprinting, until Professor Keith Simpson, the pathologist at Guy's Hospital, decided to try a chemical method to harden a decaying finger-end, and obtained a fingerprint that matched a prostitute named Gwynneth Rees, age twenty-one, of Barry in Wales.

Born in 1941, she was sixteen when her mother died, and she declined her father's suggestion that she stay at home and look after the younger children. In the following year she had been impregnated by a boyfriend and went to live with an elder sister in Essex. Her habit of staying out half the night caused a quarrel, and she returned to Wales, took a factory job and had the baby, a boy. With her sister's help she began proceedings to have the baby adopted, then changed her mind. Her sister agreed to look after the child if Gwynneth would go out to work. She took a job at a shoe factory. But when she began taking men home with her, her sister threw her out. At this point, it seems Gwynneth took up prostitution, and became a street walker in the Notting Hill area.

Legally speaking, 1959 was not a good year for what we called 'sex workers'. Until that time prostitutes were fined £2 and allowed to return to their trade. But after the Street Offences Act of that year, the fine was increased to £10 for the first conviction, £25 for the second and three months in jail for a third. This is why most of the girls had an alias, like 'Gwynneth Rees' 'Tina Smart' and Elizabeth Figg's 'Ann Phillips'; it made them harder to trace. It was also why they worked out-of-the-way places like Duke's Meadows: reducing the chance of arrest, but increasing the risk from their more dangerous punters.

The next victim, thirty-year-old Hannah Tailford, was small and slim like the previous two. (Serial killers often target small or lightly built victims. The reason is not one of personal sexual preference, but is mainly because most serial killers are scared of being injured themselves, and find smaller victims less of a physical threat.) Hannah's street name was 'Terry Lynch'. Her body was found on the foreshore of the Thames, near Hammersmith Bridge, on 2 February 1964. She was naked, her sperm-stained panties were jammed in her mouth and several of her front teeth had been knocked out. There was a bruise on her jaw and she had died of drowning in the Thames.

Two months later, on 18 April 1964, the naked body of Irene Lockwood, a twenty-six-year-old prostitute, was found at Duke's Meadows, near Barnes Bridge, only 300 yards from the place where Hannah Tailford had been found. She had been strangled and, like Hannah Tailford, she had been in the early stages of pregnancy. A fifty-four-year-old Kensington caretaker, Kenneth Archibald, confessed to her murder, and he seemed to know a great deal about the girl; but at his trial, it was established that his confession was false and he was acquitted.

There was another reason for believing in Archibald's innocence: while he was still in custody, another naked girl was found in an alleyway at Osterley Park, Brentford. This was on 24 April, only three weeks after the discovery of Irene Lockwood's body. The dead girl – the only one among the victims who could be described as pretty – was a twenty-two-year-old prostitute and striptease artist, Helen Barthelemy.

Forensic examination turned up a number of curious facts from Barthelemy's body. A pressure line around her waist showed that her panties had been removed some time after death, and there was no evidence of vaginal sexual activity. And, like Hannah Tailford, four of Helen's front teeth were missing. Oddly enough, they had not been knocked out by a blow, but had been deliberately forced out, one by one, when she was already dead; a piece of one of her broken teeth was found lodged in her oesophagus. The autopsy also revealed the presence of sperm in her throat.

Here, then, was the bizarre cause of death: she had been choked by an erect penis, probably in the course of performing oral sex. The missing teeth suggested that the killer had removed them to allow him greater ease in raping her corpse. And the elastic panty mark suggested that he had kept the body somewhere secret to do so – only removing her clothes when he was ready to dump the body. This guess was further confirmed when it was established that she had disappeared some days before her body was found. Where, then, had her body been? Flakes of paint found on her skin suggested the answer, for it was the type of paint used in spraying cars. Clearly, the body had been kept somewhere near a car-spraying plant, but in some place where it was not likely to be discovered by the workers.

The 'nude murders' became a public sensation, for it now seemed likely that they were the work of one man. Large numbers of police were deployed in the search for the spray factory, and in an attempt to keep a closer watch on the areas in which three of the victims had been picked up – around the boroughs of Notting Hill and Shepherd's Bush. Perhaps for this reason, the killer decided to take no risks for several months.

The body of the fourth victim – Mary Fleming, aged thirty-one, found on 14 July, confirmed that the same man was responsible. Her false teeth were missing, there was sperm in her throat, and her skin showed traces of the spray paint. She had vanished three days earlier.

Her body was found, in a half-crouching position, near a garage in Acton, south-west of Shepherd's Bush. The killer was perhaps taunting the police, as Fleming's naked body was dumped in plain sight, visible from the open street, in an area that the police were patrolling regularly.

But the killer probably regretted his audacity almost immediately. A motorist driving past Berrymede Road, a cul-de-sac, at 5.30 a.m., had to brake violently to avoid a van that shot out in front of him. He was so angry that he phoned the police to report the incident. If he had made a note of the number, Jack the Stripper might have been caught within hours. A squad car that arrived a few minutes later found the body of Mary Fleming in the forecourt of a garage in the cul-de-sac.

The near-miss probably alarmed the killer, for no more murders occurred that summer. Then, on 25 November 1964, another naked woman was found under some debris in a car park in Hornton Street, Kensington. She was identified as Margaret McGowan. Under the name 'Frances Brown', she had been called as a witness in the trial of Stephen Ward, involved in the Profumo scandal, and Ludovic Kennedy described her (in his book on the trial) as a small, bird-like woman with a pale face and fringe. Margaret McGowan had disappeared more than a month before her body was found, and there were signs of decomposition. Again, there were traces of paint and a missing front tooth indicated that her corpse had been secreted and raped in the same way as the previous two victims.

The last of the Stripper's known victims was a prostitute named

Bridget 'Bridie' O'Hara, aged twenty-eight. She was found on 16 February 1965, in some undergrowth on the Heron Trading Estate, Acton. She had last been seen on 11 January in the Shepherd's Bush Hotel. The body was partly mummified, which indicated that it had been kept in a cool place. As before, teeth were missing and sperm was found in her throat. Bruising finger marks on the back of her neck indicated that, like at least four of the other victims, she had died in a kneeling position, bent over the killer's groin and choking on his erect penis.

The Heron Trading Estate apparently provided the case-breaking lead that the police had been waiting for. Investigation of a paint-spray shop revealed that this was definitely the source of the paint found on the bodies – chemical analysis proved it. The proximity of a disused warehouse solved the question of where the bodies had lain before they were dumped. The powerful spray guns caused the paint to carry, with diminishing intensity, for several hundred yards. Analysis of paint on the bodies enabled experts to establish the spot where the women must have been concealed: it was underneath a transformer in the warehouse.

Yet even with this discovery, the case was far from solved. Thousands of men worked on the Heron Trading Estate. (Oddly enough, Reg Christie, the 10 Rillington Place Strangler, had once been employed there). Detective Chief Superintendent John du Rose was recalled from his annual holiday to take charge of a huge investigation in the Shepherd's Bush area. But mass questioning seemed to bring the police no closer to their suspect. Du Rose decided to throw an immense 20-mile cordon around the area, to keep a careful check on all cars passing through at night. Drivers who were observed more than once were noted; if they were seen more than twice, they were interviewed.

Du Rose conducted what he called 'a war of nerves' against the killer, dropping hints in the press or on television that indicated the police were getting closer. They knew he drove a van, they knew he must have right of access to the trading estate by night. The size of the victims, all short, suggested that the killer himself was under middle height.

As the months passed, and no further murders took place, du Rose assumed that he was winning the war of nerves. Seven thousand men were eventually interviewed by officers. Du Rose had officers check on *all* men in the country who had been jailed since mid-February; also all men with prison records who had been hospitalised since the date of the last murder; and all men who had died or committed suicide. In his book *Murder Was My Business* (1971), du Rose claimed that a list of twenty suspects had been reduced to three when one of the three committed suicide.

This man left a note saying that he could bear the strain no longer. He was a security guard who drove a van and had access to the estate. At the time when the women were murdered, his rounds included the spray shop. He worked by night, from 10 p.m. to 6 a.m. The dead man wasn't formally proved to be the killer, so his name wasn't given by du Rose. But his suicide saw the end of the murders, so investigating officers felt sure that they had got their man – if only indirectly.

The Stripper murders were clearly a case of the obsessive mentality – even more so than in the case of Christie. Reginald Christie's peculiarity was his inability to have intercourse with a woman who was fully conscious; the Stripper was interested only in oral sex. (This was not revealed at the time of the case, and it is only hinted at in du Rose's book. Even into the 1970s, a large proportion of English society regarded fellatio as a disgusting perversion that couldn't be mentioned in public for any reason.)

If, as seems likely, Jack the Stripper was the killer of Elizabeth Figg and Gwynneth Rees (the first two victims) then his homicidal obsession had still not reached a climax. We can guess this because both the above victims were strangled, not choked to death. The reason that modern psychological profiling can be so effective in catching serial killers is that such murderers typically fall into habits. Before graduating to killing they fantasise about murder so much that they create a favourite homicidal scenario, or set of scenarios, in their mind that they eventually find themselves acting out in reality. A trained psychological profiler can look at two crime scenes, and almost immediately tell if the same man, with the same obsessions, was responsible.

Detective Chief Superintendent du Rose thought Hannah Tailford was the first victim, and that her death could have been accidental: at the height of his sexual satisfaction, guiding her head with his hand on her neck, the other probably gripping her hair, he may have lost control, and choked her with the glans of his penis – as if 'an apple had been jammed in her throat', as du Rose rather graphically explained in an article written after his retirement. But such an accident is unlikely, otherwise why should the killer have stuffed her panties into her mouth, presumably to make sure she was dead?

Given the unlikelihood of there being two killers of prostitutes in the west London area – who shared an obsession with oral sex and knocked out their victims' front teeth – it seems likely that Figg and Rees were Jack the Stripper's first victims. He strangled them because he had not yet discovered his favourite fantasy about killing. Du Rose might have been right that the killer accidentally choked Hannah Tailford with his penis, but he was almost certainly planning to strangle her anyway.

Most male readers will wince at the very thought of endangering such a sensitive piece of anatomy by using it as a weapon. And anyone might wonder why Jack's victims didn't bite their attacker. But Jack the Stripper must have discovered, probably by accident, that a choking victim won't shut their mouth. They desperately need air, so all their instincts fight against closing their mouth. It would have probably taken just over a minute before Hannah was too weak, from lack of oxygen, to fight back. And before that she must have been in a state of terrified panic, and incapable of doing the one simple thing that could have saved her life . . . to bite the bastard's penis hard enough to put him in the hospital.

Certainly by the time he choked Irene Lockwood, 'Jack' knew in advance what he intended to do. The serial killer had found his fantasy method of killing, and probably spent much of his days self-glorifying over Hannah Tailford's death in his mind, or dreaming about doing it again to another victim. He picked up Irene on the night of 7 April and the murder almost certainly took place in the back of his van. After this he stripped her and threw her body in the river. One writer on the case has suggested that the victims were stripped to avoid identification, but this would clearly be pointless. Why should the murderer care whether the women were identified, or how soon? The stripping was a part of his ritual, the desire to feel himself to be totally dominant.

His sadistic fantasy evidently involved a helpless and terrified woman dying because of the power of his 'manhood'. But he was also, like Christie, a necrophile; keeping the corpses as long as possible to orally rape at his pleasure – hence the post mortem removal of teeth. In the later murders, the bodies were kept in the warehouse for several weeks, not because he was waiting for a favourable moment to dispose of them (after all, the longer he waited, the more chance there was that they would be discovered), but in order to repeat his rapes of the corpses.

The last corpse, Bridget O'Hara, was kept longer than any of the others, and was dumped on the Heron Trading Estate – perilously close to the killer's previous haunts and thus greatly endangering him. This may have been partly out of fear of being stopped with her in his van – after his near miss dumping the body of Margaret McGowan. But the police cordon had not been formed at that time. It is more likely that the same indifference that eventually overtook Heath and Christie started to get to Jack the Stripper – murder had become a habit, and that level of destructiveness involved an element of self-destruction. Many serial killers fall into this state of *ennui* – a sense of unreality starts to eat at them, so that they make the stupid mistakes that lead to their capture. Sometimes, in this state, they kill themselves, but this is very rare – the typical serial killer type is both too egocentric and too scared of physical pain to commit suicide.

The identity of Jack the Stripper remains unknown to this day. Several candidates have been suggested, including the champion British heavy-weight boxer Freddie Mills. In Mills's case, the only 'evidence' that he was Jack the Stripper seems to have been his brutal boxing style, the fact he lived in London during the murders and that he shot himself (or was murdered) in July 1965. There have also been rumours that the killer was actually a policeman, who either used inside knowledge of the investigation to escape capture, or was covered up for by his colleagues. But, again, there is no proof against any of the named suspects.

All we know for certain is that the murders around Notting Hill and Shepherd's Bush seemed to stop in February 1965. Whether this was because the killer was dead, or had moved to some distant part of the globe, we can't be certain. The former is the most likely because of two factors: first, he was a serial killer – and such murder addicts rarely stop killing unless they are caught or they die themselves. The second reason we can be fairly sure Jack the Stripper died – or was otherwise incapacitated – in 1965 is that his bizarre method of killing would have highlighted his presence, no matter where in the world he started killing again.

Chapter 20

Hunting Monsters

At the time of Heath, Christie and the Stripper, the term 'serial killer' was still unknown. It was coined at the Bramshill Police Academy in Harlesden, London, in 1977, as an indirect result of a series of murders in the north of England committed by a killer who became known as the 'Yorkshire Ripper'.

This man murdered thirteen women between 1975 and 1980. He would knock them unconscious, in isolated public areas, with a ball-peen hammer. Then he would stab them to death. The police investigation into the murders was chaotic, largely because of the wide area covered by the killer, leading to there being many thousands of potential suspects. And the investigation relied on card filing, rather than computers, to co-ordinate the vast amounts of data collected. Thus the killer, Peter Sutcliffe, was interviewed three times by police; but was released each time because his interviewers did not know that he had been suspected before. The Yorkshire Ripper was eventually caught, almost by luck, in a random police sweep.

The term 'serial killer' was invented by a visiting American Federal agent called Robert Ressler, who had been at a talk when the lecturer used the term 'serial burglar', which Ressler thought would be a useful coinage to refer to mass-murderers like the still-unidentified Yorkshire Ripper.

The concept of a serial criminal (killer, burglar, stalker, arsonist or rapist) signifies more than a repeat or habitual offender. A serial criminal has a psychological addiction to committing their crimes – often with an underlining sexual obsession attached to the act. They will generally have a cooling-off period immediately after a crime, followed by a gradually increasing need to commit another felony. They also suffer the law of diminishing returns like other, less antisocial, types of addict. They find their crimes less satisfying over time and tend to commit greater crimes to make up the difference; thus serial rapists often become serial killers. After recognising this psychological criminal category, Robert Ressler would go on to become one of the founding inventors of the discipline known as psychological profiling.

An expert in psychological profiling – also called 'offender profiling' – can make highly accurate predictions about an otherwise unidentified criminal. This skill is based on a knowledge and understanding of previous criminals who have committed similar crimes, who have then been captured and have given detailed confessions and outlines of their overall lives.

Although psychological profiling was being practiced as early as the 1950s (most notably in the New York Mad Bomber case in 1956) the consistent gathering of data only began systematically with the FBI's *Violent Criminal Apprehension Program* (ViCAP) in 1985. The programme was originally just meant to be a police database that allowed across-the-board availability of data from unsolved homicides and missing-person cases where homicide was suspected. But ViCAP, and its results, eventually became one of the most important advancements in the war on crime since the invention of fingerprinting.

It was decided, as part of the ViCAP programme, to interview imprisoned violent offenders, in the hopes of gathering extra data. Perhaps not much was expected from this arm of the programme: why, after all, should criminals cooperate with the authorities any more than they had to? But, in fact, most interviewed criminals proved very talkative. Habitual criminals can be like children, in that they often like nothing better than to talk about themselves, if only to brag.

A great mass of data was collected over just a few years, and when the different criminals' depositions were compared, it was realised that people who commit certain types of crime were very likely to share background details and personality features. Looking at it another way, an unsolved crime of a specific type was probably committed by someone sharing characteristics with previous, known criminals who committed just that sort of crime. And in the case of those addicted to committing murder – serial killers – they always seemed to have a 'signature' to their crimes. This is a clue to their personal obsessions that might be echoed by previous, similar serial crime cases. For example, Reg Christie's habit of raping his victims only after he had strangled them, born at least partly out of his impotence with conscious women. If a profiler can identify this characteristic signature, they can get a powerful insight into an unidentified killer and this, in turn, greatly increases the chance of catching them.

Of course the very idea of psychological profiling flies in the face of one of our most heartfelt personal beliefs: that we are all highly complex individuals, governed by our own free will, and are thus beyond simple quantification. But humans can in fact be very easy to profile, and from that our actions and habits can be accurately predicted. Psychological profiling simply wouldn't work if this were not so – and it does. Like it or not, many of our life decisions are entirely predictable to anyone who had studied our previous pattern of decision-making. (This is why shops and supermarkets are so keen for you to carry discount 'store cards'. These record the history of all of your purchases, and allow prediction of your likely future buying habits.)

This psychological predictability has proved doubly true of the sort of people who commit violent crimes. Each of us faces only a limited number of options when deciding the course of our lives at any key juncture. Our choices – both our conscious decisions and those forced on us by our ongoing circumstances – connect up over time to make a pattern of behaviour that indicates not only our past influences, but also our likely future behaviour. And a person who has lived a life of violence is likely to come from a more restricted set of circumstances than someone who has lived a violence-free life.

Many people come from an impoverished background, have been subject to physical and psychological abuse, or have a disposition that's prone to fits of hot rage or cold sadism. But only a very small part of the population regularly give in to negative influences to the extent that they live a life of violent crime. That limited set of life circumstances and, more importantly, the highly limited set of life choices that led to crime, give a psychological profiler a much less intimidating field in which to build their predictions of an unidentified criminal.

The upshot of this is that a good psychological profiler can walk on to a crime scene, examine the clues, and then make a confident prediction about the perpetrator. For example, they might tell homicide investigators: 'You're looking for a heterosexual man in his early thirties, almost certainly Caucasian. Probably married, but likely estranged from his family. He will almost certainly have a previous criminal record for petty theft, and may also have been arrested for domestic violence. He doesn't live in the local area and has a menial job involving a lot of travelling. He has also killed before at least twice, and when he kills again it will be a similar sort of victim but in another part of the country.'

This may sound akin to a Sherlock Holmes-like deduction, and to a large extent it is. Doctor Arthur Conan Doyle wrote the early Sherlock Holmes stories partly because he was frustrated by what he saw as the unscientific methods of the British police. A large part of Sherlock Holmes's magic is that he has an extensive expert knowledge and observes clues carefully – only making his brilliant deductions after carefully considering all the facts that he can collect and cross-index in his mind. Doyle felt that this was what all investigating policemen should do. The annoyance that Holmes habitually shows for the clodhopping methods of policemen, like Inspector Lestrade, is largely what Doyle felt himself.

At the time of the first Sherlock Holmes story (A Study in Scarlet, published in 1887), the British police – and police everywhere – relied heavily on paid informants and what was called 'shoe-leather police work'. That is, perambulating around the local area asking if anyone knew who the criminal was. This worked fine if you were only looking for 'the usual suspects':

uneducated criminals who lived near or in the areas where they committed their crimes. But with the increasing sophistication and the spread of education in the nineteenth century, Conan Doyle realised that sooner or later the police would be facing educated criminals who knew how to cover their tracks. The early Sherlock Holmes stories were therefore something of a personal campaign by Doyle – one that was picked up and supported by his readership. But if the police were annoyed by this upstart doctor criticising their simple but tried-and-trusted methods, they were soon to be shown the error of their thinking. The year after the publication of *A Study in Scarlet*, London – and then the world – was riveted by the Jack the Ripper murders.

Even today, Jack the Ripper is the most iconic serial killer in the public mind. When asked to name infamous serial killers most people will mention him, even though nobody knows his real name or very much about him. Some believe (incorrectly) that 'Jack' was the first known serial killer. Others suppose that the Ripper crimes took place over many years and that his victims ran into dozens; whereas, in actual fact, the murders took place over just a few months in 1888 and the victims were possibly no more than five in number.

At 2.30 a.m. on Friday 31 August, a woman friend saw a prostitute named Mary Ann Nicholls (aged forty-three and known as 'Polly') at the corner of Osborn Street; she admitted to having had 'no luck'. Three-quarters of an hour later, her body was found by a cart driver named Cross on Bucks Row, lying in the entrance to the Old Stable Yard at the west end of the street. In the mortuary of the Old Montague Street Workhouse it was discovered that she had been disembowelled. Death was due to severing of the windpipe, which took place before she was gutted. A bruise on her face indicated that the murderer clamped his hand over her mouth before cutting her throat. A woman sleeping in a bedroom only a few yards from the murder had heard no sound.

It was revealed that Nicholls had been staying at a doss-house in Thrawl Street, where a bed could be had for fourpence a night. On the previous evening she had been turned away from the doss-house because she had no money. She commented: 'Don't worry, I'll soon get the money. Look what a fine bonnet I've got.'

The next Ripper murder took place on 8 September. Annie Chapman, aged forty-seven, was turned away from a lodging house in Dorset Street, having no money to pay for a bed. It seems probable that the murderer picked her up outside the yard where the murder took place at 29 Hanbury Street. She accompanied him down a passageway at the side of the house some time after 5 a.m. The body was found shortly after 6 a.m. The head had been almost severed from the body. The body was eviscerated, as in the case of Mary Nicholls. Two brass rings and some coppers were laid neatly at her feet.

Again, the murderer had carried out the crime with extreme coolness and had made no sound. There were sixteen people living at 29 Hanbury Street and a scream would have quickly brought help to the victim.

On 28 September a letter was sent to the Central News Agency threatening more murders: 'I am down on whores and shant quit ripping them till I do get buckled.' It was signed 'Jack the Ripper'.

The murders, and the letter, caused public hysteria. Meetings were held in the streets, criticising the police and the Home Secretary. Bloodhounds were suggested but, when used, they promptly lost themselves in the borough of Tooting. The newspapers gave extensive reports of the murders and inquests – concentrating on the grim details – and were tireless in offering theories.

A description of 'the murderer' was offered by someone who saw Annie Chapman talking to a man outside 29 Hanbury Street. It mentioned a large moustache and a 'foreign appearance'. This description was widely circulated and unfortunately played directly to Londoners' bigotry, many of whom would have liked to believe that only a foreigner was capable of such monstrous crimes.

On the morning of 30 September two more murders were committed in Whitechapel. The first was of a Swedish woman called Elizabeth Stride, aged forty-four. A hawker named Louis

Deimschutz drove his horse and cart into the back yard of the International Workers' Educational Club in Berner Street. He saw a woman's body on the ground and rushed into the club to give the alarm. Stride's throat had been cut and she had died very recently – so recently that it is likely that the killer had been interrupted, and was hidden in the shadows of the yard as Deimschutz ran past him. He then made his escape in the following confusion. This was at 1 a.m.

At around the same time, a forty-three-year-old prostitute named Catherine Eddowes was released from Bishopsgate Police Station, where she had been arrested for drunkenness. She was almost immediately picked up by the Ripper – who must have still been red handed from the killing of Elizabeth Stride. Eddowes was taken into a narrow alleyway that extends between Mitre Square and Duke Street, known as Church Passage. Police Constable Watkins passed through the passage on his beat at 1.30 a.m. A quarter of an hour later he again passed through the square, and found the body of Catherine Eddowes in the corner of the square near Church Passage. Her face had been badly mutilated and her body cut open; the left kidney and some of her entrails had been removed and taken away. A householder who lived in nearby Berner Street testified that she saw a young man carrying a shiny black bag away from the scene of the crime.

It was some time before Eddowes was identified and, in the meantime, one of the newspapers published a report that she was a certain 'Mary Anne Kelly' – this being the false name she had given the police when she was arrested for being drunk and disorderly. This is a remarkable coincidence, since the name of the final known victim was Mary Jane Kelly.

After the Eddowes murder the Central News Agency received another letter signed 'Jack the Ripper', regretting that he had been interrupted with his victims, and had not been able to send the ears to the police. (There *had* been an attempt to cut off the ear of Catherine Eddowes, although this fact had not been made public at that time.) He also mentioned that 'number one squealed a bit', which is borne out by a witness in Berner Street who heard a cry. The letter, the most likely to have been written by 'Jack' himself, was posted only a few hours after the murders and was written in red ink.

Bands of vigilantes now patrolled the streets of Whitechapel at night, but as weeks passed without further crimes, the panic died down. Then, on 9 November, the last of the known murders took place at a house in Millers Court, which ran off Dorset Street. Mary Jane Kelly was younger than the other victims. She was only twenty-four.

On the morning of 9 November, at 10.45 a.m., a man knocked on the door of Mary Kelly's one-room, ground-floor flat to collect the rent. Getting no reply, he peered in at the dirty, broken window. Jack had evidently spent a long time in there. The walls of the room were spattered with blood and what remained of Mary Kelly lay on the bed. Her throat had been slashed so deeply that her head had been almost severed from her body. Her lower face had been slashed to ribbons. Her heart had been cut out and placed on the bed pillow. Her belly had been torn open and her entrails pulled out and draped over a picture frame. One of the thighs of her spread-eagled legs had been filleted to the bone.

As usual with the Ripper, he had swiftly killed his victim by cutting her throat, then he mutilated her corpse. He had apparently worked by the light of a pile of rags, the ashes of which were lying burnt out in the grate. The probable time of the killing was set by neighbours' reports of hearing a cry of 'Murder!' at about 3.30 a.m. It goes some way to show just how frightened the people of the East End were by the Ripper murders that none of the dozen or so inhabitants of Millers Court investigated the cry.

By this stage, the whole of London was bordering a state of mass panic over the murders. Nobody had ever seen this sort of savage and apparently motiveless killing outside a war, and had no idea what might follow next. Would the killer stop murdering 'women of the night' and start attacking ordinary, 'decent' people? Might he start breaking into respectable houses, rather than killing in the street or in slum flats? It is somewhat indicative that Jack the Ripper very soon became the bogeyman used to frighten English children into behaving: 'If you're naughty, Jack the Ripper will come and get you.'

The police investigators remained stumped. An elusive and daring killer – with no connection to his victims and no evident connection to the local area of the murders – utterly defeated the old 'shoe-leather' investigation technique – just as Conan Doyle had warned that he would. But the science of forensic policing was in fact developing, almost despite itself.

A police surgeon, Doctor Thomas Bond, had been asked to compile a medical assessment of the murders after the killings of Elizabeth Stride and Catherine Eddowes. The main aim of this request was to ascertain whether Jack the Ripper had had any surgical training; but, on the day after the discovery of Mary Kelly, Bond handed in what was almost certainly the first offender profile in history. His basic conclusion was:

> In each [murder] the mutilation was inflicted by a person who had no scientific nor anatomical knowledge. In my opinion he does not even possess the technical knowledge of a butcher or horse slaughterer or any person accustomed to cut up dead animals.

But then Bond went on to say:

> The murderer must have been a man of physical strength and of great coolness and daring. There is no evidence that he had an accomplice. He must in my opinion be a man subject to periodical attacks of Homicidal and erotic mania. The character of the mutilations indicate that the man may be in a condition sexually, that may be called satyriasis. It is of course possible that the Homicidal impulse may have developed from a revengeful or brooding condition of the mind, or that Religious Mania may have been the original disease, but I do not think either hypothesis is likely. The murderer in external appearance is quite likely to be a quiet inoffensive looking man probably middle aged and neatly and respectably dressed. I

think he must be in the habit of wearing a cloak or overcoat or he could hardly have escaped notice in the streets if the blood on his hands or clothes were visible.

Assuming the murderer to be such a person as I have just described he would probably be solitary and eccentric in his habits, also he is most likely to be a man without regular occupation, but with some small income or pension. He is possibly living among respectable persons who have some knowledge of his character and habits and who may have grounds for suspicion that he is not quite right in his mind at times.

At the time Bond's report was largely ignored by investigators, and with some reason: beyond his medical conclusions he was evidently speculating – and there was already far too much wild speculation going on about Jack the Ripper. But, in hindsight, we can see that Bond's profile is a reasonable match with what a modern, professional profiler might produce.

The Ripper stopped killing after the Mary Kelly murder – at least, as far the investigating police believed – and his identity has never been verified, despite a legion of suspects and theories offered up over the intervening decades. So we may never know how close Dr Thomas Bond was in his psychological profile of Jack the Ripper.

Although it remains a single tool in an investigator's repertoire, psychological profiling has often proved vital in a key task in any serial crime case – to sift and reduce the sheer number of suspects. But it remains far from a perfect science; if the profiler gets it wrong, he or she can send an investigation off on entirely the wrong track. The expert evidence of psychological profilers is seen, at best, as purely circumstantial by the courts. And a good defence lawyer can paint it as nothing more than hearsay, dressed up in pseudo-scientific mumbo-jumbo. Yet, when it works and allows the police to zero in on a single suspect, it can greatly increase the chance of a conviction. After all, the police are much more likely to find damning evidence when investigating a single suspect, rather than spreading their efforts investigating dozens or perhaps hundreds of people.

In the case of serial killers, the celebrated FBI profiler John Douglas created a pair of definitions (mentioned in the last chapter) that have proved very useful to subsequent investigations. He noted that all the serial killers on the ViCAP books seemed to roughly fall into two psychological categories: asocial/disorganised and non-social/organised.

Asocial/disorganised serial killers tend to be below average intelligence. They generally kill on impulse and in a frenzy, with little or no previous planning; and the victim may be some random person who just happened to be in the wrong place at the wrong time. They almost always leave the body where it fell, and make little or no effort to cover their tracks. If they have killed multiple times, then they probably travel a lot (either for their work or as a drifter) simply because an asocial/disorganised serial killer will be caught quickly if they kill on their home turf. Their only hope of escaping justice for any length of time is to keep on the move, and thus keep the police busy with thousands of potential suspects. Jack the Ripper was almost certainly in this category; as were Peter 'the Yorkshire Ripper' Sutcliffe and Neville Heath.

The non-social/organised serial killer is the type most often portrayed by movies and feared by the public. They are generally above average intelligence, but are highly unlikely to have made much of a success with that cleverness. Some, like John Wayne Gacy Junior (who killed at least thirty-three youths and boys in Texas between 1972 and 1978) may have had some small success in business, but most bounce from one job to another because of their lack of commitment and general dishonesty. Like many sociopaths they are often charming on first acquaintance, but rarely maintain good long-term relationships, simply because they will only disguise their lack of empathy and conscience for a limited period. They often meticulously plan their murders and may target a specific victim. They will attempt to hide or otherwise dispose of dead bodies and cover their tracks carefully. However, as we will see below, they are also prone to sadistic delusions of grandeur. These may lead them to leaving the bodies in plain sight (to horrify and shock people) and to sending jeering correspondence to the police or to grieving relatives. 'Jack the Stripper' and Reg Christie were non-social/organised serial killers.

Tidy as these categorisations may seem, they are at best guidelines. Most serial killers will show traits from both lists, or may even start moving from one type to another as their lives (and list of victims) progress. Yet categorisation tools like this have proved fantastically successful in helping investigations track down unidentified killers.

One of psychological profiling's earliest, and fastest, successes was the case of a fourteen-year-old schoolgirl named Julie Wittmeyer of Platte City, Missouri, whose body was found in September 1977, two days after her disappearance. A local police officer rang the FBI profiler in Quantico, Virginia, and was told: 'The kind of person you are looking for is a heavily-built teenager, known to be interested in sex but lacking the social skills to form a relationship . . .'

The policeman interrupted him, saying: 'I know the person you're talking about.' The suspect was Mark Sager, aged seventeen, who was subsequently found guilty of killing Julie Wittmeyer. However, he was only sentenced for manslaughter (and served just five years in jail) because the jury was uncomfortable over the expert witness evidence used to convict him.

Four years earlier, in June 1973, a seven-year-old girl, Susan Jaeger, vanished from her tent near Farmington, Michigan, when an intruder sliced the canvas; her parents were in a tent a few feet away. A team of profilers concluded that the abductor was a 'peeping Tom' who lived somewhere near the campsite, and had spotted the child and her family when they arrived. Their analysis of the crime scene, cross-indexed with similar cases that had previously been solved by ordinary policing methods, suggested a relatively young white male, with a previous criminal record, who was well-organised in his *modus operandi*. They added that this level of organisation suggested that he had probably kidnapped, and probably killed, before. If so, he would likely have kept body parts or victims' clothes as souvenirs.

A local man called David Meirhofer, aged twenty-seven, was

mentioned as a possible suspect after the psychological profile had been delivered; but the lead was not adequately followed up. The fact was that nobody then had much reason to believe that a lot of eggheads, using unproven scientific methods, had any chance of pinpointing the kidnapper.

Shortly afterwards, on the anniversary of Susan's kidnap, Mrs Jaegar received a phone call from a soft-spoken man who said Susan was still alive and in Germany. Mrs Jaegar responded gently, without reproach, and reduced the anonymous caller to tears.

The police had advised the Jaegars to keep a tape recorder by the phone, and the voice on the tape was tentatively identified as Meirhofer. But that was still not strong enough evidence to convince a judge to issue a search warrant for his apartment. Knowing himself under suspicion, Meirhofer offered to meet the parents in the office of his own lawyer, and maintained such a facade of innocence that the Jaegars were convinced he was the wrong man. But soon after, the Jaegars received a long-distance phone call from someone who said he had kidnapped Susan, and called himself Mr Travis. But Marietta Jaegar recognised the voice and evidently shook the caller when she suddenly said: 'Well hello, David.'

The police were now able to obtain a warrant, and in Meirhofer's flat found 'souvenirs' of Susan, and of three other victim. Two of the victims were boys: Bernard Poelman, aged thirteen and Michael Raney, aged twelve. Meirhofer, then aged nineteen, had shot Bernard Poelman from a distance, like a sniper, on 19 March 1967, then run away before the police arrived. He had killed Michael Raney on 7 May 1968, clubbing then stabbing the boy to death as he was camping. Then Meirhofer kidnapped and murdered seven-year-old Susan Jaeger on 24 June 1974. He strangled her, dismembered the body, and then burned the remains. But he kept her head as a keepsake.

The fourth victim was a young woman, nineteen-year-old Sandra Dykman Smallegan, who Meirhofer had once dated. He suffocated her in her apartment on 10 February 1974, then took her body to the same deserted ranch house where he had killed

Susan Jaeger. He dismembered her and disposed of the body. He kept her hands in his freezer, however, as mementos.

David Meirhofer did not live to be tried. He committed suicide by hanging himself in his cell.

Why did Meirhofer invite his own arrest by contacting Susan's parents? The answer is that this is by no means unusual. Many profilers would regard the need to indulge self-congratulation – which is what it amounts to – as an integral part to the organised/non-social serial killer type. Ever since Jack the Ripper, in 1888, serial killers have enjoyed taunting investigating police and victims' families, from what they consider a safe distance.

This sort of grotesque sadism at least partially stems from the god complex that many serial killers seem to develop after their first murders. They kill, at least partially, in order to battle their own innate feelings of inadequacy. The psychosexual high that they get from murder is underlined by the 'god-like' power of death that they feel that they have granted to themselves. Many captured serial killers have confessed to a transcendent illusion of superiority enjoyed after a murder – of looking at passing people as if they were mere insects, to be crushed or let go at the serial killer's whim.

But, as with all highs, the exultation fades away over time. One obvious answer to this is to kill again – to renew the feeling – but (as we discussed in Chapter 7) the law of diminishing returns will eventually reduce the sense of euphoria brought on by killing. Even the monstrously extraordinary can finally become unexciting through habit and repetition. Plus, committing a murder is an extremely dangerous activity. Only the most Yahweh-like god complex could completely eradicate the serial killer's own fear of being injured by a victim, or of being caught by the police . . . literally red handed. (This fear is one of the reasons why serial killers often go for months or even years between murders – they have to build up their addictive need, and the courage, to kill again.)

Taunting apparently hapless police officers and the frightened relatives of victims is therefore a sort of palliative for a serial killer; like a baby sucking its thumb to simulate breast feeding when no breast is available. Indeed, some serial killers seem to have been as addicted to taunting as they were to murder itself. And if their god complex grows, their delusion that they are 'uncatchable' might grow too. This fantasy for a serial killer – that taunting is a risk-free sadistic high – is very far from the truth. All that they are really doing, besides causing suffering, is giving more clues to those hunting them.

(It is a common pop-psychology/Hollywood trope that this behaviour is a subconscious act of confession by the killer: an unconscious attempt to get themselves caught and end the horror. 'Catch me before I kill again!' But this is entirely wishful thinking. Sociopathic killers don't want to be caught, any more than muggers or burglars want to go to prison. They taunt because they want to taunt. No more. No less.)

On the afternoon of 31 May 1985, the father of seventeen-year-old high school student Sharon 'Shari' Smith saw her car pull up in front of the distant mailbox at the end of the drive of their home in Lexington County, South Carolina. Minutes later, when Shari had still not appeared, Bob Smith went to investigate and found the car with the engine running and the door open, but no sign of Shari. The police who were summoned also found no clue, and the neighbours had apparently noticed nothing unusual.

Shari's elder sister Dawn was Miss South Carolina and a well-known singer. There was some speculation that the abductor had been after Dawn.

The kidnapper soon called the Smiths, declaring that Shari was still alive and would be writing. Police tried to trace the calls, without success. There were more calls, making it clear that the abductor was enjoying this power game. He also turned up the psychological pressure by saying that he intended to send the Smiths Shari's last will and testament. This duly arrived, written on note paper, and in Shari's own handwriting. Shari said she was writing with a sense of foreboding as if she knew she was going to die: 'I love you Mommy, Daddy, Robert, Dawn and Richard and everyone else and all other friends and relatives. My thoughts will always be with and in you. Casket closed. I am sorry if I ever disappointed you in any way. I only wanted to make you proud of me because I have always been proud of my family.'

Five days after her disappearance the kidnapper telephoned them again to tell them she was dead, how he had killed her and where to locate the body; she had been strangled and was found where he indicated.

But Shari's 'will' contained the clue the police needed to catch the killer. It was written on the kind of notepad kept by a telephone. And examined under an Esta machine, for magnifying and studying documents, the police were able to distinguish a telephone number that had been written on an earlier sheet and whose pressure had carried through the paper. They rang the number and its owners were at first unable to help. But a little sleuthing tracked the number down to some people who had used a house-sitter called Larry Gene Bell. (Indeed, he had been house-sitting for someone else when he kidnapped Shari Smith.)

Larry Bell was arrested as he was driving his car, and the arresting sheriff said his face turned the colour of whitewash when he was told that he was under arrest for suspected murder. Probably the bubble of Bell's sadistic fantasy world – in which he was the all-powerful arbiter of life and death – burst at that moment, as he found himself in the hands of the authorities and facing an almost certain death sentence himself.

In the four weeks since he had kidnapped Shari Smith, Bell had claimed another victim, a nine-year-old girl called Debra May Helmick who had been snatched from her lawn. So Bell was, legally speaking, a multiple-murderer but not a serial killer, because he did not (as far as we know) kill three or more people over a protracted period of time. But there seems little doubt that, if he hadn't given himself away by taunting the Smith family, he would have gone on to kill again before he was caught.

It was for Debra May Helmick's rape and murder that Bell was found guilty and sentenced to death. Various appeals were turned down. Allowed to choose between lethal injection and the chair, Bell chose the latter, and was electrocuted on 4 October 1996.

The parallels between the case of Larry Gene Bell and that of the multiple rapist Maury Travis, which follows, are too obvious to need underlining. Travis is what Bell would probably have become, if the police had missed the clue on Shari Smith's farewell note to her family.

Has serial killing always been with us? Were there Cro-Magnon cavemen who were addicted to murder? The answer is almost certainly that serial crime is a modern phenomenon. Although not quite as modern as may initially be thought . . . The following section is from my 2008 book *Serial Killers* (co-written with my son Damon).

It is a matter of historical debate over who can be described as history's first known and recorded serial killer. The most commonly mentioned name that fits the serial killer mould is that of a fifteenth-century French nobleman. He was a warrior for his people's freedom; he was a famously handsome man of exquisite taste; he was a gifted courtier and diplomat; he was comrade-in-arms to a famously virtuous woman who would later be canonised as a saint. And he was also one of the most monstrous serial killers on record.

Gilles de Rais was born in 1404, the eldest son of the Baron of Rais (now known as Retz, in the area bordering Brittany called Machecoul). France, at the time of his birth, had already suffered greatly in what was later to be called the Hundred Years War with England, but worse was to come.

Gilles was orphaned when he was eleven and was afterwards raised by his maternal grandfather. In that same year the English king, Henry V, unexpectedly won a stunning victory at the Battle of Agincourt. French knights charged a well dug-in English battle line and were cut to pieces by the armour-piercing arrows of the English longbowmen. It seems possible that Gilles' father died in the bloody mud at Agincourt, along with a large proportion of the French military aristocracy.

Accurate biographical details about the young Gilles de Rais are hard to come by, but we know that his grandfather found it difficult to marry him off when the time came. This

*was not because Gilles was in any way ugly – not that that
mattered much in aristocratic matchmaking. He was actually
quite striking, sporting a dapper beard so black that people
swore that in certain lights it looked bluish. This earned Gilles
the nickname 'Bluebeard'.*

*Gilles' early marital misfortunes were entirely a matter of
bad luck. Two potential brides dropped dead before marriage
alliances could be cemented, but sudden death was not uncommon in disease-ridden Europe at that time. Certainly there is
no suspicion that the then teenaged Gilles had anything to do
with the deaths. However, it has been suggested that the fairy
story 'Bluebeard' – in which the eponymous villain marries
repeatedly, only to murder his new wives the morning after
the honeymoon – might be the result of a confused mixing up
of Gilles' story: the dying fiancés, his striking nickname, and
his later murders.*

*The third marriage attempt proved more fortunate. In
1420, de Rais married a very wealthy heiress, Catherine de
Thouars, and so became one of the richest men in Europe.
That said, the courtship did not go entirely smoothly –
Catherine had to be kidnapped at one point in order to get the
deal settled. But France was in a very chaotic state at that time
– with the English 'Goddamn' armies conquering or laying
waste to large swathes of the north – so the bandit matchmaking tactics of Gilles' grandfather were probably seen as in-step
with the times.*

*We first see Gilles acting on his own account when he
arranged the release of the captured John VI, Duke of Brittany.
He did this with such diplomatic aplomb that the Breton
parliament awarded the young baron with a sizable monetary
reward, thus making him even richer. We can also see from
this that, even in his early twenties, Gilles de Rais was
evidently a smooth talker and a diplomatic courtier. We next
hear of him attending the court of the Dauphin Charles, the
heir to the French throne.*

*Gilles was taking a chance by siding with Charles. The
Dauphin was a singularly ineffectual man – disowned as a*

bastard by his own mother and, despite the death of his 'father', unable to get the military and political backing to have himself crowned King of France. In the 1420s most sensible money was on Charles's destruction and the total conquest of France by England.

Then something extraordinary happened. In 1428, a young woman called Joan of Arc (the daughter of a well-off farmer, not a lowly peasant as is often stated) heard voices in her head that she believed to be the messengers of God. The voices told Joan to go to the Dauphin and declare that Heaven was on his side. Charles, bankrupt and terrified, was willing to try anything, so he sent Joan to 'lead' his armies. In fact, capable generals did most of the actual commanding, although Joan did prove to be something of a genius in the use of artillery. She also excelled at rallying the flagging morale of the French armies. With her at their head they started a fight-back that was eventually to hurl the English out of France completely. Joan did not live to see this; she was captured by the Burgundians, sold to the English and then burned as a heretic by the Church in 1431. That same Catholic Church canonised her as Saint Joan in 1920.

Not surprisingly, much has been made of the relationship between Gilles de Rais and Joan of Arc: the savage monster and the saintly virgin. But much of this seems to have been wishful thinking by later chroniclers. De Rais certainly knew Joan, and probably fought alongside her in some battles, but he was not her bodyguard, as some have claimed, or even one of her key supporters. In fact de Rais is on record as only commanding twenty-five men-at-arms and eleven archers, so he was hardly one of Joan's generals.

Even his military title, Marèchal, was largely an honorary designation. It was bestowed by Charles VII after his coronation, more in thanks for Gilles' financial loans than for his marshal prowess. After the coronation, despite the fact that the war was still raging, de Rais retired to his estates, gadding between castles at Machecoul, Malemort, La Suze, Champtoce, and Tiffauges.

He lived with immense extravagance: he kept a bodyguard of two hundred knights, a private chapel, and one of the finest manuscript libraries in Europe. But soon these huge expenditures ate up even his vast fortune and forced him to start to sell land. When they heard of this his relatives (and potential heirs) obtained an injunction from King Charles to prevent Gilles selling more. This order was ignored in semi-autonomous Brittany, however, where Bishop Malestroit and Duke John VI were happy to acquire more of De Rais' lands.

Nevertheless, Gilles was still facing bankruptcy; so he turned to alchemy to mend his fortunes, seeking the fabled 'Philosopher's Stone' that could turn all base metals to pure gold. He employed Father Gilles de Sille, a priest, to conduct more-or-less scientific researches into the possibility; but when he failed, de Rais became prey to a series of charlatans, ending, in 1439, with a defrocked priest, Francesco Prelati of Florence. It was probably Prelati who turned Gilles from the scientific pursuit of the Philosopher's Stone to black magic and invocation of the Devil using the blood of young children.

Over the next six years de Rais is said to have used his position as a baron to secretly kidnap dozens, perhaps hundreds of children, all of whom he tortured and killed. It seems likely that he originally started as a would-be devil worshiper but, in the light of our knowledge of serial killer psychology, we can confidently say that he must have soon become addicted to murder. The sheer numbers of children involved, and the cruel methods said to have been used to murder them, do not point to a man whose only interest was the production of magical gold.

De Rais' downfall began with, what would have been to a baron, a minor misdemeanour. He sold his estate at Malemort to the Treasurer of Brittany, Geoffroi le Ferron, but then refused admission to Geoffroi's brother, Jean le Ferron. When this man insisted on his family's rights, de Rais had him beaten and then imprisoned. But Jean le Ferron was a priest, and Bishop Malestroit seized on this pretext to try to have Gilles declared a heretic.

Preliminary hearings began on 28 September 1440, and his accusers were so certain of finding him guilty that some of his lands were actually disposed of before the trial began. He was charged with the abuse of a priest, with conjuring demons, and with sexual perversion involving children. Gilles laughed at these charges and declared them too silly to deny. One of the charges declared that 'spurning the natural way of copulation', Gilles had committed sodomy with young boys and girls . . . and that his victims were sometimes alive, sometimes dead, and sometimes even in their death throes when he mounted them.

The formal trial opened on 15 October, 1440; the key evidence being the dismembered, rotting bodies of about fifty children that had been found in an abandoned tower at de Rais' estate at Machecoul. Gilles de Rais was himself tortured on 19 October; as were his servants and four alleged accomplices. Judicial torture, it should be noted, was then so common as to be a virtual formality in all capital trials – many, for example, were shocked at Joan of Arc's trial when she was not tortured, but was merely intimidated by being 'shown the instruments [of torture]'.

One servant, under this extreme duress, declared that Gilles rubbed his penis against the thighs and bellies of children and, having achieved orgasm, then took pleasure in seeing their heads cut off, or in decapitating them himself. It was also alleged that he took great pleasure in watching the death throes of children, sometimes sitting on their chests while they were dying. It was said that, on one occasion, de Rais tortured and killed one child in front of his brother, then did the same to the other boy.

His own torture apparently had less effect on Gilles than the threat of excommunication: this latter made him break down completely and 'confess everything'. On 26 October 1440, de Rais was hanged, using a knot that garrotted him slowly while his feet dangled and seared in a blazing fire; a fate he shared with two of his associates. Although it is hard not to appreciate the cold irony of such a savage method of execution, it is also plain that casual sadism was a norm in fifteenth-century Europe, even within the judicial system.

No final figure was ever arrived at for the number of children tortured and murdered by Baron Gilles de Rais – estimates ranged between eighty and two hundred.

It is almost certain that Gilles de Rais was not the first serial killer in history – many others, like the Roman Emperor Caligula, were evidently addicted to murder. Most tyrants have used the terror of random acts of murder as a prop to their power, and any number of bandits and outlaws in history must also have become habitual killers. But 'Bluebeard' de Rais was one of the first powerful men to be specifically executed for his crimes. His death was not so much the end to the first serial killer, but evidence that the forces of the law were coming to recognise that noble birth and prestige were not immunities to justice.

Chapter 21

'Tyger Tyger'

We are conditioned to think, by endless TV dramas and horror movies, that serial killers are a threat to us all. This is simply not true. Serial killers are rare monsters to begin with and tend to target a very limited section of the population. Most people are more likely to be killed by a gas explosion or a lightning strike than by a serial killer.

As already noted, serial killers tend to prefer small or lightly built victims, simply because they are scared of being injured themselves. Young women are certainly more at risk than most people – as are, to a lesser extent, young men. But most potential victims are safe from serial killers if they are not the sort to go off, out of sight of other people, with a total stranger.

The reduction or outlawing of hitchhiking in many countries, and the practice of 'safe' prostitution – in which street walkers travel in pairs to order to watch out for each other – has greatly reduced the number of available victims to a prowling serial killer. And those countries like Germany, Mexico and Turkey that have legal and regulated brothels – getting many prostitutes off the streets – have gone even further in limiting opportunities for random murder. But a serial killer, by their very nature, will be searching for potential victims all the time. Sooner or later, they will find an undefended victim.

On 1 April 2001, the corpse of a young black woman was found in Washington Park, St Louis, Missouri. She had been beaten and strangled. Her fingerprints identified her as Alysia Greenwade, a known prostitute and drug addict.

Thirty miles away, across the border in Illinois, another black prostitute was found strangled a month later; she was identified through her dental plate as Teresa Wilson, another drug addict who walked the streets to support her habit. Yet another black prostitute, Verona Thomson, was found close to the site of the previous body a month after this. And still the police were unable to generate a lead.

A fourth body was found in St Louis, another black prostitute with a drug addiction. Betty James also had a tyre print on one of her lower legs, presumably caused as the serial killer made a hurried getaway.

But the next two victims, found in East St Louis on 25 August and 8 October 2001, provided the police with their first important clue: both had semen in them, from which identical DNA profiles were obtained. They were Yvonne Cruise and Brenda Beasley – and, like the others, they were drug-addicted black prostitutes.

Since the murders had been occurring approximately every six weeks, police expected another in December. But it apparently never happened.

Then, in May 2002, a reporter on the *St Louis Post-Dispatch*, Bill Smith, wrote a piece on the first known victim, Alysia Greenwade. Five days later, he received an anonymous letter ironically congratulating him on his 'sob story', and suggesting that he should go on and write more profiles of victims – in which case, said the writer, he would provide him with plenty more material. And he enclosed a map, with the position of another body marked on it at West Alton.

The police followed up its instructions, along Highway 67, and located a woman's skeleton on some remote open ground. The letter had claimed she was victim number seventeen.

The letter itself, in computer-generated 'handwriting', failed to yield any clues – either fingerprints or DNA. But the map had clearly been taken from a website, and although the edges had been cut off, the Cyber Crimes Unit was able to track it down to holiday-booking website Expedia.com. And the website, in turn, had a record of computers that had logged on to it. Using the IP address. the police were able to track the computer that had printed the map. It belonged to a man called Maury Travis, a thirty-six-year-old waiter who lived alone in a house in nearby Ferguson, Missouri, and had a criminal record for armed robbery. On 7 June 2002, two detectives knocked on the door of Maury Travis at 7 a.m.

The black man who opened the door asked them indignantly: 'Do you know what time this is?' Special Investigator Bob Morton, an FBI profiler, told Travis that it was his computer that had printed the map showing the body's location.

'He was very controlling,' said Morton. 'He indicated where we should sit and also tried to steer the conversation.' They showed him photographs of the prostitutes and Travis said he had never set eyes on any of them. Ten minutes later he said: 'Could I see those pictures of the dead girls again?' and Morton asked him: 'Who said they were dead?' Travis's calm demeanour cracked and he hung his head.

But it was when he was told that a forensic team was on its way to examine his bungalow that Travis began ranting, during which he said 'That damn computer . . .' and the agents knew this was virtually an admission.

In fact, Travis made no further admissions. But an aluminium can from which he drank a Diet Coke while being questioned yielded his DNA, which was identical to the semen samples. And the tyre mark on Betty James's leg matched the tyre of Travis's car.

The basement of his duplex proved to be a torture chamber, the floor and walls spotted with blood. Videotapes showed him subjecting his victims to rape and beatings, and forcing them to show total submission, repeating 'You are the master'. He had also videotaped himself murdering some of them.

Travis was described by neighbours and colleagues as a quiet, polite man. At the age of twenty-two, as a college student in Atlanta, he had become hooked on cocaine and acquired a $300-a-day habit. And the following year, 1988, he committed a series of hold-ups in St Louis to support the habit. He was sentenced to fifteen years in prison, but was paroled after five. He worked as a waiter in restaurants and served several shorter periods in jail on drug-related charges.

On 10 June, soon after his arraignment, Maury Travis hanged himself with a bed sheet in his cell. The number of his victims is unknown. He himself confessed to seventeen murders, of which the police were able to confirm only twelve. Some believe he killed as many as twenty women.

As noted in Chapter 19, it is very rare for serial killers to commit suicide . . . provided they remain unidentified and free. The very fact that they have become addicted to murder is a sign that they are living in a sadistic fantasy world that is divorced from most of the norms of everyday society. It would be nice to believe that they suffer terrible guilt and remorse, but evidence from serial killer confessions and memoirs suggests that they really don't. Their fantasy world buoys them up, aggrandises them and is self-maintaining . . . until they find themselves facing an arresting policeman.

A serial killer is a sort of twisted Walter Mitty character – living as much of their time as they can in a fantasy world, in which reality is an unwelcome guest. For example, Jeffrey Dahmer – the 'Milwaukee Cannibal' who drugged, raped, killed, dismembered and partially ate seventeen men and boys between 1978 and 1991 – commented after his arrest that he had spent much of his time gloatingly remembering his past murders and feverishly imagining future murders. The actual killings, he said, were rather grim and grisly things that he hadn't enjoyed fully until he looked back on them – doubtlessly embellishing them in his imagination.

Andrei Chikatilo – the 'Rostov Ripper' who mutilated and killed at least fifty-two women and children between 1978 and 1990 – admitted in his confession that he spent a large proportion of his time hunting victims. That is, he would lurk around railway and bus stations, looking for vulnerable people who he might persuade to go with him into the woods. So, over a twelve-year period, Chikatilo spent almost all his spare time, and much of the time he was supposedly at work, wandering about 'hunting'. As such, even the horrifying figure of fifty-two murders is a very low strike rate. The fact is that Chikatilo, one of the most prolific serial killers of the twentieth century, spent an inordinate amount of time hunting, *and generally failed to catch anyone.*

This might seem, to an outside observer, to be a frustrating purgatory – if Chikatilo's only aim was to kill. But what he was actually doing, when hunting, was *fantasising* about killing. As he wandered around the dreary stations, Chikatilo was happily indulging in his favourite murder daydreams – much as a sex maniac might fantasise about picking up and copulating with every girl he sees, but with little intention of even speaking to most of them.

Jeffrey Dahmer said that he had fantasised about violent killing and dismemberment for years before he committed his first murder; then one day he acted out one of his fantasies to the full. This seems to be another typical serial killer trait – that they fantasise about murder so much that their fantasy eventually consumes their lives – and, indirectly, the lives of their victims.

Yet, the moment a killer is caught, that fantasy and any associated delusions of grandeur vanish. During subsequent police interviews the killer may reluctantly see himself, possibly for the first time in his life, through the eyes of others – as a heartless, murdering monster. And he ironically finds himself in a parallel situation to where he put his victims: captured, controlled by force, and threatened with life imprisonment or a death sentence.

It is a fairly well-documented fact that serial killers often become as quiet as lambs when imprisoned. Bereft of their self-indulgent fantasy worlds by the brutal reality of capture and imprisonment, the serial killer is generally less capable of dealing aggressively with prison life than other inmates. Far from being the terrifying takers of life portrayed in the movies, they often become the victims of other prisoners. For example, Jeffrey Dahmer was beaten to death in the prison gym, and Peter Sutcliffe – the Yorkshire Ripper – was partially blinded when another inmate slashed at his eyes with a pen.

But only a few serial killers – like David Meirhofer, Maury Travis and Britain's Fred West – commit suicide in their cells. It might be nice to believe that they killed themselves out of sudden, crushing remorse over their crimes – but given the fact that most or all serial killers are almost certainly clinically sociopathic (that is, physically and psychologically incapable of developing a conscience) they almost certainly killed themselves out of towering self-pity and resulting despair.

It *is* possible to stop a potential serial killer before their fantasy life goes too far, they commit their first murder and then evolve into a fully fledged killing-junkie. It may not be possible to cure the sadism and self-indulgent fantasy that leads them in that direction, but arrest and treatment could shatter their delusions enough to save them, and their potential victims. Take the case of the Canadian 'terrorist', Roger Charles Bell.

A series of pipe-bombings began in October 1988 in Charlottetown, Prince Edward Island, and at first offered no clues to law enforcement. The first homemade bomb exploded outside the Sir Louis Henry Davies Law Courts in Charlottetown in October 1988. The bomb was obscured in a flowerbed and exploded at 6 a.m., causing no casualties or structural damage; although windows were broken and the law library was superficially damaged.

On 20 April 1995, a powerful pipe bomb exploded beneath a wooden wheelchair ramp on the north side of Province House, Charlottetown, destroying glass in windows and causing some minor structural damage. Several passers-by were injured and the explosion occurred only five minutes after an entire class of schoolchildren had passed through the area. The bombing also occurred a day after the Oklahoma City bombing, when Timothy McVeigh, with the assistance of Terry Nichols, destroyed the Alfred P. Murrah Federal Building in downtown Oklahoma City. The Canadian police had to consider the possibility that they might have a would-be copy-cat killer on their hands, if their unknown bomber had been 'inspired' by the Oklahoma atrocity.

The bomber's next exploit had the police even more worried. They received a threat that a bomb had been placed in a large storage facility of propane gas. If it exploded it could blow a vast crater and devastate the neighbouring residential area. It took an enormous operation to locate the device, isolate it and detonate it harmlessly.

Responsibility for the Province House bomb had been claimed by a group calling itself 'Loki 7', who used a swastika with pointed arms as its symbol. (Loki is the Norse god of mischief who can be found in Wagner's *Rheingold*.) The letter contained references to 'venal injustice officials' and 'crypto-Zionist producers' but revealed little about potential motives. Despite the neo-Nazi rhetoric, police were not led to believe that Loki 7 represented a real white supremacist group. The letter seemed to be a deliberate distraction to the investigation; but if it *was* written by the real bomber, it was potentially a valuable clue.

One of the exploded bombs was part-reassembled, and the pipe proved to be four inches across – unusually wide for household plumbing. Plumbing stores that would sell it were checked. Such a piece of pipe would be less than a foot long, and would need to have a screwtop, or nipple, at either end. Two caps would be unusual – most plumbers would only need one. Finally, a purchaser was tracked down who had bought two.

His signature read 'John Macleod' – almost certainly an alias. But was there some way of comparing it with dozens of other suspects' signatures? The chief investigator took the correspondence of Loki 7 to a university professor, who quickly concluded that the group was highly educated. That enabled them to reduce the suspect list to five. And one of those signatures matched a former high-school science teacher named Roger Bell. He was on the suspect list because Customs and Excise had tipped off the authorities that Bell had purchased three books on bomb-making from an American publisher.

Bell proved to be a recluse who seldom spoke to neighbours. A member of his old science class told how Bell had supervised one session and stared out of the window the whole time without speaking. He obviously saw himself as a loner, an outsider. A relative who had formerly been close to him told police that he was obsessed by the idea of his own superiority – that he was a uniquely gifted human being.

Bell, who had been under constant surveillance (so skilful that he had not noticed) was arrested and his flat searched. At first nothing incriminating was found. Then, on a notepad, the searchers came upon the outline of a cut-out swastika with pointed ends. This evidence was conclusive; but because, by sheer luck, nobody had been killed, Bell was only sentenced to nine years in jail.

Why did he do it? Before his release on parole he dropped his only hint. 'I think my motive was revenge at society.'

Bell's hesitational mode of speaking is significant. For a person who takes pride in logic, it betrays underlying doubts. British Prime Minister Margaret Thatcher once said that there is no such thing as society – only individuals. What individual was Bell seeking to punish? If the propane bomb had wiped out half the town, did Bell want to make them suffer as opposed to the other half? Such dubious logic reminds us that the criminal is generally self-divided and does not know his own mind.

We can be fairly sure, however, that Bell's delusions of superiority motivated him towards potential murder. In his personal fantasy world – indulged in his self-imposed isolation and, before that, during the times when he was supposed to be teaching – he apparently saw himself as a god-like figure and the rest of the world as holding him back. His attempted 'revenge', in this light, seems the act of a delusional sociopath having a prolonged temper tantrum. Yet now that Bell has been released (in 2006) it should be possible to help him overcome his homicidal tendencies. It should simply require continuous psychiatric evaluation and treatment for the rest of his life.

We have noted that many serial killers seem at some point to have had an experience of such intensity that it turns them into 'monsters' by instantly and permanently forming an obsession. It is easy to imagine it happening to Jack the Stripper (*see Chapter 20*) the first time he realised a girl had choked to death on his penis. And to Reg Christie as he watched Muriel Eady becoming passive as she breathed the gas, and he knew that nothing now stood between him and the sexual assault he would never have dared commit when she was conscious. A lifetime of frustration was over; no wonder he experienced 'that quiet, peaceful thrill' and had no regrets. Christie could have no regrets because, as a sociopath, he only really cared about himself. Muriel's death meant nothing to him, but her corpse held wonderful opportunities.

An interesting and chilling fact is that serial killers can also 'reactivate' if they are ever released from jail and left fully to their own devices. There are several examples of this, seen when serial killers are arrested and imprisoned for other crimes, but without being identified as a serial killer. They obviously stop killing when in jail, but they then start again almost as soon as they are released. This phenomenon has happened often enough that if a series of murders just stops, the investigators should automatically check who in the region was jailed for other, apparently disconnected crimes just after the last murder. If they can't pinpoint the serial killer in jail, however, they can be sure the murders will begin again, as soon as the unidentified killer is paroled.

Probably the most striking example of this 'reactivation' of a released serial killer was the case of Jack Unterweger. The following account is taken from my 2008 book *Serial Killers* (co-written with my son Damon).

Jack Unterweger – poet, dramatist and serial killer – qualifies as one of the strangest criminals of the twentieth century.

From the point of view of law enforcement, his case began on 14 September 1990, when the naked body of a shop assistant, Blanka Bockova, was found on the banks of the Vltava River, near Prague. She had been beaten and strangled with stockings. Although lying on her back with legs apart, a tampon was still in place, and there were no traces of semen. She had been out drinking with friends in Wenceslas Square the previous evening, but had decided not to leave with them at 11.45 p.m. The police were baffled; there were simply no leads.

On New Year's Eve 1991, in a forest near Graz, Austria, nearly 300 miles south of Prague, another woman was found strangled with her pantyhose. She was Heidemarie Hammerer, a prostitute who had vanished from Graz on 26 October 1990.

Although fully clothed, there were signs that she had been undressed and then re-dressed after she was dead. Bruises on her wrist suggested rope or handcuffs. Again, no semen was present. Some red fibres found on her clothes were preserved as forensic evidence, as were minute particles of leather, probably from a jacket.

Five days later, a badly decomposed woman was found in a forest north of Graz. She had been stabbed and strangled – again, probably with her pantyhose. She was identified as Brunhilde Masser, another prostitute.

There was another disappearance from Graz on 7 March 1991, a prostitute named Elfriede Schrempf. Her decomposed body was found eight months later, on 5 October, in a forest near Graz. And still the police had no clue to this multiple killer of prostitutes.

When four more prostitutes, Silvia Zagler, Sabine Moitzi, Regina Prem and Karin Eroglu, disappeared in Vienna during the next month, it looked as if the killer had changed his location. Although the police claimed there was no established connection between the crimes, the press began to speak of a serial killer. They called him 'the Vienna Courier'.

And at that point, investigators found a vital lead. Ex-policeman August Schenner, retired for five years from the Vienna force, was reminded of the MO of a murderer he had met seventeen years earlier, in 1974. His name was Jack Unterweger, and he was now a famous writer and media personality.

The case dated back to the time when Unterweger was twenty-three. Two women had been strangled. The first, Margaret Schaefer, aged eighteen, was a friend of Barbara Scholz, a prostitute, who had turned him in. She told how they had robbed Schaefer's house, then taken her to the woods, where Unterweger had strangled her with her bra after she refused to give him oral sex. He had left her naked and covered with leaves – just as in most of the more recent killings.

The second 1970s victim, a prostitute named Marcia Horveth, had been strangled with her stockings and dumped in a lake. Unterweger was not charged with this murder, because he had already confessed to the first and had been sentenced to life. Nevertheless he had pleaded guilty to the murder of Horveth, claiming that as he was making love to her, he had seen the face of his mother before him. This, apparently, was his reason to kill her. A psychologist diagnosed him a sexually sadistic sociopath with narcissistic tendencies.

Unterweger, a good-looking youth who was the son of a prostitute and an American GI, had been illiterate when he went to jail. He had already been in prison fifteen times, for offences like rape and car theft. He had even been a pimp. But in prison for life, he set about learning to read and write. Then he edited the prison newspaper, started a literary review, and wrote his autobiography, a book called Purgatory *('Fegefeur'), which professed that he was totally rehabilitated, and had killed Marcia Horveth because he hated his mother.*

The book made him an overnight literary icon and celebrities on the Austrian intellectual scene began to lobby for his release. He was paroled on 23 May 1990, after sixteen years. And he was now a celebrity himself, who quickly became rich when his book was made into a movie. Since then he had written plays, had given readings of his poetry, and was a regular guest on TV talk shows. He habitually wore a white suit and drove expensive cars. Moreover, as a magazine writer, he had even interviewed the police about the 'Vienna Courier', and had been critical of their failure to catch him. Could this charming, brilliant new literary celebrity be a serial killer?

As they reviewed the evidence, the Vienna police – and especially a detective called Ernst Geiger – decided the answer had to be yes.

To begin with, when they checked his credit card receipts, to establish his whereabouts at the times of crimes, they learned that Unterweger was in Graz in October, when Brunhilde Masser was killed. And he was there again in March when Elfriede Schrempf vanished. He was also in Bregenz, from where Heidemarie Hammerer was taken, in December and, moreover, resembled the last person with whom she was seen.

Unterweger had been in Prague the previous September, and when the police contacted their counterparts in Prague, they learned about the murder of Blanka Bockova. Of course, all this could hardly be coincidence. After months of secretly investigating the celebrity, investigators finally decided that it was time to show their hand.

They interviewed Unterweger on 2 October 1991. Naturally, he denied everything. Moreover, he renewed criticism of the police for their failure to catch the Vienna Courier. Support for him among the Viennese celebrity set and his society friends remained strong. (But how could they admit that their enthusiasm for his writing had unleashed a killer on Vienna? Was it not more likely, as Unterweger told them, that the authorities were persecuting this ex-criminal who had now become their journalistic scourge?)

Undeterred, investigator Ernst Geiger went on with his search. Prostitutes who had been with Unterweger testified that he liked to handcuff them during sex – which was consistent with some of the marks on the wrists of the Vienna Courier's victims. Police tracked down the BMW that Unterweger had bought on his release from prison, and found in it a dark hair with skin on the root. It was tiny, but using the PCR technique to make multiple copies of DNA, they were able to identify it as belonging to victim Blanka Bockova.

A search of Unterweger's apartment revealed a red scarf whose fibres matched those found on Bockova, as well as a leather jacket, and receipts from California, where Unterweger had gone to research a magazine article on prostitution in Hollywood. A check with the Los Angeles Police Department revealed that there had been three murders of prostitutes in the five weeks Unterweger was there; while the 'Courier's' activities in Vienna ceased over that same period. All three women – Irene Rodriguez, Shannon Exley and Sherri Long – had been strangled with their bras and left out in the open.

It turned out that Unterweger had gone to the LAPD and introduced himself as a European writer researching red light

*areas. He went out with police in patrol cars, and was treated
as a distinguished guest.*

*It was time to arrest the suspect. In February 1992 a judge
signed a warrant. But when the police arrived at his apartment, Unterweger was gone. They learned from his friends
that he had gone on holiday with his latest girlfriend, eighteen-year-old Bianca Mrak, whom he had picked up in a
restaurant, and with whom he had been living since the previous December.*

*It seemed they had gone to Switzerland, and then, when
friends tipped him off by telephone that there was a warrant
out for him, to New York.*

*Before leaving Europe, Unterweger had telephoned Vienna
newspapers to insist that the police were trying to frame him.
He also made an offer: if the officer in charge of the case would
drop the warrant for his arrest, he would return voluntarily to
'clear his name'. He had alibis, he said, for all the murders – on
one occasion he had been giving a reading of his work.*

*Unterweger and Bianca moved to Miami, Florida, and
rented a beach apartment. They were running short of money,
and Bianca took a job as a topless dancer. Bianca's mother also
kept them supplied with cash by telegraph.*

*When the police learned about this, they called on the
mother, and prevailed on her to inform them next time her
daughter made contact. And when Bianca asked her mother to
telegraph more cash to the Western Union office in Miami, two
agents were waiting for them. The alert Unterweger spotted
them and fled, urging Bianca to go in another direction. But
he was caught after running through a restaurant, causing
havoc, and out at the back, where an agent with a gun arrested
him. When told he was wanted for making a false customs
declaration in New York – he had failed to admit his prison
record – he looked relieved. But when they added that he was
also wanted in Vienna for murder, he began to sob.*

*Learning that he was also wanted in California, where his
semen had been found in one of the dead victims, Unterweger
decided to resist extradition to Europe and opt for trial in Los*

Angeles. Then he was told that California – unlike Austria – had a death penalty. So he immediately changed his mind.

Back in Vienna, the final outcome was inevitable. The strength of the evidence against him was overwhelming. As the trial – which began in April 1994 – dragged on for two and a half months, his support among journalists and former admirers began to ebb away. He failed to produce any of the unshakeable alibis he had promised. On 28 June 1994, the jury found Unterweger guilty, and he was sentenced to life imprisonment.

American agent Gregg McCrary, who had been actively involved since 1992 as a psychological profiler, advised the Vienna police to keep a suicide watch on Unterweger, since he had frequently boasted that he would never spend another day in prison. They failed to heed his warning, and a few hours after being sentenced to life imprisonment, he hanged himself in his cell with the cord from his jumpsuit.

Jack Unterweger was a sexual sadist who liked to utterly dominate, then kill his victims. That urge led him to his first two murders in 1974. If he had not been caught then, he would almost certainly have killed again. Prison 'froze' his violent tendencies, and he may have been able to redirect some of the energy that normally went into his sadistic fantasy life into his campaign to educate himself and win early release.

Paroled and out from under the eye of the authorities, Unterweger's fantasy existence fell back into its old, pre-prison tendencies. And his inclination to become an egotistical, organ-ised/non-social serial killer must have been boosted by the plaudits of the Viennese celebrity crowd, who regarded his early release as a triumph of their own humanity and decency. They could not have known, until it was too late, what an unrepentant monster he was.

The final message of the Jack Unterweger case is that fully fledged serial killers can never be trusted to reform. Like alco-holics or drug addicts, they can never be completely cured. At best, they will spend the rest of their lives as 'recovering serial killers'. Releasing a former serial killer into the public again is like locking a former alcoholic in a room with a crate of booze. But where the alcoholic might fight with all their will not to drink, a serial killer is unlikely to put up much of a fight against reasserting their homicidal habits.

We will look more closely in a later chapter at the subject of sociopathy – also called pschopathy and antisocial personality disorder. Here it should only be noted that a high proportion of, and perhaps all, serial killers are sociopaths. In reading the details of serial crime cases, it is easy for the average reader to be shocked at the cruelty, lack of conscience, and the simple monstrosity of a serial killer. But all this can be at least partially explained by the fact that they are sociopathic.

A sociopath – for reasons that are still a matter of scientific debate – seems to be unable to develop a conscience. Other people – even a parent, spouse or their own children – have no value to a sociopath, other than to serve their personal interests. The people around them are used and misused as and when a sociopath feels that they can get away with it. They can display convincing affection, sympathy and even charm, but it is almost entirely an act. Their inherent lack of any genuine personal bonding to others, and of any feeling of social responsibility, makes them capable of appalling acts of cruelty. And, if questioned about it afterwards, they might honestly reply that their only reason for that cruelty – and the only justification that they feel is necessary – was that they simply wanted to do it.

Other people are just unreal playthings to a fully fledged sociopath – like expendable characters in a video game. The only control on their antisocial behaviour is their strong sense of short-term self-preservation: they do the right thing not because they feel it to be right, but because they want to avoid being punished for doing the wrong thing. A sociopath is quite aware of society's rules and punishments, but they only respect the latter. And if a sociopath has, for whatever reason, developed a psychosexual sadistic streak, then they might eventually become a serial killer. Fantasies about dominating, hurting, raping and killing the 'worthless drones' that surround them grow to dominate their everyday thinking. Until, as Jeffrey Dahmer ruefully noted, they suddenly 'discover' that they have acted out one of their fantasies . . . and that they have a corpse to get rid of.

Certainly not all sociopaths are serial killers. If the estimates of experts are correct, then between 1 per cent and 4 per cent of the total human population are sociopathic to some degree. If they were all addicted to murder, that would mean the world should have between 73 million and 292 million serial killers. So the United States, with 4.3 per cent of the world population, should then have, at the time of writing, between 3.2 million and 12.7 million serial killers – as opposed to the thirty to fifty murder-addicted individuals (0.00001 per cent of the total population) as once estimated by FBI profiler John Douglas.

So what makes a person become a serial killer? Certainly it is not animalistic stupidity. A significant minority of serial killers have a high intelligence quotient (IQ). Ted Bundy had an IQ of 136, Dr Harold Shipman scored 140, and Jeffrey Dahmer scored 145. The typical medical doctor, by comparison, has an IQ in the 120 to 140 range. But studies suggest that most serial killers have an average or slightly lower than average IQ. (A study of 174 tested serial killers showed an average IQ of 93, where 100 is the mid-range IQ result.) But then half the general population are, by definition, on or below average IQ score.

Certainly some serial killers can pass themselves off as very intelligent when they are not, but this is often an illusion, created by the cunning charm that is so often a characteristic of a dangerous sociopath. On the other hand, very few serial killers have had a low intelligence quotient – and most of those that we know of were caught before the 1980s, when techniques for detecting and preventing serial crime were, necessarily, less precise than today. To manage to kill three or more people nowadays, and hope to escape detection, a monster has got to be clever as well as lucky.

A sociopathic lack of conscience (that is probably inherent at birth and is beyond their control) is another potential factor in motivating someone to become a serial killer. So, too, we know from studying the life histories of captured serial killers, is childhood and adolescent trauma or abuse. This can often be a matter of being sexually and or violently abused by adults or even other children. Or it can be something more psychologically subtle . . .

In his adolescence, Andrei 'the Rostov Ripper' Chikatilo was both horrified and fascinated by a family tale of a cousin who, during the Ukrainian famine in the late 1930s, had been kidnapped, murdered and eaten in the woods by bandits.

Ted Bundy (who raped and murdered at least thirty young women across the USA between 1974 and 1978) may have discovered that his abusive maternal grandfather might also have been his father.

Aileen Wournos (one of the rare female serial killers, who murdered seven men in Florida between 1989 and 1990) was shocked to discover that her supposed parents were actually her grandparents, and her supposed sister was really her mother.

The parents of Jeffrey 'the Milwaukee Cannibal' Dahmer simply argued with each other all the time, making his childhood home life unbearable.

And Henry Lee Lucas (who killed between three and eleven people, including his own mother, between 1960 and 1983) was bullied and ridiculed at school for having a glass eye.

When an adolescent passes puberty their brain is rewiring its neural network pathways to form the adult psychological connections, most notably sexual, that will stay with them for the rest of their lives. This is why so many of us unconsciously try to recreate – for good or bad – the relationship that we saw between our parents or carers; it is the mould into which our malleable young minds flowed as we grew up. If a person is abused or traumatised during this period, they may eventually become programmed to think that sex and violence are intrinsically connected – they feel genuine sexual pleasure when causing or feeling pain. Thus they become sadists and/or masochists, depending on their temperament and their circumstances.

The primitive human pack instinct also has a part to play in this process; an enjoyment of domination, or being dominated, is a key part of the pleasure/pain of sadomasochism. (The once deliberately brutal English public school system used to produce these sexually maladjusted people by the hundred. So much so, that the French used to call sadomasochism 'the English disease'.)

So a potential serial killer might be a person with an average to high IQ; has the sociopath mind type; was psychologically traumatised during adolescence; and became a sexual sadist. At the same time, or before adolescence, they learned to hide from reality by enveloping themselves in a fantasy world – a world that was necessarily sadistic in nature after they became sexually fixated on the misery and subjugation of others. But even then they might live a relatively normal life – after all, most sadomasochists live responsible and harmless lives – but the avid fantasy life of a potential serial killer is an ever present danger and temptation.

Their early bad experiences gave them a nagging sense of inferiority, that they compensate for with grandiose daydreams. And the easiest way to boost their own ego is to fantasise about crushing and dominating others – usually those that the person finds sexually attractive. These fantasies may continue, harmlessly, for years or decades; but one day an over-tempting situation presents itself and the fantasist kills somebody.

As noted above this first murder – imagined and probably masturbated over for years by the fantasist – may have something of a feeling of revelation about it: like Reg Christie's 'quiet, peaceful thrill' on killing a fellow human being and raping her corpse. After that, and enjoying the thrill of getting away with murder, the fledgling murder junkie's urge to commit subsequent murders will be as tempting as a teenager's need for sex after losing their virginity. And after the third homicide the murderer is a serial killer, both legally and psychologically. They have shown that they are permanently addicted to killing; prison will render them harmless – as, of course, will execution – but they can never be considered cured and safely paroled into the public, as they will immediately feel the temptation to kill again.

So are serial killers here to stay? Will our great grandchildren be as afraid of serial murderers as we are? It is easy to think so, as we all grew up in the shadow of Jack the Ripper, so to speak. But, as noted in Chapter 20, Jack the Ripper himself came as a horrific revelation to the Victorians. As late as the summer of 1888, very few people would have believed that a person could be as hooked on killing strangers as a drug addict could be to opium.

The increase in serial killer numbers worldwide in the past two hundred years – from effectively zero in the early nineteenth century to its peak in the 1980s – suggests that there is a cultural or historical element that has influenced that growth. Something started to happen around the late nineteenth century that had not happened before. We can largely leave out national culture from the equation, as serial killers have occurred in almost all societies in that time – although it may be worth noting that the United States and Europe suffer significantly more serial crime than other cultures.

Urbanisation is almost certainly a factor, if only because big towns offer a greater number of potential victims than rural villages; and people can disappear in towns and cause less comment or investigation. Improved living standards are also a factor: even the most dedicated sadistic sociopath fantasist will have trouble becoming a serial killer if he is working flat-out, from dawn to dusk, just to feed himself. (This is why the idle and pampered Baron Gilles de Rais (*see Chapter 20*) was a serial killer, but none of the overworked peasants on his estates could have been.) And automobiles have proved nearly essential tools for serial killers: to kidnap victim, to kill in areas well away from their own homes, transport bodies and afterwards to make their escape undetected in the stream of other vehicles.

Seen in this light, serial crime should have become much easier to get away with in the past few decades. This is because human life has generally become more urbanised and imper-sonal: people – especially prostitutes, transients and teenage runaways – disappear from areas all the time. The authorities generally pay little heed, as the 'disappeared' have usually just moved to another area for their own reasons and are probably unharmed. But that also means that a murder victim might go unmissed until the body is found . . . if that ever happens. And road transport – both for escaping killers and any dead bodies they might want to hide – is easier and more universal than ever before.

So why have serial killers become noticeably less prevalent since the 1980s? Although figures are notoriously hard to determine for the probable number of uncaptured serial killers, it seems clear that active serial killer numbers, worldwide, have been falling in the past quarter of a century.

In their book *Extreme Killing: Understanding Serial and Mass Murder* (2005) Professors James Alan Fox and Jack Levin give their estimate of serial killer numbers in the United States between 1900 and 2005. Up until 1960, they believe, there were only around a dozen known serial killers. During the decade of the 1960s they count nineteen serial killers – more than in the previous sixty years put together. Then the rocket took off: 119 known serial killers in the 1970s. A horrifying peak of 200 in the 1980s. Then a drop to 141 serial killers in the 1990s, and just sixty-one in the first five years of the new millennium. (Those serial killers who spanned two decades are dated to the mid-point of their killing career, to avoid double counting.)

So the tendency of serial killing closely follows that of rape and other violent crime from 1960 to the present day: a bell curve that peaks in the 1980s, but drops steadily in the past twenty years (*see Chapter 15*). My own five-decade study of serial crime (my first non-fiction book investigating the subject was *Encyclopedia of Murder*, written with Pat Pittman and published in 1961) tends to indicate a similar rising and then falling pattern around the globe. Unfortunately we are far from returning to the comparatively happy days of the 1960s (and before) but the statistical trend of serial killing is unarguably heading downward at the moment. Why is this?

One element is almost certainly the recent drop in media interest. During the peak time of serial killer activity, newspaper editors regarded serial crime as the perfect way to fill the front page. The television news also joined the media feeding frenzy whenever a new serial killer investigation was announced. Then TV dramas, Hollywood movies and novelists followed suit. And here I have to hold my hands up and admit that my own writing – as both a novelist and as a criminologist – fed the seemingly perennial public hunger for true crime stories about serial killers. As noted above, all this coverage – about real and especially fictional serial killers – convinced many people that serial killers were a major threat to society. Where, in fact, serial murderers were a hazard to individuals so small that it wouldn't appear on the most obsessive list of potential risks on a life insurance application.

But serial killers read and view serial killer-related material too – obsessively in the case of the organised serial killer type. Stephen Griffiths started killing in 2009, and murdered at least three prostitutes in the town of Bradford, in West Yorkshire. He killed forty-three-year-old Susan Rushworth on 22 June 2009; thirty-one-year-old Shelley Armitage on 26 April 2010; and thirty-six-year-old Suzanne Blamires on the following 21 May. The police arrested Griffiths three days later, after it was found that a security camera had caught the moment he killed Suzanne Blamires as she tried to escape his flat. He confessed immediately and bragged about the killings to detectives.

On his first appearance in court, Griffiths gave his name as 'The Crossbow Cannibal'; much to the annoyance of the presiding magistrate and to the delight of attending journalists. Not surprisingly, after introducing himself in this darkly flamboyant fashion, he pleaded guilty to all three murders. He claimed that he had killed his victims with a hunting crossbow, dismembered them, and had cooked and eaten parts of their bodies before dumping their remains in the River Aire. It was almost as if Griffiths, a forty-year-old part-time psychology PhD student, had deliberately designed the perfect *modus operandi* to win him world infamy as a real-life Hannibal Lecter.

In the 1980s the case would have made headlines around the world, and would have spawned documentaries, books and TV movies. In 2006, even the British tabloid media were comparatively low key about the case (and barely covered Griffiths's three subsequent attempts at prison suicide). The world media barely twitched. The *New York Times*, for example, gave the entire case one paragraph on an inside page. It is certainly true that people don't become serial killers simply to become infamous. But the loss of the media glamour factor in recent years will certainly have reduced the copy-cat attraction that is a motivating factor for some potential serial killers.

But there's been a more powerful reductive effect on serial killer numbers in recent years: the fact that would-be serial killers are rarely stupid.

Anyone who has sat to the end of a late-night debate in the British parliament will have heard the two doorkeepers of the House call the traditional question: 'Who goes home?' This apparently whimsical habit had a very practical origin: it dates from the eighteenth century when the area around the parliament buildings was unlit and partly rural. The question was a warning to MPs that they better get together into defensive groups to travel home. Otherwise they might find themselves walking through the dark on their own and would very likely fall prey to the many horse-mounted highwaymen who stalked the local area. These highway robbers would just as often shoot a victim, rather than just rob them; so not reacting to the call of 'Who goes home?' could be a matter of life and death to some unlucky parliamentarian. And there were so many highwaymen because it was such a profitable trade.

Yet a hundred years later, by the early nineteenth century, the criminal profession of highwayman was all but extinct in Britain: the last recorded highway robbery, by a lone mounted man, took place in 1831. Why the change? Because the invention of street lighting, better maintained and guarded roads, and an ever more efficient police force all meant that a highwayman would usually be caught, tried and executed after completing only one or two robberies. Under such appalling odds, nobody in their right mind would risk entering the profession; and criminals found safer, if less flamboyant ways to rob people.

As noted before, most legal authorities categorise a person as a serial killer if they are convicted of killing three or more people, for no specific motive other than sadism, over a protracted period of time. But with modern forensic techniques, it is very hard for any killer to get away with three murders before they are caught and sent to prison or a mental institution for the rest of their lives. Or, in increasingly rare jurisdictions, end up facing execution themselves.

A wide range of risks face the modern would-be serial killer. Risks that would have ended Jack the Ripper's criminal career before his third murder. Psychological profiling can give an excellent indication of who police investigators should question, based on sometimes the smallest crime-scene clues and indications. Forensic laboratories can lift readable fingerprints from almost any surface, including feathers or human skin. Minute, almost microscopic clothes fibres, or specks of dirt from a killer's shoe, can be analysed and categorised; and then computerised cross-referencing of huge numbers of databases can identify a suspect almost as accurately as a photograph. DNA experts can lift identifiable samples from a single human hair, or from dust fragments from a killer's skin. So getting DNA samples from spots of semen or blood – clues very often accidentally left behind by a serial killer on their victims – is child's play to a modern police force.

Soon, the only way a killer could be reasonably sure of not leaving such clues is to commit his crimes while wearing a sealed biohazard suit, and to radically change his *modus operandi* with each new crime. But then, as seen in the case of Stephen 'the Crossbow Cannibal' Griffiths, the growing plethora of security and traffic cameras in the world (and the impossibility of spotting and avoiding every one) would make even such a carefully planned crime rather difficult to get away with.

Some sociopathic sadists will continue to obsessively fantasise about murdering people; and some of those, in turn, will lose control and actually do it. But very few of those killers will be fortunate or clever enough to avoid capture in order to do it two more times, and thus be designated as serial killers. Most countries are also improving their violent offender assessment, control and, where possible, rehabilitation programmes – thanks partly, again, to the developments in psychological profiling. So a captured killer – if he or she is secretly or even unconsciously unrepentant and is likely to kill again – will find it increasingly hard to receive parole to the outside world – and to unguarded potential victims.

When a judge passes a life sentence on a convicted killer (the most common and often the minimum sentence allowed for murder) it usually means that the convict will be released after ten or maybe twenty years – dependent on local jurisdiction rules and on the practical necessities produced by prison overcrowding. This fact predictably and understandably infuriates the public, the tabloid newspapers and relatives of the victim. But it is easy to forget what the term 'life sentence' actually means. It indicates that the state can keep a person in jail until they die, provided the state's experts judge that the person is unsafe to be released. And thanks to improving psychological techniques, potential serial killers will find it increasingly hard to avoid that judgement, once they are already serving a life sentence for murder.

The combination of factors that have vastly improved violent criminal detection, apprehension and control, are hardly likely to loosen in the future. Indeed with continuing development in these fields – and with new forensic techniques as yet undeveloped – 'getting away with it' will prove more and more difficult for the would-be Jack the Ripper or Hannibal Lecter. And, as noted above, potential serial killers are rarely stupid. As they see the increasing likelihood that indulging their urge to kill another human being will end their own existence as a free individual, they will be less likely to indulge it. And even if they do, they will probably be caught before they can do it again.

I believe that it is entirely possible, in the next decade or two, that the twenty-first-century serial killer will go the way of the eighteenth-century highwayman. Driven to functional extinction by the forces of civilisation, and by social and scientific development.

Chapter 22

The Essence of Sex

On Christmas Day in 1954, I sketched out a plan for a philosophical book called *The Outsider* in my journal. It was, in a sense, the most significant day of my life so far. A day or two later the British Museum Reading Room opened again after the holiday and I cycled there to make a start on the book.

It was on the way there that I recalled a book I had read about in the introduction to the Everyman edition of Henri Barbusse's war novel *Under Fire*. Barbusse (born 1873) fought in the First World War before he became a Communist and went to Moscow. By that time he had already achieved fame with a novel called *Hell* (*L'Enfer*, published in 1908) in which a young man living in a Paris boarding house discovers a small hole in his wall through which he can observe the people who come and go in the next room. The book is based on a true scandal in which two men took it in turn to spy on girls undressing in the honeymoon suite next door. The hole in the wall struck me as such a marvellous symbol of 'outsiderism' that I ordered up the book as soon as I got to the museum, and read it through in a morning and afternoon. Then I copied a paragraph from it into my notebook:

> *In the air, on top of a tram, a girl is sitting. Her dress, lifted a little, blows out. But a block in the traffic separates us. The tramcar glides away, fading like a nightmare.*
>
> *Moving in both directions, the street is full of dresses which sway, offering themselves airily, the skirts lifting; dresses that lift and yet do not lift.*

In the tall and narrow shop mirror I see myself approach-
ing, rather pale and heavy-eyed. It is not a woman I want
– it is all women, and I seek for them in those around me,
one by one . . .

This became virtually the first paragraph of *The Outsider.* I
saw at once that this observation is of far greater significance
than at first appears. All normal males respond to the stimulus of
a lifting dress, yet most are rational enough to recognise an
element of absurdity in the reaction, since sexual desire cannot,
by its very nature, be totally satisfied. Barbusse's narrator recognises this:

Defeated, I followed my impulse casually. I followed a woman
who had been watching me from her corner. Then we walked
side by side. We said a few words; she took me home with
her . . . Then I went through the banal scene. It passed like a
sudden hurtling-down.
    Again, I am on the pavement, and I am not at peace as I
had hoped. An immense confusion bewilders me. It is as if I
could not see things as they were. I see too deep and too much.

In other words, the actuality of sex has an element of a confidence trick. She hands us something; a moment later our hands
are empty again. And it happens every time a pretty girl walks
past in the street. Think of a case mentioned in the last chapter:
the American serial kidnapper and killer Ted Bundy. He
became so obsessed by watching college girls undress through
their lighted bedroom windows that he turned it into a 'project',
and the number of his murder victims may have reached thirty
or more. Bundy was executed in the Florida electric chair in
January 1989.

There is an element of absurdity in all this. Bundy was not
stupid; on the contrary, he had been a brilliant student and was
strikingly charismatic . . . when he wasn't kidnapping, raping and
murdering young women. Judge Cowart, who sentenced Bundy
to death, had heard a grimly detailed catalogue of the man's

cruelty and savagery. Yet he concluded the death sentence by saying ruefully:

It is an utter tragedy for this court to see such a total waste of humanity as I've experienced in this courtroom. You're a bright young man. You'd have made a good lawyer, and I would have loved to have you practice in front of me, but you went another way, partner. Take care of yourself.

But it was Bundy's very intelligence that was part of the problem. He recognised the intensity of the erotic experience – of peeping in at undressing college girls – as greatly superior to the monotonous quality of most human consciousness. He decided, in his 'project', to pursue this intensely alive feeling, and attempt to pin it down by taking it to the greatest extreme – by kidnapping, raping and killing women. But his pinning it down is the part where it began to go wrong and began his downhill slide to the electric chair.

Something similar happened to the philosopher Bertrand Russell. Young women attracted him so much that he wanted to bed them all and found it hard to keep his hands off them. The underlying urge was certainly the philosopher's craving to learn the secrets of the universe, to become a kind of magician. But Russell learned no secrets except that most women are much the same when undressed. Unfortunately, he made no attempt to focus his *philosophical* intelligence on the problem. It demanded a different *kind of thinking* from anything he had become accustomed to.

But as I copied down the paragraph from *L'Enfer,* I could suddenly see that it *is* a basic logical problem that should yield to reason. It had led, for example, to the executions of Neville Heath and Reg Christie on the scaffold. But what kind of intelligence would be required to solve it?

There is a story by Edgar Allan Poe called 'A Descent into the Maelstrom' that conveys the point I am trying to make. The narrator describes how he has been led to the top of a peak called Hellseggen, on the coast of Norway, to witness the giant whirlpool named the Maelstrom, created daily by the clash of two currents. We are then told how a survivor and his two brothers were trapped on their boat after being driven into its vicinity by a hurricane. Soon they are being sucked down into a giant funnel of water which towers above them like a mountainside. One brother falls overboard; the second goes insane. The third clings on and waits. Finally, he notices that barrel-shaped objects take far longer to descend, and decides that his best chance of survival is to tie himself to a barrel and throw himself into the sea. And in fact, long after his two brothers and the ship have vanished, he is picked up by fishermen.

The point, of course, is that the hero survives by refusing to panic and maintaining his power of detached observation. His survival lies in the fact that he has become, so to speak, an existential thinker, one in whom thinking and being are united. On the other hand, what Bundy has in common with Heath and Christie is that he has willingly surrendered himself to this sexual force simply for the pleasure of abandoning control – then had to learn that it cannot be recovered by a simple act of will.

It was when I noted that *L'Enfer* came out in 1908, I was struck by a coincidence. This was in the midst of a great advertising war in the London newspapers.

In effect, it had all started in 1888 when a brilliant young businessman named Alfred Harmsworth decided to launch a magazine called *Answers to Correspondence,* an imitation of the magazine *Tit-Bits,* launched by George Newnes. It became a huge success when it started a competition in which the prize was £1 a week for life for anyone who could guess how much gold there was in the Bank of England in December 1889. On the success of *Answers to Correspondence*, Harmsworth launched the *Daily Mail*, in 1896. This newspaper's success was largely based on advertising, paid for by London's new department stores.

In 1906 the American businessman Gordon Selfridge had come to London to survey British stores and was not impressed. He decided that what London needed was a massive 'department store' – a shop, divided into many different departments, that catered to almost any shopper's needs from tin tacks to ball-gowns. Gordon Selfridge's genius was to see that women were becoming more empowered and thus had more money to spend; so he oriented his new design of shop towards the female shop-per. His creation was Selfridges of Oxford Street, and it made him very rich very fast. Among many other innovations, he decided on what was then a scandalous novelty: to advertise ladies' underwear – although by modern standards his offerings would have been regarded as anything but sexually stimulating. Even so, it was a breakthrough that was universally criticised . . . and then hurriedly imitated by competitors.

Up to that point in history, female underwear was – where it was worn at all – a largely functional item: principally designed to warm and cover up body parts, not to titillate. Most early Victorian bloomers were crotchless, for example, not to allow ease of access to men, but to allow a woman go to the privvy without having to spend half an hour removing her dress, farthingale and corset, in order to be able to then remove her drawers. But Selfriges' knick-ers adverts suddenly made something public that had previously been essentially private. As a result, ladies' underwear started to become less pragmatic, but more revealing and sexy.

So when Barbusse's 'outsider' speaks of 'dresses that lift and yet do not lift' (i.e not far enough) what he had in mind were knickers designed to appeal to the lustful male. The connection was made explicit a decade later in James Joyce's *Ulysses* (1922) when the teenage Gerty Macdowell displays her underwear as she leans back to watch the fireworks, and Leopold Bloom's fevered response is to secretly masturbate with his hand in his trouser-pocket.

I am suggesting that when Barbusse wrote that sentence 'It is not a woman I want, it is all women . . .' he had stumbled upon something quite new about the twentieth century.

Let me immediately qualify that. I am not claiming that this vision of what one might call 'the infinite desirableness of all women' had never been glimpsed by other writers or philoso-phers. I suspect that Goethe meant something of the sort when he wrote that 'the eternal womanly draws us upward and on'.

Moreover, a younger contemporary, Heinrich von Kleist, had undoubtedly been expressing the same vision in a story called *The Marquise von O*, in which the young widow of the title is baffled to discover she is pregnant when, to her certain knowledge, she has never been anyone's mistress. She goes to the length of advertising for the unknown father. And when a sheepish young Russian officer appears, she suddenly understands what has happened . . .

Many months earlier, her home, a citadel in northern Italy, had been under siege by an invading army. She had been on the point of being raped when she was rescued by the handsome young officer, after which she lost consciousness. And it is he who now presents himself to admit responsibility for her condition, and to confess that as he had knelt beside the beautiful young lady whose dress had lifted as she fainted on the couch, he had caught a glimpse up the skirt. The sight of her naked pubis was too much; fortunately she remained unconscious during the next minute or so, during which he completed his purpose. And the grateful lady, whose hand he then kissed, was quite unaware that she was now *enceinte*.

The story caused a great scandal at the time of its publication in 1808 (although Kleist gives it a happy ending), the objection being that no officer and gentleman would behave like such a scoundrel. Kleist's reply, in effect, was that most young men might behave like this when looking up the skirts of an unconscious girl – at least if they could be certain that she would remain unconscious for a few more minutes.

And so, exactly a century after the publication of Kleist's story, Henri Barbusse's hero finds himself in a Paris street understanding precisely what Kleist's antihero had felt in 1808: 'Moving in both directions, the street is full of dresses which sway, offering themselves airily, the skirts lifting.' The central difference is that the women of 1808 wore no knickers under their skirts – a hundred years later all women wore knickers and men were then sexually attracted to the knickers as well as the women wearing them.

The fact is that humans are aroused by the idea of sex, almost more than they are by sex itself. It was simply honest, not pornography, for literary heroes to be described as being aroused when surrounded by the tempting 'skirts that lift and do not lift'. James Joyce was reporting a truth when he described the titillating nature of what Gerty Macdowell inexpertly concealed during a firework display.

But, as we saw above, Henri Barbusse's hero's encounter with the prostitute revealed that it is not sex he is looking for. Rather, it is as if the swaying skirts are offering the *essence* of sex, just as an expensive Parisian perfume might offer the essence of spring flowers.

It is in this first decade of the twentieth century that the human spirit continues the exercise of bursting its Victorian bonds. Ibsen's play *A Doll's House* had sowed the seed in 1879, with its assertion that a woman has a right to individual self-development apart from her duties as a housewife. H. G. Wells's *Ann Veronica* caused a tremendous scandal in 1909, with its thesis of a girl who goes to science school, falls in love with her teacher – the anonymous-sounding Capes who is separated from his wife – and sets out to seduce him into running away with her. Wells admitted to being inspired by a novel called *The Woman Who Did* by Grant Allen (1895) about an unmarried girl who decides to bring up a baby without the benefit of a husband – another *suces de scandale*.

What immediately strikes a modern reader of *Ann Veronica* is the absence of sex; its hero and heroine do not even kiss. But then, we have to bear in mind that it was not until the coming of D. H. Lawrence's *Sons and Lovers* (1913) that novelists dared to speak openly of physical contact between male and female, and that the price Lawrence paid for his frankness was the banning of his next novel, *The Rainbow* (1915).

What most shocked the readers of Wells's *Ann Veronica* was that when Capes asks her 'What do you want?' she brashly replies: 'You.' Nowadays this dialogue wouldn't shock even the most hidebound religious fundamentalist. But in 1909, Wells' depiction of a (mildly) sexually aggressive woman caused feathers to fly. Decent women (in novels) were simply not supposed to *initiate* sexually charged scenes. At best they were expected to be the swooning recipient of romance from a man.

Wells himself had married – his cousin Isabel – when he was twenty-five, but it had not been successful. She lacked his own highly romantic sexuality and he found their love life bitterly disappointing. Then came an experience that changed his life:

> *Quite soon after my marriage indeed came an adventure, that did much to restore my baffled self confidence. There was a certain little Miss Kingsmill who came to Haldon Road first as a pupil to learn retouching and then as a helper with the work. She was cheerfully a-moral and already an experienced young woman. She was about the house before and after my marriage; the business stirred her; she may have had confidences from my cousin and a quickening interest became evident in her manner towards me. I found myself alone with her in the house one day; I was working upon a pile of correspondence books, my aunt was out shopping and my wife had gone to London with some retouched negatives. I forget by what excuse Ethel Kingsmill flitted from her retouching desk upstairs, to my study. But she succeeded in dispelling all the gloomy apprehensions I was beginning to entertain, that love-making was nothing more than an outrage inflicted upon reluctant womankind and all its loveliness a dream. The sound of my returning aunt's latch-key separated us in a state of flushed and happy accomplishment. I sat down with a quick-ened vitality to my blottesque red corrections again and Ethel, upstairs, very content with herself, resumed her niggling at her negatives . . .* [1]

After this discovery, Wells was committed to further sexual experimentation, and in later life acquired a reputation as a Don Juan that undermined his reputation as a serious social thinker. But Wells had only made the same discovery that was beginning to permeate the air of the new century: that combined with

---

1 H. G. Wells, *Experiment in Autobiography*, (page 352) (1934)

imagination and intellectual excitement, sex could throw a dazzling light on human evolution and man's future possibilities. Like Barbusse's outsider he was also aware that some deep fundamental change had occurred.

In *L'Enfer*, a lawyer describes at a dinner party the case of a man who has raped and strangled a little girl and, listening, 'a young mother with her daughter at her side, has half got up to leave, but cannot tear herself away. And one of the men, simple, placid, I heard distinctly panting . . .' That is to say that the barrier that normally separates men and women from sexually explicit knowledge – and had previously kept society stable like the safety catch on a gun – has slipped into the 'off' position; a barrier as fragile and light, as it turns out, as a woman's summer dress. Everyone around the dinner table is instinctively aware of what has happened – the lawyer's story has temporarily stripped away a social norm – but they cannot protest because they are also fascinated. But in another sense nothing has happened; everything is exactly as it was before.

This passage from *L'Enfer* also indicates an interesting change between 1905 and our own time. It immediately strikes us that there is something psychologically inaccurate about Barbusse's description. Today a 'placid-looking man' would not audibly begin to pant over the dinner table on hearing a salacious story. Nor would a mother, protecting her child, be so fascinated that she is unable to leave. But perhaps this is because we have become so accustomed to the idea of sex crime in the intervening century that the shattering of a conversational taboo no longer has the same riveting impact on us. Barbusse is describing people so unaccustomed to the idea of rampant and, in this case, murderous sex that they are drawn to listening about it just as we might gawp when driving past a traffic accident.

This presents an interesting paradox. *Ann Veronica* was not a well-written book by H. G. Wells's usual standard; yet it is nevertheless an important novel. How so? The answer is that, at that point in history, it was waiting to be written. Before *Ann Veronica's* publication, Wells was regarded as a proponent of Dickensian social radicalism, with a strong touch of Jules Verne thrown in; but his work was still firmly within the mores of Victorian values. Up to the publication of *Ann Veronica*, nobody saw him as remotely scandalous. Yet here he was, writing a novel about a sexually unfulfilled girl who decides to do something about it, and so virtually demands that her teacher takes her virginity.

The answer begins to appear as soon as we take an overall view of nineteenth-century literature. From Byron to Swinburne; from Balzac to Flaubert; from the Brönte sisters to George Eliot; in all this work there was a deep vein of sensuality to their writing that was nevertheless kept below the surface for fear of upsetting public morals. Even Tennyson seethes with the same languid sensuality that inspired Swinburne. But it was a risk to go too far. For example, Swinburne himself ran into controversy when he published *Dolores: Our Lady of Pain* (a lengthy symbolist poem with a sadomasochistic and religious theme, published in 1866). And so did Oscar Wilde with his novel *The Picture of Dorian Gray* (a philosophical horror story about a decadent rake who can load his sins onto a magic painting hidden in his attic – an allegory echoing Wilde's own shame at his philandering and secret homosexuality – published in 1890). In both cases there was furious burst of indignation from critics and readers. Victorian writers had to mind their Ps and Qs.

Then a play like *A Doll's House*, or a novel like *Ann Veronica*, comes along, and everything changes. The word has been spoken and it cannot be unsaid. Once the genie has been uncorked it can take up residence where it likes. Ibsen said: 'Women have a right to individual self-development,' and suddenly it was obviously true. Wells said: 'Women have a right to choose where they bestow their maidenhood,' and again it seems self-evident. When an idea has escaped from its cage, anything can happen. It acts as an *agent provocateur* that leads an uprising.

The amazing thing is that mere words have ever been able to catalyse such a change. It had happened before, in the year 1740, as a result of the publication of a book called *Pamela, or Virtue Rewarded* – penned by Samuel Richardson, a rotund and retired middle-aged printer. Yet this book, his first excursion into fiction writing, should be acknowledged as the original modern novel.

The book's theme seems plain and simple enough by modern standards. *Pamela* is written in the form of letters from a young servant girl, describing her master's attempts to seduce her; finally, shamed by her goodness and innocence, he decides to marry her instead. Richardson stretches this straightforward tale over two lengthy volumes.

Having presented his portrait of Christian virtue rewarded, Richardson then set out to complete the picture with an attempt to portray wickedness and libertinism: *Clarissa* (1748). This time the middle-class heroine, Clarissa Harlowe, refuses to yield her virtue to the spoilt aristocratic playboy Lovelace, who then drugs and rapes her. He then tries to salvage a little self-respect from his moral failure by offering her marriage, which she angrily refuses. Lovelace dies in a duel with one of her relatives. So Clarissa – who also dies, but of 'wounded chastity' – again proves the superiority of goodness.

Richardson's third and final novel, *The History of Sir Charles Grandison* (1753) begins by borrowing from the first two, and showing the heroine, Harriet Byron, about to be abducted in a coach; the miscreant is the unscrupulous Sir Hargrave Pollexfen, whose aim is forced marriage. Her screams bring rescue from Sir Charles Grandison who, having ascertained that she is being taken against her will, offers her refuge with his sister, 'the most virtuous and prudent of women', and she is soon restored to her own home.

Inevitably, Harriet finds herself falling in love with her rescuer and he with her. But the conclusion is not yet achieved, for it seems Grandison has another moral dilemma, an Italian lady named Clementina who at some time in the past has fallen in love with him, and to whom he regards himself engaged. Naturally, he is willing to sacrifice his future happiness (and Harriet's) for the sake of doing the right thing, but ultimately is not called upon to do so when Clementina decides against marriage to a Protestant. Richardson's biographers Duncan Eaves and Ben Kimpel express dissatisfaction at the time it takes to bring about this conclusion (most of two volumes), but Richardson's admirers, including as Jane Austen and George Eliot, do not share their impatience.

It is worth noting that the second part of *Clarissa*, after her betrayal and rape, sold as well as the first part, even though readers had now satisfied their curiosity about what happened. The same is true of the second part of *Pamela*. All the attacks, satires and parodies only increased the popularity of the two books, and the critics continued to be enthusiastic. Doctor Johnson declared that Richardson had 'enlarged the knowledge of human nature', while Diderot said that *Pamela* made him feel as if he had actually lived through the experiences described in it – a comment that, more than any other, explains Richardson's popularity.

Yet from the perspective of the twentieth century, we can see that even Richardson's greatest admirers failed to grasp the extraordinary nature of his achievement. Dr Johnson had the warmest regard for Richardson, but if anyone had told him the retired printer was one of the greatest innovators in literary history, he would have dismissed it with one of his bear-like growls. ('Your feeling does you more credit than your intelligence, sir.') Today, we can see that what made Richardson so remarkable was not that he enlarged our knowledge of human nature – he didn't – but that he *freed the human imagination.*

Nowadays, when we can switch on a television and be instantly transported to Ancient Rome or the other side of the galaxy, it is almost impossible to imagine what it was like to be born three or four centuries ago. The words 'Will Shakespeare's England' or 'Sam Johnson's London' evoke a colourful picture of majestic sailing ships on the Thames, rowdy taverns and, for the latter, buzzing coffee houses. But in fact the chief characteristic of life in that period must have been its sheer dullness.

We can gain some idea of it from some of those Russian novels of the nineteenth century, with their small villages and shabby towns in which nothing ever seems to happen; *that* was closer to the truth of Shakespeare's England, even for the tiny number of intellectuals in that society. There were theatres, of course, but only in the major cities. There were books – and even works of fiction – but only the rich could afford them; and, in any case, most people could not read. The majority of people lived and died without ever seeing beyond the same daily routine that their parents and grandparents had known. It was as if they were born in a yard with high walls, and they never saw over the walls.

Gradually, through the Renaissance and into the Enlightenment, standards of general education slowly improved, and more people learned to read. But still there was nothing much *to* read. This explains the immense success of Addison and Steele's *Spectator*, which began to appear – daily – in 1711. It was not a newspaper in our sense, as it rambled cheerfully from subject to subject. But it *was* a breakthrough in communication; one single voice was speaking to several thousand Englishmen at the same time, as they drank their coffee or mulled ale.

And the most unexpectedly popular of those *Spectator* articles were those dealing with the absent-minded old knight Sir Roger de Coverley. They were in a low key; they talked about his everyday life, his relations with his servants and tenants. His creators intended him to be an example of the kind of amiable old Tory landowner they generally approved of – a convenient starting point for discussions about morality and social duty. To everyone's surprise, the articles became a roaring success; readers could not get enough of him. Addison and Steele had stumbled on a discovery that is known to every television producer: that people enjoy reading about everyday events, because they can 'identify' with the characters involved. In effect, Addison and Steele had sowed the seeds that would eventually bloom into the modern novel.

Most critics would give that credit to Daniel Defoe, whose *Robinson Crusoe* appeared eight years later, in 1719. But *Robinson Crusoe* really belongs to that earlier picaresque tradition of books like *Lazarillo de Tormes* and *Don Quixote*. Besides, Defoe was a reporter rather than an inventor – Crusoe was based on Alexander Selkirk, an actual castaway whose life story was purchased by Defoe for a few crowns. But the popularity of *Crusoe* certainly demonstrates that the reading public was ready for the advent of the novel. If it had not been immediately pirated by other publishers, it would have made Defoe a rich man.

Literature had never been so much in demand. There was a new audience of female readers, middle-class women with time on their hands. In that age of cheap domestics, the wives of country gentlemen had little to do but embroider cushion covers and read whatever happened to be available. Volumes of sermons sold out on publication day. There was a wide demand for newspapers, and for journals like the *Spectator* and Dr Johnson's *Rambler.*

There were also novels, with titles like *The Royal Slave, Ornatus and Artesia, The Jamaica Lady,* but they were about far-away places and far-fetched events. By present-day standards, most of them were little more than extended short stories. Few had any literary merit; they were mostly Grub Street productions, churned out by hacks for money. Still, they were eagerly snatched up by a public that was developing an increasing appetite for journeys of the imagination.

And at this point, Richardson, the retired printer, with his passion for psychological analysis, wandered on to the scene. *Pamela* was the book everyone had been waiting for. It satisfied a deep, urgent demand that had been building up for decades. It differed from earlier novels as much as cutting-edge theatre differs from B-movie cinema. The reader could become *totally involved* in it, like entering another, but believable, world and living someone else's life.

We must try to make an imaginative effort to grasp what that meant. Imagine the daughter of a country clergyman, on a wet afternoon, with nothing much to do but stare at the rain. She opens *Pamela* . . . and it is as if she has walked out of her own home into Mr B's country house. For the next few hours, she *is* Pamela. She is moved to tears by the indignities and shocked by the attempts at rape. At certain points she lays down the book and drifts into a daydream, wondering how she would react to being kissed by Mr B . . . In two hours, she lives through more experience than in two years of daily routine. *Pamela* may be long, but for her it is not long enough; she would like it to go on forever. She has made the discovery that 'living' is not necessarily a matter of physical experience, that the imagination is also capable of voyages.

Today, this sounds utterly banal; in 1740, it was as startling as discovering you could fly by flapping your arms. Richardson had taught the European mind to daydream with a purpose.

Perhaps the oddest part of the story is that historians do not seem to have noticed the revolutionary significance of *Pamela*. They recognise it as a literary landmark, of course. They also observe that there was an immense gulf – psychological and cultural – between the age of Swift and the age of Dickens. But they are inclined to set it down to social causes – wars, upheavals, the Industrial Revolution. A glance at the history books shows this to be untrue; there was nothing very revolutionary happening in Europe around the mid-eighteenth century. As to the Industrial Revolution and the French Revolution, they came fifty years later, when the imaginative revolution had already transformed Europe. They were the consequences, not the cause.

No, it was Richardson's *Pamela* that was the falling pebble that stated the avalanche that brought about one of the greatest developments in the history of the human intellect. To grasp what happened, you only have to turn to Samuel Pepys's diary, written a hundred years earlier. Pepys is always describing what he *does* – a trip on the river, a visit to the theatre – but never what he thinks or feels. It doesn't strike him that a sheet of paper is a medium for *talking to yourself*.

In Pepys's time and before, only a few philosophers and theologians had the time or inclination to contemplate themselves and their existence to any great degree. Most people thought of themselves, if they thought about that subject in any depth at all, as an extension of their social position and job. They were a noble, a priest, a butcher, a baker or a candlestick-maker. They were a wife, a seamstress or a prostitute. (This is why so many surnames – like Smith, Fisher and Thatcher – are essentially job titles.)

But if you then turn to almost any diary written in the century after Richardson, you will find it, by contrast, full of reflections and meditations. Human thinking had become deeper and more imaginative, right across the spectrum of literate people. And the number of people who wanted to become literate had increased dramatically in that century. Before *Pamela* few servants, manual workers or even prosperous middle-class burghers had little reason to learn to read beyond the very basics – most available books were simply too dull to attract any level of effort. After *Pamela* – and the huge number of me-too novels following immediately in the wake of its success – many semi-literate and illiterate people realised that knowing how to read fluently was the only gateway to a fantastic new form of entertainment.

By comparison think of modern computers. For most of my career as an author, I was one of the few people I knew who could type reasonably fast – it was a necessity of my career. For almost everyone else, typing was a job that you gave to secretaries or, if a typing pool wasn't available, you typed things out painstakingly yourself. But you avoided doing such a tedious job when at all possible.

With the advent of home computers and the internet, however, everyone has an abundant reason to be able to type efficiently and fast. Today my grandchildren regard professional typing to be as natural as fluent reading – how else can they get full access to a world of wonders?

The creation of the modern novel had a similarly catalysing effect on the people of the early Industrial Revolution: it provided a tempting reason for them to get an education. That, in turn, catalysed the education revolution and eventually led to universal education being seen as an essential part of any developed society. For that reason alone there should be plaques commemorating the chubby and moralising Samuel Richardson outside every public library. In his own way, he was as important to the modern world as Newton or Darwin.

It is no coincidence that when President Abraham Lincoln met Harriet Beecher Stowe – the author of the novel *Uncle Tom's Cabin; or, Life Among the Lowly* – he reportedly said: 'So this is the little lady who started this great war.' Stowe's heart-rending depiction of the misery of the southern states slaves, published in 1852, had greatly enthused the abolitionist movement in the northern states. That, in turn, led the resentful and unrepentant South to secede and spark the American Civil War. That war blazed between 1861 and 1865, ending with the total defeat of the South and the abolition of slavery. One might argue – and Lincoln plainly thought – that if *Uncle Tom's Cabin* had not been written, slavery might have survived another few decades in the 'freedom-loving' United States.

But what was it about *Pamela*, *Clarissa* and *Sir Charles Grandison* that marked such a boundary between Richardson's writing and what had come before? Richardson was the first to treat prose as a medium for expressing thoughts and feelings – what he and his contemporaries called 'sentiments' – rather than just actions. His novels are immensely long, but never boring, because Richardson himself was never bored by them. The ideas and reflections flow out in a slow, broad, majestic stream like the largo of a symphony. Johnson said that anyone who read Richardson for the story would hang himself, and it is true there is very little external action. The drama takes place *inside* the characters. In effect, he had taught his contemporaries that the written word can be used as a vehicle for inner voyages. Eighty years later, the mystical painter Caspar David Friedrich expressed the essence of the discovery when he said: 'Shut the living eye; then you begin to see with the spiritual eye.'

So, what has all this to do with sociopathic sex murderers like Ted Bundy? The freeing of the human imagination during the Enlightenment had another effect: it made people value their individuality more than they ever had before. A browbeaten maid servant could escape into the world of fiction in her few hours off; but when she emerged from her reading she might examine the elements of her own life just as the characters in the novel did theirs. This level of introspection, on a society-wide level, was bound to have a powerful effect. Early movements for civil rights, like the British nineteenth-century Chartists, were driven by this feeling that people had intrinsic value in and of themselves, whatever their social or financial position. Or – after another hundred years or so – whatever their age, sex or race.

But the emphasis on the value of the individual has a darker side. People before the Enlightenment no more believed that they were each 'special' and had a 'right to be happy' than they thought that they had a right to fly by flapping their arms.

Afterwards, when modern novels had given them the illusion that they could fly, or do anything else the author could convincingly describe, they became necessarily more self-centred. A growing sense of self will do that to a person.

Sex killers like Jack the Ripper, Ted Bundy, and Jeffrey Dahmer have this self-centredness in abundance. They want to experience the 'ultimate high' through their sexual obsession and are quite willing to sacrifice their victims in order to try to achieve it. Sex killers pursue the idea of sex – the essence of sex – as if it were some sort of perfectly satisfying holy grail. And because of the modern conviction of the value of the individual, they subconsciously convince themselves that they have a *right* to achieve that goal, whatever the cost to other people.

But it never quite works. The rush of sadistic exultation that they feel on raping and killing – Reg Christie's 'quiet peaceful thrill' – ebbs away too fast. And it leaves them feeling as desperately unfulfilled as the protagonist in Barbusse's *L'Enfer*; when he goes with a prostitute after getting worked up watching girls' dresses tantalisingly flip in the summer breeze. The prosaic usually disappoints when compared with the imaginary.

I have said elsewhere that sex is a spiritual elevator that does not go all the way to the top. It cannot provide lasting happiness or enlightenment, any more than eating can. To achieve any real intellectual satisfaction and inner growth, a person has to get out and slog on up the steps of self-development. But sex killers are simply too selfish and lazy to see this.

Chapter 23

The Man Who Invented Pornography

I must admit to having always been fascinated by the impact Richardson made on his age, but also by the way it has reverberated down to our own time. This was due to a large extent to the influence of a writer who was born in the same year *Pamela* was published. Aldonse-Donatien Louis de Sade, better known as the Marquis de Sade, was born on 2 June 1740, five months after Volume One of *Pamela* appeared on 6 November 1740.

The wealthy, aristocratic de Sade family was already sliding downhill by the eighteenth century. They were relatives of the Prince de Condé, whose mansion overlooked the Luxembourg Gardens; de Sade's father, the Comte Jean-Baptiste de Sade, was an ambassador and soldier whose chief hobby was the seduction of teenage girls. His charm and good looks (which his son came to inherit) brought him many amorous successes.

The count's downfall began when still a bachelor. He conceived an overwhelming lust for a beautiful fifteen-year-old German princess named Caroline. That she was the wife of his main patron, the Prince de Condé, only made her more desirable.

Since her husband was jealous, Count de Sade needed to find a way of gaining ready access to her, and hit on the device of pretending to fall in love with one of her ladies-in-waiting, the teenage Maillé de Carman, and offering to marry her. Moreover, since Maillé – who was pretty but otherwise undistinguished – was terrified of the pain involved in losing her virginity, Princess

Caroline obtained her husband's permission to sit by the marriage couch and hold her hand while the operation was taking place. The cunning Count de Sade reasoned correctly that witnessing her maid-in-waiting being deflowered would sexually excite the princess and make her eager to join in; the result was that the Count acquired two new bed partners within days.

The sequel proved problematic. The princess soon objected to sharing her new lover with her maid and did her best to make him forswear his wife's bed; he objected, as did his wife, who also threatened to let the cuckolded husband in on the secret. The Count was saved from a painful choice only when war broke out, in 1740, and he was sent to join his regiment. In due course, Princess Caroline would give birth to a royal heir and the maid-in-waiting to the Marquis de Sade.

This story is worth telling because it makes us aware of how much importance an obsessive seducer like de Sade senior attached to the conquest of the Princess de Condé; to possess whom he was willing to marry a girl without prospects or fortune. The surprising thing is that a moralistic bourgeois like Samuel Richardson should also understand the mentality so well. We can see this in his creation of characters like Lovelace or Sir Hargrave Pollexfen; men who are clearly enslaved by the sexual obsession. In due course, de Sade junior would display the same characteristic.

De Sade's maternal parent was, in fact, about as hopeless a mother as it possible to be: erratic, capricious, flighty, self-centered and unstable. She lived on in the Condé palace, acting as governess and guardian to her own son and to the son of the prince, who was four years older. But the young Donatien (the name by which most biographers call de Sade junior) was about to get himself evicted from the Condé palace. He was utterly spoilt and expected to get his own way in everything. Then one day when he got into a dispute about a toy with his playmate, he yelled and screamed so loudly that every servant within half a mile came to see what was going on, and tried to separate the two. Donatien was so convinced that it was *his toy* that he began hitting and slapping the prince as he screamed. This was simply

too much – for the son of the maid-in-waiting to assault the heir
to the title – and serious punishment was demanded. Donatien
was packed off to one of his other homes. (To live with his grandmother, which was not, after all, such a severe punishment. His
paternal grandmother adored and spoiled him still further).
What became of the disputed toy is not recorded.

His grandmother lived in a fifteenth-century mansion in
Avignon, where the child remained only for a few months before
being moved on to the castle of his uncle, Jacques-François. This
was in the town of Saumane, twenty miles from Avignon. Here
the Comte de Sade's younger brother, a forty-year-old priest,
spent most of his days when he was not in a small abbey in the
Auvergne. Although a priest, Uncle Jacques was not in the least
religious, regarding himself as a humanist, like his friend Voltaire.
His many mistresses included the two sisters who were his body
servants and various ladies whose beds he visited regularly. He
was also a connoisseur of Paris brothels, so clearly his sexual
appetite was voracious.

He was also a scholar, among whose interests was the Italian
Renaissance poet Petrarch, whose inamorata Laura, surnamed
de Sade, happened to be an ancestor. Universally liked for his
amiable temperament, the priest was the ideal guardian for his
nephew, who revelled in his uncle's vast library and his illustrated
collection of pornography; and did not miss the royal Palais de
Condé in the least. And as if one amiable abbé were not enough,
Donatien had a young tutor who was studying for the priesthood
and therefore also known, like Donatien's uncle, as L'Abbé, and
noted for the sweetness of his temper. Donatien's environment
certainly lacked those hostile factors that might otherwise explain
his later obsession with cruelty.

Things began to change when he was ten years old and he was
sent away to school – the Jesuit College Louis-le-Grand, not far
from the Condé palace. But he was still a noble, so had private
rooms and his own private tutor. He left at fourteen and spent
the next year at the military academy at Versailles, where he was
finally commissioned as a subaltern in the foot guards.

Donatien was just in time to see another outbreak of war, this time against the British, whose King George II was a Hanoverian and reacted violently to France's invasion of Hanover. De Sade was under fire for the first time at Sondershausen, where the French were victorious. By the age of nineteen he had been promoted to a captaincy in the cavalry, and a travelling companion named Castéra remarked that he was showing himself to be highly susceptible to German girls and gambling away twenty livres a day – to the disgust of his father, who was increasingly short of money.

When the war ended, in 1762, Donatien had acquired a taste for wine and women – not the kind of women he could easily pick up, but successful actresses, whom his good looks and social position convinced him ought to be his by right. His father became even more unhappy after creditors seized much of his property.

From Maurice Blanchot's chronology of de Sade's life, we learn:

Late February 1763: Sade, it would appear, is engaged to two young ladies simultaneously: Mademoiselle Renée-Pelagie de Montreuil and Mademoiselle Laure de Lauris. Of the two, Sade prefers the latter, with whom he is wildly in love, but his father is intent on arranging an alliance between his son and the wealthy Montreuil family, doubtless because of the seemingly delicate financial situation in which he then finds himself. (He wrote to his brother, the Abbé: 'Everything here has been seized.)

Fortunately, Laure then found herself another lover, abandoning de Sade junior. This was just as well; as under a law passed by Louis XV a son who declined to marry the woman nominated by his father was liable to go to jail until one side or the other relented. So Donatien, like it or not, was betrothed to his father's choice, Renée-Pelagie de Montreuil. Renée's family – unlike the very blue-blooded de Sades – were mere (but wealthy) tax collectors with no royal connections, so it seems likely that Donatien felt that he was being sacrificed to social ignominy, in order to solve his father's financial problems.

They were married on 17 May 1763 and the young couple

went to the Montreuil's Normandy estate for their honeymoon. At this stage Donatien's mother in law, Marie-Madeleine de Montreuil, who was still a beautiful woman, was apparently more than a little in love with her aristocratic son-in-law. This was perhaps not surprising as Donatien was handsome and (apart from his imperious temper) had perfect manners, though he only was 5 feet 3 inches tall.

The honeymoon period did not last for long. By October 1763 Donatien was in trouble. At the time, he was due to make an official visit to the Burgundian *parlement* at Dijon, to be installed as the king's *Lieutenant-Generale*. In fact, he was already rather tired of his marriage to his shy and easily shocked wife, and was looking forward to a session in Paris. There a procuress named Rameau had arranged for him to spend the night with a twenty-year-old fan-maker named Jeanne Testard – who supplemented her income with a little prostitution on the side.

De Sade had rented himself a small house on the Rue Mouffetard, which he furnished on credit. He offered the girl the considerable sum of forty-eight livres for her services, which was about forty times what she would normally expect for sex.

We are told in a police report:

The marquis, wearing a bright-blue cloth jacket, red cuffs and collars trimmed with silver buttons, had driven Mlle Testard by coach to a little house with a bright-yellow carriage gate, and led the girl to a second-floor room, and locked and bolted the door.

He asked her if she was religious; she answered that she believed in God, Jesus, and the Virgin Mary and abided by all practices of the Christian religion. The marquis then blurted out a stream of atrocious insults and profanities. After telling her that he had proved that God did not exist, he masturbated into a chalice, referred to the Lord as a 'motherfucker' and to the Holy Virgin as a 'bugger', and asserted that he had recently taken two Communion hosts, placed them in a woman's vagina, and entered her, shouting, 'If thou art God, avenge thyself.' After that, Sade and Mlle Testard went into another

room, containing a curious collection of objects hanging from
the wall: four cane whips and five sets of cat-o'-nine-tails –
three of hemp, two of iron and brass. Alongside them hung
several religious articles – ivory crucifixes, engravings of
Christ and the Virgin – which in turn were intermingled with
several prints and drawings that Mlle Testard testified were 'of
the greatest obscenity'.

De Sade then told Jeanne that she must whip him with the
cat-o'-nine-tails after heating it in the fire until it glowed red, and
he then would beat her with whatever other whip she wished.
Although he pressed her hard, Jeanne flatly refused to be
whipped herself. After that he took two of the crucifixes off the
wall, one of which he trampled, while masturbating over the
other; after which he ordered her to do the same. Then, while
showing her two pistols that lay on the table and holding his hand
on his sword – threatening to stab her with it – he told Jeanne to
further blaspheme her God by shouting: 'Bugger! I don't give a
fuck about you.'

After having refused the marquis's orders to commit a few
more such sacrilegious acts, Mlle Testard – who appears to have
been genuinely devout and truly shocked – was forced to spend
the night with her tormentor. Between more mundane sexual
acts, he read her poetry 'filled with impieties and totally contrary
to religion'. In the dawn hours the marquis announced that he
intended to sodomise Mlle Testard, a mode of congress she
adamantly refused. He then made her promise that she would
return the following Sunday morning, when they would go to a
nearby church, steal two Communion hosts, burn one and use
the other as 'an instrument of sexual pleasure'.

At nine the next morning, when the procuress came to fetch
her, the two women went straight to a high-ranking police official. De Sade was arrested ten days later.

As we read this account, we note that there is something about
it that fails to make sense. It would not take an intelligent man
long to notice that a working girl like Jeanne was evidently half-
educated and terrified to boot. So why did he treat her like a

lecture audience? Was de Sade just showing off? Was he not wasting his own time as well as hers? And why did he pay her so much? Was he hoping to win her willing assent to playing his silly games of stealing Communion hosts, and thus becoming his permanent partner in blasphemy?

It's hard not to conclude that Donatien was an extremely muddled young man who, at twenty-three, was still a long way from any real sense of his own identity. He was evidently intellectually lonely and not a little deluded. Why else hope that the girl that he had sermonised at and terrorised all night might be willing to consider another date? A classic rebel without a cause, de Sade was desperately fighting his childhood Christian indoctrination but, at that stage, had no real idea why.

After his arrest, he was sent to the prison at Vincennes, where the amenities were not of the best – the toilet was a gutter in the cell floor and the bed straw was filthy. De Sade was soon expressing his deep repentance and regret. After three weeks he was allowed to rejoin his mortified wife, who was pregnant. (Sadly, the baby, a girl, lived only two days after her birth.)

It was not until the following May (1764) that de Sade was given permission to go to Dijon to be installed as the king's Lieutenant-General and to make a speech. He told parliament that this was one of the happiest days of his life, and since he was at last playing a small part in government. He may well have been telling the truth but, if he was, his conventional mood did not last long.

By June he was indulging in his usual infidelity to his wife, telling a pretty actress named Colet that he wanted to die at her feet. She became his mistress – for a fee of 500 livres a month (paid from his wife's money). There is no evidence that he treated her sadistically, although he probably sodomised her – he had decided that this method of sexual entry to be more insulting to God than normal sex. At this point, his mother-in-law, whose police spies kept her informed, succeeded in making him break up the affair. His response was to take another beautiful actress named Beauvoisin as his mistress.

Apart from Echauffour, the Normandy château owned by his in-laws, de Sade possessed his own château in Provence; it was called Lacoste and had a magnificent view from a mountain top. Since the staff at Lacoste had not yet seen his wife, he decided to continue his pattern of deliberately scandalous behaviour by taking Beauvoisin there with him. He also invited his uncle the Abbé as a guest. Always willing to accept free hospitality, the Abbé hastened there and thus became his nephew's accomplice in infidelity. Soon after this his long-suffering wife Renée, back in Paris, gave birth to a son, christened Louis-Marie.

In January 1767, de Sade's father died. Donatien, despite his generally distant and abrasive relationship with his father, was unexpectedly upset. He now inherited the title 'count' (which he never used). He consoled himself by taking a ballet dancer called Mlle Riviére as his mistress. He had also rented himself a small house at Arcueil, an hour outside of Paris, where he held orgies with both men and women. One evening in early February his valet picked up four girls in the Faubourg Sainte-Antoine, and de Sade gave them dinner, whipped them and was whipped by them. He gave the valet twenty livres to pay them, but the man kept three for himself as a pimp's commission. There were evidently many such 'parties'.

If de Sade had confined himself to these arranged orgies, all would have been well. But at Easter 1768 he again landed himself in severe trouble by picking up a beggar named Rose Keller, aged thirty-six – in the Place des Victoires, in Paris – and asking her to go with him to clean his house.

He took her out to Arcueil by carriage – where, in fact, two prostitutes brought by his valet were already awaiting his attention. He locked Rose in a room, then went off to attend to the two ladies; getting them to 'fluff' him by stimulating him manually or orally. Then, fully excited by his sexual *hors d'oeuvres*, he returned to Rose and ordered her to undress 'for fun'. When she protested he told her he would kill her and bury her in the garden if she didn't shut up, then left her alone to remove her clothes.

When he returned, naked but for a vest, she was still wearing her chemise. He tore this off and pushed her face downward on the bed. He then began to flog Rose frantically, alternating between a cane and a cat-o'-nine-tails. When she bled he dripped hot candle fat on her wounds.

As the strokes became more rapid, he began to cry out and then, with a final terrifying shriek, he achieved orgasm. (De Sade always had problems reaching a climax.) With his victim also screaming, the racket must have been horrific.

De Sade then took Rose a bowl of water and told her to wash and dress. He brought her dinner – bread, boiled beef and a carafe of wine – then led her to an upstairs room with two beds. He locked her in, ordering her to stay away from the window, and left her alone. She lost no time in forcing open the wooden shutters with a knife, knotting together two sheets, and scrambling down them to the garden.

The valet, spotting her, rushed after Rose with a purse full of money but she ignored him. Half an hour later she had reached comparative safety in the house of the local bailiff, where she told her story between sobs.

Back in Paris, de Sade poured out his tale to his wife, who recognised that he would be lucky to escape prison unless they acted instantly. She despatched Donatien's abbé uncle, plus a lawyer, to find out how much would buy Rose Keller's silence. She demanded 3,000 livres – a small fortune considering seventeen livres could buy three prostitutes for a whole night of whipping. The negotiators got this down to 2,400 livres; and Mme de Sade, on being consulted, told them to settle for this. De Sade's need to force an unwilling woman to join one of his orgies had cost him, and his wife, very dearly. Not least because the Rose Keller scandal had an extraordinary and unexpected consequence: it made de Sade infamous. Within a week the story was all over France, and then all over Europe.

This in itself is rather odd. There had been dozens of shocking aristocratic scandals in previous years, but all were kept silent simply because they involved aristocracy. The king's brother, the Comte de Charolais, was another notorious sadist and in a recent episode he had invited a Mme de Saint-Sulpice to supper, got her utterly drunk, then undressed her and inserted a lit firework into her vagina. She was seriously burnt and injured. In another sadistic scandal, an innocent peasant had been seized by a crowd of drunken aristocratic merrymakers. They had held a mock trial and then held a very real execution by hanging him from a tree.

On the whole to be a sadistic and homicidal noble was considered shocking but acceptable in eighteenth-century France – provided it was only women or peasants who were harmed. And that suitable hush-bribes were paid; taken from the taxes levied by those same nobles from the pockets of peasants and tradesmen.

But in the de Sade case there was also a suspicion of blasphemy: that the scourging of Rose Keller, at Easter, was intended to sacrilegiously parallel the flogging of Christ. That placed the incident beyond the pale of well-bred acceptability. That de Sade actually meant to insult the Church sounds plausible, but is probably untrue – kidnapping and sexual assault on a helpless beggar was a typically thoughtless act by a bored and spoiled aristocrat. Besides, if de Sade had wanted to insult Christ by whipping Rose, he would almost certainly have mentioned the fact to her. He wasn't the type to keep that sort of inspiration quiet. The fact is that Donatien, at twenty-eight , had outgrown his earlier need to give the church such a blatant two-fingered salute.

Yet the fact remains that the 'sacrilegious' Rose Keller case became a symbol for the wickedness of the French aristocracy, and the widespread notion that people like the Marquis de Sade could do whatever they liked with impunity. And this in itself was about the worst thing that could have happened to the French nobility at this point in the eighteenth century. It would be no exaggeration to say that a direct powder trail leads from the flogging of Rose Keller in 1768 to the French Revolution of 1788, and that Donatien de Sade played a central part in lighting it. And he, a born iconoclast and upper-class rebel, would have been delighted by this judgement of history.

To grasp how this came about, we need to know how France had got into this explosive state. The Thirty Years' War, that devastated Europe from 1618–48, was essentially a turf war between Christian sects – the Catholics and Protestants. Yet, oddly enough, it was the Catholic Cardinal Richelieu of France who prevented the Protestants from losing; for he had no desire to see a Spanish Habsburg royal clan dominating Europe.

Thanks to Richelieu – accurately portrayed as a ruthless

political mastermind in the novel *The Three Musketeers* – France came out of the Thirty Years' War stronger than ever. So the next French king, Louis XIV, could behave like a Roman emperor – militarily aggressive, anti-reform and utterly self-indulgent. Louis had so much money that he was able to bribe half of Europe to do whatever he wanted and then to build the fabulously expensive Palace of Versailles outside Paris.

The 'Sun King's' continued wealth was also due to his good sense in choosing as his chief minister Jean Baptiste Colbert, a shopkeeper's son, who revolutionised French industry. But Colbert disagreed with his master on one vital point; he thought the rich should pay taxes like anyone else, while Louis just wanted the aristocrats to decorate his court. And they couldn't do that to his satisfaction unless they too were fabulously wealthy. Thus they couldn't be ordered to pay taxes.

This hole in the treasury, and the king's regular wars, drained the national wealth as fast as Colbert made it – and hence the increasing gap between the lives of the noble rich and the struggling poor. By the time of the Donatien de Sade scandal – another feckless King Louis later – this inequality was a gaping chasm. De Sade's behaviour seemed to sum up everything that was wrong about French society. Indeed, one might argue that England had no revolution because it had no Marquis de Sade – but that would be like blaming the pebble that starts an avalanche. England had no revolution because its aristocrats were just a little more circumspect in their self-indulgent lifestyles than their French counterparts.

After becoming a household name, de Sade's behaviour went on getting worse. Every time he got near a city, he sent out his manservant to round up a few prostitutes to have an orgy. Many of these street-walkers were destitute children; but this reflects the state of France as much as it does de Sade's sexual tastes.

In 1772, four years after the Rose Keller scandal, he and a manservant named Latour went to Marseilles to collect a debt. Latour also collected four young prostitutes. De Sade and Latour then spent the morning having vaginal and anal sex with the girls while flogging them (and one another). The girls were also given

sweets containing Spanish Fly: this was a concoction of the dried
and mashed green beetle of the same name (scientific designation: *Lytta vesicatoria*). Spanish Fly was supposedly aphrodisiac,
as eating it increased blood flow to both male and female geni-
tals, causing automatic erection in the former and increased
sensitivity to the latter. But, in large doses, Spanish Fly was also
a dangerous emetic.

That evening Latour procured another prostitute, and gave
her more of the Spanish-Fly-spiked sweets. This time he overdid
it, and as a result she was violently ill in the night. A doctor
suspected she had been given arsenic, but later analysis disproved
this. An arrest warrant was issued for de Sade and Latour, who
had by then hurried back home.

As soon as de Sade got the news that he was probably going to
be thrown in jail, again, he prepared to flee. He took Latour – his
servant, flogging-partner, aphrodisiac-administrator and pimp –
with him. (That must have been a memorable job interview.) At
this point, to his surprise, his sister-in-law declared she was
coming too. Anne-Prospére was nine years younger than de
Sade's wife Renée and had been in love with Donatien ever since
she first saw him. Indeed, de Sade had originally wanted to marry
her, although this may have been because of his paedophile
tendencies. It seems likely she had become his mistress as soon
as she went to live at Lacoste. Anne was a canoness – that is, a
kind of apprentice nun who had not yet taken her vows. That
alone was enough to excite de Sade's lust. But why Renée was
willing to allow her sister to steal her husband remains a mystery.

At all events, by the time the bailiffs arrived with the arrest
warrants, the birds had flown. De Sade and Latour were tried in
their absence in Marseilles, found guilty of poisoning and
sodomy, and both sentenced to be beheaded. Of course, if it
hadn't been for the earlier Rose Keller Easter flogging scandal,
the sentence would almost certainly have been lighter. But, then,
if de Sade's name hadn't already become mud across Europe, he
probably would never have been charged for so minor a crime as
maltreating and almost killing a prostitute.

For reasons that are unknown to us, Anne did not find her

brother-in-law a satisfactory lover – perhaps she found his enthusiasm for flogging or sodomy too much for her – and by November
had returned to Lacoste. But her brief period as her brother-
in-law's mistress was enough to arouse her mother's violent
hostility, and Mme Montreuil became henceforth de Sade's most
bitter enemy and the bane of his life.

She now applied to the King of Savoy for a *lettre de cachet*
('order of imprisonment') for her son-in-law. He was arrested
that December in his house in Paris and removed to the twelfth-
century fortress of Miolans, near Chambéry. There he remained
for four months, until 30 April 1773. On that date de Sade,
together with Latour and a fellow prisoner, the Baron de l'Allée,
(in jail for debt) succeeded in escaping, with the aid of a local
farmer. They managed to cross the Swiss border by dawn.

Once more his mother-in-law spent months procuring a court
order to have him imprisoned. The bailiffs who went to Lacoste
on 6 January 1774, to launch a 'Commando attack' planned by
Mme de Montreuil, could find no sign of the marquis, but only
of his wife. De Sade had been warned by a villager.

On 10 May, 1774, King Louis XV died of smallpox, and was
succeeded by his son, who would be the last of the pre-
revolutionary kings of France. It was traditional for a new king
to listen to pleas for pardon by convicted felons – especially
aristocratic felons. So the Marquise Renée hastened to Paris,
hoping to get the *lettre de cachet* revoked, but was too late –
her mother had got in first. So for the next six months or so, de
Sade was obliged to remain on the run in Italy and Switzerland.
By November 1776 he was home at Lacoste. And, as if he had
not got problems enough, he immediately launched into
another bout of debauchery – an episode that became known as
'the young girls scandal'.

It seems that, as he prepared to get used to the idea of another
fairly dull period at Lacoste, he had also decided to enliven it
with a few orgies. So he ordered his wife to engage five fifteen-
year-old girls, to return with them to Lacoste, nominally as
maids. All were innocent young women, who had no history as
child prostitutes and were probably all virgins.

And at this point another bizarre development took place: his wife Renée Pelagie, who had spent years trying to get him out of trouble, quite suddenly decided she may as well join him in misbehaviour. We do not know why, unless it was something to do with her sister Anne's brief decision to become her husband's mistress and the resultant legal row with her mother. Whatever the reason, Renée threw herself into the deflowering of the five young maids with apparent gusto.

We do not know exactly what the de Sades inflicted on the teen-age girls – for the simple reason that the marquis and his wife took great care to suppress the details. We only know that, six weeks later, by the time the parents began making enquiries, the de Sades had good reason for not wishing the teenagers to be examined and packed them off to stay with various local families.

De Sade now fled again to Italy, leaving his wife to cope with endless problems, including lack of money, and proceeded to write his first book, *Travels in Italy*. (He even hired an artist to illustrate it.) He hoped that authorship might bring him a new career.

Back in Lacoste, de Sade tried to organise yet another orgy. He asked a priest named Fr Durand to find him four more servant girls. He took these back to Lacoste, but they returned home to Montpellier the next day, alleging that de Sade had approached each one of them – separately – during the night and tried to persuade them to join him in his room in exchange for a purse of silver. They all, possibly by then having heard his brutal reputation, refused.

In early January 1777, the father of a kitchen maid called Trillet went to Lacoste to demand that his daughter Catherine should accompany him back home. He produced a pistol and fired at de Sade, but it proved to be loaded only with powder and no ball. Even so, it gave de Sade a nasty shock. A court ordered him to hand over the girl.

In early February, de Sade and his wife went to Paris with the notion of being reconciled with his mother-in-law. It was a major mistake. As soon as Mme de Montreuil knew he was in Paris, she had him arrested.

When de Sade appeared at the courthouse at Aix to be tried, a crowd of two hundred people had gathered to catch a glimpse of the famous evildoer, but he was in a closed sedan chair. He was then retried on the charge of poisoning the prostitute in Marseilles with Spanish Fly and was acquitted. But the court ordered a new investigation of the charges of libertinage and pederasty, and of these he was found guilty. He was fined just fifty livres – the equivalent cost of hiring a few prostitutes for a couple of flogging orgies.

However he was also kept under arrest under the terms of the *lettre de cachet*, originally obtained by his mother-in-law from the King of Savoy in 1772. Under this arbitrary document, de Sade might be held in jail for the rest of his life – on no evidence – because a king had said so. There was no chance of appeal or parole, except on the word of a king.

On the way back from Aix, escorted by police, he made his escape from an inn. Then he made the mistake of returning to Lacoste. A few days later he was once more arrested and taken to Vincennes prison. After three months in solitary confinement he was given writing materials and permission to write what he liked. But in effect, his days of freedom were now over. And the days of his authorship were about to begin.

This was in December 1780. Four years later, in February 1784, he was transferred to a cell in the Bastille prison-fortress in the heart of Paris. He was placed in the ironically named Liberty Tower, where he was kept in a room fifteen feet square.

Lady Anne, his sister-in-law and ex-mistress, had died of smallpox in May 1781. (His mother had died in January 1777.) Fortunately his wife Renée remained as devoted as ever – although what she was up to while he was locked in jail was anybody's guess. De Sade could hardly complain if she was unfaithful, considering it was he who had successfully introduced her to orgiastic behaviour.

But now, at least, he had begun to write: in 1782, he had penned a dialogue called *Dialogue between a Priest and a Dying Man*, in which a dying man indignantly rejects a priest's exhortations to virtue and repentance, and ends by persuading him (perhaps implausibly) to join an orgy.

In July 1787, he wrote (in just two weeks) the draft of his first novel, which he titled *Les Infortunes de la Vertu* (*The Misfortunes of Virtue*). The novel was later revised and retitled *Justine*.

This book, since it went on to become his best-known work, and was the ultimate cause of his permanent loss of freedom, deserves more space here. Originally meant as little more than a novella, it was intended to kick off a volume of 'stories and fables' (*contes et fabliaux*). The tale is of two sisters, Therese and Juliette, orphaned when their father, a banker, is driven to suicide by a crooked associate. De Sade's intention is to show how both sisters set out with equal chances in life, but Juliette is open-minded and adjustable, and after a brief period of crime and vice, is able to live comfortably. Meanwhile, her sister, determinedly virtuous and narrow-minded, encounters endless misfortunes.

De Sade's intention is quite clear: to indicate that he much prefers Juliette and her level-headed common sense to her sister's narrow-minded Christianity. But it soon becomes clear that de Sade so enjoys describing Therese's sufferings that he lingers over them indefinitely. Which is why Therese, and her arguably earned '*infortunes*', turned into 'Justine' in the later draft. In *Justine*, de Sade drops any real attempt at moral philosophy and even to tell much of a story. The heroine, on her way to execution, simply tells of her many undeserved sexual misfortunes . . . in titillating detail.

In 1785, de Sade spent twenty evenings hand-making a huge roll of writing paper – gluing together small strips and sheets of paper that had been smuggled into his cell. It was finally twelve metres long and twelve cm wide. He then covered it with the penned manuscript of *The 120 Days of Sodom*. In this unfinished novel an aristocrat, a judge, a banker and a bishop lock themselves in a castle with several prostitutes and forty-six teenage boys and girls – including the protagonists' own daughters – and spend the 120 days of the title trying to commit every conceivable sexual depravity – and de Sade could conceive of quite a few, most bizarre and many murderously horrific.

When he was not surreptitiously writing, de Sade hid what he plainly hoped would be his master work in a hole in his cell wall, because he knew that his jailers would confiscate his pet project if they knew about it. He must have also realised that if the authorities read its satiric as well as pornographic contents, he would lose any chance of ever being released.

Meanwhile, in the outside world, revolution was approaching. France was almost bankrupt. By 1787, the Marquis de Lafayette, who had played an active role in the American Revolution, suggested that the king should set up a parliament (constituent assembly), but Louis XVI refused – only to have to give way soon after. Parliament met, but the representatives of the people soon found themselves blocked at every turn by the representatives of the church and the aristocracy. In 1788, after a crop failure, peasants began to revolt and burn the houses of the rich.

Perhaps hoping to precipitate a revolution, de Sade took advantage of being in the Liberty Tower to shout from his window, incorrectly, that prisoners were being murdered. As a result, on 4 July 1788, he was transferred to the Charenton Asylum, transported there 'as naked as a worm'. Ten days later a revolutionary mob surrounded the Bastille. The governor agreed to surrender, then treacherously fired cannons into the crowd. He eventually did surrender, again, and as he emerged he was seized and his head hacked off with a butcher's knife. Hearing the news, de Sade's wife Renée fled Paris, abandoning other papers that he had managed to smuggle out of his tiny cell; these are now all lost to history.

Behind her, as she left, the rejoicing poor of Paris tore the hated Bastille down to the ground, brick by brick. This of course included de Sade's former cell in the Liberty Tower. He despaired and 'shed tears of blood' when he heard this, as he realised that his precious manuscript of *The 120 Days of Sodom* must have been destroyed too. He eventually went to his grave, quite unaware that his masterwork had been saved two days before the siege of the Bastille, by a guard who was sacking his cell for loot. The roll of paper, and its shocking content, disappeared for over a hundred years. Eventually it was revealed to be in the hands of a private collector and it was finally published in 1904. The book is now widely seen as a recovered treasure of French culture and one of the great satiric works of the eighteenth century. Of course, that doesn't change the fact that very few people can read the book without wanting to vomit – but that too would probably have delighted the Marquis de Sade.

On 2 April, Good Friday, 1790, de Sade finally regained his liberty – thanks to the revolution that he had indirectly helped to start. By this point his wife Renée, under the influence of her Father Confessor, had decided to separate from him. But by 1 July, de Sade had been issued his identity card as a 'citizen' of the Place Vendome section of Paris, of which he soon became secretary and chief orator.

On 3 August, the *Theatre Italien* accepted de Sade's one-act verse play *The Suborner.* And two weeks later he began an affair with a young actress, Marie Constant Renelle, whose husband had walked out on his wife and child. It was a happy relationship that would last the rest of his life.

It would be pleasant to imagine that de Sade became famous as one of the fathers of the Revolution, but nothing of the sort happened. *The Suborner* was a flop, because no audience full of revolutionary red bonnets was going to applaud the work of an aristocrat. The same was true of his play *Oxtiern,* which later received just one performance.

On 22 June 1791, the king and queen were caught trying to escape from Paris to Austria, hoping to summon an army to overthrow the revolution. The king was tried and executed, the queen soon after. Then, the following year, came 'the Terror' . . .

It is a popular misconception that a majority of the victims of the Jacobin 'Reign of Terror' were members of the French aristocracy. In fact, of the estimated forty thousand people executed between July 1793 and July 1794, only 8 per cent (3200) were aristocrats. A further 14 per cent (5,600) were middle-class *bourgeoisie,* and 6 per cent (2,400) were members of the clergy. The remaining 72 per cent (28,800) were penniless commoners accused of minor or imaginary crimes. Yet, despite being one of the most notorious aristocrat decadents in the country, de Sade was spared; largely because of his imprisonment by the old royalist regime.

It was in the year of the king's execution, in 1793, that *Justine* finally found its way into print. An updated version, it was dirtier and more violent than its original. It sold well but, because of the chaos of the times, failed to make de Sade much money. The new version tells how the innocent and virtuous Justine, having endured endless undeserved miseries, appears before a senior law lord on a murder charge, only to discover that fate has relented. Her judge proves to be the lover of her sister Juliette, who is as sinful and wicked as Justine is pure and good; the two sisters fall into one another's arms, and Justine is treated as lovingly and protectively as if her past misfortunes were a nightmare. Then a great storm descends on the house where she has finally found peace and refuge, and as she stands at an open window, a thunderbolt kills her instantly. Her horrified sister decides to repent, gives her fortune to the Church, and finally dies in an atmosphere of sanctity.

In April 1793, de Sade's father-in-law Lord Montreuil, former tax-collector, came to see him. The Montreuils had been imprisoned by the revolutionaries and, even though now free, were still in a dangerous position. Lord Montreuil's motive was probably to make sure that his son-in-law was not contemplating revenge on Mme de Montreuil; but he need not have worried – Donatien had a forgiving temper.

This visit was a proof of how respectable 'Citizen de Sade' had recently become; he was now a magistrate and had even been invited as a delegate to a convention to debate the reformation of the army. But in August 1793 – at the beginning of the Terror – de Sade resigned as vice-chairman from a government committee on the grounds that a proposal for mass executions of 'enemies of the state' was 'horrible and utterly inhuman'.

Then, in December 1793, de Sade was again arrested and this time narrowly escaped execution for being a 'moderate'. Fortunately, on 27 July 1794, the convention turned on Robespierre, the Jacobin leader and the chief instigator of the Terror. He himself was then guillotined, along with most of his cronies. The murderous Reign of Terror lapsed into normal political turmoil and a right-wing backlash ensued. That, in turn,

eventually led to the glorious and then disastrous rule of the
Emperor Napoleon. De Sade was freed in October 1794, went
back to living with his beloved Constance and her young son, and
decided to keep the Hell out of mainstream politics from then on.

In 1795, de Sade wrote one of his lighter works, *Philosophy in
the Boudoir,* in which a brother and sister set out to educate (and
corrupt) a fifteen-year-old girl, with the aid of a libertine named
Dolmancé. It has lines like: 'Masturbate your sister,' to which the
reply is: 'No I'd rather fuck her.' This book contains as its fifth
chapter a semi-satirical tract called 'Frenchmen, one more step
if you wish to become Republicans', which declares that now the
French have had the courage to execute the king, they should
take the logical next step and execute God.

Philosophy in the Boudoir, one of de Sade's most engaging
and tongue-in-cheek works, also failed to sell; perhaps because
1795 offered the reader such a profusion of romantic best-sell-
ers, like translations of Matthew Lewis's *The Monk*, and works by
Mrs Radcliffe and William Godwin. De Sade decided that what
was needed was another historical family saga in the manner of
Richardson, and returned to an idea for a vast work called *Aline
and Valcour,* partly about a judge who plans to commit incest
with his daughter. He even threw in a volume about a visit to a
socialist utopia called Toamoé, with echoes of Rousseau, but it
all proved to be too much of a mish-mash to appeal to a public
sated by real horrors, and failed to take off.

The earlier *Justine* still sold well, but de Sade must have
brooded sadly on the lost *120 Days of Sodom* destroyed, as he
thought, in the Bastille. Surely the answer was to rewrite and
expand *Justine,* his nearest approach to a best-seller? So this
became his new literary project. The result, published in 1801,
was *Juliette.* This book is another sadomasochistic *Pilgrim's
Progress*, but contains some genuinely funny scenes. For example, Juliette at one point receives an audience with Pope Pius VI
(the then sitting pontiff). She uses the opportunity to graphically
list the sexual infidelities that she alleges were committed by his
predecessors. Rather than be shocked by these accusations, the
Pope gets into the spirit of the thing and initiates an orgy.

As the reader contemplates this and the many other outrageous scenes in de Sade's books, it is almost inevitable that they will be struck by the reflection that its chief purpose is to offend and outrage the author's fellow citizens. Given that he published everything anonymously, it might be tempting to see de Sade as nothing more than a crazy, depraved and cowardly prankster. But a closer reflection may also lead, as in my own case, to the recognition that the author is neither mad nor bad, but is merely driven by rage to make a point with extreme repetition.

And the nature of the point? Surely it is the same *frustration* that Barbusse's 'outsider' feels on the Paris street as he contemplates the dozens of dresses that 'lift and yet do not lift', that offer themselves and then change their minds? He is expressing the frustration Yeats expresses in the poem 'Towards Break of Day' about the waterfall 'upon Ben Bulben's side':

> *I would have touched it like a child*
> *But knew my fingers would have touched*
> *Cold stone and water. I grew wild*
> *Even accusing heaven because*
> *It had set down among its laws:*
> *Nothing we love overmuch*
> *Is ponderable to the touch.*

In the spring of 1801, First Consul Napoleon Bonaparte instructed his chief of police, Joseph Fouché, to uncover the anonymous author of the scandalous *Justine*. On 6 March, police raided the offices of de Sade's Parisian publisher, Nicolas Massé. De Sade happened to be there at the time and was arrested too. Fouché decided against giving de Sade the publicity of a trial; instead, he was thrown in one of Paris's most crowded jails, Sainte-Pelagie, and forgotten. De Sade unhappily continued to deny that he was the author of *Justine*, but nobody was about to believe him.

The novelist and playwright Charles Nodier met de Sade in prison and noted his enormous obesity that made movement difficult; but he added 'his weary eyes still had something indescribable, something brilliant and fine which came to life like a dying spark on a dead coal . . .' He also said that de Sade was very courteous and polite – an aristocratic gentleman to the last.

After spending over a year in Sainte-Pelagie prison, de Sade was transferred to another jail, the Bicetre, in south Paris. Now he was charged with being the author of the 'infamous works' *Justine* and *Juliette*, which he still hotly denied. After six weeks, his family agreed to pay 3,000 livres a year for his keep at Charenton Asylum in the val de Marne, an institution known for its 'humane' treatment of patients by *hydropathy* – a misbehaving patient might be blindfolded and thrown into a large swimming pool, or made to sit under a pipe that gushed cold water.

But since de Sade was self-evidently not insane, by any standard assessment, it is unlikely that the old man was treated this way often or at all. Indeed, the head of the asylum successfully resisted demands from a government minister that de Sade be kept in solitary confinement. Citizen de Sade remained in Charenton until his death on 2 December 1814, when he was seventy-four years old. However, there is reason to believe that he wasn't too unhappy in his last years. For the last four years of his life he is believed to have been conducting an affair with the teenage daughter of one of the asylum employees.

I have dwelt on Aldonse-Donatien Louis de Sade's life in detail, because he is a perfect example of a sex criminal gone good. In his early life he had the makings of another Gilles de Rais (*see Chapter 20*) and for probably just the same reasons that 'Bluebeard' eventually became such a monster. De Sade and Rais were spoiled rotten by both their childhood guardians and by their social position as privileged aristocrats. As noted in Chapter 21, childhood and adolescent psychological trauma is a seeding factor that can create a sex criminal later in life – what is realised less often is that utterly spoiling a child can also be a form of psychological abuse. Denied the boundaries that all children crave, a spoilt brat can lack all sense of proportion and can feel as desperately miserable as a child who has suffered more direct abuse.

Perhaps then the key moment in de Sade's life was his decision to abduct Rose Keller during Easter in 1768. If his flogging of a helpless woman had not taken place during a religious festival, there would have been no scandal and he would have felt free to carry on his debauched lifestyle. The fact that de Sade *did* do just that after the Keller scandal broke is largely irrelevant, since his blackened reputation meant that his next brush with the law quickly removed his previous feeling of being untouchable: for much of the rest of his life, de Sade was either on the run or in jail. One can't help feeling if 'Bluebeard' de Rais had been given this sort of slap – instead of being lauded as the former body-guard of a national heroine and saint – he might not have ended up being hanged for murdering over two hundred children.

Donatien de Sade is proof that the dark energies that create a sexual obsessive can be redirected, if never actually deleted. There is no question that the young de Sade was a kidnapper, rapist and paedophile. He was also a true sadist – after all, the mental condition was named after him. All things considered he would have almost certainly become a murderer too, if left on that path. But, thanks largely to the pure boredom of the Bastille, he was forced to put his considerable creative powers into writ-ing socially satirical sadistic pornography – just to avoid going barmy. The monstrous Marquis de Sade was still there in his writings, but it had been tamed by the realisation that only crea-tivity could build the real inner development that he craved. By comparison, decadent sexuality (in the flesh) had – and had always – left him feeling disappointed and empty.

When he was freed by the French Revolution, Citizen de Sade could have become a truly hideous monster – something to have made Bluebeard de Rais seem like an under-achiever. De Sade found himself surrounded by political chaos and legalised murder, and, as his short political career showed, he could easily have exploited the situation to become a leading figure during the Reign of Terror. But he didn't – indeed he shied away from the mass executions, indicating genuine horror.

I think the reason for this humane reaction is that – in his youthful days of freedom and debauchery – he never crossed the mental Rubicon of killing another human being. As we have seen so often with serial killers, this particular Rubicon is actually more like a one-way valve: once passed, a sadistic sociopath can never be trusted not to kill again.

The Marquis de Sade has maintained his ability to shock down through more than two centuries. As late as 1957, the French publisher of a reissue of *Juliette* was prosecuted and found guilty of 'outrage of public morals'. But, anyone who knows de Sade's story after his release from the Bastille can see why is it absurd to speak of him as 'the wickedest man in the world'.[1] It is clear, for example, that de Sade had every opportunity to take revenge on his mother-in-law for his years in prison – he merely had to denounce her to Robespierre or to any revolutionary tribunal – but he never made the slightest attempt to do so.

And, as paradoxical as this sounds, his collected writings bear out this judgement. None of the works he published under the title of *Les Crimes d'Amour*, with titles such as *Miss Henrietta Stralson*, *Eugenie de Franval* and *The Mystified Magistrate*, would be banned today. But if we go on to protest that works like *La Nouvelle Justine* and *La Nouvelle Juliette* are too appalling to be read by decent people, de Sade might justifiably reply: 'Quite so. They were written for collectors of blasphemy and indecency, solely to support Constance and her son. Would you tell me I should have let them starve?' And we might admit that he had succeeded in making us feel a little guilty.

The Marquis de Sade was certainly a monster. But, towards the end of his life, he was the sort of monster that one could almost find loveable.

---

1 Quoted from the introduction to the Oxford World Classic's edition of de Sade's *The Crimes of Love: Heroic and Tragic Tales*

Chapter 24

The Man Who Hated Everybody

The killer whose name has become famous among criminologists as a symbol for irrational violence was called Carl Panzram, and his story deserves telling at some length, for reasons that will become self-apparent.

When Carl Panzram was locked into his cell in the Washington DC District Prison on 16 August 1928, no one even suspected that he was one of the world's most brutal mass-murderers. It is just possible that no one ever would have known – except for a lucky coincidence. That same week, a young guard named Henry Lesser also arrived in the jail.

The Washington prison was architecturally a long box, with tier upon tier of barred doors facing each other down either side. As Lesser climbed the iron stairs, he noticed the silhouette of a man framed against the afternoon sunlight – a big man with massive shoulders and a round, almost hairless head. There was something about the prisoner that made an immediate impression – Lesser declared later: 'There was a kind of stillness about him.' He noticed the name outside the cell door: 'C. Panzram'. Wanting to be friendly, Lesser asked him when his case was due to come up in court.

'November eleventh.' The face was so hard, the eyes so flat and stony, that Lesser assumed he must be a gangster.

'What's your racket?' he asked.

Panzram gave an odd smile. 'I reform people.'

The two other prisoners in the cell laughed.

Lesser checked, later on, why Panzram was in jail. To his surprise it was not violence or extortion – merely burgling a home and stealing a radio. When the policeman who arrested him had asked why he was smiling, Panzram had replied: 'Because a charge of stealing a radio is a joke.'

'What do you mean?'

Panzram said: 'I've killed too many people to worry about a charge like that.'

The policeman had assumed that the petty burglar was a fantasist, so had failed to follow the statement up. Panzram did have a long prison record, but it was mostly for burglary and vagrancy.

Henry Lesser soon became well liked among the prisoners. A young Jew from a poor background, he was more liberal and humane than the other guards. A few days later Lesser asked Panzram what he meant by 'reforming people'. Panzram said without expression: 'The only way to reform people is to kill them.'

Lesser hurried away. What he had just heard disturbed him profoundly. Yet there was something about Panzram that aroused a curious feeling of response.

The prison governor, William L. Peak, would have found that attitude incomprehensible. He was a tough man who regarded the prisoners as dangerous subhuman creatures who had broken the laws of society and now had to take their punishment. Sympathising with them would be as pointless as rewarding naughty children. Panzram made no secret of the fact that he hated Peak and would welcome a chance to get his hands round his throat.

Later that day, the guards were ordered to do a 'shakedown' of Panzram's tier, searching for weapons or illegal substances. Two guards entered Panzram's cell, one of them holding a short iron rod with which he tapped the window bars, while the other one watched the prisoners. One of the bars gave a dull sound instead of a clear, metallic ring. The guards looked at one another and left immediately. Ten minutes later, they were back with handcuffs, which they clicked onto Panzram. They knew better than to bother with his cellmates; only Panzram's immense hands would have had the strength to gradually loosen the bar in its cement setting.

Panzram was taken down to the basement of the jail. The iron beams of the ceiling were supported by thick pillars. Panzram was backed against one of these pillars and his hands were passed around it then re-handcuffed. Then a rope was passed through the chain of the cuffs and thrown over a beam; Panzram was heaved up until only his toes touched the floor. The angle of his arms around the pillar almost dislocated his shoulders, and the pain was agonising. For the next twelve hours he was left in this position.

The next morning, Lesser saw him lying on the floor of the isolation cell, the skin of his wrists in ribbons, and his arms covered with bruises where the guards had beaten him with blackjacks (small leather bags packed with sand). Panzram only muttered when Lesser asked if he was all right. But when one of the other guards looked into the cell, Panzram stirred himself enough to call him a son of a bitch. Soon after, four guards entered the cell; when Panzram resisted, he was knocked unconscious with a blackjack. When he woke up, he was once again standing on his toes in the basement, his arms chained around the pillar. All night he cursed and shrieked defiance at the guards; blows seemed to make no difference. One of the 'trusties' – a convict trusted by the guards – told Lesser that, in his agony, Panzram had roared that he had killed dozens of people and would kill more if he got the chance.

The next day, when Panzram was back in his own cell, Lesser handed the trusty a dollar to give to Panzram. He knew that a dollar meant extra food and cigarettes. When the trusty passed on the dollar, Panzram obviously thought it was a joke. When the trusty assured him that it was no joke, Panzram's eyes filled with tears.

Later, when Lesser passed his cell, Panzram limped to the bars and thanked him. 'That's the first time a screw has ever done me a favour.' He told Lesser that reporters had been asking to see him since word of his 'confessions' had leaked out, but he had refused to see them.

'But if you'll get me a pencil and paper, I'll write you the story
of my life.'

This was strictly against the rules; prisoners were only allowed
to write a limited number of censored letters. But Lesser decided
to break the rules. The next morning, he smuggled the pencil
and paper through the bars, and Panzram hid them under his
mattress. That evening, after midnight, Lesser slipped up to
Panzram's cell and was handed a batch of manuscript. They had
time for a short conversation, and for the first time, Lesser realised that Panzram had a powerful if uncultivated mind. He was
startled, for example, when the prisoner told him that he had
read Schopenhauer, and he agreed entirely with the German
philosopher that human life was a trap and a delusion.

Panzram's autobiography began: 'This is a true statement of
my actions, including the times and places and my reasons for
doing these things, written by me of my own free will at the
District Jail, Washington DC, 4 November 1928.'

As he began reading the account of Panzram's childhood,
Lesser had no idea that 'these things' would include twenty
brutal murders.

Just over a week later, Panzram limped into court. With his
record of previous convictions, it was likely that the burglary
charge would earn him a five-year sentence. In such circumstances, most prisoners would have done their best to seem
harmless and repentant. But Panzram seemed to be in the grip
of a demon. Having told the judge that he would represent
himself, he sat in the witness chair and faced the jury, staring at
them with his cold, baleful eyes.

When asked to plead 'guilty' or 'not guilty', he growled: 'You
people got me here charged with housebreaking and larceny. I'm
guilty. What I didn't steal I smashed. If the owner had come in I
would have knocked his brains out.'

This man was obviously a dangerous psychotic. The jurors
looked pale and shaken. Panzram went on evenly:

'While you were trying me here, I was trying all of you too. I've
found you guilty. Some of you I've executed. If I live I'll execute
some more of you. I hate the whole human race . . . I believe the

whole human race should be exterminated. I'll do my best to do it every chance I get. Now, I've done my duty, you do yours.'

Not surprisingly, the jury took less than a minute to find him guilty. The judge sentenced him to twenty-five years in Leavenworth, one of America's toughest jails.

Lesser was shocked when he heard of the sentence. But, unlike the other occupants of the Washington jail, he knew exactly why Panzram had done it. He had been reading Panzram's autobiography and it revealed a man whose bitterness was so deep that he would have cheerfully destroyed the world. Lesser's own childhood, while poverty-stricken, had been full of family warmth and affection. Now he read with horror and fascination the story of a man who had never received any kind of love, and therefore never learned to give it.

Carl Panzram had been a tramp and a jailbird since he was fourteen. He had been born one year before the worst American depression of the nineteenth century. His father was a poor German immigrant, an ex-soldier who had hoped to make his fortune in America. Instead, he was forced to work as a farm labourer until he scraped together the money to buy a small farm in Minnesota. A man with a violent temper and a brooding disposition, John Panzram saw his investment wasting away through drought and hard times. His overworked wife, Matilda, suffered from high blood pressure and dizzy spells. Carl, their fourth child, was born on 28 June 1891. One day, not long after the birth of yet another baby, John Panzram walked out and the family never saw him again.

Carl was a difficult child. He longed for adult notice, but no one had any time to give it to him. So he behaved badly to get attention; but even then he was only spanked and then ignored again. His first appearance in court was at the age of eight, on a charge of being drunk. At school he had further beatings with a strap – on his hands, because at this stage he was sickly and often ill. One day he decided to run away out west to be a cowboy; he broke into the home of a rich neighbour and stole some cake and apples, and a revolver. But before he had travelled more than a few miles he was caught. At the age of eleven he was sent to his first reform school. 'Right there and then I began to learn about man's inhumanity to man.' He was often tied, face down and naked, over a wooden block. Then salty water was poured on his back and allowed to dry. Then he was beaten with a strap with holes punched in it, so the skin came up through them as it struck the flesh, instantly causing small blisters; when these burst, under further blows, the salt caused agony.

But Panzram was a strong-minded boy. 'I began to hate those who abused me. Then I began to think I would have my revenge as often as I could injure someone else. Anyone at all would do. If I couldn't injure those who had injured me, then I would injure someone else.' This last sentence could be said to be Carl Panzram's guiding motto.

Sent home after two years, Carl was immediately packed off to a Lutheran school whose teacher detested him on sight and often beat him. One day Panzram stole a revolver. When the teacher next began to hit him, he pulled out the gun, aimed it at his suddenly terrified tormentor, and pulled the trigger. It misfired. Before he could be sent back to reform school, Panzram jumped into an empty car on a freight train and went west.

Riding the freight trains at the age of fourteen, he had another lesson in inhumanity when he invited four burly tramps into the comfortable box car he had found. Ignoring his struggles, they held him down and raped him. The same thing happened again in a small town in the Midwest when he approached a crowd of loafers sitting around a fire and tried to beg food. They got him drunk on whiskey and he only realised what had happened when he recovered consciousness. The lesson Panzram learned from this was simple: 'Might makes right.'

Panzram was a highly sexed youth, but even the cheapest whores were too expensive for a teenage tramp. Instead he developed a taste for sodomising men. On one occasion when a brakeman caught him hiding in a freight car, Panzram pulled out a revolver and sodomised him at gunpoint, then forced two other hobos to do the same.

Such an over-the-top sort of crime obviously involved more than mere sexual satisfaction: it was Panzram's crude method of taking revenge on the world as a whole. Yet this was not the rabid brutality of an enraged beast – Carl Panzram started his criminal career with the cool attitude of a general planning a war. Crime seemed the easiest way to get what he wanted – wealth and the freedom to escape the control of others. So he became a monster, quite aware that that was what he was doing.

This habit of committing rape to satisfy both his sexual tension and vindictive streak was soon ingrained in Panzram – but the decision to attack only males was apparently purely strategic. After catching gonorrhoea from a female prostitute, he decided that women were too high a risk. He picked up young boys whenever he could, because they were unlikely to be carrying venereal diseases. It was for this same reason, he claimed, that he sodomised men during the course of robberies – typically tying them to a tree to do so. Yet if someone had accused Panzram of being homosexual, he would have been astonished. Rape was merely a sexual outlet for him – and an outlet for his aggression. By committing anal rape on men and boys, he was somehow repaying what had been done to him. He called it 'the law of compensation', and saw no irony or injustice that he attacked innocent people to take revenge for crimes committed on him by others.

In a way, there were only two entities in Carl Panzram's universe – himself and an amorphous conglomerate consisting of everyone else. Revenge on one part of this vast and often malicious blob was revenge on the whole thing, as far as he was concerned. His miserable early life and his natural self-centredness meant that he couldn't or wouldn't empathise with any one person as another individual.

Back in detention for robbery, he escaped with another youth, and they teamed up. 'He showed me how to work the stick-up racket and how to rob the poor box in churches. I in turn taught him how to set fire to a church after we robbed it.' They enjoyed destruction for its own sake – even boring holes in the floor of wagons full of wheat so the grain would run away along the tracks, and emptying sand into the oil boxes of the freight cars so they would seize up.

A brief period in the army ended in court martial for insubordination, and a three-year sentence in a military jail. The sentence was signed by the Secretary of War, Howard Taft. Thirteen years later, Panzram burgled Taft's home and stole $3,000, as one of his few directed acts of revenge.

Panzram served his three years, together with an extra month for trying to escape. But he succeeded in burning down the prison workshop. 'Another hundred thousand dollars to my credit.' He wrote later: 'I was discharged from that prison in 1910. I was the spirit of meanness personified.' During the next five years his only legal employment was as a strike-breaker – which ended when he was beaten unconscious by strikers. There were also several spells in prison for burglary. But the episode that had turned him into a full-blown enemy of society had happened in 1915, when he was twenty-three.

In San Francisco, he had been arrested for burgling the home of a bank president. The District Attorney offered him a deal; if he would confess where he had hidden the loot, they would 'go easy' on him and give him a minimum sentence. The law broke its word, however; Panzram handed over the loot, but was still sentenced to seven years.

In an insane rage, Panzram succeeded in breaking out of his cell, plugging all the locks so no guards could get in, then set about wrecking the jail. He tore radiators and pipes off the walls, piled up everything that would burn and set fire to it. The guards finally broke in and 'knocked [his] block off'. Then Panzram was shackled and sent off to the Oregon State Penitentiary, one of the most inhumane in America.

He swore that he would not complete his sentence; the warden, a brutal man named Harry Minto, swore that he would.

One of Panzram's first acts was to hurl his chamber pot in a guard's face; he was beaten, then handcuffed to the door of a dark cell known as 'the Hole' for thirty days. A few weeks later he was flogged and thrown in again when he was caught trying to hack a hole in the prison roof. When released, he was made to wear a uniform of red and black stripes, recently designed to indicate dangerous troublemakers. The 'punishment' misfired;

prisoners wearing a 'hornet suit' were regarded by other convicts as heroes.

Warden Minto was shot dead in 1915, during a hunt for an escaped convict called Otto Hooker (who was himself killed by other guards soon afterwards). Minto's brother – who was equally brutal – took over his job as warden. He set out to make Panzram's life difficult – not least because it was known that Panzram had helped Otto Hooker to escape.

For his part, Panzram set out to make the new Warden Minto's life hell. He broke into the storeroom and stole bottles of lemon extract – which contained alcohol – and got a crowd of prisoners drunk; they started a riot, while Panzram, who remained sober, sat back and grinned. Next Panzram burned down the prison workshops – but was caught and thrown back into the Hole. Then he was confined in a specially built isolation block called the Bullpen.

Panzram won this round. He roared and cursed all night, beating his slop bucket on the door. Then the other prisoners joined in. Tension was already high because the warden had cut prisoner hard labour wages from a dollar to 25 cents a day. So, fearing another riot, the warden decided it would be wiser to release Panzram; and then tried to bribe him into good behaviour by assign him a plum job in the kitchen. Panzram was unmoved. Arriving in the prison kitchen he immediately went berserk with an axe, causing everyone to flee. He had smashed all the locks in an empty block of cells before he was clubbed unconscious.

Tension across the prison mounted until the guards refused to go into the yard alone. When two convicts escaped, Minto ordered that Panzram and another suspected plotter should be 'firehosed' – a punishment outlawed by the state. The two prisoners were 'water-hammered' until they were battered and bruised all over. But the news reached the state governor, who sent for Minto and ordered him to resign.

The new warden, a man named Murphy, believed that prisoners would respond to kindness. When told that Panzram had been caught sawing the bars of his cell, he asked how many times Panzram had been thrown into the Hole; the guard said eight.

'Then it doesn't seem to be working, does it?' said Murphy, and ordered that Panzram should have extra rations and be given books to read. When, a few weeks later, Panzram was again caught with a hacksaw that someone had dropped into his cell, the warden sent for him.

Murphy told Panzram that he had heard he was the wickedest man in the jail. Panzram said he quite agreed. And then Murphy gave Panzram the greatest shock of his life. He told him that he could walk out of the prison and go anywhere he liked – provided he gave his word of honour to return by supper time. Panzram gave his word – without the slightest intention of keeping it – and when supper time came, found that some curious inner compulsion made him go back.

Gradually, Murphy increased Carl's freedom and that of the other prisoners. He installed an honours system, and Panzram became virtually a 'trusty'. But one night when he was 'on leave' in the local hospital, Panzram got drunk with a pretty nurse and stayed out too late. He decided to abscond. It took a week to catch him, and then he made a determined attempt to kill the deputies who cornered him. Murphy's critics had a field day and the honours system was undermined. Panzram was given an extra ten years and thrown back into solitary confinement. But soon after that, on 12 May 1918, he succeeded in escaping and evaded recapture. At last he had won his bet with the deceased Warden Harry Minto.

The experience of Warden Murphy seems to have been a turning point in Panzram's life. So far he had hated the world, but not himself. His betrayal of Murphy's trust seems to have undermined his certainty that his hatred and violence were all justified by what had been done to him by others. But instead of changing his direction, his new self-loathing led to attempts at denial, followed by the need to further pass the blame on to innocent strangers. It was after his escape that he quite deliberately began his career of murder.

In New York Panzram obtained seaman's papers and sailed for South America. He and another sailor planned to hijack a small schooner and murder everybody on board; but the sailor got drunk and tried to carry out the plan alone. In fact, he killed six men, but was caught. Panzram sailed for Europe, where he spent some time in Barlinnie Jail in Glasgow – as usual, for theft.

Back in New York he burgled the home of Howard Taft, the erstwhile Secretary of War who had confirmed Panzram's earlier military prison sentence. (Howard Taft, while Panzram had been in jail, had served as the 27th President of the United States.) Panzram bought himself a yacht with the stolen $3,000 in cash (around $50,000 in 2015 money). This was more than a self indulgence. Carl Panzram had coolly decided to commit his first murders, in such a way as to get the maximum fun and profit out of the venture.

'Then I figured it would be a good plan to hire a few sailors to work for me, get them out to my yacht, get them drunk, commit sodomy on them, rob them and then kill them. This I done . . .'

He explained in his handwritten autobiography, written for prison guard Henry Lesser, how he would hire two sailors, take them to his yacht and wine and dine them. He would then rape them when they were too drunk to resist, blow out their brains with a revolver he had stolen, then he would drop their weighted bodies into the sea from a rowboat. 'They are there yet, ten of 'em'.

After this excursion into serial killing, Panzram hired two more sailors and sailed down the coast, piratically robbing other yachts. It had been his intention to rape and murder these latest two helpers as well, but the yacht went on to rocks and sank. So, instead of killing them, Panzram paid them off.

A return to a career in burglary ended in a six-month jail sentence. Free again, Panzram signed on as a sailor. This time he travelled to the Belgian Congo – the country of the 'Heart of Darkness', of the Joseph Conrad novel, was about to become even darker. A job with an oil company came to an end when he sodomised the boy who served food in the company mess room. Panzram observed ironically, in his autobiography, that the youth did not appreciate the benefits of civilisation. Shortly after that, Panzram picked up another Congolese boy, raped him, then battered in his skull with a rock. 'His brains were coming out of his ears when I left him and he will never be any deader.'

'Then I went to town, bought a ticket on the Belgian steamer to Lobito Bay down the coast. There I hired a canoe and six niggers and went out hunting in the bay and backwaters. I was looking for crocodiles. I found them, plenty. They were all hungry. I fed them. I shot all six of those niggers and dumped 'em in.' (Panzram explains that he shot them in the back.) 'The crocks done the rest. I stole their canoe and went back to town, tied the canoe to the dock, and that night someone stole the canoe from me.'

Back in America in 1920, Panzram returned to burglary and stick-ups. He also raped and murdered another boy. After taking a job as a caretaker at a yacht club in New Haven, Connecticut, he stole a yacht and sailed it down the coast. A man who offered to buy it tried to hold him up at gunpoint, but Panzram was ready for him; he shot him to death and dumped his body overboard.

The police soon caught up with him, but this time a good lawyer succeeded in getting him acquitted. Panzram paid him with the yacht. When the lawyer tried to register the yacht, it was promptly reclaimed by its owner. By that time, Panzram was back in New Haven, where he committed his last rape-murder, bringing the total up to twenty killings.

He now signed on as a sailor to go to China, but was fired the same day for getting drunk and fighting. The next day he was caught as he was burgling the express office in Larchmont, New York. Once again, the prosecution offered a deal; if he would plead guilty, he would receive a light sentence. History repeated itself; he received the maximum sentence of five years.

This time he was sent to America's toughest prison: Dannemora, in New York state. Enraged again by the state's injustice, he promptly attempted to escape, but fell thirty feet on to concrete and broke both ankles. There was no attempt to set them by the prison doctor; Panzram was simply left in a solitary cell and given enough food to survive each day. He was there for several months before his ankles healed. 'I was so full of hate that there was no room in me for such feelings as love, pity, kindness or honour or decency. I hated everybody I saw.' One day he jumped from a high gallery, fracturing a leg. He was given the same 'medical treatment' and, unsurprisingly, walked for the rest of his life with a limp.

Carl spent the rest of his sentence dreaming of revenge on the whole world: planning how to destroy a passenger train by setting a bomb in a tunnel, or poisoning a whole city's water supply. But, within a short time of being released from Dannemora, Panzram burgled a house in Washington DC, stole a radio, and was caught. And it was in Washington District Jail that he wrote his story of robbery, rape and murder for Henry Lesser . . .

On 30 January 1929, Carl Panzram and thirty-one other prisoners were chained together and placed on a train for Leavenworth Penitentiary in Kansas. Henry Lesser was sent along as one of the escorts; they hoped that his presence would calm the 'dingbat', as Panzram was known. It was a strange experience for Lesser – to look at this man 'under his care', and to know that he had committed more than a dozen sex murders, and that no one but he and Panzram knew the whole truth.

The problem for Lesser was that he was in no position to confirm the crimes in Panzram's autobiography, and if he showed it to his superiors Panzram could just claim that the story was fiction. All that would certainly happen was disciplinary action, against Lesser, for smuggling the paper and pencil to Panzram.

Certainly a man as clever as Carl Panzram must have realised this, otherwise he would probably never have written the confession in the first place. One might even suspect that he was sadistically toying with the humane Lesser, if it wasn't for the fact that Panzram was honest enough, on several occasions, to warn his benefactor not to trust him. This fundamental honesty is an interesting side to the serial rapist and killer. Unlike so many human predators, he made no effort to convince others that he was actually a good guy who had suffered bad luck. Panzram knew and accepted that he was a monster and he liked Lesser enough to try to save him . . . from Carl Panzram.

On the trip to Kansas Panzram was in a bad mood. He made a grab for Warden Peak's personal 'trusty', but only had time to spit on him before he was manhandled back into line. But he was heard to mutter that he intended to 'get' Peak – who was travelling with them – and hoped to wreck the train. But Peak had somehow found out that Panzram hoped to pull the emergency cord when the train was at top speed, to try to derail it; accordingly, the emergency cord was disconnected. Panzram was then flogged when he tried to carry out his plan.

Harris Berman, a doctor who checked Panzram's heart while he was being flogged, sat up all night watching the 'dingbat'. He had heard that Panzram was planning to break loose and would try to kill Peak – or possibly himself. Panzram eyed the doctor with contempt, and made jeering accusations of sodomy with his assistant. He shouted the same accusations at Warden Peak whenever he showed his face. Later, when Lesser saw Panzram staring at two small boys who were peering in through the window at a station, he shuddered as he imagined what might be going through Panzram's mind.

The train finally pulled up in the grey stone walls of Leavenworth, the ground covered with dirty snow. The Leavenworth rule book contained no fewer than ninety statutes – including total silence during meals; breaking any single one of them entailed harsh punishment.

While Lesser and his fellow guards were taken on a tour of the five-storey cell blocks – all jammed to capacity – Warden Peak paid a call on Warden T. B. White, and warned him that the most dangerous man in the new batch was Carl Panzram. He advised White to keep him in solitary. But White, a lanky Texan, had his own ideas of reform – or perhaps he felt that Panzram was only one of dozens of dangerous prisoners. He decided to ignore the warning, and assigned Panzram to the laundry. Warden Peak and his contingent of guards, including Lesser, then returned to Washington.

When Deputy Warden Zerbst gave Panzram the regulation lecture on what was expected of him, Panzram only shrugged, then said levelly: 'I'll kill the first man that bothers me.' Like so many before him, Zerbst thought this was bluff.

The laundry was one of the worst assignments in the prison: damp, badly ventilated and either too hot or too cold. The man in charge, Robert Warnke, was a short, plump civilian who was also a member of the local Ku Klux Klan (then a respected organisation across much of America . . . dedicated to bigotry and violence 'in defence of the white race'.) Warnke had been warned that Panzram was dangerous, but seems to have felt no misgivings as he directed him to work on a machine with a skinny burglar named Marty Rako.

Years later, in a tape-recorded interview, Rako described his impressions of Panzram. The big prisoner was a loner, seldom speaking to others. But he read throughout his spare time, including volumes of Schopenhauer and Nietzsche. And when he took a dislike to his dirty and illiterate cellmate, he ordered him to apply for a 'transfer'. (One of the few privileges the prisoners were allowed was to move out of a cell if they disliked their cellmate.)

Panzram received regular letters from Henry Lesser, although many of these failed to get through – the authorities were automatically obstructive concerning anything that might give prisoners any pleasure. Lesser told Panzram that he had shown the autobiography to the famous literary critic H. L. Mencken, and Mencken had been impressed by the keenness of Panzram's mind. But he thought the confessions were too horrific to publish. Mencken had told Lesser nevertheless: 'This is one of the most amazing documents I have ever read.'

Panzram was flattered, but he had other things on his mind. He hated the laundry and its plump foreman. But he had thought of a way out. If a prisoner was punished – by being thrown in the Hole – he was seldom sent back to his previous work; most supervisors had no desire to work with a man they had severely punished.

Accordingly, Panzram made no real attempt to hide the fact that he was breaking the rules by laundering extra handkerchiefs. Many prisoners were wealthy men who were serving sentences for fraud; these were willing to pay for good food and for special services. When Warnke found out, he had Panzram demoted – which meant loss of wages – and sent to the Hole.

So far, Panzram's scheme was working. But when he came out of the Hole, he learned that the second part had misfired. He was being sent back to the laundry. Possibly Warnke felt he would lose face by allowing Panzram to be transferred, since Panzram was known to hate him. Or possibly he simply saw through Panzram's scheme and decided to frustrate it. He also turned down Panzram's direct request for a transfer.

As the Kansas summer wore on the weather was becoming stifling and new batches of prisoners made the jail intolerably overcrowded. There were so many that there were no fewer than nine sittings in the dining hall. The main meal of the day consisted of boiled rice with tomato sauce.

Thursday 20 June, 1929 looked like being another blazingly hot day as foreman Warnke walked into the laundry and prepared to check on the prisoners. He walked down the aisle towards a disassembled washing machine that stood near some open packing cases, strolling past a heavy steel pillar that held up the ceiling – not unlike the one Panzram had been chained to in the Washington Jail – and stood surveying the washing machine. Then he turned, and realised that Carl Panzram had been standing behind the steel pillar and that he was holding a crowbar that had been used to open the packing cases. Warnke had no time to notice anything else as the crowbar was brought down on his head, shattering the bone. Panzram screamed with rage and satisfaction as he went on pounding the skull of the fallen man's head to a pulp. Then, when he was sure Warnke was dead, he turned on the other prisoners and guards; they fled in all directions as he flourished the blood-stained crowbar.

Like some rampaging ape, Panzram shambled down the street outside and into the office of the Deputy Warden. Fortunately for Zerbst, he was late that morning. Panzram opened the door of the mailroom and limped in, swinging the bar; yelling clerks scattered in all directions. A convict who came in with a message was chased down the street. Then Panzram made his way back to the locked gate of the isolation unit. When he got there he bellowed: 'Let me in!'

'Not with that in your hand,' said the startled guard.

Panzram threw away the crowbar and the guard unlocked the

steel door. Now Panzram's rage was all dissipated, he looked relaxed and almost serene as he walked into the nearest cell.

When Warden Peak heard the news in Washington, he lost no time in summoning the press and saying 'I told you so'. Lesser was shocked and depressed – as much by the death of a fellow prison employee as by Panzram's predicament.

Panzram himself was startled when no one tried to beat him to death, or even drag him off to the Hole. Instead, he was placed in a large, airy cell, next door to a prisoner named Robert Stroud (who would later become known as 'the Bird Man of Alcatraz') and although he was kept locked in without exercise, he was allowed to read all day long. He told the visiting Lesser: 'If, in the beginning I had been treated as I am now, then there wouldn't have been quite so many people in this world that have been robbed, raped and killed . . .'

In reply, Lesser suggested that he himself should try and raise support from influential people – like Mencken – to get Panzram a reprieve. Panzram replied: 'Wake up, kid . . . The real truth of the matter is that I haven't the least desire to reform . . . It took me thirty-six years to be like I am now; then how do you figure that I could, if I wanted to, change from black to white in the twinkling of an eye?'

Lesser declined to take no for an answer, and persuaded a famous psychiatrist, Karl Menninger, to go and see Panzram. Forty years later, Menninger recalled how he had interviewed Panzram – under guard – in the anteroom of a federal court. When he told Panzram that he did not believe he would harm someone who had never done him any harm, Panzram's reply was to hurl himself at Menninger as far as his chains would allow him, and to shout: 'Take these off me and I'll kill you before their eyes.' Then Panzram went on to describe, with gruesome satisfaction, all his murders and rapes.

Despite the fact that a Sanity Commission had ruled that Panzram was insane – and therefore not responsible for his actions – on 15 April 1930 the jury in a federal courtroom in Topeka, Kansas, found him guilty, and the judge sentenced him to death. Panzram was evidently pleased with the verdict, and interrupted his defence attorney to say that he had no wish to appeal.

One problem for the state was that executions in Kansas were illegal – remember, the death sentence was passed in a federal, not a Kansas State, court. Panzram's sentence caused indignation in anti-capital punishment groups. One such group was permitted to appear outside his cell to ask him to sign a petition for clemency. They were startled to be met with shrieks of rage and obscenity.

Subsequently Panzram wrote a long and brilliantly lucid letter to a penal reform group explaining precisely why he had no desire to escape the death sentence. He even wrote to President Herbert Hoover telling him not to interfere and reprieve him. He also managed to make an unsuccessful attempt at suicide, eating a plate of beans that he had concealed until they had gone black and poisonous, and somehow slashing a six-inch wound in his leg. However, his magnificent constitution saw him through.

Shortly before 6 a.m. on 5 September 1930, Panzram was led from his cell, singing a pornographic song of his own composition. Seeing two men in clerical garb among the spectators in the corridor, he roared an obscenity about 'Bible-backed cock-suckers', and told the warden to get them out. When this had been done, he said: 'Let's get going. What are we hanging around for?'

On the scaffold, the hangman, who was from Ohio where locals are nicknamed 'Hoosier', asked him if there was anything he wanted. 'Yes, hurry it up, you Hoosier bastard! I could hang a dozen men while you're fooling around.'

Moments later the trap fell, breaking Carl Panzram's neck.

In effect, Carl Panzram's brutal life, and his personal philosophy of undirected revenge, turned him into two persons – or rather, a man and a beast. There was the Panzram who wrote an extremely clear-sighted confession and who felt the need to honestly warn Lesser not to trust him. This might be said to be the original Carl Panzram – who might have existed as a fulfilled and decent human being, if only life and other people hadn't beaten him to a pulp so often.

Yet it would be a mistake to simply blame those other people for the monster that Panzram ultimately became. His lucid confession, and his honest refusal to believe that he could ever reform, showed that his savagery was a chosen lifestyle. He dedicated his life to brutality and destruction in much the same way that another man might decide to be a priest or a doctor. Theft, rape and murder comprised Panzram's vocation. And he followed that vocation with the same dedication that a would-be saint might pursue honesty and decency.

But Carl Panzram felt that he had a right – through the sacred principle of revenge – to do whatever he wanted to whomever he wanted; be they terrified children or a former president of the United States. Justice didn't come into it, since Panzram believed that justice was a sham, used by the strong to control the weak. What he believed was that 'might made right': so he dedicated his life to being as strong and predatory as possible.

Yet Panzram's coldly thought-out crime career singularly failed to work. His lifelong attempt to increase his freedom, through violence, only succeeded in reducing his freedom, both physically and mentally. It might indeed have been Carl Panzram versus the rest of the human race – in fact his crimes soon made that inevitable – but all his 'revenge' killing did nothing for him. Maybe the tragedy is that Panzram's high intelligence was still not quite keen enough to grasp this simple fact. Until the end, that is, when – by rejecting all offers of help or clemency – he deliberately made sure that the last victim of his criminal strategy was himself.

Chapter 25

The Bogeyman

Are violent criminals simply born that way? Or are they made into thugs by their social background and by negative upbringing factors? These questions come as close to the central theme of this book as it is possible to get: are humans violent through nature or nurture?

More to the point concerning imprisoned criminals: can a human monster mentally grow beyond his crimes, as the Marquis de Sade seemed to do? Or will that person always surrender to a mire of self-indulgence, self-delusion and, ultimately, self-destruction, like Carl Panzram?

Consider the curious case of serial killer Steven Judy.

On 4 April 1979, a twenty-one-year-old Indiana mother named Terry Chasteen was driving her three children to a babysitter when she saw another motorist signalling to her and pointing to the rear of her car; so she pulled over to find what he wanted. In fact, he wanted to rape her. While purporting to diagnose her problem, he disabled her coil wire; then, when the car refused to start, offered her a lift in his truck, which she accepted.

Her naked body was found in White Lick Creek; she had been strangled and raped. The bodies of her three children, aged three, four and five, were also found in the creek. They had died of drowning. A public appeal for information led to reports of a red and silver pick-up truck near the crime scene. Its owner, Steven Judy, was arrested on a building site where he was working.

Child of a broken home, Judy had committed his first rape at the age of twelve, stabbing the woman repeatedly and severing her finger. He now told the jury: 'You'd better put me to death. Because next time, it might be one of you, or your daughter.' And before his execution he told his stepmother that he had raped and killed more women than he could remember, leaving a trail of bodies from Texas to Indiana. Like Carl Panzram, Judy opposed every effort to appeal against his death sentence.

Stephen Michaud, a crime writer who studied the serial sex killer Ted Bundy, reported his finding that there were, in effect, two 'Teds', an intelligent human being, and an entity Michaud came to call 'the hunchback'. In the Middle Ages they might well have referred to this as the Devil and perhaps would not have been entirely wrong.

As a writer on crime, I have seen case after case in which the actual perpetrator seems to have been Michaud's 'hunchback' – rather than the Carl Panzram or the Steven Judy who ultimately takes the blame. (Indeed, in both those cases, it might be seen that it was Panzram and Judy who ultimately killed their hunchback side, by insisting on execution.) In such cases it can seem as if there are two different people inhabiting the same body. Yet, where the one ends and the other takes over can be impossible to say. Ultimately we punish 'both', so we usually just shrug and put it down to a lack of control by the non-hunchback part of the criminal. But if we are to understand our own violent natures, then we cannot ignore this odd inconsistency.

I have never been more aware of this paradox than after I made the acquaintance of one of the most well-known British serial killers of the twentieth century, the 'Moors murderer' Ian Brady.

Brady wrote to me out of the blue in the summer of 1990. Shortly before that, a girl named Christine had introduced herself to my wife as a correspondent of Brady's, and we asked her to the house. Her story was that she had been orphaned as a child and adopted by a middle-class family in the home counties. An unhappy and rebellious teenager, she had been fascinated by the Moors murders of the 1960s and fantasised about Brady as a kind of soulmate. She and Brady had begun to correspond and she claimed she had been to see him in prison; but they had since quarrelled. She was now thinking of writing a book about Brady and wanted to ask my advice about whether she could quote his letters.

I told her the answer was no – they remained his copyright. But a few weeks later I received a letter from Brady, asking if it was true I meant to collaborate with her on a book about him. I replied that this was untrue, but Brady and I began to correspond. After decades as a crime writer, I was curious about how an intelligent man – as it soon became clear he obviously was – had become a serial killer. Brady's story, as it emerged from his correspondence, is as follows:

Ian Brady – christened Ian Duncan Stewart – was born on 2 January 1938 in Glasgow: his mother, twenty-eight-year-old Margaret Stewart, worked as a waitress in hotel tearooms; his father was a Glasgow journalist, who died three months before Ian's birth. Margaret Stewart did her best to support the child, but was finally forced to advertise for a 'child minder'. He was taken by a working-class couple named Sloan, whose home has been described as 'warm and friendly'. (Brady is on record as saying he was fond of his foster family.) So it hardly seems that Ian Brady can be classified with Panzram and other criminals who were badly treated in childhood.

At the age of eleven he started attending Shawlands Academy, a school for above-average pupils, but seems to have taken a certain pleasure in misbehaving, perhaps in reaction against richer schoolmates. And at the age of thirteen he came before a juvenile court for burglary, but was bound over to keep the peace (that is, effectively, a suspended sentence). Nine months later, he was in the dock for the same thing, but was simply bound over again. At sixteen he appeared again before a Glasgow court with nine charges against him. This time he was put on probation on condition that he joined his mother in Manchester. Margaret Stewart had moved there when her son was twelve and had married a meat porter named Patrick Brady.

Brady found the teenager a job in the local fruit market, and it was at this time that Ian took on his stepfather's surname. The boy was becoming a loner however, spending most of his non-working hours in his room reading a pile of books, including the works of Dostoevsky. But, in November 1955, he was again in court, this time on a charge of aiding and abetting a crime.

A lorry driver had asked him to load some stolen lead on to his lorry. Then the scrap dealer gave them away to the police. In court, Brady pleaded guilty, expecting a fine for such a trivial offence. But because he was on probation, the judge decided that severity was called for. To his bewilderment – and rage – Brady was remanded to Strangeways prison to await his sentence.

There he spent three months among professional criminals and deliberately cultivated fences, cracksmen, even killers. He had made up his mind that society was going to get what it deserved. This reaction, as we have seen, is typical of the high-dominance male faced with what he considers outrageous injustice. Carl Panzram, for instance, made undirected revenge the theme of his life.

The two-year borstal sentence that followed only confirmed the decision – particularly when, in an open borstal at Hatfield, he found himself in further trouble. He had been selling home-distilled liquor and running a betting book, on horse and dog races. One day, after getting drunk and having a fight with a warder, he was transferred to an altogether tougher borstal housed in Hull Prison. This was where he prepared himself to become a big-time criminal. His aim was now to become wealthy as quickly as possible, so he could enjoy the freedom and pleasure that he dreamed about. This was why he studied book-keeping in prison – to learn how to handle stolen money.

He was released at the end of the two years, but remained on probation for another three. Returning home to Manchester, Brady immediately became involved in a crime ring that was handling stolen Jaguars. Fortunately, this remained unknown to his probation officer. In fact, apart from one brush with the law for being drunk and disorderly, Brady managed to officially stay out of trouble. His probation officer also obliged him to take a labouring job in a brewery, which Brady detested. In 1959, at the age of twenty-one, he succeeded in changing this for something less disagreeable; book-keeping training led to a job as a stock clerk with Millwards Ltd, a small chemical firm. He was a careful and neat worker, although inclined to be unpunctual, and to slip out of the office to place bets with a local bookmaker. But he remained a loner, spending the lunch hour alone in the office, reading books which included Adolf Hitler's *Mein Kampf* and other volumes on Nazism.

What seems clear is that Ian Brady was turned into an enemy of society by a burning sense of injustice. That this attitude was quite unjustified is beside the point; given his background, and the two years in Borstal, it later seemed to him to have been inevitable.

(It also seems possible that Brady's sexual attitudes might have been skewed by this period of incarceration. As already noted, in Chapter 21, psychological trauma during childhood and/or adolescence can permanently damage a young person's sexual outlook. This was confirmed by a report issued on 10 February 2015 by the UK's Howard League for Penal Reform. Its conclusions indicated that young people who serve time in prison are notably more likely to become sex offenders in later life. The following are extracts from the report by the Howard League Commission on Sex in Prisons, chaired by Chris Sheffield:

> *Incarcerating children at this formative time is counter-productive and may be compounding problematic behaviour and increasing their risk of sexual offending.*

> *As children approach adulthood they are exploring their relationships with others developing intimate relationships with others and learning about issues such as equality, respect, sexuality, gender identity and sexual consent.*

> *[An imprisoned child's] opportunities to form relationships and model their behaviour on adults in normal healthy relationships are severely restricted.*

> *The commission heard that boys learnt to keep their sexual behaviour secret in prison. Punishment for normal sexual*

*behaviours could evoke feelings of guilt or shame for boys in
prison and could increase the risk of sexual offending.*

As we will shortly see, Ian Brady certainly showed signs of a
sexual development that had been truncated and malformed. It
is true that he was actually sixteen, and therefore relatively old,
when he was first sent to Borstal; but the indicators are clearly
there to see. Initial shyness was followed by the need to totally
dominate his sex partner. Even his later rapes, sadism and
murders might also be seen as offshoots of a predatory, obsessively self-centred and essentially adolescent-fantasist attitude
towards sex.)

Although a loner Brady was by no means an outcast among his
contemporaries, who seem to have regarded him as a daredevil.
His brushes with the law had been infrequent, and he was
treated leniently until the stolen lead episode. In Brady's own
opinion, the judge's decision to remand him to Strangeways was
the true origin of the Moors murders.

Among writers on the case there has been a fairly concerted
effort to represent Brady as a mindless devotee of violent comics
and books with titles like *The Kiss of the Whip*. This is inaccurate, since his reading included intellectually demanding books
like *Crime and Punishment* and *Thus Spake Zarathustra*.

The journalist Fred Harrison records that Brady discovered
Crime and Punishment in the Manchester public library in 1958,
around the time of his twentieth birthday. Its hero, an intelligent
but impoverished student called Rodion Raskolnikov, tries to
justify his murder and robbery of an two old women by explaining that he asked himself what Napoleon would have done in his
place. What if, instead of having the opportunity to prove himself
at the Battle of Toulon at the age of twenty-five, Napoleon had
been a poor student in St Petersburg? Wouldn't he too have
murdered to get money? Don't gifted individuals have a right to
ascend above the rules that bind ordinary people?

This seems, in many ways, to be the key to Brady's personality.
Since childhood he had never doubted that he was a 'somebody'.
Like Raskolnikov, he saw himself as an unlucky Napoleon – or, in

Brady's case, an unlucky Adolf Hitler. Nietzsche talks about 'how one becomes what one is'. But how could he find a way of becoming a 'somebody?' Especially if your native talents don't seem to be earning the plaudits that you think that you deserve.

The answer that Brady found lay in the second major influence on his late teens: Hitler's *Mein Kampf*. Anyone who wonders how an anti-Semitic tirade could have exercised such an immense influence on a whole generation should brush aside preconceptions and try reading it. Its starting keynote is reasonableness and reminds us that when the young architect Albert Speer first went to hear Hitler speak, expecting a ranting maniac, he was amazed to discover a man who talked quietly and rationally, almost pedantically.

Hitler begins the book by speaking of his father, the son of a poor cottager, who set out from his village at the age of thirteen, with a satchel on his back and a single gold coin in his pocket, to launch himself into the strange, unknown world of Vienna. He became a civil servant, then retired and became a farmer.

Hitler's father was determined that his son should become a civil servant; Hitler was equally determined that he would not. Conflict began when Hitler was eleven and became more bitter when, at the age of twelve, he decided to become an artist.

Then, in his early teens, his father and his mother died in quick succession. He was left in poverty and he was forced to go to Vienna to seek his fortune.

By this point the reader is hooked. Hitler's descriptions of his sufferings and poverty in Vienna are simple and undramatised. And when he goes on to speak of a corrupt society, rotten with injustice and poverty, it seems that he is speaking common sense. Suddenly, it is possible to see how Hitler exercised such an immense influence on his audiences; they felt he was simply articulating what they had always felt. He goes on to conjure up a family of seven living in a dark basement, where every minor disagreement turns into a quarrel. Sometimes the father assaults the mother in a fit of drunken rage. All religious and political and humanistic values seem an illusion. The truth is simply the brutal struggle to survive. A child brought up in such an environment becomes totally anti-authoritarian. When he leaves school he is 'cynical and resentful. And he soon ends up in a reformatory, which completes his education in self-contempt and criminality . . .'

Hitler goes on to describe how, working in the building trade, he first came up against trade unionism and Marxism. When told he had to join the union, he refused. As he got to know his fellow workers better, he knew he could never 'join' them; they struck him as too stupid. Finally, when they threatened to throw him from the scaffolding, he left. By that time he had come to despise socialism, which seemed to him the glorification of the mediocre – the weak demanding protection from the strong, simply because they *are* weak and demanding. In other words, he saw socialists as a form of parasite.

According to Hitler, it took him a long time to see an apparent connection between socialism and the Jews. At first he claims that he was actually disgusted by the anti-Semitic press. Then he began to recognise what he saw as the part played by Jews in socialism, particularly Marxism. It was Marxism that aroused his most furious disgust, with its dislike of entrepreneurs and – by implication – of individual enterprise. Dostoevsky had expressed the same disgust with socialism in *The Possessed* (a novel that Brady read five times). Hitler ends his second chapter by stating ominously that 'should the Jew, with the aid of his Marxist creed, triumph over the people of this world, his crown will be the funeral wreath of humanity'. It is notable and ominous that Hitler clearly doesn't regard Jewish people as a part of humanity.

Then the rest of *Mein Kampf* descends from Hitler's initially rather humane approach to a repetitious political diatribe. He continually blames the Jews for all the woes of the modern world; lionises the German people (without giving much supporting evidence) as a race who are close to becoming Nietzsche's imagined 'supermen'; and glares darkly eastward and growls about confiscating *lebensraum* ('living space') from the 'subhuman' peoples native to Eastern Europe.

Hitler's doctrine, as put forward in *Mein Kampf*, achieved

enormous influence in the decade before the outbreak of the Second World War; but, it should be remembered that that influence came mostly *after* he had been appointed as German Chancellor by the senile President Hindenburg. And that *Mein Kampf's* success had also come after Hitler had declared a national emergency, seized total power and had made ownership of a copy of his book virtually compulsory for everyone (the latter being a private daydream of most writers).

In his Nazi doctrine, Hitler was proposing to place a concentrated German nationalism at the heart of the nation's worldview. This was partly based upon pride in German cultural heritage – most notably the works of Goethe, Schiller, Beethoven, Nietzsche and Wagner (ignoring the fact that all of these recognised world figures had been dead for some time). And as much as he bellowed hate for his designated out-groups – like the Jews, Slavs, blacks and communists – Hitler ladled (largely unearned) praise on the contemporary German people. The result was something like a narcotic: a highly potent brew which, when distilled into films like Leni Riefenstahl's *Triumph of the Will*, seems to offer a simple and deceptively seductive solution to all the problems of the modern world.

For two years Ian Brady continued to work quietly at Millwards. In his spare time he read, learned German and played records – including Hitler speeches – and almost certainly continued to keep in touch with ex-Borstal friends and plan 'jobs'.

Then, on Monday 16 January, 1961, an eighteen-year-old shorthand typist named Myra Hindley came to work at Millwards and Ian Brady dictated her first letter. She was four and a half years younger than Brady, a completely normal working-class girl: not bad-looking, with a blonde hairdo, bright lipstick, and an interest in boys and dancing. She had been born a Catholic, brought up a Protestant, and returned to Catholicism when she was sixteen. When she was four, the birth of a sister made the family home too cramped and she went to live in her grandmother's house. This was not particularly traumatic since she could spend as much time as she liked at her home around the corner. At school she had received good marks and wrote poetry and 'excellent English essays'. She played the mouth organ and was known as a high-spirited tomboy.

Hindley had been engaged but had broken it off, finding the boy 'immature'. This was one of the problems for working girls at that time, whose notions of attractive males were formed by cinema and television: hard-bitten, strong jawed, heroes or charismatic rebels like James Dean and Elvis Presley. By contrast, the youths they met at dance halls seemed commonplace and boring.

Ian Brady was certainly not that. He had slightly sulky good looks reminiscent of the young Elvis Presley, and a dry and forceful manner. His self-possession was intriguing. So was his total lack of interest in her. (Myra, of course, was unaware that he was bisexual, with a strong inclination toward homosexuality.) Her infatuation blossomed and she confided it to her red diary. 'Ian looked at me today.' 'Wonder if Ian is courting. Still feel the same.' 'Haven't spoken to him yet.' Then: 'Spoken to him. He smiles as though embarrassed.' On 1 August: 'Ian's taking sly looks at me at work.' But by November: 'I've given up with Ian. He goes out of his way to annoy me . . .' Then, on 22 December 1961: 'Out with Ian!' They went to see the film *King of Kings*, the life story of Jesus. Just over a week later, on the divan bed in her gran's front room, Ian Brady and Myra Hindley became lovers. 'I hope Ian and I love each other all our lives and get married and are happy ever after.'

Myra was overawed and fascinated by her lover. She declared later: 'Within months he had convinced me there was no God at all: he could have told me the earth was flat, the moon was made of green cheese and the sun rose in the west, I would have believed him.' Brady later told me that the relationship with Myra was so close that they were virtually telepathic. They spent every Saturday night together, went for visits to the moors on Ian's motorbike, taking bottles of German wine, read the same books, and went to see his favourite films, such as *Compulsion*, based on the Leopold and Loeb murder case.

Now he had a willing partner/disciple, but the central problem remained: how to escape the boring rut of working-class existence and find a more fulfilling way of living. According to the journalist Fred Harrison, it was early in 1963 – after they had been lovers for a year – that Brady suggested that the two of them should collaborate on robbing a bank or a shop.

For a payroll robbery it would be necessary to possess a car. Myra began to take driving lessons and passed her test at the first attempt. Also at about this time, Brady took up photography and bought a camera with a timing device. He took photographs of Myra in black crotchless panties; she, in turn, photographed him holding his erect penis; then, using the timing device, they photographed themselves having sex. The intention, apparently, was to make money selling the pictures.

In April 1963, Brady wrote to her that he would be surveying an 'investment establishment' (i.e. bank or building society) in the Stockport Road. In June 1963, Brady moved into the house of Myra's grandmother, and Myra acquired a car, a second-hand minivan. It was then, according to Harrison, that he began to talk to her about committing a murder.

In an open letter to the press in January 1990, Brady would say that the murders were 'the product of an existentialist philosophy, in tandem with the spiritualism of death itself.' What seems clear from this is that, for Brady, crime had become a form of dark romanticism; and that this philosophy was based on his personal reading of Nietzsche, Dostoevsky and de Sade.

The first 'Moors murder' happened on 12 July 1963, a month after Brady had moved in with Myra. The only account we have of the murder is from the confession Myra Hindley would make to Detective Chief Superintendent Peter Topping, quoted in his book *Topping* (1989). According to Myra, she picked up a neighbour named Pauline Reade – who was sixteen – in the minivan, and asked her to help her come and look for an expensive glove which she had lost at a picnic on Saddleworth Moor. Hindley offered her a pile of gramophone records in exchange. When they had been on the moor about an hour, Brady arrived on his motorbike and was introduced as Myra's boyfriend. Brady and Pauline then went off to look for the glove, while Myra (she claims) waited in the car. Later Brady returned to the car and took Myra to Pauline's body. Her throat had been cut and her clothes were in disarray, indicating rape. They then buried the body with the spade that Myra had brought in the back of the van.

In his open letter of 1990, Brady claimed that Myra had been involved in the actual killing and had also made some kind of sexual assault on Pauline Reade. On the whole, his account sounds the more plausible. Myra's accounts of the murders invariably have her elsewhere at the time and Detective Chief Superintendent Topping admits that Myra told the truth only in so far as it suited her.

It seems clear that Brady was now totally in the grip of the criminal-outsider syndrome. The plans for the payroll robbery – or robberies – were well advanced. And so were plans for more murders. The one thing we know for certain about serial sex crime is that the criminal is a sort of addict. Of course, the satisfaction in all sex derives partly from the 'forbidden', but the forbiddenness is diluted by the need for mutual consent; rape – possessing a person without their consent – is like undiluted corn liquor. Few rapist killers have succeeded in stopping of their own accord. But it is also important to grasp that the murders were only a part of Brady's agenda.

In October 1963, three months after the murder of Pauline Reade, Ian Brady made the acquaintance of sixteen-year-old David Smith, the husband of Myra's sister Maureen (who was now also working at Millwards). Smith was a big youth who had been a member of a street gang and had been in trouble with the law. Soon David and Maureen took a trip to the Lake District with Ian and Myra, where they sailed on Lake Windermere. While not homosexual, Smith experienced an emotional attraction to males; soon he was almost as completely under Brady's spell as Myra was.

On Saturday 23 November 1963, Ian Brady and Myra Hindley drove to the small market town of Ashton-under-Lyne. A twelve-year-old boy named John Kilbride had spent Saturday afternoon at the cinema, then went to earn a few pence doing odd jobs for stallholders at the market. It began to get dark and a fog came down from the Pennines. At that moment, a friendly lady approached him and asked him if he wanted a lift. It seemed safe enough, so he climbed in. It was the last time he was seen alive. Later, Brady was to take a photograph of Myra kneeling on his grave on the moor.

Six months later, on 16 June 1964, twelve-year-old Keith Bennett set out to spend the night at his grandmother's house in the Longsight district. His mother called to collect him the following morning, but he had failed to arrive. Like John Kilbride, Keith Bennett had accepted a lift from a kind lady. His body has never been found.

Meanwhile, David Smith's admiration for his mentor was steadily increasing. Brady took him up to Saddleworth Moor and they engaged in pistol practice – Myra had obtained two pistols by the expedient of joining the Cheadle Rifle Club.

Myra was not entirely happy about this intimacy; her attitude to Smith had an undertone of hostility. In fact both of them were getting sick of the Smiths. She was glad when her grandmother was rehoused in Wardle Brook Avenue, in the suburb of Hattersley, in September 1964, and she and Ian moved into the little house at the end of a terrace. Nevertheless, Ian continued to consolidate his influence over Smith. If he was going to rob banks, a partner would be needed. Soon Smith was recording in a notebook sentences like: 'God is a disease, a plague, a weight round a man's neck' and 'Rape is not a crime, it is a state of mind. God is a disease which eats away a man's instincts, murder is a hobby and a supreme pleasure.' Soon he and Brady were 'casing' banks and drawing up elaborate plans.

One day Brady asked him: 'Is there anyone you hate and want out of the way?'

Smith mentioned several names, including an old rival named Tony Latham. After some discussion, they settled on Tony Latham as the murder victim whose death would bind Smith to the gang. First, Brady explained, he would need a photograph. This was no problem. Smith had a Polaroid camera and he knew the pub where Latham drank. The next evening, Ian and Myra drove him to the pub, then drove away. Unfortunately, Smith had forgotten to insert the film, and when he went into the toilet to develop the photograph found the camera empty.

When he went out to Wardle Brook Avenue to confess his failure, Brady seemed to take it casually enough. In reality he did not believe Smith was telling the truth and was alarmed. Now, suddenly, David Smith was a potential risk. Now Brady began to think seriously about removing him. Oddly enough, it was Myra who dissuaded him. 'It would hurt Mo.' (Maureen).

On 26 December 1964, Boxing Day, there was another murder. Like the others, this was planned in advance. Myra had arranged for her grandmother to stay the night with an uncle at Dukinfield. At about 6 p.m., she picked up ten-year-old Lesley Ann Downey at a fair in Hulme Hall Lane. In her 'confession' to Topping, Myra gave her own version of what happened. They took Lesley back to the house in Wardle Brook Avenue and switched on a tape recorder. Myra claims that she was in the kitchen when she heard the child screaming. Brady was squeezing her neck and ordering her to take off her coat. Lesley was then made to undress and to assume various pornographic poses, while Brady filmed her. On the tape, Myra can be heard ordering her to 'put it in, put it in tighter', presumably referring to the gag that appears in the photographs. Lesley screams and asks to be allowed to go home. At this point, Myra claims she was ordered to go and run a bath; she stayed in the bathroom until the water became cold. When she returned, Lesley had been strangled, and there was blood on her thighs. The following day they took the body to the moors and buried her.

In his 1990 open letter to the press, Brady denies that Myra played no active part in the murder. She insisted upon killing Lesley Ann Downey with her own hands, using a two-foot length of silk cord, 'which she later used to enjoy toying with in public, in the secret knowledge of what it had been used for'.

Brady had killed approximately once every six months since July 1963: Pauline Reade, John Kilbride, Keith Bennett, Lesley Ann Downey. For some reason, July 1965 went by – as far as we know – without a further murder. But in September, Brady decided to kill out of sequence. The aim seems to have been (once more) to cement David Smith's membership of the 'gang' According to Smith, during a drinking session on 25 September Brady asked Smith: 'Have you ever killed anybody? I have – three or four. The bodies are buried up on the moors.'

Two weeks later, on 6 October, Smith turned up at Wardle Brook Avenue – he was now living close by, in a council flat in Hattersley – hoping to borrow some money, but they were all broke. Brady had already suggested that they should rob an electricity board showroom, and the robbery had been planned for two days later. Smith's urgent need for money to pay the rent suggested that now was the time to 'cement' him beyond all possibility of withdrawal.

Towards midnight, Myra called at her sister's flat with a message for their mother, then asked David Smith to walk her home. As he stood waiting in the kitchen expecting to be offered a drink there was a scream from the sitting room, and Myra called 'Dave, help him!' As Smith ran in, Ian Brady was hacking at the head of a youth who was lying on the floor. In spite of blow after blow, the youth continued to twist and scream. Finally, when he lay still, Brady pressed a cushion over his face and tied a cord around the throat to stop the gurgling noises. Brady handed Smith the hatchet, saying 'Feel the weight of that.' Smith's fingers left blood-stained prints on the handle.

Gran called down to ask what the noise was about and Myra shouted that she had dropped a tape recorder on her foot.

When the room had been cleaned up, the body was carried upstairs between them – Brady commented: 'Eddie's a dead weight.' The victim was a seventeen-year-old homosexual, Edward Evans, who had been picked up in a pub that evening.

They all drank tea, while Myra reminisced about a policeman who had stopped to talk to her while Brady was burying Pauline Reade. After this, Smith agreed to return with 'an old pram' the next day, and help in the disposal of Edward Evans.

When he arrived home Smith was violently sick. And when he told Maureen what had happened, it was she who decided to go to the police.

At eight o'clock the next morning, a man dressed as a baker's roundsman knocked on the door of 16 Wardle Brook Avenue. Myra answered the door, dressed ready to go to work. The man identified himself as a police officer, and said he had reason to believe there was a body in the house. Brady was on the divan bed in the living room, writing a note to explain why he was not going to work that day. The police demanded to see into a locked room. When Myra said the key was at work, a policeman offered to go and fetch it. At this, Brady said 'You'd better tell him. There was a row here last night. It's in there.' Under the window in the bedroom there was a plastic wrapped bundle. Two loaded revolvers were found in the same room. Brady later told me that if he had not left his revolver upstairs he would have liked to have shot the policeman, then himself.

David Smith told the police that Brady had stored two suit-cases in the left luggage at Manchester Central Station, and these were recovered. (The cloakroom ticket was later found where Brady described it – in the spine of a prayer book.) These proved to contain pornographic photographs – including nine of Lesley Ann Downey, the tape of Lesley Ann pleading to be allowed to leave, various books on sex and torture, and wigs, coshes and notes on robbing banks. Other photographs led them to dig on the moors, where the bodies of Lesley Ann Downey and John Kilbride were recovered.

On 6 May 1966, Ian Brady and Myra Hindley were both sentenced to life imprisonment. There had been no confession – this was to come many years later, Brady to the journalist Fred Harrison, and then Myra to Detective Chief Superintendent Peter Topping. At the time, Brady maintained that Lesley Ann had been brought to the house by two men, who had taken her away after taking the photographs. It was not until July 1987 that Brady returned to the moor, under police escort, and tried – without success – to help locate the body of Keith Bennett. Pauline Reade had already been located, with the help of Myra's confession.

It is easy to understand why the Moors murders have 'tormented the psyche of a nation' for half a century – vague stories related to the case still generate headlines in the tabloids.

Like the Jack the Ripper murders, they seem to embody some of our worst nightmares about human cruelty. Brady has often been described as 'Britain's most hated murderer'.

After she attended the trial, Pamela Hansford Johnson wrote a book about it called *On Iniquity*. Her argument was that Brady and Hindley seemed totally 'affectless'; that is, totally without feeling. This view sounds plausible enough until we recall that both killers had an enormous affection for animals and that when she learned that her dog had died in police custody, Myra burst out: 'They're just a lot of bloody murderers.' She was equally upset by the death of her sister Maureen's baby. And Brady's affection for his mother and stepmother – as well as for Myra – indicates that he possessed the same human feelings as the rest of us. Harrison reveals that after the arrest, he did his best to dissociate Myra from the crimes. (It was only years later, after her partial-sounding confession to Topping, that Brady accused Hindley of direct involvement in the murders.)

In fact, from the criminological view, the main interest of the Moors case is that it reveals so clearly the basic psychological patterns of a certain type of antisocial behaviour.

One of the fundamental problems of human beings, particularly in adolescence, is to discover 'who they are'. The certainties of childhood are behind them; they face an adult world in which they have to play an active part. But unless they happen to be lucky enough to have had clear 'role models', or to have acquired some basic enthusiasm in their early teens, their identity remains a kind of blank, like a gap on a census form, waiting for someone to fill in a name.

In the case of a dominant male, the question is particularly acute. Biological studies have established that approximately one in twenty of any animal group is 'dominant' – that is, 5 per cent. The dominant 5 per cent are, on the whole, natural leaders. They crave a means of expressing their dominance. Those of purely physical dominance may establish a place in life by sheer bullying. In childhood, Brady seems to have established this kind of dominance over his contemporaries. But in his teens, it ceased to be so simple. Fred Harrison commented:

'Ian Brady knew that he was special. He did not feel the same way as ordinary people . . .'

In describing such people, the word 'outsider' turns up with monotonous regularity. An American serial killer, Douglas Clark, expressed it in another way: 'I march to a different drummer.'

The years of Brady's late teens – when he obsessively read Dostoevsky, Nietzsche, de Sade and *Mein Kampf* – were a period of intellectual ferment in which he seems to have begun to define the outline of his 'real identity'. The influence of *Mein Kampf* can hardly be underestimated. Even its title – 'my struggle' – helps to explain the profound influence it still exercises among modern-day fascists. To these fanatics the book is a kind of archetypal Hollywood success story: the autobiography of an 'outsider', with all the cards stacked against him, yet somehow succeeding in imposing his own vision on the world. The catastrophic outcome of that imposition, of course, they blame on a world that wasn't ready for Hitler's vision.

In *Mein Kampf* Ian Brady had found a creed (ignoring – like so many sadistic neo-fascists – the fact that the prudish Hitler would have had him executed as a sexual deviant if the pair had ever actually met.) But Brady still had not built an identity. It was the relationship with Myra that seems to have caused this to crystallise. The German jurist Rosenstock-Huessy said: 'Even a man who believes in nothing needs a girl to believe in him.' Quite apart from the sexual drive – which is often overpowering in those of high dominance – the admiration of a member of the opposite sex is like a mirror in which a man can admire his own face.

Here we need to add a note again – that Brady was strongly homosexual, although capable of bisexuality. So seducing Myra on her grandmother's settee was not as important to him as it might have been if he had been totally heterosexual. This probably explains the plans to involve Smith. The tomboyish Myra told Topping that they had sex only occasionally and that Brady enjoyed anal intercourse (which she disliked) or liked to have her insert a candle into his rectum while he masturbated. Brady would probably have preferred Smith, hence his otherwise curious obsession with involving Smith in the gang that ended so disastrously. His homosexuality also explains why two of his victims were boys.

Meanwhile, Myra served as Brady's ego-boosting 'mirror' and also as his unwitting catalyst to commit crimes. There is good reason to believe that Brady's downward spiral into homemade pornography, kidnapping, rape and serial killing was at least partly fuelled by his need to constantly impress Myra. He needed to see, reflected in her admiring eyes, the idea that he was a rebel against petty social norms. If she ever showed signs of tiring of his act, then he felt the overpowering need to 'up the ante': to suggest, then ultimately to do, something that would shock her back into dreamy submission.

Hindley's confession, in Topping's book, offers an intriguing insight into Brady's divided attitude to what he was doing. She said: 'On one occasion when I was with him, he told me that he did not believe in God, that it was a nonsense to believe in a deity. He said that after the killing of John Kilbride he had looked up into the sky, shook his fist and said "Take that, you bastard!" He was talking to God and he told me he thought about it a lot afterward because it meant he was acknowledging the existence of God.'

What, after all, is the point of being a rebel, if that which you are rebelling against doesn't even notice? Brady wasn't about to confess to the police – to sacrifice his freedom just to see their horrified expressions – but he could fantasise about having shocked an all-seeing God, that he otherwise was too intelligent to want to believe in.

And it is at this point the argument reconnects with the criminal outsiders of Chapter 21, particularly the would-be serial-killing bomber from Canada, Roger Bell. Brady did not want to believe in God; yet when it came to it, he shook his fist at the sky. Bell was obviously hesitant to admit that his motive was revenge. 'I think my motive was revenge at society.' But when it was a question of winning his parole he felt compelled to acknowledge his schoolboy error in logic, even though it made him feel embarrassed.

Where morality is concerned, the pugnaciously unrepentant Brady is obviously in an impossible position. He has murdered children, yet he claims that in some way it is not wrong to murder children. How so? 'To the free-thinker or relativist' – he states in the second chapter of his book *The Gates of Janus* – 'personal belief and principles – rather than external social dogmas – dictate action. Truth be told, we owe genuine loyalty only to our loved ones and close friends. It is to whom we give our word that matters, not the giving of it.'

In other words, the typical human repugnance against killing children is an 'external social dogma', like going to church on Sunday or buying a TV licence. Because Brady believes himself to be a freethinker and relativist, he feels free to reject this custom. But his next sentence implies that owing loyalty to loved ones is not a mere social dogma, but an existential truth. He implies that only those loyalties and ideas that are personally generated have any real value. And that any behavioural rule inherited from the society that you inhabit can be rejected at will.

Myra Hindley died in prison on 15 November 2002, aged sixty, of smoking-related heart disease. Brady remains (as of this final edit in April 2015) incarcerated in the Ashworth high-security mental hospital, diagnosed with paranoid schizophrenia. He apparently remains lucid however, as when he makes occasional statements to the authorities about his wish to starve himself to death.

Ian Brady remains an alien mind to most of us. His continuing refusal to care about the damage that he has done stems from his belief that a parent's agony at the loss of a murdered child is unimportant: a mere externally enforced social dogma; a knee-jerk emotional reaction demanded by a society that he despises. But here he is merely displaying a selfish lack of imagination. He lauds his own emotional ties as being fundamentally true, yet casually belittles the emotional reactions of people he doesn't care about. The irony of this logical dichotomy seems lost on him, just as when as Myra Hindley said that, because her dog had died, the police were 'just a lot of bloody murderers'.

The essence of the disagreement between Brady and myself emerged when we discussed *Crime and Punishment*. This is the novel in which Dostoevsky dramatises the nineteenth-century 'superman' argument. The student Raskolnikov is tormented by poverty and by pity for human misery. He reflects that a Napoleon would take decisive action, and that his own solution lies in murdering a 'worthless' old pawnbrokress and stealing her money. In the event he is also forced to kill her sister. The police soon come to suspect him and the investigator plays with him like a cat with a mouse. Raskolnikov finally decides to confess and serves eight years in Siberia.

Brady was convinced that Dostoevsky had chosen this conclusion as a concession to the tsarist censor. That if Dostoevsky had possessed Brady's courage he would have recognised that Raskolnikov has nothing to repent of, and would have ended the novel by allowing him to walk free.

But in saying this, Brady seemed to me to have missed the point of *Crime and Punishment* – that Raskolnikov is quite wrong in his self-indulgent self-justification. Defining himself as an unlucky Napoleon, and his victims as 'vermin', is simply an evasion of a painful truth: that Raskolnikov is, above all else, a thieving murderer. All his clever evasions of this fact just shows the emptiness of his case: if he was self-evidently correct in his decision to kill the old ladies – as he tries to convince himself – then Raskolnikov's choice of action would need no complex justifications. If the old ladies had instead killed Raskolnikov in self-defence, nobody would have expected them to mount a complex philosophical justification of their act of homicide. Indeed, even Raskolnikov comes to this conclusion by the end of the novel, feeling that only confession and punishment can remove the stain from his soul.

To me, Brady's view of the novel left the essential dilemma unresolved. Raskolnikov's problem is his vacillating and weak will; he is poor because of this lack of a backbone as much as because of his difficult circumstances. And his attempt to escape his circumstances by violence is worthless on any philosophical level, no matter how much he tries to rationalise it. What he

must learn in Siberia is the strength to bear suffering and ultimately to rise above his own selfish and self-indulgent weakness. A
weak superman is a contradiction in terms.

That this also applies to Brady is proved by an assertion in
Fred Harrison's book, where Brady admits that after killing five
children 'I felt old at twenty-six. Everything was ashes. I felt
there was nothing of interest – nothing to hook myself on to. *I
had experienced everything.*'

It is natural for human beings to believe that the secret of
happiness lies in being allowed to have anything you like. There
can be few children who have not imagined being allowed to
help themselves in a toyshop. (The first step towards this fantasy
would be to have an unlimited supply of cash – which is why
Brady started life as a burglar.) But it is only one step from this
to recognising how easily the senses become sated with satisfaction. The trouble with being able to take anything you like from
a toyshop is that you would soon stop liking *anything*. Our
capacity for self-indulgence is limited, because desire itself can
evaporate and leave us empty-handed.

This explains what went wrong for Brady when he set out to
'do everything'. He agreed with me when I pointed out that his
comments to Fred Harrison reveal that he himself suffered from
the 'Ecclesiastes effect': the feeling that 'all is vanity'. Yet he
failed to agree that his idea of 'relativism' – turning his back on
all shared morality – is no solution because it leaves the relativist
with 'nothing to hook on to',

As I got to know Brady better – through a series of letters – it
became impossible not to feel somewhat sorry for him. It is true
that what he had done was sickeningly evil, but life imprisonment seemed to me to be somehow excessive. It meant that any
possibility of a creative outlet was denied to him. Unlike
Raskolnikov, he could not pay the penalty for his crimes and then
move on. His real penalty was to be trapped, for the rest of his
life, in the persona of 'the Moors Murderer'.

I'm in no way condoning anything that Ian Brady has done
or said: I'm quite aware that he is an unrepentant child-
murderer and a selfish egotist. But I hate to see what I believe

to be an intelligent mind going to waste. And the loss is so much greater when that mind has been sentenced, by its owner as much as by anyone else, to be a bogeyman for an entire nation, and nothing else.

Which is why I suggested that he should write a book. He was clearly intelligent enough – I've met many successful writers with less brains than Ian Brady. But obviously he should not write about himself – his case was too horrifying – the public would burn any book in which he laid out his own bleak version of events in full. But we had occasionally discussed, in our letters, certain famous murder cases – like that of Leopold and Loeb: the rich young men in Chicago who, in 1924, killed a fourteen-year-old boy in order to 'prove' that they were supermen. These cases evidently fascinated him. So why not write a criminology book about them? Or why not write about the ongoing problem of serial killers in general?

Finally Brady did it, and the result was a volume he called *The Gates of Janus: Serial Killing and its Analysis* – a title that refers to the fact that in ancient Rome the Gates of Janus were open in times of war and closed in times of peace. (Presumably Brady feels he has opened them to declare his own war on a society he regarded as utterly corrupt.) I persuaded an American publisher friend to issue it and to pay an advance of $5,000 (which Brady gave to his mother.)

Yet that publication ended any relationship I had with Ian Brady. His prison, Ashworth, insisted on seeing the typescript, and demanded some very small and unimportant changes. To save further trouble I accommodated their request in the form of a short correction slip whose tone was tongue-in-cheek:

Ashworth Hospital has pointed out a number of factual errors contained in the introduction to this book by Colin Wilson. Corrections are as follows:
Page 31, lines 6,7,8
Ashworth Hospital wish it to be known that computers were taken away from all patients and not just Mr Brady.
Page 31, lines 10

The girl of eight, referred to as 'daughter of an Ashworth employee', was in fact the daughter of an ex-patient who visited the hospital.
Page 31, line 22
Medical evidence was produced on behalf of the hospital, which showed that Mr Brady's wrist was not broken during the move from Jade Ward. [In spite of which] at the judicial Hearing held in the High Court Liverpool 10 March 2000, Mr Justice Kay in his public Summing Up spoke of 'an undisplaced crack fracture of his [Brady's] right arm. [Regina v Collins & Ashworth Hospital Ex Parte Ian Stewart Brady. Law Reports].
Page 31, line 23 and Page 32, line 10
It was a bucket handle found taped under a sink and not a knife.
Page 31, line 28,29
Ashworth Hospital Authority dispute Mr Brady's allegations that 'Guards talked in loud voices outside his door all night preventing him from sleeping'. They wish to point out that there are no guards on the wards and all staff are either registered mental nurses or nursing assistants. There was no deliberate attempt to prevent Mr Brady from sleeping.

To my surprise, Ian Brady was infuriated by this unimportant concession to the bureaucrats and (so his solicitor told me) swore and cursed for two hours. His solicitor insisted that it would eventually blow over, but I no longer gave a damn. I was sick of Brady's vindictive tantrums (this was by no means the first) and so allowed the correspondence to lapse.

Chapter 26

Contemplating a Demon-Haunted World

In late August 1990, both *Time* and *Newsweek* magazines carried the story of the slaughter of four women and a man on the Gainesville university campus, in Florida. The killer remained at large. It is infrequent for either magazine to carry stories about American murders in their European edition and the fact that they did was a sign of how far the five murders had shocked America.

On Sunday 26 August, 1990, police had been called to an apartment block on the Gainesville campus. Parents were concerned that they had not heard from their daughters – Christina Powell and Sonja Larson, both seventeen years old – who shared an apartment in the block. When officers broke down the door to the apartment they found a horrible scene. Sonja's dead body was spread-eagled on an upstairs bed. Christina they found on the stairs down to the lower floor of the apartment. Both girls were naked, had been stabbed to death, mutilated and then arranged by the killer into obscene poses. Both bodies were also putrescent, having lain for over two days in the Florida summer heat.

Early the next morning police found the body of eighteen-year-old Christa Hoyt in her apartment. She too had been stripped and stabbed to death. She had then been mutilated, decapitated and posed in an obscene fashion. Her time of death was found to have been on 25 August – the day after the Powell/ Larson killings.

The last two Gainesville Campus murder victims were Tracy Paules and Manuel Taboada – both aged twenty-three. The killer had broken into their shared apartment on the night of 27 August. He had first killed Manny Taboada after a struggle. This must have been no mean feat, as Manny was a 6 ft 3 in, 200 lb athlete.

While the killer had been stabbing Taboada to death, Tracy Paules had barricaded herself into her bedroom. The killer smashed down the door and – as with his previous female victims – he had subdued her, stripped her, and bound and gagged her. He stabbed her to death then obscenely posed the body to shock whoever found her. Taboada's body he left untouched where he had killed him.

All four female victims had been raped; Sonja Larson after she was dead. All four were similar in appearance – petite Caucasian brunettes with brown eyes. This suggested that the killer had specifically targeted them before breaking into their apartments

The killing spree spread panic on the Gainesville campus, with many parents pulling their children out of college and taking them home. But no further killings took place. The man that the press had dubbed 'The Gainesville Ripper' had simply vanished.

I had just finished writing – in collaboration with Donald Seaman – a book called *The Serial Killers,* and the last major American case I had dealt with had been the murders of the serial killer Leonard Lake, in California, which had come to light after Lake's suicide in 1985. As far as I can remember, this was the last occasion when *Time* and *Newsweek* had given such wide coverage to an American case. For this reason, I paid particular attention to the reports from Gainesville – a campus where I had once lectured. Then, as the weeks and months went by with no further reports, I assumed that the killer had escaped. In fact, no one then knew that he had been arrested (including those who made the arrest) ten days after the murders.

It was some time before I learned what had actually happened. This came about in 1993, through reading Sondra London's book *Knockin' on Joe,* a remarkable and intimate study of serial killers, including Carl Panzram, Gerard Schaefer and Ottis Toole (the partner-in-crime of Henry Lee Lucas). I had never heard of Danny Rolling, but from this I learned that at that time, he stood accused of the Gainesville murders.

It seemed that Danny Rolling had written to Sondra London from prison in June 1992, addressing her as 'Madame Sondra, Media Queen'. He was serving life for armed robbery, and had just been charged with the Gainesville murders. By Christmas of that year, Sondra London and Danny Rolling had decided they were in love. Finally she was allowed to visit him one time at Florida State Prison. The meeting apparently confirmed their feelings for one another. There was an instant and powerful attraction. Soon after this, they announced that they were engaged. This announcement, in February of 1993, was featured in newspapers next to a story claiming that Danny Rolling had confessed to the Gainesville murders to a fellow inmate, Robert Fieldmore Lewis. The local media implied – understandably – Sondra was only pretending to be in love with Danny to get his story.

Rolling's nickname for Sondra, 'Media Queen', was based on her publishing company of the same name. She had launched this company, in 1989, initially to bring out a private edition of a book called *Killer Fiction* by Gerard Schaefer, who was serving life for killing two teenage girls in Florida. Oddly enough, Schaefer had been Sondra's first lover. They had met when Schaefer was eighteen and Sondra a year younger. But Sondra was shaken by his admission of the sinister and violent impulses he experienced towards women, and walked out on him. In fact, Schaefer's sexual fantasies were all concerned with humiliating women and with hanging them. *Killer Fiction* includes sketches of women in their underwear standing on gallows.

On 22 July 1972, about seven years after the break-up, Gerard Schaefer abducted two teenage girls: seventeen-year-old Pamela Wells and eighteen-year-old Nancy Trotter. He then tied them to trees and terrorised them. It seems clear that he was intending to kill them both, but he suddenly heard a radio message from his car and had to leave. While he was gone, both girls escaped and ran to the local police station. It was there that their description of their kidnapper was found to match that of Schaefer. The police recognised it immediately, because Gerard Schaefer was working as a sheriff's deputy from that very police station. In fact the radio message that had called him away, probably saving the girls' lives, had been issued from that station.

After being arrested Schaefer was fired as a sheriff's deputy; but then, regrettably, bailed and released – regrettably, because he used his freedom to murder two more teenage girls – Georgia Jessup and Susan Place – before he was called to trial.

On 27 September 1972, Schaefer had turned up at Susan's home and had taken the two girls off in his car, telling Susan's mother they were 'going to the beach to play guitar'. They never returned home. But Susan's mother had been suspicious of this smiling man who, at twenty-six, was so much older than her teenage daughter, and noted down the number of the licence plate on his car. Unfortunately she managed to get one of the digits wrong and an innocent man was interviewed by police. Fortunately he had a watertight alibi. With no bodies and no suspect, the police let the investigation rest. This may be seen as pure incompetence – since investigators should have been aware that Schaefer had abducted two teenage girls just a few months before – but despite the similarities between the cases, he was not called in for questioning.

In December 1972, Schaefer was sentenced to a year in prison for aggravated assault on Pamela Wells and Nancy Trotter. In April 1973, the bodies of Susan Place and Georgia Jessop were found buried in woodland on the nearby Hutchinson Island. The autopsy showed that they had been tied to trees, tortured, strangled and then dismembered. A glance at his photograph told Susan's mother that Gerard Schaefer was the man who had gone to the beach with her daughter. A search of Schaefer's room at his mother's house in Fort Lauderdale revealed many personal items (including teeth) belonging to a number of girls who had also vanished. Schaefer received two life terms for the murders of Georgia Jessop and Susan Place, but police suspected that the true number of victims was around thirty-four. (Schaefer himself later told Sondra London the number was upwards of eighty.)

Though Sondra was shocked at the thought that she had lost her virginity to a future serial killer, her curiosity led her to write to him in prison. He replied and in 1990 she went to see him. He showed her the 'stories' he was writing – sadistic fantasies about raping and murdering women – and gave her permission to publish some of them. And so *Killer Fiction* appeared, in a desktop edition priced at $18. I bought my copy from a crime bookseller in New Jersey. It was only later, through Paul Woods, the British publisher of *Knockin' on Joe,* that I made Sondra's acquaintance.

Gerard Schaefer, in fact, must be one of the most disgusting serial killers of all time, although he consistently denied being a serial killer and even tried suing me once for referring to him as one. (The judge threw it out.)

His 'killer fiction' and his even more explicit letters to Sondra, make it clear that all his fantasies involved sadistic cruelty. He liked terrifying his victims, and he particularly enjoyed having two girls at his mercy, so he could make each one beg him to kill the other first. He finally died in prison in December 1995, his throat slashed and his eyes stabbed by another prisoner. Schaefer had had a reputation as a 'rat' and a troublemaker among the other inmates, so his murder did not particularly surprise anyone.

All this, then, makes it clear why Sondra London went on to present the memoirs of another self-confessed serial killer, Danny Rolling, who was clearly a different kind of killer from Gerard Schaefer. His crimes were horrific, but they lacked the obsessive sadism of Schaefer's. It is not my intention to make any excuses for Danny Rolling, for as a student of criminology, that is hardly my business. Yet one thing seems clear: that while Schaefer revelled in his sadistic fantasies, accepting them totally and unquestioningly, Danny Rolling was always more of a Jekyll and Hyde. Rolling was a man who struck many who knew him (as I did through correspondence) as sensitive, decent and arguably talented; but who was possessed periodically by an intense sexual violence.

Schaefer's writing had literally dozens of passages like the following:

I kicked her in the stomach and she doubled up. 'Teach you to
bite my dick, bitch!' Bloody vomit spewed up from her gut and
splashed from her mouth . . .

I personally think that Danny Rolling – when not in his manic
phase – would have found that passage as revolting as the rest of
us do. But, that said, Rolling was diagnosed in prison as a sociopath. And a skill often associated with sociopath syndrome is a
brilliant skill at manipulating the feelings of others; and to
pretend to humane sympathies that they don't, and indeed can't,
share with others.

Sondra London's account of Rolling in *Knockin' on Joe* makes
it clear that from the beginning, Rolling was fated to be a reject
from the society that the rest of us take for granted. Many criminals claim that their fathers are to blame, but in the case of
Danny Rolling, this is at least partly true. His father, a police
detective, was a brutal domestic tyrant. The first time Danny
dared to argue with him, his father threw him on the floor, handcuffed him and sent for a squad car to take his son to jail; Danny
spent two weeks in there.

It is hard to understand such men; their aim seems to be to
crush the ego of their children and wives, rather than, like
most fathers, doing their best to nurture a sense of security
and self-confidence. I have written at length about what A. E.
Van Vogt called 'Right Man Syndrome'. The following is a
summation of the theory from my book *A Criminal History of
Mankind* (pp. 64–65):

In 1954, Van Vogt began work on a war novel called The
Violent Man, *which was set in a Chinese prison camp. The
commandant of the camp is one of those savagely authoritarian figures who would instantly, and without hesitation, order
the execution of anyone who challenges his authority.*

*Van Vogt was creating the type from observation of men like
Hitler and Stalin. And, as he thought about the murderous
behaviour of the commandant, he found himself wondering:
'What could motivate a man like that?' Why is it that some*

men believe that anyone who contradicts them is either dishonest or downright wicked? Do they really believe, in their heart of hearts, that they are gods who are incapable of being fallible? If so, are they in some sense insane, like a man who thinks he is Julius Caesar?

Looking around for examples, it struck Van Vogt that male authoritarian behaviour is far too commonplace to be regarded as insanity. Newspaper headlines tell their own story:

HUSBAND INVADES CHRISTMAS PARTY AND SHOOTS WIFE
Grief stricken when she refuses to return to him, he claims.

ENTERTAINER STABS WIFE TO DEATH – UNFAITHFUL HE SAYS
Amazed friends say he was unfaithful, not she.

WIFE RUN OVER IN STREET
Accident says divorced husband held on suspicion of murder.

WIFE BADLY BEATEN BY FORMER HUSBAND
'Unfit mother,' he accuses. Neighbours refute charge, call him a troublemaker.

HUSBAND FOILED IN ATTEMPT TO PUSH WIFE OVER CLIFF
Wife reconciles, convinced husband loves her.

Marriage seems to bring out the 'authoritarian' personality in many males, according to Van Vogt's observation. He brought up the question with a psychologist friend and asked him whether he could offer any examples. The psychologist told him of an interesting case of a husband who had brought his wife along for psychotherapy. He had set her up in a suburban house, and supported her on condition that she had no male friends. Her role, as he saw it, was simply to be a good mother to their son.

The story of their marriage was as follows. She had been a nurse, and when her future husband proposed to her she had felt she ought to admit to previous affairs with two doctors. The man went almost insane with jealousy, and she was convinced that was the end of it. But the next day he appeared with a legal document, which he insisted she should sign if the marriage was to go ahead.

He would not allow her to read it. Van Vogt speculates that it contained a 'confession' that she was an immoral woman, and that as he was virtually raising her from the gutter by marrying her, she had no legal rights . . .

They married, and she soon became aware of her mistake. Her husband's business involved travelling, so she never knew where he was. He visited women employees in their apartments for hours and spent an unconscionable amount of time driving secretaries home. If she tried to question him about this he would fly into a rage and often knock her about. In fact, he was likely to respond to any questions he regarded as 'impertinent' by knocking her down. The following day he might call her long distance and beg her forgiveness, promising never to do it again.

His wife became frigid. They divorced, yet he continued to do his best to treat her as his personal property, determined to restrict her freedom. When this caused anger and stress, he told her she ought to see a psychiatrist – which is how they came to Van Vogt's friend.

The case is a good example of what Van Vogt came to call 'the violent man' or the 'Right Man'. He is a man driven by a manic need for self-esteem – to feel he is a 'somebody'. He is obsessed by the question of 'losing face', so will never, under any circumstances, admit that he might be in the wrong. This man's attempt to convince his wife that she was insane is typical.

Equally interesting is the wild, insane jealousy. Most of us are subject to jealousy, since the notion that someone we care about prefers someone else is an assault on our amour propre. *But the Right Man, whose self-esteem is like a constantly festering sore spot, flies into a frenzy at the thought, and becomes capable of murder.*

Van Vogt points out that the Right Man is an 'idealist' – that is, he lives in his own mental world and does his best to ignore aspects of reality that conflict with it. Like the Communists' rewriting of history, reality can always be 'adjusted' later to fit his glorified picture of himself. In his mental world, women are delightful, adoring, faithful creatures who wait patiently for the right man – in both senses of the word – before they surrender their virginity. He is living in a world of adolescent fantasy. No doubt there was something gentle and submissive about the nurse that made her seem the ideal person to bolster his self-esteem, the permanent wife and mother who is waiting in a clean apron when he gets back from a weekend with a mistress . . .

Perhaps Van Vogt's most intriguing insight into the Right Man was his discovery that he can be destroyed if 'the worm turns' – that is, if his wife or some dependant leaves him. Under such circumstances, he may beg and plead, promising to behave better in the future. If that fails, there may be alcoholism, drug addiction, even suicide. She has kicked away the foundations of his sandcastle. For when a Right Man finds a woman who seems submissive and admiring, it deepens his self-confidence, fills him with a sense of his own worth. (We can see the mechanism in operation with Ian Brady and Myra Hindley.) No matter how badly he treats her, he has to keep on believing that, in the last analysis, she recognises him as the most remarkable man she will ever meet. She is the guarantee of his 'primacy', his uniqueness; now it doesn't matter what the rest of the world thinks. He may desert her and his children; that only proves how 'strong' he is, how indifferent to the usual sentimentality. But if she deserts him, he has been pushed back to square one: the helpless child in a hostile universe. 'Most violent men are failures', says Van Vogt; so to desert them is to hand them over to their own worst suspicions about themselves. It is this recognition that leads Van Vogt to write: 'Realise that most

Right Men deserve some sympathy, for they are struggling with an almost unbelievable inner horror; however, if they give way to the impulse to hit or choke, they are losing the battle, and are on the way to the ultimate disaster . . . of their subjective universe of self-justification.'

In a letter to me, Danny described how his father had once made a scene at the checkout of the supermarket, raving and shouting until the manager came and told him that if he didn't calm down, he would have to leave. Unimpressed, James Rolling asked the manager if he knew who he was talking to – that he was a police sergeant. All this fuss, Danny recounts, was due to the fact that Danny's mother had picked out the wrong brand of chewing tobacco for her husband. It is easy to see why his children found life with James Rolling all but intolerable.

It must be admitted that Rolling senior had one reason for feeling furious with his son. When Danny was a child, a friend introduced him to voyeurism. They would watch a young cheerleader undressing and bathing. Finally, they got caught and it became general knowledge that Danny Rolling was a peeping Tom. For a father who saw himself as a war hero, and who was now a proud member of the police force, it must have been a keen humiliation. The habit of voyeurism stayed with Danny Rolling his whole life.

What is clear is that the sense of insecurity in his home life led Danny to rebellion. If he had been of more malleable material, he would have been crushed, and become merely a social inadequate. In fact, he was born a fairly dominant person (one of the dominant 5 per cent of any human cluster, who will attempt to control or even dominate the rest of the group) and he was also talented, as his writing, his songs and artwork reveal. Such people tend to rebel against bullying.

My own situation bore some relation to Rolling's: my father was an irritable, short-tempered man and if anyone had asked me as a child if I loved him, I would have answered with astonishment: 'Of course not!' The astonishment would have been due to the fact that I somehow took it for granted that no one loved their fathers. Mothers were for loving, fathers were for fearing – or at least being nervous about. Yet now it seems to me totally obvious that children – particularly boys – need a father to love; to begin with, they need him as a role model. (All this has been expressed with exemplary force and clarity in Robert Bly's 1990 book *Iron John*.)

Now, in my case, it may have been just as well that I felt totally detached from my father. I must emphasise that I didn't hate him, as Danny hated James Harold Rolling. I just didn't care much about him. My dad was not a reader and he had no interest in ideas, so it would have been a catastrophe for me to take him as a role model. But when, at the age of ten, I became fascinated by chemistry, and then by astronomy and physics, I suddenly had a purpose in life. But things were still difficult. In 1947 I left school, aged sixteen, and went to work in a factory for forty-eight hours a week, and hated it as much as Dickens had hated the blacking factory, or H. G. Wells the drapery emporium. But by then I knew I wanted to be a writer, not a scientist, and it took eight years before I succeeded in getting my first book – *The Outsider* – published. It had been a hard struggle and I had frequently plunged into total discouragement – particularly when a typescript was rejected. But I now recognise that if, on top of my other problems, I had had to deal with a father like James Rolling, I would almost certainly never have made the breakthrough. And I might now well be dead, doubtless from one of the many illnesses and self-destructive lifestyles that are so influenced by sheer resentment and frustration.

Danny Rolling had another problem I didn't have. He was living in a drug culture. I was never tempted to take drugs, probably because they were not available after the Second World War when I was a teenager. Danny was not so lucky. He was called up, but enjoyed the Air Force. Then, just before he was due to be shipped to Vietnam in 1971, he was arrested for possession of narcotics, was sent to the stockade, and given a dishonourable discharge. His father was furious and disappointed and things went from bad to worse between the pair. Danny then spent most of the next two decades drifting from one short-lived, dead-end job to another.

After a religious conversion, Rolling married a fellow member of the Pentecostal Church in 1974. But he claimed that she was sexually frigid – despite having a daughter with her – and when police caught Danny peering in through a window at a woman undressing, his wife divorced him.

From then he let his life slide further downhill. Feeling deep resentment after being served his divorce papers, he committed his first rape: a local female student. He claimed that he was immediately filled with remorse, and decided to go and apologise to her the next day. But when he saw a threatening-looking male coming out of her front door, he hurried away. Whether this attempt at confession and atonement actually happened, however, we have no proof other than Rolling's word. Not long after that he committed his first armed robbery.

Soon he was in prison – and this, it seemed to me, was a real turning point. The habitual violence of prison life shocked him. He later claimed that he came close to being gang-raped in the shower by a crowd of black prisoners. Interracial violence was, and is, endemic in the American penal system. Rolling recalled a white prisoner was killed by three blacks simply because he was white; then two months later the murdered prisoner's brother stabbed to death two of the killers. Being plunged into this violent world may have convinced him – as with so many other individuals who have been brutalised by modern, overcrowded prison systems – that violence was the answer to all his needs.

According to his autobiography, *The Making of a Serial Killer* (published posthumously in 2011), Rolling's chief compulsion after being freed from prison was an urge to commit rape. As he defensively suggested in a letter to me, the difference between a rapist and a normal male is not necessarily enormous. He referenced a study where a hundred college men, asked if they would rape a pretty girl if they were sure they could get away with it, replied 'yes'.

However, in his autobiography, Rolling describes himself as more of a cad than a rapist – at one point defining it as rape when he ejaculated inside a girl, during consensual sex, when he had promised that he would pull out in time. Of course we have to ask, if this was true, then why would he describe it as rape at all? He was either being over self-critical, or he was lying about the sex being consensual. Either he was being dishonest with himself or the reader. And, considering his life story, it isn't hard to decide which was the most likely.

After another period in prison, even more degrading than the others, he committed his first multicide – a treble murder of a girl named Julie Grissom, her eight-year-old nephew and her father. It was the day after he had been fired from a job and again the cause seems to have been a fury of misdirected resentment.

A few months before the Gainesville murders, a violent quarrel with his father ended with James Rolling trying to shoot him, and Danny shooting his father and leaving him for dead. In fact, James Rolling recovered, minus the use of one eye and one ear. But Danny Rolling was now on the run. Another rape attempt ended in sudden remorse. In another, the girl suddenly showed herself willing and after it was over, drank a beer with him.

After that, he went to Gainesville and committed the five murders that caused hundreds of students to flee the campus in terror. Then he left Gainesville and went back to armed robbery. Within ten days he was caught after robbing a grocery store in a town forty miles south of Gainesville.

It was not until January of 1991 that the murder investigators reached the point of testing his blood, and his DNA positively identified him as the man who had raped at least three of the four women in Gainesville. Even then it was not until 11 November 1991 that he was formally charged with the five murders and three rapes.

He pleaded guilty to the crimes at his trial in February of 1994. By then he had already been given four life sentences plus an additional 170 years for the armed robberies. He then received seven more life sentences for the Gainesville rape-killing spree, equalling a hundred more years, and – making all the rest redundant – five death penalties.

Danny Rolling was executed on 25 October 2006. He showed

no sign of remorse for his many crimes, but he did spontaneously confess – just before he was given the lethal injection – that he had killed three other people: the Grissom family in Rolling's native Shreveport, Louisiana. Confirmation of this brought his official number of murders to eight.

And that, it would seem, is all there is to say about it. His criminal career seems easy enough to understand. It began with the voyeurism in childhood, watching the cheerleader get undressed. Ted Bundy's career of murder started in exactly the same way. The poor relationship with his father led to social maladjustment, as well as inability to control his rage and resentment. His antisocial personality disorder (also known as sociopathic syndrome) just underlined and exacerbated these character flaws. The rest followed easily, if not naturally – his first rape, his first armed robbery, his first prison sentence . . . his first murders.

Yet Danny Rolling believed there was another cause: that he was periodically 'possessed' – either by a darker side of his own personality, or by an evil spirit.

Rolling claims to have become convinced that he had at least two demonic alter-egos, one called *Ennad*, who was a rapist and a robber but not a killer, and one called *Gemini*, an entity who thirsted for blood. Yet clearly he was not entirely in Gemini's power, for during the course of an intended rape-murder, he realised that there was a baby lying in a crib, watching him with innocent curiosity, and allowed his intended victim to escape alive.

In his autobiography he tells how, lying in bed with his wife Omatha, the room filled with an evil presence. In a letter to me, he tells of another frightening encounter, when he was in solitary confinement:

> *I was resting on my iron bunk when this thing that appeared like a gargoyle pounced on my chest, pinning me to the mattress. It had both claws pressing against my shoulders . . .*
>
> *It released its grip on one of my shoulders and clawed open my mouth, snaking a foot-long slimy tongue down my throat. I couldn't breathe . . . I was suffocating, and I began to*

struggle. I managed to push the thing far enough away from my face to get that horrible tongue out of my windpipe. It sneered and spat, 'How does it feel to kiss a snail?' I screamed and it just disappeared.

This sounds, of course, like a bad nightmare, and that may well be all that it was. Yet it seems to me possible that Danny Rolling was dealing with something more than that.

In 1980, I began to write a book about poltergeists. I had been interested in the paranormal for ten years or more, since being commissioned to write a book called *The Occult*. My approach was rationalistic. I believed tales of poltergeists were probably based on some sort of truth, but was convinced that they were probably due to spontaneous psychokinesis, or 'mind over matter' – mostly on the part of emotionally disturbed teenagers. But as I researched case after case for my book, I gradually became convinced that they were nothing of the sort – that they were, indeed, caused by the actions of disembodied entities – in other words, 'spirits'.

And several cases seemed to indicate that many of these spirits were highly unpleasant – not just disembodied juvenile delinquents, like poltergeists, but entities capable of inspiring criminal violence.

There was no abrupt change of viewpoint; I did not suddenly become a 'spiritualist'. But I came to accept that spirits could wander in and out of a human being as easily as a tramp can wander in and out of an empty house whose doors have all been left open. However, according to the authorities on this subject – men such as Allan Kardec and Carl Wickland – such spirits cannot obtain much influence over a person unless the individual happens to be on their 'wavelength'. That both share some essential attitude or state of mind. So in a sense, any such possession takes place by some form of mutual consent.

I have been struck by how many criminals come to believe that they have been possessed by some unpleasant entity. Ted Bundy said he felt like a vampire. Peter Sutcliffe, the Yorkshire Ripper, thought he was ordered to kill prostitutes by the voice that he thought was God. David Berkowitz, the killer known as 'Son of Sam' – who killed six people in New York between 1976 and 1977 – claimed that a demon, possessing his neighbour's pet Labrador dog, ordered him to commit the murders.

Little by little, I have become willing to entertain the hypothesis that some criminals are possessed by demonic entities – that once they have been accustomed to being swayed by negative emotions, they have opened themselves to the possibility of being influenced by some of the nastier denizens of the 'spirit world'. Of course it is only a hypothesis, a suspicion that creeps into my mind again and again, reading about serial killers like Ted Bundy and Pee Wee Gaskins. I have been particularly struck that men who start out as rapists, simply enjoying 'stealing' sex without the other person's consent, often drift into the most appalling sadism. In one of the worst murder cases in England, the builder Fred West, who began simply as a man who thought of little but sex (due, I suspect, to an accident that caused frontal lobe brain damage) ended by torturing girls before he killed them and only having sex with them after they were dead.

So I am perfectly willing to entertain the hypothesis that Danny Rolling was possessed by the entity he called Gemini. He claims that Gemini magically unlocked the door of Christina Powell and Sonja Larson's apartment, so that he could enter. And detectives who saw a bookcase he moved in Christa Hoyt's apartment were convinced that two men must have been involved, since it was too heavy for one man to move.

Of course, on a practical level, it hardly matters if a convicted criminal claims to be motivated by greed, hot fury, cold revenge, sexual obsession . . . or that they were possessed by demons. We throw them all into the same incarceration pit, so to speak. The only question we need ask is whether the self-convinced demon-possessed are any harder to rehabilitate than those driven by the more mundane inspirations. But it is only human to wonder if possession by spirits is a reality, or merely a manner of speaking: a kind of shorthand for a psychological condition we do not yet understand, like multiple-personality syndrome.

When I was speaking to an audience in Marion, near Boston,

Massachusetts, in 1995, the respected psychiatrist Stanislav Grof was one of my fellow lecturers. After a panel discussion about criminal psychosis, I asked him whether he had ever seen any evidence of possession. In reply, he told the following story, which can also be found in his book *The Adventure of Self-Discovery* (1988).

In the Maryland Psychiatric Research Centre he encountered a girl called Flora, who had a criminal record. She had been imprisoned for driving the getaway car in a robbery in which a watchman was murdered. After leaving prison, she had become a drug addict and alcoholic and had been imprisoned again for accidentally wounding a girl when cleaning a gun under the influence of heroin. Now she was suffering from a multitude of psychiatric problems, including suicidal violence.

Grof was treating patients with the drug LSD, and decided – after much hesitation – to try this. During the first two sessions there was minimal progress. But at the third session, she suddenly began to complain of facial cramps. Suddenly, her face froze into a 'mask of evil', and a deep male voice came from her mouth, declaring that it was 'the Devil'. The voice ordered Grof to stay away from Flora, declaring that she belonged to him and that he would punish anyone who tried to take her away. He then began to threaten Grof, describing in detail what would happen to Grof and his colleagues if he persisted.

What worried Grof was that 'the Devil' seemed to know all kinds of personal details about himself and his colleagues that Flora could not possibly have known. Although he began to experience panic, Grof forced himself to take Flora's hand – which had twisted like a claw – and held it for the next two hours while calming himself and envisaging a capsule of light embracing them both. After what seemed the longest two hours he had ever spent, her hand relaxed. When she 'awoke', she had no memory of what had taken place. From that point on, Flora began to improve, until she was discharged, joined a religious group and took a normal job.

Grof retains an open mind. But he is still puzzled about how 'the Devil' came to know so much about his personal life and that of his friends. Given my previous experiences researching *The Occult* – and later my books *Poltergeist* (1981) and *Afterlife* (1985) – it is rather easy – in the absence of any other convincing explanation – to believe that the entity Grof encountered was a genuine 'evil spirit'. And I find it just as easy to believe that the same hypothesis may explain some of the mystery of the monstrous life of Danny Rolling.

Part 3
Conclusions

Damon Wilson

Chapter 27

Why We Don't Fight

Having got the reader this far, I should now admit that there are no certain answers to the two main questions of this book: what has always made human beings so violent to each other? And why has the planet been noticeably less violent in the past fifteen to twenty years? That being said, there are interesting theories that we should now examine, some of which will certainly provide elements towards the answers that we're looking for.

Hints towards an answer to the first question are seeded throughout the earlier part of this book. For example, whether or not we accept Raymond Dart's 'killer ape' theory, it seems certain that our distant ancestors' move to regular meat-eating – from what must once have been a predominantly vegetarian diet – must have been a factor in our later violent behaviour. Hunters have to learn lethal skills in order to kill their prey, and those skills can just as easily be turned on competing members of your own species.

But wolves, lions, dolphins and other cooperatively hunting animals very rarely fight other pack members to the death. And certainly they don't kill with the almost habitual internecine violence typically displayed by humans.

The answer here seems to at least partly relate to the inter-relationship between our gut instincts, our multifaceted intelligence and our complex social structures. A male chimpanzee, for example, has no mental block towards killing males from a hostile troupe, or from snatching, killing and eating the babies carried by females from competing troupes.

But they can't bring themselves to rape those same females; not, at least, in the way that is so common to human warriors. A male chimp, still with the blood of her baby on his lips, will try to groom an 'enemy' female and to gently convince her to mate. And she herself might actually surrender to mating, even under those hideous circumstances. This is because a chimp's instincts dominate their rational minds in the area of sex and reproduction.

On the other hand, baby-eating has rarely if ever been a key feature of human conflicts. Our horrified reaction to the very idea is not just intellectual, but instinctual. Chimps share this species-protecting instinct to an extent that their males won't, under any circumstances, eat their own kids. That would be a terrible waste of shared genetic material. But in the case of children of males from other, competing troupes, they make an exception.

The history of chimp territoriality and, ultimately, chimp evolution somewhere led them to block, or never develop, an instinct against enemy infant-snacking. We retained it. Male humans, on the other hand, at some point in our evolutionary history overcame any complex mating ritual instincts, allowing them to force sex on other humans as and when they felt the occasion allowed.

Of course enforced sexual contact, as we would define it between humans, is hardly unknown in the animal kingdom: many species commit rape – heterosexual and homosexual – under everyday, natural conditions. And monkeys in the zoo do it to each other fairly regularly. Yet in that last fact we may see another clue: as we saw in Chapter 5, John B. Calhoun's experiments with rats, living in the cage equivalent of slum ghettos, clearly showed a deterioration of rat basic instincts. Mating rituals were abandoned and rape became common – as did murder, gang-fights and baby-eating. It thus seems clear that 'unnatural living' – like zoo enclosures, the experimental cages of behavioural scientists, or living on the bad side of town – can loosen or break the hold that animal instincts usually maintain under more natural conditions.

Consider the well-known fact that the female praying mantis will cannibalistically devour her mate after or often during mating. In *The Selfish Gene* (1976) Richard Dawkins gives a lucid explanation for this ghoulish behaviour. During mating the female mantis will turn and snap off the head of her partner, crunching it up while his dying body continues to try to impregnate her. Afterwards she eats his body as well. Dawkins points out that removing the male mantis's head also truncates some of his inhibitory instincts – for example, the chance that he will see something that will distract him. This actually improves his mating efficiency . . . for a while, at least. His body will survive without his head for long enough for the female's purposes – to fertilise her – and afterwards will provide a nice sustaining meal for the pregnant mother.

Indeed, on a genetic level, this situation could be seen as win-win for both of them. The female gets to pass on her genes and is strengthened by a good meal; and the male gets to pass on his genes and also does his bit to provide for his mate and their shared offspring in the near future. Several types of male creature automatically die after mating – for example, ants, salmon and some tiny types of insect-eating marsupial. So the female mantis is arguably just being a bit pro-active.

This drive to pass on our genes, whatever the cost to the host body (as discussed in Chapter 5), is what is sometimes called the 'genetic imperative'. The fact that that 'host body' is also what you usually consider to be 'yourself' is the reason that so many people have a visceral dislike of the 'selfish gene' theory of natural selection. It just feels wrong that all that we consider to be essential to our individuality – our minds, bodies, and our accumulated knowledge and experience – are expendable assets to our genetic inheritance/donation. We rebel against the idea that 'a chicken is just a way for an egg to make another egg'. Yet we cannot deny the fact of our inevitable mortality, while acknowledging that the only part of us that we *know* survives death are the genes we pass on to our children. Indeed, Richard Dawkins later said that he wished that he had named his book *The Immortal Gene*, rather than *The Selfish Gene*; as the effective immortality of genetic survival was what he was really talking about.

However, Dawkins's neat hypothesis about praying mantises is somewhat undermined by the discovery that praying mantis females are much less likely to try to eat their mates in the wild. Of course it is actually better for the mantis genes overall if the male survives mating, as he will be more likely to successfully mate again . . . if he is still alive. Thus more mantis children will be born, carrying more copies of the mantis genes. So, even on a genetic level, female mantis mate-eating is actually rather perverse.

It is in captivity that the female praying mantis is more inclined to turn pragmatically cannibalistic. This suggests that conditions and behavioural influences can subvert the natural flow of the genetic reproduction imperative: in this case the stress of incarceration and, it has been suggested, the indoor strip-lighting in laboratories and zoo insect houses.

Richard Dawkins's critics might regard this as evidence that we are not totally controlled by our genes; but, in all fairness, Dawkins never argued that we are. With typical succinctness, he points out that humans successfully, and with comparative ease, act directly against our genetic imperatives every time that we use birth control – or, indeed, whenever we *fail* to mate given any opportunity. And that sort of intellectual rebellion against unthinking instinct is something that we need to consider in relation to the matter of chimp baby-eating; and also in the matter of human rape.

In the first case humans go strongly with an instinctual reaction *against* killing and eating babies, even if they are the offspring of our worst enemies. And this feels both natural and rational to us. But – speaking entirely rationally – this is illogical. In sparing enemy children we are both increasing the risk of potential enemies growing up to later threaten us and our social group, *and* we are wasting a perfectly good source of nourishment (provided we don't eat their brains, and thus avoid the risk of prion diseases).

The revulsion that you are now feeling towards my modest

proposal is instinctual, not rational. You, and I, can certainly find rational reasons to support our instant rejection of infanticide and cannibalism; but we need to recognise that we are thus rationalising instinctual reactions. In this matter the baby-eating male chimps could be said to be less instinctually governed, and thus more rational, than we are.

In the second case – that of rape – male humans have successfully overcome any natural instincts to groom, calm and impress a potential mate, before attempting to mount them. Male chimps in the wild, on the other hand, are governed by their instincts in this matter and thus are effectively barred from raping an unwilling partner; just as our instincts bar us from eating enemy babies. But to us rape also seems a natural part of human behaviour – if not very civilised.

The point here is that we are rather bad at judging where our instincts stop and our rationality begins. Both elements are there in almost everything we think and do, yet we are convinced that all our good decisions are arrived at based on rationality alone. The bad ones we are much more likely to blame on factors outside our rational control – like our base instincts.

So, how much are our violent reactions to the world governed by our instincts? And, more to the point, how much can our intellectual powers control and subvert those violent instincts? Most of us would say that we can control our brutal side with ease. But there are still plenty of assaults and murders each year, committed by people who later wish that they had kept a better lid on their knee-jerk reactions.

And how much does the influence of the world around us play into any 'decision' whether or not to attack other people? Here we'll look at some surprising theories concerning certain environmental factors that might have caused humans, as a whole, to have become less violent in recent years.

Thomas Midgley was arguably the most terrible man in history. If the human race survives for another couple of centuries, Midgley may go down in any future histories as the man whose work destroyed civilisation and, ultimately, may lead to the death of all life on Earth. As a lesser charge, he can also be accused of causing more violence and death than any other individual in history. Yet Midgley wasn't a serial killer or a mass-murdering tyrant. He was a much-lauded chemist who dedicated his career to improving human life around the planet, and was then pathetically killed by one of his own inventions.

Born in Beaver Falls, Pennsylvania, in 1889, Thomas Midgley graduated from Cornell University in 1911 with a degree in mechanical engineering. Five years later he got a job in the research department of the prestigious General Motors Corporation and soon proved to be one of their most valuable employees.

Food preservation by mechanical cooling was still a new technology. Up to the late Victorian period, people had chilled food and made frozen desserts by hauling ice from winter frozen lakes and rivers, and then storing it in ice houses (basically brick-insulated cellars) into the warmer months – chipping off bits of ice and taking it to the kitchen as and when they needed it. This method had survived (for those who could afford the expense) from back before the days of the Roman Empire, but the invention of mechanical refrigeration slowly made it obsolete.

The problem with the original fridges and freezers was that they could quite easily kill you. Early refrigeration relied on coolant chemicals like ammonia, sulphur dioxide, or propane to provide the chilling element of the process. But leaks in the rickety systems could stink out a whole house; or the leaked gas could poison you or explode, knocking you through the wall of your kitchen. In the late 1920s, Thomas Midgley led the General Motors' team that discovered that chlorofluorocarbon was an ideal replacement for these dangerous chemicals – it was an inert gas that neither poisoned nor exploded, and worked more efficiently at cooling than the older and more volatile alternatives. General Motors patented the gas as 'Freon' – but we know it better as CFC.

Soon Freon was being used in every fridge and air-conditioner – chilling not just food and hot people, but many other processes in industry and medicine. If you ever needed a blood transfusion during the mid-to-late twentieth century, then your life was probably indirectly saved by Thomas Midgley and his General Motors team: blood storage in hospitals was almost impossible before the discovery of Freon. They also discovered that Freon was an ideal propellant for asthma inhalers – firing the needed drugs into the asthma victim's oesophagus with no poisoning side-effects. Shortly after that the spray can was invented, using CFC gas to shoot out everything from paint to hairspray.

And in all that time, waste CFC gasses were floating up into the upper atmosphere and were destroying the ozone layer. This natural layer of gas reflects cosmic rays – the radiation from outer space. With the ozone layer becoming increasingly thin and full of holes – thanks to our CFCs – that cosmic radiation is getting through and is heating the atmosphere (and is greatly increasing the risk of skin cancer on the planet surface). This extra heat energy increases the chaos effect in our weather, creating unexpected climate conditions; like flash floods, decade-long droughts, unprecedented hurricanes and the rising of sea levels as the ice caps at the poles melt.

Combined with the human release of 'greenhouse gasses' – like carbon dioxide from our vehicles, farms and industries – we are facing a rapid downward cataract of effects, deteriorating the condition of our overheated atmosphere. Greenhouse gasses effectively insulate the planet, while allowing the cosmic radiation through unhindered. Without them, much of the unwanted heat of the planet could vent into space – as it always has done. But with the amounts of human-made greenhouse gases building up in the atmosphere, we are increasingly being trapped with too much heat.

Imagine that you have been locked inside a heating oven. The walls and floor are almost cool at the moment, but you know that eventually they will be red hot. If that thought makes you feel sick with horror, then good. You are clearly envisioning the trap that we are presently building for our own descendants.

We call this problem 'global warming' – although a more accurate term would be 'global weather chaos', as hotter weather is only a part of the problem. At best, people in the late twenty-first century will probably be facing difficulties largely undreamed of today. For example a piece of grit, propelled by a 200 mph gust of wind, might kill you as easily as a bullet. And we will be seeing a lot more of that sort of storm, as the excessive energy in the atmosphere becomes more chaotic and destructive.

At worst, we may already be approaching the point of no return. If we can find no way to stop the rising heat levels in our atmosphere, then Earth may end up like the planet Venus – where a layer of greenhouse gases makes the typical ground-level temperature hot enough to melt lead. Life – human, animal or even bacterial – would be impossible to sustain under such conditions. The Earth, the only place in the universe that we know sustains life, will become just another dead rock.

Deniers of global climate change should consider the fact that a frog can be boiled to death in a shallow dish of water; a dish that the frog could easily climb out of at any time. Provided the water is heated slowly, the frog's primitive temperature judgement will not register the rising heat as a significant threat – while its instincts insist that it is safer in water than it would be climbing out. But the frog's instincts are wrong and the heating water *will* eventually kill it. Waiting until we see the bubbles of steam start to rise – or, in our case, waiting until the number of weather catastrophes have silenced the naysay-ers – might mean that it is already too late. Given the stakes involved, doing everything we can as quickly as we can to reduce global atmospheric heating would seem the only rational thing to do.

After all, even if global warming *is* a scientific myth – or, as some doubters claim, a massive anti-capitalist conspiracy – then we will still have greatly improved our environment at the cost of only money and effort. (Two things that we are otherwise quite happy to expend on less vital matters, like wars and entertain-ment.) And if – as all the scientific evidence seems to indicate – global warming and weather chaos is a genuine extinction-level threat to all life on Earth, then a loss of money, and an industrial edge over our competitors in commerce, seem rather petty issues to suggest as a reasons for inaction.

Of course it is profoundly unfair to place all this at poor

Thomas Midgley's door. He and his team were aiming to improve human life and, to their own knowledge, did that magnificently. It isn't their fault that they knew nothing of the negative side-effects of CFC gases when they discovered their practical uses. We, on the other hand, can claim no such defence for our continued use of CFCs and our massive over-production of greenhouse gases.

Something similar can be said for Thomas Midgley's other great double-edged discovery: the use, in petrol, of 'tetraethyl lead' – or 'ethyl' for short. Midgley's 'leaded' petrol – invented and marketed in the early 1920s – removed the annoying knock-ing sound that internal combustion engines had always suffered and made them much more efficient. Unfortunately – again – Midgley was unaware of the subtle negative side-effects of his invention, and remained so until his untimely death in 1944.

(Thomas Midgley was infected by polio in his early fifties. Severely disabled, he used his talents as a mechanical engineer to create a complex pulley system over his bed, allowing him to get himself in and out with at least some ease. Three years later he became trapped in the pulley ropes and was strangled to death.)

Lead is poisonous – and here Thomas Midgley *can* be faulted in his research, as he must have been aware of the fact. Since before the Industrial Revolution, it had been well known that people regularly exposed to lead – in lead mines, in industry or in the home – might die in agony due to overexposure. The cele-brated Renaissance painter Caravaggio may have died of lead poisoning, for example, simply because lead was an ingredient of some of the paints that he used.

But Midgley can't have known just how insidious low-level lead poisoning is – that was not discovered until the 1970s. Even tiny inhalations of lead particles, taken in over a protracted period, can badly damage the human body. Chronic lead poisoning attacks both the central nervous system and the gastro-intestinal system, and can cause a loss of coordination, depres-sion, poor concentration, abdominal pain, pallid skin and hair loss. The heavy metal builds up over time and the body can't easily eject it. So the effects will get worse as time goes on, even if exposure to lead is not increased.

Chronic lead poisoning is particularly horrible when seen in children – whose small bodies are more easily overwhelmed by the long-term toxic effects. As well as causing all of the above poisoning symptoms, low-level lead poisoning can greatly impede brain growth in children, with related developmental problems as a result.

This is where we get back to the subject of unnecessary human violence. One of the developmental side-effects of chronic low-level lead poisoning is a lack of normal growth to the areas of the brain that govern both impulse control and the overall executive oversight of the cognitive functions. In other words, kids exposed to even low levels of lead as they grew up were found to be more likely to have short tempers and to be less able to judge when it was a bad idea to throw a punch. Connect a series of these poor decisions within a person's life and you have a habitual violent criminal.

In May 2000, an economist called Rick Nevin published a paper titled 'How Lead Exposure Relates to Temporal Changes in IQ, Violent Crime and Unwed Pregnancy'. Nevin had been involved, in the early 1990s, in a US federal project to remove leaded products (such as old paint) from areas where it might negatively influence the physical development of children. During this work, Nevin had begun to wonder just how closely the correlation was between the use of lead in petrol and that of violent crime. His conclusion, in the 2000 paper, was shocking.

He tracked the increased use of cars – and other vehicles and industries – that used ethyl leaded fuel, over the period after the Second World War in the increasingly affluent America. Then he showed that violent crime rose in America by almost exactly the same degree, but always twenty years after the increases in environmental lead levels. In other words, Nevin's graphs showed that violent crime had been exactly shadowing the use of leaded petrol, but with a steady one generation gap in time. America and its love of the motor car had been inad-vertently brain-damaging its children and – by extension – so had the rest of the world. And those areas that had the highest degree of lead in the atmosphere – usually the inner cities – had the highest crime rates.

An economics professor called Jessica Wolpaw-Reyes confirmed Nevin's findings with a reverse study in 2001. She showed that as states started to pass legislation to force industries, motor manufacturers, oil companies and consumers to abandon the use of leaded fuel, twenty years later there was a concomitant drop in violent crime rates in those same states. The countries that reduced the use of leaded fuel the fastest have had the fastest drop in violent crime.

So, thankfully, more kids are now growing up without needing to deal with the additional problem of having lead-lined brains. But, as with the problem of human alcohol abuse (as discussed back in Chapter 6), the overall destructive effect of more than half a century of leaded petrol is probably incalculable. We can never accurately estimate just how many people, unknowingly suffering lead-restricted brain development, lost control and assaulted, raped and killed people who would have otherwise gone unharmed. But certainly the tetraethyl lead-related casualty figures must be in the many millions. This is why I suggested that Thomas Midgley may have been – inadvertently and indirectly – responsible for more unnecessary violence than any other individual in history.

Nevertheless, few experts believe that the reduction of lead in the environment is the only explanation for the twenty-year drop in violent crime that much of the world has recently been enjoying. Another suggestion (that this author, as a one-time computer game journalist, particularly enjoys) is that the crime reduction is partly due to the increasing coolness of computer games.

It is a statistical fact that almost all violent crime is committed by young people, between the ages of fifteen and thirty. Most violent crime victims are also young people between those ages. Male violent offenders also greatly outnumber female violent offenders – in 1995 in the USA for example, 5.38 men were arrested for violent offences for every one female suspect of a violent crime[1]. In criminology, this correlation between age, gender and an inclination to violence is sometimes referred to as 'Cads versus Dads'.

This theory simply suggests that young men – awash with aggressive and territorial hormones – are more likely to act like 'cads' – an old-fashioned term for a man who behaves in an ungentlemanly fashion. However, as soon as he gets out of his twenties, a man's chance of being involved in violence – as attacker *or* victim – drops dramatically.

It is suggested that this is partly a matter of the pre-mentioned hormones calming down in his system due to ageing. But it is also suggested that the greater social responsibility that typically settles on a man in his thirties also has a calming effect. In other words he is statistically more likely to be a dad after thirty. He is thus more likely to think of the effect on his family if he swings an angry punch, mugs someone or takes part in a drive-by shooting – and then gets hurt himself or arrested. 'Cads versus Dads' theory is also apparently confirmed by the fact that even men with long records of impulsive violence are quite likely to settle down and calm down as soon as they get into their thirties. This simply shouldn't happen if there was no later-life environmental break, acting against their violent inclinations.

What does all this have to do with computer games? It is a simple matter of opportunity. A very high proportion of violent crime takes place on the streets, committed by young men hanging around with nothing much to do. In extreme cases these bands of bored street youths form into gangs that then commit petty and sometimes major crimes. These territorial bands often attack neighbouring gangs in turf wars that are very reminiscent of tribal conflicts in non-state societies. For example, witness the Bloods and Crips 'war' that has made many American inner-city areas effective no-go areas, after dark, since the early 1970s. Or the Blues and the Greens – supporters of rival chariot-racing clubs – that often ran riot in Constantinople during the height of the Byzantine Empire.

---

1 Finn-Aage Esbensen and Dana Peterson, *Youth Violence: Sex and Race Differences in Offending, Victimisation, and Gang Membership* (2010)

The growing technical elaboration of computer games (or their amazing coolness, to put it another way) plus the comparative cheapness of home computers and gaming systems, means that increasing numbers of these disaffected young men spend at least some of their evenings at home playing games in front of a screen – rather than hanging around on street corners, drinking cheap alcohol and trying to impress each other. Less time in the arena means less opportunity to fight. Part-time gamers are less likely to commit violent crimes than full-time gang-bangers.

An interesting side-effect of this development is the change in the public perception of the 'nerd'. Young men, and occasionally women, with a predisposition to books and computers were traditionally bullied and ridiculed by non-nerds (especially in secondary school). In the past ten years, however, the concept of 'nerd-chic' has been developing. Even the toughest street thug can hardly claim to detest all computer nerds, when he spends the other half of his life playing computer games. And the nerds, in their wonky glasses and unfashionable clothes, are also being increasingly recognised as the ones who are creating the wonderful toys of the twenty-first century.

The Nobel Prize-winning physicist, Richard P. Feynman, commented on a similar change in social attitudes just after the Second World War. In his book of autobiographical essays – *The Pleasure of Finding Things Out* (published posthumously in 1999) – he noted that, before the war, scientists were seen by the public as tedious boffins. It was the businessmen and tycoons who were regarded as the most laudable part of American society. But after those same tedious boffins had invented the most destructive weapon in human history – the atom bomb – Feynman found that it was much easier to impress girls by saying that he was a physicist.

There is yet another theory of an environmental influence that may be drawing us away from violent crime, which bears some examination. This was first popularised in the book *Freakonomics: A Rogue Economist Explores the Hidden Side of Everything*, published in 2005 and written by (journalist) Stephen J. Dubner and (the economist of the title) Steven D. Levitt. Put simply: Levitt and an earlier collaborator – John J. Donohue III – claimed that legalising abortion eventually reduces violent crime[2].

Like the Nevin/Wolpaw-Reyes theory about environmental lead pollution influencing crime rates, the Levitt/Donohue abortion theory is based on the slow-burn effect of demographic changes. Steven Levitt has written that:

> *After abortion was legalized [in the USA by the Roe versus Wade federal case in 1973] the availability of abortions differed dramatically across states. In some states like North Dakota and in parts of the Deep South, it was virtually impossible to get an abortion even after Roe v. Wade. If one compares states that had high abortion rates in the mid-1970s to states that had low abortion rates in the mid-1970s, you see the following patterns with crime. For the period from 1973–88, the two sets of states (high abortion states and low abortion states) have nearly identical crime patterns. Note, that this is a period before the generations exposed to legalized abortion are old enough to do much crime. So this is exactly what the Donohue-Levitt theory predicts. But from the period 1985–97, when the post Roe cohort is reaching peak crime ages, the high abortion states see a decline in crime of 30 per cent relative to the low abortion states.*

Why was this? Levitt and Donohue suggested that it was a simple matter of family values. A couple (or often single mothers) forced to have a child against their wishes – because of the illegality or unavailability of abortion clinics – are likely to begrudge their situation. They are thus more likely to strike their child out of pent-up resentment. If this happens often enough, then that child may grow up believing that violence is a

---

2 John J. Donohue III and Steven D. Levitt, 'The Impact of Legalised Abortion on Crime' published in *The Quarterly Journal of Economics* (Vol. CXVI, Issue 2) (May 2001)

reasonable way to react to annoyance. And, again, string enough of these antisocial decisions together in an individual's life and you have an habitual violent criminal.

This is certainly true of other types of child abuse (*see Chapter 21*). It is statistically more likely – although thankfully by no means a certainty – that children who have been abused will grow up to be abusers. The main reason for this is the social imprinting that takes place, during childhood and/or adolescence, while the abuse was happening. Abuse a kid often enough, and they may become an adult who thinks that abuse is normal.

On the other hand, children born in nations where abortion and other types of family planning, like contraception, are legal and freely available, are more likely to have been the result of planned pregnancies. Such families may be awash with tensions and dissatisfactions from other sources; but parents are unlikely to blame these on their children, and so are less likely to strike them. So those kids are, in turn, less likely to grow up thinking that punching your problems is a viable life strategy. Thus, a generation after the legalisation of abortion in a nation, there will be fewer habitual violent criminals.

Naturally the Levitt/Donohue theory is strongly disliked by the pro-life lobby – an international conglomerate of political and religious pressure groups who strongly oppose the legalisation of abortion and, in some cases, freely available contraception and even sex education in schools. The most common reason given for their anti-abortion stance is that a post-conception foetus in a mother's womb is, in their view, a living human being; and that aborting a pregnancy is therefore effectively an act of murder.

Leaving aside the numerous religious and scientific arguments that rage around this issue, I will simply make the historian's point that killing children, born or unborn, has been a necessity of life for most of human history. As noted in Chapter 6, killing unwanted babies was commonplace in biblical times and before, simply to limit the population and to prevent mass starvation. The development of agriculture has largely removed the horrid necessity of a mother having to decide if she can afford to let her newborn live. But the rocketing global population, and the resulting environmental damage, plainly mean that high levels of childbirth are becoming increasingly unaffordable for the planet, let alone for human civilisation. Family planning is not a sin in the twenty-first century: it is a survival demand.

Chapter 28

Bad Apples

We've considered some downward environmental influences on unnecessary violence – less lead in petrol, fewer street-corner ruffians and happier families. But there is a key factor that is now worth considering: that these influences only needed to influence a small number of individuals in a given population to have a major effect.

Many of us – who grew up in the decades between the introduction of leaded petrol and its eventual abandonment (in most countries) – breathed in unhealthy amounts of lead as children. But only a very few of us became violent criminals. The same goes for all those bored teenagers with nothing to do in the evenings – despite what the tabloid newspapers like to imply, a very small proportion of young people became involved in violent crime over the past half-century. And, finally, many people have grown up in dysfunctional families where violence, great and small, was considered normal. But, again, very few of those beaten children grew up to violently inflict their unhappiness on the rest of society.

Since most of the people who suffered any, or all, of these negative early influences then grew up to be decent, non-violent citizens, then that suggests that the tiny minority who *did* become habitually violent – for whatever reason – are the key players in most violent crime. The violence in modern society is not the result of all of us committing the odd crime now and again; but of a very few individuals committing a lot of crimes.

Certainly this is what judicial records suggest: a study by the

US Federal Bureau of Justice Statistics reported in 2005 that 71.3 per cent of violent offenders (across thirty US states) had been rearrested for another crime within five years of prison release. This degree of recidivism is remarkable, but is also fairly representative of crime figures from other countries. These ex-convicts can hardly claim that they had no idea of the risks of their return to crime – they had already been caught and imprisoned at least once. Such a hazardous course of action suggests, at the very least, a lack of foresight in the individuals concerned.

The old saying – 'crime doesn't pay' – is broadly correct. A few professional criminals can become staggeringly rich of course; but the vast majority are lucky if they make a basic living from criminality. A comparison can be made with that of any art form – let's say writing. A tiny number of writers become rich, best-selling authors. A few more make a reasonable living, but contracts and royalty payments can sometimes come in perilously far apart (my father was in this category: he earned an international reputation and published more than a hundred books in his career – but spent much of his life in overdraft at the bank). Many other published authors write part-time and have another, non-creative job to support their income (I myself work for the London Underground at weekends). And then there are the vast majority of writers – who are not technically professional, as they very rarely get anyone to pay them for their efforts. These at least can always find a place to display their work on the internet, but would starve if writing was their only source of income.

So, in its financial uncertainty, a life of crime is very similar to that of a life of authorship – apart from the fact that in writing there are no brutal 'white-collar' authors, who employ others to do the work and take the risks, while they collect almost all of the profits. And, of course, writers rarely face jail sentences for following their muse. With all the risks considered, a person would have to be exceptionally imprudent and/or ruthless to deliberately become a career criminal. But the fact is that the risks are rarely, if ever, considered by career criminals.

Criminologists are well aware of this foolish short-sightedness in habitual criminals – and many regard it as a key factor in the reason why the use of the state death penalty simply doesn't work as an overall deterrent to crime. The death penalty (and, indeed, draconian judicial sentences in general) work very well as a deterrent on most citizens; but the vast majority of those citizens are also very unlikely to be tempted to commit that degree of felony under *any* circumstances. So, in the case of most people, the deterrent of cruel sentencing is redundant and unnecessary. And it is also redundant and unnecessary in the case of most habitual criminals, as they care little or nothing about the consequences of their actions – to their victims or, crucially, to themselves in the future.

The studies that led to the creation of the forensic science of psychological profiling clearly showed that habitual violent criminals live very much in the present. They often react on impulse, with little or no thought of arrest or punishment. Many, in fact, tell arresting officers that they have no idea what their likely sentence will be: they just haven't thought about it, let alone calculated the balance of the possible costs against the likely benefits of their crimes. The reasons for criminals living this short-sighted way of life are multifactorial – some of which are detailed in the last chapter. But the overall result is that nations like Iran, Iraq, Saudi Arabia, Belarus, China and the United States – that implement the death penalty fairly regularly – still manage to have a high capital crime rate.

Meanwhile most people never commit even one violent crime in their entire lives. Obviously nobody keeps records of crimes *not* committed, but we can extrapolate somewhat from other figures. In 2008, the Federal Bureau of Investigation (FBI) stated that there were198.2 reports of violent crime per 100,000 of the US population. Even if we treat each report as a single occurrence – with no multiple reports accidentally referring to the same crime – and take it that there was usually only one offender who was involved in each crime, then that's still just 0.2 per cent of the overall population who were committing (reportedly) violent crimes in 2008. The other 99.8 per cent of the population avoided criminally harming each other, despite living in one of the most violent developed nations on the planet.

So who is committing all this wrongdoing? Apart from the many influences towards violence that we have already discussed, there is another key factor that we have so far only lightly touched on (*see Chapter 21*): that is, sociopathy.

(There are several other terms that refer to the psychological disorder known as sociopathy. The most common is 'psychopath', but medical practitioners also class the syndrome within the wider description of 'antisocial personality disorder'. There is something of a tradition that those who use the term 'sociopath' are believers that the condition is largely, or totally, the result of bad social programming and environmental influences. People who use the word 'psychopath' tend to believe that the condition is the result of a physical abnormality in the brain. As we will see, the latter explanation is almost certainly the correct one, but I will use the term 'sociopath' simply because the word 'psychopath' makes many people think of the savage shower murder scene from the Hitchcock movie *Psycho*. Unfortunately sociopathy is a much more complex problem than that posed in a fictional bloodthirsty nutter like Norman Bates. And anyway, Norman wasn't even a psychopath. He seemed to be suffering paranoid schizophrenia with an attached multiple-personality syndrome.)

A pure sociopath is entirely driven by their own interests, whatever the cost to those around them. They honestly don't care about anyone else in the world; not even their own children or parents. Some sociopaths are sadists, and a very few of those are serial killers – but most operate perfectly well within the rules of society. They are just rather prone to stretching those rules if they think that they can get away with it.

For example, sociopaths feel no compunction about ruthlessly manipulating anyone around them. They will bully, cajole, seduce and deceive; whatever they think they can get away with and, at the same time, whatever will get them what they want. Neither do sociopaths feel guilt after harming another person. It has been said of sociopaths that they would happily, and with no compunction, commit a murder – provided that they were certain that they could avoid detection and punishment, and could make some sort of personal profit from the killing.

In *The Sociopath Next Door* (2006) Martha Stout of the Harvard Medical School described sociopathy in these striking terms:

> *Imagine not having a conscience, none at all, no feelings of guilt or remorse no matter what you do, no limiting sense of concern of the well-being of strangers, friends, even family members. Imagine no struggle with shame, not a single one in your whole life, no matter what kind of selfish, lazy, harmful, or immoral action you had taken. And pretend that the concept of responsibility is unknown to you, except as a burden others seem to accept without question, like gullible fools.*

Spotting sociopaths in everyday life is far from easy, just as it might be hard to recognise sociopathic tendencies in yourself – if you happen to have them. Sociopathy is in-born from birth, is presently incurable, and seems to vary in scale and symptoms. Some people may be mildly sociopathic – perhaps living off the earnings of others, committing petty crimes, or just not really giving a damn for anyone or anything other than themselves. While others are hardcore sociopaths – damaging other people's lives for fun, ruthlessly climbing to the top of whatever social structure that they inhabit, dedicating themselves to cruel vengeance on people who may have done little or nothing to deserve it, and overall living a life bordering on that of a civilised cannibal (*see Chapter 7*). But whether sociopathy syndrome is indeed on a sliding scale, or is simply a matter of the laziness or ambition of the individual sociopath in question, remains a matter of scientific debate.

If you think that you might be a sociopath, but aren't sure, then try this simple test. Ask yourself if you would die to save someone else: say a close relation or a small child. Most non-sociopaths have more than enough emotional attachments to others to say 'yes' to that question (unless they live particularly isolated lives, or have an overpowering fear of death). A sociopath doesn't have *any* genuine emotional attachments, other than to themselves, so honestly can't answer 'yes' to that question.

This may all sound close to paranoid hysteria – like a rabid

Witchfinder General preaching that all of society is riddled by devil-worshipers. But, in this case, our society really is riddled with sociopaths . . .

It is estimated that between 1 and 4 per cent of the population are sociopaths[1]. The 1 per cent takes only the pure sociopaths into account, while the 4 per cent covers the wider diagnosis of 'antisocial personality disorder' – which probably includes other mental aberrations that are not, in fact, sociopathic in the medical sense. But even so, we have to consider the likely possibility that there are between 73 million and 292 million sociopaths within the planetary population of (as I write) 7.3 billion.

Sociopathy doesn't seem to have a significant hereditary element, so it would be rare to find more than one sociopath in any one family. Male sociopaths seem to outnumber female sociopaths by a factor of roughly three to one. On the other hand sociopathy seems to be evenly spread throughout all types of population – with no racial or geographical bunching that we are aware of. So if you know a hundred people, then at least one of them is probably a sociopath. If you are unlucky, they might be a significant other or a close associate. Or it might be you. In the latter case, however, you almost certainly won't feel unlucky. Sociopaths rarely if ever see any personal problem in their condition – and non-personal problems really don't interest them. When interviewed, some sociopaths have been known to frankly reply that they believe that it is the rest of society that has the mental problem – driven and distracted as it is by petty worries about the difficulties of others. They typically hold that a person who is true to themselves naturally looks after number one, ignoring or deliberately undermining other people's interests where they don't coincide with their own.

But sociopaths are rarely so forthcoming. This is because, from young childhood on, they have to learn to disguise their true feelings, or lack of feeling, for other people. The one thing that is

---

1 Robert D. Hare, *Without Conscience: The Disturbing World of the Psychopaths Among Us* (1993); Robert D. Hare and Paul Babiak, *Snakes in Suits: When Psychopaths Go to Work* (2007)

inexcusable in any type of relationship is to say to someone else that you don't care about them in the slightest. Even in the most shattered relationship, between non-sociopaths, there usually remains what the novelist Ian Fleming called 'the quantum of solace': that tiny spark of affection or mutual regard that means you at least see the other person as a human being with basic rights, even if you hate them or are indifferent to them on every other level. A sociopath lacks even the quantum of solace; and not just for those that they hate, but for everyone else on the planet.

The result is that sociopaths tend to be very good at the emotional manipulation of others. They tell lies not only with a straight face, but with a winning smile. Indeed they may appear the most pleasant and sympathetic person that you know – until they have some reason to exploit you. This need for duplicity is typically beaten into them by their early life experiences. Showing themselves to be utterly selfish when they were small children got them very negative reactions from those around them – from family and schoolmates, for example. So they faced a choice of either becoming ogre-like but honest misanthropists, or they had to become accomplished liars. The latter course obviously offers greater rewards.

If you want to see an accurate and detailed depiction of a manipulative sociopath, then watch the Brigid O'Shaughnessy character in the 1941 movie, *The Maltese Falcon*. Better still, read Dashiell Hammett's 1930 novel of the same name. In the movie the antihero, private eye Sam Spade, is depicted as falling genuinely, if rather inexplicably, in love with the ruthless and deceitful O'Shaughnessy. In the book Dashiell Hammett depicts Spade as another sociopath type – a brilliantly manipulative 'blonde Satan' lookalike, who ultimately appears uncaring about anything or anyone. He certainly doesn't feel any love for Brigid O'Shaughnessy, or remorse for – almost certainly – sending her to the electric chair. In fact Sam Spade's only real motivation in the story seems to be a vindictive fury over the *personal* insult of his detective partner being murdered. (Although Spade casually admits that he didn't like his partner, and was in fact committing adultery with his partner's wife when the killing took place.)

Sociopaths, like the fictional Sam Spade, certainly *do* feel emotions about other people; but those emotions are gravitationally distorted by the self-centredness of their intrinsic viewpoint. Sexual partners aren't lovers, but possessions – and so are as likely to engender demonstrations of real jealousy as much as fake affection. Associates, parents, siblings and even their own children are seen as tools to get what they want; or as competition to be defeated and bent to the sociopath's will. (Indeed the sociopathic condition might well be the cause of what A. E. Van Vogt called 'Right Man' syndrome, seen in some bullying husbands and fathers (see Chapter 28).) A true sociopath feels no real grief at another's death, unless that death costs them something in the way of personal support. And a sociopath never feels guilty or ashamed, whatever they get caught doing.

There is a reason for all of this. It is an in-born malformation of the sociopath's brain. This was first suspected during testing of incarcerated sociopaths in Canada in the early 1960s. The psychologist Robert Hare tested different types of subject – some sociopathic, some with other behavioural abnormalities, and others who had no known psychological problems. He initially did this by connecting the test subject to a set of wiring that measured perspiration. He then told them that after a steady countdown from one hundred to zero, he would give them a painful electric shock.

For the non-sociopaths, the tiny amounts of perspiration on their skin gradually increased through the countdown as the tension and fear grew. Hare then gave them a painful electric shock on reaching zero. For the sociopaths, however, their perspiration levels remained the same throughout the countdown and only increased immediately after receiving the shock – they evidently felt no anticipatory fear or tension and only reacted emotionally to pain in the present moment.

But what was most interesting was when Hare repeated the same experiment on the same subjects. The non-sociopaths sweated even more profusely, due to the memory of the painful electric shock. Yet the sociopaths didn't sweat the second time either. Hare theorised that this was because they had little or no emotional memory.

When most of us recall an event, what we are mostly remembering are our emotional reactions to that event. To a certain degree we actually relive what happened as the emotions play out again in our minds; although usually in a more diluted form than when we felt them during the original event. We burn with remembered embarrassment or anger. We feel a chill of remembered fear, or enjoy a flush of recalled love or triumph. A sociopath doesn't do this; they remember the details of the event alone, without any emotional colouring. They do feel emotions, but they can't remember those emotions afterwards as anything other than a cold fact.

This phenomenon seems to result from a combination of the attention focus of the sociopath, and their brain's comparatively limited emotional processing power. Memory, by its very nature, is a secondary attention focus, while events in the immediate present are a draw of our primary attention. A sociopath's brain seems to only be able to focus emotional reaction on primary matters of attention, and so has to short-change any secondary stimuli, like memory[2]. The sociopath sees the present in emotional Technicolor, but their memories are reviewed in black and white because of brain bandwidth issues.

This odd dissociation from their own emotional memory also seems to have an overall dampening effect on a sociopath's understanding of emotions in general. In another experiment, Robert Hare measured test subjects' emotional reaction to certain words, by checking their response time and brain activity. Non-sociopaths would have a stronger emotional reaction to words like 'rape' and 'murder' than they would to words like 'table' or 'tree'. Sociopaths showed the same emotional reaction to all nouns – to them the word 'rape' meant as little, emotionally, as the word 'tree'.

---

2 Samantha J. Glass and Joseph P. Newman, 'Emotion Processing in the Criminal Psychopath: The Role of Attention in Emotion Facilitated Memory' published in *The Journal of Abnormal Psychology* (2009)

It even seems possible that sociopaths feel *all* emotions less intensely than non-sociopaths – although, of course, such a subjective idea would be difficult or impossible to prove. Robert Hare once interviewed a sociopathic rapist who said of his victims: 'They're frightened, right? But, you see, I don't really understand it. I've been frightened myself and it wasn't unpleasant.' Even given the fact that the sociopath couldn't remember what fear in his past had actually felt like, his unemotional memories could still have told him that he had found the sensation of fear 'unpleasant'; as opposed to neutral or even pleasant. That is unless the feeling was rather dull even as he felt it – just as all emotions can feel dull to someone who is exhausted.

A sociopath's lack of emotional memory, combined with lowered emotional reactivity, has one striking side-effect: that the sociopath simply *can't* develop a conscience; certainly not as the concept would be understood by non-sociopaths.

Whatever religious believers might say, humans are not born with a pre-formed knowledge of right and wrong. A conscience develops over time as the person has different experiences. For example, a toddler doesn't automatically know not to snatch sweets from babies, but the reaction of adults to that action soon teaches it that the prize is not worth the cost. Add enough of these life lessons together, and the young child will develop a mental map that it can use to guide its actions. Society allows nakedness in the school showers, for example, but not on the street. So a child can probably work out that, no matter how hot the day, stripping to the skin and splashing in a public fountain is not a good idea.

However, take away the emotional memory from a learning experience, and the pain-and-pleasure reward system of learning is also removed. Why are non-sociopaths kind to each other? It is because they remember the warm glow of happiness from all the times when someone thanked them for their help: an emotional reward that can be relived in memory. And the whip of remembered punishment, and shared empathic pain, generally prevents non-sociopaths from casually harming others.

These emotional motivations are denied to sociopaths. A

sociopath can remember that stealing from babies is punished, but they can't remember (and relive) the embarrassment of being told off for snatching. So the life lesson that they develop on the subject of stealing is not that it is fundamentally wrong; but that you should avoid being caught when you do steal.

It has even been suggested that sociopathy might be a development of human evolution. Sociopaths, both male and female, tend to have many short-term relationships, and/or cheating affairs. They also tend to have lots of children. In the case of male heterosexual sociopaths, they often get women pregnant and then walk out on them (and tend to be very bad at making child-support payments). But female heterosexual sociopaths also tend to have a lot of children – frequently by different sexual partners. Their large families are often badly mothered or, where possible, children are given out for adoption. (One female sociopath – who had connived in covering up her boyfriend's murder of one of her children – was asked how she could do such a thing. She replied: 'Why not? I can always have another kid.')

However, if sociopathy *is* an evolutionary gambit, it is a failed one. The increased number of children born to sociopaths – as compared with non-sociopaths – could theoretically mean that the majority of the human race might eventually become sociopathic. Certainly this has occurred with other regional human traits, like skin colour and body build. But the hereditary element of sociopathy – if there indeed is one – is too uncertain and uncommon to allow such a 'take-over'. Adult sociopaths do not produce entire families of second-generation sociopaths. And sociopathy has been around since before *Homo sapiens* first left Africa – we know that because it is found in all racial groups, which it would not be if it had developed after our ancestors had split into widely separated migrating bands. Yet sociopaths still only number between 1 per cent and 4 per cent of the population. If they were ever going to become the dominant human strain, they would have done it by now.

At the time of his original experiments, Robert Hare suspected that the cause of sociopathy was an in-born physical abnormality in the brain (thus his use in his books of the word 'psychopath', rather than 'sociopath'.) But with the medical equipment available in the 1960s, he simply couldn't prove it. So Hare went for a less certain, but more pragmatic approach.

He devised a set of forty interrelated statements; the 'true' or 'false' answers to which could be graded and would give an overall likelihood of whether a test subject was, or wasn't, a sociopath. Some examples of the test statements are: 'My problems are mostly the fault of others', 'I feel bad when I trick people', 'I have committed many types of crime' and 'I often get others to pay for things for me'. Three of those four, if marked 'true', are indicators of sociopathic tendencies.

What is known as Hare's Psychopathy Checklist (and is also called PCL-R) is now commonly used by mental health professionals when they need to assess a patient suspected of sociopathy. It looks for certain key personality factors: for example, glibness or manipulativeness in personal relationships; a lack of guilt and a shallowness of general emotional affect; an impulsive and irresponsible lifestyle with a proneness to boredom; and early developing of and lifelong problems with breaking rules and criminal actions.

If a person scores over thirty on the PCL-R, then they are likely to be a sociopath. Around 5.5 per cent of those tested score thirty or above, but this should not be read as indicating that 5.5 per cent of the population are sociopaths, since few people who are not suspected of sociopathy ever take the test. (The author has taken a self-administered (and thus largely unscientific) PCL-R test. I scored nine, placing me with about 3.9 per cent of those who have taken the test.)

However, there has now been a recent confirmation of Robert Hare's original suspicion: that sociopathy is the result of an in-born brain dysfunction. A 2011 magnetic-resonance imaging study, by a team from the University of Wisconsin-Madison[3], showed that sociopaths have insufficient connections between

3 Julian C. Motzkin, Joseph P. Newman, Kent A. Kiehl, and Michael Koenigs, 'Reduced Prefrontal Connectivity in Psychopathy' published in *The Journal of Neuroscience* (2011)

the ventromedial prefrontal cortex – the part of the brain responsible for emotions like empathy and guilt – and the amygdala,
which controls fear and anxiety.

The result is that a sociopath has difficulty regulating their
social and emotional behaviour. Their reduced fear reaction
undermines their ability to judge risk. Indeed, thoughtless risk-
taking is another common feature of sociopathy. This is why
sociopaths don't do well in the army: they may be willing or even
keen killers, but their recklessness will often get them killed in
combat (if their own comrades don't 'accidentally' shoot them
first, to save themselves from the sociopath's careless actions).
And the sociopath's restricted empathic sense is, of course, the
key to their sometimes heartless and even monstrous behaviour.
They simply *can't* give a damn about anyone but themselves.

However, what has all this to do with the subject of unnecessary human violence, when it has already been noted that most
sociopaths manage to keep on the right side of the law? (If not
necessarily the right side of the spirit of the law.) It is true that
between 20 per cent and 35 per cent of inmates in prisons are
likely to be sociopaths; that's between 16 per cent and 34 per
cent more than there should be on simply demographic grounds.
And a proportion of those imprisoned sociopaths seem to make
up more than half the numbers of those convicted of serious
crimes: sociopaths are twice as likely as a non-sociopath to criminally victimise a stranger, and they are seven times more likely
to murder a total stranger. But all that still doesn't change the
fact that it is only a small minority of sociopaths who ever fall foul
of the law.

What is perhaps more worrying is the necessarily unconfirmed
suspicion that many of the top people in business and politics are
sociopaths. (Unconfirmed because people in those sorts of
positions are hardly likely to take honest and publicly scrutinised
PCL-R tests.)

Consider three twentieth-century political leaders who are
widely suspected to have been sociopaths: Joseph Stalin, Adolf
Hitler and Mao Zedong.

Stalin showed many signs of being a paranoid sociopath. (It

should be noted that sociopaths seem highly prone to paranoia
– especially in later life. This may be due to the psychological
isolation produced by decades of telling, and living, lies.) His
cold 'Right Man' demeanour apparently drove his second wife to
suicide – that is, if Stalin didn't secretly murder her himself. He
also refused an offer to ransom his son from imprisonment by
the Nazis during the Second World War, mainly because he felt
that his boy's capture in combat had reflected badly on himself.
(Stalin, of course, never went anywhere near a battle, let alone
took part in any combat.) Stalin's son was later killed in the
Sachsenhausen concentration camp but, on hearing the news,
his father showed little sign of grief. And, outside the subject of
his family circle, Stalin dismissed his personal (if bureaucratic)
murder of millions of his own people as a mere 'statistic'.

Adolf Hitler probably had a sexual affair with his own niece,
and is certainly highly suspect in her 'suicide'. He was also
mendaciously expert in changing his tone to fit his audience –
one day appearing pleasant and rational to a group of university
professors, and the next day being ranting and dogmatic in front
of a bierkeller of thuggish storm troopers. It might even be questioned how much Hitler believed his own bullshit. He once told
his pet architect, Albert Speer, not to bother reading the Nazi
bible, *Mein Kampf*, because it was 'out of date'. The Führer had
no close friends and was even rather distant with his mistress,
Eva Braun. Hitler was also strikingly lazy for a wartime dictator
whose decisions affected the lives of millions: he generally
watched movies late into the night and rarely got out of bed
before 11 a.m.

Mao Zedong slept with thousands of women, willing and
unwilling, during his decades of totalitarian rule. (As noted
above, extreme sexual promiscuity is a sign of sociopathy.) He
also seems to have enjoyed the sights of death and horror: in
1927 he witnessed the bloody aftermath of savage rioting in
Hunan province, and later described the mutilated bodies as
engendering in him '[a] kind of ecstasy'. Certainly he caused his
own share of death and misery. Mao's half-baked policies – like
'the Great Leap Forward' – caused the deaths of tens of millions

of his own people. And he once remarked that he was quite willing to see half of the Chinese population dead, if it would guarantee the victory of his idea of communism.

All three men were ruthlessly ambitious in driving their careers forward, and were highly disinclined to accept any blame for their many and often earth-shattering mistakes. They also betrayed former allies (usually killing them in the process) and, between them, caused the unnecessary deaths of well over a hundred million people. Without any specific evidence other than these circumstantial facts, we can reasonably speculate that all three men were hardcore sociopaths.

Three sociopaths.

Over a hundred million deaths.

The risk of allowing a sociopath any degree of life-and-death power over others seems fairly plain. Yet sociopaths apparently rise to the top of government all the time. Being driven by entirely selfish motivations means that they can ignore the restraints that often hold back non-sociopaths. They can neglect their families and betray allies whenever they see an overall advantage to doing so. They will mendaciously grovel, ruthlessly bully and connive like Steerpike in order to improve their position, never feeling any resultant shame or guilt. The almost automatic narcissism of their sociopathic viewpoint makes them want to attain a grand position for its own sake, regardless of any idea of serving the public good. And they are willing to climb over any number of bodies to get to the top.

Once in power a sociopath might deal ruthlessly with any leadership challenge. And may wallow in corruption in order to line their own pockets. They might even commit appalling acts – like starting unnecessary wars – to feed their conceited desire for glory and praise. Or they might rule with reasonable fairness and then retire gracefully. There is no particular reason that a sociopath shouldn't be a good man or woman – or that they should be particularly tempted to dabble in monstrosity. They simply have less empathic and conscience-driven restraints against bad behaviour than non-sociopaths.

The field of business is also filled with high-flying sociopaths, if hearsay reports are to be believed. During the 1960s, capitalism took a nasty turn when it was realised that the asset-stripping (selling off the resources) of long-standing businesses could temporarily boost the stock value and make their majority stockholders very rich. Those same stockholder/managers could then exit, sometimes with financial bonus 'golden parachutes' guaranteed in their contracts, before the gutted firm collapsed and made all its workers redundant. The vampire financial managers could then use the money they had just leeched to buy up controlling percentages of other firms . . . and begin the process all over again. At the time the media and politicians lauded such parasites for 'cutting out the dead wood of industry'; while ignoring the obvious idiocy of destroying working businesses for the sake of short-term profits.

By the 1990s this ruthless form of free-market capitalism had grown to the point where it could asset-strip whole countries. The collapse of the southeast Asian 'tiger economies' in 1997 was largely caused by the imposition of 'globalisation' open-market policies. Previous opening of their trade borders to international firms had boosted those economies in the short run. But when the financial bubble burst the international companies got the hell out – loaded down with hefty profits – and left the tiger economy nations to crash and burn.

By the early twenty-first century this business version of civilised cannibalism had reached the global stage. Over the previous decade the big banks and financial firms had pressured most governments to rescind many of the laws that restricted their financial dealings – those same laws that had maintained reasonable stability in the markets since the Great Crash of 1929. Demanding greater and greater returns, the banks and financial firms indulged in dodgier and dodgier practices, and also built up a huge financial bubble of excessive borrowing. In 2008 those same questionable practices were revealed and a resulting market collapse in confidence burst the debt bubble. The whole planet went into a recession that we are (as I write seven years later) still laboriously crawling out of.

Yet the very people who caused the crash were those least

affected by it. They had made sure that governments would declare that their financial firms were 'too big to [be allowed to] fail', and would thus bail them out with billions provided by the newly impoverished tax payer. Certainly very few people have since been prosecuted for the illegal and corrupt practices that partly led to the crash; and, more worryingly, the financial markets are being allowed to return to many of the questionable financial practices that instigated the greatest global recession since 1929.

Adam Smith – the first visionary of modern capitalism – would have wept to see the corrupt mess that his descendants presently inhabit. And, knowing about sociopath characteristics, it is hard not to see certain sociopathic tendencies in the behaviour of international capitalism in the past fifty years. As with politics, a few powerful sociopaths in leading positions might have undermined the ethics of the whole system.

Chapter 29

Good Apples

So, should the 99 per cent of normal people hunt down and neutralise the sociopath menace? Do we need to get back to the good old days of the European witch hysteria? After all we now have the tools to do it where, less than five years ago, we effectively had none.

Identifying the sociopaths is an obvious starting point. In a controlled clinical setting we could do that with Robert Hare's Psychopathy Checklist (PCL-R). But of course PCL-R is only useful if the subject gives honest reactions to the test's statements. It is perfectly possible to 'game' the results if you know what is being tested for and you are willing to be dishonest. And a sociopath is always willing to be dishonest if they see a personal advantage in doing so.

But the University of Wisconsin-Madison magnetic-resonance imaging study of 2011 indicated that sociopaths can be identified from the structure of their brain alone. The technology is in the early stages at the moment, but so was DNA identification twenty years ago. And nowadays the police use DNA tests as an essential investigation tool, because the technology has become so reliable.

So, as a species, we are shortly going to face a difficult question: what are we going to do with the significant percentage of our fellow citizens who have been positively identified to have the sociopathy brain dysfunction? Will we make them wear an identification badge – like the yellow star that the Nazis forced all Jews to wear in their empire? Will we deny sociopaths access to jobs that we deem unsuitable for someone who can't develop a conscience – just as women and non-whites were once denied senior careers in the USA and in Europe? Or will we go for a 'Don't ask, don't tell' policy to sweep the whole matter under the rug? This last might seem to be the least socially divisive option; until we remember that it will essentially be going back to the days before sociopaths could be accurately identified. That vast period of history saw untold horror, misery and death – inflicted by sociopaths on others – because unidentified sociopaths saw no reason not to behave that way if nobody could stop them.

At the other end of the political scale, the good-old genocide solution is also probably impractical in this matter. Since sociopathy is so demographically widespread, even a totalitarian government might have difficulty in killing, on average, a member of one family in every fifty. Not without risking a rather bloody backlash.

The only thing we can be reasonably certain of is that in the future, suspected perpetrators of serious crimes will probably be brain-scanned on arrest – much as they are now fingerprinted, photographed and breathalysed for alcohol.

Another hard question is what will society do if a cure for sociopathy is ever found? Would we have a right to force people to take it? After all, most sociopaths might feel that there is nothing wrong with them – and the law is largely on their side, because most of them have done nothing illegal.

By the way, it should also be noted in this context that another profession that is believed to have a lot of sociopaths occupying its senior positions is that of the lawyers – and the various legal professions in general. No doubt they might make a strenuous protest against their human rights being infringed.

Just because a sociopath is statistically more likely to commit a crime than a non-sociopath, does that give us the right to meddle with up to 292 million sociopathic brains? (That's a number that's just 28.5 million less than the entire population of the USA.) On those grounds women would have the right to 'medically pacify' all men, because men are much more likely to commit serious crimes than women. (Should they go for lobotomising all men, do you think? Or maybe just castrate most of us; keeping a few prize specimens – under lock and key – as studs?)

Scary jokes aside, there is an element of hope here; specifically within the context of the global fall of unnecessary violence in the past twenty years – the main reason for the writing of this book. It should be fairly plain to the reader, by now, that the causes of the drop in human violence are multifactorial but nevertheless strong. Those influences might affect sociopaths just, or almost as much as their fellow citizens. And on every front, the violence that has been historically endemic to human life is being reduced, if not actually drained away.

Yes, wars continue. But the daily casualty figures in those conflicts are no longer counted – as they were just half a century ago – in the multiple thousands. Not even a superpower like the USA, or a dictatorial theocracy like Iran, could nowadays get away with that many filled body bags returning home from a warzone.

And the causes of war have radically changed too. The 1990 Gulf War set a new international standard – that *any* war for the permanent conquest of territory would not be allowed by the rest of the world. Saddam Hussein had honestly thought that his invasion of neighbouring Kuwait had the sanction and political protection of the United States. But he soon saw his cities devastated, and what was left of his army hurled back into Iraq, all because he was rather behind the times on matters of military expansionism.

Moreover the common, man-in-the-street population are – on the whole – much less jingoistic nowadays. Today it is almost impossible to imagine young men running happily to a military recruitment office to join up, the moment that they hear their country has declared a war. Yet that was the situation across Europe when the Great War broke out a hundred years ago.

Baruch Spinoza – one of the seventeenth century philosophical fathers of the European Enlightenment – wrote:

> *Peace is not the absence of war; it is a virtue, a state of mind, a disposition of benevolence, confidence, justice.*

And the American poet Carl Sandburg wrote in the 1930s: 'sometime they'll give a war and nobody will come'. That time no longer seems so impossibly far away.

Neither are political revolution and – its opponent and shadow – reactionism the dangerous powers that they used to be. These basic ideological forces were arguably the two biggest people killers of the twentieth century. The post-Cold War world does not turn because of great ideological movements like communism, fascism, liberalism, libertarianism or anarchism. Even free-market capitalism – the claimed victor of the Cold War – seems to prefer controlling society indirectly: through political lobbying rather than by fanatical soldiers or secret policemen. The poor and disenfranchised may often protest against globalisation and capitalist exploitation; but nobody joins counter-marches, carrying banners proclaiming their support *for* faceless big business.

The key political idea of the twentieth century was that [insert your favoured ideology here] shows the one certain way to live correctly; and those who disagree must be forced to agree. Today, in most circles, this thinking does not carry much weight. Indeed most twenty-first-century people seem to think that those old certainties were actually paper tigers – fierce political masks that covered up the uncertainties that are to be found in all (sane) human thought. And the evidence of history seems to back this assumption.

When pushed gently by such dogmatic forces in society, people tend to dig in their heels. When pushed hard (or at the point of a bayonet) they convert – apparently wholeheartedly but essentially as a matter of self-preservation – and embrace the mindset of the people forcing them. But such compulsory revolutions have always collapsed back after a few years or, at the most, a few decades. We return to the human norm: unidealistic capitalism; largely harmless tribalism; unthinking religious or scientific reverence; and unassuming charity to the visibly worst-off. Anything more ideologically complex than these bottom-line impulses tends to eventually fly apart under the pressures of its own off-centre momentum.

Nevertheless, as Galileo whispered, the world *does* move; otherwise all humans would still be living as hunter-gatherers. The 1920s Marxist philosopher, Antonio Gramsci, described what he called the 'cultural hegemony': this is the overall direction that a culture will take from say, an agricultural to an industrial lifestyle, or perhaps from a monarchist to a democratic style of government. It can also describe the status quo of a society that has, for the time being, settled on a set direction of culture.

The cultural hegemony is fashioned by a ruling power bloc, itself formed by an ad hoc and often unaffiliated collection of dominant vested-interest groups – anything from political parties and labour unions to social reform groups and, say, fast-food conglomerates. Some of these will hold widely divergent political views; yet they temporarily cooperate to achieve mutual goals.

For example, in 1960s Britain, the asset-stripping free-market-eer financial managers (*see Chapter 28*) and the newly elected socialist Labour party joined forces, nominally to modernise British industry. The financiers also got rich, a lot of people were made unemployed and the Labour party got the blame for an economy that collapsed into the doldrums; yet the overall direction of Britain's industrial development was permanently changed by a coalition of two power groups who otherwise hated each other.

To Gramsci's idea of the cultural hegemony, we will add another concept: that of the 'social hegemony'. We will consider the difference between the two concepts further on. Both types of hegemony, cultural and social, consist of a largely unthinking movement of beliefs and actions in a society: a sort of democratic conspiracy, in which that society develops in the direction that most suits the majority of the power groups within it – often in detriment to the minority power groups. And as time and power-balances change, so does the overall hegemonic direction.

Examples of cultural hegemony might be as powerful as the ideological direction of a nation – like socialism or conservatism – or as ephemeral as the level of media censorship or the dominant types of fashion.

In the latter case, did you know that the pointiness of shoes used to be a cultural power statement? The longer the point, in medieval Europe, the richer the shoe-wearer; as it took more expensive leather and craftsmanship to make the shoe. The fashion became so extreme that the toes of shoes sometimes had to be pulled up with chains attached to the knees, in order to avoid tripping. (At one battle during the Crusades, the defeated nobles had to hastily cut-off the toes of their shoes, so that they could run away faster.) Ridiculous as this may seem now, a man wearing pointy shoes – five or six hundred years ago – was actually proclaiming that he was a power to be reckoned with. He was indicating that he was part of the local power bloc or ruling class, and thus had influence on the direction of the cultural hegemony. So nobody better dare laugh at his shoes.

For another, less humorous, example; the Republic of Ireland was effectively a theocratic state in the 1950s (when my mother was a student in Trinity College, Dublin, and witnessed the unofficial rule of Catholic clerics at first hand). Éire was nominally a democracy, but the elected politicians rarely, if ever, did anything that the Catholic Church disapproved of. Yet this was not necessarily corrupt – as most voters in Éire were strict Catholics and approved of a government that showed deference to the rulings of the Pope and the College of Cardinals. Nevertheless as time has gone on, public opinion in the Republic has been swayed; most notably by the revelation of the vast amount of child-rape and child-abuse practised by politically cosseted Catholic clergy over past decades. The Catholic Church in Ireland now wields considerably less power than it once did. And thus the Church has been reduced in its influence on the hegemonic development of Éire.

The direction of a hegemony can also waver back and forth under the influence of changing historical conditions. The hegemonic direction in early 1920s Germany, for example, was towards democracy and economic stability. By the early 1930s, failure to fully achieve either goal led to a change in the German hegemonic direction: towards totalitarianism and empire-building. And, in turn, the failure of the Nazi project in the 1940s – due to what might be called internal and external forces – led at least half of the Germanic hegemony back towards democracy and economic stability. (The other half took a bit longer to realign, due to the influence of an external hegemonic force: the Soviet Army.)

However, understanding the difference between cultural and social hegemony is important; because cultural hegemony can be, and usually is, hijacked by the ruling class of a society. The rulers can use their position and power to cement their own interests against those of everyone else. They do this by vigorously remodelling the cultural norms of society. For example, they may force the idea of 'the divine right of kings', or 'the dictatorship of the proletariat', or 'the glory of unrestricted free-market capitalism', on to the majority of the population. The poor dupes may suspect that they are being sold a lemon, but have little power to say so. And, if the leadership's line is said often enough and long enough, it becomes a 'proud tradition', which is of course questioned even less (*see Chapter 7*).

Social hegemony is much harder to control, or even to predict. In many ways it resembles a force of nature – and is often taken to be one. An example is the idea of 'national character'. There is no fixed definition of any region's national character, largely because it changes from generation to generation – and almost from year to year. Yet, looking at a nation's history, anyone can spot what they will feel are clear and unchanging examples of national characteristics. And the ruling class – although it will undoubtedly have strong opinions on the subject of what the national character is – will have a much harder time changing it to more closely match their idea.

The reason for this endless changeability, and yet stability, is that any social hegemony derives from largely environmental norms: a vast array of local influences such as the geographical, climatic, aesthetic, economic, industrial, agricultural, culinary . . . and so forth. It varies to such a chaotic degree that two neighbouring countries – that share virtually identical cultural hegemonies – may still seem to have essentially different social hegemonic inclinations. Think of Britain and France; the USA and Mexico; or Japan and China.

The other difference between cultural and social hegemonies is that the cultural is always parochial and local (and thus is controllable); where the social can fill as big a frame as is wanted. To talk of European, African, Asian, or American 'culture' is to stretch the term almost obscenely, because doing so automatically eradicates so many regional variations of cultural difference. But the social structures of regions, large or small, are what they are; they don't need to fall in line or be homogenised just to make a neat and understandable picture. Any question relating to culture will tend to the specific, whereas any question relating to society will tend to the general.

The social hegemony of the human race as a whole may seem riddled with tribalism and selfishness – indeed, those are almost the definitions of the essential hegemonic drives. Yet the world is improving. Our shared social hegemony seems to be inexorably pushing civilisation towards some common principles: anti-racism; feminism; child-rights; social safety nets; ecological protection; economic fairness; egalitarian legal systems; universal education; and the worldwide brotherhood of humanity. These ideals (rather than ideologies) have all made enormous leaps forward in the past few generations. And they will probably continue to do so because it is in all of our selfish, individualist, short-sighted interests that they do. The world is a much safer and more profitable place when we add a letter 'e' to the end of the word 'human'.

So what of all the religious feuding that has shaken the world in recent times? Most noisy and attention-seeking is the form of theocratic fascism that calls itself Islamic fundamentalism. This is partly a reaction to the sometimes tactless – and often tacky – cultural impingement of western thought on to Islamic countries; and maybe also the imperialist exploitation of Islamic nations, and their resources, by the western powers for the past couple of hundred years.

But it is also a knee-jerk response by an utterly paternalistic, insular and totalitarian social hegemony to outside cultures: those who hold less reactionary attitudes to, among other things, women, satirical cartoons, democracy and religious freedom.

Young Sunni and Shiite men are presently immolating themselves – and many bystanders – in the name of an aggressive,
mean-spirited and short-sighted version of the Islamic faith. An
idea of Islam that would have, almost certainly, horrified the
Prophet Mohammed.

The Catholic Church reacted in a similar if less bloody way to
the early European Enlightenment in the seventeenth century
– creating the subtle speaking and thinking Order of Jesuits,
aiming to fight scientific and liberal thinkers on their own debat-
ing ground. In fact all that they managed to achieve was to
distance themselves even further from the development of the
modern world. At least when the eleventh-century Viking king,
Cnut, ordered the tide to turn back, he was intending to be
comically ironic. The Catholic Church still doesn't seem to have
got his joke. And in the cases of both late-medieval Catholicism
and modern Islamic fascism, the essential drive was and is the
same: to get back to the good old days when no godless smart-
arses dared to question their right to speak with divine authority.

Meanwhile, pitiable young Islamic kamikazes destroy themselves in the 'certain hope' (an oxymoronic religious term) that
they will receive a martyr's welcome in Heaven – including the
much advertised endless orgy with seventy-two virgin girls. As
the journalist Christopher Hitchens pointed out[1], there is a
strikingly pathetic truth about young, male, modern-day Islamic
suicide martyrs. Most of them are trained and brainwashed in
monastic separation from the opposite sex; and they are taught
to despise all women as weak and sinful temptresses, even their
own sisters and mothers. So most of these theologian nerds are
probably virgins too, when they terminally catapult themselves
towards Heaven.

The cancerous growth of the Islamic State of Iraq and the
Levant (also known as ISIS, or simply IS) is another matter
entirely. A pseudo-nation hacked bloodily out of regions of Syria,
Iraq and (recently, as of this writing) Libya, Islamic State is a

---

1 Christopher Hitchens, *God Is Not Great: How Religion Poisons Everything*
(2007)

bandit kingdom of the worst sort. Slave-trading, rape, looting, child-abuse, torture and mass murder are not just tolerated in IS – they are positively expected of a 'soldier for Allah'. Under the belief that they are defending (Sunni-only) Islam, recruits often live as if transported into a combination of violent computer game and porno movie. All their savage actions, they believe, are dispensated by their religion. And if they happen to be killed by one of the people that they are victimising, they also believe that they will go immediately to the same martyr's heaven as their suicide-bombing brethren. At present Islamic State is not short of young male recruits, despite taking severe battlefield losses.

The Koranic term *jihad* is usually translated into English as 'holy war'. But this is somewhat inaccurate as a better translation might be 'holy defence'. A jihad is supposed to be a directed fight-back against unbeliever incursions. A key element of the Islamic creed is that one cannot kill fellow believers. However, unfortunately, this rule has often been forgotten or circumvented by the faithful. The problem with Islamic State, and other Islamic fascists, is that they ignore the *directed* element of jihad. They do not name a specific foe and go after them, but take the attitude that anyone they choose to fight must deserve to die . . . because people targeted by holy warriors must be worthy of death. QED. This circular reasoning means that nobody can trust them, or can feel safe while they are around.

It is perhaps notable, in passing, that there has never been a purely religious war without some amount of arguably impure bribery being offered to get the troops to fight. The medieval crusaders were promised automatic dispensation for their sins and an almost automatic pass to Paradise, provided they sewed on the scarlet crucifix and slogged off in the general direction of Jerusalem to kill the unbelievers. And both the brainwashed suicide-bombers of Al-Qaeda, and the joyously homicidal juvenile delinquents of Islamic State have been promised the ever-lasting-orgy option of eternal life – provided they kill, and are killed, in the name of the twenty-first-century jihad.

The religious and military leaders who make such afterlife offers are clearly promising something that they cannot *know* is true, because they are still alive enough to make them. But they claim that their personal faith is enough of a guarantee. However, it is worth considering just how few religious leaders have strapped on bullet belts, bomb vests or broadswords, and then made the long fearful march towards the sound of the guns. The faith to send others to certain death, and the faith to go yourself, are possibly of a different order of magnitude.

Moving beyond adolescent-fantasy-style Islam, we should also consider the counter-scientific movement of Christian fundamentalism. Mark Twain once wrote that 'faith is believing what you know ain't so'. Modern Christian fundamentalists, by insisting on the 'gospel truth' of every word of the Bible, should therefore ultimately believe that the visibly functioning evidence of geology, archaeology, biology, medicine, physics and astronomy ... simply 'ain't so'. And in vigorously and politically expressing their faith – to the extent that they want to deny evolutionary education and sex education to the young – they are, at the very least, retarding the development of their local cultural hegemonies.

But such Christian true believers also seem a little lax on other elements of the gospel truth. For example, Jesus of Galilee made it quite plain that all believers in his message should give their wealth to the poor and then live themselves in simple poverty, awaiting the end of the world. Yet there still seem to be a lot of very rich people who also insist that they are fundamentalist Christians.

In the Occupied Territories of Palestine, Jewish Israeli settlers annex large areas of other people's property – often with violence and with the protection of the Israeli Defence Force. They do this based on the excuse of the 'promise made to Abraham': a bond reportedly made by the god Yahweh to a nomad tribal chief about three thousand years ago. The creator of the universe is said to have pledged that Abraham, his clan, and all their descendants had permanent rights over the whole of the area of land that Abraham could then see.

Given the curvature of the Earth's surface, even if Abraham was standing on a hill on a very clear day (and had good eyesight) he wouldn't have been able to see more than about twelve miles in each direction. Nevertheless, many Israeli settlers feel that this is quite sufficient reason to drive Palestinians off considerably more than 452 square miles of land. Of course in doing this they are ignoring the Palestinians' own belief that they are *also* descendants of Abraham. Then there is the unhappy fact that Israeli illegal occupation of Palestinian land has been a facilitator of brutal conflict in the Middle East for many decades.

And finally (perhaps literally) there is the Hindu chauvinism in India that, confronting an identical but Islamic bigotry in their neighbour Pakistan, has brought the world closer to the edge of nuclear annihilation than at any time since the collapse of the Soviet Union. Anyone who believes that a nuclear war between India and Pakistan would be in any way 'limited' – in either local scope or global impact – is kidding themselves. An exchange of nuclear weapons on the Indian subcontinent would catastrophically affect the entire planet with radioactive fallout, and might well bring on a global nuclear winter that would certainly bring all civilisation to its knees, if not ending it for good.

Once again we can turn to George Orwell, this time to shed light on the battle between the humane secular and the inhumane religious. (In the context of our wider argument, please read 'religious' where Orwell writes 'Christian'.)

Ultimately it is the Christian attitude which is self-interested and hedonistic, since the aim is always to get away from the painful struggle of earthly life and find eternal peace in some kind of Heaven or Nirvana. The humanist attitude is that the struggle must continue and that death is the price of life.

Men must endure
Their going hence,
even as their coming hither:
Ripeness is all.

– which is an un-Christian sentiment. Often there is a seeming truce between the humanist and the religious believer,

*but in fact their attitudes cannot be reconciled: one must
choose between this world and the next. And the enormous
majority of human beings, if they understood the issue,
would choose this world. They do make that choice when
they continue working, breeding and dying instead of crippling their faculties in the hope of obtaining a new lease of
existence elsewhere.*[2]

No matter how fervently the religiously inclined might
disagree with Orwell's statement, the evidence of their own lives
tends to support his contention. Even the most orthodox believer
makes constant adjustments between complexities of the (often
contradictory) demands of their religious texts, and the need to
live a reasonably happy life. It is simply not possible to gear a
modern life, seamlessly and consistently, to a set of theocratic
rules which were designed for and by people who thought that
the Earth was flat, that the stars were small holes in a giant,
opaque sky-bowl and that slavery was a perfectly decent basis for
an economic system.

This existential dichotomy, between proclaimed belief and the
practical reality of modern life, is the reason why such a tiny
percentage of religious believers – of whatever faith and whatever level of fundamentalism – actually take up arms on behalf of
their god or gods. And as our global society becomes more
peaceful, more educated and more affluent, the dichotomy of
human life versus religious duty may become all the greater; and
the calls to kill the infidel may become less strident.

And lastly there is the twenty-year drop in violent crime to
mull over. It is here tempting to go into a lengthy statistical illustration to prove that crime has indeed fallen in the past two
decades, but the effort would be both tedious for the reader and
would also be largely superfluous. Anyone with access to the
internet can view police force reports from around the world
that will confirm it. In Britain and the USA, the present per

---

2 George Orwell, *Lear, Tolstoy and the Fool* (1947); (the internal quote is from
Shakespeare's *King Lear*; Act 5, Scene 1)

capita risk of violent crime is about the same that it was in those countries in 1960. In parts of Europe it has fallen even further. The real questions are why violent crime has declined, and whether it will continue to fall.

Of course, violent crime is still something of a threat to all of us, but nowhere near as much as it was is the 1970s, the 1980s and the early 1990s. I've spoken with ageing British police officers who remembered the days when fights in pubs and clubs on Friday and Saturday nights were always half-expected, if not actually commonplace. Younger officers are almost shocked by the very idea: as if you were suggesting that fistfights might break out in restaurants or wine bars.

One obvious answer, which yet explains nothing of the mechanics of crime, is that people are simply behaving in a less criminal fashion. As noted in Chapter 28, it is only a very small percentage of any society that commits any serious crime at all, let alone violent crime. Within that small percentage there will also be striations of criminal tendency; the petty criminals who resort to violence only when desperate are on the outer margins, while the dedicated sadists and criminal sociopaths – who commit acts of violence because it is as natural to them as breathing – are at the core. The latter type are unlikely to ever reform, but they are also a tiny minority of a tiny minority. The rest of the potentially violent criminals are more open to reformation, and it is possible that this is what they are doing.

Strange as it may seem, social responsibility is actually a major factor in violent crime. Only about one in ten convicted murderers confess that they killed purely for personal profit – say, for example, in the course of a robbery, to silence a witness who might give evidence against them, or to rid themselves of an inconvenient spouse so that they can pursue someone else. The vast majority of murderers insist that they did it 'because the bastard deserved it' – or something similar.

Self-deluding rationalisation or outright lie as this may be, we cannot afford to totally discount evidence from, often, the only surviving witness of a homicide. This potential importance is underlined by the fact that the murderer often knows that their explanation won't be believed, or will make no difference to their eventual sentence. Yet that fact doesn't change their essential contention: that they have done society a favour.

Men kill others over petty arguments – then tell the police that it was a matter of personal honour. Women kill their two-timing partners – and tell police that they were protecting other women from being similarly betrayed. Gang members defend their inner-city blood-feuds by describing themselves as a last bastion against chaos, bravely defending their neighbourhood from incursions by barbarians from other gangs – those outside gangs that often seem to investigators to be identical in make-up and behaviour, and who also give identical excuses for murder.

This conviction on the part of murderers – that they had no choice, as an essentially decent person, but to pull the trigger or thrust the knife – is what criminologists sometimes call 'self-help justice', and most other people call vigilantism. It is also much more common to homicides in high-crime areas than it is to the odd murder in leafy suburbs.

Again this last point may seem obvious, but it is actually counter-intuitive if studied closely. People in bad neighbourhoods are rather more likely to offer the 'dog-eat-dog' defence if asked to explain their antisocial attitudes. Their world is often bleak, uncompromising and unfair. So they feel that they have a survival right to behave that way as well. Those who live in greater relative safety and comfort are supposed to have a more judicious attitude to life, and to show a greater commitment to social right-eousness. Yet it is the people on the wrong side of the tracks who are the most likely to be involved in what they themselves see as vigilante violence – often knowing that it will come at great cost to themselves.

The reason for this is fairly simple. People in low-crime areas have every reason to believe that the police are doing a good job. People in high-crime areas are likely to believe just the opposite. And with that belief comes the conviction that they are the only person who can deliver justice. Thus the 'bastard/bitch had it coming' defence.

It is a common belief – especially on the political right – that prison sentencing works in suppressing crime. On the simplest level this is true: prison physically prevents convicted criminals from committing further crimes for the period of their sentence . . . in the community. But – leaving aside the very high crime rate in prisons themselves and the fact that prisons are renowned for training up petty criminals into serious criminals – there is little or no evidence that the 'deterrent-effect' works in suppressing crime. Most people who are thoughtless enough to enter a career of crime are also too unthinking to consider the likely long-term consequences (*see Chapter 28*). Many governments, over the past century, have experimented with absurdly long prison sentences for convicted criminals – and have found little or no impact on the later crime rates.

However, visibly efficient policing *does* deter crime. London in the 1980s was plagued by burglars. (Having lived there through much of that period, I can attest that most people I knew had been burgled at one time or another – and these were mostly people with few possessions worth stealing.) Then, in 1991, the London Metropolitan Police initiated Operation Bumblebee. This was an intelligence-led anti-burglary crackdown that had impressive results. The police had realised that there were very few professional burglars in any one area of the city at any one time, but it was these few individuals who were responsible for most of the burglaries. Using informant networks and other surveillance methods, they targeted these 'key players', and effectively made their lives hellish.

Police would conduct dawn raids on the suspected burglar's home and, even if they found no stolen goods, made it plain that the suspect could expect to be taken in for questioning every time that there was a burglary in the neighbourhood. Faced with this targeted 'round up the usual suspects' form of policing, some burglars simply retired from the profession. Others used their many, many police interviews to inform on their professional competitors. Of course, in a classic case of the 'prisoner's dilemma' (*see Chapter 5*) that same grassed-up burglar might be in the next cell doing exactly the same to them – netting the police two arrests for the price of one. As many full-time burglars changed profession, or went to prison, many part-timers also got the hint and retired too. Either that, or they came under the same police pressure that the professional burglars had suffered. In the first year alone, Operation Bumblebee raided 3,002 premises; arrested 2,308 people; and the overall burglary rate in the city fell by 13 per cent.

This form of intelligent and targeted policing is hardly new. In the fifteenth century the Cornish port of Fowey was a centre of piracy. But this had largely been government sanctioned – Cornish pirates were issued 'letters of marque' that licensed them to attack and loot the vessels of the hated French. However, following the signing of a peace treaty between England and France, the people of Fowey failed to get the message and carried on raiding. So King Edward IV sent a representative to deal with the matter.

The king's sheriff used troops to confiscate almost every stitch of clothing from the citizens of Fowey – all but one set of clothes each for modesty's sake – and also the front door from every Fowey home. (Being solid wood – often oak – the front door was the most valuable possession that the homeowner couldn't hide away from the bailiffs.) Then, with a touch of true brilliance, it was announced that if *anyone* along the south Cornish coast indulged in further illegal piracy, the bailiffs would return to Fowey and go through the confiscation process again – regardless of whether the people of Fowey were actually responsible. This turned the Fowey pirates into anti-piracy vigilantes overnight and removed the necessity of the English crown having to stamp out any further piracy directly.

An absolute necessity to efficient policing is good publicity. The more that policing successes are spread across the media, the more the message gets across to potential criminals that they are likely to be caught. And this is the key to the whole issue. The sort of people who commit crimes are, as we have seen, generally too short-term in their outlook to care about potential prison sentences. But, ironically, they do care about being caught. Their sense of self may be very firmly anchored in the present – to the extent that a prison sentence in a few months' time means little or nothing to them. But the high likelihood that they will spend the rest of their evening – following a crime – in a police cell being badgered by a copper is a clear deterrent that is close enough to where they mentally live, so to speak.

In the twenty-first century, after over two hundred years of the 'shoe-leather detective work' that so annoyed Arthur Conan Doyle (*see Chapter 20*), the police are finally learning to be more than just foot-soldiers with alternative duties. Conan Doyle meant his creation, Sherlock Holmes, to be an example of intelligent, scientific and above all efficient forensic investigation. The police now have powerful scientific tools – like DNA identification, computer data cross-indexing and psychological profiling. They just have to learn to use them in a more Sherlock Holmesian fashion to see the crime rate fall even further.

Having previously discussed the idea of a social hegemony we can put it into use in considering the wider matter of unnecessary human violence. Other names for the social hegemony are the 'zeitgeist' or more simply 'the spirit of the time'. And, at present, the global zeitgeist seems to be moving towards greater civility and less violence.

Sudden changes in the prevailing social hegemony are hardly unknown. A surprising one, for example, was the death of the Wild West. Immediately after the end of the American Civil War, in 1865, many young men headed out to the western territories to find their fortunes. The west of the continent was then largely unsettled by Europeans and was mostly wilderness. But it was the arriving young men – many of whom had fought in the war – who made the west 'wild'.

In his 1998 book *Violent Land*, the historian David Courtwright gives some shocking figures. In the Kansas town of Abilene, the annual murder rate peaked at an average of fifty out of every 100,000 inhabitants. In the infamous Dodge City, the annual murder rate hit one hundred in 100,000. In the town of Witchita, the peak average was a staggering 1,500 murders per 100,000 citizens. This was between fifty and three hundred times higher than the average murder rate of the east coast states during the same period.

What was causing this bloodbath? Just as Hollywood has always said, it was hardboiled young men, between the ages of fifteen and thirty, getting drunk on bad whiskey; playing competitive games of chance; and killing each other over petty arguments. Steven Pinker, in *The Better Angels of Our Nature* (2011) quotes the pithy inscription on a Colorado grave marker: 'He Called Bill Smith a Liar'.

Yet, just a few years later, the murder rate in the American west had fallen to roughly the same as that of the east coast. Steven Pinker offers a surprising explanation for this drop in the wildness of the west: it was the women. During the glory days of gun smoke and cowboys (the latter word originally being used as an insult equivalent to 'gangster' today) there were very few women around. And most of those were effectively slaves – prostitutes tied to their wilderland brothels – and with nowhere else to go. These women may have offered their punters a few fruity insults, but they could hardly control their behaviour.

Then the widows and spinsters from the eastern states started to move out west. They were still heavily outnumbered by the male population, but these women were in a position to choose who they married – and sex without marriage was simply not on the table, so to speak, in the late-Victorian period. Certainly such civilised women were not going to marry a man who had just killed someone in a knife fight, and they told their suitors as much.

So the tough guys of the Wild West then had a choice: to live like *real* men – gambling, drinking and fighting every night . . . with other men. Or they could get laid. There was no contest. The Wild West didn't die, it just got married and settled down.

Indeed, the civilising effect of women – when matched with genuine female suffrage – has clearly been another key influence on the downward tendency of human-to-human violence in previous decades. There are various theories why women are less prone to violence than men, but the most commonly cited is their lengthy pregnancy period and their subsequent inclination to child-rearing rather than to combat. Battles and babies don't mix and women are rather more keen to keep them separated than men tend to be.

In all the countries where violent crime has fallen by the greatest degree, we see a greater degree of sex equality. Specifically: those countries where women get to choose their sexual partners have also won a dividend in the form of a falling violent crime rate. (And remember, even in the USA and Europe, that women not having to ask their father's permission to marry has only been generally the case since the 1960s.)

Conversely, those countries where women are still treated like chattels – often forced into arranged marriages where they have little or no influence over their husband's actions – still suffer comparatively high murder rates. Since the vast majority of criminal violence is perpetrated by males (and most males are heterosexual) the potential of the sexually civilising influence of women can hardly be over-emphasised.

Much has been made in the popular media over the apparent 'feminisation' of the male sex in recent years – stay-at-home dads, nerdy boys and that Northern Irish definition of a homosexual: a man who would rather stay in, having sex with his girlfriend, than go down the pub with his mates. But few of the blustering tabloid commentators have credited the drop in mugging and murder to the girls who would never put out for bloody-handed boyfriends.

We often forget, in both our proud individualism and our petty squabbling, just what social animals we humans are. The 'broken windows' theory of inner-city policing (*see Chapter 5*) suggests that merely improving the physical neighbourhood – often in totally cosmetic ways – will reduce the crime level and increase the social solidarity of even a slum area. This simply wouldn't be even conceivable if human beings weren't quietly (and partly subconsciously) obsessed with the social structures that we inhabit and create throughout our lives.

We define ourselves by a surname that identifies our family allegiance; by what job we do; by our political or religious affiliations; by our tribal loyalty to sport teams or social groups; by our pet interests, hobbies and obsessions; by our residence in a local area or town; and, when abroad, by the nation state that we happened to be born in, or adopted as a matter of later choice.

We also define ourselves by our race, gender and sexual preference; but these somehow say less about us than the others
because they are utterly natural dispositions and are thus less
personal to us.

All of these identifications, chosen and accidental, form an
invisible mental structure around us that interlinks with that of
each person that we come into contact with. Sometimes that
contact causes annoying or infuriating friction – especially if the
contacts fail to match in any significant degree. More often,
unless you suffer a personality or mental dysfunction, you will
find points of contact and form alliances: anything from casual
pleasantries to passionate sex.

The connections with those that we regularly come into
contact with become the local social structure that you inhabit.
If you live in a crime-ridden slum, then you are less likely to
care too much about the opinions of those around you. They,
after all, are up to their necks in the same miserable pit that
you are struggling to survive in. Social stability is weakened,
and the area goes further downhill. But if the area takes an
upturn – maybe just social services replacing broken windows
in derelict buildings – then hope enters your mental social
structure and your interaction with your neighbours is likely to
improve. This upward spiral can eventually turn a Gin Lane
into a Beer Street (*see Chapter 5*).

This and the previous chapter are titled in reference to the old
saying: 'One bad apple can spoil a whole barrel of good apples'.
But with human beings the converse can also be true; the influence of the good apples – sometimes just through proximity –
can turn bad apples healthy again. This constructive process has
been happening, I believe, on a planetary scale for several
decades. Improving affluence, increased education, amazing
technology and, not least, our shared escape from the shadow of
nuclear annihilation at the end of the Cold War, has effectively
mended some of the broken windows in our shared world view.

It is possible that – starting to be freed from many of the griefs
and privations that have dogged humanity for millions of years
– a simple 'absence of war', as Spinoza put it, might be enough to

engender a global state of mind that is more open to 'a disposition of benevolence, confidence, justice'.

However . . . the evidence of history, some of it illustrated in this book, is that the social hegemony will take a swift turn towards the violent if there is a genuine shortage of some vital resource. Our ape ancestors doubtless fought for the last groves of trees – on the drought parching plains of Africa – before being expelled to live on the savannah and on the beach. Our *Homo sapiens* ancestors were suspiciously nearby when the Neanderthals died out, perhaps competing for shelter and hunting grounds in ice-age Europe. In the past thirty thousand years, human beings have fought countless wars over scarce resources – sometimes those resources even being the enslaved bodies of other people. It was only in the twentieth century that we started fighting wars over ideologies rather than for land or gold. But those ideologies, at heart, were just competing ways to divide up scarce resources – like land or gold.

Escalating planetary weather chaos – also called global warming – is a fact. Even if we find a scientific cure for the planet's ailing atmosphere we, and our descendants, will probably still face a long period of geographical and ecological recuperation. The oceans are rising, making living space more scarce. Weather patterns are changing, drenching some regions in floods and turning other parts of the globe into deserts. On a planet hosting more than seven billion people, even finding enough clean drinking water is becoming more difficult, let alone enough food.

It is entirely possible that in a few decades the human race will look back on the present period as a lost golden age. A wonderful time when killing for a gallon of water, or for a bowl of gruel, or for shelter out of the hellish wind, was not commonplace. We have spent millions of years crawling out of the horror that is the state of nature. Now we find that our longed-for paradise is populated with man-created demons.

H. G. Wells ended his 1895 novel *The Time Machine* with the following thought:

[The Time Traveller] I know – for the question had been discussed among us long before the Time Machine was made – thought but cheerlessly of the Advancement of Mankind, and saw in the growing pile of civilization only a foolish heaping that must inevitably fall back upon and destroy its makers in the end. If that is so, it remains for us to live as though it were not so.

Dogged hope, in the end, is the only way to face a coming darkness. Pessimism and despair are worthless; as are self-deluding denial or mindless optimism. And, after all, one of the many things that humankind has proved itself so good at killing are our self-created demons.

An End

The odds against your existence were astronomical. Your parents had to meet and then make love – the latter act at just the right time for the egg with the correct genetic mix to be available. Then the right sperm had to beat thousands of others in the race to that egg. Your mother had to carry you through pregnancy, without miscarriage, and successfully deliver you. Then you had to avoid being killed – by other people, disease or accident – up to at least this point in time.

But all that is next to nothing. Four people, your grandparents, had to go through the same destruction test to allow your parents to exist; and eight great-grandparents to create your grandparents; and sixteen people in the generation before that; and thirty-two in the generation further back. By twelve generations back from your conception – roughly three hundred years – your direct forebears will have numbered 4,096 individuals. Like you, the odds against just those people existing, and living long enough to produce your next forebear, were incalculably high.

Now multiply that already unimaginable chance of your personal nonexistence by all the generations back to at least the proto-human hominid that was mutated enough to branch us away from the ancestors of the chimps and bonobos – about five million to seven million years ago. Break any part of that immeasurable chain of events, and *you* would never have existed. So, the odds against your existence were astronomical.

And that is true of every person that you have ever met, ever heard about, has ever existed. But that is even more true of every cold virus you ever suffered from, or fly you ever swatted (because of their much faster reproductive cycles). So add to the mix the unbelievable achievements of our species. Surviving the great African Miocene drought, that destroyed so many other types of primate. Part-evolving into a water mammal and thus developing our strange method of walking. Using our dangerously ungainly bipedalism, and our pack instinct, to become killer apes. Creating basic tools, and weapons. Growing an increasingly powerful, but energy-expensive brain. Learning to talk, both to negotiate and insult. Learning to think in abstract terms; thus allowing both complex feelings of love and the burning need for protracted revenge. Colonising the planet; surviving a brutal ice age and our Neanderthal cousins. And all that only takes us up to the evolution of *Homo sapiens sapiens* and the pre-dawn of civilisation.

The premature death of *anyone*, seen in these terms, is a loss to the world that is beyond our understanding. The destruction of the most precious work of art is nothing compared to it. Every human being who ever existed is irreplaceable.

George Orwell tried to express the commonplace catastrophe of that loss when he wrote about his experience – when a British Imperial Policeman in Burma – of taking a man to be hanged:

> *He and we were a party of men walking together, seeing, hearing, feeling, understanding the same world; and in two minutes, with a sudden snap, one of us would be gone – one mind less, one world less.*[1]

This is not to say that all human life is sacred. From all but a religious standpoint, such a belief is absurd and impractical. It remains true that all human life *is* unimaginably precious; but, when a person threatens another human life, the worth of the endangering life – in social comparative value – is rendered to less than nil.

---

1 George Orwell, *The Hanging* (1931)

This is the internal decision that a police sniper must make in a fraction of a second – to kill a hostage-taker in order to save the hostage. In that instant the copper effectively balances the value of each life; then kills the hostage-taker because, by threatening another person, they have undermined the value of their own life in comparison. Both lives remain precious on many levels, but the hostile person has undermined their own value to those judging them.

Sanctity, by definition, is of an eternal and unchanging value – something is either sacred or it isn't. Therefore, on a practical level, human life cannot be sacred because its value is so often relative. This is why the many societies that proclaim a belief in the sanctity of human life still kill a lot of people one way or another. Unassailable sanctity in such matters is simply an impractical proposition.

Esoteric as all this may seem, the fact is that various elements of society make balancing decisions on the relative value of human life all the time. Soldiers kill the enemy to protect themselves and their comrades. Judges decide whether to execute or imprison convicted criminals, not (generally) to punish, but to protect society from further risk of the criminal's actions. And politicians (should) consider the balance of profit and loss to the lives of different elements of their society with virtually every decision that they make.

With all this judgemental calculation going on – every day and everywhere – it is inevitable that some people will, sooner or later, be judged by those around them to be in dire need of killing. (Doubtless the reader will be able to think of several instances themselves.) We can certainly question such harsh judgements – both illegal and legal – but the fact is that civilisation has always depended on a certain amount of human death. In fact the main theme of this book has been the study of why we now seem to be reducing the demand for such sacrificed human blood.

I'm not a religious man. I believe that if God exists and is a decent being, it would have introduced itself directly to its children by now – instead of sending a series of dubious and contradictory go-betweens. And if God is not a decent being, I have no interest in meeting it.

This, however, gives me a small problem; as writing about and judging evil is traditionally in the realm of the religiously inclined. The reader will have seen that this book is crammed with evil, yet its overall aim was to try to quantify the good developing in human society: to measure if we are actually becoming civilised, instead of just saying and hoping that we are. Thomas Keneally, in his documentary novel *Schindler's Ark*, pointed out that it is horribly easy to quantify evil. You just count the murdered bodies. Quantifying good, he said, is much harder to do; as it is rare that you can accurately count the number of living bodies *saved* from murder.

Yet reading my father's many books showed me that being aware of the evil that humans do can give you a better idea of human good. Like the meaning in a Joseph Conrad novel, good cannot be found like a nut within the shell of a story – it is the glowing nimbus around the edge of the darkness. The horror, hate and darkness of our shared existence stands out all too plainly; but around it is the gentle and defining glow of human kindness and decency.

In my life I have seen the belief in racism go from being an acceptable political stance, to being seen as the worst insult that you can level at a person's outlook. When I was a child in the 1960s and 1970s, women were still largely seen as being incapable of holding important or technical jobs. My wife is an NHS consultant orthopaedic surgeon, and returns home to me every day having made her patients' lives quantifiably better. Open homosexuality was a crime in my country when I was born. Now the homosexual community is increasingly celebrated and cherished in Britain, and in many other nations. And the violent crime rate is falling around the globe. Even the once-forgotten crimes of the past are being reinvestigated with new forensic techniques, and delayed justice is being handed out to criminals who thought that they had gotten away scot free. The glow around the edge of the darkness has become perceptibly brighter in just my fifty years.

My father, Colin Wilson, died peacefully on 5 December 2013. I know that he, although also non-religious, believed in the possibility of an afterlife. And I'm in no position to argue against his views on that matter.

He was always a deeply humane and optimistic person, some of which has rubbed off on to his children. I've known him to be on perfectly happy conversational terms with some of the most celebrated people of the past half-century; and with brutal convicted murderers. When all is said and done, he always saw people as beings of fascinating potentiality; all worthy of delighted wonder, if not always respect.

So.

Whoever you are. Whatever you've done. Whatever you may become.

I, and my dad, love you.

Damon Wilson, March 2015

Bibliography

Aeschylus, *Agamemnon* (458 BCE)

Ardrey, Robert, *African Genesis: A Personal Investigation into the Animal Origins and Nature of Man* (Macmillan Publishing, 1961)

Arendt, Hannah, *Eichmann in Jerusalem: A Report on the Banality of Evil* (Penguin Books, 1963)

Babiak, Paul and Hare, Robert, *Snakes in Suits: When Psychopaths Go to Work* (Harper Publishing, 2006)

Barbusse, Henri, *L'Enfer* (1908)

Beccaria, Cesare, *On Crimes and Punishments* (1764)

Beecher Stowe, Harriet, *Uncle Tom's Cabin; or, Life Among the Lowly* (1852)

Beevor, Antony, *Berlin: The Downfall 1945* (Penguin Books, 2007)

Beevor, Antony, *Stalingrad* (Viking Press, 1998)

Beevor, Antony, *The Battle for Spain: the Spanish Civil War 1936–1939* (W&N, 2007)

Beevor, Antony, *D-Day: The Battle for Normandy* (Penguin Books, 2009)

Brady, Ian, *The Gates of Janus: An Analysis of Serial Murder by England's Most Hated Criminal* (Feral House, 2000)

Brecht, Bertolt, *Fear and Misery of the Third Reich* (1938)

Brecht, Bertolt, *Life of Galileo* (1945)

Brecht, Bertolt, *The Resistible Rise of Arturo Ui* (1941)

Bryson, Bill, *A Short History of Nearly Everything* (Doubleday, 2003)

Burnham, James, *The Machiavellians: Defenders of Freedom* (Putnam, 1943)

Burnham, James, *The Management Revolution* (Putnam, 1940)

Burrow, Ashley N. and Currence, Nichole and Lemus, Diana and DeBono, Amber and Crawford, Matthew T. and Walker, W. Richard, 'Psychopaths View Autobiographical Memories as Less Memorable, Important, and Emotional than Normal Individuals', *The International Journal of Humanities and Social Science*, Vol. 4, No. 6 (April 2014)

Chagnon, Napoleon, *Yanomamo: The Fierce People (A Case Study in Cultural Anthropology)* (Thomson Learning, 1968)

Charriere, Henri, *Papillon* (Hart-Davis, 1969)

Chatwin, Bruce, *The Songlines* (Franklin Press, 1987)

Chesterton, G. K., *The Napoleon of Notting Hill* (Bodley Head, 1904)

Conrad, Joseph, *Heart of Darkness* (1902)

Craig, William, *Enemy at the Gates: The Battle for Stalingrad* (Penguin Books, 1973)

Curtis, Adam, *The Mayfair Set* (BBC2 documentary series, 1999)

Curtis, Adam, *The Power of Nightmares* (BBC2 documentary series, 2004)

Curtis, Adam, *The Trap: What Happened to Our Dream of Freedom?* (BBC2 documentary series, 2007)

Cyriax, Oliver and Wilson, Colin and Wilson, Damon, *The Encyclopedia of Crime* (Carlton, 2005)

Dart, Raymond, 'The Predatory Transition from Ape to Man', *The International Anthropological and Linguistic Review*, Vol.1 # 4 (1953)

Davies, Norman, *Europe: A History* (Oxford University Press, 1996)

Dawkins, Richard, *The Blind Watchmaker* (W. W. Norton & Company, 1986)

Dawkins, Richard, *The God Delusion* (Boston: Houghton Mifflin, 2006)

Dawkins, Richard, *The Selfish Gene* (Oxford University Press, 1976)

De Sade, Aldonse-Donatien Louis, *Dialogue Between a Priest and a Dying Man* (1782)

De Sade, Aldonse-Donatien Louis, *Justine, or The Misfortunes of Virtue* (1791)

De Sade, Aldonse-Donatien Louis, *Juliette* (1801)

De Sade, Aldonse-Donatien Louis, *Philosophy in the Boudoir* (1795)

De Sade, Aldonse-Donatien Louis, *The 120 Days of Sodom, or The School of Libertinism*, (written 1785, first published 1904)

De Sade, Aldonse-Donatien Louis, *The Crimes of Love: Heroic and Tragic Tales* (1800)

Dickens, Charles, *Great Expectations* (1860)

Donaldson, William, *Brewer's Rogues. Villains and Eccentrics* (Cassell, 2002)

Dostoyevsky, Fyodor Mikhailovich, *Crime and Punishment* (1866)

Doyle, Arthur Conan, *A Study in Scarlet* (1887)

Du Rose, John, *Murder was My Business* (W. H. Allen, 1971)

Dubner, Stephen J. and Levitt, Steven D., *Freakonomics: A Rogue Economist Explores the Hidden Side of Everything* (William Morrow & Company, 2005)

Dyson, J. Freeman and Feynman, Richard P., *The Pleasure of Finding Things Out* (Allen Lane, 1999)

Ereira, Alan, and Jones, Terry, *The Crusades* (BBC Books, 1994)

Esbensen , Finn-Aage and Peterson, Dana and Taylor, Terrance, *Youth Violence: Sex and Race Differences in Offending, Victimisation, and Gang Membership* (Temple University Press, USA, 2010)

Fast, Howard, *Spartacus* (Blue Heron Press, 1951)

Forest, Jean-Claude (scriptwriter and original comic book author), *Barbarella* (movie) (Dino de Laurentiis Cinematografica, 1968)

Forester, C. S., *Death to the French* (Bodley Head, 1932)

Fox, James Alan and Levin, Jack, *Extreme Killing: Understanding Serial and Mass Murder* (Sage Publications, 2005)

Frazer, James, *The Golden Bough* (1890)

Furneaux, Rupert, *The Two Stranglers of Rillington Place*, (Panther Books, 1961)

George, Andrew (translator), *The Epic of Gilgamesh* (Penguin Books, 2003)

Glass, Samantha J. and Newman, Joseph P., 'Emotion Processing in the Criminal Psychopath: The Role of Attention in Emotion Facilitated Memory', *The Journal of Abnormal Psychology*, February 2009

Goldman, James, *The Lion in Winter* (1966)

Gramsci, Antonio, *Prison Notebooks* (Columbia University Press, 2011 edition)

Grimm, Jacob and Grimm, William, *Children's Household Tales* (1812)

Grof, Stanislav, *The Adventure of Self-discovery: Dimensions of Consciousness and New Perspectives in Psychotherapy and Inner Exploration* (State University of New York Press, 1988)

Gurr, Ted Robert, *Violence in America* (Bantam Books, 1969)

Hammett, Dashiell, *The Maltese Falcon* (Alfred A. Knopf, 1929)

Hansford Johnson, Pamela, *On Iniquity: Some personal reflections arising out of the Moors murder trial* (Macmillan, 1967)

Hardy, Alister Clavering, 'Was Man More Aquatic in the Past?', *New Scientist Magazine*, (March 1960)

Hare, Robert, *Without Conscience: The Disturbing World of the Psychopaths Among Us* (Guilford Press, 1999)

Haritos-Fatouros, Mika, *The Psychological Origins of Institutionalized Torture* (Routledge, 2002)

Hasford, Gustav, *The Short-Timers* (Harper and Row, 1979)

Herodotus, *The Histories of the Persian Wars* (circa 420 BCE)

Hitchens, Christopher, *God is Not Great* (Twelve Books, 2007)

Hitler, Adolf, *Mein Kampf* (Eher Verlag, 1925)

Hobbes, Thomas, *Leviathan*, (1651)

Homer, *The Iliad* (circa 750 BCE)

Horizon, *Stone Age Columbus* (BBC2 documentary, 2002)

Huston, John (writer and director), *The Maltese Falcon* (movie) (Warner Brothers, 1941)

Ibsen, Henrik, *A Doll's House* (1879)

Josephus, Flavius, *Against Apion* (circa. 200 CE)

Joyce, James, *Ulysses* (Sylvia Beach, 1922)

Keeley, Lawrence H., *War Before Civilisation: The Myth of the Peaceful Savage* (Oxford University Press, 1997)

Keneally, Thomas, *Schindler's Ark* (Hodder and Stoughton, 1982)

Kennedy, Ludovic, *Ten Rillington Place* (Gollancz, 1961)

Kraymer, Heinrich and Sprenger, Jacob, *Malleus Maleficarum* (1486)

Kubrick, Stanley (scriptwriter), *Full Metal Jacket* (movie) (Stanley Kubrick Productions, 1987)

Kurosawa, Akira (scriptwriter and director), *Seven Samurai* (movie) (Toho Company, 1954)

Lewis, Wyndham, *Rotting Hill* (Methuen, 1951)

Lifton, Robert Jay, *Thought Reform and the Psychology of Totalism* (Norton, 1962)

Lombroso, Cesare, *Crime: Its Causes and Remedies* (Little Brown, 1899)

London, Sondra, *Knockin' on Joe* (Nemasis Publications, 1993)

Macdonald Fraser, George, *Flashman and the Redskins* (Collins, 1982)

Macdonald Fraser, George, *Flashman at the Charge* (Barrie and Jenkins, 1973)

Machiavelli, Niccolo, *Discourses on Livy* (1531)

Machiavelli, Niccolo, *The Prince* (1532)

Mandel, Loring (scriptwriter), *Conspiracy* (a dramatic recreation of the Wannsee Conference based on the official Nazi transcript) (BBC Television, 2001)

Marshall, S. L. A., *Men Against Fire* (University of Oklahoma Press, 1947)

Masters, Brian, *Killing for Company: The Case of Dennis Nilsen* (Random House, 1995)

Milius, John and Coppola, Francis Ford (scriptwriters and director), *Apocalypse Now* (movie) (Zoetrope Studios, 1979)

Miller, Frank, *The Dark Knight Returns* (DC Comics, 1986)

Moon, Paul, *This Horrid Practice: The Myth and Reality of Traditional Maori Cannibalism* (Penguin NZ, 2008)

Moore, Alan, *Watchmen* (DC Comics, 1987)

Morgan, Elaine, *The Aquatic Ape Hypothesis* (Souvenir Press, 1997)

Morgan, Elaine, *The Aquatic Ape* (Stein & Day, 1982)

Morgan, Elaine, *The Descent of Woman* (Souvenir Press, 1972)

Morgan, Elaine, *The Scars of Evolution* (Sounenir Press, 1990)

Morris, Desmond, *The Naked Ape: A Zooologist's Study of the Human Animal* (Jonathan Cape, 1967)

Motzkin, Julian C. and Newman, Joseph P. and Kiehl, Kent A. and Koenigs, Michael , 'Reduced Prefrontal Connectivity in Psychopathy', *The Journal of Neuroscience* (November 2011)

Noelle-Neumann, Elizabeth, *The Spiral of Silence: Public Opinion – Our Social Skin* (University of Chicago Press, 1984)

Orwell, George, *1984* (Secker and Warburg, 1949)

Orwell, George, 'A Hanging', *The Adelphi Magazine* (August 1931)

Orwell, George, *Down and Out in Paris and London* (Victor Gollancz, 1933)

Orwell, George, *Essays* (Everyman Library, 2002)

Orwell, George, *Homage to Catalonia* (Secker and Warburg, 1938)

Orwell, George, 'Lear, Tolstoy and the Fool', *Polemic Magazine* #7 (March 1947)

Orwell, George, *The Road to Wigan Pier* (Gollancz, 1937)

Paine, Thomas, *The Age of Reason* (1794)

Paine, Thomas, *The Rights of Man* (1791)

Parenti, Michael, *The Assassination of Julius Caesar: A People's History of Ancient Rome* (The New Press, 2004)

Parrish, J. M. and Crossland, John (editors), *The Fifty Most Amazing Crimes of the Last 100 Years* (Odhams Press, 1936)

Peake, Mervyn, *Gormenghast* (Eyre & Spottiswoode, 1950)

Peake, Mervyn, *Titus Groan* (Eyre & Spottiswoode, 1946)

Pinker, Steven, *The Better Angels of Our Nature* (Penguin Books, 2011)

Pitman, Pat and Wilson, Colin, *Encyclopedia of Murder* (Putnam, 1962)

Poe, Edgar Allen, *A Descent into the Maelstrom* (1841)

Richardson, Samuel, *Clarissa* (1748)

Richardson, Samuel, *Pamela, or Virtue Rewarded* (1740)

Richardson, Samuel, *The History of Sir Charles Grandison* (1753)

Rolling, Danny and London, Sondra, *The Making of a Serial Killer: The Real Story of the Gainesville Student Murders in the Killer's Own Words* (Feral House, 2011)

Ronson, Jon, *The Psychopath Test* (Macmillan, 2011)

Rousseau, Jean-Jacques, *The Social Contract* (1862)

Sagan, Carl, *The Demon-Haunted World* (Random House, 1995)

Sandburg, Carl, *The People, Yes* (Harcourt, Brace & Company, 1936)

Schaefer, Gerard, *Killer Fiction* (Media Queen, 1989)

Schott, Ian and Wilson, Damon, *World Famous Dictators* (Constable & Robinson, 2004)

Seaman, Donald and Wilson, Colin, *Encyclopedia of Modern Murder 1962–82* (Littlehampton Books, 1983)

Seaman, Donald and Wilson, Colin, *The Serial Killers: A Study in the Psychology of Violence* (BCA, 1990)

Shute, Nevil, *On the Beach* (Heinemann, 1957)

Smith, Adam, *An Inquiry into the Nature and Causes of the Wealth of Nations* (1776)

Speer, Albert, *Inside the Third Reich* (Macmillan, 1970)

Spinoza, Baruch, *Tractatus Politicus* (1676)

Steel, Mark, *Vive La Revolution* (Scribner, 2003)

Steinbeck, John, *Once There Was a War* (Viking Press, 1958)

Steinbeck, John, *The Moon is Down* (Viking Press, 1942)

Steinbeck, John, *Travels with Charley: In Search of America* (Viking Press, 1962)

Stout, Martha, *The Sociopath Next Door* (Broadway Books, 2005)

Swift, Jonathan, *A Modest Proposal for Preventing the Children of Poor People From Being a Burthen to Their Parents or Country, and for Making Them Beneficial to the Publick* (1729)

Thucydides, *History of the Peloponnesian War* (431 BCE)

Thurber, James, 'The Secret Life of Walter Mitty', *The New Yorker* (March 1939)

Topping, Peter, *Topping: The Autobiography of the Police Chief in the Moors Murder Case* (Angus & Robertson, 1989)

Trumbo, Dalton (scriptwriter), *Spartacus* (movie) (Bryna Productions, 1960)

Twain, Mark, *Following the Equator* (1897)

Twain, Mark, *The Adventures of Huckleberry Finn* (1884)

Van der Post, Laurens, *The Seed and the Sower* (Hogarth Press, 1962)

Von Kleist, Heinrich, *The Marquise von O* (1808)

Vonnegut, Kurt, *Slaughterhouse-Five, or The Children's Crusade: A Duty-Dance with Death* (Delacorte, 1969)

Wells, H. G., *An Experiment in Autobiography* (Gollancz, 1934)

Wells, H. G., *Ann Veronica* (Unwin, 1909)

Wells, H. G., *The Croquet Player*, Chatto & Windus, 1936

Wells, H. G., *The Outline of History*, Garden City Publishing, 1931

Wells, H. G., *The Time Machine*, 1895

Wilde, Oscar, *A Picture of Dorian Gray* (Lippincott's Monthly Magazine, 1890)

Wilson, Colin and Wilson, Damon and Wilson, Rowan, *World Famous Robberies* (Magpie Books, 1994)

Wilson, Colin and Wilson, Damon, *A Plague of Murder* (Robinson Publishing, 1995)

Wilson, Colin and Wilson, Damon, *Crimes of Passion* (Carlton, 2006)

Wilson, Colin and Wilson, Damon, *Serial Killers* (Constable & Robinson, 2008)

Wilson, Colin, *A Casebook of Murder* (Mayflower, 1969)

Wilson, Colin, *A Criminal History of Mankind* (Granada Books, 1984)

Wilson, Colin, *A Ritual in the Dark* (Gollancz, 1960)

Wilson, Colin, *Afterlife: An Investigation of the Evidence of Life After Death* (The Leisure Circle, 1985)

Wilson, Colin, *Order of the Assassins: The Psychology of Murder* (Harper Collins Publishing, 1972)

Wilson, Colin, *Poltergeist! A Study in Destructive Haunting* (New English Library, 1982)

Wilson, Colin, *The Corpse Garden* (Pan Books, 1998)

Wilson, Colin, *The Devil's Party: A History of Charlatan Messiahs* (Virgin Books, 2000)

Wilson, Colin, *The Glass Cage* (Barker, 1966)

Wilson, Colin, *The Janus Murder Case* (Harper Collins, 1984)

Wilson, Colin, *The Killer* (Harper Collins, 1970)

Wilson, Colin, *The Misfits: A Study of Sexual Outsiders* (Grafton Publishing, 1988)

Wilson, Colin, *The Occult: A History* (Random House, 1971)

Wilson, Colin, *The Outsider* (Gollancz, 1956)

Wilson, Colin, *The Schoolgirl Murder Case* (Harper Collins, 1974)

Wilson, Colin, *The World of Violence* (Grafton, 1963)

Wilson, Colin, *Written in Blood: A History of Forensic Detection* (Harper Collins Publishing, 1995)

Wilson, Edward O., *The Social Conquest of the Earth* (Liveright Publishing, 2012)

Wilson, Robert Anton, 'The Semantics of "Good" & "Evil"', *Critique: A Journal Questioning Consensus Reality* #28

Wood, Michael, *In Search of the Trojan War* (BBC Books, 1985)

Index